SOCIETY FOR NEW TESTAMENT STUDIES
MONOGRAPH SERIES

GENERAL EDITOR
MATTHEW BLACK, D.D., F.B.A.

17

HEROD ANTIPAS

TO GINI

MY BELOVED

AND

DEVOTED WIFE

HEROD ANTIPAS

BY

HAROLD W. HOEHNER

Assistant Professor,
Dallas Theological Seminary

CAMBRIDGE
AT THE UNIVERSITY PRESS
1972

Published by the Syndics of the Cambridge University Press
Bentley House, 200 Euston Road, London NW1 2DB
American Branch: 32 East 57th Street, New York, N.Y.10022

Library of Congress Catalogue Card Number: 79–158548

ISBN: 0 521 08132 7

Printed in Great Britain
at the University Printing House, Cambridge
(Brooke Crutchley, University Printer)

CONTENTS

PART 3: ANTIPAS' REIGN

PREFACE

There are several books on Herod the Great, many of which have a short section on his sons. Most of those have no more than ten to twenty pages on Herod Antipas and yet he was the tetrarch who ruled over the domains in which John the Baptist and our Lord were ministering. The subject of this book was suggested to me by my New Testament Research Supervisor Dr E. Bammel.

The work was originally presented to the University of Cambridge in 1968 for the degree of Doctor of Philosophy. I have attempted to read the literature relevant to the subject which appeared subsequently and have updated the work until it went to the Press. Since the time of my original study several works (e.g. Jaubert, Jeremias, Kittel, Lohse, Reicke) have been translated into English and I have for the benefit of the English readership changed the bibliographical data accordingly. Of course, the works in the original language were retained where there had been substantial revision subsequent to the English translation (e.g. Schürer, Blinzler). Since the debate on the synoptic problem has been renewed, I have attempted where relevant not to assume one position dogmatically.

It is a delightful task for an author to express his appreciation. I owe a debt of gratitude to the Provost and Fellows of King's College, Cambridge for their substantial grants; to the Trustees of the Bethune-Baker Fund; the Alasdair Macpherson Fund; and the Hort Memorial Fund in Cambridge for their financial assistance. Also, I wish to thank Mr and Mrs K. S. Lamb and Grace Bible Church of Dallas for their financial aid. I want to express my appreciation to one who wishes to remain anonymous (even to me) for the assistance which enabled me to spend part of the summer of 1970 for research in Cambridge.

I am especially indebted to Dr E. Bammel for directing me, for encouraging me at every stage of the work, and for constantly giving new insights into the problems connected with Herod Antipas' day. He has been a true *Doktorvater*. I would like to express my thanks to the late Professor A. H. M. Jones, Professors W. H. C. Frend, and M. Black for reading the original manuscript and to Professor R. McL. Wilson for making helpful suggestions in preparation for its publication. None of the above men will agree with all that I have written but their help has been valuable and whatever conclusions and errors remain rest solely upon me.

Finally, a word of thanks is due to Mrs W. G. Lister who typed the original manuscript; to Mrs Lucille Bieger for typing one of the indices; to Mr Ernest Fox and Drs Charles G. Ozanne and John A. Witmer for helpful stylistic criticisms; to Mr Larry Myers, Mrs Sandi Ekholm and Jane Roundy for helping in the proofreading; to many of my students for proofreading the indices; to SCM Press for their permission to reprint pages 233–9; to the readers and printers of the Cambridge University Press for their skill and accuracy; and above all to my wife and family who all suffered through the long birth-pangs of research and publication.

H. W. H.

Dallas, Texas
September 1971

ABBREVIATIONS

AASOR	*The Annual of the American School of Oriental Research*
AGG	*Abhandlungen der königlichen Gesellschaft der Wissenschaften zu Göttingen – Philosophisch-historische Klasse*
AJP	*The American Journal of Philology*
ALUOS	*The Annual of Leeds University Oriental Society*
Appian *BC*	Appian *Bella Civilia*
ASTI	*Annual of the Swedish Theological Institute*
ATR	*Anglican Theological Review*
BA	*The Biblical Archaeologist*
BASOR	*The Bulletin of the American School of Oriental Research*
Bauer/AG	W. Bauer, *A Greek–English Lexicon of the New Testament and Other Early Christian Literature*, trans. and adaptation of the 4th rev. and augmented ed. by W. F. Arndt and F. W. Gingrich (Cambridge, 1957)
BC	*The Beginnings of Christianity*, 5 vols., ed. by F. J. Foakes Jackson and K. Lake (London, 1920–33)
BDB	F. Brown, S. R. Driver, and C. A. Briggs, *A Hebrew and English Lexicon of the Old Testament* (Oxford, 1906)
BD/Funk	F. Blass and A. Debrunner, *A Greek Grammar of the New Testament and Other Early Christian Literature*, trans. and rev. of the 9–10th German ed. by R. W. Funk (Cambridge, 1961)
BJRL	*The Bulletin of the John Rylands Library*
BS	*Bibliotheca Sacra*
BW	*The Biblical World*
BZ	*Biblische Zeitschrift*
CAH	*The Cambridge Ancient History*, 12 vols., ed. by S. A. Cook, F. E. Adcock and M. P. Charlesworth (Cambridge, 1923–39)
CIG	*Corpus Inscriptionum Graecarum*
CIS	*Corpus Inscriptionum Semiticarum*
CJT	*Canadian Journal of Theology*
Cod. Iust.	*Codex Iustinianus*
CQR	*The Church Quarterly Review*
D	*Iustiniani Digesta*
Dalman, *SSW*	G. Dalman, *Sacred Sites and Ways*, trans. by P. P. Levertoff (London, 1935)
EB	*Études Bibliques*

EJ	*Encyclopaedia Judaica*, 10 vols., ed. by J. Klatzkin and I. Elbogen (Berlin, 1928–34)
EncB	*Encyclopaedia Biblica*, 4 vols., ed. by T. K. Cheyne and J. S. Black (London, 1899–1903)
Eng. trans.	English translation
ET	*The Expository Times*
Exp	*The Expositor*
Eus.	Eusebius
Chron.	*Chronica*, 2 vols., ed. by A. Schoene (Berlin, 1867–75)
DE	*Demonstratio Evangelica*
HE	*Historia Ecclesiastica*
Onomast.	*Onomasticon*, ed. by E. Klosterman (Leipzig, 1904)
FGH	*Die Fragmente der griechischen Historiker*, 3 pts., 14 vols., ed. by F. Jacoby (Berlin, 1923–58)
FRLANT	*Forschungen zur Religion und Literatur des Alten und Neuen Testaments*, ed. by W. Bousset, H. Gunkel, *et al.*
Gai Inst.	*Gai Institutiones*
HDB	J. Hastings, *A Dictionary of the Bible*, 5 vols. (Edinburgh, 1898–1904)
HNT	*Handbuch zum Neuen Testament*, ed. by H. Lietzmann
HTR	*The Harvard Theological Review*
HUCA	*The Hebrew Union College Annual*
ICC	*The International Critical Commentary*, ed. by S. R. Driver, A. Plummer, and C. A. Briggs
IDB	*The Interpreter's Dictionary of the Bible*, 4 vols., ed. by G. A. Buttrick, *et al.* (Nashville, 1962)
IEJ	*Israel Exploration Journal*
Itin.	*Itineraria Antonini Augusti et Burdigalense*
Ius. Inst.	*Iustiniani Institutiones*
JBL	*Journal of Biblical Literature*
JE	*The Jewish Encyclopedia*, 12 vols., ed. by I. Singer, *et al.* (New York and London, 1901–6)
JJS	*The Journal of Jewish Studies*
Jones	A. H. M. Jones
CERP	*Cities of the Eastern Roman Provinces* (Oxford, 1940)
GC	*The Greek City from Alexander to Justinian* (Oxford, 1940)
Herods	*The Herods of Judaea* (Oxford, 1938)
Jos.	Josephus
Ant.	*Antiquitates Judaicae*
Ap.	*Contra Apionem*
BJ	*Bellum Judaicum*
JPOS	*The Journal of the Palestine Oriental Society*
JQR	*The Jewish Quarterly Review*

JRS	*The Journal of Roman Studies*
JSS	*The Journal of Semitic Studies*
JTS	*The Journal of Theological Studies*
Just.	Justin Martyr
Apol.	*Apologiae*
Dial.	*Dialogus cum Tryphone Judaeo*
KEK	*Kritisch-exegetischer Kommentar über das Neue Testament*, ed. by H. A. W. Meyer, *et al.*
KNT	*Kommentar zum Neuen Testament*, ed. by T. Zahn
KS	*Kleine Schriften*
LCL	*The Loeb Classical Library*
LSJ	H. G. Liddell and R. Scott (comps.), *A Greek–English Lexicon*⁹, new ed. rev. and augmented by H. S. Jones (Oxford, 1940)
MGWJ	*Monatsschrift für Geschichte und Wissenschaft des Judenthums*
MM	J. H. Moulton and G. Milligan, *The Vocabulary of the Greek Testament* (London, 1930)
Moulton	J. H. Moulton, *A Grammar of New Testament Greek*, I, *Prolegomena*³ (Edinburgh, 1908)
Moulton–Howard	J. H. Moulton and W. F. Howard, *A Grammar of New Testament Greek*, II, *Accidence and Word-Formation* (Edinburgh, 1929)
Moulton–Turner	J. H. Moulton and N. Turner, *A Grammar of New Testament Greek*, III, *Syntax* (Edinburgh, 1963)
MPG	J.-P. Migne (ed.), *Patrologia Graeca* (Paris, 1857–1936)
MPL	J.-P. Migne (ed.), *Patrologia Latina* (Paris, 1844–1963)
MW	*The Muslim World*
NKZ	*Neue kirchliche Zeitschrift*
NovT	*Novum Testamentum*
NTD	*Das Neue Testament Deutsch*, ed. by P. Althaus and G. Friedrich
NTS	*New Testament Studies*
OGIS	*Orientis Graeci Inscriptiones Selectae*
Otto	W. Otto, *Herodes: Beiträge zur Geschichte des letzten jüdischen Königshauses* (Stuttgart, 1913)
PCB	*Peake's Commentary on the Bible*², ed. by M. Black and H. H. Rowley (London, 1962)
PEFQS	*Palestine Exploration Fund, Quarterly Statement*
PEQ	*Palestine Exploration Quarterly*
Philo	Philo
Flacc.	*In Flaccum*
Leg.	*Legatio ad Gaium*
PJB	*Palästinajahrbuch*
Pliny *NH*	Pliny *Naturalis Historia*
PO	*Patrologia Orientalis*

P. Oxy.	*The Oxyrhynchus Papyri*
PW	A. Pauly and G. Wissowa, *Realencyclopädie der klassischen Alter-tumswissenschaft* (Stuttgart, 1894–)
QDAP	*The Quarterly of the Department of Antiquities in Palestine*
RB	*Revue Biblique*
RES	*Répertoire d'Épigraphie Sémitique*
RHR	*Revue de l'Histoire des Religions*
Rostovtzeff	M. Rostovtzeff
SEHHW	*The Social and Economic History of the Hellenistic World*, 3 vols. (Oxford, 1941)
SEHRE	*The Social and Economic History of the Roman Empire²*, 2 vols., rev. by P. M. Fraser (Oxford, 1957)
Rostowzew [= Rostovtzeff], *Kolonates*	M. Rostowzew, *Studien zur Geschichte des römischen Kolonates*. Beiheft 1 to *Archiv für Papyrusforschung und verwandte Gebiete* (Leipzig and Berlin, 1910)
RQ	*Revue de Qumrân*
SAB	*Sitzungsbericht der königlich preussischen Akademie der Wissen-schaften zu Berlin – Philosophisch-historische Klasse*
SBT	*Studies in Biblical Theology*, ed. by T. W. Manson, *et al.*
Schürer	E. Schürer, *Geschichte des jüdischen Volkes im Zeitalter Jesu Christi⁴*, 3 vols. (Leipzig, 1901–9)
SE	*Studia Evangelica*, ed. by F. L. Cross
SH	*Scripta Hierosolymitana*
SJ	*Studia Judaica*, ed. by E. R. Ehrlich (Berlin, 1961–).
Smith, *HGHL*	G. A. Smith, *The Historical Geography of the Holy Land*²⁵ (London, 1931)
SS	*Synoptische Studien*, ed. by J. Schmidt and A. Vögtle (München, 1953)
SSP	*Studies in the Synoptic Problem*, ed. by W. Sanday (Oxford, 1911)
Strack–Billerbeck	H. L. Strack and P. Billerbeck, *Kommentar zum Neuen Testament aus Talmud und Midrasch*, 6 vols. (München, 1922–61)
Suet.	Suetonius
Aug.	*Divus Augustus*
Calig.	*Gaius Caligula*
Claud.	*Divus Claudius*
Tib.	*Tiberius*
Tit.	*Divus Titus*
Ves.	*Vespasian*
Vit.	*Vitellius*
Tac.	Tacitus
Ann.	*Annales*
Hist.	*Historiae*
TAPA	*Transactions and Proceedings of the American Philological Association*

Taylor	V. Taylor
Behind	*Behind the Third Gospel* (Oxford, 1926)
Jesus	*Jesus and His Sacrifice* (London, 1959)
Life	*The Life and Ministry of Jesus* (London, 1954)
Mark	*The Gospel According to St Mark*² (London, 1966)
TB	The Babylonian Talmud
TDNT	*Theological Dictionary of the New Testament*, trans. of *TWNT* by G. W. Bromiley (Grand Rapids, 1964–)
THNT	*Theologischer Handkommentar zum Neuen Testament*, ed. by E. Fascher
TJ	The Jerusalem Talmud
Tos.	Tosephta
TU	*Texte und Untersuchungen zur Geschichte der altchristlichen Literatur*, ed. by O. von Gebhardt and A. von Harnack, *et al.* (Leipzig and Berlin, 1883–)
TWNT	*Theologisches Wörterbuch zum Neuen Testament*, ed. by G. Kittel and G. Friedrich (Stuttgart, 1932–)
Ulp. Reg.	*Ulpiani Liber singularis Regularum*
ZDPV	*Zeitschrift des deutschen Palästina-Vereins*
ZNW	*Zeitschrift für die neutestamentliche Wissenschaft*

JEWISH LITERATURE

Mishnah

Ab.	Aboth
A.Z.	Abodah Zarah
B.B.	Baba Bathra
Bek.	Bekhoroth
Ber.	Berakhoth
Bik.	Bikkurim
B.K.	Baba Kamma
B.M.	Baba Metzia
Ed.	Eduyoth
Er.	Erubin
Git.	Gittin
Hag.	Hagigah

Hul.	Hullin
Kel.	Kelim
Ket.	Ketuboth
Kid.	Kiddushin
Maas.	Maaseroth
Maks.	Makshirin
Meg.	Megillah
Men.	Menahoth
M.K.	Moed Katan
Naz.	Nazir
Ned.	Nedarim
Oh.	Oholoth

Pes.	Pesahim
R.H.	Rosh ha-Shanah
Sanh.	Sanhedrin
Shab.	Shabbath
Sheb.	Shebiith
Sot.	Sotah
Suk.	Sukkah
Taan.	Taanith
Ter.	Terumoth
Toh.	Tohoroth
Yeb.	Yebamoth

Midrash

Gen. R.	Genesis Rabbah	Ecc. R.	Ecclesiastes Rabbah
Cant. R.	Canticles Rabbah	Est. R.	Esther Rabbah

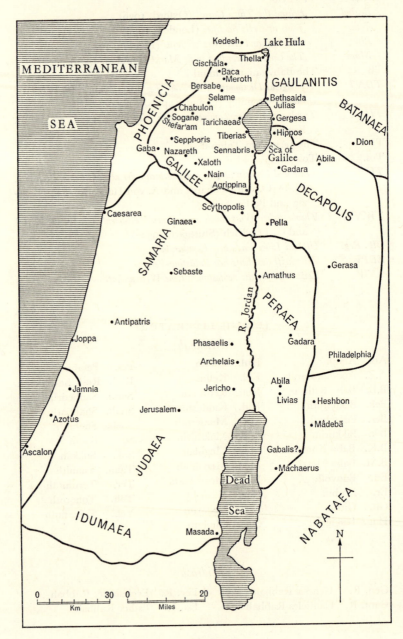

xvi

INTRODUCTION

Today, in the study of the Gospels there is an attempt to understand the evangelists on a theological plane. Although this approach has some validity, a full understanding of the message of Jesus will require also a careful linking of the events described in the Gospels with a reconstruction of the historical context of the life and times of those who surrounded him.

Jesus' relationships with Caiaphas, Pilate, Pharisees, and Sadducees are important. However, equally important is the illumination of his relationship with his governmental head, Herod Antipas. This is not only desirable but also possible, for the sources at one's disposal are greater than those for the study of Caiaphas, Pilate, and the Rabbis of the Sanhedrin. First, there are the direct sources which describe Antipas' actions, and second, there are the historical, archaeological, and circumstantial contexts which all testify to the type of rule he had established. A prosopographical method seems likely to prove the most worthwhile approach to the study of a person who was the tetrarch of Galilee and Peraea, where most of the ministries of Jesus and John the Baptist took place.

Understandably there has been interest in Pilate but there has been a great neglect of Herod Antipas during the last century. In 1873 Brann made a study on the sons of Herod.[1] However, it was Otto who first introduced a historical approach to the Herods but the scope of his presentation was limited within the scheme of an encyclopedia.[2] Further, Otto's main concern was Herod the Great, and this is also true of the works of Jones[3] and Perowne,[4] where little space is given to Antipas.

The first theologian to deal with Herod Antipas is Blinzler,

[1] M. Brann, 'Die Söhne des Herodes', *MGWJ*, xxii (1873), 241–56, 305–21, 345–60, 407–20, 459–64, 497–507.
[2] W. Otto, 'Herodes', PW, Supp. ii (1913), 1–200. This was with a few alterations printed as a separate work, *Herodes: Beiträge zur Geschichte des letzten jüdischen Königshauses* (Stuttgart, 1913).
[3] *Herods.*
[4] S. Perowne, *The Life and Times of Herod the Great* (London, 1957); *The Later Herods* (London, 1958).

yet the study, valuable as it is, is only a sketch.[1] The first full length monograph on the subject was written by Harlow;[2] he attempted to give a vivid picture of the life of Antipas, and the work is semi-popular in manner. The most recent work, by Schofield,[3] is on a popular level. It is clear that there is room for an independent study on the life of Herod Antipas.

The approach of this study is an attempt to reconstruct the background as well as the life of Antipas. It is divided into three parts: the first treats his youth and struggle for the kingdom, the second deals with the geography, inhabitants, and economics of his realm, and the third discusses the early years of his reign, his relationship with John the Baptist, Pilate, and Jesus, and the last years of his reign. After the conclusion there are appendices and tables, and a map of his territories is to be found on p. xvi.

[1] J. Blinzler, *Herodes Antipas und Jesus Christus* (Stuttgart, 1947).

[2] V. E. Harlow, *The Destroyer of Jesus: The Story of Herod Antipas, Tetrarch of Galilee* (Oklahoma City, 1954).

[3] G. Schofield, *Crime before Calvary: Herodias, Herod Antipas, and Pontius Pilate; a New Interpretation* (London, 1960).

PART 1

ANTIPAS' BACKGROUND

CHAPTER I

ANTIPAS' YOUTH

FAMILY BACKGROUND

The dynasty of the Herods became prominent during the confusion which resulted in the decay of the Hasmonaean dynasty, the transference of Syria and Palestine to the rule of the Romans, and the civil wars which marked the decay of the nation. The first of the Herodian dynasty was Antipater (or Antipas) who was appointed governor of Idumaea.[1] His son was also named Antipater and Josephus considers him an Idumaean by race and of great wealth.[2]

[1] Jos. *Ant.* xiv. 10. For the Herodian genealogy, see Table I.

[2] Jos. *BJ* i. 123. From different sources there are three stories regarding the origin of the Herodian dynasty. One story is that given by Nicolaus of Damascus who states that Antipater (Herod the Great's father) was from a family belonging to the leading Jews who came to Judaea from Babylon (*Ant.* xiv. 9). This would make Herod a full-blooded Jew and a member of the returning remnant. Since Nicolaus was a trusted friend and counsellor of Herod the Great, Josephus feels that he gave this story in order to please Herod (*ibid.*). This seems to be a plausible criticism. Reference may be made to *FGH*, II a, 381 (90 frag. 96), II c, 255, where Jacoby argues that Nicolaus really did invent a Babylonian Jewish ancestry for Herod, and he believes that Hölscher in his article 'Josephus', PW, ix (1916), 1971–3, is incorrect in thinking that Nicolaus' account was falsified by a Jewish polemicist. The second story is that given by Justin Martyr, who states in *Dial.* lii. 3 (*MPG*, vi, 592) that it was reported among the Jews that Antipater was an Ascalonite (or Ashkelonite). A fuller treatment of this same story is given by Julius Africanus in his *Epistola ad Aristidem* which is mentioned by Eusebius (*HE* i. 6. 2; 7. 11). He states that Antipater's father, whom he calls Herod, was only a temple slave in the temple of Apollo. When he was a little child Antipater was taken captive by Idumaean robbers at the time they attacked the city of Ascalon. Antipater lived with the Idumaeans because his father being poor was not able to pay a ransom for him. As a result he was brought up in the customs of the Idumaeans and was befriended by Hyrcanus, the high priest of Judaea. This would mean that Herod's dynasty was of Philistine origin and therefore not Jewish at all. This story was probably an invention of the Pharisees and/or the Christians who wanted to make Herod a Philistine because the family was hated by them. The Pharisees might have done this because they were strict in the Law and did not accept Herod as a rightful heir to the throne, while the Christians disliked him because they

5

Antipater married an illustrious Arabian lady, Cypros, by whom he had four sons – Phasael, Herod, Joseph, and Pheroras – and a daughter, Salome.[1] Of these children Herod, called the Great (in the sense of the eldest[2]), was proclaimed king of the Jews by the Roman Senate[3] in late 40 B.C.[4] by nomination of

blamed him for the massacre of the children (Mt. 2: 16). For support of his story, Africanus mentions that he received his information from kinsmen (συγγενεῖς) of Jesus Christ. At any rate Africanus' attitude of bitter hatred against Herod results in prejudice against him in his writings. The third story is that stated by Josephus, who makes Herod an Idumaean by race. This would mean that he was a half-Jew descended from Esau, Jacob's brother. This is the most likely solution, for there is no reason for Josephus' having invented his story as the others seemingly had done. Certainly if he had wanted to discredit Herod he could have repeated the same story or one similar to that given by Justin Martyr, or like the Talmud have made Herod a slave of the Hasmonaeans (cf. TB: B.B. 3 *b*–4 *a*; Kid. 70 *b*). If he had wanted to make the Herodian dynasty purely Jewish, being himself a Jew, he could have accepted Nicolaus of Damascus' story without comment. But this he did not do and so it is probable that his story is the most correct. At least both Africanus and Josephus state that Antipater had his origin in Idumaea, though Africanus would make it very poor, while Josephus makes it distinguished. For a more detailed study, see Otto, cols. 17–19; Schürer, I, 292 n. 3; A. Schalit, 'Die frühchristliche Überlieferung über die Herkunft der Familie des Herodes', *ASTI*, I (1962), 109–60; and a subsequent article by W. Wirgin, 'Bemerkungen zu dem Artikel über "Die Herkunft des Herodes"', *ASTI*, III (1964), 151–4; cf. also A. Schalit, 'Die "herodianischen" Patriarchen und der "davidische" Herodes', *ASTI*, VI (1968), 114–23; A. Schalit, *König Herodes: Der Mann und sein Werk*, *SJ*, IV (Berlin, 1969), 4–5, 677–8; S. Zeitlin, 'Herod: A Malevolent Maniac', *JQR*, LIV (1963), 4–7.

[1] Jos. *Ant.* xiv. 121; *BJ* i. 181.

[2] The title ὁ μέγας is only in Jos. *Ant.* xviii. 130, 133, 136. Since this title is not found elsewhere (e.g. on inscriptions or coins), H. Ewald, *Geschichte des Volkes Israel*, IV[3] (Göttingen, 1864), 546 n. 2, conjectures with a high degree of probability that ὁ μέγας merely indicates that he was 'the elder' in comparison with his sons. This title was used by Agrippa I, as found in Josephus (*Ant.* xvii. 28; xviii. 110, 142; xx. 104) and on coins, cf. below, p. 108 n. 5.

[3] Jos. *Ant.* xiv. 381–5; *BJ* i. 282–5. This is also confirmed by Strabo xvi. 2. 46; Appian *BC* v. 75; Tac. *Hist.* v. 9.

[4] Josephus states in *Ant.* xiv. 389 that Herod was pronounced king in the 184th Olympiad. But this seems to be incorrect, for the 184th Olympiad ended in the summer of 40 B.C., and Herod did not even go to Rome until the winter. Moreover, since Octavian and Antony did not reach Rome until the autumn of 40 B.C., they could not have appointed Herod as king until after the 184th Olympiad (cf. Schürer, I, 355 n. 3). That Herod was accustomed to reckon his accession from 40 rather than from 37 B.C. when his reign became *de facto*, is plausibly argued on the basis of numismatic

Antony and Octavian.[1] Herod entered the possession of his sovereignty in the summer of 37 B.C. when, with the help of the Roman army, Jerusalem was captured[2] and Antigonus removed,

evidence by B. Kanael, 'The Coins of King Herod of the Third Year', *JQR*, XLII (1952), 261–4.

[1] A mere survey of Herod's life is given here. For a more detailed study of his life and rule, cf. Schürer, I, 360–418; Otto, cols. 1–164; H. Willrich, *Das Haus des Herodes* (Heidelberg, 1929); A. Momigliano, 'Herod of Judaea', *CAH*, x (Cambridge, 1934), 316–39; Jones, *Herods*; Perowne, *Herod the Great*; A. Schalit, *König Herodes*; S. Sandmel, *Herod: Profile of a Tyrant* (Philadelphia, 1967); S. Zeitlin, *The Rise and Fall of the Judaean State*, I (Philadelphia, 1962), 393–411; II (Philadelphia, 1967), 3–99; cf. also W. Foerster, 'Herodes und seine Nachfolger', *Die Religion in Geschichte und Gegenwart*[3], III (1959), 266–9; S. Sandmel, 'Herod (Family)', *IDB*, II (1962), 586–90; B. Reicke, 'Herodes', *Biblisch-historisches Handwörterbuch*, II (1964), 696–700; J. S. Minkin, *Herod, King of the Jews* (New York, 1936); B. Reicke, 'Herodes der Grosse', *Reformatio*, IX (1960), 24–34; S. G. F. Brandon, 'Herod the Great', *History Today*, XII (1962), 234–42.

[2] Jos. *Ant.* xiv. 470–80; *BJ* i. 349–52. This is confirmed by Tac. *Hist.* v. 9; Dio xlix. 22. 6. The conquest of Jerusalem is conflictingly dated. According to Dio it occurred in the consulship of Claudius and Norbanus in 38 B.C. But according to Josephus it occurred under the consulship of Marcus Agrippa and Caninius Gallus in the 185th Olympiad on the day of the fast (τῇ ἑορτῇ τῆς νηστείας), on which day Pompey had captured Jerusalem twenty-seven years earlier (Jos. *Ant.* xiv. 488). The limits of the 185th Olympiad would be from 1 July 40 to 30 June 36; cf. J. Finegan, *Handbook of Biblical Chronology* (Princeton, 1964), p. 113. The sabbatical year is assumed by most scholars to have occurred from 1 Tishri 38 B.C. to the same date in 37 B.C. Thus the year is limited from the autumn of 38 to the autumn of 37. It is known that Pacorus was conquered by Ventidius on 9 June 38 B.C., cf. T. Lewin, *Fasti Sacri* (London, 1865), p. 57. After this Ventidius campaigned against Antiochus of Commagene and besieged him in Samosata. It was after this siege had begun (Plutarch *Antonius* xxxiv. 2–4), in July 39 B.C. at the earliest, that Antony arrived at Samosata. It was only after Samosata was captured that he returned to Athens and dispatched Sossius to assist Herod (Jos. *Ant.* xiv. 439–47). This could not have been before the autumn of 39 B.C. Because of the weather (cf. Jos. *Ant.* xiv. 453, 461, 465, 473) Herod would not have been able to capture Jerusalem before the summer of 37. Thus if Pompey conquered Jerusalem in 63 B.C., according to Jewish reckoning (or twenty-seven years after Pompey's capture of Jerusalem), it would mean that Herod had taken over Jerusalem in 37 rather than 38 B.C. It seems, then, that Dio is incorrect in dating the fall of Jerusalem as having occurred in 38 B.C. Regarding the length of the siege, Josephus states in *BJ* i. 351 that it lasted into the fifth month, and in *Ant.* xiv. 487 that it lasted into the third month. Schürer (I, 358–60 n. 11) explains these two dates as having reference to the length of the siege rather than to the third and fifth months of the Jewish calendar, and that the three months are to be reckoned back to the

he being the last of the Hasmonaean rulers of the Jews, who with the support of the Parthians acted as the priest-king during the preceding three years.[1]

During his reign of thirty-four years Herod was unreservedly loyal to Rome. Up to the Battle of Actium (31 B.C.) he enjoyed friendly relations with Antony which even Cleopatra's covetous ambitions towards Judaea could not destroy.[2] After Actium he convinced Octavian (now Augustus) that his loyalty to Rome would be most beneficial to him,[3] and as a result his kingship was confirmed.[4] Among certain national groups Rome preferred

commencement of the operations – no doubt, as Lewin thinks (cf. p. 60), when Sossius joined Herod after his marriage to Mariamme. The five months, then, are to be reckoned from the beginning of the siege which occurred before his marriage to Mariamme. Where these two events are to be placed presents another problem, for some think that the capture of Jerusalem occurred at the time of the fast or the Day of Atonement (as Lewin, pp. 59–62; A. Dupont-Sommer, 'Le "Commentaire d'Habacuc" découvert près de la Mer Mort', *RHR*, CXXXVII [1950], 160, 169 n. 1), whereas others think that it occurred in July (cf. Schürer, I, 358–60 n. 11; M. B. Daget, 'The Habbakuk Scroll and Pompey's Capture of Jerusalem', *Biblica*, XXXII [1951], 547–8). The latter view seems to be more probable. The tradition that Herod captured Jerusalem on the Day of Atonement was intended to discredit him by making him invade the city on that most sacred of days (cf. Otto, cols. 33–7 n., esp. cols. 35–6). Most probably, therefore, Jerusalem was captured by Herod around July 37 B.C.

[1] Jos. *Ant.* xiv. 481; *BJ* i. 353. Josephus states that Antigonus fell beneath the axe as a result of a large bribe which Herod gave Antony (*BJ* i. 357; *Ant.* xiv. 490). This is confirmed by Plutarch *Antonius* xxxvi. 2 who states that Antony had Antigonus beheaded (ἐπελέκισε) although no other king before him had been so punished. Dio xlix. 22. 6 states that Antony had Antigonus bound to a cross and flogged, and that he afterwards slew him or had his throat cut (ἀπέσφαξεν), a treatment that no other king had suffered at the hands of the Romans.

[2] Cleopatra actually wanted Antony to get rid of both Malchus king of Arabia and Herod king of Judaea, but Antony did not concede; instead (so as not to refuse her altogether) he gave her land from both kings, including the district of Jericho with its palm trees and balsam – the most fertile territory of Herod's kingdom (Jos. *Ant.* xv. 93–6; *BJ* i. 360–1). In addition, Malchus and Herod each had to pay her a tribute of 200 talents for the lease of the land (*BJ* i. 362; *Ant.* xv. 96, 132). Cleopatra hoped that at least one of these kings would not be able to pay. She could then engage the other to overthrow the defaulter and so she would become the mistress of his land (*Ant.* xv. 106–7; *BJ* i. 365).

[3] Jos. *Ant.* xv. 188–93; *BJ* i. 387–90. Josephus' account of Herod's speech is doubted to be a true account by Otto, cols. 50–1.

[4] Jos. *Ant.* xv. 194–5; *BJ* i. 391–3; Strabo xvi. 2. 46.

client kingdoms to ruling them direct through provincial governors. A native ruler could conciliate the idiosyncrasies of his subjects far better than an outsider whose position was only temporary.[1] The Jews were ideally suited to be a client kingdom on account of their strong religious convictions. Moreover, Herod's domain was ideally located to act as a buffer state between Rome and Parthia.

During the spring preceding the capture of Jerusalem, Herod married Mariamme (hereafter designated Mariamme I) to whom he was already betrothed.[2] This was both a contemptuous move towards Antigonus, the uncle of Mariamme I, as well as a shrewd political gesture, designed to ingratiate the Jews at the beginning of his reign by marrying someone in the Hasmonaean family. This marriage only lasted until late 29 B.C. when Herod, being suspicious of her loyalty, ordered her execution.[3] From this marriage there were two notable sons, who bore the good Hasmonaean names of Alexander and Aristobulus. These, in 22 B.C., were sent to Rome to receive a proper education under the tutelage of one of Herod's friends, Pollio,[4] and it was probably at this time that they were nominated as Herod's heirs.[5] However, Herod became suspicious of them, and finally had them executed in 7 B.C.[6]

Herod's suspicion of these two sons was partly caused by their elder brother, Antipater, Herod's son by his first wife Doris, whom he had put away when he married Mariamme I.[7] In

[1] Cf. Strabo xiv. 5. 6.   [2] Jos. *Ant.* xiv. 467; *BJ* i. 344.
[3] Jos. *Ant.* xv. 202–36. The execution most likely occurred in late 29 B.C. though this is problematic (cf. Otto, cols. 54–5).
[4] Jos. *Ant.* xv. 342–3. Josephus makes this journey coincide with the rebuilding of Caesarea (*Ant.* xv. 341–2). According to *Ant.* xvi. 136, the building of Caesarea was completed in Herod's twenty-eighth year, or 10 B.C. The latter passage states that it took ten years to complete the city but the former that it took twelve years. This is to be preferred (Schürer, i, 368–9, 389). This would mean that he began to rebuild it in 22 B.C. In addition, Josephus states that the arrival in Rome of Herod's sons was the occasion of Augustus' bestowing upon Herod the territories of Trachonitis, Batanaea, and Auranitis (*Ant.* xv. 343). According to *BJ* i. 398, this took place after September, 24 B.C. Therefore, as Otto (cols. 70–1 and n.) rightly concludes, the journey could not have been earlier than 22 B.C.
[5] For a discussion on Herod's wills, cf. Appendix I.
[6] Jos. *Ant.* xv. 361–404; *BJ* i. 538–51.
[7] Jos. *BJ* i. 241, 432–3.

9

approximately 12/11 B.C.[1] Antipater was made joint heir with Alexander and Aristobulus;[2] but after their death he became the sole heir and co-ruler with his father.[3] In due course Herod became suspicious of Antipater also, and appointed heir to the throne his youngest son, Antipas, whom Malthace, a Samaritan, had borne to him (*ca.* 5 B.C.).[4] He passed over the two elder brothers – Philip, a half brother to Antipas by Cleopatra of Jerusalem, and Archelaus, his full brother – because Antipater had raised suspicions against them in Herod's mind.

Finally, after a severe illness, Herod passed away in March/ April 4 B.C.[5] Only four or five days before his death, he ordered

---

[1] Cf. Schürer, I, 371; T. Corbishley, 'The Chronology of the Reign of Herod the Great', *JTS*, XXXVI (1935), 30–2.

[2] Jos. *Ant.* xvi. 133; *BJ* i. 458.

[3] Jos. *Ant.* xvii. 3.

[4] Jos. *Ant.* xvii. 146; *BJ* i. 646.

[5] Jos. *Ant.* xvii. 191–2; *BJ* i. 665–9. Regarding the date, see Schürer, I, 415–17 n. 167 and Corbishley, *JTS*, XXXVI, 32. According to Finegan (p. 231) Herod's death took place between 12 March and 11 April in the year 4 B.C. Lewin states that it occurred on 1 April 4 B.C. (cf. Lewin, p. 125). For an ingenious but unconvincing chronology of the reign of Herod the Great, see W. E. Filmer, 'The Chronology of the Reign of Herod the Great', *JTS*, N.S. XVII (1966), 283–98. According to Filmer (pp. 296–8), Herod died in January 1 B.C., but this is improbable for the following reasons. First, in order to fit the nine or ten year reign of Archelaus (Jos. *Ant.* xvii. 342; *BJ* ii. 111), Filmer has Archelaus begin his rule while Herod was still alive, this being based on the very weak evidence that Archelaus had long exercised royal authority (*BJ* ii. 26). Other things said by Josephus, especially regarding the sorting out of Herod the Great's will, do not substantiate this view. Secondly, Filmer has to charge Josephus with error in stating that Philip died both in the twentieth year of Tiberius and 'after' thirty-seven years of his own rule over his tetrarchy (*Ant.* xviii. 106). It is true that Josephus does not place this information in the right chronological order, but this he fails to do in other places as well (cf. below, pp. 93–4). Finally, the latest coins of Antipas are dated with the year ΜΓ or 43 (for a discussion of this date, cf. below, pp. 262–3 n. 4). According to Filmer's conjecture, Antipas would have been exiled in A.D. 42. This would mean that Claudius and not Gaius banned Antipas, though for this there is no evidence whatever (cf. Jos. *Ant.* xviii. 252; *BJ* ii. 183). Also, Antipas' territory was given to Agrippa during Gaius' and not Claudius' reign (Jos. *Ant.* xviii. 252; xix. 351; Philo *Leg.* 326). For these reasons, Filmer's theory will not stand. Most probably Herod's death was in the spring of 4 B.C. Subsequently and independently this was confirmed by an article, which goes into more detail in refuting Filmer's thesis, by T. D. Barnes, 'The Date of Herod's Death', *JTS*, N.S. XIX (1968), 204–9.

Antipater's execution and once again changed his mind about the succession. Rather than having Antipas as the sole heir, he divided his domain among his three sons, Archelaus, Philip, and Antipas. The will stating this had to be ratified by the emperor before it became effective. This ratification will be discussed in Chapter 2.

BIRTH

The approximate date of the birth of Herod Antipas can best be determined by a process of elimination. First to be considered is the date of Herod the Great's marriage to Malthace, the Samaritan mother of Archelaus and Antipas.[1] Since Josephus never mentions when Herod's marriage to Malthace occurred, it is essential to note when he was married to the wife before and the wife after her, and in this way to work from the known to the unknown.

According to Josephus, Herod's wife before Malthace was a second Mariamme (hereafter designated Mariamme II), daughter of Simon the high priest.[2] The date of this marriage can be determined with fair precision. It occurred about the same time as he built the royal palace, that is, in 23 B.C.[3] From this marriage was a son Herod (Philip) who may well have been born sometime in 23.

The wife after Malthace was, according to Josephus' list, Cleopatra of Jerusalem.[4] Apparently he married her while he

---

[1] Jos. *Ant.* xvii. 20; *BJ* i. 562.

[2] *Ibid.* Cf. also *Ant.* xv. 319–21.

[3] Jos. *Ant.* xv. 317–21; cf. Otto, cols. 71 n., 131; F.-M. Abel, *Histoire de la Palestine*, EB, 1 (Paris, 1952), 365.

[4] Jos. *Ant.* xvii. 21; *BJ* i. 562. That one can consider Josephus' list of wives as being chronological is doubted by Otto (cols. 131–2, 200). He argues that when Herod made his fifth will, he passed over his eldest sons (τῶν πρεσβυτάτων), Archelaus and Philip, and appointed his youngest son (τῷ νεωτάτῳ), Antipas, as his successor (Jos. *BJ* i. 646; *Ant.* xvii. 146 [regarding the order of Herod's wills, see Appendix I]). Therefore, since the eldest sons were Archelaus and Philip, Otto concludes that Mariamme II was not married to Herod before Malthace and Cleopatra. The argument is not as strong as it first appears. First of all, when Archelaus and Philip are designated as the eldest sons, this would refer only to those candidates who would be eligible as his successors. Since this would automatically have cancelled out Antipater and Herod (Philip) (he was excluded from the fourth will because of his involvement in the plot against Herod the Great, cf. *Ant.* xvii.

was still married to Malthace, for one receives the impression from Josephus that both Archelaus and Philip were older than Antipas.[1] Herod, therefore, seems to have married Cleopatra soon after he married Malthace. Thus, if he married Mariamme II early in 23 B.C., he may well have married Malthace in late 23 or early 22 and Cleopatra in 22. This would mean that Archelaus may have been born sometime in 22 B.C. and Philip, at the earliest, later in the same year. The words τῶν πρεσβυτάτων, used in conjunction with Archelaus and Philip, and the words τῷ νεωτάτῳ,[2] used in conjunction with Antipas, would imply that there was at least a noticeable age gap between Archelaus and Philip on the one hand and Antipas on the other. In all probability, therefore, Antipas was not born earlier than 20 B.C.

EDUCATION

How do the above dates for the three brothers fit with other considerations? They seem to fit very well. One must ask at

78; *BJ* i. 600), Archelaus and Philip would have been left as the oldest valid candidates. Therefore, just because Herod (Philip) is not mentioned in this context, one cannot conclude that he was younger than Archelaus and Philip. If this were true then one could also use this same argument to prove that Antipater was younger than Archelaus and Philip. Secondly, there is no good reason for denying that Josephus' lists of Herod's wives are in chronological order. The order in both lists agrees except for the two wives who are unknown. Since nothing is known of them and they had no offspring, they were unimportant to Josephus. This may be the reason for his placing them at the end of the list in *BJ*. In *Ant.* they are mentioned immediately after Mariamme II, which may indicate that they were married to Herod during the same period that he was married to Mariamme II. Or possibly since they were so insignificant, he may have remembered only that they were married sometime around Herod's marriage to Mariamme II. Or may it be that they were married to him during the seven-year interval between Mariamme I and Mariamme II, but that, when listing the wives, he forgot to include them? On coming to Mariamme II's name it may have entered his mind that Herod had married two other wives also without offspring. He may not have been sure when exactly this happened. In conclusion, then, it is reasonable to believe that Josephus' lists are chronologically correct. Naturally he never mentions Mariamme I because he had just finished a long narrative concerning her and her two sons, the latter having just been executed by Herod.

[1] Jos. *BJ* i. 646; *Ant.* xvii. 146.

[2] Nicolaus of Damascus designates Antipas as only νεώτερος; *FGH*, IIa, 424 (90 frag. 136. 9).

what age Herod sent his sons to Rome and how long they stayed there. It was about 22 B.C.[1] when he sent his sons, Alexander and Aristobulus, to Rome.[2] This would mean that they were about thirteen years old, the age at which a boy became Bar Mitzvah, that is, of an age to assume religious duties. According to Josephus, they had completed their studies when Herod fetched them from Rome.[3] This occurred around 17 (or 16) B.C.[4] which would mean that they stayed in Rome for about five (or six) years.

A similar programme of education in Rome can be outlined for Archelaus and Philip. For them to have gone to Rome when they were thirteen years old would mean that they would have needed to leave Palestine around 10 B.C.[5] This fits well, for it was at about that time that Archelaus, king of Cappadocia, came to Jerusalem and reconciled Herod with his sons, Alexander and Aristobulus.[6] After the reconciliation, Herod made a full report to Augustus, apparently going to Rome himself.[7] What better time would there have been to send Archelaus and Philip to Rome? Thus, that Herod sent them for schooling in Rome about 10 B.C. is plausible. They were called back to

[1] Above, p. 9 n. 4.   [2] Jos. *Ant.* xv. 342–3.

[3] *Ant.* xvi. 6.

[4] Schürer (I, 370) states that it occurred in 18 or 17 B.C. This he bases on the fact that it had to occur between the summer of 19 B.C. and the summer of 16 B.C. because Augustus was outside of Italy before and after those dates. It is felt by Corbishley (*JTS*, XXXVI, 27–9) that it occurred in the years 17 or 16 B.C., and this for three reasons. First, since Herod did not marry Mariamme I before the spring of 37 B.C., her eldest son could not have been born much before the end of the same year, and her second son not earlier than 35. They would, therefore, have been twenty-one and nineteen years of age respectively on completing their studies. Secondly, he feels, on the basis of *BJ* i. 427, that Herod accepted the post of president for the quadrennial celebration, which coincided with his visit to Rome. Corbishley shows that 16 or 12 B.C. are the only possible years, and that 16 is the most likely. Thirdly, in *Ant.* xvi. 11, Josephus states that the two sons were married soon after their return to Judaea, yet before they were estranged from their father. Because of the quarrels with his two sons, Herod brought Antipater, son of Doris, back into favour, this occurring in the autumn of 14 B.C. Hence, he concludes that their marriages took place in 15. These, then, are the reasons for placing Herod's first journey to Rome in 17 (or 16) B.C.

[5] *Contra*, Schürer, I, 408.

[6] Jos. *Ant.* xvi. 261–70; *BJ* i. 498–512.

[7] Jos. *Ant.* xvi. 271; cf. also Schürer, I, 373.

Palestine about seven months after Herod had heard of Antipater's plot which was uncovered in the middle or end of 5 B.C.[1] This would mean that they, like their two older brothers, were in Rome for about five years and were about seventeen years of age when they returned to Palestine.

But what about Antipas? His early education was at home[2] where from an early age[3] great emphasis was laid on the Scriptures and the Law for every Jewish boy.[4] After this he went for the completion of his education to Rome,[5] where he would gain a knowledge of Hellenism and Roman policies. He would have been too young to have departed for Rome at the same time as Archelaus and Philip, since at that time he would have been only ten years of age. However, an incident occurred later which provided an opportune time for Antipas to journey to Rome for his education. At Rome, in 8 B.C., Syllaeus, the Arabian administrator, unjustly accused Herod of invading Arabia, and was able thereby to bring Herod into grave disfavour with Augustus.[6] After receiving a harsh letter from the emperor, Herod sent him envoys to plead his case but they were sent back home unsuccessful. Finally, Herod sent Nicolaus of Damascus to Rome, and he gained for Herod reconciliation with Augustus.[7] Nicolaus' departure from Rome may well have been in late 8 or early 7 B.C. Since Antipas would have been twelve or thirteen years old when Nicolaus departed, what better time could there have been for Antipas to leave Palestine for Rome in order to complete his education?

[1] Jos. *Ant.* xvii. 80–2; *BJ* i. 603.

[2] According to Acts 13: 1 Manaen was the σύντροφος Ἡρῴδου τοῦ τετράρχου. The term σύντροφος can have the meaning of 'foster brother' but it is better understood as 'courtier' or 'intimate friend' (MM, p. 615). It carries the idea of 'playmate' or 'companion in education', meaning that they attended the same schools for their education, cf. A. Deissmann, *Bible Studies*[2], trans. by A. Grieve (Edinburgh, 1903), pp. 311–12.

[3] Jos. *Ap.* ii. 178: 'From our first consciousness' (ἀπὸ τῆς πρώτης εὐθὺς αἰσθήσεως); Philo *Leg.* 210: 'From the earliest age' (ἐκ πρώτης ἡλικίας).

[4] Cf. Jos. *Ant.* iv. 209–11; *Ap.* i. 60; TB: B.B. 21 a. For implications of this, cf. Ket. ii. 10; Kid. iv. 13; Shab. i. 3.

[5] Jos. *Ant.* xvii. 20.

[6] Jos. *Ant.* xvi. 280–92. For the date, cf. Schürer, I, 373; B. Z. Wacholder, *Nicolaus of Damascus*, vol. LXXV of the *University of California Publications in History* (Berkeley and Los Angeles, 1962), p. 32.

[7] Jos. *Ant.* xvi. 293–9, 335–56; cf. also *FGH*, IIa, 423 (90 frag. 136. 1).

When Herod sent his eldest sons to Rome they stayed in the house of Pollio.[1] Feldman has argued, with a high degree of probability, that this was the celebrated orator, poet, and historian, Asinius Pollio, and that he was friendly towards Judaism.[2] It may be that Pollio or Herod hired a Jewish attendant to look after them, but Pollio would have been their instructor. This would confirm the incidental remark of Josephus that Archelaus and Antipas were brought up by a certain Jew.[3] For them to have been brought up while in Rome in a home that was hostile to Judaism would, as Willrich suggests, have aroused a scandal in Palestine.[4] Hence, it is possible that while in Rome Antipas was brought up by a certain Jew, and was instructed by Asinius Pollio, as his brothers had been.

Since Josephus only once mentions Antipas' being in Rome, Willrich believes that this was an error on Josephus' part, and that he did not receive his education in Rome at all.[5] It is true, as Willrich points out, that Josephus has erred with regard to the Herod family,[6] but this does not prove that he was in error at this point. Josephus does not contradict himself here. Willrich points out that Antipater always made his accusations against Archelaus and Philip, passing over Antipas, from which he concludes that Antipas was not in Rome.[7] However, there are reasons for this. During Antipater's first stay in Rome,[8] he made no accusations against anyone except against his rivals Alexander and Aristobulus.[9] This led to the trial, and finally to the execution, of these two men in 7 B.C. After their death Herod the Great made a new will, and shortly after, in

---

[1] Jos. *Ant.* xv. 342–3.

[2] L. H. Feldman, 'Asinius Pollio and his Jewish Interests', *TAPA*, LXXXIV (1953), 73–80. For a study of Pollio, although there is no mention of his relationships with the Herods, see J. André, *La vie et l'œuvre d'Asinius Pollion*, vol. VIII of *Études et Commentaires* (Paris, 1949).

[3] *Ant.* xvii. 20: παρά τινι Ἰουδαίῳ τροφὰς εἶχον.

[4] P. 117. Willrich believes that Pollio was not Asinius Pollio but probably a Jew of that name (cf. Minkin, pp. 173, 257; Otto, cols. 106–7).

[5] P. 189.

[6] E.g. once he states that Philip was a full brother of Archelaus (*Ant.* xvii. 189).

[7] P. 189.

[8] Antipater went to Rome in 13 B.C. accompanying Agrippa (Jos. *Ant.* xvi. 86; Dio liv. 28. 1).

[9] Cf. Jos. *Ant.* xvi. 78–90; *BJ* i. 448–51.

about 6 B.C., Antipater returned to Rome.[1] As far as Antipater was concerned, his new rivals were Archelaus and Philip. Consequently, both before and after his arrival in Rome, he invented devious ways to injure them.[2] Since they were now sixteen or seventeen years old,[3] they would have been more of a threat to Antipater than Antipas, who was a couple of years younger and had arrived in Rome only a year or two before. Archelaus' and Philip's return to Palestine in 5 B.C. caused Antipater the greatest uneasiness.[4] For now it would be difficult for him to slander them. With Antipas still remaining in Rome for his education, Antipater had no cause to worry about him.

In conclusion, then, Willrich has given a conjecture that is not acceptable. The reason for Antipater's passing over Antipas was the fact that he was too young to be considered a serious rival. Rather were his rivals Archelaus and Philip, and on them he now concentrated as formerly, when they were alive, he had concentrated on Alexander and Aristobulus. No doubt, if Archelaus and Philip had returned to Palestine, Antipater could keep a close watch on him and had no need to worry. His great concern was that the other two brothers had returned, and this as he well knew could be troublesome. In this situation it seems reasonable for him to have passed over Antipas.

After discovering Antipater's intrigues against him, Herod recalled him to Palestine. Upon his return he was tried and cast into prison, and the matter was reported to the emperor.[5] Before Herod received a reply, he fell ill and made his fifth will,[6] in which he passed over Archelaus and Philip against whom Antipater had poisoned his mind, and chose Antipas as his sole successor.[7] This all occurred in 5 B.C.[8]

---

[1] Jos. *Ant.* xvii. 52–3; *BJ* i. 573.

[2] Jos. *Ant.* xvii. 80–2; *BJ* i. 602–5.

[3] Josephus (*BJ* i. 602) describes Archelaus and Philip as 'growing lads with full manly spirits' (μειράκιά τε ἤδη καὶ φρονήματος μεστοί).

[4] Jos. *BJ* i. 603: καὶ τοῦτο ἦν τὸ μάλιστα ταράσσον ᾿Αντίπατρον. For chronological data, cf. above, pp. 12–14.

[5] Jos. *Ant.* xvii. 60–133, 144–5; *BJ* i. 582–640. Regarding the trial and its sources, see E. Täubler, 'Zur Beurteilung der constantinischen Excerpte', *Byzantinische Zeitschrift*, xxv (1925), 33–6.

[6] Cf. Appendix I.

[7] Jos. *Ant.* xvii. 146; *BJ* i. 464.   [8] Schürer, I, 374.

At what time Antipas returned home is unknown. He was home at the time of his father's death in the spring of 4 B.C.[1] Possibly, on making the will in which he nominated him as his sole successor, Herod recalled him to Palestine in order to talk with him. He, being sick and nearly seventy years old, may have realized he had not long to live. This would mean that Antipas returned in late 5 or early 4 B.C. If this is the case, he would only have been in Rome for about two and a half to three years (only half the length of his brothers) and would have been only sixteen years old when he returned to Palestine.

Only four or five days before his death, Herod again changed his will and included Archelaus and Philip in addition to Antipas. Possibly he realized that he had been unjust to them. Also, now that death was close at hand, he may have felt that Antipas was too young to be the sole ruler of such a large domain, an arrangement which in any case would probably have been unacceptable to the Roman government.

Antipas, then, though born of a Samaritan mother, was chosen as one of Herod the Great's successors. This only needed to be ratified by the emperor.

[1] Cf. Jos. *Ant.* xvii. 198, 224; *BJ* i. 672; ii. 20.

CHAPTER 2

ANTIPAS' STRUGGLE FOR
THE KINGDOM

Both Antipas and Archelaus struggled to be the sole heir of
Herod the Great. This chapter will discuss Antipas' attempt to
obtain this position.

HEROD'S RIGHT TO MAKE A WILL

The basic requirement before a Roman tribunal for the validity of a will made in accordance with Roman law was that the
author of the will be a Roman citizen.[1] Although it is nowhere
explicitly stated, it can be assumed that Herod the Great had
Roman citizenship, on the grounds that he must have inherited
it[2] from his father, Antipater.[3] Certainly, to have been designated
by Antony and Octavian with the Senate's approval as king in

---

[1] According to Roman law the fundamental prerequisite for making a will
and thus choosing one's successor was that of being a Roman citizen up to
the time of death (*Gai Inst.* ii. 112; ii. 147; *Ulp. Reg.* xx. 10–16; *Ius. Inst.* ii.
17. 6).

[2] Legally the rights of citizenship passed only to the son if he were con-
ceived after the father became a citizen, or if at the time of conferment this
addition was applied for and included in the concessions (cf. *Gai Inst.* i. 93,
94; ii. 135 a; iii. 20). There is no specific record either of Antipater applying
for this or later of Herod the Great applying for it. Hence it seems best to
assume that the emperor included the children as citizens along with their
father. This gave Antipater *potestas* over his children, but it did not end there;
it included also his grandchildren by all descendants through the male line
(cf. *Gai Inst.* iii. 2), though not through the female line (cf. *Gai Inst.* iii.
71).

[3] Roman citizenship was granted to Antipater in 47 B.C. by Julius Caesar
in Syria after the latter had won the war against the Egyptians with Antipater's help (cf. Jos. *Ant.* xiv. 127–37; *BJ* i. 187–94; this is again reiterated
in *Ant.* xvi. 53, where it states that the citizenship was approved by the
Senate). Since the latter reference comes in an address by Nicolaus of Damascus to Agrippa on behalf of the Jews of Ionia, it may well be that Nicolaus
here condenses the history, combining both Antipater's being given Roman
citizenship by Caesar and his being designated ruler over Palestine by both
Caesar and the Senate.

40 B.C.[1] and to be considered one of the emperor's best and most loyal friends,[2] it would seem unlikely for Herod not to have been a Roman citizen.

Herod's citizenship being only assumed, the best indication of his right to make a will is that on several occasions Augustus specifically told him that he could designate his successor.[3]

THE DISPUTE OVER HEROD'S WILL[4]

Introduction

As soon as Herod died, Ptolemy, to whom the king had entrusted his signet-ring, read the codicils[5] which designated Archelaus as king and Philip and Antipas as tetrarchs. All that was needed was the emperor's ratification.[6] Realizing that Herod's last will and testament did not have the emperor's ratification, Archelaus did not accept the title of king or allow himself to be crowned.[7] He did however assume the leadership. This being the situation, the people began to make demands, with which Archelaus complied in order to ingratiate himself with them. There were, however, revolutionaries among the crowd who were out to revenge the blood of those whom Herod had killed

---

[1] Jos. *Ant.* xiv. 382–5; *BJ* i. 282–5; Strabo xvi. 2. 46; Appian *BC* v. 75; Tac. *Hist.* v. 9.

[2] Jos. *Ant.* xv. 199. According to *Ant.* xv. 361 and *BJ* i. 400, Augustus gave Herod first place in his friendship after his deputy Agrippa (cf. also *Ant.* xvi. 61). Although it is not expressly stated, he may have had the official title of φίλος τοῦ καίσαρος or *amicus principis* (for a discussion of this, see J. Crook, *Consilium Principis* [Cambridge, 1955], pp. 21–30). This may be deduced from the fact that when Augustus believed Syllaeus' false report about Herod's attack on the Arabs (Jos. *Ant.* xvi. 286–9), Augustus wrote Herod a harsh letter to the effect that he could no longer treat him as a friend but only as a subject (ὅτι πάλαι χρώμενος αὐτῷ φίλῳ, νῦν ὑπηκόῳ χρήσεται), cf. *Ant.* xvi. 290. Nicolaus went to Rome in order to reconcile Augustus and Herod (*Ant.* xvi. 338), and this was finally accomplished when Augustus apologized for writing so harshly to one who was his φίλος (cf. *Ant.* xvi. 352). For a discussion of Herod's relationship to the emperor, see E. Bammel, 'Die Rechtsstellung des Herodes', *ZDPV*, LXXXIV (1968), 73–9.

[3] Jos. *Ant.* xv. 343; xvi. 92–9, 129, 133 (cf. *BJ* i. 454, 458).

[4] Josephus' source for the trial is undoubtedly Nicolaus of Damascus, cf. G. Hölscher, *Die Quellen des Josephus* (Leipzig, 1904), pp. 31–2; Hölscher, PW, IX, 1977; cf. also Täubler, *Byzantinische Zeitschrift*, xxv, 36–40.

[5] Jos. *BJ* i. 668; *Ant.* xvii. 195.

[6] Jos. *Ant.* xvii. 194–5; *BJ* i. 668–9.

[7] Jos. *Ant.* xvii. 202–3; *BJ* ii. 2–3.

for cutting down the eagle from the temple gate. Archelaus, wanting to prevent an uprising of the mob at the Passover, sent out his army and killed 3,000 people.[1]

He then departed for Rome, taking with him his mother (Malthace), Poplas (or Ptollas), Ptolemy, Nicolaus, and Salome who brought also her children and many of Archelaus' relatives. This she did ostensibly to support his cause but in reality to accuse him of the recent incidents in the temple.

While they were in Rome, Philip took care of the home front.[2] Although halted momentarily by Varus, Sabinus, imperial procurator (or finance officer) of the province of Syria, journeyed to Jerusalem and took possession of the palace. There he tried to search into the accounts and take possession of the citadels, but Archelaus' men, who guarded these, would not submit to him on the pretext that they were guarding them for the emperor.[3]

Antipas also sailed to Rome with the claim that Herod's fifth will had greater validity than the codicils. His supporters were his mother, Ptolemy (brother of Nicolaus and not the same one who read the codicils) who had been won over to him, Salome who promised her support,[4] and Irenaeus his advocate.[5]

---

[1] Jos. *Ant.* xvii. 206–18; *BJ* ii. 5–13. Nicolaus of Damascus likewise records the number of Jews massacred by Archelaus, only he states that more than 10,000 participated in the revolt, see *FGH*, iia, 424 (90 frag. 136. 8–9).

[2] Jos. *Ant.* xvii. 219–20; *BJ* ii. 14–15.

[3] Jos. *Ant.* xvii. 221–3; *BJ* ii. 16–19.

[4] It must be remembered that Salome and her relatives went to Rome with the express purpose of opposing Archelaus, hoping thereby to improve their position at his expense. She and the relatives only joined up with Antipas because they felt that it would be impossible to be under Roman rule without one of the two brothers, and Antipas was the lesser of two evils (cf. Jos. *Ant.* xvii. 220, 227; *BJ* ii. 15, 22). In *Ant.* xvii. 227 and *BJ* ii. 22 Josephus states that Salome joined up with Antipas before he went to Rome. Otto (col. 176) suggests that this is a later development placed in an earlier context. But is it not more likely that she made an agreement with Antipas before going to Rome, thus securing some advantage in case her cause was lost? It was in fact her encouragement which prompted Antipas to try for the throne.

[5] Jos. *Ant.* xvii. 224–6; *BJ* ii. 20–1. According to Nicolaus of Damascus, Antipas went to Rome on the same ship as Archelaus, and already on the ship all the relatives were siding with Antipas against Archelaus. It may be here that Salome began to intrigue for her own ends, cf. *FGH*, iia, 424 (90 frag. 136. 9).

Antipas' confidence in obtaining the throne rested on Irenaeus' skill as an advocate. On arriving in Rome, he was advised to yield to Archelaus on the grounds of the latter's rights of seniority and his being named king in the final will, but this advice Antipas refused. Due to his persistence, many came over to his side. This they did only because they preferred Antipas to Archelaus in the event that they were unable to secure autonomy under the administration of a Roman governor.[1]

Reconstruction of the trial

Preliminaries before the trial

Before the actual trial, Augustus had received letters from Sabinus[2] and Salome and her friends containing indictments against Archelaus. Antipas also sent letters in his own defence. To this Archelaus responded by sending to Augustus both the statements of his right to the throne and his father's testament. He also sent Ptolemy with the accounts of Herod's property sealed with Herod's own seal. Varus and Sabinus submitted accounts of the amount of property and the size of the annual revenue. With all these reports Augustus privately reflected on the whole situation. After this he summoned a council of leading Romans to give a hearing to the two parties.[3]

Antipas' case

In reconstructing the trial only those things will be considered which are relevant to Antipas' attempt to gain the throne. It is Antipas' case which must be considered for it was he who was contending for a position which once he had been promised. He believed he had good reasons for contending for this position. The reasons why he believed he had a good case, and why he lost it, will now be stated.

---

[1] Jos. *Ant.* xvii. 226–7; *BJ* ii. 21–2.

[2] Sabinus' dislike for Archelaus is due probably to an incident at Caesarea just prior to Archelaus' departure for Rome. Being the imperial financial officer for Syria, Sabinus intended to confiscate the property of the deceased king. Due, however, to Archelaus' friend Varus (Jos. *Ant.* xvii. 303; cf. also *BJ* ii. 83) he was prevented from carrying out his purpose (*Ant.* xvii. 221–3; *BJ* ii. 16–19). It would be natural, on this account, for Sabinus to send an unfavourable report on Archelaus to the emperor.

[3] Jos. *Ant.* xvii. 228–30; *BJ* ii. 22–5.

The reasons for contending against Archelaus. If Antipas had not believed he had good reasons for making a claim for the throne, he would not have come all the way to Rome. From the narrative one can deduce several reasons why Antipas believed he could win the case. First, Salome and Irenaeus had convinced him that the will in which Herod designated him as king had greater validity than the codicils which designated Archelaus as king.[1] This was also mentioned by Antipater, the son of Salome, who defended Antipas against Archelaus.[2] Actually it was only a small part of Antipater's defence. He also stated that when Herod designated Antipas as king, he was in good physical and mental health, whereas when he named Archelaus as king he was stricken both in mind and body, and was incapable of sound reasoning. He knew that Roman law specified that a lunatic or one out of his mind (*furiosus*) could not make a valid will, whereas a will made prior to insanity was deemed valid.[3] Antipater did not state it so strongly since this would have been dangerous; nevertheless the implication was clear, and Nicolaus of Damascus, in his rebuttal, caught the significance of it.[4]

Although *Pauli Sententiae*, *Ulpiani Liber Singularis Regularum*, and *Iustiniani Institutiones* are works of the second and third century A.D., many of the laws contained therein must embody either law or custom going back several centuries.[5] Certainly Nicolaus of Damascus, in his defence, strongly argues that Herod was of a sound mind when he wrote the codicils, in that he was sane enough to cede his authority to Augustus, and not to be mistaken over his selection of an heir. From the importance attached to proving Herod's sanity, it seems clear that this part of the Roman law was in effect at that time.[6]

[1] Jos. *Ant.* xvii. 224–6; not as explicit in *BJ* ii. 20–1.

[2] Jos. *Ant.* xvii. 238; *BJ* ii. 31–2.

[3] *Pauli Sententiae* iii. 4*a*, 5, 11; *Ulp. Reg.* xx. 13; *Ius. Inst.* ii. 12. 1; cf. W. W. Buckland, *A Text-Book of Roman Law from Augustus to Justinian*[3], rev. by P. Stein (Cambridge, 1963), p. 289.

[4] Jos. *Ant.* xvii. 246–7; *BJ* ii. 35–6.

[5] Cf. Buckland, pp. 52–5; H. F. Jolowicz, *Historical Introduction to the Study of Roman Law*[2] (Cambridge, 1952), pp. 5–6.

[6] *The Twelve Tables* (v. 7) which were written *ca.* 450 B.C. state that the property of a lunatic was to be managed by a guardian. Thus, a man lost control over his property when he was not in his right mind. This may be the origin of the Roman law specifying that insanity invalidated a man's will.

The second reason why Antipas considered that he had a strong case was that he apparently had more support behind him than had Archelaus. Nicolaus' brother, Ptolemy, had been won over to his side.[1] He was one of Herod the Great's closest friends, and Antipas expected his influence to be especially beneficial. Another influential person was the advocate, Irenaeus,[2] in whose reputation for eloquence Antipas had great confidence. He also had the support of Salome and all the relatives. Though really favouring direct Roman rule, because they did not want Archelaus as king, they were content to join forces with Antipas. This was more out of hatred for Archelaus than out of love for his rival. Finally, Sabinus favoured Antipas and to this effect wrote a letter to Augustus.[3]

The third reason was Archelaus' questionable conduct after the death of Herod. Both Josephus in his record[4] and Antipater in his speech before Augustus state that he badly mishandled the uprising in Jerusalem at the Passover festival.[5] Much of the accusation hinged on the question of Archelaus' acting as king before the emperor had conferred this title upon him. Nicolaus of Damascus came to his defence by saying that the revolt was against the emperor rather than Archelaus, and that the opposition had done nothing to help the situation.[6]

These, then, are the reasons that Antipas believed he had a good case against Archelaus.

The reasons for losing the case. Augustus finally decided that Archelaus should receive the higher title and Antipas that of tetrarch. Why did this happen? There would seem to be at least seven reasons.

The first is that Salome's purpose in going to Rome was not to put Antipas on the throne but to keep Archelaus off the throne. Ostensibly she went to Rome together with other of Herod the Great's relatives, to help Archelaus, but actually to work against him and to accuse him of the recent illegal actions at the temple.[7] It is interesting to notice that none of Antipas'

---

[1] Jos. *Ant.* xvii. 225; *BJ* ii. 21.   [2] Jos. *Ant.* xvii. 226–7; *BJ* ii. 21–2.
[3] Jos. *BJ* ii. 23.   [4] *Ant.* xvii. 206–18; *BJ* ii. 5–13.
[5] Jos. *Ant.* xvii. 230–9; *BJ* ii. 26–32.
[6] Jos. *Ant.* xvii. 240–2; *BJ* ii. 34–5.
[7] Jos. *Ant.* xvii. 220; *BJ* ii. 15.

relatives went to his defence out of goodwill for him but only because they hated Archelaus. What they wanted most of all was autonomous rule under a Roman governor.[1] A situation such as this could not have been of any benefit to Antipas. It is probable that the relatives mentioned as travelling with Salome and the relatives who wanted autonomous rule were the same people, and that their leader was Salome.

How were Salome and her party to accomplish their end? First, it must be remembered that the odds were in favour of Archelaus, for Herod's last will had designated him as king. In this same will Salome was given Jamnia, Azotus, and Phasaelis, and 500,000 pieces of coined silver, and all the relatives were given expensive gifts and the assignment of revenues. All these assignments notwithstanding, still Archelaus was king! Salome did not like him for he had himself taken complete control in Palestine, while she was not at all involved in the running of affairs. Moreover, she and her husband had been compelled to relinquish to Archelaus the control of the army which they had enjoyed after Herod's death.[2] Also, she did not like his performance as a leader in the way he handled the revolt during the Passover, when 3,000 were killed at the temple which her brother had rebuilt.[3] After all, there had been no trouble when she was in control. Furthermore, her attitude may have been influenced, in some degree, by Antipater, son of Doris, who had denounced Archelaus, along with Philip, when he was receiving his education in Rome.[4] The fact is, one of Antipater's wives was a grand-daughter of Salome![5] Josephus' statement that Salome's son, Antipater, was very

---

[1] Jos. *Ant.* xvii. 227; *BJ* ii. 22. It may be contended that the relatives mentioned in this section were not the same as Herod the Great's relatives mentioned in former passages. However, Antipas and Archelaus being full brothers would have had only one set of relatives and only those from their father's side would have gone to Rome. Their mother, Malthace, was a Samaritan and there is no mention of her family being involved in the present dispute.

[2] Jos. *Ant.* xvii. 194; *BJ* i. 666.

[3] Jos. *Ant.* xvii. 213–18; *BJ* ii. 10–13.

[4] Jos. *Ant.* xvii. 79–81; *BJ* i. 602–3.

[5] Jos. *Ant.* xvii. 18; *BJ* i. 565. This is guilt by association. Only Philip and Archelaus were mentioned by Antipater and Antipas' name was never mentioned in this context.

hostile to Archelaus[1] further indicates that this family had no love for Archelaus.

The best way she could obtain power for herself was by having a contender for the same title as that for which Archelaus was contending, and who could serve better than Antipas, who had been so named in the previous will? He was furious at being stripped of his power and was thus a willing tool in Salome's hands.[2] By furnishing him with promises (ὑποσχέσεσι Σαλώμης ἡρμένος), she convinced him that he could have the government on the grounds that the will which named him was more valid than the codicils (or the sixth will).[3] He, for his part, realized that Salome had much influence in Rome due to her friendship with the empress, Livia.[4] He was also much influenced by Irenaeus.

It is interesting to notice in the first trial that Antipas' advocate was not Irenaeus the brilliant orator, but Antipater, Salome's son.[5] This switch was probably caused by Salome, whose son may have been a part of the conspiracy to gain autonomous rule. In the trial[6] itself Antipater's primary point was Archelaus' conduct after the death of Herod, and his secondary point the last two wills of Herod. It was to convince Augustus of Archelaus' incompetence as the proper successor of Herod and of the invalidity of Herod's last will. In his speech he twice mentioned the slaughter of the 3,000, first in the main body of the speech[7] and then in concluding remarks.[8] This was certainly due to Salome's influence (for such was her purpose in coming to Rome).[9] One other indication of Salome's prodding may be found in Antipater's accusation that Archelaus made revelry during the days of mourning for Herod,[10] for few others would have cared about Archelaus' conduct during that

---

[1] *Ant.* xvii. 230.

[2] Otto (col. 176) also believes that in order for Salome to gain advantage for herself, she desired the two brothers to fight each other. Cf. also, Jones, *Herods*, p. 159.

[3] Jos. *Ant.* xvii. 224; cf. also *BJ* ii. 20.

[4] Jos. *Ant.* xvii. 10, 134–41; xviii. 31; *BJ* i. 566, 641–3; ii. 167.

[5] Jos. *Ant.* xvii. 226, cf. 230; *BJ* ii. 21, cf. 26.

[6] Jos. *Ant.* xvii. 230–47; *BJ* ii. 26–36.

[7] Jos. *Ant.* xvii. 237; *BJ* ii. 30.   [8] Jos. *Ant.* xvii. 239; *BJ* ii. 32.

[9] Jos. *Ant.* xvii. 220; *BJ* ii. 15.

[10] Jos. *Ant.* xvii. 234; *BJ* ii. 29.

time of mourning for the wicked king. Thus the first trial was noticeably influenced by Salome. She was even close to achieving her ends, for Augustus now hesitated to give the kingdom to Archelaus alone, and even contemplated giving it to the whole family.[1]

After Nicolaus' defence of Archelaus, Josephus records the revolt which was occurring in Palestine at that time.[2] After the revolt, Varus allowed a Jewish delegation of fifty to plead for the autonomy of their nation and for its union with the province of Syria. When they arrived in Rome, Josephus states that they were joined by 8,000 Roman Jews. Philip was also sent to help Archelaus, and to seek a share of Herod's estate if Augustus were to divide it among all the descendants.[3] Augustus summoned a new council in the temple of Apollo to hear the Jewish delegation and to make a decision about the distribution of the land.[4] There are three interesting facts in this case. First, Herod's relatives, who had formerly adopted the same policy as this Palestinian delegation, did not side with them, at least publicly, because they feared that Augustus might punish them as he had so recently punished those of Herod's relatives who had revolted in Palestine.[5] Secondly, the Jewish envoys did speak against Herod's rule,[6] which was designed to satisfy the need of an

---

[1] Jos. *Ant.* xvii. 249; *BJ* ii. 38.

[2] Jos. *Ant.* xvii. 250–98; *BJ* ii. 39–79.

[3] Jos. *Ant.* xvii. 299–303, 314; *BJ* ii. 80–3, 91. According to Josephus, the Jewish delegation demanded direct Roman rule, though according to Nicolaus, they preferred Roman rule but were willing to accept Antipas if that were not possible, cf. *FGH*, IIa, 424 (90 frag. 136. 9). Wacholder (p. 63) thinks that Nicolaus' account is here the more accurate.

[4] According to Crook (cf. pp. 20–36, 104–14), Josephus here illustrates what must have been common in Roman policy. There were two council meetings: the first, in which the *amici* of Caesar gave him advice on the case in point, was more judicial in nature, and the second more public and administrative.

[5] Cf. Jos. *Ant.* xvii. 302 and 298; *BJ* ii. 81–2 and 78.

[6] Jos. *Ant.* xvii. 304–10; *BJ* ii. 84–7. No doubt they only dared to speak so violently against Herod's rule because it was a public meeting (cf. Jos. *Ant.* xvii. 249; *BJ* ii. 38). Who were included in the Jewish delegation it is impossible to know; but, since such vehemence was expressed against Herod the Great's rule, it is possible that a great number of them were the Herod-despising Pharisees. This is beyond the scope of this work, but for an interesting discussion, see G. Allon, 'The Attitude of the Pharisees to the Roman Government and the House of Herod', *SH*, VII (1961), 70–2.

autonomous rule, at the same time accusing Archelaus of the massacre of the 3,000.[1] Moreover, according to Nicolaus of Damascus, the Jewish delegation was willing to consent to Antipas' rule if direct Roman rule were impossible.[2] This was the identical aim of Salome. Therefore, although Salome may not have publicly endorsed the envoys, it seems very likely that she worked behind the scenes. This is not to say that she fully endorsed everything that was said, especially against her brother. Thirdly, there was no defence by Antipas. It may be that Salome advised him not to defend himself because Livia had informed her that the emperor favoured Archelaus. But could it not be that Salome, feeling that she did not need him any more and that now she had a large enough delegation which shared her views, prevented him from having a hearing?

In conclusion, Salome was a main factor in preventing Antipas from winning his position as stated in Herod's fifth will. Although she only used him to counteract Archelaus and to achieve her own ends of gaining more power under the guise of autonomous rule, she nevertheless convinced him that he could win the case. If she could not gain autonomous rule, she preferred Antipas to Archelaus as king. The result of the trial was not autonomous rule, but she did gain more than originally stated in Herod's will (i.e. Jamnia, Azotus, Phasaelis, and 500,000 pieces of coined silver). Augustus gave her the royal palace at Ascalon and the annual revenue of sixty talents.[3] No doubt he gave her estates that were in the territory ruled by Archelaus in order that he would keep her in hand, and so prevent civil war.

The second reason for Antipas losing his case concerns Antipater's defence. In this he demonstrated that Archelaus was not fit to succeed his father, but did not make a strong positive case for Antipas.[4] This fact complements that which is stated above, namely, that it would not have been in Salome's interest to back him too strongly. Antipas, in addition, was too young to

---

[1] Jos. *Ant.* xvii. 311–13; *BJ* ii. 88–90.

[2] *FGH*, IIa, 424 (90 frag. 136. 9).

[3] Jos. *Ant.* xvii. 321; *BJ* ii. 98.

[4] *FGH* IIa, 424 (90 frag. 136. 9): οὐ τῷ νεωτέρῳ [i.e. Antipas] συναγωνι-ζόμενοι. Only Sabinus highly commended him, though of course this would have been of little help, cf. Jos. *BJ* ii. 24.

have established a reputation for leadership. If he had felt that it was his right to rule, certainly he did not manifest it when the Jews revolted; although he may have been suppressed by Archelaus. Or is it possible that at the time of the revolt he had no illusions of this nature, the codicils having been read publicly, and that it was not till later that Salome prodded him into making a bid for the throne?

The third reason for his losing his case is that Archelaus had a stronger one. As regards the revolt, Augustus must have realized the awkward position in which Archelaus had found himself, and that the people had taken advantage of the situation. Archelaus' youth would not have commanded respect. He may not have handled the situation in the best possible manner but he had, after all, been forced to act quickly.[1] As regards Archelaus' conduct after Herod's death, it is not true that he had posed as king, for according to Josephus' narrative, he had been careful not to wear the diadem and would not accept the title of king until the will had been ratified by the emperor.[2] Thus Antipater's accusation that Archelaus had posed as king by wearing the diadem was a lie; while his accusation that he had given orders and had changed the ranks of the army as if he were king, or were making the emperor only a dispenser of titles,[3] was at best an exaggeration. As for the will, Augustus seems to have accepted Nicolaus of Damascus' arguments that Herod was not insane when he made the codicils, and consequently the previous will was invalid.

The fourth reason for Antipas' failure was that Archelaus had more influential support, whereas his own support, though numerous, was of little influence. First, there was Nicolaus of Damascus. He was an 'intimate friend of both Herod the Great and Augustus'.[4] It was he who finally reconciled them when their friendship broke down over Augustus' misunderstanding

---

[1] In the last resort the revolt was against the Roman government, for it was the emperor who gave Herod permission to choose his successor (cf. Jos. *Ant.* xvii. 241; *BJ* ii. 34).

[2] Jos. *Ant.* xvii. 202; *BJ* ii. 2-3.

[3] Jos. *Ant.* xvii. 231-3; *BJ* ii. 26-8.

[4] H. St J. Thackeray, *Josephus: The Man and the Historian* (New York, 1929), p. 40. According to Nicolaus of Damascus' own testimony with regard to the outcome of the trial, Augustus honoured Nicolaus and made Archelaus ethnarch, cf. *FGH*, IIa, 425 (90 frag. 136. 11).

regarding Herod's treatment of the Arabs.[1] He it was who charged Antipater, Herod's son, with his great crimes against his father.[2] He had never lost a case yet! He was a great asset to Archelaus.[3] Then there was Varus, the governor of Syria.[4] He had sat in the trial when Herod accused Antipater of his crimes, and was considered largely responsible for the results of that trial. He too it was who reported it to Rome.[5] It was from Varus, during the hearings in Rome of Herod's wills, that Augustus received news concerning the new revolt of the Jews,[6] and he it was who sent to Augustus the leaders of the revolt.[7] The ringleader was Sabinus[8] who supported Antipas; and Augustus may have suspected that Antipas was a revolutionary like his supporter. Also, the fact that Varus had married a grand-niece of Augustus[9] may have told in Archelaus' favour. His third influential supporter was Ptolemy. He was one of Herod's most honoured friends[10] as well as being his finance minister[11] and later his executor.[12] Although he had no official part in the trial it was he who gave Augustus the accounts of Herod's seal.[13] Thus, among Archelaus' few supporters were

[1] Jos. *Ant.* xvi. 335–50.

[2] Jos. *Ant.* xvii. 99, 106–24; *BJ* i. 637–8.

[3] In fact, according to Nicolaus of Damascus (*FGH*, IIa, 425 [90 frag. 136. 11]), Augustus praised Nicolaus' defence of Archelaus, and certainly the impression one receives from the trial narratives is that Nicolaus was eminently successful in his advocacy. On the other hand, 'Nicolaus' advocacy was not as successful as he or Josephus would like one to believe' (Wacholder, p. 35, cf. also pp. 107–8 n. 206). Archelaus had come to Rome hoping to receive the ὅλη ἀρχή (*FGH*, IIa, 424 [90 frag. 136. 8]) and to be designated as king (Jos. *Ant.* xvii. 188, 226, 317; *BJ* i. 668) but he left Rome only an ethnarch of half of Herod's territory (Jos. *Ant.* xvii. 317, 319, 339; *BJ* ii. 93, 96, 111; *FGH*, IIa, 424–5 [90 frag. 136. 11]).

[4] Jos. *Ant.* xvii. 303; *BJ* ii. 83.

[5] Jos. *Ant.* xvii. 89–91, 93, 120, 127, 131–3; *BJ* i. 617–18, 622–8, 636, 639–40.

[6] Jos. *Ant.* xvii. 250; *BJ* ii. 40.   [7] Jos. *Ant.* xvii. 297; *BJ* ii. 77.

[8] Jos. *Ant.* xvii. 252–3; *BJ* ii. 41. Also Sabinus' escape from Varus gives the impression that he would have had to answer to Varus (*Ant.* xvii. 294; *BJ* ii. 74).

[9] Tac. *Ann.* iv. 66; *Prosopographia Imperii Romani*[2], ed. by E. Groag and A. Stein, II (Berlin and Leipzig, 1936), 268 no. 1116; cf. also W. John, 'P. Quinctilius Varus', PW, XXIV (1963), 964–5.

[10] Jos. *BJ* i. 473; cf. also *Ant.* xiv. 377; *BJ* i. 280.

[11] Jos. *Ant.* xvi. 191; cf. Otto, col. 63.

[12] Jos. *Ant.* xvii. 195; *BJ* i. 667.   [13] Jos. *Ant.* xvii. 228; *BJ* ii. 24.

men who had not only great influence but prior contact with the emperor.

The fifth reason for Antipas' defeat is that he was not favoured by Augustus. According to Josephus, Augustus concluded after the first trial that Archelaus deserved to succeed his father, although he did not pronounce his verdict until later.[1] Could factors other than the trial itself have influenced him? It seems very likely. It must be remembered that while both Archelaus and Antipas were educated in Rome,[2] Archelaus had been there for five years, having presumably completed his education,[3] whereas Antipas seems to have been there for little more than half that time. It is likely that Archelaus was better known to the emperor, not only because of his longer stay in Rome, but also because towards the end of his educational tour, he would probably have attended more of the imperial social gatherings. He may also have been friends with Gaius, Augustus' adopted son, who was not only about his own age but was favoured to succeed the emperor.[4] Although very young he was a very influential person. In addition, Archelaus having completed his education in Rome, Augustus may have felt that he was better versed in Roman politics.

The sixth reason for Antipas' failure is that he was still very young. Augustus most likely would have preferred a distribution of property rather than giving complete control to one so young. He was in fact only sixteen or seventeen years old at Herod's death.

The seventh reason for Antipas losing the case is the probability of an agreement between Nicolaus of Damascus and his brother Ptolemy,[5] who were on opposite sides.[6] In preference

---

[1] Jos. *Ant.* xvii. 248; *BJ* ii. 37. One must, of course, remember Nicolaus' and Josephus' bias, Nicolaus being Archelaus' defence attorney.

[2] Jos. *Ant.* xvii. 20, 80; *BJ* i. 602.

[3] When Alexander and Aristobulus were fetched by Herod the Great, they had been in Rome about five years, and Josephus states that they had completed their education (*Ant.* xvi. 6), cf. above, pp. 12–14, 17.

[4] Jos. *Ant.* xvii. 229; *BJ* ii. 25. Cf. Crook, pp. 32, 110.

[5] He is not to be confused with the other Ptolemy mentioned above (p. 29). Ptolemy, Nicolaus' brother, was also, according to Josephus, one of Herod's 'most honoured friends', and was in Herod's service, cf. *Ant.* xvii. 225; *BJ* ii. 21; cf. also *FGH*, IIa, 326 (testimony 8), 420–1 (90 frag. 131); IIc, 290.

[6] As suggested by Nicolaus, see *FGH*, IIa, 424 (90 frag. 136. 10).

to losing everything to Salome or the relatives,[1] the two attorneys may have agreed between themselves, and with Augustus, to give half of Herod's kingdom to Archelaus, designating him ethnarch and not king, and to appoint Antipas and Philip as tetrarchs of the other half. Jones thinks that this would have been very acceptable to Augustus. Not only would it have reduced friction between the brothers, but it would have reduced Archelaus' responsibility of ruling the entire kingdom of which he had not proved capable initially.[2] Thus this agreement may have prevented Antipas from being named king; it may have also prevented him from losing everything to Salome or the relatives.

In conclusion, although Antipas lost his claim to kingship, he did gain by asserting his cause, and in so doing prevented Archelaus from becoming king of Herod's entire realm.

Results of the trial

Whereas in his last will Herod had specified that Archelaus was to be king over the whole realm, with Antipas and Philip as subordinate tetrarchs, Augustus divided the kingdom between the three brothers. Archelaus received Judaea and Samaria with the title of ethnarch and the promise to be made king if he proved capable of that position. Antipas and Philip became tetrarchs as specified in the codicils.[3]

Usually it is thought that the only significance in Archelaus' title of ethnarch was that he ruled a larger domain than his brothers, and that it was an honour somewhere between tetrarch and king. However, since *ethnarch* means the leader of an ἔθνος, he may have been the representative of all the Jews before Rome and possibly before the Sanhedrin.[4] Hence he may have had oversight of Antipas' and Philip's territories. Nothing of this is specifically mentioned by Josephus, but after 4 B.C. his history of the Herods is rather sketchy. There is a curious statement made by Justin Martyr to the effect that

---

[1] Otto, col. 176. [2] Jones, *Herods*, p. 164.
[3] Cf. Jos. *Ant.* xvii. 188 and 317–18; *BJ* i. 664 and ii. 93–4; *FGH*, IIa, 424–5 (90 frag. 136. 11); Tac. *Hist.* v. 9.
[4] Solomon points out that an ethnarch was not only responsible for the political but also the spiritual leadership of his people, D. Solomon, 'Philo's use of ΓΕΝΑΡΧΗΣ in *In Flaccum*', *JQR*, LXI (1970), 128–30.

Herod (Antipas) succeeded Archelaus and received the authority that was allotted to him.[1] Although this statement is generally regarded as inaccurate, there may be an element of truth
in it. For one thing the source is very early. For another,
Eusebius, in his *Chronica*, reckons the first year of Antipas'
reign from Archelaus' deposition,[2] and in his *Historia Ecclesiastica* states that after Archelaus' death Herod (Antipas) and
Philip administered their own territories.[3] Although the historical validity of Josippon is open to question,[4] there also it is
mentioned that Antipas ruled in Archelaus' stead when the
latter was deposed.[5] Is it not possible then that Archelaus had
oversight of Antipas' and Philip's domains, and acted as
Rome's representative in Palestine? If this be the case, then
Antipas and Philip would not have been entirely free in their
administration until Archelaus' deposition.

On the other hand they were not responsible to Archelaus
alone as seems to have been the case with Herod the Great's
brother, Pheroras, who became the tetrarch of Peraea.[6] Herod
seems to have had complete control over even his brother's
private life,[7] and there is no suggestion that Pheroras could
have appealed to the Roman emperor directly. Since he was
only an ethnarch, Archelaus may have exercised oversight on
his brothers without being allowed to control the tetrarchies as
if they were a part of his kingdom. The line of authority would
have been emperor–ethnarch–tetrarch, but this does not mean

---

[1] *Dial.* ciii. 4 (*MPG*, VI, 717): Ἡρῴδου δὲ τὸν Ἀρχέλαον διαδεξαμένου,
λαβόντος τὴν ἐξουσίαν τὴν ἀπονεμηθεῖσαν.

[2] II, 146–7.

[3] *HE* i. 9. 1: τὰς ἑαυτῶν διεῖπον τετραρχίας. The verb διεῖπον is an
imperfect of the verb διέπω. Since there seems to be no aorist form of this
verb it may well mean that they did not begin to administer their territories
until after Archelaus was ousted. This is borne out by the genitive absolute
which seems to indicate that their rule began when Archelaus was deposed.
Finally, this is substantiated by Eus. *Chron.* II, 146–7, where it states that the
first year of their reign began after Archelaus' deposition.

[4] Cf. Wacholder, pp. 10–13; below, p. 124.

[5] Cf. Joseph ben Gurion, trans. into Latin by S. Münster (Basel, 1559),
p. 191; Joseph ben Gurion, *The Wonderful and Most Deplorable History of the
Latter Times of the Jews*, trans. by P. Morwyn from Hebrew of Abraham ben
David's abridgement ed. by J. Howell (London, 1671), p. 88.

[6] Jos. *Ant.* xv. 362; *BJ* i. 483.

[7] Cf. Jos. *Ant.* xvi. 194–200, 212; xvii. 14, 16, 48–51, 58; *BJ* i. 483–4,
557, 572, 578–9.

that the tetrarchs could not appeal to the emperor directly if the need arose. At the time of Archelaus' deposition, the brothers, according to Strabo, were suing one another.[1] Since only Archelaus was deposed, Antipas and Philip being allowed to return to their realms, it seems that the two brothers united against Archelaus. Possibly they opposed his oversight in Palestine.

Besides what was assigned in Herod's will, Salome gained the royal palace in Ascalon and an annual revenue of sixty talents.[2] The three Greek cities, Gaza, Gadara, and Hippos, were to be detached from Herod's territory and annexed to Syria.[3] This was because Nicolaus did not think it worthwhile to contest for these against the Greek delegation.[4]

Certainly Antipas' attendance at the trial benefited him. It prevented Archelaus from receiving the coveted title of king. Although he did not himself acquire what he had hoped for, he did at least receive what was specified in the last will.

CHRONOLOGICAL CONSIDERATIONS OF THE TRIAL

It is the object of this section to determine the time spent in Rome sorting out Herod's will, and the date of Antipas' return to Palestine.

The journey to Rome

The Passover festival in 4 B.C. fell on 11–18 April,[5] but before it was over Archelaus had already ordered the people to return

---

[1] Strabo xvi. 2. 46.　　　　　　[2] Jos. *Ant.* xvii. 321; *BJ* ii. 98.

[3] Jos. *Ant.* xvii. 320; *BJ* ii. 97. Josephus gives no reason why these three Greek cities should be detached from Herod's territory, whereas Nicolaus of Damascus states that there was a Hellenistic delegation at the trial asking for their independence, cf. *FGH*, IIa, 424 (90 frag. 136. 9).

[4] *FGH*, IIa, 424 (90 frag. 136. 10). The results of the trial may be considered accurate for the following reasons. (1) Josephus is consistent with himself with regard to their territories (although Philip's territory is variously stated in different contexts, cf. *Ant.* xvii. 319; *BJ* ii. 95 with *Ant.* xviii. 106; cf. also Lk. 3: 1). (2) Literature outside of Josephus is in agreement with him (cf. Mt. 2: 22; 14: 1; Lk. 3: 1, 19; Tac. *Hist.* v. 9). (3) Since Nicolaus of Damascus was Archelaus' defence attorney, it is natural for the story given by Nicolaus and Josephus to be biased in Archelaus' favour, and to credit him with all possible victories (cf. above, p. 29 n. 3). However, since the results for Archelaus were not as favourable as had been hoped, it is probable that the details of the trial are authentic and accurate.

[5] This is calculated on the basis of R. A. Parker and W. H. Dubberstein, *Babylonian Chronology 626 B.C.–A.D. 75*[2] (Providence, 1956), p. 45.

to their homes.[1] After that he immediately left for Rome via Caesarea. Since Caesarea is approximately sixty-eight Roman miles from Jerusalem,[2] it would have taken him and his party about four days to make the journey.[3] Thus if Archelaus left Jerusalem around 20 April, he would have arrived at Caesarea on 23 April. Upon his arrival in Caesarea he encountered Sabinus, the imperial finance officer for Syria, who had designs on Herod's property. Through Ptolemy, Archelaus urgently solicited Varus to obstruct Sabinus' activities, with which request Varus complied.[4] This would have involved the dispatch of a message to Antioch and then a journey by Varus from Antioch to Caesarea, a distance of 357 miles.[5] Friedländer reckoned that the special couriers travelled at ten miles an hour, or 160 miles a day;[6] but his calculations have been subjected to severe criticisms.[7] Friedländer's figure may be valid, it is argued, in special cases of comparatively short distances, but for long distances one cannot reckon on more than fifty miles a day. In the present case, however, the message was urgent and the distance relatively short. Hence it is a reasonable estimate that three to five days elapsed before Varus received the message, say, on 25 April. It would have taken Varus at least four to six days to reach Caesarea – in the first week of May. After Varus had prevented Sabinus from following his original plan, Archelaus sailed for Rome while Varus went to Jerusalem before returning to Antioch.[8]

---

[1] Jos. *Ant.* xvii. 218; *BJ* ii. 13.

[2] Although *Itin.* 589. 5 suggests a distance of 116 miles between Jerusalem and Caesarea (possibly the figure CXVI is a scribal error for LXVI), the itemized list in *Itin.* 600. 1–6 which totals 68 miles seems far more plausible.

[3] This is based on the calculation of Ramsay, who estimates that one may cover seventeen Roman miles (= fifteen to sixteen English miles) of road travel a day, cf. W. M. Ramsay, 'Roads and Travel (in NT)', *HDB*, Extra Volume (1904), 386.

[4] Jos. *Ant.* xvii. 219–22; *BJ* ii. 14–16.

[5] *Itin.* 147. 2 – 150. 1.

[6] L. Friedländer, *Darstellungen aus der Sittengeschichte Roms*[10], 1 (Leipzig, 1922), 334.

[7] Ramsay, *HDB*, Extra Volume, 387–8; A. M. Ramsay, 'The Speed of the Roman Imperial Post', *JRS*, xv (1925), 60–74; C. W. J. Eliot, 'New Evidence for the Speed of the Roman Imperial Post', *The Phoenix*, ix (1955), 76–80.

[8] Jos. *Ant.* xvii. 222, 251; *BJ* ii. 17–18, 40.

It is probable that Archelaus did not have to wait for a ship, but had one prepared, this being official and urgent business. Although between 11 March and 26 May was considered a doubtful period for sailing,[1] because of the urgency of his mission Archelaus probably sailed about the first of May. The distance to Rome by sea is about 1,600–1,700 nautical miles,[2] and an average sailing time westward (which was more difficult than the opposite direction) from Caesarea to Rome was around fifty-five to seventy-three days.[3] Since for part of the voyage he was travelling during the doubtful period, it is probable that it would have taken sixty-five to seventy days, arriving in Rome in early July. Antipas sailed about the same time, if not, as suggested by Nicolaus of Damascus, on the same ship, as Archelaus.[4] Hence he also arrived in Rome in early July. After their arrival there seems to have been a brief interval before the trial itself began, during which time Augustus reviewed the claims of the two sides.[5] The trial may have started around the middle of July.

The revolt in Palestine

How long the trial lasted is not known, but after the first part of it there arrived in Rome a dispatch from Varus concerning the Jewish outbreak at Jerusalem during the feast of Pentecost.[6] It seems probable that Varus sent this dispatch immediately after he received news of the revolt from Sabinus.[7] It need have taken only four to seven days for Sabinus' message to have arrived in Antioch from Jerusalem (a distance of only 425 Roman miles),[8] and Varus' dispatch to Rome would have

---

[1] Vegetius Renatus *De re militari* iv. 39.

[2] These figures are based on H. Fullard (ed.), *The Mercantile Marine Atlas*[16] (London, 1959), maps 17, 18; R. W. Caney and J. E. Reynolds (comps.), *Reed's New Marine Distance Tables* (Sunderland, 1965), pp. 87–9.

[3] L. Casson, 'Speed under Sail of Ancient Ships', *TAPA*, LXXXII (1951), 145–6.

[4] *FGH*, IIa, 424 (90 frag. 136. 9).

[5] Jos. *Ant.* xvii. 228–9; *BJ* ii. 24–5.

[6] Jos. *Ant.* xvii. 250–98; *BJ* ii. 39–79.

[7] This is implied in Josephus' narrative in *Ant.* xvii. 250; *BJ* ii. 40. If one looks at the context there is only mention of Augustus receiving a letter about the revolt. The description of the revolt in the same context is only an explanation of the letter. It seems to have been supplied by Josephus, and was not therefore a part of the letter itself.

[8] Above, p. 34 and nn. 2, 5.

taken another forty to forty-five days[1] (the distance by land from Antioch to Rome being about 1,988 Roman miles).[2] Since Pentecost fell approximately on 1 June,[3] Varus' dispatch would have arrived in Rome around the middle of July. This fits well with the time calculated for the two brothers to have travelled to Rome, the preliminaries to the trial, and the trial itself. Augustus no doubt would immediately have sent a dispatch to Varus to find out more about the revolt, and to hear of its outcome before he proceeded with the trial. This, at least, is a reasonable assumption due to the fact that Varus seems to have known in which direction the trial was proceeding.[4] A message from Rome to the East via Alexandria would have taken approximately fifteen to twenty days,[5] arriving in Palestine in early August.

A consideration of the length of the revolt in Palestine is now in order. Due to its being quite extensive, Brann thinks that it would have taken at least a year for the occurrence of all the events.[6] For several reasons, however, it does not seem likely that it would have lasted such a long time. In the first place it seems to have been well organized. At the Pentecost festival the Jews, who were divided into three groups, seem to have been immediately effective, because Sabinus, against whom they had revolted, panicked and immediately summoned help from Varus.[7]

[1] Cf. W. M. Ramsay, *HDB*, Extra Volume, 385; A. M. Ramsay, *JRS*, xv, 73; Eliot, *The Phoenix*, ix, 76, 80.

[2] The distance is based upon *Itin.* and is roughly as follows: Antioch to Byzantium 765 miles (*Itin.* 139. 1 – 147. 1); Byzantium to Dyrrachium 854 miles (*Itin.* 317. 7); Dyrrachium to Brundisium 1,400 stadia = 140 nautical miles or one or two days travel by sea (*Itin.* 497. 5); Brundisium to Tarentum 43 miles (*Itin.* 119. 1); Tarentum to Beneventum 157 miles (*Itin.* 120. 1); Beneventum to Capua 33 miles (*Itin.* 111. 6); Capua to Rome 136 miles (*Itin.* 612. 5).

[3] Based on Parker and Dubberstein, p. 45. Cf. also Lewin, p. 134.

[4] E.g. he sent Philip to receive a portion of the kingdom, for he had heard of the autonomy desired by many (Jos. *Ant.* xvii. 303; *BJ* ii. 83).

[5] Beginning with 19 July the etesian (ἐτησίαι) or annual winds blow for thirty days (Pliny *NH* ii. 47. 124), and one is able to sail from Puteoli to Alexandria in about nine days (Pliny *NH* xix. 1. 3). From Rome (Ostia) to Puteoli (about 120 nautical miles) would have taken one or two days. Therefore, a journey from Rome to Alexandria would have taken about ten to thirteen days. From Alexandria it should not have taken more than five to seven days to reach Varus if he were still in Palestine.

[6] Brann, *MGWJ*, xxii, 254.   [7] Jos. *Ant.* xvii. 254–6; *BJ* ii. 42–5.

Thus no long period elapsed before the revolt actually commenced. Secondly, although Josephus gives a lengthy description of the fight, at least the first part of the struggle was concentrated around the temple and palace.[1] Thirdly, the majority of the royal troops sided with the rebels.[2] This seems to indicate a confusion in the fighting, which in turn may indicate that everything happened very rapidly. Fourthly, the Jewish rebels offered to let Sabinus escape without harm; but this offer he refused, because he did not trust their promises and because he expected very soon to receive from Varus the help which he had requested.[3] Fifthly, Varus acted promptly on receiving the dispatches from Sabinus.[4] This indicates not only the urgency of the situation but also that it was not a long drawn out struggle. Sixthly, when, as a result of the revolt in Jerusalem, there were disturbances throughout Judaea and Galilee, Varus, with the aid of the people of Berytus and Aretas of Petra, was able to come quickly to Jerusalem. The evidence for this is that the Jews fled on his arrival with the siege-work half completed (ἡμίεργον τὴν πολιορκίαν).[5] If the revolt had been a long drawn out affair the siege-work around Jerusalem would certainly have been completed. Seventhly, when Varus questioned the Jews on their conduct in Palestine, they used the festival as an alibi.[6] This would seem to indicate that the festival had occurred very recently.

With such a vast amount of military aid at his disposal, it is probable that Varus had the entire revolt under control within one and a half to two and a half months. Since Pentecost fell on about the first of June, he may well have been in full control by late July or early August. Varus then returned to Antioch, whence he allowed a delegation of fifty Jews, accompanied

[1] Jos. *Ant.* xvii. 257–64; *BJ* ii. 46–50.

[2] Jos. *Ant.* xvii. 266; *BJ* ii. 52. The only exception were the 3,000 Sebastenians who remained on the Roman side. These were troops drafted in the region of Sebaste (Samaria). They could have been summoned quickly to Jerusalem; very probably a large proportion were already stationed in Jerusalem for the festival to prevent a recurrence of what had happened at the Passover festival.

[3] Jos. *Ant.* xvii. 265, 268; *BJ* ii. 51, 54.

[4] Jos. *Ant.* xvii. 286; *BJ* ii. 66.

[5] Jos. *Ant.* xvii. 292; *BJ* ii. 72.

[6] Jos. *Ant.* xvii. 293; *BJ* ii. 73.

by Philip, to go to Rome.[1] If they left Antioch in mid or late August they would have arrived in Rome some fifty to seventy days[2] later, that is, in mid or late October.[3]

The time of the second trial

The second trial could have taken place at the end of October or the beginning of November. The decision was given a few days later[4] and thus the whole proceeding would have been easily finished by the second week of November.

An interesting incident occurred after the trials which confirms the above conclusion. There appeared on the scene a pseudo-Alexander.[5] When he arrived in Dicaearchia (or Puteoli),[6] he won over the Jews, just as he had previously won them over in Crete and Melos. Being brought to the emperor, he was questioned as to why he had left behind his brother Aristobulus. His reply to the emperor was that he had left him in Cyprus out of fear of shipwreck and to protect the posterity of Mariamme supposing some evil were to befall himself.[7] The important point is his mention of the danger at sea. Could not this have reference to the fact that he was sailing during the doubtful period, so affording an excuse that would carry weight with Augustus? This may also be the reason why he disembarked at Puteoli at a distance from Rome of 133 Roman miles.[8] If it can be assumed that he arrived in Puteoli on the closing date of sea travel (11 Nov.),[9] or shortly after, he would have arrived in

---

[1] Jos. *Ant.* xvii. 299–300, 303; *BJ* ii. 80, 83.

[2] Since there were so many people travelling at one time, it is reasonable to assume that they went by sea. According to Casson it took a ship ten to twelve days to travel from Gaza to Rhodes (via Syria and the coast of Asia Minor) and about seven to nine days from Berytus to Rhodes. Antioch is about the same distance again from Berytus as Berytus from Gaza. Thus the journey would have taken some four to six days from Antioch to Rhodes and forty-five to sixty-three days from Rhodes to Rome, a total of about fifty to seventy days (Casson, *TAPA*, LXXXII, 145–6).

[3] Crossing the Mediterranean was considered doubtful during the period 15 Sept. to 10 Nov. (Vegetius iv. 39) and so only the last portion of their trip would have been risky. The risk varied of course from year to year.

[4] Jos. *Ant.* xvii. 317; *BJ* ii. 93.   [5] Jos. *Ant.* xvii. 324–38; *BJ* ii. 101–10.

[6] Jos. *Vita* 16.   [7] Jos. *Ant.* xvii. 335; cf. also *BJ* ii. 108.

[8] Puteoli to Terracina 77 miles (*Itin.* 122. 4 – 123. 1) and Terracina to Rome 56 miles (*Itin.* 611. 10 – 612. 4).

[9] Vegetius iv. 39; Pliny *NH* ii. 47. 125.

Rome about eight days later[1] (or the latter half of November). He would have had to leave Cyprus some forty-six to sixty-five days[2] prior to that. Indeed, since his entire journey was during the doubtful period, it is better to allow sixty to seventy days. This means that he would have left Cyprus in mid-September. Since from 15 September to 10 November was considered doubtful, pseudo-Alexander's excuse would have been legitimate. This was never questioned. If, moreover, he arrived at Rome in the latter half of November, that is, two or three weeks after the trial had ended, this would fit in well with Josephus' narrative.

It is concluded that Archelaus and Antipas knew of Augustus' decision about the middle of November. Whether or not the three brothers returned home immediately cannot be known. It is unlikely, however, that they would have travelled in the winter; hence it is probable that they returned in the spring of 3 B.C.[3] The length of time between Herod's death and his sons' return to Palestine could be outlined as follows:

Herod's death	Mar./Apr. 4 B.C.
Passover	12–19 Apr.
Archelaus in Caesarea	*ca.* 23 Apr.
Archelaus and Antipas departed for Rome	*ca.* early May
Pentecost and dispatch to Rome	May/June
Archelaus and Antipas arrive in Rome	early July
First trial	middle of July
Dispatch from Varus arrived in Rome	middle of July
Dispatch to Varus arrived in Palestine	early Aug.
End of revolt	July/Aug.
Delegation and Philip left for Rome	middle/late Aug.
Delegation and Philip arrived in Rome	middle/late Oct.
Second trial	Oct./Nov.
Decision of Augustus	early/middle Nov.
Pseudo-Alexander arrived in Rome	late Nov.
Three brothers returned to Palestine	spring, 3 B.C.

[1] Cf. above, p. 34 n. 3.

[2] This is obtained by reckoning the time spent from Cyprus to Rhodes (four to five days), from Rhodes to Rome (forty-five days to sixty-three days), less that spent from Puteoli to Rome (three days), cf. Casson, *TAPA*, LXXXII, 143, 145–6.

[3] Though Gaius gave Agrippa I Philip's territory in A.D. 37, Agrippa did not visit it until around August 38 (Jos. *Ant.* xviii. 238; *BJ* ii. 181; cf. below, p. 260.

PART 2

ANTIPAS' REALM

CHAPTER 3

THE GEOGRAPHY OF
ANTIPAS' REALM

On returning to Palestine Antipas was immediately involved in the administration of the territories committed to him by Augustus. It is the purpose of Part 2 to consider these territories geographically and economically.

Since Antipas had two territories it is proposed to define briefly the borders of each of them[1] and then to discuss the relationship between them.

THE TERRITORY OF GALILEE[2]

Its name

The term *Galilee*[3] comes from the Hebrew גָּלִיל or גְּלִילָה and the Aramaic גְּלִילָא (in Greek Γαλιλαία), literally *circle* or *district*. Really it is גְּלִיל הַגּוֹיִם a *district of the Gentiles* (τῶν ἐθνῶν)[4] or *of foreigners* (ἀλλοφύλων).[5]

Its boundaries

This was a small region in northern Palestine which had a vague and variable boundary until defined by the Roman administration. When Herod the Great ruled it, it was only a small part of his domain, but after his death when Antipas became the tetrarch of this region it became both necessary and important to define its boundaries.

These boundaries as outlined by Josephus at the time of the

---

[1] The delimitations of Galileee and Peraea are treated more fully in Appendix II. Cf. also map, p. xvi.

[2] There is great interest in Galilee today. For a popular yet good presentation of the land of Galilee, see K. MacLeish, 'The Land of Galilee', *National Geographic Magazine*, cxxviii (1965), 832–65.

[3] For a discussion of the origin of the name, see A. Alt, 'Galiläische Probleme', *PJB*, xxxiii (1937), 52–64, or *KS* (München, 1953), ii, 363–74.

[4] Isa. 8: 23 [9: 1]; Mt. 4: 15.

[5] 1 Macc. 5: 15.

revolution of A.D. 66–70 would probably be the same as in the time of Antipas.[1] Schürer rightly insists that Josephus gives not the political borders but a description of those places inhabited by Jews.[2] Consequently one has to be careful in trying to reconstruct Antipas' political borders. It seems that Josephus' mention of Galilee's fortresses[3] more probably refers to political Galilee than to mere centres of Jewish population. Moreover, since borders are apt to change and especially after wars, Talmudic and later references, though valuable at times, cannot be depended on to establish the boundaries of Galilee before the war of 66–70. Hence this study will be concerned primarily with Josephus' account.[4]

Josephus mentions a Lower and Upper Galilee, which met in the Plain of Ramah on a line roughly between the northern end of the Sea of Galilee and the city of Ptolemais (Acre).[5]

For Galilee's boundaries a good starting point is the town of Gaba[6] which would mark the southwestern corner. Proceeding eastward, the southern border would pass through the middle of the Great Plain of Esdraelon, running south of Xaloth,[7] Nain,[8] and possibly Agrippina, but north of Ginaea[9] (of Samaria) and the city-state of Scythopolis. Northeastward the border ran towards the Sea of Galilee with Sennabris[10] and Philoteria[11] as

---

[1] BJ iii. 35–40. Oehler is right in stating that it is a risky endeavour to reconstruct the territory of Antipas solely on the basis of Josephus. Since, however, there are no other sources for that time, except a few Talmudic references, it is worth making the attempt. Cf. W. Oehler, 'Die Ortschaften und Grenzen Galiläas nach Josephus', ZDPV, xxviii (1905), 65.

[2] Schürer, ii, 8 n. 11.

[3] BJ ii. 573–4; Vita 187–8.

[4] For geographical references from Talmudic and other sources, see A. Neubauer, La Géographie du Talmud (Paris, 1868); M. Avi-Yonah, Map of Roman Palestine² (London, 1940); P. Thomsen, Loca Sancta (Halle, 1907); S. Klein, 'Zur Topographie des alten Palästina', ZDPV, xxxiii (1910), 26–43.

[5] BJ iii. 35–40. This is also confirmed by the Mishnah, which states that Upper Galilee (i.e. that portion above Kefar Hananiah) is the place where the sycamore is not found, and Lower Galilee the region below Kefar Hananiah where the sycamore flourishes. It also states that the neighbourhood of Tiberias is the valley (Sheb. ix. 2).

[6] Jos. Ant. xv. 294; BJ iii. 36; Vita 115.

[7] Jos. BJ iii. 39.

[8] Lk. 7: 11.

[9] Jos. BJ iii. 48; Ant. xx. 118.

[10] Jos. BJ iii. 448.

[11] Polybius v. 70. 3–4.

a part of Galilee. Probably it followed first the Scythopolis–Damascus road and then the Jordan River to the Sea of Galilee.

From Sennabris the eastern border of Galilee ran northward along the Sea of Galilee, the Jordan River, and Lake Hula, Thella being a northeastern boundary point.[1] The northern boundary proceeded westward from the most western tip of Lake Hula to somewhere between Kedesh of Tyre[2] and Gischala of Galilee[3] (possibly the *Wādi 'Ōba* served as the boundary line), and ended somewhere north of Galilee's most northwesterly village, Baca or *el Jermak*.[4]

The western border seems to have started near *el Jermak* and to have run west of Meroth,[5] Bersabe,[6] Selame,[7] Chabulon,[8] and *Shefar'am*, and continued southward until it joined the southern border west of Gaba.

Assuming that these were the boundaries of Galilee, its area would have been approximately 750 square miles.

Its divisions

For Galilee Josephus mentions only two toparchies, Tiberias and Tarichaeae.[9] Both of these are located near to each other on the Sea of Galilee, in the eastern half of Lower Galilee. Since Josephus speaks of Tiberias, Tarichaeae, and Sepphoris as cities of Lower Galilee, in contrast to various villages, Jones argues that he probably means toparchic capitals, especially since Tarichaeae was never a city at all in the proper sense.[10] With respect to Sepphoris this would seem reasonable, for though replaced by Tiberias as the capital of Galilee, it still remained Galilee's largest city.[11] Furthermore, Josephus implies that it was a toparchic capital, for he says that many villages were round about it.[12] Avi-Yonah's suggestion that Araba or Gabara (*Arrabat el-Battuf*) may have been another toparchic capital in Lower Galilee seems plausible.[13] This is strengthened by the fact

---

[1] Jos. *BJ* iii. 40.
[2] Jos. *BJ* ii. 459; cf. also *BJ* iv. 104; *Ant.* xiii. 154, 162.
[3] Jos. *BJ* ii. 575; iv. 84–96.   [4] Jos. *BJ* iii. 39.
[5] Jos. *BJ* iii. 40.   [6] Jos. *BJ* iii. 39.
[7] Jos. *Vita* 188; *BJ* ii. 573.   [8] Jos. *BJ* iii. 38; *Vita* 234.
[9] *BJ* ii. 252.   [10] *CERP*, pp. 275–6.
[11] Jos. *BJ* iii. 34; *Vita* 232.   [12] *Vita* 346.
[13] M. Avi-Yonah, *The Holy Land* (Grand Rapids, Michigan, 1966), p. 97.

that Josephus considers it one of the three chief cities of Galilee;[1] while its position ten to twelve miles due north of Sepphoris is an ideal situation for the toparchic capital of the northwestern area of Lower Galilee. Since there are no toparchies mentioned for Upper Galilee, the whole area may have been a toparchy in itself.[2]

To sum up: Josephus mentions two toparchies in the eastern half of Lower Galilee, and it seems likely that there were three others, making a total of five toparchies in Galilee.

THE TERRITORY OF PERAEA[3]

Its name

The name ἡ Περαία (or Περαῖος, Περαΐτης), though constantly used by Josephus, is never found in either the Old or New Testaments,[4] where instead it is represented by עֵבֶר הַיַּרְדֵּן in the Old Testament,[5] and πέραν τοῦ Ἰορδάνου in the Septuagint and New Testament.[6]

Its boundaries

Even in the times of the Mishnah it was considered by the Jews a province distinct from Galilee and Judaea.[7] Prior to Antipas, Herod gained control of this territory on defeating the Arabs,[8] at about the same time as the Battle of Actium took place. Josephus mentions that Herod a short time after that rebuilt Heshbon in Peraea.[9] At any rate Herod set up his brother as tetrarch over the whole Transjordanic region[10] which after Herod's death became Antipas' territory.[11]

---

[1] *Vita* 123. [2] Avi-Yonah, *Holy Land*, p. 97.

[3] For a detailed study of Peraea as given by Josephus, see L. Haefeli, 'Samaria und Peräa bei Flavius Josephus', *Biblische Studien*, ed. by O. Bardenhewer, XVIII (Freiburg, 1913), 66–120.

[4] Except for the variant reading given by ℵ* and W in Lk. 6: 17.

[5] Isa. 8: 23 [9: 1].

[6] Mt. 4: 15; 19: 1; Mk. 3: 8; Jn. 1: 28; 3: 26; 10: 40.

[7] Sheb. ix. 2; Ket. xiii. 10; B.B. iii. 2.

[8] Jos. *Ant.* xv. 108–60; *BJ* i. 364–85.

[9] *Ant.* xv. 294. Hildesheimer concludes that Heshbon was still a Jewish town at the time of Herod the Great, cf. H. Hildesheimer, *Beiträge zur Geographie Palästinas* (Berlin, 1886), pp. 65–6.

[10] Jos. *BJ* i. 483. In *BJ* i. 586 it can be observed that Pheroras went to Peraea which may indicate that it was his own territory.

[11] Jos. *Ant.* xvii. 188, 318; xviii. 240; *BJ* ii. 95.

With the same proviso as mentioned above, the borders of Peraea may also be learned from Josephus. Not being a centre of Jewish activity, there is not as much information about Peraea as about Galilee. Josephus gives a general statement about its boundaries as extending in length from Machaerus to Pella and in breadth from Philadelphia to the Jordan.[1]

Its western border is presumably the Jordan River. It seems that the Herodian fortress Machaerus was the most southern point of the region.[2] It is probable that the River Arnon and its tributary, the River Wala, served as the southern boundary.

The eastern boundary touched Philadelphia, Gerasa, Arabia, and Heshbon.[3] Since however these were districts rather than specific towns it is difficult to establish the eastern boundary with exactness. As the north–south line west of Mâdebā (a town east-southeast of the north end of the Dead Sea) formed the eastern boundary of the former Moabite territory,[4] there is no reason for believing it was different in Antipas' time.

It is probable that Pella was not a part of Peraea.[5] The Jabesh River may have served as the northern boundary.

Assuming these to have been the approximate borders, Peraea would have been around 850 square miles. This would mean that it was larger than Galilee, as in fact Josephus states.[6]

Its divisions

Peraea seems to have comprised five toparchies. After Herod the Great's death there was the destruction of the governmental offices (Βασίλεια) at Betharamphtha or Ammatha,[7] later renamed Livias (or Julias).[8] This was the capital of a toparchy[9]

---

[1] *BJ* iii. 46.   [2] This is certainly implied in Jos. *BJ* iv. 439.
[3] Jos. *BJ* iii. 46–8.
[4] N. Glueck, 'Explorations in Eastern Palestine, III', *AASOR*, xviii–xix (1937–9), 140.
[5] Cf. Appendix II.   [6] *BJ* iii. 44.
[7] Jos. *BJ* ii. 59; *Ant.* xvii. 277. For a discussion of this city, see below, pp. 87–91, especially p. 88 n. 6. Jones makes these into two separate cities and identifies Ammatha with Amathus, cf. A. H. M. Jones, 'The Urbanization of Palestine', *JRS*, xxi (1931), 79; Jones, *CERP*, p. 275. He gives no explanation, however, for this distinction and identification. If one reviews the context of the two passages in Josephus, it seems more natural to assume that he is referring to one and the same place.
[8] Jos. *Ant.* xviii. 27; cf. below, p. 89.
[9] Jos. *BJ* ii. 252.

comprising fourteen villages.[1] Gadara, besides being the capital of Peraea, could have been a toparchic capital as well.[2]

The third toparchic capital may well have been Amathus. It was regarded as the most important fortress east of the Jordan at the time of Alexander Jannaeus[3] and was destroyed by him.[4] Later, under Gabinius, five councils (συνέδρια) were set up as governmental centres, and Amathus (as well as Gadara) was selected as one of them.[5] Hence it could have been constituted as a capital of a toparchy. This is strikingly confirmed in the sixth century A.D. when the area east of the Jordan was still divided into the three regions (ῥεγεῶνες) of Livias, Gadara, and Amathus.[6] Due to its identification with *Tell el-Ammata*,[7] on the east bank of the Jordan (thirty-two to thirty-five miles north of the Dead Sea and eighteen to twenty miles south of Pella), Amathus would have been the northern region of Peraea, with Gadara as north-central, and Livias the central region. The distribution, then, is fairly even in the northern half of the territory.

Nero granted to Agrippa II, Julias and Abila.[8] There are three places with the name Abila but the one in Peraea is probably to be identified with that mentioned by Josephus as being near Livias and the Dead Sea[9] and about sixty stadia from the Jordan.[10] This is to be identified with *Khirbet el-Kefrein*[11] which is only about two miles north of Livias. Jones identifies the toparchy of Abila with the extension of Peraea east of the Dead Sea, and thinks that Josephus alludes to this district as Esbonitis (i.e. Heshbon).[12] This suggestion stems from the need for a toparchic capital in south Peraea; but the conjecture proves too much besides having no historical or archaeological founda-

---

[1] Jos. *Ant.* xx. 159. [2] Jones, *JRS*, xxi, 79.

[3] Jos. *Ant.* xiii. 356; *BJ* i. 86. [4] Jos. *Ant.* xiii. 374; *BJ* i. 89.

[5] Jos. *Ant.* xiv. 91; *BJ* i. 170.

[6] Georgii Cyprii *Descriptio Orbis Romani*, ed. with commentary H. Gelzer (Leipzig, 1890), 1016 (Ἀπάθους = Ἀμαθοῦς, cf. comment on pp. 190–1), 1018, 1019; cf. Jones, *JRS*, xxi, 79.

[7] Eus. *Onomast.* pp. 22: 23–8; 23: 25–31; N. Glueck, 'Explorations in Eastern Palestine, IV', *AASOR*, xxv–xxviii (1945–9), 353–4.

[8] Jos. *BJ* ii. 252; *Ant.* xx. 159.

[9] *BJ* iv. 438. [10] *Ant.* v. 4; cf. iv. 176.

[11] Glueck, *AASOR*, xxv–xxviii, 376–8; N. Glueck, 'Some Ancient Towns in the Plains of Moab', *BASOR*, No. 91 (1943), 13–15.

[12] *CERP*, p. 275.

tion. Is it not more probable that Livias was the capital of the land north of itself up to the district of Gadara and that Abila was the toparchic capital of the land south of itself? Capitals need not necessarily be in the centres of their districts.

In preference to Jones' advocacy of Abila, it may be conjectured that the fifth toparchic capital was Machaerus. Machaerus was destroyed by Gabinius,[1] but was rebuilt by Herod the Great, who made it a πόλις and established there the palace or governmental offices (Βασίλεια).[2] When Antipas' wife fled to her father, Aretas IV, the preparations for the flight were made by the governors (στρατηγοί).[3] The Nabataean inscriptions mention officers with the titles στρατηγός and ἔπαρχος. These are transliterated into Nabataean אסרתג and הפרך[4] respectively, which shows that the titles were of foreign origin. Jones suggests that the Nabataean kings tried to organize their kingdom on the regular Hellenistic model, but that the centralized system broke down and they gave the local sheikhs the title of 'governor'.[5] A parallel may be found in the governing of about 108 Hellenistic cities in Asia Minor where there were organized magisterial boards of στρατηγοί consisting usually of five members and frequently headed by a 'first στρατηγός'.[6] Thus it would seem that Machaerus was governed much like a Hellenistic city, and may well have been the toparchic capital east of the Dead Sea from the district of Abila to Peraea's southern border.

Thus, the five toparchies of Peraea from north to south were Amathus, Gadara, Abila, Livias, and Machaerus.

[1] Jos. *Ant.* xiv. 83, 89; *BJ* i. 167; vii. 171.

[2] Jos. *BJ* vii. 172–7. According to Pliny (*NH* v. 15. 72) Machaerus was, next to Jerusalem, the strongest fortress in Palestine.

[3] Jos. *Ant.* xviii. 112.

[4] אסרתג = *CIS*, II, i, 160: 2; 161: 3, 6; 169: 2; 195: 2, 4; 196: 2, 3, 5; 213: 2; 214: 1; 224: 7; 234: 3; 235: A; 238; 387; *RES*, II, 1104: 1; 1108: 8. הפרך = *CIS*, II, i, 173: 5; 207: 2, 4; 214: 2; 221: 1; 790: 2; *RES*, II, 1104: 2; 1108: 1; 1196; 2024: 2. Cf. R. Savignac and J. Starcky, 'Une inscription Nabatéenne provenant du Djôf', *RB*, LXIV (1957), 200–2, especially p. 201 n. 3.

[5] Jones, *CERP*, p. 292. Cf. also L. Mowry, 'A Greek Inscription at Jathum in Transjordan', *BASOR*, No. 132 (1953), 38; cf. also M. Gihon, 'Idumea and the Herodian Limes', *IEJ*, XVII (1967), 29–30.

[6] D. Magie, *Roman Rule in Asia Minor*, I (Princeton, 1950), 643–4; II, 1508 n. 29.

THE RELATIONSHIP BETWEEN GALILEE AND PERAEA

When attempting to establish the boundaries of Galilee and Peraea, it can be observed that these areas do not adjoin but are separated by the Decapolis. In order to escape this conclusion, Harlow conjectures that the cities of the Decapolis, with the exception of Damascus, were within Antipas' and Philip's domains.[1] He would then extend the border of Galilee to include Scythopolis, and the northern border of Peraea to include the Decapolis cities of Pella and Gadara (he also includes Philadelphia and Gerasa within the eastern border). As is argued below, the Gadara to which Josephus refers as being the capital of Peraea is not to be identified with the Gadara of the Decapolis but rather with a city just south of Pella.[2] Certainly Harlow has difficulty in explaining the Decapolis Gadara as a part of Peraea in face of Josephus' statement that Pella is on the northern boundary of that region. Further support for Peraea's northern boundary being at the Yarmuk river rather than the Jabesh may be found in the dispute between Antipas and Aretas over the boundary limits of Gamalitis or Gamala.[3] Since this area was in Philip's territory, even Harlow has to shift the location of Gamalitis away from the northeast corner of Peraea.[4] There is no basis for this, however, and consequently there is no foundation for the extension of Peraea's northern boundary.

Thus, Harlow's attempt to avoid the separation of the two areas is unfounded. This separation is not in fact as great a problem as it may at first appear. To begin with, Augustus may have deliberately separated the two areas so as to prevent Antipas from becoming too powerful. In particular this was necessary immediately after the ratification of Herod the Great's will so as to avoid a revolt on Antipas' part against either his brother, Archelaus, or the Roman government. Thus Augustus may have intentionally made this division in order to keep a

[1] Harlow, pp. 243–6; see also the map on p. 78.

[2] Below, Appendix II.

[3] Jos. *Ant.* xviii. 113–15. Gamala is problematic and probably should read Gabalis, which is a district south of Moabitis in Idumaea, cf. *Ant.* ii. 6; Jones, *CERP*, p. 449 n. 19. This will be treated when dealing with that border dispute (below, pp. 254–5 n. 4).

[4] Harlow, pp. 244–5.

proper balance of power. Secondly, it must be remembered that though there were different rulers over the various parts of Palestine, Rome's control of the entire region gave it an essential unity. Each ruler received his authority from Rome, and this could be withdrawn if he did not promote the interests of Rome. Palestine was under the supervision of the Roman government and the need of free movement between Antipas' two areas would certainly have been recognized.[1]

There is no basic need, therefore, for Galilee and Peraea to be physically joined for the smooth operation of Antipas' administration and economy. The freedom of movement which was permitted between the two territories was of benefit not only to Antipas but also to the Roman Empire.

SUMMARY

Antipas became tetrarch over Galilee and Peraea. The area of Galilee was about 750 square miles and of Peraea about 850 square miles, in all 1,600 square miles. Each area was divided into five toparchic districts. Although the territories were not joined physically, it is reasonable to suppose that there was freedom of movement between them.

[1] G. E. Wright and F. V. Filson (eds.), *The Westminster Historical Atlas to the Bible* (London, 1946), p. 85.

CHAPTER 4

THE INHABITANTS OF
ANTIPAS' REALM

THE POPULATION

To attempt to come to a definite conclusion about the population in Antipas' realm is impossible because of the lack of necessary data. Josephus' figure of 3,000,000 inhabitants for the land of Galilee[1] is grossly exaggerated. It would imply about 4,000 persons to the square mile. This is an extremely high density, for today in the same approximate area there is only a population density of 253 persons to the square mile.[2] However, taking into consideration the various factors that are necessary for attempting an estimation of the population, it seems reasonable that there would have been about 25,000 inhabitants in each of Galilee's four main cities (Tiberias, Sepphoris, Gabara, and Tarichaeae) and about an average of 500 persons for each of the 200 Galilaean villages.[3] For Galilee it would mean a population of 200,000 or about 266 persons to the square mile.

There is a greater shortage of necessary information for the estimating of Peraea's population. Josephus specifically states that although Peraea was larger than Galilee, it was mostly desert and rugged mountains with only a few places of good productivity.[4] However, it does not seem unreasonable to estimate a population of 80,000 to 85,000 for the rural Peraea in Antipas' day and a total of 45,000 to 50,000 inhabitants for the cities/towns of Julias, Machaerus, Gadara, and Amathus.

---

[1] *BJ* iii. 43; *Vita* 235.

[2] State of Israel, Central Bureau of Statistics, *The Division of the State of Israel into Regions for Statistical Purposes. Population and Housing, 1961*, publication no. 20 (Jerusalem, 1964), pp. 22–3. This calculation includes the demographic regions of Eastern Upper and Lower Galilee, Western Upper and Lower Galilee, Hazor, Kinerot, Kokhav Plateau, and Nazareth–Tiran Mountains which gives a total area of 797 square miles and a population of 201,876 persons.

[3] This is worked out in more detail in Appendix III.

[4] *BJ* iii. 44–5; cf. also Pliny *NH* v. 15. 70.

52

This would mean a population density of somewhere between 147 and 159 persons to the square mile in Peraea.[1]

To sum up: if the population of Galilee were around 200,000, and 130,000 for Peraea, it would mean a total population of 330,000 for Antipas' domain and an average of 206 persons to the square mile.

THE NATIONALITY

Galilee

In the time of the Judges Galilee's territory was primarily that of the tribes of Zebulon and Naphthali[2] but the Canaanites and the Sidonians were still among them in considerable numbers.[3] In the days of Isaiah Galilee was the 'circuit' or district of the Gentiles (גְּלִיל הַגּוֹיִם)[4] which may suggest that it was surrounded by non-Jewish people such as the Phoenicians and the Syrians. In the eighth century B.C. there was the Assyrian conquest and the deportation of many people who were replaced by peoples of other lands.[5] After the fall of Jerusalem in 586 B.C. the North and South seem to have been drawing together; however, after the return from the Babylonian captivity, the southern people again suspected the purity of the Hebrew stock among the northerners.[6]

During the Maccabaean times the genuine Jews were only a small portion of the total population of Galilee who were brought to the vicinity of Jerusalem.[7] Galilee, then, was considered heathen.[8] Under John Hyrcanus (134–104 B.C.) or his successor Aristobulus I (104–103 B.C.) there was an extension of the Jewish state and Galilee was reconquered. This gave opportunity for many Jews to return to their native land without persecution, during which time the former inhabitants of Galilee had the option of expulsion or incorporation by circumcision.

---

[1] Cf. Appendix III. [2] Judg. 1: 30, 33.

[3] Judg. 18: 7, 28.

[4] Isa. 8: 23 [9: 1].

[5] 2 Kgs. 15: 29; 17: 24–7; Jos. *Ant.* ix. 235; cf. A. Alt, *PJB*, xxxiii, 67–9 (*KS*, ii, 409–11).

[6] L. E. Elliott-Binns, *Galilean Christianity*, *SBT*, No. 16 (London, 1956), pp. 18–19.

[7] 1 Macc. 5: 14–17, 20–3, 55.

[8] 1 Macc. 5: 15. Alt, *PJB*, xxxiii, 73–4 (*KS*, ii, 414–15); W. Bauer, 'Jesus der Galiläer', *Festgabe für Adolf Jülicher* (Tübingen, 1927), p. 18.

Most of them chose the latter alternative.[1] Certainly in Alexander Jannaeus' reign (103–76 B.C.) the Jewish element was so predominant that Ptolemy Lathyrus found it difficult to capture Asochis, and impossible to take Sepphoris.[2] Since there is no mention of the Jews in Jannaeus' time except in Sepphoris and Mt Tabor,[3] it may be that only southern Galilee was predominantly Jewish at that time. By New Testament times Galilee seems to have been quite thoroughly Judaized. This was probably accomplished by the Pharisees in their establishment of the synagogues and schools. Several times in the New Testament it is mentioned that Jesus went through the cities and villages of Galilee teaching in the synagogues.[4] Again at Capernaum there were Pharisees and teachers of the law from every village (κώμη) of Galilee, Judaea, and Jerusalem.[5] It seems, therefore, that in Herod Antipas' time Judaism was quite widespread in Galilee. What proportion of the population was Jewish is difficult to say. Moulton thought the Gentiles were in the majority[6] and although this seems to be an exaggeration, Strabo does state that Galilee contained Egyptians, Arabians, and Phoenicians[7] as well as Greeks,[8] which indicates that a large element of the population was Gentile.

Peraea

Peraea's territory comprised the former territories of Reuben, Gad, and possibly a small southern portion of Manasseh.[9] At the disruption of the kingdom these eastern tribes fell to the northern kingdom.[10] The eastern tribes, who sometimes are identified *en bloc* as Gilead,[11] suffered the Assyrian deportation as

---

[1] It is most likely that the conquest of the Ituraean territory northeast of Galilee (Jos. *Ant.* xiii. 318) would have been undertaken after the conquest of Galilee (cf. also *BJ* i. 76). Schürer (i, 276 n. 10) thinks that the Judaizing of Galilee was accomplished during Aristobulus I's reign, whereas Smith (*HGHL*, p. 416 n. 3) believes it was acccomplished during Hyrcanus' reign.

[2] Jos. *Ant.* xiii. 337–44.

[3] Jos. *Ant.* xiii. 338–44, 395–6.

[4] Mt. 4: 23; 9: 35; 12: 9; Mk. 1: 39; Lk. 4: 15–16, 44; 13: 10.

[5] Lk. 5: 17.   [6] Moulton–Howard, pp. 12–13.

[7] Strabo xvi. 2. 34.   [8] Jos. *Vita* 67.

[9] Josh. 12: 6; 13: 8–28; 18: 7; 20: 8; 22: 1–4, 9; 1 Sam. 13: 7.

[10] 1 Kgs. 11: 31. In fact Jeroboam's building of Penuel in the eastern territories (1 Kgs. 12: 25) may have served as his capital.

[11] 2 Kgs. 10: 33.

did Galilee.[1] After this time one does not hear of their existence or activity in the land of Palestine.

During the period of Alexander the Great there was an immigration of Greek settlers, and the towns of Pella and Dion may have been founded by Alexander.[2] In the earlier days of the Maccabees Peraea was inhabited chiefly by the Gentiles, and the Jewish minority was conveyed for safety into Judaea.[3] The policy of Judaizing the province was not introduced before the time of Hyrcanus and/or his successors who brought the area under their complete control and who attempted to extinguish the Greek culture by replacing it with Jewish manners and ideas or by destroying those places where the inhabitants would not submit to these ideals.[4] From that time until at least the war of A.D. 66–70 Peraea seemed predominantly Jewish.[5] The Mishnah always assumes that Peraea (עֵבֶר הַיַּרְדֵּן) is a land inhabited by Jews.[6] It was probably here that the Pharisees tempted Jesus concerning divorce,[7] that Jewish mothers brought their children to Jesus that he might lay his hands upon them,[8] and a Jewish ruler who knew the Law came to Jesus.[9] It seems that John the Baptist's main centre of activity was in Peraea.[10]

Conclusion

Philip the tetrarch was the first Jewish prince to have images of the emperor on his coins.[11] No trouble resulted from this action, and this would seem to point to a small Jewish minority in his realm. On the other hand Antipas' avoidance of human images on his coins seems to indicate a predominant Jewish element in his domain.

---

[1] 2 Kgs. 15: 29; 1 Chron. 5: 26; Jos. *Ant.* ix. 235.

[2] This is suggested by a somewhat corrupt text of Stephanus Byzantinus, Δῖον, annotations by L. Holstein, A. Berkel, and T. de Pinedo, 1 (Leipzig, 1825), 155. For a discussion of this text, see Schürer, 11, 175 n. 334.

[3] 1 Macc. 5: 45–54.   [4] Jos. *Ant.* xiii. 396–7.

[5] Jos. *Ant.* xx. 2 (the dispute of the Jews with the Philadelphians); *BJ* iv. 419–39 (the Jews of Peraea share in the war of 66–70).

[6] Sheb. ix. 2; Ket. xiii. 10; B.B. iii. 2; cf. also Bik. i. 10; Taan. iii. 6; Ed. viii. 7; Men. viii. 3.

[7] Mt. 19: 1–12 = Mk. 10: 1–12.

[8] Mt. 19: 13–15 = Mk. 10: 13–16.

[9] Mt. 19: 16–22 = Mk. 10: 17–22.

[10] Jn. 1: 28; 10: 40; cf. Smith, *HGHL*, p. 496 n. 1; below, pp. 146–7.

[11] Cf. F. W. Madden, *History of Jewish Coinage* (London, 1864), pp. 100–2;

In the Jewish literature Galilee and Peraea were considered Jewish territories along with Judaea.[1] Although there was no geographical connection between Galilee and Peraea one can see the wisdom of rule by the same tetrarch.

THE CHARACTER OF THE PEOPLE

Again most of the information concerning the character of the people is about Galilee, since it was more the centre of activity than was Peraea.

Their temperament and reputation

The temperament of the Galilaeans has often been characterized as having a frequent tendency to 'flare up' in the manner of the typical Galilaean, Peter.[2] But what about the other ten Galilaean disciples? Were they untypical Galilaeans?

Because of their courage and patriotism,[3] it is thought that the Galilaeans were fanatics and always causing riots.[4] For example, Hausrath states that Josephus calls the Galilaeans 'the usual disturbers of the peace of the country' and that they were the ones who incited tumults at the feasts in Jerusalem.[5] How-

Coins of the Jews (London, 1881), pp. 123–7; A. Reifenberg, Ancient Jewish Coins (Jerusalem, 1947), pp. 19, 43–4, pl. iv; Israel's History in Coins (London, 1953), pp. 10, 24; J. Meyshan, 'The Coins of the Herodian Dynasty', The Dating and Meaning of Ancient Jewish Coins and Symbols, Vol. II of Numismatic Studies and Researches (Jerusalem, 1958), pp. 30, 115; B. Kanael, 'Ancient Jewish Coins and their Historical Importance', BA, XXVI (1963), 51. For the coins of Antipas, see below, p. 99 n. 2.

[1] E.g. Sheb. ix. 2; B.B. iii. 2; Ket. xiii. 10; TB: Sanh. 11 b.

[2] Cf. T. Keim, The History of Jesus of Nazara, trans. by E. M. Geldart, II (London, 1876), 11.

[3] Cf. Jos. BJ iii. 41–2. In the war of 66–70 the Galilaeans showed their courage (cf. BJ iii. 1–8, 64–9, 289–306; Vita 230). Both Vespasian and Titus acknowledged their courage (BJ iii. 320, 471–84).

[4] H. Graetz, Geschichte der Juden³, III (Leipzig, 1878), 508. Graetz states that among the enthusiasts were Judas, the founder of the Zealots, and Jesus of Nazareth. Keim (II, 9–10) claims that the contempt of the Jews for the Galilaeans, implied even by the more recent historians such as Graetz, is not deserved, and that to some extent it is 'an artificial coinage at the expense of Jesus'.

[5] A. Hausrath, A History of the New Testament Times, trans. by C. T. Poynting and P. Quenzer, I (London, 1878), 12. Similar statements about the Galilaeans are made by J. Klausner, Jesus of Nazareth, trans. H. Danby

ever, this is not fair to the evidence. Josephus' mention of the disturbers of the peace refers to those robbers in the caves whom Herod subdued early in his reign.[1] To blame the Galilaeans for the uprising after Herod's death[2] is unfair, for people from Idumaea, Jericho, Transjordan, and Judaea were also involved. Indeed Judaea is described as having been overrun with robbers.[3] In the first century A.D. one can cite many instances of troubles in Judaea[4] whereas there is no record of any rebellion or anarchy in Galilee or Peraea during Antipas' reign. Although this is an *argumentum ex silentio*, it does carry some weight because of Josephus' interest in Galilaean affairs in that he had been a military and political leader in Galilee during the war of 66–70.

There are two main reasons for the troubles in Judaea and the tranquillity in Galilee. First, much of the trouble in Judaea was because of unwise moves by the procurators. Secondly, Antipas seems to have been a good ruler, for even though he did things which annoyed Jews (e.g. building Tiberias upon a former cemetery) he was in control and ruled for a long period of time, and this length of rule is, in itself, evidence of the Roman government's satisfaction with his authority. The discontinuity of rule in Judaea tended to encourage anarchy. Also, one gains insight into Antipas' rule in his handling of John the Baptist. He imprisoned John before his activities could lead to an uprising.[5] If this be typical of his handling of such situations it seems that it was his policy to act promptly to preclude trouble.

On the whole one can conclude that Antipas' subjects were a

(London, 1929), pp. 143–4; S. W. Baron, *A Social and Religious History of the Jews*[2], II (New York, 1952), 47–8; S. E. Johnson, *Jesus in His Own Times* (London, 1957), pp. 18–23; S. G. F. Brandon, *Jesus and the Zealots* (Manchester, 1967), pp. 54, 65.

[1] *Ant.* xiv. 420–30; *BJ* i. 309–13.
[2] Cf. Jos. *Ant.* xvii. 254–64; *BJ* ii. 45–8, 55–6.
[3] Jos. *BJ* iv. 400–9; ii. 264–5, 271; *Ant.* xx. 124, 160, 185, 214–15.
[4] E.g. at the time when Pilate brought the standards to Jerusalem (Jos. *Ant.* xviii. 55–9; *BJ* ii. 169–74); when he took money from the temple treasury (*Ant.* xviii. 60–2; *BJ* ii. 175–7); when he set up the gilded votive shields (Philo *Leg.* 299–305); at a Passover during Cumanus' rule (*Ant.* xx. 105–12); the quarrel between the Jews and Syrians at Caesarea (*Ant.* xx. 173–8); when Florus extracted money from the temple (*BJ* ii. 293–5).
[5] Jos. *Ant.* xviii. 118.

courageous people and yet, at the same time, law abiding citizens. Antipas' wise administration contributed to a tranquil life in Galilee and Peraea.

Their religious zeal

In a study of the religious zeal of the people, available information again concerns only the Galilaeans, and such comparisons as may be drawn between them and the Judaeans. Graetz holds that since the Galilaeans were a great distance from the temple, they were backward in their understanding of the Law and as a result they were more strict in morality and more rigidly enforced the laws and customs than the Judaeans.[1] In other words ignorance in the understanding of the Law made them fanatical dogmatists in matters of the Law. Neubauer goes so far as to suggest that Galilee possessed no wise men, still less a school.[2] But such statements reflect more prejudice than facts about the Galilaeans. It was during the reign of Queen Alexandra (*ca.* 76–67 B.C.) that the Pharisees rose to power and excelled all others in the 'accurate' interpretation of the Law.[3] The instruction was given in the synagogues which were the schools of piety and virtue.[4] As mentioned above there are several references in the New Testament to Jesus going through the cities and villages of Galilee teaching in the synagogues[5] and on one occasion at Capernaum there were Pharisees and teachers of the Law from every village (κώμη) of Galilee, Judaea, and Jerusalem.[6] This seems to indicate that the teaching of the Law in Galilee was quite widespread. Finally, it must be remembered that the Judaean Jews always looked down upon the Galilaean Jews. This prejudice is seen as early as New Testament times[7] and was held in the era of the Mishnah and Talmud.[8]

---

[1] III, 297–8; cf. also L. Finkelstein, *Akiba: Scholar, Saint and Martyr* (Philadelphia, 1936), pp. 13–14.

[2] P. 75.   [3] Jos. *BJ* i. 110; *Ant.* xiii. 408.

[4] Philo *De Vita Mosis* ii. 216; *Quod Omnis Probus Liber Sit* 81–5.

[5] Mt. 4: 23; 9: 35; 12: 9; Mk. 1: 39; Lk. 4: 15–16, 44; 7: 5; 13: 10. Hausrath (I, 89) states that 'the synagogue was a true school for the nation'.

[6] Lk. 5: 17.

[7] Jn. 7: 41, 52. This may be partially implied in Acts 4: 13; cf. also J. A. T. Robinson, 'The Destination and Purpose of St John's Gospel', *NTS*, VI (1960), 125.

[8] Ned. ii. 4; TB: Ned. 18*b*, 19*a*; Er. 53*a*; Baron, I, 277–80. The strongest statement against the Galilaeans was made by R. Johanan b. Zakkai (d. *ca.*

This same prejudice is continued by such Jews as Neubauer and Graetz as a polemic against Jesus, for if he came from a place where ignorance was rampant, especially ignorance of the Law, he could not be compared with the doctors of the Law who resided in Jerusalem.[1]

Probably a more correct distinction to be made is that the Jerusalemites were champions of tradition whereas the Galilaeans were the champions of the Law.[2] The Galilaeans were characterized as being adherents to the strict letter of the Law (at times the Pharisaic law).[3] This may be one reason why Jesus was more acceptable to the Galilaeans than to the Judaeans. He stated that he did not come to break the Law but to fulfil it.[4] On the other hand he spoke heavily against the traditions (Pharisaic) which in many cases misrepresented the Law.[5] The Sermon on the Mount, whether it is one discourse or

---

A.D. 80). He lived in Galilee for eighteen years and during that time he was asked only twice for consultation on the Torah. He then stated, 'O Galilee, Galilee! Thou hatest the Torah! Thine end will be to be besieged' (TJ: Shab. xvi. 8). The last sentence is problematic and there are various translations (cf. Strack–Billerbeck, I, 157). For a discussion of this, see J. Neusner, *A Life of Rabban Yohanan ben Zakkai ca. 1–80 C.E.*, *Studia Post-Biblica*, ed. by P. A. H. DeBoer, *et al.*, VI (Leiden, 1962), p. 29 n. 2. This same Rabbi looked down on his contemporary, R. Hanina b. Dosa who remained in Galilee, even though the latter's prayer saved the former's son from death (TB: Ber. 34*b*). Apparently R. Johanan b. Zakkai was soured towards Galilee because he was consulted so seldom.   [1] Graetz, III, 297–9.

[2] A. Geiger, *Urschrift und Uebersetzungen der Bibel* (Breslau, 1857), pp. 150–8. Geiger plausibly suggests that the Galilaeans being new settlers accepted Pharisaism, which was beginning at that time, rather than the established Judaean Sadducaeanism. The Pharisees indoctrinated them in the Law.

[3] Graetz, III, 298. Graetz believes that they were fanatical dogmatists, but there is no evidence for this whatever. This is typical of Graetz' habit of downgrading the Galilaeans and elevating the Judaeans. Neubauer (*Géographie*, p. 184) thinks that the Galilaeans' strictness in the Law would be applicable to Jesus' statement in Mt. 5: 18.

[4] Mt. 5: 17–18; Lk. 16: 17. Despite the fact that many regard Mt. 5: 17 as a Judaeo-Christian addition, its authenticity has been recently defended, cf. W. D. Davies, *Christian Origins and Judaism* (London, 1962), pp. 34–7; R. Schnackenburg, *The Moral Teaching of the New Testament*[2], trans. by J. Holland-Smith and W. J. O'Hara (Freiburg, 1965), pp. 57–9, esp. pp. 58–9 n. 5.

[5] Mt. 15: 1–20 = Mk. 7: 1–23. That he 'taught with authority and not as the scribes' (Mt. 7: 29) may have reference to the fact that Jesus did not appeal to the traditions as did the scribes.

the substance of many discourses, and certainly if it were in the earlier part of his ministry, could not have been preached in Judaea. Without question Jesus' ministry was predominantly in Galilee and secondarily in Peraea.[1] It is very doubtful that Jesus could have had such a protracted ministry in Judaea as he had in Galilee and Peraea.

Furthermore, the Galilaeans were more prone to accept miracles and faith healing than were the Jews of Judaea. Even among the Rabbis this was known. R. Hanina b. Dosa (ca. A.D. 70) was known for receiving answers to prayer with regard to healings[2] and to the cessation and starting of rain as well as other fantastic miracles.[3] It is said that men of good deeds (or workers of miracles or men of might) ceased to exist when R. Hanina b. Dosa died.[4] It is interesting to notice that of the thirty-three miracles recorded in the four Gospels, twenty-three or twenty-four were performed in Galilee and only six (three of which are in John) were performed in Judaea. It could possibly be concluded by some that Jesus was more acceptable in Galilee than in Judaea because of his miracles or because he was 'a man of good deeds'.[5] However, this hardly would be a fair conclusion, since Jesus' ministry in Judaea was of such a short duration compared with that in Galilee. Besides, Jesus' miracles are quite different in character from those of R. Hanina b. Dosa.

The Galilaean indifference to the Judaean traditionalism is sometimes attributed not only to their distance from the temple but also to their being less sensitive to the heathen influence. It is thought that a Gentile city like Tiberias would not have been

---

[1] Meeks gives an interesting analysis of Jesus staying (μένων) in Galilee as far as John's gospel is concerned, cf. W. A. Meeks, 'Galilee and Judea in the Fourth Gospel', *JBL*, LXXXV (1966), 163–9.

[2] Ber. v. 5; TB: Ber. 34*b*. It is interesting to notice that though R. Johanan b. Zakkai looks down upon his contemporary R. Hanina b. Dosa, he did ask R. Hanina b. Dosa to pray that his own son might live when he was on the verge of death. His prayers were answered.

[3] TB: Taan. 24*b*–25*a*.

[4] Sot. ix. 15. Büchler believes that 'a man of deeds' is not to be interpreted as meaning a 'miracle worker' but rather as a man doing acts of kindness or love toward other men, cf. A. Büchler, *Types of Jewish-Palestinian Piety* (London, 1922), pp. 79–91.

[5] Klausner (p. 266) believes that the miracles were the only way Jesus could attract the 'simple folk of Galilee'.

tolerated in Judaea.[1] Actually this assertion has no real grounds. Although Tiberias had a stadium,[2] there were theatres and amphitheatres in many of the large cities in Palestine. In fact the heathen games known in Italy and Greece were played in Jerusalem[3] and Caesarea.[4] The Galilaeans may have been less sensitive to the heathen influence in their commercial and social contacts but this was not so in their basic religious views. The devout Jews of Galilee believed that it was improper to mix with the Gentiles.[5]

On the whole then, it seems that the Judaeans were more traditionally minded while Galilaeans were more strict to the letter of the Law and its moral applications. There is, therefore, no concrete evidence for the claim that the Galilaeans understood the Law less than the Judaeans nor that they were necessarily less loyal to the Hebrew religion.

Their language and dialect

There is little doubt that Aramaic was the popular speech in Galilee[6] and perhaps in Peraea. Moore believes that neither Jesus nor his disciples spoke Greek and that in general the Galilaeans were not bilingual; certainly the discussions on religious topics would be only in Aramaic.[7] It is generally believed, though, that Greek was used and this would be more

---

[1] Hausrath, I, 11.

[2] Jos. *BJ* ii. 618; *Vita* 92, 331.

[3] Jos. *Ant.* xv. 267–76; xix. 332–4.

[4] Jos. *Ant.* xvi. 137–41.

[5] Acts 10: 9–29; 11: 1–11, 18; Gal. 2: 11–14.

[6] M. Black, *An Aramaic Approach to the Gospels and Acts*[3] (Oxford, 1967), pp. 15–20, 47–9. See the Qumran discovery of the *Genesis Apocryphon* which gives a witness to the Aramaic language and literature in the time of Christ; cf. M. Black, *The Scrolls and Christian Origins* (London, 1961), Appendix C, pp. 192–8; cf. also A. Neubauer, 'On the Dialects Spoken in Palestine in the Time of Christ', *Studia Biblica*, I (Oxford, 1885), 49–62; G. Dalman, *The Words of Jesus*, trans. D. M. Kay (Edinburgh, 1902), pp. 1–12; *Jesus-Jeshua*, trans. P. P. Levertoff (London, 1929), pp. 7–27; T. W. Manson, *The Teaching of Jesus*[2] (Cambridge, 1935), pp. 46–50. For a discussion which brings up to date the whole problem regarding which language Jesus spoke, see H. Ott, 'Um die Muttersprache Jesu; Forschungen seit Gustaf Dalman', *NovT*, IX (1967), 1–25; J. A. Fitzmyer, 'The Languages of Palestine in the First Century A.D.', *Catholic Biblical Quarterly*, XXXII (1970), 501–31.

[7] G. F. Moore, *Judaism*, I (Cambridge, Mass., 1927), 184; III (Cambridge, Mass., 1930), 53–4.

true of the Galilaeans than the Judaeans.[1] How much Greek was used by the Galilaeans is not known. Moulton thinks that the Galilaeans were definitely bilingual and that the Greek used by the members of Jesus' own circle, Peter, James, and Jude, reveals that their Greek may well have been better than their Aramaic![2] No doubt Moulton has gone too far, for Josephus, who had the educational opportunities, wrote his *Bellum Judaicum* in Aramaic and later translated it into Greek for the benefit of those under the Roman rule;[3] this he did with the help of assistants because his knowledge of Greek was inadequate.[4] Generally it is felt that Jesus made use of both Hebrew and Aramaic in his formal disputations[5] and would have known

[1] Cf. J. H. Moulton, 'New Testament Greek in the Light of Modern Discovery', *Cambridge Biblical Essays*, ed. by H. B. Swete (London, 1909), p. 488; J. N. Sevenster, *Do You Know Greek? How much could the First Century Jewish Christians have Known?*, Supplements to *NovT*, XIX (Leiden, 1968); S. Lieberman, 'How Much Greek in Jewish Palestine?', *Biblical and Other Studies*, ed. by A. Altmann (Cambridge, Mass., 1963), pp. 123–35.

[2] Moulton–Howard, pp. 25–7. Taylor argues that Jesus spoke mostly in Greek instead of Aramaic, cf. R. O. P. Taylor, 'Did Jesus Speak Aramaic?', *ET*, LVI (1945), 328. Turner is reopening the discussion on whether or not Jesus spoke Greek. He believes that Jesus normally spoke, at least in Galilee, biblical Greek which was 'rather a separate dialect of Greek than a form of Koine, and distinguishable as something parallel to classical, Hellenistic, Koine and Imperial Greek', cf. N. Turner, *Grammatical Insights into the New Testament* (Edinburgh, 1965), p. 183. Because of so many occurrences of μὲν...δέ and the genitive absolute, Turner believes that the Gospels were originally written in Greek, *ibid.* pp. 176–83; cf. also Moulton–Turner, pp. 3–9. *Contra* Turner's view see M. Black, 'Second Thoughts. IX. The Semitic Element in the New Testament', *ET*, LXXVII (1965), 20–3; A. J. B. Higgins, 'The Words of Jesus according to St John', *BJRL*, XLIX (1967), 375–6.

[3] *BJ* i. 1–3.

[4] Jos. *Ap.* i. 50. There are different views on how much influence these assistants may have had on the compositions of Josephus' Greek version, cf. Thackeray, *Josephus*, pp. 100–24; R. J. H. Shutt, *Studies in Josephus* (London, 1961), pp. 59–78; H. Petersen, 'Real and Alleged Literary Projects of Josephus', *AJP*, LXXIX (1958), 260–1 n. 5.

[5] Manson, *Teaching*, pp. 46–57; Black, *Aramaic Approach*, pp. 16, 41–9; M. Black, 'The Recovery of the Language of Jesus', *NTS*, III (1957), 305–6; Higgins, *BJRL*, XLIX, 365–70; H. P. Rüger, 'Zum Probleme der Sprache Jesu', *ZNW*, LIX (1968), 113–22. Birkeland believes that the common language in Jesus' day was Hebrew – not of the Mishnaic variety but a dialect nearer to the classical language of the Bible and that some of the words were 'Aramaized', cf. H. Birkeland, 'The Language of Jesus', *Avhandlinger Utgitt*

Greek due to the fact that Nazareth was so close to Sepphoris.[1]
It is also probably true that on the whole the Galilaeans, if not
the Peraeans, were trilingual[2] owing to their contact with the
Greek-speaking districts such as the Decapolis cities, and to the
fact that Greek was the language of the official administration
and of international commerce.[3]

On the other hand there is a general impression that the
Jews of Jerusalem regarded the dialect or the pronunciations of
the Galilaeans with contempt and were at times provoked to
laughter over it.[4] The Talmud states that it was basically
because the Galilaeans constantly interchanged the gutturals
(ה, ח, א, ע).[5] It is true that in one place the Babylonian Talmud
does give several amusing stories with regard to the Galilaean
dialect.[6] However, this seems to be the exception rather than
the rule. Maybe the defective pronunciation of gutturals was
prevalent in the third and fourth century but it is probable that
it was not so markedly developed in the earlier period of
Galilee.[7]

The dialect of Galilee is referred to only twice in the New
Testament, once in connection with Peter at Jesus' trial[8] and

av det Norske Videnskaps-Akademi, 1 (Oslo, 1954), 6–40. Grintz argues that
Mishnaic Hebrew, not Aramaic, was spoken in Palestine at the time of the
Second Temple, cf. J. M. Grintz, 'Hebrew as the Spoken and Written
Language in the Last Days of the Second Temple', *JBL*, LXXIX (1960), 32–
47. Against these two views, see J. A. Emerton, 'Did Jesus Speak Hebrew?',
JTS, N.S. XII (1961), 189–202; J. Barr, 'Which Language did Jesus Speak?—
Some Remarks of a Semitist', *BJRL*, LIII (1970), 9–29.

[1] Dalman, *Jesus-Jeshua*, pp. 3–4; *SSW*, p. 75; cf. also A. W. Argyle, 'Did
Jesus Speak Greek?', *ET*, LXVII (1955), 92–3. Against this, cf. H. M. Draper,
'Did Jesus Speak Greek?', *ET*, LXVII (1956), 317; a reply to this objection by
A. W. Argyle, 'Did Jesus Speak Greek?', *ET*, LXVII (1956), 383.

[2] Gundry argues from archaeological evidence that not only the Jews of
northern Palestine were trilingual but this was also true of those in southern
Palestine; R. H. Gundry, 'The Language Milieu of First-Century Palestine',
JBL, LXXXIII (1964), 404–8.

[3] Dalman, *Jesus-Jeshua*, p. 4; Manson, *Teaching*, p. 46.

[4] Graetz, III, 298; Hausrath, I, 13–14; Keim, II, 5; A. Edersheim, *The Life
and Times of Jesus the Messiah*[3], I (London, 1886), 225–6; Elliott-Binns, p. 21.

[5] TB: Er. 53a–b; Meg. 24b; Ber. 32a; cf. also, Strack–Billerbeck, I, 156–7;
Neubauer, *Studia Biblica*, I, 49–62; G. Dalman, *Grammatik des jüdisch-
palästinischen Aramäisch*[2] (Leipzig, 1905), pp. 56–61, 96–9.

[6] TB: Er. 53a–b. [7] Dalman, *Grammatik*, pp. 43–4.

[8] Mt. 26: 73; Mk. 14: 70; Lk. 22: 59. Only Matthew records the fact that
Peter was detected as a Galilaean by his speech.

the other time on the Day of Pentecost.[1] But there is no hint of ridicule here, but only the fact that their accent gave them away. No doubt Jesus and his disciples were recognized because of their accent, but there is no implication of dishonour or ridicule.[2] It would seem that if the dialect were a point of ridicule, certainly the enemies of Jesus would have used it against him or at least would have scorned his preaching if it had been couched in the inexactitudes which the Talmud suggests were characteristic of the Galilaeans' language. This could also have been applied to the disciples on the Day of Pentecost if the Talmudic criteria were true in that period.

On the contrary, there is no evidence from the New Testament or from any early Jewish literature[3] that the Galilaean dialect was treated with contempt or was the object of ridicule.

Conclusion

Although often criticized as being an unruly people whose tempers were easily roused, it is seen that there is no real basis for such claims. Their love of the Law is demonstrated by their strict adherence to its precepts and they were not steeped in the traditions of men as were the Judaeans. Many times they have been looked down upon by the Judaeans because of their religious convictions and because of their peculiar accent, but especially in Jesus' time there appears little foundation for the accusations. All in all it has been seen that these people in Antipas' territories were an honourable people. It has been said that the Galilaeans thought more of their honour while the Judaeans thought more of their money.[4] What higher compliment can be paid to any people?

[1] Acts 2: 7. [2] Cf. Dalman, *Words*, pp. 80–1.

[3] Hausrath (I, 13) states that Josephus narrates with self-enjoyment the good joke from which Cabul (1 Kgs. 9: 13) received its name (*Ant.* viii. 141–3). If Josephus is in fact enjoying himself over the joke, is it not over a particular incident of naming an area Cabul, rather than with any thought about the Judaeans laughing at the Galilaeans?

[4] TJ: Ket. iv. 12.

CHAPTER 5

THE ECONOMICS OF ANTIPAS' REALM

PRODUCTIVITY

There have been several works on the productivity of Palestine as a whole,[1] but the following is an attempt to assess the productivity of Antipas' two areas outlined in Chapter 3.

Agriculture

Again there is much more information about Galilee than about Peraea in this area of study. Josephus gives a picture of Galilee as being very fertile and productive[2] and Peraea, although mostly desert, as having tracts of good soil.[3] Although Josephus gives an exceptionally favourable picture, it is true that Galilee had a better water supply than Judaea and even in the present century its soil is deep and rich.[4]

There was an abundance of produce. Next to Judaea, the best wheat in the country was produced at such places as Chorazin, Capernaum,[5] and the valley of Arbel.[6] Large quantities of grain were stored in the towns of Upper Galilee belonging

---

[1] Cf. S. Krauss, *Talmudische Archäologie*, II (Leipzig, 1911), 148–247; H. Vogelstein, *Die Landwirtschaft in Palästina zur Zeit der Mišnâh* (Berlin, 1894), pp. 1–78; F. M. Heichelheim, 'Roman Syria', *An Economic Survey of Ancient Rome*, ed. by T. Frank, IV (Baltimore, 1938), 127–44; G. Dalman, *Arbeit und Sitte in Palästina* (Gütersloh, 1928–42), 7 vols.; C. R. Conder, 'The Fertility of Ancient Palestine', *PEFQS*, VIII (1876), 128–31; J. Juster, *Les Juifs dans l'empire Romain*, II (Paris, 1914), 291–310; W. Grundmann, 'Das palästinensische Judentum im Zeitraum zwischen der Erhebung der Makkabäer und dem Ende des jüdischen Krieges', *Darstellung des neutestamentlichen Zeitalters*, vol. I of *Umwelt des Urchristentums*, ed. by J. Leipoldt and W. Grundmann (Berlin, 1965), pp. 180–4.

[2] *BJ* iii. 42–3, 516–21; cf. also, Gen. R. xcviii. 17 (xlix. 21); xcix. 12 (xlix. 20).   [3] *BJ* iii. 44–5.

[4] E. W. G. Masterman, *Studies in Galilee* (Chicago, 1909), p. 17.

[5] TJ: Taan. iv. 5.

[6] TB: Men. 85a; cf. also Neubauer, *Géographie*, pp. 220–3. Yâkût (A.D. 1225) states that Peraea was noted for its wheat crops, cf. G. Le Strange, *Palestine Under the Moslems* (London, 1890), p. 35.

to the imperial family.[1] There were also grain stores for the Herodian family in Lower Galilee.[2] During the siege at Jotapata there was no lack of anything except salt and water.[3] Galilee was well known for fruit[4] such as date-palms, figs, and walnuts.[5] Galilee also produced Palestine's best wine as well as being its largest producer.[6] Abu-l Fidâ (A.D. 1321) states that the pomegranates from *es Salt* (Gadara) Peraea were celebrated in all countries.[7]

Most of all, Galilee was renowned for the production of olive oil.[8] It was said that it was easier to raise myriads (i.e. a forest) of olives in Galilee than to rear one child in *Eretz Yisrael*.[9] Gischala was renowned for the abundance of its oil. Once when the people of Laodicea wanted oil they sent their agent to Jerusalem and to Tyre, but the quantity desired could be found only in Gischala, Galilee.[10] The best oil came from Tekoa[11] and the second best from Peraea,[12] while Gischala occupied third place in regard to both the quantity and quality of the oil produced.[13] Great quantities of oil were stored in Upper

---

[1] Jos. *Vita* 71–3; cf. below, p. 70.

[2] Jos. *Vita* 118–19.   [3] Jos. *BJ* iii. 181.

[4] Jos. *BJ* iii. 517; TB: Ber. 44*a*; Pes. 8*b*; Meg. 6*a*; cf. TJ: Maas. iii. 2.

[5] Jos. *BJ* iii. 45, 517. Livias was also very famous for its dates; cf. Pliny *NH* xiii. 9. 44.

[6] Jos. *BJ* iii. 45, 519; TB: Naz. 31*b*; Shab. 147*b* (Perugitha = Pelugto? south of Tiberias); Meg. 6*a*.

[7] Le Strange, p. 529.

[8] Gen. 49: 20; Deut. 33: 24; Midrash Tannaim: Deut. 33: 24 (Hoffmann, pp. 220–1); Sifre: Deut. 33: 24; Mishnah: Men. viii. 3; Tos.: Men. ix. 5 (p. 526); TB: Men. 85*b*; Pes. 53*a*; Shab. 47*a* (by implication); Sanh. 11*b*; Hag. 25*a* (it is interesting to notice that the custom of leaving a portion of the olive harvest for the poor was learned from the Galilaeans!); Jos. *BJ* ii. 592. Cf. also, I. Löw, *Die Flora der Juden*, II (Wien und Leipzig, 1924), 289–90; Dalman, *Arbeit*, IV (Gütersloh, 1935), 177–82; Krauss, II, 215.

[9] Gen. R. xx. 6 (iii. 16).

[10] TB: Men. 85*b*; Midrash Tannaim: Deut. 33: 24.

[11] Men. viii. 3; TB: Men. 85*b*; 72*a*; Pes. 53*a*; B.B. 145*b*; Shab. 147*b*; Er. 91*a*. Tekoa is identified by some as being in Galilee, cf. Krauss, II, 215, 594 n. 475; Heichelheim, p. 137.

[12] Men. viii. 3, Regeb (רגב) is east of the Jordan River and is identified with modern Rāgib which is eight miles east of the Jordan River and fourteen miles west of Gerasa (Jos. *Ant.* xiii. 398; F. M. Abel, *Géographie de la Palestine*, EB, II [Paris, 1938], 427); cf. also, Jos. *BJ* iii. 45; Bik. i. 10.

[13] Tos.: Men. ix. 5. Gischala from Gush Heleb = 'fat soil'. (Cf. also Midrash Tannaim: Deut. 33: 24.)

Galilee. Josephus shows that both the demand and the supply were great and that the revenues from it were large. Such, for example, were those of John, the rival of Josephus, who once had the monopoly.[1] Oil was so abundant in Jotapata that they heated it and poured large quantities upon the Romans who soon broke their ranks and scattered.[2] In New Testament times, oil was commonly used for the treatment of the sick.[3] Herod the Great in his last sickness was almost killed by being plunged into a tub of oil.[4]

Antipas' territories, then, were very rich in agricultural produce. Galilee could rightly be called a land of milk and honey[5] though its fertile tracts were more suited for produce than for pasturing cattle. Indeed, there were only a few small cattle (i.e. sheep and goats)[6] raised in Galilee because the rich pasture could be used more profitably. Such were raised in abundance in the waste area of Judaea and Syria.[7]

Industry

The largest industry was fishing. Both the Jordan[8] and the Sea of Galilee[9] were widely known for their fish.[10] Countless fishing boats dotted the Sea of Galilee, which in turn was surrounded with villages inhabited by fishermen. For this reason the most important town in the area bore the Hebrew name Magdala or Magdal Nunia (מגדל נוניה)[11] 'fish tower'.[11] In Greek it was called 'Tarichaeae' from the word τάριχος used of salted or pickled fish which were sold all over Palestine.[12] According to

[1] *BJ* ii. 590–3; *Vita* 74–6.   [2] Jos. *BJ* iii. 271–5.

[3] Mk. 6: 13; Lk. 10: 34; Jas. 5: 14.

[4] Jos. *Ant.* xvii. 172; *BJ* i. 657.

[5] As was the country around Sepphoris, TB: Meg. 6 a.

[6] TB: B.K. 79 b–80 a.   [7] *Ibid.*

[8] TB: Yeb. 121 a; TJ: Yeb. xvi. 4.

[9] Jos. *BJ* iii. 508, 520; TB: B.K. 81 a.

[10] Cf. Masterman, pp. 37–48; Dalman, *Arbeit*, vi (Gütersloh, 1939), 343–70.

[11] TB: Pes. 46 a; such is the conclusion of S. Klein, *Beiträge zur Geographie und Geschichte Galiläas* (Leipzig, 1909), pp. 76–84, Dalman, *SSW*, p. 126.

[12] Strabo xvi. 2. 45; TB: Meg. 6 a. In the time of Pliny the lake was sometimes called 'Lake Tarichaeae', cf. Pliny *NH* v. 15. 71. Grant states that fish from Tarichaeae were shipped not only to Jerusalem 'but to Alexandria, Antioch, and even Rome'. His sources are A.Z. ii. 6; Ned. vi. 4; Herodotus ix. 120; Strabo xvi. 2. 45 (F. C. Grant, *The Economic Background of the Gospels*

Josephus it had a population of 40,000 and a fishing fleet of
230 (or 330) boats.[1] In Jesus' time the Jews distinguished between clean and unclean fish.[2] This is probably the meaning of
the phrase 'they gathered the good into vessels, but cast the
bad away'.[3] Certainly the Gospels furnish sufficient evidence to
show that this business in New Testament times was extensive
and profitable.[4] Another important industry was the weaving of
linen[5] and silk.[6] There was also the making of coarse cloth and
mats.[7]

Galilee seemed to have had a monopoly of the manufacture
of a peculiar kind of vessel that was necessary for preserving
oil.[8] Kefar Hananya (Kefr 'Anān)[9] and Kefar Shihin (modern
Asochis)[10] were most noted for the making of these vessels.[11]
These two places had black earth suited for their construction.
This was the principal business of these places and it was very
lucrative. A proverbial saying, 'To bring vessels to Kefar
Hananya'[12] was almost equivalent to the French proverb,
'porter de l'eau à la riviere',[13] or the English proverb, 'to bring
coals to Newcastle'.

Thus Galilee had important industries to boost its economy.
These brought in considerable revenue; nevertheless the inhabitants of both Galilee and Peraea were primarily agricultural.[14]

[London, 1926], p. 56). But these references give no evidence of shipments
outside of Palestine. Elliott-Binns (p. 17) makes the same sweeping statement.

[1] *BJ* ii. 608, 635.

[2] Ter. x. 8; Hul. iii. 7; Bek. i. 2; Maks. vi. 3; TB: Hul. 63*b*.

[3] Mt. 13:48.

[4] Mk. 1: 16–17; Mt. 4: 17–22; 13: 47–8; 17: 27; Lk. 5: 1–11.

[5] B.K. x. 9; TB: B.K. 119*a*; Ecc. R. i. 18. Pausanias mentions the flax of
the Hebrews, Pausanias *Descriptio Graeciae* v. 5. 2; cf. also Krauss, I, 139.

[6] Ecc. R. ii. 8. 2.

[7] These were made in Tiberias and Uscha, TB: Suk. 20*a–b*. Uscha was
a village in Galilee, Neubauer, *Géographie*, pp. 199–200.

[8] Kel. ii. 2.

[9] About four miles south of Meroth, cf. Avi-Yonah, *Map*, p. 37, see also
map p. xvi. This village marked the mid-point between Upper and Lower
Galilee, cf. Sheb. ix. 2.

[10] About eighteen miles west of Tiberias, cf. Avi-Yonah, *Map*, p. 32, see
also map p. xvi. Cf. Jos. *BJ* i. 86.

[11] TB: B.M. 74*a*; Shab. 120*b*.   [12] Gen. R. lxxxvi. 5 (xxxix. 3).

[13] Neubauer, *Géographie*, p. 226.

[14] There was a city-ward movement which was deplored by the author of
the *Letter of Aristeas* (108–13).

Commerce

Galilee had numerous roads which criss-crossed the state, including the trade routes from Damascus to Egypt and from Damascus to the sea coast of Palestine.[1]

Just east of Peraea was a main trade route which ran from the Jordan (opposite Scythopolis) through Pella, and then south-eastward over the hills of Gilead to Gerasa, there joining the main road from Damascus to Philadelphia.[2] There was also a north–south road which left Gadara of Decapolis and followed the Jordan west of Pella through Tell Ammata and Beth Nimrin,[3] and probably continued south to Machaerus.[4] The main west–east road was from Bethel, or Jerusalem, to Jericho, across the Jordan and over the plateau to Rabboth Ammon[5] (i.e. Philadelphia). Apparently there was also a road from Jericho to es Salt leading to Gerasa.[6]

There were many religious restrictions on Jewish business dealings with the Gentiles.[7] The Galilaeans may not have been so meticulous in such matters as the Judaeans, though according to the Talmud the Galilaeans were not so concerned with worldly prosperity. Unlike the Judaeans they were more concerned with honour than with Mammon.[8] The influence of Hellenism and their closeness to the Gentiles must in general

---

[1] Smith, *HGHL*, pp. 373–4, 427–32; Masterman, pp. 10–11; Y. Aharoni and M. Avi-Yonah, *The Macmillan Bible Atlas* (New York, 1968), p. 17.

[2] G. A. Smith, 'Trade and Commerce', *EncB*, IV (1903), 5167.

[3] Dalman, *SSW*, p. 237.

[4] As shown on the maps in Wright and Filson, map xiv; L. H. Grollenberg, *Atlas of the Bible*, trans. and ed. by J. M. H. Reid and H. H. Rowley (London, 1956), p. 116.

[5] D. Baly, *The Geography of the Bible* (London, 1958), p. 115.

[6] Cf. maps of Smith, *EncB*, IV, 5165–6; Dalman, *SSW*, p. 234.

[7] E.g. A.Z. i. 1, 'For three days before the festivals of the gentiles it is forbidden to have business with them – to lend to them or borrow from them, to lend them money or to borrow money from them, to repay them or to be repaid by them'; i. 5, 'These things it is forbidden to sell to the Gentiles: fir-cones, white figs with their stalks, frankincense, or a white cock'; i. 8, 'None may hire houses to them in the land of Israel or, needless to say, fields'; ii. 1, 'Cattle may not be left in the inns of the gentiles'; ii. 3, 'It is forbidden to have business with them that are going on an idolatrous pilgrimage, but with them that are returning it is permitted' (trans. from *The Babylonian Talmud*, by I. Epstein, XIII (London, 1961), *ad loc.*).

[8] TJ: Ket. iv. 12 [or 14].

have caused the Galilaeans (as also the Peraeans) to deal more easily with the rest of the world. Galilee was a rich land and had much to offer in the way of trade.

ECONOMIC CONSIDERATIONS
The distribution of wealth

Although most of the eastern provinces had a middle class, it seems that in Antipas' realm this class was almost non-existent, and that in practice there were only the very rich and the poor.[1]

The rich

The rich were either large landowners[2] or merchants. The imperial family had estates,[3] in some of which was stored the imperial corn.[4] The Palestinian royal family owned much of the land. It is probable that Herod the Great privately owned half to two-thirds of his kingdom.[5] Land ownership by the royal family continued after his death, for when Archelaus was deposed the Roman government had to liquidate his estates,[6] and at Antipas' deposition the emperor gave not only his tetrarchy but also his property (χρήματα) to Agrippa.[7] Antipas undoubtedly owned much of the land in his realm. For example,

[1] A. N. Sherwin-White, *Roman Society and Roman Law in the New Testament* (Oxford, 1963), p. 139.

[2] Cf. J. Herz, 'Grossgrundbesitz in Palästina im Zeitalter Jesu', *PJB*, XXIV (1928), 98–113.

[3] Jos. *Vita* 119. Hyrcanus II had estates (*Ant.* xiv. 209). To Livia (Augustus' wife) Salome bequeathed Jamnia and its territory, together with Phasaelis and Archelais with its rich palm-groves (*Ant.* xviii. 31; *BJ* ii. 167). There was, even after the war of 66–70, a Roman military colony established by Vespasian at Emmaus (*BJ* vii. 217). How much land the imperial family owned within Antipas' realm is difficult to ascertain. For a helpful discussion of this problem (although in relation to Asia Minor), see B. Levick, *Roman Colonies in Southern Asia Minor* (Oxford, 1967), Appendix VI, pp. 215–26.

[4] Jos. *Vita* 71–3. Rostovtzeff (*SEHRE*, II, 664 n. 32) thinks it more probable that the imperial corn stored in the villages of Upper Galilee was the produce of the imperial estates of Galilee rather than the proceeds of a tax in kind paid to the Roman government. *Contra* this, cf. Jones, *CERP*, p. 461 n. 62.

[5] Otto, cols. 72, 92.

[6] Jos. *Ant.* xvii. 355; xviii. 2, 26; *BJ* ii. 111.

[7] Jos. *Ant.* xviii. 252.

he was able to build a city like Tiberias and give the adjacent land at his own expense to those who occupied it.[1]

In addition to the royal family, Josephus gives a picture of a native aristocracy of large landowners,[2] as well as officers of the king. The latter included such men as Capellus,[3] John of Gischala,[4] Crispus,[5] and Josephus himself,[6] as well as others.[7] It seems that most of the land was in the hands of the Sadducees.[8]

Some of Jesus' parables allude to those owning estates. There is the parable of the rich fool;[9] the vineyard owner who had several slaves and leased out his land;[10] another vineyard owner, who, although he had a steward, went himself to the market square to hire labourers;[11] and the father of the prodigal son who had also a few servants.[12]

Besides the owners of estates, the merchants were also among the rich. One such man was John of Gischala who made enormous profits by selling corn to the wealthy citizens,[13] and by selling oil to Caesarea.[14] The New Testament mentions two businessmen of more moderate means: the fisherman Zebedee who had hired servants,[15] and the jeweller who bought a costly pearl.[16] This and other parables[17] point to the presence of the extremely rich in Jesus' day.

[1] Jos. *Ant.* xviii. 38. Salome, another member of the royal family, owned Jamnia, Azotus (Ashdod), Phasaelis, and Archelais (*Ant.* xvii. 321; xviii. 31; *BJ* ii. 98).

[2] The land was not entirely owned by the royal family, for Quirinius, after Archelaus' deposition, had not only to liquidate Archelaus' estate but also to assess the private property of the Jews (Jos. *Ant.* xviii. 2, 26).

[3] *Vita* 32, 66–7, 296.   [4] *BJ* ii. 575, 585–94; iv. 564–8; *Vita* 70–6.

[5] Owned estates east of the Jordan, *Vita* 33.   [6] *Vita* 422–5, 429.

[7] Rostovtzeff, *SEHRE*, I, 270; II, 664 n. 32; Baron, I, 414 n. 35. There were large estates in the time of Herod the Great – Costobarus, Salome's husband, had one (Jos. *Ant.* xv. 264). Herod himself expropriated estates (*Ant.* xvii. 305–7).

[8] Cf. L. Finkelstein, 'The Pharisees: their Origin and their Philosophy', *HTR*, XXII (1929), 188–9; W. H. C. Frend, *Martyrdom and Persecution in the Early Church* (Oxford, 1965), p. 103 n. 91.

[9] Lk. 12: 16–21.   [10] Mt. 21: 33–42 = Mk. 12: 1–11 = Lk. 20: 9–17.

[11] Mt. 20: 1–14.   [12] Lk. 15: 11–23.   [13] Jos. *BJ* ii. 590; *Vita* 70–3.

[14] Jos. *BJ* ii. 591–3; *Vita* 74–6.   [15] Mk. 1: 20.

[16] Mt. 13: 45–6.

[17] E.g. the parables of the great supper (Lk. 14: 15–24 = ?Mt. 22: 1–14); of the unjust steward whose lord was rich (Lk. 16: 1–12). Jesus also spoke about and to the rich (cf. Lk. 6: 24–5; 7: 41–3; Mt. 19: 16–23 = Mk. 10:

The poor

The vast majority of the people were poor.[1] The peasants probably had little parcels of land, either by inheritance from Maccabaean times when the allotments were made in the Galilaean territory,[2] or by the older traditional tribal rights, or by leasing land from the rich landowners. It was difficult for the peasants to compete against the large landowners who had cheap slave labour under the direction of stewards,[3] and hence were able to produce at low prices.[4] Josephus makes a few references to the poor[5] while the New Testament gives ample illustrations of them.[6]

Conclusion

Little is known of a middle class. Much is given on the rich and the poor. In fact some of Jesus' parables make a contrast between these two classes. There is the rich man with his

17–23 = Lk. 18: 18–24); cf. J. Jeremias, *Jerusalem in the Time of Jesus*, trans. from the 3rd German ed. (with the author's rev. to 1967) by F. H. and C. H. Cave (London, 1969), pp. 109–19.

[1] The great number of very small coins indicates the diminutive character of most commercial transactions and the poverty of the majority of the people (cf. Smith, *EncB*, IV, 5190). For a full discussion of the term πτωχός, cf. F. Hauck and E. Bammel, 'πτωχός', *TDNT*, VI (1968), 885–915. Also, for a study of the problem of the *'am ha-ares* one should consult A. Büchler, *Der galiläische 'Am-ha 'Ares des zweiten Jahrhunderts* (Wien, 1906); I. Abrahams, "Am Ha-Arec', Appendix to *The Synoptic Gospels* by C. G. Montefiore, II (London, 1927), 647–69; L. Finkelstein, *The Pharisees*[3], II (Philadelphia, 1962), 754–61; A. Burgsmüller, 'Der Am hā 'ares zur Zeit Jesu' (unpublished dissertation, 1955 – the present writer has not been able to locate this work).

[2] Grant, p. 64.

[3] For a discussion on labour in New Testament times, cf. Grant, pp. 64–71.

[4] Baron, I, 277.

[5] E.g. Tiberias was composed of sailors and the destitute class (Jos. *Vita* 66) as well as the peasants (*Ant.* xviii. 37–8); cf. Rostowzew, *Kolonates*, pp. 305–6.

[6] E.g. Mt. 5: 3 = Lk. 6: 20–1; Lk. 14: 13; Mk. 12: 42–4 = Lk. 21: 2–4 (widow's mite); cf. Jeremias, *Jerusalem*, pp. 109–19. Chrysostom speaks of the poverty in Antioch during the fourth century, where the rich exploited the poor tenants by leasing the land at high prices with high interest rates, cf. Chrysostom, *Commentarii in Matthaeum* homily lxi. 2–4 (*MPG*, LVIII, 591–4).

steward who was owed by two peasants 100 measures of oil and wheat;[1] and the man who owed 10,000 talents while his own debtors owed him a mere 100 δηνάρια;[2] the debtors who owed the money-lender 50 and 500 δηνάρια;[3] and the rich man and Lazarus who vividly contrast the two extremes.[4] If Jesus' parables had not reflected the economics of the day they would have been pointless to his hearers. It can be safely concluded that there existed both the extremely rich and the miserably poor, the latter being the lot of the majority of the people.

The taxation of the people

Introduction

Palestine came under the Roman tribute for the first time under Pompey. Later, under Gabinius,[5] it was divided into five synods (σύνοδοι or συνέδρια), two of which were Sepphoris of Galilee and Amathus of Peraea.[6] The tax in Palestine, along with that in Syria, seems to have been collected by Roman *publicani*.[7] There were complaints in various parts of the Roman Empire of exploitation by high taxes and expenses.[8]

Julius Caesar was the first to introduce reforms in 47 B.C. In 44 B.C. he ordered the abolition of the farming of taxes on land and persons in Palestine.[9] He also changed land taxation by

[1] Lk. 16: 1–7.

[2] Mt. 18: 23–30.

[3] Lk. 7: 41.

[4] Lk. 16: 19–22.

[5] Jos. *Ant.* xiv. 74; *BJ* i. 154; Velleius Paterculus *Historiae Romanae* ii. 37. 5; Plutarch *Pompeius* xxxix. 2–3.

[6] Jos. *Ant.* xiv. 91; *BJ* i. 170.

[7] Cicero *De Provinciis Consularibus* v. 10–11; cf. also M. Rostowzew, 'Geschichte der Staatspacht in der römischen Kaiserzeit bis Diokletian', *Philologus*, Supplementband IX (1904), 476.

[8] Cicero *In Verrem* iii. 207–8. This record presents the exaggerations of an orator pleading his case against a notorious offender. It represents the worst era of Roman misgovernment, but is all too characteristic of the exploitation of Roman rule. Cf. also Tac. *Agricola* xv; *Ann.* ii. 42.

[9] Jos. *Ant.* xiv. 190–206; cf. Schürer, I, 345–50, esp. 346–8 nn. 24–5. In the rest of the Roman Empire the farming of taxes continued, but beginning with Julius Caesar it seems to have been gradually suppressed, Appian *BC* v. 4. Rostovtzeff, *SEHRE*, II, 559 n. 7; Rostowzew, *Philologus*, Supp. IX, 378–80; K. Wieseler, *Beiträge zur richtigen Würdigung der Evangelien* (Gotha, 1869), pp. 78–9.

taxing a fourth of the harvest[1] 'in the second year',[2] with the exception of the sabbatical year, and ordered that they should continue to pay tithes to the leader of their nation.[3] Although the changing of the tax structure did relieve the Jews to some extent, soon after the Herods came into power they again demanded heavy taxes. As far as Antipas was concerned, Augustus allowed him to receive 200 talents[4] for Galilee and

[1] In addition to this tax, Heichelheim (pp. 231, 235) tentatively suggests that Appian's reference to the Syrian 1 per cent annual tax on the assessed value of property (Appian Συριακή viii. 50) can also be applied to the Jews in the Gabinius–Pompey era.

[2] Jos. *Ant.* xiv. 203. This is very difficult to interpret. Heichelheim (pp. 231, 235) thinks it refers to every second or every other year, and thus there would be a 12 per cent annual tax with the exception of the sabbatical year. Grant (pp. 90–1 n. 3) views it as meaning that there was a 25 per cent tax to be paid in the second year of the sabbatical period. Mommsen contends that the land was freed from tribute from the second year onward and that only Joppa was to give a fourth of its produce to the Romans at Sidon (T. Mommsen, *The Provinces of the Roman Empire*, trans. W. P. Dickson, II [London, 1909], 175 n. 1). Mommsen's view is unlikely, for Josephus is apparently stating that all Jews, with the exception of Joppa, were to pay tax for the city of Jerusalem of a fourth of their produce 'in the second year'. Josephus then elaborates on the special requirements for the citizens of Joppa. An interesting theory is presented by Reinach, who substitutes μηνί for ἔτει (T. Reinach [ed.], *Œuvres complètes de Flavius Josèphe*, trans. by J. Chamonard, III [Paris, 1904], 241 n. 7). This would mean a 25 per per cent annual tax. Certainly the latter part of the decree (*Ant.* xiv. 206) states that the district of Joppa had to pay a lump sum annually. The only difficulty with this view is that there is no textual evidence for it whatsoever; cf. B. Niese, *Flavii Iosephi Opera*, III (Berlin, 1892), 277. Jones thinks it could have been as little as 5 per cent since the Jews at this time were a favoured community; cf. A. H. M. Jones, 'Review and Discussion of "Ricerche sull'organizzazione della Giudea sotto il Dominio Romano (63 a.C. – 70 d.C.)", by A. Momigliano', *JRS*, xxv (1935), 229.

[3] Jos. *Ant.* xiv. 200–10. Cf. Rostowzew, *Philologus*, Supp. IX, 476–7, esp. n. 315; F. Rosenthal, 'Die Erlässe Cäsars und die Senatsconsulte im Josephus Alterth. XIV, 10 nach ihrem historischen Inhalte untersucht', *MGWJ*, XXVIII (1869), 176–83, 216–28, 300–22; cf. also, Jones, *JRS*, xxv, 228–9.

[4] This would be approximately 182,892 pounds sterling or 438,333 American dollars. This is based on the fact that during Augustus' reign the average *aureus* was around 121·9 grains and thus one denarial talent would be 60·956 troy oz., cf. F. Hultsch, *Griechische und römische Metrologie*[2] (Berlin, 1882), pp. 308–11, esp. p. 309 n. 1; T. Mommsen, *Geschichte des römischen Münzwesen* (Berlin, 1860), pp. 752–3 nn. 41–2; A. R. S. Kennedy, 'Money', *HDB*, III (1900), 426–9. This is also based on the current price of gold in May 1970 at 299/1·25 shillings or $35·95487 per troy oz. (according to the

Peraea.[1] It is probable that the money for running the government, for his building programme, and for Roman tribute[2] was
collected in a form of taxation over and above the 200 talents
he was allowed to receive.

Subjects of taxation

At the time of the debating of Herod's will, people complained
of his exorbitant taxes;[3] this was a regular feature at the accession of a new monarch.[4] Herod's building programme was so
immense that taxes must have been heavy. High taxes may
have been also a part of Archelaus' unbearable tyranny.[5]

Herod collected poll and land taxes from his private property.[6]
Also no doubt Antipas collected taxes from the people to whom
he leased his land. Those who had their own land would have
had to pay heavy taxes as well.

Items of taxation

One source of revenue was land tax. In Syrian times it had been
customary, at least for a while, to exact a tax of a third part of the
corn and half of the wine and oil.[7] In the time of Caesar a fourth
part of the harvest 'in the second year' was demanded, with the
exception of the sabbatical year.[8]

report of Sharps, Pixley Limited, Bullion Brokers [London, May, 1970]).
There is some disagreement over the weight of the talent. Mommsen
(*Provinces*, II, 187 n. 1) believes that Josephus is referring to the Hebrew talent
rather than the denarial talent as calculated by Hultsch (pp. 605–6). If this
is true, then the talent would be worth 50 per cent more than calculated
above and Herod Antipas' revenue would have been about 274,338 pounds
or 657,500 dollars per annum. For further discussion on the talent, see
F. Hultsch, 'Das hebräische Talent bei Josephus', *Klio*, II (1902), 70–2;
Lehmann-Haupt, 'Talent', PW, Supp. VIII (1956), 834–5.

[1] Jos. *Ant.* xvii. 318; *BJ* ii. 95.   [2] Cf. Appendix IV.
[3] Jos. *Ant.* xvii. 308; *BJ* ii. 86.   [4] Jones, *Herods*, pp. 87–8.
[5] Jos. *Ant.* xvii. 342; *BJ* ii. 111. This should not be pressed, for his deposition is adequately explained by the fact that he was a bad ruler.
[6] Josephus gives numerous examples of the Jewish royal family collecting
revenues from their own property (cf. *Ant.* xiv. 206; xvii. 25–8, 204, 320; *BJ*
i. 483; ii. 97; cf. also Strabo xvi. 2. 41; Heichelheim, p. 161).
[7] 1 Macc. 10: 30; Jos. *Ant.* xiii. 49–50.
[8] Jos. *Ant.* xiv. 203; xvii. 204; cf. above, p. 74 n. 2. This form of taxation may have continued in the tetrarchies of Antipas and Philip, but have
been altered in the case of Judaea when it became a province. This tax was
payable to the leader of the land and not to the treasury of Rome.

By implication it seems that there was a poll tax, at least during Herod the Great's reign.[1] In Roman times the government seems to have claimed the fishing rights in the rivers and lakes,[2] and to have gained revenue from this source. Customs were also collected on the trade routes.[3] Levi was such a collector in Capernaum,[4] this city being on the route from Damascus to the Mediterranean Sea.[5] It may also have been a place for port duties and fishing tolls. Levi, then, was a customs collector not for Rome but for Herod Antipas. Every city was a frontier in itself and Pliny states that at every stopping place by land or sea some tax was levied.[6] This resulted in goods being sold at a much higher price than their original cost. Klauser states that the increase in price would have been 100 per cent on its original price, in spite of a fixed duty of only $2\frac{1}{2}$ per cent for the province of Asia (including Palestine) imposed by the Roman government.[7]

No doubt in Antipas' administration, as in his father's,[8] there were other taxes such as purchase and sales taxes. During the first and second centuries there was a sales tax on slaves, oil, clothes, hides, furs, and other valuable commodities in Palmyra. Also, taxes were imposed on leather workshops, on butchery, on prostitution, on the use of water in the city, and a pasturing tax on the beasts of foreigners in that city.[9] 'It is probable, if not almost certain, that similar taxes were levied throughout the whole Roman Near East.'[10] Since this was an independent city not under direct Roman taxation, a similar system may have existed in Antipas' cities and lands.

Over and above these taxes were the religious dues. These were no less than 10 per cent and sometimes as much as 20 per

[1] Jos. *Ant.* xvii. 308.

[2] Rostowzew, *Philologus*, Supp. IX, 414; Rostovtzeff, *SEHRE*, II, 689 n. 100.

[3] E.g. Strabo xvi. 1. 27.

[4] Mt. 9: 9; Mk. 2: 14; Lk. 5: 27.   [5] Smith, *HGHL*, p. 430.

[6] *NH* xii. 32. 63–5.   [7] P. 188.

[8] Jos. *Ant.* xvii. 205; *BJ* ii. 4. These were removed in the case of Jerusalem in A.D. 37 by Vitellius (*Ant.* xviii. 90).

[9] *CIS*, II, iii, 3913. An Eng. trans. and commentary is given by G. A. Cooke, *A Text-book of North-Semitic Inscriptions* (Oxford, 1903), pp. 313–40; M. Rostovtzeff, 'Seleucid Babylonia', *Yale Classical Studies*, III (1932), 74–91; Heichelheim, p. 239.

[10] Heichelheim, p. 239.

cent of a man's income as calculated before the governmental tax had been deducted, since it was to be given to God.[1] Grant believes that the total taxation of the Jewish people in Jesus' time approached the intolerable rate of 30 to 40 per cent, and perhaps even higher.[2]

Although in A.D. 17 Judaea, along with Syria, complained of the Roman burden and asked for a reduction of taxes,[3] there are no recorded complaints or riots on this issue within Antipas' domain. This need not mean that his taxes were lower, but that his government was more stable and could cope more easily with any attempts at rebellion.

Collection of taxes

In the Ptolemaic era taxes were farmed out to the *publicani*. These people were leased a particular district for which they had made the highest bid, and whatever was collected in excess of their bid was to their gain.[4] The *publicani* were usually quite wealthy. This system continued under the Roman Republic. Later (during the Roman Principate), the *publicani* in the Roman Near East collected custom tolls and similar taxes, but the land and poll taxes were collected by the local government.[5]

The so-called 'publicans' (τελῶναι) in the New Testament were mere tax collectors having no connection with the wealthy *publicani* of the Roman Republic. The latter farmed the taxes of an entire province and were nearly always foreigners.

---

[1] For a discussion of the religious dues, cf. Grant, pp. 92–100.

[2] Grant, p. 105. Baron (I, 279) states that according to Jewish Law 'the farmer was to put aside about 12 per cent of the remainder of his crop for priestly tithe and heave-offering, plus a "second tithe" for the poor or for spending in the distant city of Jerusalem. There may actually have been a third tithe for the poor every third year.' If there was a yearly governmental tax of 25 per cent, then the total tax would have been 41 per cent, and every third year 48 per cent, of the total income. On top of this, the strict observance of the sabbatical year resulted in the loss of at least another year and a half of agricultural produce (*ibid.*).

[3] Tac. *Ann.* ii. 42.

[4] Jos. *Ant.* xii. 167–85; cf. M. Rostovtzeff, 'Ptolemaic Egypt', *CAH*, VII (Cambridge, 1928), 129–30. Rostovtzeff thinks that Joseph, the tax farmer, collected from the city authorities (cf. Rostowzew, *Philologus*, Supp. IX, 359–61). On the other hand, Jones (*CERP*, p. 448 n. 18) believes that the tax farmers in the Ptolemaic period collected taxes directly from the populace.

[5] Heichelheim, p. 233.

The publicans, on the other hand, were Jews who prayed in the temple[1] and with whom Jesus and his disciples ate.[2] One of them, Levi, lived in Antipas' territory at Capernaum.[3] So numerous were they that it is improbable that they were all very rich. In fact Luke had to specify that Zacchaeus was not only an ἀρχιτελώνης but also very rich.[4] They seem for the most part to have been contractors or small farmers, collecting one form of tax in a town or small district. From the example of Levi it would seem that each had his own tax office where he collected his particular tax.

By law they were permitted to collect a certain duty, but in many instances they illegally collected more than the proper amount.[5] Though not permitted to exact arrears, they could denounce and accuse defaulters before the officers of the state, and sometimes they gained money illegally by false accusations.[6] Hence, their powers were fairly limited in comparison with the old republican *publicani* and their agents. These τελῶναι were natives and were hated by their countrymen, being classified with sinners,[7] harlots,[8] robbers,[9] and Gentiles.[10] They were hated because they used unscrupulous means for extorting more money than allowed, and pocketing the excess amount. This is why they were so often classified as robbers. The Jews especially resented them for being native Jews.[11] Not only

---

[1] Lk. 18: 10–13.   [2] Mt. 9: 10–11; Mk. 2: 15–16; Lk. 5: 29–30.

[3] Mt. 9: 9; Mk. 2: 14; Lk. 5: 27.

[4] Lk. 19: 2.   [5] Lk. 3: 12–13; TB: B.K. 113a; Sanh. 25b

[6] Lk. 19: 8; Rostowzew, *Philologus*, Supp. IX, 343–4. The word συκοφαντέω means 'to accuse falsely' or 'to extort by false charges or threats', cf. A. Plummer, *A Critical and Exegetical Commentary on the Gospel according to St Luke*[4], ICC (Edinburgh, 1905), pp. 92–3; LSJ, p. 1671; MM, p. 596; Bauer/AG, p. 784.

[7] Mt. 9: 10–11; 11: 19; Mk. 2: 15; Lk. 5: 30; 7: 34; 15: 1; TB: A.Z. 39a; Bek. 31a. This category is broad and would include harlots, robbers, and Gentiles. For a discussion of publican and sinners, cf. I. Abrahams, 'Publicans and Sinners', *Studies in Pharisaism and the Gospels*, 1 (Cambridge, 1917), pp. 54–61; J. Jeremias, 'Zöllner und Sünder', *ZNW*, xxx (1931), 293–300.

[8] Mt. 21: 31.

[9] TB: Shab. 78b; Hag. 26a; Sheb. 39a; Sanh. 25b–26a; B.K. 113a; cf. also Ned. iii. 4; Toh. vii. 6.

[10] Mt. 18: 17; TB: Er. 36b.

[11] Cf. A. Büchler, *The Political and Social Leaders of the Jewish Community of Sepphoris in the Second and Third Centuries* (London, n.d.), pp. 13, 40 n. 1.

were they cheating their own people but also were collecting for a cause other than the temple. In Galilee and Peraea they were exacting taxes from their brethren only to line the coffers of the Herodian household. This was hardly calculated to make them popular!

Conclusion

Taxation under Antipas' administration was a burden to the people of Galilee and Peraea. Yet there was never a rebellion on this account or any record of outward resentment towards Antipas. Besides land and poll taxes, taxes were exacted from many sources such as trade routes, ports, fishing tolls, produce, and sales. On top of this were the religious dues. In short, not less than 30 to 40 per cent of one's income went on taxes and religious dues. These were collected for Herod Antipas by native Jews who were known to exact more than they should, and were thus despised by their own countrymen.

PART 3

ANTIPAS' REIGN

CHAPTER 6

THE EARLY YEARS OF ANTIPAS' REIGN

When Antipas returned to Palestine, his domain was ravaged by war. An unusually large number of Jewish pilgrims from Galilee, Peraea, and Idumaea, as well as from Judaea, had come up to the feast of Pentecost in 4 B.C. There appears to have been a co-ordinated military strategy, for the Jews had divided themselves into three camps, completely surrounding Jerusalem. The Romans burned the porticoes of the temple and pillaged the treasury, making the Jews even more furious and causing them to lay siege to the palace where Sabinus was residing.[1]

The rebellion began to spread through the surrounding countryside. In Judaea the revolts were led by Achiab (a cousin of Herod),[2] Athronges, and other unnamed leaders.[3] The Peraeans placed themselves under the leadership of Simon, a former slave of Herod (who destroyed the palace at Jericho) and they were severely defeated by a combination of the royal troops under Gratus, and Romans and the troops of the Sebastenians. East of the Jordan a different group of Peraeans destroyed the royal palace at Ammatha or Betharamatha.[4]

In Galilee, Judas, son of Hezekias (the celebrated brigand-chief in the days of Herod the Great), seized the arms in the arsenals of the royal palace at Sepphoris.[5] Sepphoris apparently was then made the headquarters of the rebellion, for it was attacked and completely burnt by a detachment of Varus' force, and the inhabitants were reduced to slavery.[6]

[1] Jos. *Ant.* xvii. 254–68; *BJ* ii. 42–54.

[2] Jos. *Ant.* xvii. 269–70; *BJ* ii. 55.

[3] Jos. *Ant.* xvii. 278–85; *BJ* ii. 60–5. Athronges' approach was similar to that of the Maccabaean family over 150 years before, cf. W. R. Farmer, 'Judas, Simon, and Athronges', *NTS*, IV (1958), 152–5.

[4] Jos. *Ant.* xvii. 273–7; *BJ* ii. 57–9; Tac. *Hist.* v. 9.

[5] Jos. *Ant.* xvii. 271–2; *BJ* ii. 56. Judas may have been linked to the royal Maccabaean family which was suppressed by Herod the Great (cf. Farmer, *NTS*, IV, 150–2).

[6] Jos. *Ant.* xvii. 288–9; *BJ* ii. 68. In *BJ* it is Gaius, a friend of Varus, who is in command of the detachment, though in *Ant.* both Varus' son and Gaius are in command.

THE BUILDING OF HIS CITIES

When Antipas returned to his newly acquired domain he had to restore order and to rebuild what had been destroyed. Following the example of Alexander the Great, Herod and his sons founded twelve cities in conformity with Hellenistic ideals. Herod himself founded six cities, Archelaus one village (κώμη), Philip two cities, and Antipas three cities. Two of the last three, namely, Sepphoris and Tiberias, were in Galilee, while the third, Livias, was in Peraea. Tiberias alone of these was an entirely new city. If it was built in honour of Tiberius, it probably was not built until after his accession in August A.D. 14. As for Sepphoris and Livias, it is likely that they had been rebuilt soon after Antipas' return from Rome because: (1) they had been recently destroyed; (2) they were fortresses; and (3) Sepphoris was Antipas' capital city until he founded Tiberias. A discussion on Sepphoris and Livias is now in order.

Sepphoris

Its name and rebuilding

Although not mentioned in pre-exilic sources, the ancient town of Sepphoris was designated most frequently in post-Biblical sources by צפורי[1] and Σέπφωρις.[2] It is six miles northwest of Xaloth, and is largely buried under the modern Arab village of Ṣaffuriyye, which is similar to that name.

The first mention of Sepphoris is in Josephus. Reference is there made to the early part of Alexander Jannaeus' reign (103–76 B.C.) at the time Ptolemy Lathyrus unsuccessfully attempted to take the city *circa* 100 B.C.[3] When Gabinius (75–55 B.C.) divided Palestine into five administrative councils (συνέδρια)[4] Sepphoris became the Sanhedrin (highest court) of Galilee.

During Herod the Great's reign, Sepphoris was apparently an important military post where arms and provisions were

---

[1] S. Yeivin, 'Historical and Archaeological Notes', *Preliminary Report of the University of Michigan Excavations at Sepphoris, Palestine, in 1931*, L. Waterman, director (Ann Arbor, 1937), p. 17.

[2] Schürer, II, 209–10.

[3] *Ant.* xiii. 338.

[4] Jos. *Ant.* xiv. 91. For συνέδρια, *BJ* i. 170 has σύνοδοι.

stored, for after his death the revolutionary leader, Judas, equipped his followers with weapons from the royal palace there and it became the main seat of the rebellion.[1] Varus, with the help of Aretas of Arabia, captured and burned the city, and made slaves of its inhabitants – a high price for seditious activity.[2]

As mentioned above, in all probability Antipas began to re-build Sepphoris soon after returning from Rome,[3] for it was his residence[4] until he founded Tiberias.[5] Since Nazareth was only four miles south-southwest of Sepphoris, Joseph, husband of Mary, may have there plied his trade as a carpenter.[6] If the building commenced immediately after Antipas' return from Rome it would have continued well into the first century A.D., possibly until A.D. 8 or 10.[7] It may be that Jesus himself helped in the later stages.

[1] Jos. *Ant.* xvii. 271; *BJ* ii. 56.

[2] Jos. *Ant.* xvii. 289; *BJ* ii. 68.

[3] Case believes that he built it at the same time as he rebuilt the Pereaan city of Betharamphtha. This would have been before Tiberius' death since it was built in honour of his wife, Livia, before she was admitted into the *gens Julia* (below, p. 89). Hence from the order of events in Jos. *Ant.* xviii. 26–8, Case believes that these two cities were not built before A.D. 7. However, as even he admits in the same footnote, Josephus does not always arrange his history chronologically, cf. S. J. Case, 'Jesus and Sepphoris', *JBL*, XLV (1926), 18 n. 4; *Jesus* (Chicago, 1927), p. 204 n. 1.

[4] Dalman (*SSW*, p. 75) believes that Antipas took up residence at Sepphoris around 2 B.C.

[5] Although Sepphoris later became subordinate to Tiberias (Jos. *Vita* 37), its distinction was not seriously impaired. For one reason it continued to be the largest city of Galilee (*BJ* iii. 34; *Vita* 232). In the time of the revolution of 66–70 it still remained prominent (this is emphasized by Josephus, cf. *Vita* 30, 37–9, 64, 82, 103–4, 111, 123–4, 188, 203, 232–3, 346–7, 373–4, 379–80, 384, 394–6, 411; *BJ* ii. 511, 574, 629, 645–6; iii. 30–4, 59, 61, 129; cf. also Schürer, II, 212–13). Because of its pro-Roman policy it again became the capital of Galilee (*Vita* 38). After the war during Trajan's reign it became a true city, for it produced coins (Jones, *CERP*, p. 277; G. F. Hill, *Catalogue of the Greek Coins of Palestine* [London, 1914], pp. xi–xii, 1–3; B. V. Head, *Historia Numorum*² [Oxford, 1911], p. 802). It remained prominent in the Talmudic period (for Talmudic references, cf. Schürer, II, 209 n. 489; Büchler, *Political and Social Leaders...of Sepphoris*; Klein, *Beiträge*, pp. 26–45).

[6] Mt. 13: 55; Mk. 6: 3.

[7] Yeivin, p. 19 n. 14. It seems hardly conceivable that the building of Sepphoris continued until A.D. 25, as suggested by Case (*JBL*, XLV, 18; *Jesus*, p. 204).

Following his father's Hellenistic zeal, Antipas restored
Sepphoris so splendidly that it became the 'ornament of all
Galilee' (πρόσχημα τοῦ Γαλιλαίου παντός) and was called
αὐτοκρατορίς.[1] From archaeological evidence it is probable
that Antipas built there a theatre and an elaborate water-works.[2]
In building a theatre, he may have been emulating his father,
for Herod was known as a theatre builder.[3] There was also of
course a wall for the purpose of fortification.[4] Although the
name Diocaesarea was never used of this place until Antoninus
Pius (A.D. 138–61), Dalman believes Antipas so designated the
city at the time of its reconstruction.[5]

Its composition

Sepphoris was pro-Roman during the war of 66–70.[6] What,
therefore, was its allegiance in Antipas' reign? Due to the sur-
vival of the Sanhedrin, Yeivin believes that the city remained
wholly Jewish.[7] For its pro-Roman attitude during the revolu-

[1] Jos. *Ant.* xviii. 27. To determine the exact meaning of αὐτοκρατορίς is
difficult. Since αὐτοκράτωρ may have the meaning of Imperator or Emperor
(cf. Polybius iii. 86. 7; Plutarch *Pompeius* viii. 2; *Galba* i. 5; Aristides *Apologia*,
preface; Justin Martyr *I Apol.* i. 1 [*MPG*, VI, 328]; *II Apol.* ii. 8 [*MPG*, VI,
445]; for further references, cf. LSJ, pp. 280–1; G. W. H. Lampe, *A Patristic
Greek Lexicon* [Oxford, 1961], p. 270), αὐτοκρατορίς may in some way have
honoured Augustus. It may have conveyed the idea of an imperial city or
possibly a capital city. Schürer (II, 211 n. 496) believes that it indicates
nothing more than that Sepphoris was granted autonomy. Subsequent
history, he says, makes it probable that already at that time the rest of
Galilee was subordinate to it.
[2] For a description of these buildings, cf. N. E. Manasseh, 'Architecture
and Topography', *Preliminary Report of the University of Michigan Excavations at
Sepphoris, Palestine, in 1931*, L. Waterman, director (Ann Arbor, 1937),
pp. 6–12, 14–16. For its historical setting, cf. Yeivin, pp. 23–6, 29–30.
Albright believes that there is no evidence for the building of the theatre
before the second or third century A.D., cf. W. F. Albright, 'Review of
*Preliminary Report of the University of Michigan Excavations at Sepphoris, Palestine,
in 1931*', by L. Waterman, *et al.*, *Classical Weekly*, XXI (1938), 148.
[3] Jos. *Ant.* xv. 267–76.
[4] Jos. *Ant.* xviii. 27. For an identification and description of this wall, see
Yeivin, pp. 28–9.
[5] Dalman, *SSW*, p. 75. Of course, during the reign of Antoninus Pius the
coins issued from this city bore the designation of Diocaesarea (cf. Hill,
pp. xii, 3–4).
[6] Cf. Jos. *Vita* 30, 38, 104, 232, 346; *BJ* iii. 31, 61.
[7] P. 19.

tion, he argues that Sepphoris had an external water supply which could easily be stopped by the Romans, and that consequently the city would have been defenceless in a siege.[1] But one wonders if this is sufficient reason for their being so strongly pro-Roman. Later, when coins were minted there, Trajan's image appeared on them,[2] and later still, in the Talmudic period, there is evidence that the city, or at least its government, was not wholly Jewish.[3]

In Antipas' day, however, the city seems to have been predominantly Jewish, although influenced no doubt by Antipas' policy of hellenization. Despite its being pro-Roman during the war of 66–70, Josephus appealed to the Galilaeans to spare the city for the reason that its inhabitants were of the same stock as themselves.[4] If then its population was chiefly Jewish, why was it pro-Roman during the revolution? One reason would have been, as mentioned above, that the water supply could easily have been stopped by the Romans; but the realization of how futile it had been to rebel against the Roman government in 4 B.C., when their inhabitants were reduced to slavery, would have been a stronger reason. Also, having laboured long and hard for the city to be called the 'ornament of all Galilee', they would not have wanted to risk its being burned, as it had been in 4 B.C. It was not therefore because its inhabitants were mainly non-Jewish that Sepphoris leaned towards the Romans, but because (notwithstanding the predominance of Jews) experience had shown the futility of rebelling against the Roman government.

In summary: Sepphoris was rebuilt by Antipas and was the residence of the government until Tiberias replaced it. Even after this, it remained the largest city of Galilee[5] and maintained a great influence in the affairs of that territory.

Livias (or Julias)

Probably the second city to be rebuilt by Antipas was Livias. Since this was in Peraea and not therefore in the centre of Jewish activity, little is known of it in comparison with the cities of Antipas' Galilee. The only fact recorded of this city is

---

[1] Pp. 23–4.   [2] Hill, pp. xi–xii, 1–3.
[3] Kid. iv. 5; see Schürer's comment on this passage (II, 211 n. 495).
[4] Jos. *Vita* 376–7; cf. also *BJ* iii. 32.   [5] Jos. *Vita* 37.

that it was burnt sometime between Herod the Great's death and its receiving its new name.

Its name and location

Josephus states that Antipas built a wall round Betharamphtha (Βηθαραμφθᾶ)[1] which he then named Julias after the emperor's wife. Betharamphtha is to be identified with a place called בֵּית חָרָם[2] or בֵּית הָרָן[3] in the realm of the Amorite king of Heshbon. In the Talmud it is designated בית רמתה[4] which is supposed to be the more modern name. Both Eusebius and Jerome identify the scriptural Βηθαράμ and Betharam with Βηθραμφθᾶ and Bethramtha respectively.[5] Undoubtedly this is the Βηθαράμαθα[6] where, shortly after his death, Herod the Great's palace was burned to the ground by some Peraean insurrectionists. Hence there was a need for Antipas to rebuild this city. It is conceded by most scholars that Βηθαραμφθᾶ is to be identified with modern *Tell er-Râmeh* which is about six miles north of the head of the Dead Sea and east of the Jordan[7] opposite Jericho.[8]

---

[1] *Ant.* xviii. 27. The variant in the Epitome reads Βηθαραμφά. In the parallel passage Josephus states that Antipas built the city (not just a wall) and named it Julias (*BJ* ii. 168).

[2] Josh. 13: 27. The LXX reading is Βαιθαράμ (or Βηθαράμ).

[3] Num. 32: 36. The LXX reading is Βαιθαράν (or the codex Alexandrinus variant Βαιθαρρά). [4] TJ: Sheb. 38d; in Sheb. ix. 2 it reads בית חורון.

[5] Eus. *Onomast.* pp. 48: 13; 49: 14.

[6] Jos. *BJ.* ii. 59. Niese has Βηθαράμιν εὔθα as a variant in codices Parisinus and Ambrosianus of Βηθαραμάθου. In the parallel passage, *Ant.* xvii. 277, it is designated 'Αμμάθοις (variants in codex Ambrosianus 'Αμάθοις and Epitome 'Αμαθοίς), but this is problematic. Schürer (II, 214 n. 513) believes it is corrupt, and Harder that 'Αμαθά should be allowed as a by-form of Beth-Ramatha. He states that Josephus had incorporated the excerpts word for word in the three obvious places (i.e. *Ant.* xvii. 277; xviii. 27; *BJ* ii. 59) in the style of his source without bringing them into harmony, cf. G. Harder, 'Herodes-Burgen und Herodes-Städte im Jordangraben', *ZDPV*, LXXVIII (1962), 60–2 n. 25.

[7] Jerome *Commentarii in Joelem* 3: 18 (*MPL*, xxv, 987); Eus. *Onomast.* pp. 48: 4; 49: 4; Abel, *Géographie*, II, 273; Glueck, *BASOR*, no. 91, p. 21; *AASOR*, xxv–xxviii, 289–91; cf. also F. M. Abel, 'Exploration du sud-est de la vallée du Jourdain', *RB*, XL (1931), 217–23; A. Mallon, 'Deux forteresses au pied des monts de Moab', *Biblica*, XIV (1933), 401–5; J. Simons, *The Geographical and Topographical Texts of the Old Testament* (Leiden, 1959), p. 122.

[8] Eus. *Onomast.* pp. 12: 24–5; 13: 24–5; 16: 26 – 18: 1; 17: 27.

Josephus designates the city once Ἀμμαθά, once Βηθαράμαθα, and once Βηθαραμφθᾶ;[1] the first two being before Antipas' rule, and the last after he had become tetrarch. Josephus states here that he called the city Julias, after the emperor's wife. Whenever else this city is mentioned by Josephus it is always designated Ἰουλιάς.[2] Nowhere else, however, is it designated Julias, but rather Livias (Λιβιάς).[3] It may be, as suggested by Schürer[4] and Jones,[5] that Antipas originally refounded Betharamphtha as Livias in honour of Livia, the wife of Augustus, and that later (A.D. 14) when Livia was adopted into the *gens Julia*,[6] he changed its name to Julias. This name remained in official use during the first century but was ultimately replaced once again by Livias.

Its foundation date

As regards its foundation date, one can only conjecture. Avi-Yonah has shown that the Herods did not haphazardly fix foundation ceremonies for the cities they founded but that they coincided with important dates in the lives of the emperors.[7]

---

[1] *Ant.* xvii. 277; *BJ* ii. 59; *Ant.* xviii. 27.

[2] *Ant.* xviii. 27; xx. 159; *BJ* ii. 168, 252; iv. 438. The only exception to this arises if Λίββα, one of the twelve Arabian states, is construed as Λιβιάς, as it is in some MSS (codices Leidensis, Ambrosianus, Medicaeus, Vaticanus) in *Ant.* xiv. 18 (called Λεμβά in *Ant.* xiii. 397), cf. Schürer, II, 215 n. 517; Haefeli, pp. 102–3. Haefeli feels certain of this. But today Λίββα or Λεμβά is identified with *Khirbet Libb*, a village twelve miles east of the Dead Sea (cf. Abel, *Géographie*, II, 148).

[3] E.g. Pliny *NH* xiii. 9. 44 (*Liviade*); Ptolemy *Geographia* v. 16. 9 (Λιβυάς); Eus. and Jerome *Onomast.* pp. 48: 15 and 49: 14 respectively. For a more complete list, see E. Kuhn, *Über die Entstehung der Städte der Alten. Komenverfassung und Synoikismos* (Leipzig, 1878), p. 426; Schürer, II, 214–15 n. 515.

[4] II, 214–15.

[5] *CERP*, p. 275.

[6] Regarding the testament of Augustus and Livia's adoption into the Julian family, cf. Tac. *Ann.* i. 8, 14; Dio lvi. 32. 1; 46. 1; lvii. 12. 2; Suet. *Aug.* ci. 2; G. Grether, 'Livia and the Roman Imperial Cult', *AJP*, LXVII (1946), 233–4. Josephus used Julia rather than Livia in *Ant.* xvi. 139; xvii. 10, 141, 146, 190; xviii. 31, 33; *BJ* ii. 167 (Livia, however, is used in *BJ* i. 566, 641) as well as other writers such as Tac. *Ann.* i. 14; v. 1; Suet. *Calig.* xvi. 3; Dio lvi. 46. 1; Pliny *NH* x. 76. 154. On Jewish coins Julia is used, cf. Madden, *History of Jewish Coinage*, pp. 141–51; *Coins of the Jews*, pp. 177–82; Reifenberg, *Ancient Jewish Coins*, pp. 55–6.

[7] M. Avi-Yonah, 'The Foundation of Tiberias', *IEJ*, I (1950–1), 168–9.

Otto has shown, for example, that Sebaste was founded in
27 B.C.[1] – rather than 25 B.C. as formerly assumed – the year in
which Octavian became Augustus (in Greek: Σεβαστός =
Augustus).[2] Avi-Yonah has argued, with a high degree of
probability, that Caesarea's foundation date was 13 B.C. – the
year of Augustus' fiftieth birthday and the thirtieth anniversary of his assuming command of the army (*imperatoria potestas*).[3]
Although the actual building of Caesarea would have lasted
several years, the official foundation date could be placed
whenever the king desired.[4]

As mentioned above, the date of Livias' 'official' foundation
seems to have been before Livia was adopted into the *gens
Julia* in A.D. 14. Livia was very active and was much honoured
so long as Augustus was alive.[5] She had erected a temple to
Concordia which honoured the imperial marriage, apparently.[6]
The dedication of the *Ara Numinis Augusti* in either A.D. 5 or 9
was on the wedding anniversary of Augustus and Livia.[7] In
9 B.C. the *Ara Pacis Augustae* was dedicated on Livia's birthday.[8]
Her birthday continued to be celebrated after Augustus'

---

[1] Cols. 56 n., 79 n. For these and the following dates, cf. H. F. Clinton,
Fasti Hellenici (Oxford, 1834).

[2] Dio liii. 16. 8.

[3] *IEJ*, I, 169. Avi-Yonah states: 'The case of Caesarea is somewhat more
complicated: the foundation ceremony is assigned by Josephus to the 192nd
Olympiad and the 28th year of Herod's reign. The 192nd lasted from the
summer of 13 to that of 9 B.C. Though it is usually considered that the regnal
years of Herod should be calculated from 37 B.C., when he had captured
Jerusalem, there is no doubt that Josephus, following the official reckoning,
calculated Herod's reign from 40 B.C., the year in which Herod was nominated by the Senate as "King of the Jews". The official year for the foundation of Caesarea would therefore have been in 13–12 B.C. Now in 13 B.C.
Augustus had reached his fiftieth birthday as well as the thirtieth anniversary
of the year in which he had first assumed (on 7 January, 43 B.C.) command
of the army (*imperatoria potestas*), a power which he held to his death. It
could have been no mere coincidence that Caesarea was founded in the
same year.'

[4] Herod the Great began building Caesarea in 22 B.C. and completed it
twelve years later (Jos. *Ant.* xv. 341; cf. above, p. 9 n. 4). It was officially
founded in 13 B.C., nine years after the building commenced.

[5] Cf. Grether, *AJP*, LXVII, 223–33.

[6] *Ibid.* p. 226.

[7] L. R. Taylor, 'Tiberius' *Ovatio* and *Ara Numinis Augusti*', *AJP*, LVIII
(1937), 185–93.

[8] *Ibid.* p. 190.

death (e.g. in A.D. 18 at Forum Clodi)[1] and even after her own death until the time of her consecration.[2] All this shows that she played an important part in Roman affairs. In general she was also highly venerated in the East.[3]

Assuming that the Herodians did not select the foundation dates of their cities haphazardly, the most probable date for Livias' 'official' foundation is A.D. 13. The date 17 January of this year marked Augustus' and Livia's fiftieth wedding anniversary.[4] It was also the year of Livia's seventieth birthday,[5] and a very significant year for Augustus, for in it he accepted the empire a fifth time for a further ten years.[6] In addition, it was the fifty-fifth year (19 Aug. A.D. 12 to 19 Aug. A.D. 13) from his first consulship,[7] and his thirty-fifth year (27 June A.D. 12 to 27 June A.D. 13) of *tribunicia potestas*.[8] Therefore, it seems highly probable that the official founding of Livias was in A.D. 13. This would help explain the confusion between the names Livias and Julias, for A.D. 13 was approximately only a year before Livia was adopted into the *gens Julia*. Politically it would have been a well-timed move to name a city after the empress now that Livia's good friend Salome had died, for this would have endeared her to Antipas. This date, moreover, allows Antipas plenty of time for the building of Livias. If he commenced the building soon after the completion of Sepphoris, that is, sometime between A.D. 8 and 10,[9] it would allow three to five years for its completion. This is sufficient for a city which seems to have been quite small.

Tiberias

The third and last city to be considered is Tiberias. This city[10] should be considered one of the most important of all those built by the Herods for it was the first city in Jewish history founded within the municipal framework of a πόλις.[11]

---

[1] Grether, *AJP*, LXVII, 227, 238.   [2] Tac. *Ann.* vi. 5.
[3] Grether, *AJP*, LXVII, 229–33.   [4] Dio xlviii. 43. 6 – 44. 5.
[5] She was eighty-six when she died (Dio lviii. 2. 1), which was in A.D. 29 (Tac. *Ann.* v. 1).   [6] Dio lvi. 28. 1.
[7] His first consulship began 19 Aug. 43 B.C. (cf. *Res Gestae Divi Augusti* i. 1; Livy *Epitomae* cxix; Appian *BC* iii. 13. 94; Dio xlvi. 43. 1 – 46. 2; lv. 6. 7; lvi. 30. 5; Suet. *Aug.* xxxi. 2.
[8] His tribunician power began 27 June 23 B.C. (cf. Dio liii. 32. 5; Tac. *Ann.* i. 9; cf. also Dio liii. 17. 10).   [9] Above, p. 85 n. 7.
[10] Jos. *Ant.* xviii. 36; *BJ* ii. 168.   [11] Avi-Yonah, *IEJ*, I, 161.

Its location and name

It was built on the western slope of the Sea of Galilee[1] near the famous warm springs of Ammathus.[2] According to the Talmudic traditions, the site of Tiberias was identical with the Biblical Rakkath.[3] It was easily accessible, being located on the great trade route joining Syria and Egypt.[4] Moreover, for Antipas it was more suitably situated than Sepphoris, in that it occupied a more central position in his two territories. From Tiberias, Peraea was easily accessible by the various trade routes.

Avi-Yonah thinks that Antipas did not choose Arbel and Migdal-Tarichaeae as possible locations for his new capital because of their being hot-beds of zealot activity against his rule and dynasty.[5] The only evidence for this is Arbel's revolt against Herod the Great in 40–37 B.C.,[6] and that the men of Tarichaeae resisted Vespasian's army in the war of A.D. 66–70.[7] These actions, however, were respectively fifty to sixty years previous, and forty to fifty years subsequent, to the time Antipas considered building his new city, and one cannot tell what their attitudes were at that time. Attitudes change with time

---

[1] The New Testament designates this lake by three different names, viz., 'Sea of Galilee' (Mt. 4: 18; 15: 29; Mk. 7: 31; Jn. 6: 1); 'Lake of Gennesaret' (Lk. 5: 1); 'Sea of Tiberias' (Jn. 6: 1; 21: 1). On linguistic grounds Nestle argues that 'Sea of Tiberias' is more correctly rendered 'Sea of Tiberius'; cf. E. Nestle, 'The Lake of Tiberius', *ET*, xxiii (1911), 41; 'Stadt und See des Tiberius', *Berliner philologische Wochenschrift*, xxxi (1911), 1486–7; 'Der Name des Sees Tiberias', *ZDPV*, xxxv (1912), 48–50.

[2] Jos. *Ant.* xviii. 36; *BJ* iv. 11. Ἀμμαθούς = חמתה which was originally חַמַּת, Josh. 19: 35; cf. TJ: Meg. i. 1 (70a line 42). Cf. also Jos. *BJ* ii. 614; *Vita* 85; Pliny *NH* v. 15. 71; Shab. iii. 4; xxii. 5; Maks. vi. 7; TB: M.K. 18a. The Herods liked and used warm springs. There were hot springs at Machaerus (Jos. *BJ* vii. 186–9) and at Callirrhoe, the place where Herod the Great tried to find a cure in his last days (*Ant.* xvii. 171; *BJ* i. 657); cf. also Pliny *NH* v. 16. 74; 1 Enoch 67: 8.

[3] TJ: Meg. i. 1; cf. Josh. 19: 35.

[4] From Syria this trade route crossed the Jordan below Lake Hula (at *Jisr Banat Ya'qub* = Bridge of the Daughters of Jacob), continued southward through the Plain of Gennesaret and on to the western shore of the Sea of Galilee, and from there went to Philoteria and Scythopolis and on to Egypt (cf. Smith, *HGHL*, p. 428).

[5] *IEJ*, i, 161.

[6] Jos. *Ant.* xiv. 415–30; *BJ* i. 305–6.   [7] Jos. *BJ* iii. 462–505, 522–42.

and circumstance. Moreover, there is no evidence that the inhabitants of these places displayed any hostility during Antipas' reign. Is it not more probable that Antipas selected the actual site with a view to starting something new and developing it just as he wished, instead of having to destroy the ancient customs and governmental system of a former village?

During the Hellenistic period it was the custom of kings to name cities after themselves or after their closest relatives. Herod the Great had named a little town after his father, Antipater;[1] a fortress after his mother, Cypros;[2] a little city and tower after his brother, Phasael;[3] a tower in his palace after his wife, Mariamme I;[4] and two fortresses he had named Herodion after himself.[5] Archelaus had a little town named after himself.[6] It is interesting to note, however, that the Herods were not so brazen as to name the important places after themselves or their relatives, but preferred to name them after the Roman emperor or his family.[7] Antipas named his new city after the reigning emperor, Tiberius.[8] Since this was a new city, it retained its name, whereas the other Hellenistic town names reverted to their former names. Scythopolis, for example, reverted to Beth-shan.

Its foundation date

The date of its foundation is debated. It was built during the reigns of Antipas (4 B.C. to A.D. 39), and Tiberius (A.D. 14–37). Eusebius places it in the fourteenth year of Tiberius (A.D. 27–8).[9] This however is not reliable since Eusebius lumps the whole of Antipas' reign into this one year, and he is only following Josephus' account in *Bellum Judaicum* ii. 168.[10] Many historians have tried to establish the date of the city's foundation by careful attention to Josephus' order of events.[11] Since the

---

[1] Jos. *BJ.* i. 417.   [2] Jos. *BJ* i. 417; *Ant.* xvi. 144.
[3] Jos. *BJ* i. 418; ii. 46; *Ant.* xvi. 144–5; xvii. 257.
[4] Jos. *BJ* ii. 439; v. 170.   [5] Jos. *BJ* i. 265, 419; *Ant.* xiv. 361.
[6] Jos. *Ant.* xvii. 340.
[7] E.g. Herod the Great named Caesarea after Caesar (Jos. *BJ* i. 414; *Ant.* xv. 331–41; xvi. 136–8) and Sebaste in Samaria after Augustus (in Greek: Σεβαστός = Augustus), *BJ* i. 64, 403; *Ant.* xiii. 275; xv. 296.
[8] Jos. *Ant.* xviii. 36; Gen. R. xxiii. 1 (iv. 17).
[9] *Chron.* II, 148–9.   [10] Schürer, II, 217 n. 524.
[11] *Ant.* xviii. 35–54.

mention of the city's foundation comes after Pontius Pilate's appointment to Judaea, they conclude that it was founded in A.D. 26 or later.[1] But it is uncertain whether Josephus at this point abides by a strict chronology, for immediately after this, in the same context, he speaks of the deaths of Phraates IV king of Parthia (which occurred in 2/1 B.C.) and of Antiochus of Commagene (which occurred in 71 B.C.), before returning to Pilate. Besides, in *Bellum Judaicum* Pilate's appointment is placed after the founding of Tiberias.[2]

Avi-Yonah believes that the city was founded in A.D. 18.[3] He narrows down the date to the years 17–22 by showing, on the one hand, that coins of Hadrian struck in the year 100 of Tiberias could not have been made before Hadrian's accession in 117 (117 − 100 = A.D. 17) and, on the other hand, that coins of Commodus struck in the year 170 of Tiberias could not have been dated after Commodus' death in 192 (192 − 170 = A.D. 22). Since the Herods did not select foundation dates haphazardly, Avi-Yonah thinks that the most outstanding year was A.D. 18, in that it was Tiberius' sixtieth birthday and the twentieth anniversary of his holding the *tribunicia potestas* or coregency. Thus Antipas could have started the construction of the city on Tiberius' accession in A.D. 14 and have founded it officially four years later, A.D. 18.

However, the present author thinks a more plausible date to be A.D. 23. He feels that the numismatic evidence is reckoned incorrectly by Avi-Yonah. In the first place, the first year of a coin should be reckoned as year one and not as year nought. Hence, Hadrian's coins struck in the year 100 of Tiberias[4] should not have been dated before 117 – Tiberias was not founded before A.D. 18. The coins of Commodus struck in the year 170 of Tiberias should not have been dated after Commodus' death on 31 December 192 – Tiberias was not founded later than A.D. 23. Thus the city was founded sometime between the years 18 and 23. Secondly, A.D. 23 was a more outstanding year for Tiberius than 18. Thus it would mark his

---

[1] Schürer, II, 217. [2] ii. 168–9.

[3] *IEJ*, I, 168–9.

[4] For coins struck at Tiberias, see Hill, pp. xiii–xv, 5–10; F. De Saulcy, *Numismatique de la Terre Sainte* (Paris, 1874); Head, p. 802; A. Kindler, *The Coins of Tiberias* (Tiberias, 1961), pp. 35–65.

sixty-fifth birthday, the twenty-fifth anniversary of his holding the *tribunicia potestas*, and the tenth anniversary of his becoming emperor.[1] Thirdly, it would have given Antipas nine years to construct Tiberias before its official founding, this being a much more reasonable figure.[2] Fourthly, this would place it nearer the time of Pilate's arrival in Judaea. The founding of Tiberias and Pilate's arrival in Judaea are in both accounts of Josephus in close proximity to one another, possibly indicating that these two events occurred about the same time. It is reasonable to conclude, then, that Tiberias was founded in A.D. 23.

Its composition

Antipas wanted to build a city so as to carry on the tradition of his father. Although it is uncertain whether or not he walled this city, it is more probable that he did.[3] But there is abundant

---

[1] For these dates, see H. F. Clinton, *Fasti Romani*, I (Oxford, 1845); T. Lewin, *Fasti Sacri*.

[2] It took Herod the Great twelve years to build Caesarea (cf. above, p. 9 n. 4), and it was officially founded in 13 B.C. or nine years after the building commenced. This shows that a nine-year period for the building of a city before its foundation is not out of the ordinary.

[3] In *IEJ*, I, 164 Avi-Yonah conjectures that Antipas did not build a wall. He states: 'under Roman rule, special permission had to be obtained from the emperor before a wall could be constructed, a permission that was only grudgingly granted. For example, Claudius was to order Agrippa I to halt the building of the Third Wall of Jerusalem, even though the two rulers had been the best of friends. Thus, and considering too that the mere collection of arms was to be fatal to Antipas, it can be assumed that permission was not granted for the erection of a wall; so that Tiberias was originally an open city. As further proof, Josephus states on several occasions that it was he himself who fortified the town in the early days of the First Revolt. Certainly, the ease with which the Romans entered the city, shows that the fortifications had been only provisional. The extant wall of Roman Tiberias was built much later, in the days of the Patriarch Judah II and the dynasty of Septimius Severus.' It seems that Avi-Yonah's conjecture rests on slender evidence. First, in the case of Agrippa I, the order to halt the building was given by a different emperor (Claudius) and at a different time (A.D. 44), and there is no indication of this having been true in Antipas' time under Tiberius. In fact, Antipas had fortified Sepphoris and walled Betharamphtha or Julias (Jos. *Ant.* xviii. 27) and there were no repercussions from the Roman government regarding these activities. Secondly, Agrippa I was ordered to cease building the wall only because he was suspected of sedition (*Ant.* xix. 327) whereas there is no indication of this on the part of Antipas. Thirdly, that Josephus had to fortify it during the war of 66–70 is no valid

evidence that he did build a stadium,[1] and a large synagogue which held a great number of people.[2] He also built a beautiful palace with a gold roof, containing many valuable items including representations of animals,[3] though these were forbidden by the Jewish Law.[4] Here he followed his father who had erected a golden eagle on the temple gate, so causing a revolt just before his death.[5] Just as his father had a reputation for building beautiful cities, so Antipas attempted to do the same with respect to Tiberias, only on a smaller scale.

Since it was a new city, Antipas had to populate it. This was not an easy thing to do, for while building the city he had struck a cemetery. This he had destroyed and built the city on its rubble, for which reason the devout Jews considered the city unclean.[6] However, a mixed company, of which the majority were Galilaeans, were compelled to move in from the surrounding area, as well as some poor immigrants from abroad.[7] These he

argument that there was no wall before that time. As mentioned above, Antipas had fortified Sepphoris, yet Josephus had to fortify it again during the war (*BJ* ii. 574; *Vita* 188). Fourthly, Avi-Yonah assumes that since the Romans entered the city with such ease (*BJ* ii. 632-3), the fortifications were only provisional. He implies that these fortifications were demolished. But is this the case? There is nothing in the above mentioned passage about the destruction of any fortification or wall. It seems that there was no battle, but that the Tiberians defected to the Romans (*BJ* ii. 634). In fact, in the same context the Tiberians peered over their 'wall' (*BJ* ii. 637). This was in the winter of 66/7. There were walls still there when Vespasian captured Tiberias in the summer of 67 (*BJ* iii. 460-1). There is, then, no evidence for or against Antipas' construction of a wall at Tiberias. However, if he followed his policies in the other two cities, it is probable that he walled Tiberias at the time of its construction.

[1] Jos. *BJ* ii. 618; iii. 539; *Vita* 92, 331. From *BJ* iii. 539-40 Klein (*Beiträge*, p. 60) estimates that the stadium held over 10,000 people.

[2] Jos. *Vita* 277, 280, 293.

[3] What little description there is of the palace is given in connection with its destruction by Josephus, *Vita* 65-6, 68, 295.

[4] Exod. 20: 4; Jos. *Vita* 65. For a discussion of these animal representations in relation to the war of 66-70, see C. Roth, 'An Ordinance against Images in Jerusalem, A.D. 66', *HTR*, XLIX (1956), 173-6.

[5] Jos. *Ant.* xvii. 151-6; *BJ* i. 648-50.

[6] Jos. *Ant.* xviii. 38. Anyone who came into contact with a grave was unclean for seven days according to Exod. 19: 11-16. For more details, see Oh. xvii-xviii.

[7] Hart believes that Jesus made reference to this immigration to Tiberias in the parables of the wedding garment (Mt. 22: 1-14) and the marriage of

offered free houses and lands, and may also have exempted from paying taxes for the first few years,[1] thereby attracting the poor. He even liberated slaves on the condition that they settled in Tiberias.

The Jews seem to have been in the majority as well as being the ruling class, at least at the time of the revolution.[2] There were only a few Greeks.[3] The Jews were nevertheless affected by Antipas' policy of hellenization. They raised no objection to the representations of animals in Antipas' palace; in fact, they were at first opposed to the iconoclastic actions suggested by the Jerusalem assembly (ὑπὸ τοῦ κοινοῦ τῶν Ἱεροσολυμιτῶν).[4] Furthermore, at the time of the revolution of 66–70 they did not support the nationalistic policies of the insurgents, but surrendered at the first appearance of the Roman army.[5]

As to the size of the city, Avi-Yonah estimates 0·8 square kilometre with a population between 30,000 and 40,000.[6]

Its government

In government and constitution it seems to have followed the pattern of the Greek πόλις. There was the council (βουλή) of 600 members[7] which seems to have included almost all the leading citizens, the board of δεκάπρωτοι,[8] and the head

the king's son (Lk. 14: 16–26). This is an interesting theory but there are too many facts that do not do justice to the parables, cf. J. H. A. Hart, 'Possible References to the Foundation of Tiberias in the Teaching of Our Lord', *Exp*, 8th series, I (1911), 74–81.

[1] Jos. *Ant.* xviii. 37–8.

[2] Jos. *Vita* 33–6, 382. There is no indication of pagan shrines in Tiberias which may indicate that the predominant Jewish element would not allow it, cf. L. H. Vincent, 'Chronique', *RB*, xxx (1921), 440. Kindler (p. 41) states: 'The coin-types of Herod Antipas were continued almost unaltered under Roman rule 14 years after his banishment, with only his name replaced by that of the emperor. This may point to the great influence exercised by the dominant Jewish element in the population of the city.'

[3] Jos. *Vita* 67. [4] Jos. *Vita* 65–6.

[5] Jos. *Vita* 34; *BJ* iii. 453–61. [6] *IEJ*, I, 164–5.

[7] Jos. *BJ* ii. 641. This is also mentioned in *Vita* 64, 169, 284, 300, 313, 381. There is nothing unusual in having so many council men, for Gaza had 500 (cf. *Ant.* xiii. 364).

[8] Jos. *Vita* 69, 296. Although the technical term δεκάπρωτοι is not used in *BJ* ii. 639 (= *Vita* 168), Josephus does mention the principal men in Tiberias, and they would be the δεκάπρωτοι. They seem in the first century A.D. to have been the finance committee of the council and the tax collectors in

who was also an ἄρχων.[1] There were also lieutenants (ὕπαρχοι)[2] who seem to have been entrusted with the city's administration,[3] and the office of ἀγορανόμος to which Antipas appointed his nephew and brother-in-law, Agrippa I, who later supplanted him.[4] As the overseer of the market, the ἀγορανόμος controlled the supplies of the city.[5] In other words, he was the city's economist. He would have regulated the prices and seen that there was fair play among the citizens. Thus, Tiberias' autonomous government and constitution conformed to those of a Greek πόλις.[6]

the second century. By the fourth century this council was abolished (Jones, *GC*, pp. 139, 153). Schürer (II, 218–19 n. 529) believes that they were tax collectors even at this early date, but there is no evidence of this in Tiberias. In fact, since Tiberias was both the capital of Galilee (Jos. *Vita* 37) and the seat of the royal bank (*Vita* 38), it meant that even in the immediate vicinity of Tiberias the revenues were collected by royal officials and not by the city (cf. Jones, *JRS*, XXI, 81).

[1] Jos. *Vita* 134, 271, 278, 294; *BJ* ii. 599. In all the references Jesus, son of Sapphias, was the chief magistrate at the time of the war of 66–70. This Jesus was certainly a Jew, for he killed all the Greeks of the city (*Vita* 67). He was also a ringleader of the lower class, namely, sailors (ναῦται) and the destitute (ἄποροι), cf. *Vita* 66. One of his duties was to preside at the meetings of the council (*Vita* 276–9, 300).

[2] Jos. *BJ* ii. 615.

[3] Jos. *BJ* ii. 615 = *Vita* 86. Avi-Yonah makes the ὕπαρχοι singular and equal to a στρατηγός who was a royal commissioner supervising the city's affairs (*IEJ*, I, 165). This may be a valid equivalent though the text indicates a plurality in the office. Certainly ἔπαρχος seems to be interchangeable with στρατηγός and, as mentioned above (p. 49), there was a plurality of membership, usually of five, in the Hellenistic cities. It is interesting to observe that Herod the Great placed an ἄρχων in Idumaea (Jos. *Ant.* xv. 254); Agrippa I an ἔπαρχος in Tiberias (*Vita* 33); and Agrippa II an ἔπαρχος in Gamala (*Vita* 46), and a viceroy in Caesarea Philippi (*Vita* 74). On the one hand, one notices that there had been an ἔπαρχος in Tiberias, and, on the other, none of the Herods ever appointed a ὕπαρχος. It could be that ὕπαρχος should be read ἔπαρχος. But, since the context is the war of 66–70 and ὕπαρχος has a more military flavour, it may well be that the ὕπαρχοι replaced the ἔπαρχοι under Josephus' command during the war.

[4] Jos. *Ant.* xviii. 149. It is used several times in the Talmudic literature. For such, see S. Krauss, *Griechische und lateinische Lehnwörter im Talmud, Midrasch und Targum*, II (Berlin, 1899), 11–12.

[5] Jos. *Ant.* xiv. 261; Magie, I, 645–6; II, 1511–13 nn. 41–2.

[6] Although there is here no mention of a constitution as there is for Sebaste (Jos. *BJ* i. 403), Tiberias was organized as other Greek cities of the Roman rule, cf. Kuhn, *Über die Entstehung der Städte*, pp. 427–34; *Die*

Also characteristic of a Greek city were two additional privileges held by Tiberias, namely, the right to reckon its own era, that is, to date records from its founding, and the right to issue coins.[1] The existence of coins dated from its foundation date gives evidence of the first right. This, however, was not always the case, for Antipas himself dated his coins not from the foundation date of the city but from the beginning of his reign, even though all his coins were minted in Tiberias.[2]

In only one thing did Tiberias differ from a true Greek πόλις.

städtische und bürgerliche Verfassung des römischen Reichs bis auf die Zeiten Justinians, II (Leipzig, 1865), 352–4.

[1] Avi-Yonah, *IEJ*, I, 166.

[2] For a study of the coins of Herod Antipas, see Madden, *History of Jewish Coinage*; F. De Saulcy, 'Catalogue raisonné de monnaies judaïques recueillies à Jérusalem en novembre 1869', *The Numismatic Chronicle*, N.S. XI (1872), 253–5; F. W. Madden, 'Jewish Numismatics', *ibid.* N.S. XV (1875), 47–9; F. De Saulcy, *Mélanges de Numismatique*, II (Paris, 1877), 92–4; Madden, *Coins of the Jews*, pp. 118–22; Hill, pp. 229–30; Reifenberg, *Ancient Jewish Coins*, pp. 19, 44–5; Meyshan, 'Coins', p. 34; Kindler, pp. 15–17, 35, 37, 48, 50, 53, 54. Schürer (I, 434 n. 16) rightly divides Antipas' coins into two classes: (1) those with the inscription ΗΡѠΔΟΥ ΤΕΤΡΑΡΧΟΥ, with the years 33, 34, 37 and 38 (there is also the year 36), and on the reverse ΤΙΒΕΡΙΑΣ; (2) those with the inscription ΗΡѠΔΗΣ ΤΕΤΡΑΡΧΗΣ and on the reverse ΓΑΙѠ ΚΑΙΣΑΡΙ ΓΕΡΜΑΝΙΚѠ, with the year number ΜΓ or 43 = A.D. 39–40. Although there has been a claim for the year 44, it has been discredited (cf. below, pp. 262–3 n. 4). Another interesting fact regarding the second class of coins is that the figure on the obverse side does not resemble the palm branch for the years 33–8. Goodenough implies that this was a symbol of a palm tree, this being the first indication of such a symbol, cf. E. R. Goodenough, *Jewish Symbols in the Greco-Roman Period*, I (New York, 1953), 274 n. 45. But Simon Maccabaeus did have a palm tree as a symbol (136–135 B.C.), cf. Hill, p. 185; pl. xx. 8; P. Romanoff, *Jewish Symbols on Ancient Jewish Coins* (Philadelphia, 1944), pl. 1. Most numismatists also refer to it as a palm branch (for a short study of the palm branch figure on Antipas' coins, see W. Wirgin, 'A Note on the "Reed" of Tiberias', *IEJ*, XVIII [1968], 248–9). Nevertheless, there is a difference between the palm branches of 33–8 and of 39. Why there is a change in the style of the palm branches and why the title *Herod the Tetrarch* changes from the genitive to the nominative case, no one seems to know. Since Antipas had to change the reverse from Tiberius to the new emperor's name, Gaius, it would have been an ideal time to refashion both sides of the coin. But this does not really explain the change. For a study of the size and metallic content of the Herodian coins, cf. I. Meyshan, 'The Monetary Pattern of the Herodian Coinage', *The Patterns of Monetary Development in Phoenicia and Palestine in Antiquity*, *International Numismatic Convention*, proceedings ed. by A. Kindler (Tel-Aviv, 1967), pp. 220–6.

A true Greek city was an autonomous entity having territory[1] over which it was sovereign. This sovereignty it exercised over the external as well as the internal affairs of the city-state, and in war as well as peace. The region surrounding Tiberias was not governed by the city (as a city-state) but by the royal officials residing in the city. In other words, the new settlers were not subject to the βουλή but to Antipas.[2] Tiberias was a Greek city in the sense that it had municipal autonomy and could elect its local officials, but it was not a true Greek city-state in that it did not control the surrounding territory and was not completely independent of Antipas' rule.

In conclusion, Tiberias was founded by Antipas as a completely new city and the official foundation date was most likely A.D. 23. Antipas built a stadium, synagogue, and a palace. Although the Jews resented its being built upon a cemetery,[3] it was still predominantly a Jewish city. It had a Greek constitution and was a Greek city municipally, but was nevertheless subject to the federal government of Antipas. It was renowned in Antipas' day as the capital of Galilee.[4]

THE STRUCTURE OF HIS GOVERNMENT

While nothing is known about the governmental structure of Sepphoris and Livias, a fair amount is known about that of Tiberias. This may be a coincidence, but such is unlikely. If Livias and Sepphoris had also been set up on the pattern of a Greek city, it is probable that some mention would have been made of their governmental functions and/or their officers, especially in the case of Sepphoris, Galilee's largest city. Hence, it seems either that Antipas did not set up their governments according to the Greek constitution, or, if he did, that the

---

[1] According to Sheb. ix. 2, Tiberias did have the valley as its territory. This may have been true later.

[2] Jos. *Ant.* xviii. 37.

[3] Interestingly enough, in the third and fourth centuries it became the centre of rabbinic scholarship (cf. Neubauer, *Géographie*, pp. 208–14). For priestly communities in the first and second centuries, see S. Klein, *Neue Beiträge zur Geschichte und Geographie Galiläas*, Heft 1 of *Palästina-Studien* (Wien, 1923), pp. 32–4.

[4] For the subsequent history of Tiberias during the reigns of Agrippa I and II and its involvement in the war of 66–70, see Schürer, II, 219–21.

Greek city concept was not as fully developed in these places as it was in Tiberias. At least three reasons may account for this. First, Livias and Sepphoris, not being new foundations, may have resisted Antipas' attempt to establish their governments along the Greek city lines whereas Tiberias, being a newly created city, had no say in the matter. Secondly, Antipas may have thought it wise to set up a government that was more Hellenistic in its operation on account of Tiberius' repressive measures against the Jews in Rome.[1] Thirdly, because of his association with Sejanus,[2] Antipas may have decided to pursue a policy that was more pro-Hellenistic or pro-Roman, and therefore less pro-Jewish (though not necessarily anti-Jewish). It seems, then, that Antipas' emphasis on hellenization was more in evidence in the later part of his reign.

The freedom which the Greek city-state had formerly enjoyed was curtailed by the kings of the Hellenistic period.[3] Though still enjoying freedom, the cities had now to yield to the king's wishes and interests.[4] Thus Tiberias' citizens were not subject to the βουλή but to Antipas.[5] During the war of 66–70 its most respected citizens wanted to *continue* their allegiance to Rome and King Agrippa II,[6] which shows its close ties with Rome and Agrippa. Strikingly, among these respected citizens was Crispus, a prefect of Agrippa! Moreover, Tiberias, as Jones suggests, was far more interested in being the centre of the bureaucratic administration than having the status of an autonomous city.[7] Thus Tiberias, though closest to the concept of the Greek city, was nevertheless subject to Antipas.

[1] Jos. *Ant.* xviii. 81–4; Tac. *Ann.* ii. 85; Suet. *Tib.* xxxvi; Dio lvii. 18. 5 *a*; Seneca *Epistulae Morales* cviii. 22; cf. E. M. Smallwood, 'Some Notes on the Jews under Tiberius', *Latomus*, xv (1956), 314–22.

[2] Jos. *Ant.* xviii. 250.

[3] For a discussion on the Greek cities, their relationship to the Hellenistic kings and their subsequent existence in Roman times, see Rostowzew, *Kolonates*, pp. 306–12.

[4] Jones, *GC*, pp. 111–12.

[5] Jos. *Ant.* xviii. 37.

[6] Jos. *Vita* 33–4.

[7] *CERP*, p. 277. Jones states: 'The Tiberians bitterly resented their transference to Agrippa II's kingdom, not because they thereby had become subject to a king while the Sepphorites remained free, but because the royal bank and governmental offices of Galilee had been transferred to Sepphoris.' Cf. Jos. *Vita* 36–7.

In conclusion, it seems that Antipas continued the strong centralized system of government which he had inherited from his father and from his predecessors, the Hasmonaeans. One can almost trace the hierarchy of authority. Antipas was the head of the realm, which in turn was divided into two areas, each probably comprising five toparchies. These were again subdivided into villages. Betharamphtha (or Julias) of Peraea, for example, comprised fourteen villages.[1] Possibly each village had its clerk who was responsible to the leaders of the toparchic capital.

Zeitlin suggests that at the head of each toparchy was a στρατηγός.[2] Possibly the μεγιστᾶνες mentioned in Mark 6:21 were the toparchic leaders, while the πρῶτοι mentioned in the same verse were the aristocracy, who may have had some governmental function under the μεγιστᾶνες.[3] This bureaucratic form of government may have been needed to keep order in Palestine. Possibly Antipas, like his father, 'did not think that the Jews were to be trusted with autonomy'.[4] Finally, a strong centralized government was gratifying to Antipas, for it meant that he was the 'big chief' of his domain.

---

[1] Jos. *Ant.* xx. 159.   [2] *Judaean State*, II, 96.

[3] The word μεγιστάν is a late Greek word meaning 'a great one' or 'grandee'. It is found in the plural in the later books of the LXX, in the papyri (MM, p. 393) and twice in the NT (Rev. 6: 15; 18: 23; it is also used in Jos. *Ant.* xi. 37; xx. 26; *Vita* 112, 149). Tacitus uses the term to describe the Armenian nobles who resisted the Roman presence (Tac. *Ann.* xv. 27). In Daniel (5: 23, LXX) it is used with reference to the feast of Belshazzar ('you and your lords') in a context which is similar to that of Mk. 6: 21. This indicates that the term is appropriate in an oriental environment (Sherwin-White, p. 137). οἱ πρῶτοι is a more general term than μεγιστάν, for it is used of the leading men of a group (cf. Lk. 19: 47; Acts 25: 2; 28: 17; Jos. *Ant.* xi. 141; xvii. 342; xx. 180) or of a locality (Acts 13: 50; 28: 7; Jos. *Ant.* vii. 230), the latter being more applicable to Mk. 6: 21. Here they are the leading men of Galilee as distinct from the μεγιστᾶνες who are qualified by the personal possessive pronoun αὐτοῦ. Antipas' μεγιστᾶνες were the inner circle of his government (Sherwin-White, p. 137), whereas the πρῶτοι τῆς Γαλιλαίας were *l'aristocratie du pays* (M.-J. Lagrange, *Évangile selon Saint Marc*[4], EB [Paris, 1928], p. 160). Against this, Bammel wonders if the πρῶτοι τῆς Γαλιλαίας can 'be taken to imply that Gabinius' σύνοδοι constitution continued in Galilee?' (E. Bammel, 'The Organization of Palestine by Gabinius', *JJS*, XII [1961], 160 n. 19). To sum up: the μεγιστᾶνες may have been the head of the toparchies, whereas the πρῶτοι seem to have been the aristocracy, who had possibly some governmental function.

[4] Jones, *Herods*, p. 85.

THE ACQUISITION OF HIS TITLE

The deposing of Archelaus

The only important political event recorded early in Antipas' career was the downfall of his brother Archelaus in A.D. 6.[1] There are three different accounts of this event. According to Josephus the Jews and Samaritans combined to make a formal complaint to the emperor.[2] Upon hearing this the emperor summoned Archelaus to Rome, and the accusations being substantiated, deposed and banished him to Vienna in Gaul (modern Vienne on the Rhône, south of Lyons). The second account is given by Strabo.[3] According to him, Augustus honoured (τιμάω) Herod's sons, his sister Salome and her daughter Berenice by giving them portions of Herod's kingdom. His sons however, in the words of Strabo, 'were not successful, but became involved in accusations', and out of this Archelaus was banished. His brothers, however, escaped with difficulty, and after paying 'great court' (θεραπεία πολλῇ μόλις) to gain the emperor's favour were able to return to their respective tetrarchies. Strabo does not state the charges against them.[4] The third account is given by Dio Cassius who states that Archelaus was accused by his brothers[5] of some wrongdoing, and in consequence was banished.[6]

[1] For a brief discussion on the problem of the length of Archelaus' rule, see Appendix V.

[2] Jos. *Ant.* xvii. 342–4; *BJ* ii. 111.

[3] Strabo xvi. 2. 46.

[4] Jones (*Herods*, p. 168) considers Strabo's account 'implausible' because his story is unsupported by other authorities and because he was not familiar with Jewish affairs. However, this does not preclude that Strabo may have drawn from reliable sources, as the rest of his work gives evidence.

[5] There does occur in Jos. *Ant.* xvii. 342 the reading τῶν ἀδελφῶν ἀνδρῶν, in codices Medicaeus and Vaticanus in the sentence: οἱ πρῶτοι τῶν ἀδελφῶν ἀνδρῶν ἔν τε Ἰουδαίοις καὶ Σαμαρείταις...κατηγοροῦσιν. This would corroborate Dio but is of doubtful authority (cf. Brann, *MGWJ*, xxii, 311 n. 4). Even Naber who favours codex M (cf. Shutt, p. 114) does not accept ἀδελφῶν as the true reading, cf. S. A. Naber, Flavii Josephi *Opera Omnia*, *Ant.* (Leipzig, 1888–96), *ad loc.*

[6] Dio lv. 27. 6. It is interesting to note that Jones does not use the same argument against Dio as he does against Strabo. Dio's argument is also unsupported by other authorities and is far removed in time from Strabo (63 B.C. – A.D. 22 ?).

Although there are divergencies in these accounts, they may present different aspects of the same situation. The matter which triggered off the affair seems to have been, as Josephus records, the formal complaint which the Jews and the Samaritans made to Augustus concerning Archelaus' cruelty and tyranny. The co-operation of these two communities, normally bitter enemies, indicates the seriousness of the grievances.[1]

Not only were the grievances serious, but the Jews and the Samaritans had knowledge of the exact moment (μάλιστα ἐπεὶ ἔγνωσαν) when Archelaus had disobeyed Augustus' instructions to show moderation in dealing with them. Possibly they received this information from a member of the Herodian family. Antipas and Philip (also Salome) were under his oversight, and, in view of the unrest, they may have thought it an opportune moment to oust Archelaus. Indeed, it is possible that they were among the πρῶτοι ἄνδρες (mentioned by Josephus) who brought the charges against Archelaus in Rome. This would agree well with Strabo and Dio who state that Archelaus' brothers were in Rome accusing him. While the Jewish–Samaritan delegation complained about Archelaus' rule, Antipas and Philip may have complained about his oversight of them.[2] Archelaus, in his capacity as ethnarch, or Roman representative for Palestine, may have placed his two brothers in a bad light. Possibly Augustus was actually debat-

---

[1] Jones, *Herods*, p. 167. Archelaus was another Rehoboam. Even before he became ethnarch his handling of affairs was inept (Jos. *Ant.* xvii. 206–18; *BJ* ii. 4–13). With good reason did the Jews not want the Herodian family, and Archelaus in particular (*Ant.* xvii. 299–314; cf. also 227; *BJ* ii. 81–92; cf. also 22. This is also intimated in the parable of Lk. 19: 12–27). After becoming ethnarch he treated both Jews and Samaritans with great brutality (Jos. *BJ* ii. 111). This is corroborated by the Gospels, for Joseph, after returning from the flight to Egypt, heard that Archelaus was ruler of Judaea, ἐφοβήθη ἐκεῖ ἀπελθεῖν, and so withdrew to Galilee (Mt. 2: 22). Furthermore, Archelaus removed the high priest Joazar, the son of Boethus, on the pretext that he had sided with the insurgents, and appointed in his stead Joazar's brother Eleazar, who in turn was later replaced by Jesus, the son of See (Jos. *Ant.* xvii. 339–41). He divorced his wife Mariamme to marry Glaphyra, the daughter of King Archelaus of Cappadocia and the former wife of Alexander (Herod the Great's son and Archelaus' half brother), and thus transgressed the ancestral law (*Ant.* xvii. 341, 350–3; *BJ* ii. 114–16). Either or both of these last mentioned events may have caused unrest in the country, and if so, Archelaus' methods of suppression of unrest, as has already been indicated, were oppressive.   [2] Cf. Dio lv. 27. 6.

ing whether or not to continue the client kingdoms in Palestine. This was a form of government he may not have favoured, in which case it was only out of respect for Herod the Great that he agreed to honour his sons with the tetrarchies in Palestine.[1] At least, according to Strabo, Antipas and Philip were able to return to their respective tetrarchies only with great difficulty (μόλις) and after showing considerable subservience to the emperor.[2]

Salome, whose dislike for Archelaus was described in Chapter 2, may have been another cause of Archelaus' downfall. Being close to Livia, she could have been an informant for the emperor. For her services Augustus may have rewarded her with Archelais,[3] known for its palm-groves. This would have been a handsome addition to her estates at Phasaelis.

In summary: the unrest resulting from Archelaus' rule led to a climax. A Jewish–Samaritan delegation went to Rome to bring charges against him. It seems that Antipas and Philip were a part of the Jewish delegation. After the brothers had accused each other Archelaus was exiled. After great difficulty and paying 'great court', Philip and Antipas were allowed to go back to their domains.

The acquiring of the dynastic title

One of the probable results of Antipas' voyage to Rome in A.D. 6 is that he then acquired the dynastic title of Herod. It seems that the name *Herod* became a dynastic title after Herod the Great's death. The first clue to this is in the context of Archelaus' deposition where Josephus specifically states that Antipas was now called Herod.[4] Up to this time he is always called Antipas,[5] whereas after this time he is always designated

---

[1] Josephus (*Ant.* xvii. 317) states that if Archelaus proved himself worthy he was to have been honoured (τιμάω) with the title of βασιλεύς. In 4 B.C. it seems that Augustus honoured Herod's sons by conferring on them the tetrarchies as well as on Archelaus the title of king if he had met the conditions.

[2] Strabo xvi. 2. 46; cf. also Otto, col. 179.

[3] Cf. Jos. *Ant.* xviii. 31.

[4] *BJ* ii. 167: Ἡρῴδης ὁ κληθεὶς Ἀντίπας. Cf. also Hegesippus (Pseudo) *Historiae* ii. 3. 2.

[5] Jos. *Ant.* xvii. 20, 188, 224, 227, 229, 238 (Antipater), 318; *BJ* i. 562, 646, 664, 668; ii. 20, 22, 23, 94.

Herod.[1] It could be argued that this is due to a change of source on the part of Josephus, but other factors make this conjecture improbable. It is more likely that Antipas received the dynastic name *Herod* after Archelaus' deposition. He is so designated on his coins[2] and in inscriptions.[3] Although Josippon's reliability as a historian is questionable,[4] he confirms that Antipas received the designation *Herod* after Archelaus' deposition.[5]

[1] Jos. *Ant.* xviii. 27, 36, 102, 104, 105, 106, 109, 111, 112, 114, 115, 116, 117, 118, 119, 122, 136, 148, 150, 240, 243, 247, 248, 250, 251, 255; xix. 351; *BJ* ii. 168, 178, 181, 183; *Vita* 37, 65. Also he is so designated by Eus. *HE* i. 7. 12; 10. 1; 11. 1, 2, 3, 5, 6, 7; ii. 4. 1; 10. 9.

[2] Madden, *History of Jewish Coinage*, pp. 95–9; *Coins of the Jews*, pp. 118–22; Head, p. 808; Hill, pp. 229–30; Reifenberg, *Ancient Jewish Coins*, pp. 44–5. Since there are no extant coins of Antipas before the deposition of Archelaus, it is not known if he had *Herod* on his coins. It is probable that he did not, because of what has been said above and because Philip did not do so on his coins (cf. below, p. 107 n. 10). It seems that only one man could use the name at a time.

[3] The inscriptions of Antipas are as follows. One on the island of Cos (*OGIS*, 1, 416):

Ἡρῴδην
Ἡρῴδου τοῦ βασιλέως υἱόν,
τετράρχην,
Φιλίων Ἀγλάου, φύσει δὲ Νίκωνος,
τὸν αὐτοῦ ξένον καὶ φίλον.

One on the island of Delos (*OGIS*, 1, 417):

Ὁ δῆμος ὁ Ἀ[θηναίων καὶ οἱ]
κατοι[κ]ο[ῦντες τὴν νῆσον]
Ἡρῴδην βασιλέ[ως Ἡρῴδου υἱὸν]
τετράρχην ἀρετῆ[ς ἕνεκεν καὶ εὐνοί-]
ας τῆς εἰς ἑαυτοὺ[ς ... ἀνέθηκαν].

Since Antipas was the only one who bore both the name *Herod* and the title *tetrarch*, these inscriptions, no doubt, refer to him (cf. Schürer, 1, 431–2 n. 1).

[4] Wacholder, pp. 10–13; cf. below, p. 124.

[5] According to Josippon, Augustus, after Archelaus' deposition, made Antipas king and called him 'Herod', cf. a trans. of the Cambridge UL T.S. 8K. 17 MS by M. Sanders and H. Nahmad, 'A Judeo-Arabic Epitome of Yosippon', *Essays in Honor of Solomon B. Freehof* (Pittsburg, 1964), p. 285; Joseph ben Gurion, trans. into Latin by Sebastian Münster (Basel, 1541), chap. 46; cf. also J. Wellhausen (trans.), 'Der arabische Josippus', *AGG*, N.F. 1 (1897), 33. There is another tradition in which Augustus came to Jerusalem to depose Archelaus, installed Antipas in his stead, changed his name to Herod, and then returned to Rome, cf. Joseph ben Gurion, trans. into Latin by S. Münster (Basel, 1559), p. 191 (cf. also Joseph ben Gurion,

The second clue is on the coins of Archelaus where the obverse side had HPωΔOY (not APXEΛAOY).[1] This is further corroborated by the fact that Archelaus is designated Herod by the Roman historian Dio Cassius.[2] It is probable that Herod became a dynastic title after Herod the Great's death and that Archelaus held this title until his deposition, at which time Antipas acquired it. Furthermore, as mentioned above,[3] Justin Martyr's curious statement that Archelaus was succeeded by Herod (Antipas) and received the authority allotted to him[4] must not be overlooked. In this context it may mean that he succeeded Archelaus in carrying on the dynastic name. The fact that Eusebius begins the reign of Antipas at the time of Archelaus' deposition[5] may confirm this. Antipas, having received the dynastic title, then came into his own.

The third clue is the negative one that Philip the tetrarch is never called by the title *Herod*, but is always called Philip the tetrarch by Luke,[6] Josephus[7], Philo[8] and Eusebius,[9] and on his coins.[10] Furthermore, this title is never used by Antipas' or Philip's successors. Neither Agrippa I nor II is so called by Josephus,[11] Philo,[12] Mishnaic and Talmudic literature,[13]

The Wonderful and Most Deplorable History, p. 88). The present writer is indebted to Dr E. Bammel for pointing out to him the two traditions in the two Basel editions of Josippon.

[1] Cf. Madden, *History of Jewish Coinage*, pp. 91–5; *Coins of the Jews*, pp. 114–18; Head, p. 808; Hill, pp. 231–5; Reifenberg, *Ancient Jewish Coins*, pp. 45–6.

[2] Dio lv. 27. 6.   [3] Pp. 31–2.

[4] *Dial*. ciii. 4 (*MPG*, VI, 717).

[5] *Chron*. II, 146–7. Possibly Eusebius' chronology is based on a scheme describing the succession of Rome's Jewish representatives (this was suggested to the present writer by Dr E. Bammel).

[6] Lk. 3: 1.   [7] *BJ* iii. 512.

[8] *Flacc*. 25.

[9] *HE* i. 10. 1; ii. 4. 1; 10. 9.

[10] Madden, *History of Jewish Coinage*, pp. 100–2; *Coins of the Jews*, pp. 123–7; Head, p. 808; Hill, p. 228; Reifenberg, *Ancient Jewish Coins*, pp. 43–4; 'Unpublished and Unusual Jewish Coins', *IEJ*, I (1950–1), 176.

[11] Josephus mentions Agrippa I 106 times and Agrippa II 86 times.

[12] Philo has reference only to Agrippa I, cf. *Flacc*. 25, 39, 103; *Leg*. I 79, 261, 263, 269, 325, 332, 333.

[13] King Agrippa is mentioned in Bik. iii. 4; Sot. vii. 8, and in TB: Pes. 64b, 107b; Yoma 20b; Suk. 27a; Ket. 17a; Sot. 41b; A.Z. 55a. It is difficult to know with certainty which Agrippa is meant in the various references in

Tacitus,[1] or Dio Cassius.[2] Although Luke designates Agrippa II as Agrippa,[3] he does use the name Herod for Agrippa I.[4] Possibly the latter was known as one of the Herods and was thus called King Herod in contrast to Herod the tetrarch mentioned in the next chapter (Acts 13:1). Apart from Luke's usage it seems that the titular name Herod was used only from the death of Herod the Great until the deposition of Antipas. It may be that it was given by special permission of the emperor and was granted as a concession to Archelaus and Antipas because they were not allowed to use the title *king*. This is confirmed by the fact that both Agrippa I[5] and Agrippa II[6] received the title *king*.

the Talmud. For confirmation of this and for other references in Jewish literature, see Strack–Billerbeck, II, 709–10, 769.

[1] Agrippa I: *Ann.* xii. 23. Agrippa II: *Hist.* ii. 81; v. 1; *Ann.* xiii. 7.

[2] Dio has references only to Agrippa I, cf. lix. 8. 2; 24. 1; lx. 8. 2.

[3] Acts 25: 13, 22, 23, 24, 26; 26: 1, 2, 19, 27, 28, 32.

[4] Acts 12: 1, 6, 11, 19, 21.

[5] Jos. *Ant.* xviii. 237; *BJ* ii. 181, 182; Philo *Flacc.* 25. He is also called *king* in Jos. *Ant.* xv. 405; xvii. 31; xviii. 242, 273, 289; xix. 236, 265, 274, 279, 288, 295, 309, 310, 313, 317–49, 354, 357; xx. 1, 104; Philo *Flacc.* 103; *Leg.* 179, 261; Dio lix. 24. 1; on coins, cf. Madden, *History of Jewish Coinage,* pp. 103–11; *Coins of the Jews,* pp. 131–9; Head, p. 808; Hill, pp. 236–8; Reifenberg, *Ancient Jewish Coins,* pp. 46–8. An interesting observation is that Agrippa is called Ἀγρίππας ὁ μέγας (Jos. *Ant.* xvii. 28; xviii. 110, 142; xx. 104), a title that was used only by Herod the Great (Jos. *Ant.* xviii. 130, 133, 136). This may show that Agrippa achieved the same status as his grandfather, Herod the Great, namely, king and φιλόκαισαρ (as seen on some of his coins and in an inscription (*OGIS,* I, 419), and not merely that of ethnarch or tetrarch in that he regained the whole of Herod the Great's domain. But one must be careful here, for Herod the Great is not designated 'the Great' anywhere else, and it may be a case of Herod the elder in contrast to the younger, that is, his sons, and the same may be true of Agrippa I, namely, to distinguish him from his son Agrippa II (above, p. 6 n. 2). Agrippa I has on his coins the designation βασιλεὺς μέγας Ἀγρίππας (cf. Madden, *Coins of the Jews,* pp. 133–4; Reifenberg, *Ancient Jewish Coins,* pp. 46–7), which is very much like that which is given in Jos. *Ant.* xx. 104. Since this designation is only on the coins dated between A.D. 43 and 45, it further confirms that he wanted to distinguish himself as the elder from his son Agrippa who was the younger. An article which may be helpful, but which the present writer has been unable to locate, is E. Klimowski, 'Agrippa I as ΒΑΣΙΛΕΥΣ ΜΕΓΑΣ', vol. I of *Numismatic Studies and Research* (Jerusalem, 1954), pp. 91–5.

[6] Eus. *HE* ii. 19. 2; implied in Jos. *Ant.* xx. 104, 138, 159; *BJ* ii. 223, 247, 252; called *king* in *Ant.* xx. 179, 189, 193, 203, 211; *BJ* ii. 309, 335, 405, 520, 556, 632; iii. 29; iv. 14, 81, 498; v. 152; *Vita* 39, 46, 114, 154, 180, 182, 343,

Having received a better title, neither of them adopted the name *Herod*.[1]

Three conclusions can be drawn: (1) that the name Herod was probably some sort of title or dynastic name; (2) that it could be used by only one person at a time – Antipas did not use it until Archelaus' deposition and Philip never used it at all; (3) that it was given to Archelaus and Antipas by special permission of the emperor as a concession for their not being allowed to use the title king.

In light of the above why was it necessary to retain the title? First, it provided continuity as far as the subjects of their rule were concerned. Secondly, it served to carry on a traditional name, esteemed in political and social circles. The sons would have thought it an honour to perpetuate the family name which was so well known in the Roman world. This is seen in Antipas' inscriptions, where he states that he is the son of Herod the King.[2]

Conclusion

It seems that Antipas received the dynastic title *Herod* after Archelaus' deposition. He now represented the Herod family and rule. Since he was not promoted to a higher rank than tetrarch, it is probable that he was never an overseer of the Jewish nation as seems to have been the case with Archelaus. It would for him have been more difficult so to act since Judaea had become a Roman province. Probably with Augustus' permission, however, he was permitted to continue the Herodian name. To him this was a great honour.

345, 349, 351–4, 355, 359, 362, 364, 365, 366, 407, 408, 409; *Ap.* i. 51; Eus. *HE* iii. 10. 10; Tac. *Ann.* xiii. 7; on coins see Madden, *History of Jewish Coinage*, pp. 113–33; *Coins of the Jews*, pp. 144–60; Head, p. 809; Hill, pp. 239–47; Reifenberg, *Ancient Jewish Coinage*, pp. 49–54; called φιλόκαισαρ and φιλορώμαιος in some inscriptions (cf. *OGIS*, I, 419, 420, 424).

[1] Agrippa I had a brother who was named Herod and had the title *king*, cf. Jos. *Ant.* xix. 279, 288; xx. 13, 103, 158; *BJ* ii. 221; for coins with the inscription 'King Herod', see Madden, *History of Jewish Coinage*, pp. 111–13; Head, p. 808; Reifenberg, *Ancient Jewish Coinage*, pp. 47–8. In this case, however, the name Herod, like Agrippa, is not a title but a common name. He ruled, moreover, the small territory of Chalcis which, not being a part of Herod the Great's territory, had no interest in the Herodian title.

[2] Above, p. 106 n. 3.

CHAPTER 7

ANTIPAS AND JOHN THE BAPTIST

The episode for which Antipas is remembered is his involvement in the imprisonment and death of John the Baptist. The
main sources of information for these are, first, the New Testament and, secondly, the account in Josephus' *Antiquitates
Judaicae*. This chapter discusses Antipas and John the Baptist's
imprisonment and death.

THE CONTEXT OF THE ACCOUNTS

The Synoptics

Matthew and Mark briefly mention the fact of John's imprisonment at the conclusion of his ministry,[1] and then later in their
Gospels they reintroduce the story, stating the reasons for his
imprisonment and death.[2] In these later sections both have the
same general order, namely, (1) Antipas hears the rumours
about Jesus and believes that John whom he beheaded was
raised from the dead,[3] (2) John's imprisonment and death,
and (3) Jesus' withdrawal and the feeding of the 5,000.

Luke, on the other hand, tells of both the fact and the cause
of John's imprisonment at the conclusion of his ministry before
introducing the ministry of Jesus.[4] He only mentions in passing
the fact of John's death in connection with Antipas' hearing of
Jesus and his perplexity at who he might be.[5] In other words,
Luke seems to finish John's career in 3:19–20.[6]

---

[1] Mt. 4: 12; Mk. 1: 14.   [2] Mt. 14: 3–12; Mk. 6: 17–29.

[3] Mt. 14: 1–2; Mk. 6: 14–16. Most commentators read ἔλεγον for ἔλεγεν
in Mk. 6: 14 making it the opinion of the people rather than of Antipas, cf.
C. H. Turner, 'Markan Usage: Notes, Critical and Exegetical, on the
Second Gospel', *JTS*, xxv (1924), 380–1; H. Ljungvik, 'Zum Markusevangelium 6. 14', *ZNW*, xxxiii (1934), 90–2; E. Lohmeyer, *Das Evangelium des Markus, KEK*[12] (Göttingen, 1953), p. 115 n. 4; Taylor, *Mark*, p. 308;
E. Haenchen, *Der Weg Jesu* (Berlin, 1966), p. 235; cf. below, p. 185.

[4] Lk. 3: 19–20.   [5] Lk. 9: 7–9.

[6] Conzelmann also thinks Luke here provides a dividing point between
John's and Jesus' ministries and believes that it 'is in the sense of drawing

In looking at the broader context it seems that Mark and Luke agree against Matthew in that they have: (1) Jesus' sending out the twelve, (2) Antipas' hearing of Jesus and the mention of John's beheading, and (3) the return of the twelve and Jesus' withdrawal with them, followed by the feeding of the 5,000; whereas Matthew has: (1) the parables of chapter 13, (2) Antipas' hearing of Jesus and John's beheading, and (3) as a result of John's beheading, Jesus' withdrawal and his feeding of the multitude.

Therefore, for Mark and Luke, Antipas' hearing of Jesus, and, in the case of Mark, the mention of John's death, fills in the pause between the commissioning of the twelve and their return, whereas this is absent from Matthew, probably because he had treated the commissioning of the twelve in an earlier context.[1] Furthermore, Mark's pericope on the Baptist's beheading (6: 17–29) is a parenthetical flashback (to the immediately preceding verse where Mark states that Herod had beheaded John), digressing only to explain how and why John was beheaded. On the other hand Matthew's pericope (14:3–12) begins with a parenthesis but never closes it, verse 12 serving as an editorial bridge for Jesus' withdrawals.[2]

Josephus

Josephus gives the story of Antipas' defeat by Aretas.[3] According to Josephus, the people believed that the reason for his

a distinction between the epochs of salvation, for which xvi 16 provides the clue'; cf. H. Conzelmann, *The Theology of St Luke*, trans. G. Buswell (London, 1960), p. 21; cf. also p. 26. For a critique of Conzelmann's view, see W. Wink, *John the Baptist in the Gospel Tradition*, Society for New Testament Studies Monograph Series, ed. by M. Black, vii (Cambridge, 1968), pp. 46–57; cf. also B. Weiss, *Die Evangelien des Markus und Lukas*, KEK[9] (Göttingen, 1901), p. 308; M. Dibelius, *Die urchristliche Überlieferung von Johannes dem Täufer*, FRLANT, xv (Göttingen, 1911), 84. Interestingly enough Luke finished off John's era even before Jesus was baptized. The reason for this, undoubtedly, is that Jesus' baptism was already a part of the new era. Also in Acts 13: 24–5 Luke records Paul's sermon in the same manner – as John was finishing his course, he spoke of Jesus who was to follow him.

[1] Mt. 10: 1 ff. Matthew nowhere specifically mentions their ministry nor their return.

[2] Cf. W. Trilling, 'Die Täufertradition bei Matthäus', *BZ*, N.F. iii (1959), 273; E. Lohmeyer, *Das Evangelium des Matthäus*[3], ed. by W. Schmauch, KEK (Göttingen, 1962), p. 234; W. Grundmann, *Das Evangelium nach Matthäus*, THNT, i (Berlin, 1968), 360.   [3] Jos. *Ant.* xviii. 116–19.

defeat was God's judgement upon him for having killed John. Thus, like the Gospels, Josephus' story of John's death serves as a flashback explaining the reason for Antipas' defeat.

THE INTRODUCTORY MATTERS TO THE VARIOUS ACCOUNTS

The Synoptics

The literary considerations of the pericope

The Lucan omission. Bultmann thinks that the synoptic accounts of John's imprisonment and death could hardly have had a place in the Christian tradition as it was originally formulated.[1] His view is based upon Bussmann's analysis that where Luke uses Mark as a source, he expands him, and this is especially true with regard to the Herods, in whom he had a special interest. Therefore, since Luke omits Mark's story of John the Baptist's death, Mark could not have had the story in his original narrative but rather it was inserted by a later editor.[2] This, however, is not necessarily so. One reason for Luke's omission of the story may have been that he had already included a great deal about the Baptist, as for example his birth narrative. Secondly, since Luke had concluded the content of John's preaching near the beginning of his Gospel culminating in the Baptist's imprisonment (3:19–20), it would be unnatural for him to follow Mark in mentioning it again here.[3] This is

[1] R. Bultmann, *The History of the Synoptic Tradition*, trans. J. Marsh (Oxford, 1963), p. 301.

[2] W. Bussmann, *Synoptische Studien*, I (Halle, 1925), 30–4. Bussmann argues that Luke liked to omit doublets (*ibid.* pp. 6–66), but Grundmann rightly points out that Luke does in fact include many examples of duplicate material such as the double mission passages, cf. W. Grundmann, *Das Evangelium nach Lukas*[2], *THNT*, III (Berlin, 1961), 8.

[3] V. H. Stanton, *The Gospels as Historical Documents*, Pt II (Cambridge, 1909), 156. One could argue that John's imprisonment was mentioned by the other two synoptists (Mt. 4:12; Mk. 1:14) right after John's preaching. Actually John's imprisonment is placed after Jesus' temptation to serve as a transition from the end of John's ministry to the beginning of Jesus'. Also, Matthew and Mark only state the fact of his imprisonment whereas Luke states the cause of his imprisonment, viz., John's reproving of Antipas' actions. There was no purpose in Luke picking up again the narrative of John's reproving of Antipas and its results when he had already done so previously.

not the only example of an incident omitted by Luke because he had already included a similar story before having seen Mark.[1] Thirdly, having finished with John in 3:19–20, Luke may not have wanted to mix up the Baptist and Jesus stories. Fourthly, it may be that he thought it less important,[2] either because it did not appeal to him, or because he thought it unsuitable for his special purpose.[3] Fifthly, in every case Luke's interest in Herod Antipas was in relationship to Jesus,[4] and since this pericope shows no direct relationship to Jesus this may explain its omission.[5]

Thus, it seems that Luke's omission of John's death is justifiable and not necessarily a result of Mark's not having it originally.

The Marcan pericope. As stated above, Bussmann thinks that Luke's omission of the story of John's death was due to Mark's omission of it in his original narrative, and that it was inserted into Mark's Gospel by a later editor. However, would there have been an adequate motive for a later editor to insert this story into Mark? It is unlikely. It is more probable that Mark himself included it in his Gospel than a later editor. Lohmeyer

[1] E.g. the great commandment (Mk. 12: 28–34 = Mt. 22: 34–40) is omitted in the same context of Luke because he already had a similar story in 10: 25–8; the anointing at Bethany (Mk. 14: 3–9 = Mt. 26: 6–13) is omitted by Luke in his passion narrative because of a similar story earlier in his Gospel (7: 36–50).

[2] J. C. Hawkins, 'Three Limitations of St Luke's Use of St Mark's Gospel', *SSP*, p. 62.

[3] Taylor, *Behind*, p. 138.

[4] Cf. Lk. 9: 7–9; 13: 31–2; 23: 7–15. One may question the claim that Lk. 3: 1 mentions Antipas with no reference to Jesus. But this passage is in another category since Luke is giving a chronological note and includes other rulers besides Antipas.

[5] Bultmann (p. 301 n. 4) gives as reason for its omission from Luke that it was not included in Ur-Markus. Whether or not this story was included in Ur-Markus is a debatable point and cannot be proved one way or the other. If one assumes Marcan priority, then Matthew has used this story, and this would necessitate that Matthew used the edited form of Mark and not Ur-Markus (D. Guthrie, *New Testament Introduction*[3], [London, 1970], pp. 136–7). However, this seems highly unlikely. In general the Ur-Markus theory is not a satisfactory solution of Luke's omission (W. G. Kümmel, *Introduction to the New Testament*[14], trans. by A. J. Mattill [London, 1966], pp. 49–50).

thinks that Mark took it from a written source as it was without altering it.[1] He feels that the layout of the story deviates from other sections of Mark in that it is a well rounded composition rather than a collection of small isolated units. But this cannot be pressed, for a story is told as a whole and not as a collection of fragments.

Lohmeyer points out that there is an abundance of unusual words, and, more significantly, that the style is quite different.[2] Taylor thinks that 'the presence of many unusual words is accounted for by the subject-matter',[3] and from this he infers that Mark used a source.[4] However, Marcan style and words are not lacking.[5] For example, the phrase ἡδέως αὐτοῦ ἤκουεν in 6:20 is peculiarly his, being used one other time in his Gospel.[6] On the average Mark has 1·85 characteristic words per verse but in this particular pericope he has an average of 3·6.[7] It seems, on the one hand, that the difference in style and words may be accounted for by the subject-matter and by Mark's faithfulness in following his source; on the other hand there are stylistic and linguistic peculiarities which are characteristic of Mark.

It seems reasonable to assume that this pericope was originally in Mark and thus had its place in the early Christian tradition.

The Matthaean pericope. Styler argues that this pericope is a clear case of Marcan priority, 'where Matt. goes astray through

---

[1] Lohmeyer, *Markus*, pp. 117–18. See also P. J. Achtemeier, 'Toward the Isolation of Pre-Markan Miracle Catenae', *JBL*, LXXXIX (1970), 270.

[2] E.g. there are no historic presents, and in their place there are more aorists and a few imperfects. The longer sentences are readily introduced by participles followed by the predicate, and there is an abundance of genitive absolutes. He also claims that in spite of its popular character the story has a cultivated form through which an Aramaic basis can clearly be traced (Lohmeyer, *Markus*, p. 118).

[3] Taylor, *Mark*, p. 311.   [4] *Ibid.* p. 311 n. 1.

[5] *Ibid.* p. 311; cf. also Trilling, *BZ*, N.F. III, 272 n. 2.

[6] Mk. 12:37; cf. J. C. Hawkins, *Horae Synopticae*[2] (Oxford, 1909), p. 160.

[7] This is based on the criteria established by Hawkins (*ibid.* p. 10), viz., that in Mark the characteristic words and phrases are those 'which *occur at least three times* in Mark, and which either (*a*) are not found *at all in Matthew or Luke*, or (*b*) occur in Mark more often than in Matthew and Luke together'. The most distinctive characteristic words in Mark are the adverbial uses of πολλά and εὐθύς which appear twice.

misunderstanding, yet betrays a knowledge of the authentic version – the version which is given by Mark'.[1] In analysing this pericope there are good reasons for thinking that Matthew had its own tradition and that it was not based upon Mark. First, in the materials common to both, Matthew has on average 91 per cent of Mark's words excluding (and 88 per cent including) the passion narrative, whereas in this pericope Matthew (14:3–12) has only 54 per cent of Mark's words in 6:17–29. Secondly, the verbal correspondence in the common material of Matthew and Mark, excluding the passion narrative, is 49 per cent (51 per cent if one includes the passion narrative),[2] whereas in this pericope there are only eighty-three words[3] out of Mark's 252[4] – or 33 per cent.[5] Furthermore, the first verse of the pericope (Mt. 14:3; Mk. 6:17) seems to indicate clearly either that the evangelists borrowed from one another or that there is one tradition behind all of them (out of Matthew's nineteen words and Mark's twenty-four words, they have seventeen in common). If one excludes the first verse of the pericope then there would be only a 29 per cent verbal correspondence with Mark. Thirdly, if one reviews the

---

[1] G. M. Styler, 'The Priority of Mark', Excursus IV in *The Birth of the New Testament*, by C. F. D. Moule (London, 1962), p. 229.

[2] With the aid of W. G. Rushbrooke, *Synopticon* (London, 1880), the present writer arrived at a total of 8,687 words in Mark and 7,643 words in Matthew, excluding the passion narrative (including the passion narrative the total is 10,680 and 9,715 words respectively), in the material common to each. The verbal correspondence in the common material, excluding the passion narrative, is 4,208 words (including the passion narrative it is 5,406). It was not until after counting up the words that the writer found the work of H. Marriott, *The Sermon on the Mount* (London, 1925), who also counts the words in the Gospels on pp. 34–41. Although the totals are different, the reckoning of percentages never varies by more than 1 per cent – which confirms the present writer's results.

[3] Out of the eighty-three words, forty-five are accounted for by proper names, pronouns, articles, and conjunctions. Excluding these, there is only a 15 per cent verbal correspondence with Mark.

[4] This is counting from K. Aland (ed.), *Synopsis Quattuor Evangeliorum*[4] (Stuttgart, 1965), pp. 203–4.

[5] Hawkins (*Synopticae*, p. 160) argues that Matthew and Luke abbreviated Mark. He gives seven examples. However, two of these are the two parts of this pericope. These two examples have significantly greater variance in the number of words between the Marcan and the Matthaean accounts than any of the other examples given. The variance is striking enough to suggest that the issue is not as clear cut as Hawkins supposes.

pericope, the verbal correspondence is especially high in four verses, namely: Matthew 14:4 with Mark 6:18, Matthew 14:8–9 with Mark 6:25–6, and Matthew 14:11–12 with Mark 6:28–9. This is normal, since the first two references are treating the speeches and the last reference is the conclusion to the story; all of these would naturally be similar in the various traditions. Often in other pericopes the words of Jesus and their concluding statements tend to be similar in the parallel accounts. It is the details of the story that are expressed differently or left out by Matthew. Fourthly, on the average Matthew has 1·18 characteristic words per verse whereas here there are 2·23.[1] This would seem to indicate a Matthaean hand in the writing of the story. Fifthly, Mark's lack of historic presents robs one of a useful criterion for isolating a Matthaean alteration of Mark. Sixthly, there are several linguistic and stylistic peculiarities which seem to indicate that Matthew did not depend upon Mark.[2] Possibly some of these characteristics were from his source.

[1] This is based on the criteria established by Hawkins (*Synopticae*, p. 3). Since Matthew is longer than Mark, characteristic words or phrases are those 'which *occur at least four times* in this Gospel, and which either (*a*) *are not found at all in Mark or Luke*, or which (*b*) *are found in Matthew at least twice as often as in Mark and Luke together*'. The most distinctive characteristic word in this pericope in Matthew is προσέρχομαι.

[2] Lohmeyer (*Matthäus*, p. 233 n. 1) lists some of these peculiarities when he writes: 'Sprachliches: ἀποτίτεσθαι [*sic*] nur hier – ὡς προφήτην wie 21:26 s. dort – ἐν τῷ μέσῳ gut griechisch – ὅθεν = ὥστε nur hier – προβιβάζειν nur hier – φησίν = *inquit*, nur hier.

Stilistisches: V. 3 *om.* ἀποστείλας, *add.* ἀπέθετο und *om.* ὅτι ἐγάμησεν αὐτήν, Mt denkt wohl an ein Konkubinat. – V. 4 *om.* γυναῖκα τοῦ ἀδ. σου vgl. zu 4: 18. – V. 5 ganz verändert: Herodes hier nur der blutdürstige Tyrann, der vor dem Volke sich fürchtet; dieses (nicht Herodes) hält Johs für einen Propheten (Mk ἀνὴρ δίκαιος καὶ ἅγιος). Vgl. indes Pallis zu Mk. 6: 20. Andere Form der Erzählung oder nach at.lichem Vorbild? – V. 6 Mk. 6: 21. 22 stark verkürzt, es fehlt das Gelage (in V. 9 nachgetragen), auch die direkten Worte des Königs. Merkwürdig der Dativ γενεσίοις, vielleicht eine Fusion von Mk γενομένης (ἡμέρας) τοῖς γενεσίοις. – V. 7 Mk 6: 23. 24 stark verkürzt. ὁμολογεῖν versprechen nur hier, aber auch Preuschen, Agrapha Nr. 18; vgl. Bauer[4] *s.v.* Schwur verkürzt "um die Hälfte des Königreiches". Zu ὃ ἐάν vgl. 11: 27 und Allen z. St. – V. 8 Neuer Zug nur bei Mt: προβιβάζειν nur hier, Zeichen, dass Mt eine Variante der Geschichte benutzt, wie bei ἀπέθετο, ὁμολογεῖν. Vgl. Bauer[2] *s.v.* Worte der Tochter fast genau wie bei Mk. Zusatz ὧδε; aus V. 11 zu schliessen, dass also auch die Mutter ὧδε sein muss, d.h. hier sind König und Königin bei einem

Seventhly, although lacking many of the details, Matthew's account is substantially complete in itself.[1] Mark's version is fuller and gives it more colour as is typical of him. It may be that Matthew's readers were familiar with the story and did not need the details, while Mark's audience, presumably far away from the Palestinian scene, needed to be informed of the details.

There is, then, a strong cumulative case for considering that here are two separate traditions of the Baptist's death.

To sum up: It seems that the stories of the Baptist's death belong to two independent traditions which were taken over by the evangelists using many of their own characteristic words and phrases. On the other hand, each of them shows peculiar linguistic and stylistic characteristics in this pericope. This may be due to the nature of the subject, but it also may indicate their faithful following of their sources.

The origin of the pericope

Bultmann thinks that the story was taken over from the Hellenistic Jewish tradition, and this is rendered feasible by the existence of heathen parallels.[2] He cites three such parallels.[3] The story in Herodotus has some similarities with that of the Gospels, but, as Haenchen points out, it cannot be claimed as a true parallel.[4] On review, the other two parallels mentioned by

Mahle mit Gästen zusammen. Freilich nicht zwingend, da in V. 11 ἤνεγκεν (Mk. ἔδωκεν). – V. 9.10 Wieder verkürzt: λυπηθεὶς ὁ βασ. bei Mt nicht mehr begründet. – V. 11 Henker gestrichen von Mt; passivisch (wie 4: 1; 9: 25; 14: 11; 16: 26; 18: 8; 19: 13; 24: 22 (bis); 26: 57; 27: 58). S. Allen p. XXIII. – V. 12 προσέρχεσθαι statt ἦλθαν (bei Mt 52 mal, Mk 6 mal, Lk 10 mal). Wichtig ist der Schlussatz καὶ ἐλθόντες ἀπήγγειλαν τῷ Ἰησοῦ. 1. Nachgebildet nach Mk 6: 30 (cf. ἀπήγγειλαν). Aber hier ein anderes Subjekt und anderes Objekt. 2. Bei Mk deutlich ein Intermezzo aus kompositionellen Gründen: Der Erzähler füllt eine Pause zwischen Aussendung und Rückkehr aus. Mt verknüpft den Tod mit der Geschichte Jesu: Jesus hörte es und entwich (V. 13). Also ist für ihn 14: 1–12a eine Art Botenbericht an Jesus; daher wohl auch die Aoriste. Vgl. Allen p. 159 f.'

[1] *Ibid.* p. 233.

[2] P. 301; cf. also Lohmeyer, *Markus*, p. 121; Ergänzungsheft, p. 11 (Lohmeyer in his Ergänzungsheft changes the possible sphere of its origin from Rome to Syria).

[3] Bultmann (p. 301 n. 5) cites Herodotus ix. 108–13; Livy xxxix. 43; and Plutarch *Artaxerxes* xvii.   [4] *Der Weg Jesu*, pp. 240–1.

Bultmann are far less similar; in fact, there is hardly any similarity at all. Thus Bultmann's claim that these heathen parallels make it feasible that Mark's story is of Hellenistic Jewish origin is unfounded. If any tradition influenced the story, the Old Testament tradition gives far closer parallels.[1] On the other hand, as Scobie states, 'The Old Testament parallels are not close enough to warrant the conclusion that the New Testament story is a pure fiction'.[2]

There are several cases of semitism in Mark, which suggests that it is of Palestinian origin, either in a written or oral form.[3]

[1] E.g. the boldness of John's proclamation before Antipas is paralleled by Nathan before David (2 Sam. 12: 1–12) and by Elijah before Ahab (1 Kgs. 21: 17–24). The promise of up to half of the kingdom by Antipas in the context of a banquet is paralleled by the story of Esther before King Ahasuerus (Est. 7: 1–10).

[2] C. H. H. Scobie, *John the Baptist* (London, 1964), p. 180 n. 1.

[3] Here are some of the semitisms noted by various scholars in this field of study: (1) The use in 6: 17 of the redundant personal pronoun to strengthen the definition of the noun: αὐτὸς γὰρ ὁ Ἡρῴδης and in A C K Θ Π of 6: 22 αὐτῆς τῆς Ἡρῳδιάδος; cf. J. Wellhausen, *Einleitung in die Drei ersten Evangelien*[2] (Berlin, 1911), p. 19; Moulton–Howard, Appendix on 'Semitisms in the New Testament', p. 431; C. F. D. Moule, *An Idiom Book of New Testament Greek*[2] (Cambridge, 1959), p. 176; Black, *Aramaic Approach*, pp. 96–7. With regard to the last passage Allen thinks its does not matter which reading of the pronoun one accepts (αὐτῆς or αὐτοῦ), for its inclusion is probably due to an over-exact translation of an Aramaic idiom, בְּרַתֵּהּ דְּהֵרוֹדְיָא or בַּת הֵרוֹדְיָא, which simply means 'the daughter of Herodias'; cf. W. C. Allen, 'The Aramaic Element in St Mark', *ET*, XIII (1902), 330; W. C. Allen, *The Gospel according to Saint Mark* (London, 1915), p. 98. The redundant pronoun is also used in D of 6: 18 αὐτὴν γυναῖκα τοῦ ἀδελφοῦ σου (cf. Moulton–Howard, p. 431; Black, *Aramaic Approach*, pp. 97–100). (2) The use of πολλά may be due to the translation of the Aramaic שַׂגִּיא (or סַגִּי) as seen in 6: 20, cf. Allen, *ET*, XIII, 330; Moulton–Howard, p. 446; Wellhausen, *Einleitung*, pp. 21–2. (3) The participle used virtually as a proper name may be due to Hebraic influence, as ὁ βαπτίζων in 6: 14, 24, cf. Moulton–Turner, pp. 150–1. (4) The word order of a prepositional phrase coming after the subject (which itself is after the verb) has affinity to Hebrew where the preposition is followed by a noun rather than having a pronominal suffix (e.g. Gen. 24: 2); thus 6: 26 καὶ περίλυπος γεγόμενος ὁ βασιλεὺς διὰ τοὺς ὅρκους καὶ τοὺς ἀνακειμένους, cf. Moulton–Turner, pp. 349–50. There are two other semitisms in the variant readings of this passage. (5) The semitic usage of 'the repetition of a preposition before every noun of a series which it governs; the construction is intolerable in literary Greek' (Black, *Aramaic Approach*, pp. 114–15), is found in D lat in 6: 26 ὁ βασιλεὺς διὰ τοὺς ὅρκους καὶ διὰ τοὺς ἀνακειμένους. (6) The semitic form of expression given in

ANTIPAS AND JOHN THE BAPTIST

Also, the fact that Mark uses the term βασιλεύς four times (6:22, 25, 26, 27) in this pericope would point to a semitic origin. It is the only time in his work that he uses this designation for a ruler. If it were of Roman origin probably the term τετράρχης would have been used. The fact that Matthew does use τετράρχης in 14:1 but uses βασιλεύς in this pericope (14:9) would seem to indicate that his source used the latter term and that he himself faithfully reproduced it.

On the other hand, there are some terms in Mark's account which have a Roman and/or Hellenistic flavour. These terms are used of governmental positions or functions. Several are listed in Mark 6:21: δεῖπνον ἐποίησεν τοῖς μεγιστᾶσιν αὐτοῦ καὶ τοῖς χιλιάρχοις καὶ τοῖς πρώτοις τῆς Γαλιλαίας. By repetition of the article the three groups are distinguished.[1] First mentioned are the two civilian groups, the μεγιστᾶνες and the πρῶτοι τῆς Γαλιλαίας.[2] Then there are the two military terms, χιλίαρχοι and σπεκουλάτωρ (Mk. 6:27).[3] The presence of these words

---

A C D K Π in 6: 20 ἀκούσας αὐτοῦ πολλὰ ἐποίει, which has the idea of πολλάκις ἤκουεν, he listened to him often', Wellhausen, *Das Evangelium Marci*[2] (Berlin, 1909), p. 46, considers to be 'zwar gut semitisch'; cf. also Wellhausen, *Einleitung*, p. 21; Moulton–Howard, pp. 445–6; BD/Funk, §414 (5). In Mt. semitisms are fewer but two items cited above would be applicable, namely, no. 4 in Mt. 14:9 and no. 5 in D it of Mt. 14:9. The insertion of the definite article to denote an object hitherto unknown appears in D of Mt. 14:11 ἐπὶ τῷ πίνακι (θ = ἐν τῷ). This also is Hebraic (cf. Moulton–Howard, p. 430).

[1] A. T. Robertson, *A Grammar of the Greek New Testament in the Light of Historical Research*[3] (London, 1919), p. 786.

[2] Above, p. 102.

[3] The word χιλίαρχος in early usage had the literal meaning of 'the leader of 1,000 soldiers' (Herodotus vii. 81), but it became later the equivalent of *tribunus militum*, the commander of a cohort. In Polybius' time (second century B.C.) this consisted of about 700 men (a legion was 4,200 men – Polybius vi. 20. 8 – and there were six χιλίαρχοι for each legion – vi. 27. 4). In Josephus' day there was any number from 600 to 1,000 men under each χιλίαρχος (*BJ* iii. 67), which therefore was roughly equivalent to a major or colonel (Bauer/AG, p. 890). This was the situation under Antipas' rule (Sherwin-White, p. 137). Haenchen (p. 241) disagrees, by saying that the mention of χιλίαρχοι makes it look as if Antipas had a very large kingdom. But Haenchen is inaccurate in demanding 1,000 men under each χιλίαρχος. The term σπεκουλάτωρ (Mk. 6: 27) is a Latin loan word *speculator* which was also used in Jewish literature (ספקלטור, cf. Krauss, *Griechische und lateinische Lehnwörter*, II, 92–3, 409; Strack–Billerbeck, II, 12). It had the meaning of a *spy* or *scout* and then *courier* and also *executioner* (Bauer/

does not detract from the Palestinian character of the pericope. On the contrary, if oriental governmental terminology and offices had been used, it would arouse suspicion as not being true to life. It is only natural to have the Graeco-Roman governmental vocabulary for Antipas' administration. 'It shows the court and establishment of a petty Jewish prince under strong Roman influence.'[1]

Therefore the claim that this story is solely from Hellenistic origins will not stand.[2] There are a number of items in this pericope which seem to point to a Palestinian origin.

The sources of the pericope

It is extremely difficult to know exactly from where this story is derived. As mentioned above there are good reasons to think that it was of Palestinian origin. Rawlinson suggests that the Marcan story is 'an account written with a certain amount of literary freedom, of what was being darkly whispered in the bazaars or market places of Palestine at the time'.[3] Although there may have been rumours of this event, the early Christians surely would have used more reliable sources. There are at least two persons who might have divulged reliable information. The first is Joanna who was one of the women who ministered to Jesus and his disciples.[4] Her husband, Chuza, was the ἐπίτροπος or the financial minister of Antipas and

---

AG, p. 769; cf. also Schürer, I, 471–3 nn. 89–91; A. H. M. Jones, *Studies in Roman Government and Law* [Oxford, 1960], pp. 161, 207 n. 66; V. Skånland, 'Spiculator', *Symbolae Osloenses*, Fasc. XXXVIII [1963], 94–119). They are pictured in Tacitus (*Hist.* i. 24–5; ii. 73) as 'a special body of imperial guards who tend to appear in moments of military intrigue. The Latin term is used appropriately by Mark for the Herodian soldier who executed the Baptist' (Sherwin-White, pp. 109–10).

[1] Sherwin-White, p. 137. Brandon's remark (*Jesus*, pp. 268–9 n. 6) that σπεκουλάτωρ shows that this pericope is of Roman origin is untenable in the light of what is stated above. It seems incredible that one word should determine the origin of an otherwise semitic pericope.

[2] One can appreciate the recent emphasis in NT studies to the effect that the Hellenistic and Palestinian worlds are not two entirely separate entities, cf. W. D. Davies, *Paul and Rabbinic Judaism* (London, 1955), pp. 1–16.

[3] A. E. J. Rawlinson, *St Mark*[5], Westminster Commentaries (London, 1942), p. 82; cf. also R. Schütz, *Johannes der Täufer* (Zürich and Stuttgart, 1967), pp. 20–2.

[4] Lk. 8: 3 and also mentioned in 24: 10.

may have been among the μεγιστᾶνες or οἱ πρῶτοι τῆς Γαλιλαίας of Mark 6:21. As such he would have been an eyewitness of the events. The second person is Manaen, the σύντροφος of Antipas,[1] meaning a person who was a companion in education or one who was an intimate friend.[2] Since both of them were close to Antipas, it may explain why the Gospel accounts put the blame not so much on Antipas as on Herodias. The fact that the church was persecuted by Herodias' brother, Agrippa I, who was himself a major factor in Antipas' deposition, may be the reason for Antipas appearing in a more favourable light in this pericope. If these two persons represent the sources behind the separate Gospel accounts, this may explain the several differences between the two accounts.[3]

The character of the pericope

Bultmann claims that the synoptic narrative is a legend exhibiting no Christian character.[4] By this he implies that it is an unhistorical story, the creation of the religious imagination.[5] However, the characteristics of the story are very lifelike. The banquet for Antipas and his lords, the intrigue of Herodias, and the momentary remorse of the tetrarch are all natural in an oriental setting, and true to the life of the Herodian family.[6] The vivid description of the scene and of the actors gives it an authentic touch. On the whole 'the narrative has precisely the same colourful character as other Markan stories, notably that of the Gerasene Demoniac'.[7]

---

[1] Acts 13:1.

[2] For a further discussion on these two persons as the possible sources for this story, see Appendix VI.

[3] It is generally held that it is unusual for the evangelists to have had a direct source (cf. D. E. Nineham, 'Eye-Witness Testimony and the Gospel Tradition', *JTS*, N.S. IX [1958], 13–25, 243–52; XI [1960], 253–64; N. Perrin, *Rediscovering the Teaching of Jesus* [London, 1967], pp. 27–30). However, this is a unique story, i.e. it is not directly related to Jesus.

[4] P. 301. That the synoptic narrative of John's death is legendary and unhistorical is stressed by Dibelius, *FRLANT*, xv, 77–81; cf. also Schütz, pp. 20–2.

[5] Taylor, *Mark*, p. 310.

[6] E.g. the Herodian family were known for their birthday parties (Persius *Satura* v. 180). Intrigues and momentary lapses of remorse were common among the Herodian family.

[7] Taylor, *Mark*, p. 310.

If the story down to its details had not been believed by the early church, the improbable features would have been recognized, and either explained or ejected.[1] Moreover, having concluded that the story has two separate traditions, the principle of multiple attestation[2] may be invoked in favour of its historicity.

That this pericope exhibits no Christian characteristics, as Bultmann points out, is true. From this, however, one cannot conclude that it is legendary. The Gospels allow considerable space for the person and ministry of John, and the early Christians would certainly have been interested in his fate.

To sum up: There is no good reason for thinking that the story was a legend created out of a religious imagination and fantasy, nor that its lack of Christian characteristics points to its unhistoricity. There is no good reason, therefore, for not believing that the story is true.[3]

Josephus' account

Hölscher believes that the source of Josephus' account of John the Baptist[4] is a high priest's notice.[5] Certainly some source would seem to be required by the peculiarities of this section. These are noted by Thackeray in the following passage:

The phraseology of this passage betrays the unmistakable marks of the hack employed for this portion of the *Antiquities*. His love of periphrasis is illustrated by the phrase 'come to' or 'consort with' baptism, for 'be baptized,' his avoidance of the commonplace vocabulary by the strange words which he uses for 'punish,' 'kill,' and 'sin'; and there are other words found only in this portion of the work.[6]

The conclusion Thackeray draws is that 'the hand is the hand of the secretary; the voice that prompts it is that of Josephus'.[7] However, would it not be simpler to say that Josephus wrote it but that the idiom of the original document shows through?

---

[1] J. D. M. Derrett, 'Herod's Oath and the Baptist's Head', *BZ*, N.F. IX (1965), 49.

[2] Cf. C. H. Dodd, *History and the Gospel* (London, 1938), pp. 84–6; Manson, *Teaching*, pp. 10–11; H. K. McArthur, 'A Survey of Recent Gospel Research', *Interpretation*, XVIII (1964), 47–8.

[3] Cf. E. Bammel, 'Salome', *Encyclopædia Britannica*, XIX (1970), 952.

[4] *Ant.* xviii. 116–19.   [5] Hölscher, *Quellen*, p. 63.

[6] Thackeray, *Josephus*, p. 132.   [7] *Ibid.*

The story as given by Josephus is quite different from that of the Gospels, both in the event itself and in many details surrounding the event. Most scholars conclude that the authenticity of Josephus' account is beyond question.[1]

Other accounts

Justin Martyr has only a short passage on the Baptist's death,[2] of which only twelve words out of fifty-six (or 21·4 per cent) have verbal correspondence with Matthew and Mark. All twelve words appear in both synoptic accounts.[3] However, his story has more affinity with Mark in that both accounts mention that the daughter consulted her mother before replying to Antipas' offer.

The Slavonic version of John's ministry and death has some details not given by either Josephus or the Gospels.[4] It is a translation dating from about the middle of the thirteenth century.[5] Most scholars have discounted the authenticity of the Slavonic account as being a Byzantine interpolation.[6] The

---

[1] *Ibid.* p. 131; cf. also Dibelius, *FRLANT*, xv, 124–7; M. Goguel, *Au seuil de l'Évangile: Jean-Baptiste* (Paris, 1928), pp. 17–19; Wink, p. 109. Against this, Knox claims that Josephus at this point is unreliable, cf. W. L. Knox, *The Sources of the Synoptic Gospels*, I (Cambridge, 1953), 50; Schütz, pp. 20–7. Schütz (p. 17) thinks that Josephus had Mark at his disposal as a possible source.

[2] *Dial.* xlix. 4 (*MPG*, VI, 584).

[3] For a study on Justin's use of the New Testament, see L. W. Barnard, *Justin Martyr, His Life and Thought* (Cambridge, 1967), pp. 53–74; cf. also E. Bammel, 'Die Täufertradition bei Justin', *Studia Patristica*, VIII, *TU*, XCIII (Berlin, 1966), 53–61.

[4] Although other men such as A. Berendts and J. Frey have worked on the Slavonic version of Josephus, it was R. Eisler who made it well known and attempted to establish its authenticity over the account given in Josephus *Ant.* xviii. 116–19. See R. Eisler, ΙΗΣΟΥΣ ΒΑΣΙΛΕΥΣ ΟΥ ΒΑΣΙΛΕΥΣΑΣ, 2 vols. (Heidelberg, 1929), and the English condensed version *The Messiah Jesus and John the Baptist*, trans. A. H. Krappe (London, 1931).

[5] Cf. Eisler, I, 367–9 (Eng. trans. p. 148). Creed dates it as early as the beginning of the twelfth century, cf. J. M. Creed, 'The Slavonic Version of Josephus' History of the Jewish Wars', *HTR*, xxv (1932), 291–303.

[6] See J. W. Jack, *The Historic Christ: An Examination of Dr Eisler's Theory according to the Slavonic Version of Josephus* (London, 1933); W. Bienert, *Der älteste nichtchristliche Jesusbericht Josephus über Jesus* (Halle, 1936). Some contend that the language is not Slavonic but old Russian, cf. S. Zeitlin, 'The Slavonic Josephus and the Dead Sea Scrolls: An Exposé of Recent Fairy Tales', *JQR*, LVIII (1968), 173–7.

Slavonic Josephus will be discussed only when it gives a different interpretation or a significant alteration of the standard Josephus.

There is also the account by Hegesippus, whose name is only a corruption of 'Josephus'.[1] This is a free Latin translation of *Bellum Judaicum* into five books written in the second half of the fourth century. Finally, there is the account by Josippon, which is a Hebrew history beginning with the table of nations and ending with the destruction of the temple in A.D. 70. The author is supposed to have been Joseph ben Gurion Ha-Kohen, commonly known as Flavius Josephus. Actually the work was written about the middle of the tenth century.[2] Although the accepted view is that it is based on Latin sources only,[3] Wacholder argues that the writer knew Greek and drew upon Nicolaus of Damascus and Josephus.[4] Since the events of John the Baptist come after Herod's death, when Nicolaus ceased his work, he must have followed Hegesippus. Since however he does not follow his sources closely, the deviations in his story may be partly attributed to his fertile imagination.[5]

In the case of both Hegesippus and Josippon, references will be made to them only when they differ from the text of Josephus.

THE DIFFERENCES BETWEEN THE TWO ACCOUNTS

As mentioned above, the New Testament and Josephus are the main sources for John's death, though several differences arise

[1] For the development of the name Hegesippus, cf. Schürer, I, 96–7.

[2] U. Cassuto, 'Josippon', *EJ*, IX (1932), 420–5; Baron, IV (New York, 1958), 195. For a discussion on Josippon, see A. A. Neuman, 'Josippon: History and Pietism', in *Alexander Marx Jubilee Volume* (New York, 1950), pp. 637–67.

[3] Wellhausen, 'Der arabische Josippus', *AGG*, N.F. I, 48–9; Schürer, I, 160; Otto, col. 16.

[4] Wacholder, pp. 12–13. Wacholder (pp. 11–12) points out that Josippon is more favourable to the Herods than Josephus, thus agreeing with Nicolaus of Damascus.

[5] *Ibid.* p. 13. Cf. also A. A. Neuman, 'A Note on John the Baptist and Jesus in *Josippon*', *HUCA*, XXIII (1950–1), 140–3. For a discussion on the transmission of Josephus into the various forms, cf. E. M. Sanford, 'Propaganda and Censorship in the Transmission of Josephus', *TAPA*, LXVI (1935), 127–45.

from a comparison of these accounts. The other accounts also (e.g. Hegesippus, Josippon, the Slavonic version of Josephus, etc.) vary significantly from the two main sources. To all these differences reference will be made in this discussion.

The differences chronologically

The first difference is both obvious and minor. On the basis of Luke 3:1 the death of John must have occurred between A.D. 28 and 30. From Josephus' account, however, it seems that John's death occurred not much before the defeat of Antipas' army by Aretas in A.D. 36. In fact, his defeat is represented as God's judgement upon Antipas for having killed John.

One attempt to solve this problem is suggested by Keim,[1] followed by Hausrath[2] and Lake.[3] Since John's death was remembered by the populace in connection with Antipas' defeat, the execution, they say, must be placed as close as possible to the year 36. More precisely, in view of Pilate's deposition before the Passover of A.D. 36,[4] Jesus could not have been put to death later than Easter A.D. 35, and consequently the execution of John must have occurred at the end of 34. As Schürer states however, Keim's chronology (the same as Hausrath's and Lake's) breaks down on Luke's statement in 3:1; for even if Luke was mistaken he would hardly have erred by as much as five years.[5] It is further argued that the people might still have viewed the defeat of Antipas in A.D. 36 as a judgement of God although he had married Herodias several years before. The Pharisees no doubt would look for causes of defeat to explain this judgement, as they supposed, on the Herods. One cannot necessarily maintain that as soon as Antipas divorced Aretas' daughter and married Herodias the war with Aretas

---

[1] T. Keim, *The History of Jesus of Nazara*, trans. by A. Ransom, IV (London, 1879), 223, 227; Christ's death, IV, 222–3 n. 2; VI (1883), 234–44; Keim, 'Herodes Söhne und Enkel', *Bibel-Lexicon*, III (1871), 44–5.

[2] Hausrath, II, 122 n. 4.

[3] K. Lake, 'The Date of Herod's Marriage with Herodias, and the Chronology of the Gospels', *Exp*, 8th series, IV (1912), 462–77.

[4] This is the older view which has been rightly challenged by E. M. Smallwood, 'The Date of the Dismissal of Pontius Pilate from Judaea', *JJS*, V (1954), 12–19.

[5] I, 444.

began.[1] Josephus clearly states that the divorce was the beginning of hostility (ὁ δὲ ἀρχὴν ἔχθρας ταύτην ποιησάμενος),[2]
and that other incidents such as the boundary disputes finally
led to war.[3] Certainly Aretas would await the most opportune
time, and that was in A.D. 36, shortly after the time when the
Romans had been engaged in a struggle against Artabanus III,
king of Parthia. At that time Aretas would have had little fear
of defeat.[4]

With regard to the date of the marriage, even Keim allows
the possibility of its occurring in A.D. 32–3.[5] Since, anyway,
there is a gap of several years, why not allow it to be a few
years earlier?[6]

In conclusion, the date proposed by Keim is based on an
inference from Josephus that the Baptist's death must have
occurred very shortly before the time of Antipas' defeat by
Aretas. Since however this is only an inference it is inconclusive.
Keim's theory makes havoc of the Gospels' chronology, whereas
the latter does not affect Josephus' chronological framework.
Hence, it is better to base one's chronology on the Gospels
than on what in effect is *only* an inference from Josephus.

Another approach to this problem is that of Eisler, who also
dates the death of John in A.D. 35.[7] Eisler adduces some of the
same arguments as Keim, but adds that the Baptist's death was
a year after Philip's death in the spring of A.D. 34.[8] He derives

---

[1] The Jews felt that God's revenge did not always occur immediately at
the time of the misdeed, as seen in Antiochus Epiphanes' death which was
a result of his desecration of the temple three years previously (cf. Jos. *Ant.*
xii. 248–53, 357; 1 Macc. 1: 29, 54; 6: 8–13; for a discussion on the chronological difficulties of Antiochus' reign and death, see S. Zeitlin, 'Appendix C'
in *The First Book of Maccabees* [New York, 1950], pp. 252–65); Pompey's
death in 48 B.C. was thought to be the result of his entering the holy of holies
sacrilegiously fifteen years before (cf. Jos. *Ant.* xiv. 71–2; Psalms of Solomon
2: 30–5); and Jerusalem's destruction in A.D. 70 was considered a divine
punishment for the murder of Jonathan the high priest and other contemporary acts of bloodshed during Felix' reign of A.D. 52–60 (Jos. *Ant.* xx.
160–7).

[2] Jos. *Ant.* xviii. 113.   [3] Schürer, I, 444–5.

[4] Below, p. 255.   [5] Keim, *Jesus of Nazara*, II, 397.

[6] Schürer, I, 445.

[7] Eisler, ΙΗΣΟΥΣ, II, 123–33 [Eng. trans. pp. 288–94]. For a concise
statement of his chronology, see R. Eisler, 'Recherches sur la chronologie
Évangélique', *Revue Archéologique*, série V, XXXII (1930), 116–26, esp. 121–6.

[8] Jos. *Ant.* xviii. 106.

this from the Slavonic version of the *Bellum Judaicum*, which says that Philip died on the evening of the day on which John had interpreted to him his dream about the eagle.[1] But the Slavonic version is hopelessly confused in its chronology. It says, for example, that John the Baptist was preaching during Archelaus' reign[2] and that Jesus' death was in A.D. 21.[3] Moreover, according to Eisler, Jesus was put to death for a violent messianic doctrine,[4] and this was also the reason for John's death.[5] If Jesus was put to death for this reason in A.D. 21, how could John have eluded the authorities so long – from Archelaus' reign until A.D. 35?[6] Eisler attempts to explain the report that the Baptist had risen in the person of Jesus (Mt. 14:2; Mk. 6:14; Lk. 9:7) by saying: (1) that it was only a popular opinion and not a statement of Herod's; (2) that Jesus must have worn a similar garb to John and so they were confused; (3) that the texts of the Gospels are in a state of confusion and must be altered.[7] The first two points may be valid although the confusion by the people may have been because they had not seen or intimately known John and/or Jesus but based their opinion on popular rumour.[8] However, the need of several textual alterations is only necessary if one accepts Eisler's chronology. As Jack observes: 'surely, a theory is groundless which requires textual alterations to support it'.[9]

Finally, Eisler seems to imply that the late date of John's death agrees with the order of events in *Antiquitates Judaicae*.[10] The order is Jesus' death,[11] Philip's death,[12] and then John's death.[13] But, first, Josephus is not always chronological[14] and,

---

[1] Josephus, with an English trans. by H. St J. Thackeray, vol. III of *LCL*, Appendix: Slavonic Version, pp. 646–8.

[2] Eisler, ΙΗΣΟΥΣ, II, 77, 132 [Eng. trans. pp. 259, 293].

[3] *Ibid.* I, xxxiii; II, 165 [Eng. trans. pp. 16–21, 313]; specifically 15 or 16 April A.D. 21, cf. Eisler, *Revue Archéologique*, série V, XXXII, 126.

[4] Eisler, ΙΗΣΟΥΣ, II, 254–70, 439–529 [Eng. trans. pp. 363–70, 457–512].

[5] *Ibid.* II, 66–114 [Eng. trans. pp. 252–80].

[6] Jack, p. 245.   [7] Eisler, ΙΗΣΟΥΣ, II, 149–56 [Eng. trans. pp. 302–8].

[8] Cf. below, pp. 187–9.   [9] P. 245; cf. also p. 246.

[10] Eisler, ΙΗΣΟΥΣ, II, 126–8 [Eng. trans. pp. 290–1].

[11] Jos. *Ant.* xviii. 63–4.   [12] *Ibid.* xviii. 106.

[13] *Ibid.* xviii. 118–19.

[14] As one may see from the fact that the accession of Pilate is mentioned before the building of Tiberias (*Ant.* xviii. 35–54), whereas the opposite was the case.

secondly, his account of John's death is a flashback explaining why Antipas was defeated by Aretas.

Hence, Eisler's attempt to build a chronology on the Slavonic version creates more problems than it solves.[1] His theory requires re-arrangement of the historical framework and is built upon suppositions that will not stand.[2]

There are other factors which may help to pinpoint the date of John's imprisonment. Josephus states that Antipas went to Rome, and that it was during this journey that he and Herodias agreed to marry.[3] Herodias only stipulated that Antipas was to get rid of his present wife, Aretas' daughter. As a Hasmonean, no doubt, she did not want to share the house with an Arab, a long-term enemy of the Hasmonean dynasty. She may also have wanted to avoid the household troubles of her grandfather, Herod the Great, in which there were constant rivalries between his wives and between their various sons.

Antipas then went on to Rome[4] and returned having accomplished what he had planned (ἐπεὶ δὲ ἐπανεχώρει διαπραξάμενος ἐν τῇ 'Ρώμῃ ἐφ' ἅπερ ἔσταλτο).[5] What was it he accomplished in Rome? To claim certainty would be a bold assertion. There is however one consideration worth pondering. Josephus states that Antipas was 'in great favour with' or 'had a high place

---

[1] For a refutation of other points of Eisler's chronology, see W. F. Howard, 'John the Baptist and Jesus. A Note on Evangelic Chronology', *Amicitiae Corolla*, ed. by H. G. Wood (London, 1933), pp. 125–32.

[2] A good example of this is that since Jesus died in A.D. 21 Pilate must have come to Judaea, according to Eisler, in A.D. 18 (ΙΗΣΟΥΣ, I, 127 n. 2; II, 164 [Eng. trans. pp. 17–20, 313]). But numismatic evidence proves this to be wrong; cf. P. L. Hedley, 'Pilate's Arrival in Judaea', *JTS*, xxxv (1934), 56–8.　　　　　　　　　[3] Jos. *Ant.* xviii. 109–10.

[4] Herodias did not live in Rome as is assumed by so many writers (cf. N. Glueck, *Deities and Dolphins: the Story of the Nabataeans* [London, 1966], p. 40). This idea was rightly rejected as early as Brann, *MGWJ*, xxii, 408 n. 2 (cf. also F. J. Foakes Jackson and K. Lake [eds.], *BC*, I [London, 1939], 16–17 n. 1). It is probable that she and her former husband lived at or near a Jewish port because Antipas seems to have boarded a ship for Rome directly after seeing her (Jos. *Ant.* xviii. 111). Brann thinks it was Azotus (*MGWJ*, xxii, 408) – a town near the sea coast – which was given to her grandmother Salome by Herod the Great (Jos. *Ant.* xvii. 189, 321; *BJ* ii. 98) but was not listed among the dominions Salome bequeathed to Livia (*Ant.* xviii. 31; *BJ* ii. 167). She must therefore have kept it to be given to her heirs. Otto (cols. 201–2) agrees with Graetz that Herodias lived in Caesarea.

[5] Jos. *Ant.* xviii. 111.

among the friends of' Tiberius.[1] On the other hand, he also states that Antipas was conspiring with Sejanus against the government of Tiberius.[2] A solution to this apparent contradiction is possible in the light of the situation at Rome.

Since Sejanus, from A.D. 27 onwards, was virtually in full control,[3] it is reasonable that Antipas should want to have had a conference with him. It may be that Sejanus' selection of Pontius Pilate had already caused a stir and that Antipas wanted to talk to him about it. Could it not have been on this visit that Antipas agreed with him to conspire against Tiberius? If this were so it would have necessitated a personal confrontation. It would hardly have been done through intermediaries.

Also while in Rome Antipas may have asked for permission to marry Herodias. This, probably, was not too difficult to obtain, especially since Herodias' mother, Berenice, had been one of the closest friends of Antonia (sister-in-law to Tiberius and mother of the future emperor, Claudius).[4] To procure permission was no doubt desirable, especially since he wanted to divorce Aretas' daughter. Aretas' territory served as a buffer state between Rome and Parthia, and if he had been displeased by an insult of this sort, he could undoubtedly have caused trouble for Rome in the East. In fact, it is probable that Antipas married Aretas' daughter as a sort of peace treaty. This is confirmed by three facts. First, there was always animosity between the Arabs and the Herods. This came to the fore when the Arabs invaded Herod's territory,[5] when before Augustus

---

[1] *Ibid.* xviii. 36.

[2] Jos. *Ant.* xviii. 250. For two reasons this accusation by Agrippa should not be pressed too far: (1) Josephus being pro-Agrippa places Antipas in a bad light, cf. Hölscher, PW, ix, 1987; (2) this accusation is never challenged. But it is never disproved either. This is an argument from silence but it has some validity for it would seem unlikely that Agrippa would make up an accusation that would prove him wrong. Also, Agrippa went to Rome the year before Tiberius died to accuse Antipas before Tiberius (cf. Jos. *BJ* ii. 178; *Ant.* xviii. 126). He would probably have accused Antipas of conspiring with Sejanus, but was unable to do so because he fell out of favour with Tiberius. Subsequently he became friends with Gaius (*Ant.* xviii. 161–204; *BJ* ii. 178–80).

[3] Tac. *Ann.* iv. 41, 67; Dio lviii. 1; Suet. *Tib.* xxxix–xl; cf. F. B. Marsh, *The Reign of Tiberius* (London, 1931), pp. 181–3.

[4] Cf. Jos. *Ant.* xviii. 143–4, 164–5, 179–86, 202.

[5] Jos. *Ant.* xv. 349–53.

the Arabs falsely accused Herod of invading their territory, and when they refused to repay a loan to Herod.[1] There was also the occasion immediately after Herod the Great's death when Varus called on Aretas for help in order to subdue the brigands, and Aretas burned and plundered the villages in Judaea out of hatred toward Herod.[2] So there was a need to restore harmony between these two nations. Strikingly, after the settlement of Herod the Great's will there is no record of any dispute between the Herods and the Arabs until A.D. 36. Secondly, Josephus states that Antipas had been married to Aretas' daughter for a long time (συνῆν χρόνον ἤδη πολύν).[3] Thirdly, there is no doubt that Augustus had heard from Varus about Aretas' plundering and devastating Herod's territory. For the sake of the Roman Empire Augustus would want peace, and he was known to favour intermarriages among the various rulers to accomplish this end.[4] Probably, therefore, they were married before Augustus' death and sometime near the beginning of Antipas' reign.[5] To divorce Aretas' daughter, then, was not only a personal insult to Aretas but also a breach of a political alliance.

Possibly another business transaction was the obtaining of permission to strike his own coins. Significantly, there are no coins of Antipas before A.D. 29.[6]

Since it is probable that Antipas went to confer with Sejanus when he was at the height of his power, one can circumscribe the date between A.D. 27 and 18 October 31 (the date of Sejanus' death). If John started preaching in the autumn of 27[7] or early in 28, then Antipas' journey could have been accomplished in the summer of 27, and he could have arrived back in Palestine in the late summer or autumn of 27, when also Aretas' daughter fled. He married Herodias after the flight of Aretas' daughter, possibly in the autumn 27/spring 28, and John would have been imprisoned shortly after, possibly in the spring of 28. However, if John's preaching did not begin

---

[1] *Ibid.* xvi. 271–99, 335–55.
[2] *Ibid.* xvii. 287–97; *BJ* ii. 68.
[3] *Ant.* xviii. 109.
[4] Suet. *Aug.* xlviii.
[5] Otto, col. 186.
[6] Cf. Madden, *History of Jewish Coinage*, pp. 97–8; *Coins of the Jews*, p. 119; Hill, p. 229; Reifenberg, *Ancient Jewish Coins*, p. 44; Kindler, p. 54.
[7] For the date of the commencement of John's ministry, see Appendix VII.

until A.D. 28 or 29, then it is not difficult to place Antipas'
journey to Rome in those years. The present author thinks that
the latter date is more plausible. Although Sejanus had gained
great power in A.D. 27, he had risen to even greater heights in
A.D. 29 and it was voted in that year to observe publicly his
birthday.[1] Hence, it is highly plausible that Antipas went to
Rome in A.D. 29, possibly to be there personally at the celebration of Sejanus' birthday, and returned in the late summer or
autumn of that same year with permission to marry Herodias
and to be able to strike his own coins which he had not done
before A.D. 29. Aretas' daughter would have fled in A.D. 29
(which makes for only seven years before Aretas' revenge upon
Antipas). Only shortly after this, possibly in the autumn of
29/spring 30, Antipas married Herodias and John's imprisonment probably would have occurred in A.D. 30 or 31.

The differences over Herodias' former husband

The Gospels say that Herodias was the wife of Antipas' brother
Philip,[2] whereas Josephus states that she was married to Herod.[3]
Philip was tetrarch of the northern part of Herod the Great's
kingdom, Gaulanitis, Auranitis, Batanaea, Trachonitis, Paneas,
and Ituraea,[4] and was the son of Herod the Great by Cleopatra
of Jerusalem.[5] Herod the Great had two sons with the name
Herod: one who was born of Cleopatra of Jerusalem and was
therefore a full brother of Philip the tetrarch,[6] and the other
born of Mariamme II, the daughter of Simon the high priest.[7]
Herodias married the second Herod in accord with an arrangement by Herod the Great.[8] It was this Herod who was to be
heir of Herod the Great's throne in the event of Antipater's
death[9] but was later struck out of Herod's will because of his

---

[1] Dio lviii. 2. 7.   [2] Mt. 14: 3; Mk. 6: 17.

[3] Jos. *Ant.* xviii. 109.

[4] Jos. *Ant.* xvii. 189, 319; xviii. 106, 136; *BJ* i. 668; ii. 95; Lk. 3: 1.

[5] Jos. *Ant.* xvii. 21; *BJ* i. 562.

[6] *Ibid.*

[7] Jos. *BJ* i. 562, 573, 588; *Ant.* xvii. 19; xviii. 109, 136. Simon the high
priest was the son of Boethus, an Alexandrian (*Ant.* xv. 320; xvii. 78). For
the family of Boethus, see E. M. Smallwood, 'High Priests and Politics in
Roman Palestine', *JTS*, N.S. xiii (1962), 32–4.

[8] Jos. *Ant.* xvii. 14; *BJ* i. 557.

[9] *Ibid.* xvii. 53; *BJ* i. 573.

mother's plotting against Herod.[1] It would seem therefore that two different persons were married to Herodias.

There have been several attempts to explain the differences between the two accounts. These will now be considered.

Many scholars hold that the Gospel accounts are incorrect: since the Herodian family was hopelessly confused, Matthew and Mark incorrectly named Philip as Herodias' former husband rather than Herod. Since Herodias' daughter married Philip the tetrarch the Gospel writers may have confused Herodias' husband and son-in-law.[2] This is confirmed by the fact that Luke (3:19) drops the name Philip,[3] and so avoids the same error.[4] This is the easiest explanation, but if the Christian community included such people as Joanna and Manaen a blunder of this nature ought to have been avoided.

The other view is that both accounts are correct. There are three possible alternatives. The first is that the Gospel accounts did not originally have the name Philip.[5] In Matthew it is omitted by D it [a, c, d, e, ff1, g1, k, l], Vulgate, Augustine. In Mark, Philip is omitted by $\mathfrak{P}^{45}$. Certainly the weight of manuscript evidence is in favour of its inclusion. In the case of

---

[1] Jos. *Ant.* xvii. 78; *BJ* i. 600.

[2] E. Klostermann, *Das Markusevangelium*[3], *HNT*, III (Tübingen, 1936), p. 58; B. H. Branscomb, *The Gospel of Mark*, *The Moffatt New Testament Commentary*, ed. by J. Moffatt (London, 1937), p. 109; Rawlinson, *Mark*, p. 81; Taylor, *Mark*, p. 312; Lohmeyer, *Markus*, p. 118; W. Grundmann, *Das Evangelium nach Markus*[2], *THNT*, II (1959), 128; Haenchen, *Der Weg Jesu*, p. 238 n. 1; Grundmann, *Matthäus*, p. 361; cf. also Schürer, I, 435 n. 19; Dibelius, *FRLANT*, xv, 79; Otto, cols. 199–200; W. Foerster, *Palestinian Judaism in New Testament Times*, trans. from 3rd rev. German ed. by G. E. Harris (Edinburgh, 1964), p. 94 n. 2; S. Zeitlin, 'The Duration of Jesus' Ministry', *JQR*, LV (1965), 185; B. Reicke, *The New Testament Era*, trans. D. E. Green (Philadelphia, 1968), p. 125; Schütz, p. 20.

[3] Philip is included in C A K W 33 565 al sy^p sa^pt bo which harmonizes Luke with Matthew and Mark. It is an inferior reading which is clearly to be rejected.

[4] Scobie, p. 181; J. M. Creed, *The Gospel according to St Luke* (London, 1930), p. 54; M.-J. Lagrange, *Évangile selon Saint Luc*[8], *EB* (Paris, 1948), p. 113.

[5] This is suggested as a possible solution by C. E. B. Cranfield, *The Gospel according to Saint Mark*[2], *The Cambridge Greek Testament Commentary*, ed. by C. F. D. Moule (Cambridge, 1963), pp. 209, 483; Taylor, *Mark*, p. 312; H. J. Cadbury, 'The Family Tree of the Herods', *BC*, v (London, 1933), p. 488 n. 2.

Matthew the earliest witness for its exclusion is the codex Bezae of the fifth or sixth century, which, as shown by the rest of its readings, was confined to the western church, whereas its inclusion is widespread in all areas of the church.[1] With regard to Mark, it is incorrect to say that $\mathfrak{P}^{45}$ omits his name[2] because in the only extant fragment of this manuscript there is nothing but αυτου γυν on the relevant line. Hence, the manuscript evidence would favour inclusion of Philip in both Matthew and Mark. It seems that its exclusion points to a scribal correction.

A second alternative is suggested by Parrot: that Herodias was married to Herod and had Salome and later she married Philip and finally she married Antipas.[3] However, Josephus never mentions a former marriage with Philip, in fact, he makes it quite clear that the marriage immediately preceding her marriage with Antipas was with Herod who presumably lived near the Mediterranean Sea and not in the area of Philip the tetrarch's territory.[4]

The third alternative is that Herod, son of Mariamme II, was named Herod Philip, and so both Josephus and the Gospels are correct. Several scholars state that this solution is not impossible,[5] while others feel that it is the most probable.[6]

There are several reasons for this view. First, if the Gospels

---

[1] ℵ B C K L W X Δ Θ Π 0119 $f^1 f^{13}$ 28 33 565 700 892 1009 1010 1071 1079 1195 1216 1230 1241 1242 1253 1344 1365 1546 1646 2148 2174 Byzantine Lectionaries 883^m, it-aur (b) f (ff^2) h q, Syr-c s p h pal^{vid}, cop-sa bo fay, arm eth geo Origen, Chrysostom.

[2] As does Taylor, *Mark*, p. 312 and Cranfield, pp. 209, 483.

[3] A. Parrot, *Land of Christ*, trans. J. H. Farley (Philadelphia, 1968), pp. 53–4.

[4] Jos. *Ant.* xviii. 109–11; cf. also above, p. 128 n. 4.

[5] Taylor, *Mark*, p. 312; H. A. W. Meyer, *Critical and Exegetical Handbook to the Gospel of Matthew*, trans. from 6th German ed. by P. Christie, rev. and ed. by G. Crombie, I (Edinburgh, 1877), 378 n. 1; Haenchen, *Der Weg Jesu*, p. 238 n. 1; A. H. M'Neile, *The Gospel according to St Matthew* (London, 1915), p. 208; Grundmann, *Matthäus*, p. 361.

[6] Weiss, *Markus und Lukas*, pp. 95–6; A. L. Williams, *St Matthew* in *The Pulpit Commentary*, ed. by H. D. M. Spence and J. S. Exell, II (London, 1906), 61–2; H. B. Swete, *The Gospel according to St Mark*[3] (London, 1909), p. 122; Lagrange, *Marc*, p. 158; cf. also Edersheim, I, 672–3 n. 2; S. Sollertinsky, 'The Death of St John the Baptist', *JTS*, I (1900), 513–14; L. de Grandmaison, *Jesus Christ*, trans. by D. B. Wheelan, A. Lane, D. Carter, II (London, 1932), note K, pp. 105–6; A. Schlatter, *Der Evangelist Matthäus* (Stuttgart, 1948), pp. 458–9.

were wrong then, as Edersheim points out, the evangelists
were guilty of two gross errors: (1) that they confused this Herod
with his half-brother Philip, and (2) that they made Philip the
tetrarch husband of Herodias instead of husband of her daughter
Salome – two blunders in matters of well-known history with
which the evangelists otherwise show familiarity.[1] There would
also be a third historical blunder in that Salome would have
been the daughter of Philip the tetrarch who, according to
Josephus, had no children.[2] It seems incredible that the
evangelists who had access to reliable sources would have made
so many gross historical errors.

Secondly, the details of the Gospels which speak of a daughter
of Herodias before she was married to Antipas[3] harmonize
exactly with Josephus' reference to Herod having a daughter
named Salome.[4] There are too many factors involved for this to
be mere coincidence, and consequently it is improbable that
the evangelists confused the Philips.

Thirdly, it is frequently held that since he is called Herod
by Josephus and since there is another son of Herod the Great
named Philip, Herodias' first husband could not also have had
the same name Philip. However, although they had the same
father, they had different mothers. There were others in the
family of Herod the Great that had the same name but were
born of different mothers, namely, Antipater of Doris[5] and
Antipas (the diminutive form)[6] of Malthace.[7] There were also
two sons named Herod, namely, the first husband of Herodias

---

[1] Edersheim, I, 672 n. 2.   [2] Jos. *Ant.* xviii. 137.

[3] Mt. 14: 6, 8–11; Mk. 6: 22, 24–6, 28.

[4] Jos. *Ant.* xviii. 136.

[5] *Ibid.* xiv. 300; xvii. 68; *BJ* i. 241, 433, 448, 562, 590.

[6] Schürer argues strongly that Antipas and Antipater are not to be considered the same name (I, 435 n. 19). But the name Antipas is well known as
an Ionic abbreviation or diminutive of Antipater, cf. U. Wilcken, 'Antipatros', PW, I (1894), 2509; W. Schulze, 'Ahd. *suagur*', *Zeitschrift für vergleichende Sprachforschung*, XL (1906), 409 n. 3. Even Josephus makes the remark
about Herod the Great's father, Antipater, that he was apparently at one
time called 'Antipas' (*Ant.* xiv. 10). Besides, Herod Antipas is called Antipater by Josephus (xvii. 238) and several passages have a variant reading of
Antipater for Antipas, cf. *BJ* i. 668; ii. 22, 94; *Ant.* xvii. 20, 188, 224, 227,
238 (has a variant for Antipater), 318, which shows that they were one and
the same name.

[7] Jos. *BJ* i. 562.

and son of Mariamme II,[1] and the son of Cleopatra of Jerusalem.[2] A situation of this kind was not infrequent in Hellenistic times.[3]

Fourthly, it is possible that he was properly called Herod Philip. Otto states that double names were not in use,[4] but he gives no evidence for this. No one objects to Luke, in Acts 12:1, 6, 11, 19, 20, 21, calling Agrippa I Herod. Most say that this is Herod Agrippa I and leave it at that.[5] There is never a suggestion that Luke was confusing Agrippa with Herod, king of Chalcis (A.D. 41–8), since he used the name Herod and since this Herod married Agrippa I's daughter Berenice. The same is true of Archelaus who is so called by Josephus and Matthew,[6] and thus would have had the double name Herod Archelaus.

Fifthly, if they had meant Philip the tetrarch, they would almost certainly have styled him in the same way as Luke,[7] especially in the light of the Matthean and Marcan contexts where Herod Antipas is styled tetrarch and king.[8] 'For Philip the tetrarch was universally popular, and the Evangelist could hardly have called the worse tetrarch, Antipas, 'king' and have left the better [tetrarch] without a title at all.'[9]

[1] Jos. *Ant.* xviii. 136; *BJ* i. 562, 573, 588, 599–600; cf. also *Ant.* xvii. 14, 53; xviii. 109; *BJ* i. 557.

[2] Jos. *Ant.* xvii. 21; *BJ* i. 562.

[3] Otto, col. 199 n.

[4] *Ibid.* col. 199.

[5] The present author has looked at fourteen different commentaries on the Acts of the Apostles and they sum it up as Haenchen, 'Gemeint ist Herodes Agrippa I. (geb. 10 v. Chr., gest. 44 n. Chr.), Enkel Herodes' des Grossen' (E. Haenchen, *Die Apostelgeschichte*, KEK¹⁵ [Göttingen, 1968], p. 324 n. 2). Only Otto (PW, Supp. II, 167–8) states that Luke must have been in error partly because the New Testament writers preferred the dynastic name. Otto provides no evidence for his claim, only that he wants to maintain his own theory that there cannot be double names. This theory breaks down in the case of Archelaus (cf. Otto, col. 170).

[6] Mt. 2: 22. Josephus designates him Archelaus more than 130 times.

[7] Lk. 3: 1. The term *Philip* is used of a member of the Herodian family three times in the NT (Mt. 14: 3; Mk. 6: 17; Lk. 3: 1) but only in Lk. 3: 1 is he, as well as Antipas, styled tetrarch in the same verse. In Lk. 3: 19 Antipas is designated tetrarch but his brother is not named and has no designation, which seems to indicate that here Luke is not thinking of the same Philip as in 3: 1.

[8] Tetrarch in Mt. 14: 1 and king in Mt. 14: 9; Mk. 6: 14, 26.

[9] Sollertinsky, *JTS*, I, 514.

Sixthly, it must be remembered that a name is only a means of identification. This Herod may have been known in Galilee as Philip whereas his official name was Herod. It may be that Herod was his original name given him by his father, but that when the name Herod became a dynastic title, he became known as Philip.[1] This would apply equally to Archelaus who would have been known officially as Herod[2] but otherwise as Archelaus.[3] This can also be applied in the case of Agrippa I. It is probable that he was known as one of the Herods, and thus called King Herod in contradistinction to Herod the tetrarch in Acts 13:1. With regard to Philip, he may well have been known in Galilee as Philip but to Josephus as Herod. Thus there is reason to think that both accounts are speaking of one and the same person. Gams thinks that Josephus called him by his family name while the evangelists called him by his proper name.[4]

In conclusion, there is no over-riding reason for not considering the Herod of Josephus and the Philip of Matthew and Mark to be one and the same person. In fact, to do otherwise would seem to create inextricable confusion. To say that because Josephus mentions Herod, and the Gospels Philip, one of them must be wrong, may be the easiest solution to the problem but hardly the most cogent.

The different accounts of Antipas' motives for John's arrest

Both the evangelists[5] and Josephus[6] state Antipas' motives for John's imprisonment. Josephus' account is brief. He indicates that Antipas feared John's hold upon the people whom he

---

[1] Is it possible that since Herod became a dynastic title, this Herod had to relinquish his name? Or could he have relinquished it so as not to be identified with Antipas?

[2] Cf. Dio lv. 27. 6.

[3] As seen both in Josephus and Matthew.

[4] B. Gams, *Johannes der Täufer in Gefängnisse* (Tübingen, 1853), pp. 9–12.

[5] Mt. 14: 3–5; Mk. 6: 17–19; Lk. 3: 19–20. The Slavonic version of Josephus also gives the same reasons for John's arrest (Josephus with an English trans. by Thackeray, *LCL*, iii [1928], 647–8); Hegesippus (Pseudo) *Historiae* ii. 5. 3; Joseph ben Gurion, *The Wonderful and Most Deplorable History*, p. 88; Sanders and Nahmad, p. 285; Wellhausen, *AGG*, N.F. 1, 33.

[6] Jos. *Ant.* xviii. 118–19.

greatly incited[1] to the point of sedition.[2] Hence, Antipas thought it politically expedient to strike at the root of the matter before an uprising occurred. Consequently, John was imprisoned at Machaerus and there put to death.

The evangelists, on the other hand, give an entirely different picture of Antipas' motives for imprisoning John. According to them, it was because John had denounced the marriage of Antipas and Herodias[3] as being contrary to the Law, as indeed it was since Herodias had already been married to Antipas' half-brother.[4] In addition to this, she had divorced her former

---

[1] Ἤρθησαν ἐπὶ πλεῖστον is to be preferred to ἤσθησαν ἐπὶ πλεῖστον (highly elated, overjoyed). It has the support of all the MSS except E[pitome] of Josephus and the codices T^c (= Laurentianus 70, 7), E (= Laurentianus 70, 20), R (= Mosquensis), B (=Parisinus 1431), D^cm (= Parisinus 1433), Σ (= Syriac version) in Eus. *HE* i. 11. 6 while the latter has only the support of A (= Parisinus 1433), T^1 in Eusebius. Therefore the manuscript evidence is overwhelmingly for the first reading. Also, Eisler (ΙΗΣΟΥΣ, ΙΙ, 56 [Eng. trans. pp. 246–7]) points out that a Christian interpolator would have inserted ἤσθησαν (only a change of a single letter: ρ to σ) in order to avoid connecting John with political insurrection. Finally, it seems hardly plausible that Herod, if the people were only highly elated, would have had any suspicion of a sedition. Just to be charmed does not incite to insurrection (this was suggested by Dr E. Bammel in his seminar, Cambridge, Michaelmas Term, 1966).

[2] Στάσει is to be preferred to ἀποστάσει (to revolt). The former reading is in M[edicaeus], W (= Vaticanus), and E while the latter is in only A[mbrosianus]. Again Eisler (ΙΗΣΟΥΣ, ΙΙ, 57 [Eng. trans. p. 248]) points out that ἀποστάσει 'is a Christian correction to make Herod's alarm appear as based on a fear of a *religious* apostasy from orthodox Judaism and not a political insurrectionary movement (στάσις)'. This would also account for Eusebius' adoption of ἀποστάσει (*HE* i. 11. 6).

[3] How this denunciation by John reached the court of Antipas is impossible to determine. It may be that he went to Antipas' court at Machaerus and directly denounced him, or Antipas may have heard of John's denunciation through intermediaries. For a discussion of this, see A. T. Robertson, *John the Loyal* (London, 1912), pp. 183–5.

[4] Lev. 20: 21; 18: 16. Antipas was denounced because he married his brother's wife. John was not rebuking Antipas for the divorce of his earlier wife in order to marry Herodias, for this seems to have been allowable (TB: Ket. 57 b; Jeremias, *Jerusalem*, p. 371 n. 60), nor for taking another wife, for polygamy seems to have been very common in high places. Herod the Great had been married many times (*Ant.* xvii. 19–22; *BJ* i. 562–3). The Talmud reports a bigamous marriage by Agrippa's ἐπίτροπος (TB: Suk. 27 a). Among the priestly members similar marriages were recorded, such as Alubai, Caiaphas, and Josephus (Tos.: Yeb. i. 10; TB: Yeb. 15 a; TJ: Yeb. i. 4 [or 6]; Jos. *Vita* 414–15; cf. L. Ginzberg, *Eine unbekannte jüdische Sekte* [New

husband, which however, although forbidden by Jewish Law,

York, 1922], p. 183 n. 4). This was also true of the educated class, for Abba, son of Rabban Simeon ben Gamaliel I, a member of the Sanhedrin, had two wives at the same time (TB: Yeb. 15a; Ginzberg, p. 184 n. 1). Josephus told the Roman world that it was an ancient custom of the Jews to have many wives at the same time (*Ant.* xvii. 14; *BJ* i. 477). Justin Martyr accused the Jews of having four or five wives and for marrying as many wives as they wished, *Dial.* cxxxiv. 1; cxli. 4 (*MPG*, vi, 785, 799). Also, there was no odium attached to the fact that Antipas was marrying his niece (she was the daughter of his half-brother Aristobulus). Marrying a niece was forbidden by the Zadokite sect (*Fragments of a Zadokite Work*, p. 5, lines 7–8 in vol. 1 of *Documents of Jewish Sectaries*, ed. with an Eng. trans., intro., and notes by S. Schechter [Cambridge, 1910]), as well as by the Sadducees, Samaritans, Falashas, and Karaites, cf. S. Krauss, 'Die Ehe zwischen Onkel und Nichte', *Studies in Jewish Literature. Issued in Honor of Professor Kaufman Kohler* (Berlin, 1913), pp. 167–8. This was also true of non-Jews such as the early Arabs (Krauss, p. 168). There is an Islamic account which says that Jesus and John forbade the marriage of nieces (cf. J. C. K. Gibson, 'John the Baptist in Muslim Writings', *MW*, xlv [1955], 344), and the marriage of uncles and nieces was not approved by the Roman law until A.D. 44 (cf. Tac. *Ann.* xii. 6–7; Suet. *Claud.* xxvi. 3; F. R. B. Godolphin, 'A Note on the Marriage of Claudius and Agrippina', *Classical Philology*, xxix [1934], 143–5). Although there seems to have been a popular sentiment against the marriage of uncles to nieces (Ned. viii. 7; ix. 10) which was contested by some (TB: Yeb. 55a, b), 'the Pharisees thought that marrying a niece was permitted, and not only permitted, but meritorious' (L. M. Epstein, *Marriage Laws in the Bible and Talmud* [Cambridge, Mass., 1942], p. 251). Certainly in high places there was an abundance of uncles and nieces marrying, for Josephus mentions one case of it in the priestly family of Tobias (*Ant.* xii. 186–9) and several within the Herod family: Herod with the daughter of his brother and a daughter of his sister (*Ant.* xvii. 19; *BJ* i. 563); his son, Philip the tetrarch, with Salome, daughter of Herodias (*Ant.* xviii. 137); Herodias with two uncles successively (*Ant.* xviii. 110); Agrippa I's daughter Berenice with her uncle Herod of Chalcis (*Ant.* xix. 277). This was also true among the religious leaders (for references, see C. Rabin, *Qumran Studies* [London, 1957], p. 92; Epstein, pp. 252–5). John very carefully stated that it was unlawful for Antipas to marry his brother's wife and he completely ignored everything else. There is one exception to this spelled out in the Mosaic Law, and that is that when a man died who left no offspring, the surviving brother was responsible for raising children to his deceased brother by levirate marriage (Deut. 25: 5; Mk. 12: 19; Strack–Billerbeck, I, 886–7; cf. Epstein, pp. 77–144). However, this is not the case in the present narrative. To marry a brother's wife was a direct contravention of the ordinance (Lev. 20: 21; 18: 16; Archelaus transgressed the same law, Jos. *Ant.* xvii. 341; *BJ* ii. 116) and would be characterized as incest. But it was even a more blatant breach of the law to marry the brother's wife while the brother was still alive as in this story (cf. F. F. Bruce, *New Testament History* [London, 1969], p. 153). Therefore,

was allowed by Roman law,[1] an action to which Jesus may have alluded when he declared that if a woman divorces her husband and marries another, she commits adultery.[2] As a

according to Jewish Law, John's charge was strictly in order. Josephus confirms this by saying Herodias wanted to violate the traditions of the fathers (*Ant.* xviii. 136).

[1] Jewish Law states that a bill of divorcement must be issued by the husband (Deut. 24: 1). The Mishnah: Git. (esp. ix. 1–3) states that when a man divorced his wife, she was free to marry any man with the exceptions recognized by Jewish authorities. Epstein concludes that 'the woman cannot divorce her husband according to the Jewish law' (L. M. Epstein, *The Jewish Marriage Contract* [New York, 1927], p. 200). The Roman law permitted the wife to take the initiative in securing a divorce (cf. *Cod. Iust.* v. 17. 5–6; viii. 38. 2; cf. also, F. Schulz, *Classical Roman Law* [Oxford, 1951], pp. 132, 134; Buckland, pp. 116–17; P. E. Corbett, *The Roman Law of Marriage* [Oxford, 1930], pp. 239–43). Since the Herods were Roman citizens they seem here to have followed the Roman law and customs. Herodias would have had to initiate the divorce, which was against the Jewish Law, as mentioned by Josephus (*Ant.* xviii. 136). She did however have a precedent set by her grandmother, Salome, who divorced Costobarus, an action which according to Josephus was incompatible with Jewish Law (*Ant.* xv. 259–60). Already early in the second century the Jewish rabbis recognized the validity of a Gentile divorce instituted by the wife through a *repudium* (cf. B. Cohen, 'Concerning Divorce in Jewish and Roman Law', *Proceedings of American Academy for Jewish Research*, xxi [1952], 10–12); but neither of these divorces would come under this category, for even Costobarus, who was an Idumaean, had adopted the Jewish Law and customs (Jos. *Ant.* xv. 253–4). Therefore, Herodias, like Salome, in divorcing her husband was acting contrary to Jewish Law and custom.

[2] Mk. 10: 12. This verse is not only exegetically difficult but it also has textual complications (cf. Taylor, *Mark*, p. 420). However, the main point is not altered: the woman who leaves her husband to marry someone else is as guilty as the man who divorces his wife (for a discussion of Mk. 10: 12, cf. D. Daube, *The New Testament and Rabbinic Judaism* [London, 1956], pp. 365–8). Burkitt points out that Jesus was following in the footsteps of his precursor who lost his life on protesting against Antipas' marriage. On hearing the news of John's death Jesus retired to a 'desert place' (Mk. 6: 31) and soon after he and his disciples took an extended journey in the territory of Tyre (Mk. 7: 24 ff.). Shortly after his return he again went on a journey in the district of Caesarea Philippi (Mk. 8: 27 – 9: 29). After that he went through Galilee on his way to Jerusalem, but he did not wish anyone to know it (Mk. 9: 30). This secrecy ceased when he entered Judaea (Mk. 10: 1). The question of divorce was a good test question with which to entangle him. If the Pharisees expected Jesus to speak against Antipas now that he was safe in Judaea, they were disappointed. Jesus was more concerned with the relationships of man and wife than with the love affairs of the half-heathen princelet. But when alone with his disciples (Mk. 10: 10–12) he made clear

result John was imprisoned and later put to death.[1] Although the two accounts differ greatly, the divergence is not so great as may appear at first sight.

The interest and intention of Josephus were different from those of the evangelists. Josephus' main interest was political. He was tracing the cause and effects of political events up to and including the war of A.D. 66–70. The question was, 'Why was Antipas defeated by Aretas?' The answer is that God judged Antipas because he killed a good[2] man named John. Why did he do this? Because of the political implications of insurrection that may have been initiated by John's ministry.

The evangelists' interests and intentions were to explain to the Christian community what had happened to John and why it had happened. It was, they said, because of John's denunciation of Antipas' and Herodias' marriage that Herodias bitterly resented him.[3] The Gospels give little if any hint of a political element in John's preaching. Manson thinks that a political element is contained in John's announcement of the imminent advent of the Messiah, for it was a function of the

what he had meant, by saying that a man who divorces his wife and marries another commits adultery against her, while a woman who divorces her husband and marries another also commits adultery. This may have been a reference to Herodias' and Antipas' divorces and marriage (F. C. Burkitt, 'St Mark and Divorce', *JTS*, v [1904], 628–9; *The Gospel History and its Transmission*[3] [Edinburgh, 1911], pp. 98–101). Manson states that the weak point of this argument is that there is no evidence that Herodias divorced her husband (T. W. Manson, *The Sayings of Jesus* [London, 1949], p. 137). This is true, but neither is there evidence that she had not divorced him. It is more probable that she would have divorced her husband according to Roman law, for such a divorce was quite easy to obtain (cf. Buckland, p. 117; Corbett, pp. 241–3). This may give fuller content to her 'violating the way of the fathers' and to her separation from her living husband (Jos. *Ant.* xviii. 136). The one objection to Burkitt is that Jesus probably did not depart to a desert place on account of John's death but because Jesus wanted to be alone with his disciples and secondarily because Antipas wanted to see Jesus (cf. below, Appendix IX, pp. 317–18).

[1] According to a version of Josippon (Sanders and Nahmad, p. 285), John is associated with 'the sages of the Jews' who also disapproved of Antipas' marriage. Many of these were put to death by the tetrarch.

[2] ἀγαθόν, according to Eisler (ΙΗΣΟΥΣ II, 58 n. 1 [Eng. trans. p. 248]), was changed by the church from ἄγριον or 'wild' man. Feldman says that this is a reckless suggestion (L. Feldman [trans.] *Josephus*, vol. IX of the *LCL* [London, 1965], p. 81 n. c). It is typical of Eisler to alter the words if they will not fit his theory.   [3] Mk. 6: 19.

Messiah to put an end to foreign government in Israel. Moreover, John's baptism might be construed as the rite of initiation
into the Messianic community, and thus be considered by
Herod a treasonable activity.[1] This fear on the part of Antipas
was supplemented, says Manson, by the fact that John attracted
the rank and file of the population, including some of the least
reputable elements, while the upper echelons stood aloof or
were openly hostile (Mk. 11:27–33 = Mt. 21:23–7 = Lk.
20:1–8; Lk. 7:29f.; Mt. 21:28–32; Lk. 3:12, 14).[2] No doubt
there is an element of truth in these statements, but there is no
evidence of any tendency to sedition during John's ministry. In
Josephus there is no suggestion that John was imprisoned for
preaching the immediate appearance of the Messiah. Even if
Antipas knew that John was preaching this message, it is
unlikely that he would have put him to death for it, because a
little later Jesus preached the same message and Antipas merely
wanted to see him.[3] If Antipas did not execute Jesus, who
proclaimed not only the imminence of the kingdom, but himself as the Messiah,[4] why would he execute the lesser man,

---

[1] T. W. Manson, 'John the Baptist', *BJRL*, xxxvi (1954), 406. Eisler
carries this element to extremes by trying to picture the whole of John's
ministry in political terms. Eisler associates John and his disciples with the
'fourth sect' of the Jews, which was founded by the rebel Judas of Galilee.
These were the *barjonîm* who are identified as extremists and were a part of
the later sect of Dosithean Ṣadoqites who produced the Damascus Document (Eisler, ΙΗΣΟΥΣ, ΙΙ, 66–71 [Eng. trans. pp. 252–5]). Since John's
ministry began during Archelaus' reign, he is connected with the revolts of
Judas of Galilee, Simon of Peraea, and Athronges. John was elected high
priest of the insurgents and preached a field sermon (as seen in Lk. 3: 14)
before marching into battle. The time of the revolt was after Herod the
Great's death (Eisler, ΙΗΣΟΥΣ, ΙΙ, 83–90 [Eng. trans. pp. 252–65]). John's
baptism had political significance, for being baptized ἐν ὀνόματι κυρίου
was a soldier's oath of allegiance on his enrolment in the army of the new
Israel. The people entered into a new covenant with the national God
through the baptism of John. They were devoted as soldiers to the coming
Messiah who was the war-lord and army commander (Eisler, ΙΗΣΟΥΣ, ΙΙ,
92–6 [Eng. trans. pp. 267–70]). Eisler's theory is so fantastic that it defeats
itself. The whole historical perspective is contrary to Josephus and the
Gospels. He rejects the most reliable sources and builds his theory on unreliable Byzantine interpolations of the Greek version of Josephus (cf. Jack,
pp. 119, 187–91; Scobie, pp. 86–9).

[2] Manson, *BJRL*, xxxvi, 406.   [3] Lk. 9: 9; 23: 8–9.

[4] Jn. 6: 15. Also the difficult verses Mt. 11: 12 and Lk. 16: 16 should be
considered. For a comment on these, see Manson, *BJRL*, xxxvi, 406–7 n. 2.

John? There is nothing in the messages of John and Jesus of a military nature. Antipas may not have known exactly what John's message was, but after imprisoning and questioning him, he must have discovered that it had no political motives.[1]

Yet if one looks at John's denunciation of Antipas' and Herodias' marriage, as presented in the Gospels, there may have been more political overtones than one would suspect. It must be seen from two points of view. First, from the viewpoint of John's followers: John was urging the people to repent and be baptized because Messiah's kingdom was at hand. He counselled the crowds, tax collectors, and those in the army to prepare themselves morally and spiritually for the coming One. But he also made a scathing denunciation on their ruler for violating the commandments of God. Such a denunciation is significant, for at the climax of Messianic expectation the laws of God are heightened, and believers far less tolerant towards those who oppose the Law.[2]

Antipas would have known full well that religious fanaticism is far more dangerous than political zeal. From the point of view of John's followers, therefore, Herod had defiled not only man's law but God's, and this was not to be tolerated.

From the viewpoint of Antipas the facts take on a different slant. It is important in this connection to have a clear picture of Antipas' first marriage and of the effects of its dissolution. As previously stated, Antipas' first wife was the daughter of the Nabataean king Aretas IV. Of the smaller kingdoms of the Near East, the Nabataean kingdom was without doubt one of the strongest, and it reached the height of its power either just before, or during, Aretas IV's reign.[3] The Nabataean territory

---

[1] Sollertinsky, *JTS*, I, 511; cf. also C. H. Kraeling, *John the Baptist* (London, 1951), pp. 85–6.

[2] This was suggested by Dr E. Bammel in his seminar, Cambridge, Michaelmas Term, 1966.

[3] On the history of the Nabataean kingdom, see A. Kammerer, *Pétra et la Nabatène*, 2 vols. (Paris, 1929); G. and A. Horsfield, 'Sela-Petra, the Rock, of Edom and Nabatene', *QDAP*, VII (1938), 1–42 + lxxiii Pls., VIII (1938), 87–115 + Pls. xliii–lvi; IX (1941), 105–204 + Pls. vi–xlix; Glueck, *Deities and Dolphins*. Glueck states that the greatest flowering of the economy was before Aretas IV (p. 521). This is disputed by P. C. Hammond in his review of Glueck's book ('Review of *Deities and Dolphins: The Story of the Nabataeans*, by N. Glueck', *JBL*, LXXXV [1966], 92). Glueck seems to disagree with himself earlier in his book (cf. p. 120).

was very extensive. It reached to the frontiers of Egypt and Palestine on the south, included most of what is now the Hashemite kingdom of Jordan, stretched northward to the region of Damascus save only the free cities of the Decapolis, encompassed Antipas' Peraea and Philip's domain east of the Sea of Galilee. Because of its location, the Nabataeans were able to control the trade routes of the entire area[1] and became extremely wealthy, as evidenced by their capital city of Petra.[2] The Nabataeans fought and befriended the Judaeans irregularly over the centuries.[3] As mentioned above,[4] there had been serious disputes between the Herods and the Nabataeans. Certainly, since Herod's kingdom was divided, it was a wise move for Antipas to ally himself by marriage to the Nabataean royal house, this being the best guarantee of stability in his rule.[5] Thus, marriage was equivalent to a treaty of friendship between the two nations, but 'by the same token, the dissolution of such a union sounded the tocsin of war'.[6]

Antipas' decision to marry Herodias and to divorce[7] Aretas' daughter is spelled out clearly in Josephus.[8] Apparently Aretas' daughter got wind of the arrangements between Antipas and Herodias, and she out-manoeuvred him by asking him if she could go to Machaerus. This was granted, and she was escorted by στρατηγοί[9] of Aretas from Machaerus to the Nabataean

---

[1] M. Rostovtzeff, *Caravan Cities*, trans. D. and T. Talbot Rice (Oxford, 1932), pp. 28–31; G. E. Wright, 'Herod's Nabataean Neighbor', *BA*, 1 (1938), 4.

[2] Rostovtzeff, *Caravan Cities*, pp. 50–1.

[3] Glueck, *Deities and Dolphins*, pp. 40, 375.   [4] Above, pp. 129–30.

[5] Kraeling, *John*, p. 89.   [6] Glueck, *Deities and Dolphins*, pp. 40.

[7] Josephus (*Ant.* xviii. 110) states that Herodias stipulated that Aretas' daughter was to be ousted (ἐκβάλλω). Daube points out that the LXX renders 'to divorce a wife' by ἐκβάλλω where the Hebrew is גָּרַשׁ (only in three passages: Lev. 21: 14; 22: 13; Num. 30: 10); but this is never so used in the NT or Philo. In general ἐκβάλλω is used only where the husband proceeded with some vehemence or particular inconsiderateness. This term is used only once by Josephus, and this is the particular case (Daube, pp. 369–71). Therefore, Herodias is indicating vehemence toward Aretas' daughter, i.e. it was covenanted that Antipas would 'throw her out' or 'get rid of her'.

[8] Jos. *Ant.* xviii. 100–25.

[9] Jos. *Ant.* xviii. 112. As mentioned above (p. 49), the Nabataean inscriptions mention officers with the title στρατηγός and ἔπαρχος. In Asia Minor a board of στρατηγοί, headed by a 'first στρατηγός', was responsible

territory.[1] She reported the intention of Antipas to her father. This was taken as an insult to the Nabataean royal family which could not be left unrevenged. Within a few years war developed between Aretas and Antipas in which Antipas' lands were invaded and his troops defeated. He would have been expelled from his territory had not the Romans stepped in.

Hence in view of the political situation John's denunciation 'was not only embarrassing, it was politically explosive'.[2]

The question must now be asked, 'Is John's denunciation of Antipas' and Herodias' marriage something that is wholly foreign to Josephus' account?' Josephus gives the account of Antipas' and Herodias' marriage immediately before the

for the administration of 103 centres in the province of Asia and about 5 in Bithynia (Magie, I, 643–4; II, 1508 n. 29). It seems that the Nabataean kings tried to organize their kingdom on the regular Hellenistic model, but that when the centralized system broke down they gave the local sheikhs the title of 'governor' (cf. Jones, *CERP*, p. 292; G. M. Harper Jr, 'Village Administration in the Roman Province of Syria', *Yale Classical Studies*, I [1928], 120–1). In the present passage of Josephus, Aretas' daughter is taken under the protection of one στρατηγός after another until she reaches her father, a custom which is still practised among the Arabs in the present day (A. M. Hyamson, K. Mason, and J. L. Myres, *Palestine and Transjordan* [Oxford, 1943], p. 443). This gives an indication that the στρατηγοί were local sheikhs and were in control of, and had authority over, their own particular region. It seems, then, that these local sheikhs dignified their own office by using the foreign title στρατηγός (cf. Mowry, *BASOR*, no. 132, 38–9). Furthermore, στρατηγός seems to have been a permanent title and office which was handed down from father to son (cf. *CIS*, II, i, 161, 196, 213, 214, 224, 234, 235, 238; this may be suggested in Strabo xvi. 4. 25). It is suggested by Cooke, pp. 247–8, that the two στρατηγοί Ya'amru in *CIS*, II, i, 195: 2–4 and 'Abd-'obedath in *CIS*, II, i, 196: 2 may have assisted the wife of Herod Antipas in her flight to her father Aretas IV at Petra.

[1] On the basis of archaeological investigation of the area, Glueck states: 'Josephus describes Machaerus as being on the border of the dominions of the two kings, which is correct, but he wrongly places it in the territory of Aretas. To escape from Machaerus to the security of her father's kingdom meant for the daughter of Aretas a flight of only a few miles. Numerous Nabataean controlled settlements existed immediately south and east of that small, more or less rectangular part of Peraea which stretched along the n.e. side of the Dead Sea' (*AASOR*, XVIII–XIX, 140; cf. also Smith, *HGHL*, p. 598 n. 8). Schürer (I, 436 n. 20) suggests that the idea that Machaerus belonged to Aretas arises from a faulty reading of ὑποτελῆ instead of ὑποτελεῖ in Jos. *Ant.* xviii. 112.

[2] Kraeling, *John*, pp. 90–1.

record of John's preaching.[1] This makes it possible for the reader to suppose that the unlawful marriage was the effective cause of Antipas' fear of a popular uprising.[2] Josephus, being interested in the political causes and effects, did not relate the immediate cause which involved personal considerations.[3]

It is highly probable that Antipas was closely watching the Baptist's movements. When John denounced the marriage of Antipas and Herodias this could have been the 'straw that broke the camel's back'. At least, it furnished a good excuse for Antipas to say that it could have started a revolt. John's grip upon the people was sufficiently strong to be noticed by both Antipas[4] and the religious leaders.[5] It was better to nip it in the bud than to wait until it was too late.[6] From Antipas' viewpoint this movement could have led to serious consequences.

It is not impossible, therefore, that the evangelists and Josephus are reporting the same incident from different angles. The former was interested in personal relationships and the cause of John's death; the latter in political causes and effects. Both accounts are necessary in order to get the full picture. Kraeling has summed it up well when he writes:

It meant aligning the pious Jewish inhabitants of Peraea with those of the Arabic stock against the sovereign and thus fomenting sedition and encouraging insurrection. John's denunciation of Antipas as

---

[1] Jos. *Ant.* xviii. 109–15.

[2] Sollertinsky, *JTS*, I, 512.

[3] Sollertinsky (*JTS*, I, 512) suggests that Josephus does not report John's denunciation of Antipas' and Herodias' marriage because that would have shed unfavourable light on Herodias, who with her brother Agrippa I and Josephus himself were all of the Hasmonean family. Instead he makes Antipas solely responsible for John's death. It is true that Josephus favoured Agrippa I over Antipas, as mentioned by Sollertinsky (*JTS*, I, 509) and confirmed by Hölscher (PW, IX, 1987), but Josephus does not protect Herodias as Sollertinsky suggests. Sollertinsky states that Antipas' deposition was accounted by Josephus as God's punishment upon Antipas, whereas actually Josephus states that God's punishment was upon both Herodias and Antipas (*Ant.* xviii. 255). In fact, God's punishment upon Antipas was for listening to the frivolous chatter of Herodias.

[4] Both Josephus and the Gospels emphasize this: Jos. *Ant.* xviii. 118; Mt. 14: 5. Mk. 6: 20 states that Herod Antipas feared John, instead of fearing the people as in Matthew (cf. below, pp. 162–4).

[5] Mt. 21: 26 = Mk. 11: 32 = Lk. 20: 6; Mt. 21: 46 = Mk. 12: 12 = Lk. 20: 19.

[6] As suggested by Jos. *Ant.* xviii. 118.

reported in Mark, far from contradicting Josephus, provides the one detail necessary to make Josephus' account of the political threat involved in the Baptist's exhortation intelligible.[1]

John's personal denunciation had potential political implications[2] and it was most advantageous for Antipas to imprison him.

The differences in the location of John's execution

Taking the Gospel narratives by themselves it would appear that John's execution took place at Tiberias. This is suggested by the fact that the banquet was attended by τοῖς μεγιστᾶσιν αὐτοῦ καὶ τοῖς χιλιάρχοις καὶ τοῖς πρώτοις τῆς Γαλιλαίας.[3] Also the story of the delegation sent by John to Jesus[4] might suggest that John was imprisoned in Galilee. On the other hand, Josephus specifically states that John was imprisoned and executed at Machaerus.

In neither Josephus nor the Gospels is there record of any activity of John in Galilee. Due to Matthew 3:1, it is often thought that his work was ἐν τῇ ἐρήμῳ τῆς Ἰουδαίας. But this is unsupported by the other two evangelists who locate him ἐν τῇ ἐρήμῳ[5] and say that ἦλθεν εἰς πᾶσαν τὴν περίχωρον τοῦ Ἰορδάνου.[6] Furthermore, the fourth Gospel places John's activity on the far side of the Jordan.[7] The people flocked to him

[1] Kraeling, *John*, p. 91.

[2] It may be added that 'political ends and the anger of an insulted woman cannot be regarded as mutually exclusive' (Taylor, *Mark*, p. 311).

[3] Mk. 6: 21.   [4] Mt. 11: 2–6 = Lk. 7: 18–23.

[5] Mk. 1: 4.

[6] Lk. 3: 3. Conzelmann (p. 19) thinks that Luke could not place John in either Galilee or Judaea because these were both spheres of Jesus' activity. Therefore, John is placed in a marginal location – the region of the Jordan. Jesus had to come to John's territory to be baptized, but since the Jordan was John's territory Jesus afterwards had no more contact with the Jordan or even its surroundings. Luke later states that Jesus did come to Jericho (18: 35; 19: 1); but Conzelmann questions whether Luke knew that this town was in the region of the Jordan. However, as Bruce rightly points out: 'Even if Luke was personally unacquainted with that district of Palestine, he had presumably read Joshua and 2 Kings, where Jericho's proximity to the Jordan is made plain' (F. F. Bruce, 'History and the Gospel', *Faith and Thought*, XCIII [1964], 131 n. 2).

[7] Jn. 1: 28; 10: 40. For a discussion of Bethany beyond Jordan, see C. Kopp, *The Holy Places of the Gospels*, trans. R. Walls (Freiburg, 1963), pp. 113–29.

from Judaea, Jerusalem, and the plain of Jordan.[1] Although he may have had some ministry in Samaria,[2] the evidence suggests that his main centre of activity was in Peraea.[3] Because of Antipas he may have crossed over to the west of the Jordan at times. Antipas probably caught him in the territory of Peraea, and in this event it would be logical to imprison him at Machaerus.

Although Antipas' main place of residence was undoubtedly Tiberias, this does not preclude his living part of the time in Peraea. During the summer Tiberias was not only hot, but being situated on the western side of the Sea of Galilee, 685 feet below sea level, and enclosed by cliffs, the air was stagnant and close, and it was feverish and unbearable to live and sleep in.[4] Machaerus was situated on one of the highest places, if not the highest place, east of the Jordan, rising to a height of 2,360 feet above sea level.[5] Although also quite warm, at least there would be breezes which would make it bearable to live. Moreover, at or near Machaerus there was the attraction of hot and cold springs of water.[6]

On the other hand, it is more probable that Antipas would have gone to Machaerus because of its position in relation to the Arabs. Because of his offending Aretas he would have been anxious to keep a close eye on them and their movements from Machaerus. Machaerus was fortified by Alexander Jannaeus

[1] Mt. 3: 5; Mk. 1: 5.

[2] This depends on one's view of the location of Aenon near Salim mentioned in Jn. 3: 23. It is a knotty problem with no definite solution. For a review of the different positions, see W. A. Stevens, 'Aenon near to Salim', *JBL*, III (1883), 128–41; cf. also M. Avi-Yonah, 'Aenon', *IDB*, I (1962), 52; Kopp, pp. 129–37. For the view that Aenon near Salim was southeast of Nablus, see B. W. Bacon, 'Aenon Near to Sâlim', *BW*, XXXIII (1909), 223–38; W. F. Albright, 'Some Observations Favoring the Palestinian Origin of the Gospel of John', *HTR*, XVII (1924), 193–4; 'Recent Discoveries in Palestine and the Gospel of St John', *The Background of the New Testament and its Eschatology*, ed. by W. D. Davies and D. Daube (Cambridge, 1956), pp. 159–60.

[3] T. W. Manson, *The Servant-Messiah* (Cambridge, 1953), pp. 40–1. For the area of John's ministry, see also B. W. Bacon, 'The Baptism of John – Where was it?', *BW*, XXX (1907), 39–50; C. C. McCown, 'Scene of John's Ministry and its Relation to the Purpose and Outcome of His Mission', *JBL*, LIX (1940), 113–31.

[4] Smith, *HGHL*, p. 449; Dalman, *SSW*, p. 198.

[5] Jos. *BJ* vii. 166–7; G. A. Smith, 'Callirrhoe and Machaerus', *PEFQS*, XXXVII (1905), 228; Kopp, p. 141.   [6] Jos. *BJ* vii. 186–9.

and later destroyed by Gabinius.[1] Herod the Great rebuilt it because he realized its strategic position in relation to the Arabs,[2] and made it in strength second only to Jerusalem.[3] In addition to this, on the mountain slope Herod founded a πόλις and built there a palace (βασίλειον) with spacious and beautiful apartments.[4] This is confirmed by the fact that when Aretas' daughter asked Antipas if she might go to Machaerus, Antipas was not suspicious of her, which it seems he would have been if Machaerus had been only a fortress. She out-foxed him. Although this is based on an *argumentum ex silentio*, it is here a strong one. If it had been only a fortress, either Antipas' suspicion would have been aroused, or Josephus would have pointed out how stupid he was in not having suspected, especially since Josephus had little use for Antipas.

It is perfectly conceivable then that Antipas resided at various times at Machaerus, and that the nobilities of Galilee may have sent him a deputation on his birthday.[5] The fact that there is no mention of a Peraean delegation being sent may indicate that Antipas was already in Peraea. Although from Mark 6:21 it might appear natural that Tiberias was the place of the banquet, this is not (*pace* Keim)[6] implied by the evangelists. In fact, the evangelists are silent on the matter of location, and hence there is nothing in the Gospels to contradict Josephus on this point.[7] It seems, then, reasonable to conclude that John was imprisoned[8] and executed in Machaerus.

[1] Jos. *BJ* i. 161, 167; vii. 171; *Ant.* xiv. 83, 90; Kopp, p. 142.
[2] Jos. *BJ* vii. 172.   [3] Pliny *NH* v. 15. 72.
[4] Jos. *BJ* vii. 174–7.   [5] Kopp, p. 142.
[6] Keim, *Jesus of Nazara*, IV, 217–18 n. 4. Christie also argues that since Jesus crossed the Sea of Galilee soon after he heard of John's execution, John was probably executed somewhere near the Sea (cf. W. M. Christie, 'Ḳuṣr bint el-Melek', *Glasgow University Oriental Society Transactions*, v [1930], 37). But Jesus' withdrawal was due to his popularity. Even if he withdrew on account of John's death, he did so *after* John's disciples had reported their master's execution, and they would have come just as well from Peraea. The point of the withdrawal was to be alone with his disciples and to get out of Antipas' territory. The Sea of Galilee furnished the easiest means to accomplish this goal.
[7] Schürer, I, 441 n. 28; cf. Grundmann, *Matthäus*, p. 361.
[8] Tristram found two dungeons among the ruins of Machaerus, in one of which John may have been (cf. H. B. Tristram, *The Land of Moab*[2] [London, 1874], p. 259.

In conclusion, the differences between Josephus and the evangelists are not great. Sometimes, indeed, that which seems contradictory actually furnishes a key to the understanding of the narrative.

THE DIFFICULTIES IN THE SYNOPTICS

The problems of designation

The first problem of designation is one of Antipas' title. Antipas was the τετράρχης of Galilee and Peraea but is also called βασιλεύς by Matthew and Mark.[1] Few commentators hold that the evangelists were in error;[2] most feel that although the term βασιλεύς may be technically inaccurate there are several reasons for its use here. First, the usage may reflect a local custom or a courtesy title.[3] Luke, in the present context, does call him by his correct title,[4] a thing not uncommon to Luke.[5] On the other hand, Mark always calls Antipas *king*,[6] whereas Matthew calls him once *tetrarch*[7] and once *king*.[8] Since in Matthew these two designations are only nine verses apart, it seems that the evangelist knew of Herod Antipas' technical title but used the popular title in this pericope. Again, Matthew uses popular language when mentioning Archelaus' succession.[9] The

---

[1] Mt. 14: 9; Mk. 6: 22, 25, 26, 27. Herod Antipas was called *king* in Just. *Dial.* xlix. 4 (*MPG*, vi, 584); *Gospel of Peter* 2; *Acts of Pilate*, prologue.

[2] B. W. Bacon, *The Gospel of Mark* (New Haven, 1925), pp. 72, 75; Haenchen, *Der Weg Jesu*, pp. 240, 241; Dibelius, *FRLANT*, xv, 79.

[3] E. Klostermann, *Das Matthäusevangelium*[2], *HNT*, iv (Tübingen, 1927), p. 126; M'Neile, p. 208; Swete, p. 120; Rawlinson, p. 79; Lagrange, *Marc*, p. 155; Lohmeyer, *Markus*, p. 115 n. 3; D. E. Nineham, *The Gospel of St Mark*[2] (London, 1968), p. 174; Taylor, *Mark*, p. 308.

[4] Lk. 3: 19.

[5] Luke always called Antipas *tetrarch*, cf. Lk. 3: 1, 19; 9: 7; Acts 13: 1; as well as Philip, Lk. 3: 1. He rightly calls Herod the Great, *king* in Lk. 1: 5 as well as Agrippa I (Acts 12: 1) and Agrippa II (Acts 25: 13, 14, 24, 26; 26: 2, 7, 13, 19, 26, 27, 30).

[6] Mk. 6: 14, 22, 25, 26, 27. This does not mean that Mark was ignorant of the fact that Antipas received only part of his father's kingdom. On the contrary, only the officials of Galilee came to the banquet and not any from such places as Jerusalem – the most likely place if it were a part of Antipas' domain.

[7] Mt. 14: 1.   [8] Mt. 14: 9.

[9] Mt. 2: 22 – Ἀρχέλαος βασιλεύει τῆς Ἰουδαίας ἀντὶ τοῦ πατρὸς αὐτοῦ Ἡρῴδου.

same thing is done by Josephus, who specifically states that Archelaus received the titles *ethnarch* and *king*, but the latter only in anticipation.[1] He states, however, that Archelaus ruled as king (βασιλεύοντος)[2] and calls him βασιλεύς outright in a different context.[3] Again, Hyrcanus II was called *ethnarch* by the Romans[4] and *king* by the Jews.[5] Among the Palestinians it would seem that the title *king* did not drop out of popular usage between the death of Herod the Great and the conferring of the title on Agrippa I.[6] Secondly, Philo speaks of Herod the Great's sons as those 'who in dignity and good fortune were not inferior to a king'.[7] Hence the people would have considered and called Antipas king. Thirdly, in Aramaic '*malka* is a term with a wider range of meaning than Latin *rex* or even Greek βασιλεύς'.[8] Fourthly, since the name *Herod* became a dynastic title after Herod the Great's death, the people may have associated the title *king* with the name *Herod*, something which neither Archelaus nor Antipas would have wished to discourage. Finally, 'a tetrarch was in fact a petty king, and...he possessed a jurisdiction with which the Imperial authorities were ordinarily reluctant to interfere (Lc. xxiii. 7)'.[9]

In conclusion, therefore, it seems that Matthew and Mark in calling Herod Antipas βασιλεύς may not have been technically accurate (as was Luke). Either they used the popular terminology of the day or they spoke out of courtesy, as also did Josephus. The use of the dynastic name *Herod* may have assisted the continuation of the title *king*.

The second problem of designation is closely related to the preceding one, namely, Antipas' promise to give to Herodias' daughter ἕως ἡμίσους τῆς βασιλείας μου.[10] Some commentators have dismissed this as legendary on the grounds that Antipas

---

[1] Jos. *Ant.* xvii. 317; *BJ* ii. 93.

[2] Jos. *Vita* 5.   [3] Jos. *Ant.* xviii. 93.

[4] Jos. *Ant.* xiv. 191, 194, 196, 200, 209, 211, 226.

[5] Jos. *Ant.* xiv. 157, 165, 172, 174, 178; *BJ* i. 202, 203, 209, 212.

[6] T. Zahn, *Introduction to the New Testament*, trans. from 3rd German ed. under the direction of M. W. Jacobus and C. S. Thayer, II (Edinburgh, 1909), 503 n. 3.

[7] *Leg.* 300: οὐκ ἀποδέοντας τό τε ἀξίωμα καὶ τύχας βασιλέων.

[8] F. F. Bruce, 'Herod Antipas, Tetrarch of Galilee and Peraea', *ALUOS*, v (1963–5), 9.

[9] Swete, p. 120.   [10] Mk. 6: 23.

could never have said it. Not only did he have no kingdom to give away, but as a vassal of Rome his dominions were not even his.[1] 'But is the extravagant offer of an Oriental potentate excited by wine to be taken thus *au pied de la lettre?*'[2] In the Septuagint, Ahasuerus twice promised Esther ἕως τοῦ ἡμίσους τῆς βασιλείας μου[3] and it has been suggested that this story influenced the present narrative.[4] More probably, it was a proverbial saying even in the days of Ahasuerus.[5] Certainly to offer a half of one's possessions was a familiar expression.[6] No one at the banquet would have taken it literally, for all of them (including Antipas) knew Antipas' position. They would have accepted it as a proverbial saying. Justin Martyr interpreted it as αἰτήσασθαι ὃ ἐὰν βούληται[7] which is the essence of the proverbial statement. Neither Esther nor Herodias' daughter held the rulers to their promise, but only requested a favour which did not involve them in the surrender of any part of their domains. The promise, therefore, was not to be taken literally; it merely indicated that the ruler in question was willing to do a reasonable favour for the person to whom he uttered this saying.

The problems connected with Herodias' daughter

There are three questions in connection with Herodias' daughter: (1) whose daughter was she? (2) is she correctly designated a κοράσιον? (3) would she have danced before men?

The identity of the dancing girl

The root cause of the difficulty is the problematic pronoun in Mark 6:22. There are three suggested solutions to the problem. First, that there was originally no pronoun at all, the reading being θυγατρὸς τῆς Ἡρῳδιάδος. This has weak manuscript

---

[1] H. J. Holtzmann, *Die Synoptiker*, vol. 1 of *Hand-Commentar zum Neuen Testament* (Freiburg, 1889), p. 174; Lohmeyer, *Markus*, p. 120; Grundmann, *Markus*, p. 130; Haenchen, *Der Weg Jesu*, p. 240.

[2] Rawlinson, pp. 81–2.

[3] Est. 5: 3; 7: 2. This promise is repeated a third time in 5: 6, both in the MT and in LXX A.

[4] Taylor, *Mark*, p. 315.

[5] Rawlinson, p. 82.

[6] Cf. 1 Kgs. 13: 8; Lk. 19: 8. A similar statement is given in Homer *Iliad* ix. 616 (ἴσον ἐμοὶ βασίλευε καὶ ἥμισυ μείρεο τιμῆς).

[7] *Dial.* xlix. 4 (*MPG*, VI, 584).

attestation.[1] Although it would read more easily with the omission of the pronoun, its inclusion, as suggested by Allen[2] and later by Burney,[3] Torrey,[4] and Black,[5] may have been an attempt to reproduce the Aramaic construction בְּרַתָּה דְּהֵרוֹדְיָם ('the daughter of her, of Herodias'). Since, therefore, the omission of the pronoun has little support and since a too literal rendering of the Aramaic gives a plausible reason for its inclusion, it is probable that the pronoun is original.

Having established the probability of the pronoun, the next step is to determine its gender. Hence, the second suggestion is that the pronoun was originally masculine – θυγατρὸς αὐτοῦ Ἡρῳδιάδος, or 'his daughter (named) Herodias'. This reading has a few very important manuscripts in its support (אBDLΔ 238 565). It is accepted by some because of its weighty attestation, and because Salome, who was in her late teens, would hardly have been the little girl (κοράσιον) described in Mark.[6] Lillie states:

This, of course, would mean that the alliance of Antipas and Herodias had taken place six or more years before. There are two slight indications confirming this. (a) Josephus' statement that Herodias' second marriage took place 'after' the birth of Salome is most naturally interpreted as 'shortly after', which would indicate a date before A.D. 20. (b) The words ἡμέρας εὐκαίρου in Mk 6²¹ (which Weymouth translates, 'At length Herodias found her opportunity';...) suggest that Herodias had waited some time before her chance of taking vengeance on John came.[7]

The chief difficulty with this view is that it does not fit well with the rest of Josephus because (1) Josephus mentions no child born to Antipas and Herodias; (2) he implies that Aretas' revenge on Antipas was not too long after Antipas' and Herodias' marriage.[8] It seems that if they were married in A.D. 20 there would be a time lapse of sixteen years before

[1] f¹, 22 131, it-aur b c f, syr-s p pal, cop-sa bo, goth, arm, eth, geo.
[2] Allen, ET, XIII, 330; Allen, Mark, p. 98.
[3] C. F. Burney, The Aramaic Origin of the Fourth Gospel (Oxford, 1922), pp. 85–6.
[4] C. C. Torrey, The Four Gospels (London, n.d.), pp. 299–300.
[5] Black, Aramaic Approach, p. 97.
[6] Bruce, ALUOS, v, 12–13.
[7] W. Lillie, 'Salome or Herodias?', ET, LXV (1954), 251.
[8] Jos. Ant. xviii. 112–13.

Aretas struck back. Among other things the narrative of Mark suggests that Antipas and Herodias were not married very long, and thus a child of this marriage would have been too young to dance. Thus neither Josephus nor the evangelists give any hint that Antipas and Herodias had a child of their own, while Josephus at least specifically states that Herodias had a daughter, named Salome, from her former marriage.[1] Finally, Justin Martyr says that it was Salome, Herod's grandniece, and not his daughter, who danced.[2]

Finally the third suggestion is that the pronoun was originally feminine and the phrase should read θυγατρὸς αὐτῆς τῆς Ἡρῳδιάδος. This is supported by many manuscripts[3] and is adopted by most commentators.[4] There are several reasons for adopting this reading: (1) The Gospel narrative implies that the illicit marriage was a recent one and so the child could not have been more than two years old. (2) The context of Mark indicates that the girl was Herodias' daughter.[5] (3) The parallel verse in Matthew has ἡ θυγάτηρ τῆς Ἡρῳδιάδος.[6] (4) It fits well with Josephus who states that Herodias by her first marriage had a daughter called Salome.[7] (5) It is in agreement with Justin Martyr's τῆς ἐξαδέλφης αὐτοῦ τοῦ Ἡρῴδου and ἡ μήτηρ τῆς παιδός.[8] The inclusion of αὐτῆς may be for emphasis, to make clear that it was Herodias' own daughter who danced;[9] or it may have the relative force of the German *dieser*[10] and should

---

[1] *Ant.* xviii. 136, 137.

[2] *Dial.* xlix. 4 (*MPG*, vi, 584). It may be that Justin is wrong but why postulate this when everything else is in favour of the other possibility?

[3] A C K (W *omits* τῆς) Θ Π*f*[13], 28 33 700 892 1009 1010 1071 1079 1195 1216 1230 1241 1242 1253 1344 1365 1546 1646 2148 2174, *Byz Lect*-m, it-a d ff[22] i l q r[1], vg, syr-h.

[4] Weiss, *Markus und Lukas*, p. 97; E. P. Gould, *A Critical and Exegetical Commentary on the Gospel according to St Mark*, *ICC* (Edinburgh, 1896), p. 113; Swete, p. 125; Lagrange, *Marc*, pp. 160–1; Lohmeyer, *Markus*, p. 119 n. 6; Taylor, *Mark*, pp. 314–15; Cranfield, pp. 211–12; cf. also Schürer, i, 441–2 n. 29.

[5] Mk. 6: 24, 28. [6] Mt. 14: 6; cf. also 14: 8, 11.

[7] Jos. *Ant.* xviii. 136, 137. [8] *Dial.* xlix. 4 (*MPG*, vi, 584).

[9] Cranfield, pp. 211–12.

[10] This form is found in *P. Holm* and the relative idea of it is suggested by O. Lagercrantz, *Papyrus Graecus Holmiensis. Recepte für Silber, Steine und Purpur* (Uppsala and Leipzig, 1913), p. 157. This view is confirmed by H. Riesenfeld, 'Nachträge I. Lagercrantz' Beiträge zum N.T.', *Coniectanea Neotestamentica*, iii (Uppsala and Leipzig, 1938), 24.

be translated 'the daughter of the one who is called Herodias' (or it could be translated 'the daughter of the aforementioned Herodias');[1] or it may be an Aramaism – a redundant pronoun anticipating a noun.[2] The explanation for its inclusion is a result of a too literal rendering of Aramaic. It is possible that αὐτῆς was meaningless to some copyist at a very early date and was changed to αὐτοῦ.[3] This may explain the inclusion of αὐτοῦ in some manuscripts.

In conclusion, it is best to take the pronoun as αὐτῆς and to conclude that the dancing girl was Salome, Herodias' daughter from her former marriage. Though not supported by some of the more important manuscripts, this interpretation is favoured by the overall evidence.

The designation as κοράσιον

The second problem leads on from the first, namely, if she were Herodias' daughter from her former marriage, is the designation κοράσιον[4] a proper one for her? Herodias was the daughter of Aristobulus (the son of Herod the Great and Mariamme I) and Berenice (daughter of Herod's sister, Salome and Costobarus), who were married around 17 or 16 B.C.[5] It seems from Josephus that Herodias was either the youngest or second youngest child,[6] or at any rate younger than her brother Agrippa I who was born in 10 B.C.[7] Since Aristobulus was killed in 7 B.C., Herodias would have been born sometime between 9 and 7 B.C. She was certainly alive in 6 B.C. when

[1] BD/Funk, § 277 (3).   [2] Black, *Aramaic Approach*, p. 97.

[3] Torrey, p. 300.

[4] Mk. 6: 22, 28 (bis); Mt. 14: 11.

[5] Jos. *Ant.* xvi. 11; *BJ* i. 446; Otto, PW, Supp. II, col. 163; Zeittafel für Herodes I; cf. also Schürer, I, 407–8.

[6] In one list Herodias is placed before her sister, Mariamme (*BJ* i. 552), and after her in other places (*Ant.* xvii. 14; *BJ* i. 557); but in the lists, Aristobulus' sons are listed before the daughters (cf. *Ant.* xvii. 12; *BJ* i. 552) which may have been a normal procedure.

[7] In Jos. *Ant.* xix. 350, Josephus states that Agrippa was 54 years old when he died in A.D. 44. This is confirmed by the fact that when his father died in 7 B.C. (*Ant.* xvi. 394; *BJ* i. 551) Agrippa and his brothers were designated νήπιοι (*Ant.* xviii. 134). This could apply to any age up to puberty (cf. G. Bertram, 'νήπιος', *TDNT*, IV [1967], 912). Possibly it refers to the same category as παιδίον, or up to the age of 7, as suggested by A. Oepke, 'παῖς', *TDNT*, V [1967], 637.

Herod the Great betrothed her to Herod Philip.[1] If she were born about 8 B.C. she would have been of marriageable age in A.D. 6–10[2] but may not have married until later. Certainly she would have married before A.D. 26 and probably before A.D. 14/15.[3] The most probable time is between A.D. 6 and 15, when she was between fourteen and twenty-three years of age.[4]

At what time Herodias' and Herod Philip's daughter, Salome,[5] was born is difficult to determine. There are, however, some limits to be observed. First, she was old enough to be married to Philip the tetrarch before he died in A.D. 34.[6] Secondly, she must have been young enough to qualify for the title of κοράσιον and to be dependent on her mother for advice.[7] The exact meaning of κοράσιον is uncertain, but it is a diminutive of κόρη meaning *girl* or *maiden*.[8] This term is used sixteen times in the canonical books of the Septuagint.[9] Twice it is a translation of יַלְדָּה and has the meaning of young girl.[10] The other fourteen times it represents נַעֲרָה. Of these, six carry the idea of maiden,[11] implying an age of responsibility,

---

[1] Jos. *Ant.* xvii. 14; *BJ* i. 557.

[2] This is very difficult to determine. The marriageable age for a man was eighteen according to Mishnah: Ab. v. 21, but there is much debate over this in the Talmud, which variously states that it would be somewhere between eighteen and twenty-four or even as early as fourteen (TB: Kid. 29 b–30 a). Probably the marriageable age for women would be slightly younger than for men.

[3] Otto, col. 201.

[4] If Herodias married Antipas in A.D. 27/8 she would have been between thirty-four and thirty-seven years of age and he would have been around forty-eight.

[5] Jos. *Ant.* xviii. 136. According to the Slavonic Josephus, Herod Philip and Herodias had four children (after *BJ* ii. 168 in the regular Josephus, cf. Josephus, *LCL*, III, 647–8). Josippon also mentions that they had children rather than one child (cf. Joseph Ben Gurion, *The Wonderful and Most Deplorable History*, p. 88; M. Sanders and H. Nahmad, p. 285).

[6] Jos. *Ant.* xviii. 137, 106, cf. below, p. 251 n. 1.   [7] Mk. 6: 24.

[8] Bauer/AG, p. 445; cf. also F. Solmsen, 'Eigennamen als Zeugen der Stammesmischung in Böotien', *Rheinisches Museum für Philologie*, LIX (1904), 503–4.

[9] This excludes the use of κοράσιον in 1 Kgs. 12: 24 l which, along with 12: 24 b–z, has no counterpart in the MT.

[10] Joel 4: 3; Zech. 8: 5.

[11] Ruth 2: 8, 22, 23; 3: 2; 1 Sam. 9: 11, 12 (although verse 12 is not in the MT, it was legitimate for the LXX translators to use the word since it was used in verse 11).

and eight one who is of marriageable age[1] or has been married.[2] The predominant meaning of נַעֲרָה seems to be a young woman of marriageable age.[3] In the New Testament κοράσιον is used of Jairus' daughter[4] who was twelve years old.[5] It is possible for the term to mean a small child but it seems to be used more characteristically of a young girl at or near marriageable age. If John was beheaded sometime between A.D. 29 and 32[6] and the girl was twelve to fourteen years old, all the pieces fall into place. Salome would have been born between A.D. 15 and 19. She would have qualified to be called a κοράσιον at the time of John's death, and would have been of marriageable age before Philip's death in A.D. 34. Furthermore, her running to her mother does not necessarily imply naïveté, as stated by Bruce.[7] A girl of twelve to fourteen years old asked to state such a wish would quite naturally seek her own mother's advice, especially before a crowd of adult officials. Secondly, since Herodias was the scheming person, it is possible that she instructed Salome to come to her for advice should Antipas fall into the trap. Thirdly, αἰτέω is changed from an active in Mark 6:22–3 to a middle in 6:24–5. This 'is quite subtle, since the daughter of Herodias, after the King's pronouncement, stands in a sort of business relationship to him'.[8] This would seem to indicate that she was old enough to have such a relationship. It is highly improbable that this would apply in the case of a naive young girl. Finally, if she had been so young and naive, Antipas would not have felt obliged to do what she asked.[9] He could easily have diverted her to something else if she had been a mere child.

The problem of the dance

The third problem is whether or not Salome would have danced before a banquet gathering such as is pictured in the Gospels.[10] Does it make the story a popular fiction, because there is no

---

[1] Est. 2: 2, 3, 7, 8, 9, (bis), 12.

[2] 1 Sam. 20: 30. This is problematic in the MT but probably נַעֲרָה is the correct word, cf. S. R. Driver, *Notes on the Hebrew Text and Topography of the Books of Samuel*[2] (Oxford, 1913), p. 171.

[3] BDB, pp. 654–5.
[4] Mt. 9: 24, 25; Mk. 5: 41, 42.
[5] Mk. 5: 42; Lk. 8: 42.
[6] Below, p. 171.
[7] Bruce, *ALUOS*, v, 12–13.
[8] BD/Funk, § 316 (2).
[9] Mk. 6: 27.
[10] Mt. 14: 6; Mk. 6: 22.

other example of a princess performing a shameless dance in front of a company of men?[1] It is thought that only a harlot or a girl of loose morals would perform such a dance, and that the story could only be believed by someone who has not seen an oriental solo dance.[2] The text could certainly refer to an immoral or sensual dance, but it does not demand this interpretation.[3] In fact, Dalman, who lived in Palestine, states that there is no reason why Salome should not have danced before men, for he had seen such a dance himself and gives a description of it.[4] Moreover, Jewish literature reveals that there were several kinds of dancing,[5] and that it could be a perfectly respectable exercise in which eminently respectable people took part.[6] The dance of Salome is no less credible than the scene at the court of Orodes after the defeat of Crassus,[7] 'and there is no reason to suppose that the Herods were in general more civilized than the Arsacids, or more orthodox in their Judaism than the Arsacids in their Mazdaism'.[8]

Hence, it is reasonable to believe that Salome also 'could have appeared before the guests, singing and dancing, without any loss of dignity; and perhaps just such a graceful dance was enough to stimulate Herod in his cups to utter his careless oath'.[9]

[1] Lohmeyer, *Markus*, p. 120; cf. also E. Schweizer, *Das Evangelium nach Markus*, *NTD*, I (Göttingen, 1967), p. 74.

[2] A. Merx, *Das Evangelium Matthaeus* (Berlin, 1902), p. 228. Against this Bussmann (I, 33) states that the longer one lives in the Orient the more one knows that such dances, even before strange men, do occur.

[3] It is interesting to note that Tacitus thought that the Jews had very low moral standards amongst themselves (*Hist.* v. 5). Although an Islamic account does not have Salome's dance she nevertheless wins over the king by her sensual appeal (cf. Gibson, *MW*, XLV, 345).

[4] G. Dalman, 'Zum Tanz der Tochter der Herodias', *PJB*, XIV (1918), 44–6; cf. also H. Windisch, 'Kleine Beiträge zur evangelischen Überlieferung', *ZNW*, XVIII (1917), 73–5; E. Stauffer, *Jerusalem und Rom* (Bern and München, 1957), pp. 94–7; Jeremias, *Jerusalem*, p. 362.

[5] Krauss, *Talmudische Archäologie*, III (Leipzig, 1912), 99–102; Strack–Billerbeck, I, 682–3.

[6] Suk. v. 1–4; Tos.: Suk. iv. 1–4.

[7] Plutarch *Crassus* xxxiii. 1–3.

[8] Knox, I, 50–1.

[9] Kopp, p. 139.

The problem of change in persons

Who desired to kill John

Whereas Matthew states that Antipas desired to kill John, Mark states that it was Herodias who so desired,[1] since she 'had it in' for him, that is, she was on bad terms with him (ἐνεῖχεν αὐτῷ).[2] It is assumed by some that Matthew made an erroneous abbreviation, especially in the light of verse 9 where Antipas was grieved because he felt obligated to kill John.[3] But Antipas was not so much grieved at the killing of John as διὰ τοὺς ὅρκους καὶ τοὺς (συν)ἀνακειμένους. Up to this point[4] he had avoided killing John out of fear of the people, but now Antipas would make John a martyr to his own shame.[5] Matthew is not so much contradicting Mark's account as trying to come immediately to the point of the narrative, namely that it was Antipas who assigned or directed the killing.[6] Although Herodias may have done the scheming, it was Antipas who was finally responsible for the Baptist's death. This is borne out by Luke.[7]

[1] Mt. 14: 5; Mk. 6: 19.

[2] A. Plummer, 'Review of *The Gospel according to St Mark, the Greek Text, with Introduction, Notes and Indices*', by H. B. Swete, *JTS*, I (1900), 619. Field contends with Bois 'that these are *effects* of malevolence, not ill-feeling itself, which the writer intended to express, and could not have been expressed better than by ἐνεῖχεν, *had a grudge against him*... There is no example of this use of the word in classical writers except in Herodotus, with the addition of χόλον, which is necessary to bring out the proper force of ἐνέχειν, *to hold* or *keep within, to cherish an inward feeling*; e.g. Herod. vi. 119: ἐνεῖχέ σφι δεινὸν χόλον. viii. 27: ἅτε σφι ἐνέχοντες αἰεὶ χόλον' (F. Field, *Notes on the Translation of the New Testament*[2] [Cambridge, 1899], pp. 28-9). Another reference of its use with χόλος is Herodotus i. 118. The best example of its use in the LXX is in Gen. 49: 23: καὶ ἐνεῖχον αὐτῷ [Joseph] κύριοι τοξευμάτων where it is corresponding to שָׂטַם 'to bear a grudge, cherish animosity, against' (BDB, p. 966).

[3] Klostermann, *Matthäusevangelium*, p. 127; cf. also R. Walker, *Die Heilsgeschichte im ersten Evangelium*, FRLANT, XCI (Göttingen, 1967), 40.

[4] Mt. 14: 9; Mk. 6: 26.

[5] Lohmeyer, *Matthäus*, p. 233. Lohmeyer develops the idea that John's martyrdom was already inherent in his message, cf. E. Lohmeyer, *Das Urchristentum: I. Johannes der Täufer* (Göttingen, 1932), pp. 119-20. An account of Josippon (Sanders and Nahmad, p. 285) identifies John with sages of Israel who also disapproved of Antipas' marriage and were likewise put to death by him (cf. also Neuman, *HUCA*, XXIII, 140).

[6] Trilling, *BZ*, N.F. III, 274-5.　　　　　　[7] Lk. 9: 9.

This is also true of the imprisonment; for although Antipas is pictured by Josephus and Luke as responsible for John's imprisonment,[1] in Matthew and Mark he does it διὰ Ἡρῳδιάδα τὴν γυναῖκα Φιλίππου τοῦ ἀδελφοῦ αὐτοῦ.[2] One must distinguish what appeared to happen in the eyes of the public from what actually happened behind the scenes. These are often difficult and sometimes impossible to distinguish, especially since there is so little knowledge of the events.

One receives the impression that Antipas was ambivalent towards John whereas Herodias was bent on getting rid of him. Because of John's denunciation of his marriage as well as all the rest of his evil deeds,[3] Antipas may have considered him potentially a political hazard. Antipas may have desired not only to imprison him but also to kill him,[4] but he feared the people and/or John. While keeping him safe[5] in prison, possibly from Herodias,[6] he had on occasion heard him. He was greatly perplexed, or had many questions he wanted to raise,[7] and yet

[1] Jos. *Ant.* xviii. 119; Lk. 3: 20.

[2] Mt. 14: 3; Mk. 6: 17.

[3] Mt. 14: 4; Mk. 6: 18; Lk. 3: 19.

[4] Derrett (*BZ*, N.F. ix, 50–1) states that Antipas could by constitutional law decapitate John because of his 'contempt of convention in dealing with the lawfully constituted authority, and in stirring up popular discontent with Antipas', and this is supported by Josh. 1: 18; 2 Sam. 16: 5, 7, 9; TB: Sanh. 49a; Tos.: Sanh. ix. 3; The Code of Maimonides: Mishnah Torah xiv. 5. 3. 8. But surely all these references relate to those who disobey constituted authority and not to those who pronounce moral judgments against a ruler, especially when those pronouncements were in accord with biblical principles. Otherwise all the OT prophets would have to be categorized as law breakers.

[5] Mk. 6: 20 – συνετήρει has not the idea of observing him, as indicated in the AV, but 'to keep safely'. The preposition σύν compounded with verbs has a perfectivizing function, i.e. 'to keep *safe*' (Moulton, pp. 112–13, 116).

[6] J. A. Bengel, *Gnomon of the New Testament*,[7] trans. J. Bandinel and A. R. Fausset, I (Edinburgh, 1873), 523; Robertson, *John the Loyal*, p. 187.

[7] There is a textual problem which is difficult to resolve. The word ἐποίει is attested in A C ℜ D N Σ and by a great host of ancient versions while ἠπόρει is attested in ℵ B L (W) Θ. Field (pp. 29–30) favours the former reading and thinks that there was some concession which Antipas made, John being a sort of spiritual adviser to him. He suggests that ἠπόρει is a correction influenced by διηπόρει in Lk. 9: 7 (cf. also C. A. Webster, 'St Mark vi. 20', *ET*, xlix [1937], 93–4; Lohmeyer, *Markus*, p. 119 n. 5). Wellhausen suggests that it is too literal a rendering of a semitic original and states that ἐποίει is 'gut semitisch' (Wellhausen, *Marci*, p. 46). If this is the true

he heard him gladly. Antipas not only liked to hear him but also granted him privileges such as allowing his disciples to visit him.[1]

Still Herodias' ambition was to get rid of him. For Mark continues by saying καὶ γενομένης ἡμέρας εὐκαίρου ὅτε Ἡρῴδης τοῖς γενεσίοις αὐτοῦ δεῖπνον ἐποίησεν.[2] Although it has been suggested that εὐκαίρου has the meaning of 'empty', in other words, it was a day without work such as a festal day,[3] it seems far more convincing to take it as 'an opportune time'.[4] But for whom was it an opportune time – Antipas (i.e. was his birthday[5] a suitable occasion to give a banquet?) or Herodias?

reading, what were the 'many things' Antipas did? It does not make much sense. The word ἠπόρει 'to be perplexed' should probably be preferred (Taylor, *Mark*, p. 313). The problem with this word is that it seems to contradict the following words καὶ ἡδέως αὐτοῦ ἤκουεν. Milligan suggests that this shows Mark's vivid style by depicting the struggle in Antipas' mind in a double series of contrasts:

'Herod feared John,
And kept him safe.

He was greatly perplexed,
And heard him gladly.'

(W. Milligan, 'Some Recent Critical Readings in the New Testament', *Exp*, 1st series, VII [1878], 137). A better suggestion seems to be that of Bonner who observes that ἀπορέω has the idea 'to be at a loss' or 'to be in doubt'. It had the meaning in the schools and among the more educated 'to raise a question' in dialectic especially when it was difficult or debatable. This passage could be translated 'after hearing him he was wont to raise many questions, and he took pleasure in hearing him' (C. Bonner, 'Note on Mark 6. 20', *HTR*, xxxvii [1944], 41–4; 'Addition and Corrections, Mark 6. 20', *HTR*, xxxviii [1944], 336).

[1] Mt. 11: 2, 4; Lk. 7: 19–20, 22.

[2] Mk. 6: 21.

[3] A. Pallis, *A Few Notes on the Gospels according to St Mark and St Matthew* (Liverpool, 1903), pp. 11–12. This view is supported by Byzantine and modern Greek (cf. MM, p. 262).

[4] Weiss, *Markus und Lukas*, p. 97; Swete, p. 124; Lagrange, *Marc*, p. 159; Lohmeyer, *Markus*, p. 119 n. 7; Taylor, *Mark*, p. 314; Grundmann, *Markus*, p. 130; Cranfield, p. 210.

[5] τοῖς γενεσίοις αὐτοῦ. The plural form is often used of festivals (Robertson, *Grammar*, p. 408). The meaning of γενέσια (Mt. 14: 6; Mk. 6: 21) is debated. A few commentators understand it to mean the anniversary day of Antipas' accession to the throne (cf. K. Wieseler, *A Chronological Synopsis of the Four Gospels*[2], trans E. Venables [London, 1877], pp. 286–90;

The second makes better sense. In that case, the genitive absolute (καὶ γενομένης ἡμέρας εὐκαίρου) is temporal and is further defined by ὅτε ἱρῴδης τοῖς γενεσίοις αὐτοῦ δεῖπνον ἐποίησεν.[1] In English the entire genitive absolute should be made a separate sentence, as does the Weymouth translation: 'At length Herodias found her opportunity.' This conveys the best sense in relation to the context.[2] This is further substantiated later when Herodias' daughter comes to her mother and inquires about what request she should make. Herodias replies so promptly, 'the head of John the Baptist', that prior calculation is obvious.[3] The picture is that Herodias was intent on killing John, but that Antipas was keeping him safe from her grasp. At last Herodias' opportunity came when Antipas was celebrating his birthday.

Later Mark states: 'But I tell you that Elijah has come and

Keim, *Jesus of Nazara*, IV, 223 n. 1; Hausrath, II, 122 n. 4). Most scholars think the evidence points to Antipas' birthday (cf. Schürer, I, 438–40 n. 26; MM, p. 123; M'Neile, p. 209; Lagrange, *Marc*, p. 160; Taylor, *Mark*, p. 314). Some of those holding to the first view think that it may serve as a chronological landmark. If this were true it would be difficult to determine when Antipas would celebrate his accession, i.e. would it have been on the date of his father's death or when Augustus appointed him as tetrarch? If it indicates a birthday then some interesting things are to be observed. The celebration of birthdays was abhorred by the Jews and was considered a Gentile festival (A.Z. i. 3). It was celebrated by the Egyptians (Gen. 40: 20; Jos. *Ant.* xii. 196; *P. Oxy.* 736: 56, 57; *P. Fayum* 114: 20), the Persians (Herodotus i. 133; ix. 110), Greeks (in classical Greek τὰ γενέσια was a day kept in memory of the dead – Herodotus iv. 26 – as distinct from τὰ γενέθλια which was a birthday feast for a living man, but this distinction disappears already in Plato *Leges* vi. 784d and in later Greek, and in the papyri τὰ γενέσια is always a birthday feast – MM, p. 123), Seleucids (2 Macc. 6: 7), and the Romans (Persius *Satura* ii. 1–3; Dio xlvii. 18. 6; lix. 11. 3; cf. also lviii. 2. 7; *Epitomae* lxxviii. 12. 6; Tac. *Hist.* ii. 95; *Ann.* vi. 18). Herod the Great kept the day of his accession which, according to Josephus, was a normal procedure (Jos. *Ant.* xv. 423). But the NT shows that Herod Antipas (Mt. 14: 6; Mk. 6: 21), and Josephus states that King Agrippa I (*Ant.* xix. 321), celebrated their birthdays. It may be that Herod the Great did also celebrate his birthday. Whatever the case may be it seems that the Herods celebrated their birthdays with such magnificence that the 'birthdays of Herod (*Herodis dies*)' had passed into a proverb at the time when Persius (A.D. 34–62) wrote (Persius *Satura* v. 180).

[1] Taylor, *Mark*, p. 314.
[2] J. C. G. Greig, 'εὔκαιρος', *ET*, LXV (1954), 158.
[3] Mk. 6: 24; Taylor, *Mark*, p. 316.

161

they did to him whatever they wished as it is written of him.'[1]
This reference is obviously to John's death caused by Antipas
and Herodias. Furthermore, it refers back to the intended fate
of Elijah[2] which had overtaken John: 'he had found his Jezebel
in Herodias'.[3] Although there are several divergencies in
the present story from that of the Old Testament,[4] some of the
main features are similar in both. Elijah was denouncing the
actions of the royal household and Jezebel was out to kill him,
while Ahab was ambivalent. These same attitudes of Ahab
and Jezebel are portrayed in the seizure of Naboth's vineyard.[5]
The two husbands (Ahab and Antipas) may have wanted at
first to accomplish their designs, but later they became ambivalent. The two wives, however, accomplished their designs by
means not always known to their husbands.

It has also been suggested that Antipas wanted to kill John
because Herodias exerted pressure on him. On the other hand,
he was human enough to fear John and the people.[6]

Therefore, the divergence between Matthew and Mark may
be explained on the supposition that in Matthew's abbreviated
account there is a desire to come to the point of the narrative,
namely, that it was Antipas who in the end was responsible for
John's death. Or it may be that although at first Antipas
wanted to kill John, later he came to fear him and/or the people
and was satisfied with having him imprisoned. But Herodias
wanted more than imprisonment – she was determined to get
rid of him.

Whom Antipas feared

The second problem arises out of the first. According to Matthew, Antipas did not want to kill John because he feared the
people; but according to Mark it was because he feared John,

---

[1] Mk. 9: 13; cf. also Mt. 17: 12–13; Just. *Dial.* xlix. 5 (*MPG*, VI, 584).
Swete has pointed out that the phrase ποιεῖν ὅσα (ἃ) θέλω (τινί) is
'frequently used in the O.T. to represent irresponsible or arbitrary action
(e.g. 3 Regn. ix. 1, x. 13, Ps. cxiii. 11 (cxv. 3), Dan. viii. 4 (Th.), 2 Macc. vii.
16)' (Swete, p. 194).

[2] 1 Kgs. 19: 2, 10, 14.

[3] Swete, p. 194.

[4] Derrett (*BZ*, N.F. IX, 54–5) has outlined the divergencies of the two
stories.

[5] 1 Kgs. 21: 1–29.   [6] Gams, pp. 217–18.

whom he knew to be a righteous and holy man.[1] Josephus states that John was a good man[2] and that Antipas feared his apparent control over the crowds.[3] These are not contradictory but are complementary to one another. Antipas was not afraid of John personally, for he seized and imprisoned him, but he was afraid of his influence upon the crowd. In the same way the chief priests and elders were afraid to answer Jesus' question about John's baptism because the crowd considered John a prophet.[4] Likewise, Antipas would be afraid of what the crowd might have done if he had killed John. Matthew, in his abbreviated account, again comes to the point of the narrative, namely, that Antipas feared the crowd because of their regard and devotion for John.[5] The case of Jesus is analogous in that the leaders of the Jews feared to kill him because of what the multitude thought, or might do to them.[6]

The leaders of a people cannot be separated from the people themselves. Only a few years ago one could hear in the U.S.A. of some being afraid of what Khrushchev might do and others of what the Russians might do. When analysed, the people of the U.S.A. were not afraid of Khrushchev personally or of the Russians as a nation, but only of what Khrushchev might have caused the Russians to do against the West. Thus to be afraid of the leader and to be afraid of the people are one and the same thing.

It was bad enough for Antipas to have imprisoned John on such a flimsy excuse, but to have killed him immediately might have put his own position in jeopardy. To kill a leader of a group who was a danger to society is one thing, but to kill a

---

[1] Mt. 14: 5; Mk. 6: 20.

[2] The Slavonic version of Josephus speaks of John as wild man. Eisler suggests that the church changed ἄγριος to ἀγαθός (Eisler, ΙΗΣΟΥΣ, II, 58 n. 1 [Eng. trans. p. 248]). Feldman observes that this is a reckless suggestion on the part of Eisler (cf. Feldman, *Josephus*, LCL, IX, 81 n. c).

[3] Jos. *Ant.* xviii. 117–19.

[4] Mt. 21: 26; Mk. 11: 32; Lk. 20: 6. 'Not only was the movement one of no mean proportions but its founder was an outstanding personality' (E. W. Parsons, 'John the Baptist and Jesus. An Essay in Historical Reconstruction', *Studies in Early Christianity*, ed. by S. J. Case [New York and London, 1928], p. 163).

[5] Cf. Trilling, *BZ*, N.F. III, 274.

[6] Cf. Mk. 11: 18 = Lk. 19: 47; Mt. 21: 46 = Mk. 12: 12 = Lk. 20: 19; Mt. 26: 4–5; Mk. 14: 1–2 = Lk. 22: 2.

man who was holy and righteous and considered a prophet is quite another. Here, Antipas' fear after imprisoning John is understandable.

Whose idea it was to ask for John's head

The third problem is closely allied with the two former ones. When Antipas asked Herodias' daughter what she would like, Matthew states that she immediately made known her request, whereas in Mark she went to her mother for advice and returned to ask Antipas.[1] Justin Martyr's version is similar to Mark.[2] Matthew seems to have the same course of events but omitted the details in his condensed account. This is supported by two factors. (1) The word προβιβάζω had the meaning in classical Greek 'to cause to step forward' or 'to lead on'[3] but in the Septuagint it means 'to give instruction'.[4] Here it clearly bears the latter meaning.[5] (2) The head was brought to Salome who gave it

[1] Mt. 14: 8; Mk. 6: 24–5. With regard to εὐθύς in Mk. 6: 25 Daube states: 'Whether the meaning is nearer "immediately" – she came while the King was still at the table – or "accordingly" – in pursuance of her mother's advice – is hard to say. D omits the adverb' (D. Daube, *The Sudden in the Scriptures* [Leiden, 1964], p. 54). The former is more likely for it seems that Antipas was still at the banquet table when the embarrassing request came to him. The prepositional phrase μετὰ σπουδῆς would further substantiate this suggestion. There is also ἐξαυτῆς (Mk. 6: 25) which has the meaning of 'at once', and ὧδε 'here' (Mt. 14: 8), which support the idea that Salome's wish was to be completed before the banquet was dismissed (cf. Swete, p. 126).

[2] Cf. *Dial.* xlix. 4 (*MPG*, vi, 584). One Islamic account of this is altogether different from the above narrative. According to it, both Herodias and her daughter made the king promise to grant her whatever she asked. She asked to be allowed to interview the prisoners, and the king agreed, thinking she was sorry for them and wished to help them. The prisoners paraded before the queen and when she saw John she demanded his execution. She placed his head on a dish and her daughter presented it to the king (cf. Gibson, *MW*, xlv, 344).

[3] LSJ, p. 1471. This is its probable sense in Acts 19: 33.

[4] It is only used twice in the LXX (although also in Aquila Ps. 42 [41]: 5; Isa. 38: 15). In Exod. 35: 34 it is translated from the hiph'il of יָרָה (הוֹרֹת) meaning 'to direct, teach, instruct' (BDB, p. 435) and in Deut. 6: 7 it is translated from the pi'el of שָׁנַן (שִׁנֵּן) meaning 'to teach incisively' or the German 'einschärfen' (BDB, p. 1042).

[5] Cf. M'Neile, p. 210; cf. also MM, p. 538; Bauer/AG, p. 710. The AV has 'being before instructed' but Field has stated, 'instead of "before instructed" perhaps "instructed" would be sufficient, the instruction neces-

to her mother, Herodias. The same procedure is in Mark.[1] A severed head in those days was evidence that the person was killed,[2] and who but Herodias wanted proof of this? Apparently Matthew thought the detail of the girl running to her mother was not sufficiently important to be included. Even without this detail it is clear that Herodias was the schemer,[3] for she instructed her daughter. Antipas was grieved that he was caught in an embarrassing situation, and that the head was given to Herodias was evidence that her scheme had succeeded.[4]

MISCELLANEOUS CONSIDERATIONS

Antipas' oath

It has been pointed out that Antipas' lavish oaths are similar to those made by the Emperor Gaius to Herod Agrippa at a feast to which Agrippa had invited him.[5] Agrippa requested Gaius to abandon all further thought of having a statue of himself erected in the Jerusalem temple.[6]

Between the stories there are three similarities. First, the oaths seem to have been repeated. In Mark, Antipas twice asks Salome to make a request, and although in Matthew's condensed version Antipas' promise with an oath is only given once,[7] he agrees with Mark that Antipas was grieved διὰ τοὺς

sarily preceding the action' (p. 11). Lohmeyer believes that προβιβάζω indicates more than merely being instructed; it discloses a plot between the mother and daughter (Matthäus, p. 233).

[1] Mt. 14: 11; Mk. 6: 28.

[2] When Aretas made war on Antipas, Tiberius commanded Vitellius either to bring Aretas to him in chains if he were captured alive, or if he were killed to send him his head (Jos. Ant. xviii. 115).

[3] Against this are Trilling (BZ, N.F. III, 272) and Lohmeyer (Matthäus, p. 233) who feel that Matthew is only understandable when one is familiar with the story. It may be that those who read Matthew were familiar with the story, but even without a previous knowledge Matthew is understandable. If Luke had given a fuller account than the other evangelists, it is probable that commentators would say that without the third account the other two would not be understandable!

[4] It seems incredible that such a thing would be allowed at a banquet! Yet Herodias' ancestor, Alexander Jannaeus, while holding a feast with his concubines, commanded 800 rebels to be crucified in full view, and their wives and children to be slain before their eyes (Jos. Ant. xiii. 380).

[5] Gams, pp. 239–40; Bruce, ALUOS, v, 13.

[6] Jos. Ant. xviii. 289–304.   [7] Mk. 6: 22, 23; Mt. 14: 7.

ὅρκους.[1] The plural suggests repeated oaths[2] unless it is meant as a generalizing plural.[3] In Josephus, Gaius twice asks Agrippa to make a petition.[4] In both accounts the one who extended the offer was sorry when the request was made. Although Josephus does not state specifically that Gaius made a ὅρκος, nevertheless he could not go back on his word without incurring the charge of falsehood.[5]

The second similarity grows out of the first: both accounts emphasize the fact that the promise was made before so many witnesses,[6] and thus could not be broken with propriety. Derrett feels that the main emphasis is not on the promise, but rather on the oath.[7] But this is improbable for several reasons. (1) It is doubtful that Mark 6:26 (οὐκ ἠθέλησεν ἀθετῆσαι) suggests that the Pharisees present at the banquet (Derrett's assumption that Pharisees were present cannot be proved) were urging him to release himself from his oath.[8] Rather, it suggests that Antipas did not personally want to disappoint Salome on account of his dilemma.[9] (2) It is doubtful if the guests were placed in an embarrassing situation.[10] Rather, it was Antipas who was embarrassed before his guests, as is clearly indicated by both Matthew and Mark. (3) Derrett seems to contradict himself. On the one hand he rejects the interpretation that Antipas was afraid to compromise himself before witnesses, and on the other hand he states that if Antipas broke

---

[1] Mt. 14: 9; Mk. 6: 26.   [2] Taylor, *Mark*, p. 316.

[3] Cf. J. Jeremias, 'Beobachtungen zu neutestamentlichen Stellen an Hand des neugefundenen griechischen Henoch-Texts', *ZNW*, XXXVIII (1939), 115–16.

[4] Jos. *Ant*. xviii. 293, 296. Josephus states that when Agrippa refused to ask a favour after the first offer, Gaius all the more insisted (πλειόνως ἐνέκειτο). Josephus states that with zeal he actively constrained Agrippa to make a request (προθύμως ἐβιάζετο αἰτεῖσθαι τὸν Ἀγρίππαν μετὰ τοῦ ὀξέος), cf. *Ant*. xviii. 299.

[5] Jos. *Ant*. xviii. 299.

[6] Mt. 14: 9; Mk. 6: 26; Jos. *Ant*. xviii. 299; Bruce, *ALUOS*, v, 13.

[7] Derrett, *BZ*, N.F. IX, 51.

[8] *Ibid*. p. 232. An Islamic account has Antipas trying to release himself from killing John by asking the daughter to make another request. She refused to do so and so he was obliged to kill John (H. Schützinger, 'Die arabische Legende von Nebukadnezar und Johannes dem Täufer', *Der Islam*, XL (1965), 115–16; cf. also 128).

[9] Below, p. 167.

[10] Derrett, *BZ*, N.F. IX, 235–9.

the oath before these witnesses there would be far-reaching consequences.[1] (4) It seems unlikely that there was a discussion on whether or not Antipas should be released from his oath.[2] It is more likely that the guests waited quietly to see how he was going to get out of his dilemma. In conclusion, while the oath in itself presented a problem, it was really the making of this oath before so many witnesses that gave rise to his embarrassment. Had he broken the oath, especially if it were to save the life of John, he would have lost face in the eyes of the distinguished guests to a degree which he was not disposed to endure.[3]

The third similarity between the two stories is the way each of the rulers got out of the dilemma. Gaius reasoned that the promise should not be broken because of Agrippa's good character and the motive behind the request.[4] Antipas, for his part, did not want to disappoint Salome[5] and accordingly (εὐθύς)[6] gave orders for the execution. Both rulers pleaded honourable motives to escape their dilemma.

In conclusion, the three similarities bear on the attitudes of two men in face of promises which they did not want to honour, their attitudes towards the distinguished witnesses around them, and towards those to whom the promises were made. In both cases the ruler was obliged to fulfil his promise due to the presence of important witnesses. To have done otherwise would have raised doubts as to his integrity as their leader.

---

[1] *Ibid.* pp. 236–9.   [2] *Ibid.*

[3] Bruce, *ALUOS*, v, 13.   [4] Jos. *Ant.* xviii. 300.

[5] Mk. 6: 26: οὐκ ἠθέλησεν ἀθετῆσαι αὐτήν. The word ἀθετέω has the idea of 'setting aside' but here it seems to mean 'to disappoint' or 'to break faith'. Field (p. 30) cites Ps. 15 (14): 4: ὁ ὀμνύων τῷ πλησίον αὐτοῦ καὶ οὐκ ἀθετῶν and gives the prayer book translation, 'He that sweareth unto his neighbour and *disappointeth* him not'.

[6] Mk. 6: 27. It is difficult to determine whether εὐθύς means 'immediately' in the light of the context (cf. above, p. 164 n. 1) or the idea of 'accordingly' or 'as it had to happen'. Daube prefers the latter and states: 'The action in question here is preceded by reluctance, conflicting feelings, though finally the King decides he has no choice. The adverb, it is evident, does not signify "immediately"; it signifies "accordingly", "duly", "as had to happen"' (Daube, *Sudden*, p. 54).

Characterizations in the story

Briefly stated, are the characterizations of Herodias and Antipas true to life? With regard to Herodias, the present pericope gives an excellent characterization of her as 'an opportunist, a wily schemer, a woman motivated by deep-seated jealousies and overvaulting ambitions, a veritable Lady Macbeth'.[1] This same picture of her is presented by Josephus when she divorces her former husband to marry Antipas,[2] and when she is roused to envy at her brother Agrippa I receiving the title *king*. She insisted that Antipas should go to Rome to ask for a similar advancement, which in the end brought about his and her downfall.[3]

With regard to Antipas, the characterization given in this pericope is also true to him. 'Der galiläische Kleinfürst ist kein Löwe, sondern ein Fuchs, und nicht einmal das, er ist feig und träge, misstrauisch und abergläubisch, unentschieden und unentschlossen, immer passiv, immer Geschobene.'[4] In the present pericope John seems to have denounced Antipas' and Herodias' marriage for quite a while before Antipas took any action.[5] He imprisoned John because of Herodias, and rather than kill him, he kept him safe from Herodias. Though perplexed he kept on hearing him.[6] Again it was Herodias who took the decisive step in killing John. When Salome made the request for John's head, Antipas again was hesitant. Antipas, hearing of Jesus, wanted to see him.[7] Although it is said of Antipas that he wanted to kill Jesus, nothing ever came of this. In fact it is later stated in the same Gospel that Antipas only desired to see Jesus.[8] The reason for Antipas not killing Jesus may be that he never spoke directly against the royal family or offended Herodias. This is significant, since Jesus had a greater following than John, and his followers were quite ready to make

---

[1] Kraeling, *John*, p. 86.   [2] Jos. *Ant.* xviii. 110.

[3] *Ibid.* xviii. 240–55.

[4] Stauffer, *Jerusalem*, p. 94; cf. also 151 n. 58.

[5] In both Mt. 14: 4 and Mk. 6: 18 the ἔλεγεν is probably an iterative imperfect (cf. Stauffer, *Jerusalem*, p. 151 n. 52; M'Neile, p. 209; Robertson, *John the Loyal*, p. 183).

[6] Again in Mk. 6: 20 the verbs ἠπόρει and ἤκουεν seem to be iterative imperfects.

[7] Lk. 9: 9.   [8] Lk. 23: 8.

him their king.[1] This ambivalence or indecisiveness on the part of Antipas is also portrayed in four incidents in Josephus. (1) Antipas went to Rome to make a claim for his father's throne only after he had been encouraged by Salome's promises to support him.[2] (2) When Antipas returned from Rome after his compact with Herodias it is Aretas' daughter who took the initiative to leave.[3] It is nowhere mentioned that he made any attempt to tell her of his compact with Herodias. It may be that information concerning his intentions was deliberately permitted to leak so that he would not have to tell her directly. (3) Antipas seems to have hesitated over the imprisonment of John the Baptist. He did so only out of fear of a possible uprising.[4] Perhaps Herodias tried to impress upon him the danger. (4) Antipas was ambivalent in seeking the title of king, though Herodias was urging him to do so, and finally succeeded in persuading him.[5]

Chronological considerations

The time of John's death

The time of John's death is impossible to determine with certainty. Even if one accepts the interpretation that γενέσια has reference to Antipas' accession, there are differences of opinion when this would have been celebrated. For example, Wieseler thinks it would have been in the spring, at the time of Herod the Great's death;[6] Hausrath thinks it was in late summer,[7] and Keim in autumn or winter.[8] Schofield thinks a clue is given by the fact that the feeding of the five thousand comes immediately after the news of John's death was conveyed to Jesus. According to John's Gospel, this was near the time of the Passover, while the other evangelists record that the people sat on the grass. Grass is not much in evidence except in the spring. Thus the beheading must have been just before the Passover in A.D. 29.[9] But the sequence may not be chronological. Even if it

---

[1] Jn. 6: 15.   [2] Jos. *Ant.* xvii. 224; *BJ* ii. 20.
[3] Jos. *Ant.* xviii. 111–12.
[4] Jos. *Ant.* xviii. 117–18; Stauffer, *Jerusalem*, pp. 151–2 n. 60.
[5] Jos. *Ant.* xviii. 240–6.
[6] Wieseler, *Chronological Synopsis*, p. 290.
[7] Hausrath, II, 122 n. 4.   [8] Keim, *Jesus of Nazara*, IV, 223 n. 1.
[9] Schofield, p. 144.

is, what part of the pericope should be considered as occurring at that time – his arrest, or his death, or both? Finally, and foremost, this chronological calculation is invalid because the present pericope is only a flashback of the discussion about Antipas' hearing of Jesus. Thus it would have no necessary link chronologically with the feeding of the 5,000. In conclusion, it is impossible to determine the exact time of John's death from extant sources.

The length of John's imprisonment

How long was John in prison before he was beheaded? Josephus gives the impression that John was beheaded immediately, or very soon after his imprisonment.[1] On the other hand, Josephus' account does not demand this interpretation. There are some hints in the Gospels that there was an interval between his imprisonment and decapitation. (1) Right after the arrest Antipas desired to kill John but was fearful of the crowd.[2] (2) Antipas kept him safely (συντηρέω), presumably from Herodias' reach.[3] (3) Antipas kept on asking John questions, and though continually perplexed yet gladly kept on hearing him. These probably are iterative imperfects which imply at least some interval of time.[4] (4) The words ἡμέρας εὐκαίρου seem to imply that after some interval Herodias found her opportunity to do away with John.[5] It would seem, then, that a considerable time elapsed between Herodias' desire to kill John and its accomplishment. (5) Immediately after John's imprisonment, Jesus withdrew to Galilee.[6] Later, John sent his disciples to Jesus to enquire if he were the expected One or if they should look for another.[7] The interval between these two events seems to have been quite extensive. In both Matthew and Luke a large portion of Jesus' Galilaean ministry is included between these two points. Besides, John had heard of the many good works which Jesus had done, and this again would imply a considerable interval of time. Finally, John's question implies

---

[1] *Ant.* xviii. 119.   [2] Mt. 14: 5; Mk. 6: 19–20; above, pp. 162–4.
[3] Mk. 6: 20; above, p. 159.
[4] Mk. 6: 20; cf. above, p. 168 n. 5.
[5] Mk. 6: 21; cf. above, pp. 160–1.
[6] Mt. 4: 12; Mk. 1: 14; cf. also Lk. 4: 14.
[7] Mt. 11: 2–6; Lk. 7: 18–23.

that if Jesus were to usher in the Messianic age, why had he not done so already? John may have thought that Jesus had defaulted, and consequently that someone else was to be expected. How much time elapsed after John's enquiry is impossible to determine, for the pericope of John's death is only a flash-back of Antipas' hearing of Jesus' fame and thus of no significance for chronology.

In conclusion, then, it seems that there was a considerable interval between John's imprisonment and death. Although it is possible that it was only a few months, it seems more probable that it was nearly a year or longer. If one accepts A.D. 30 as the date of crucifixion, then one would probably place John's imprisonment in the spring of 28 and his death early in 29. However, if one accepts A.D. 33 as the year of crucifixion, as the present author does, then one would probably place John's imprisonment sometime between 30 and 31 and his death probably either in 31 or 32.[1]

---

[1] Above, pp. 130–1; cf. also Appendix VII.

CHAPTER 8

ANTIPAS AND PILATE

Although Pilate's career in Palestine began before John's ministry, the incidents therein which may have had some bearing on his relationship with Antipas probably had not occurred until after John's death. Hence the location of the present chapter.

Pilate arrived in Judaea[1] in A.D. 26[2] as the fifth Roman procurator and was in office for a period of ten years.[3] His pre-

[1] Jos. *Ant.* xviii. 35; *BJ* ii. 169.

[2] This is the probable date of Pilate's entrance into office. Valerius Gratus, Pilate's predecessor, held office for eleven years (Jos. *Ant.* xviii. 35), A.D. 15–26. An entirely different type of coin for the years 29/30 to 31/2 is attributed to Pilate (cf. Madden, *Jewish Coinage*, pp. 147–51; *Coins of the Jews*, pp. 182–3; Hill, pp. 257–60; Hedley, *JTS*, xxxv, 57; E. Stauffer, 'Zur Münzprägung und Judenpolitik des Pontius Pilatus', *La Nouvelle Clio*, I/II (1950), 496, 501. Kindler thinks that there was a coin in Pilate's era as early as A.D. 27/8 if one reads IΔ rather than IH (as does Madden, *Coins of the Jews*, p. 183). This would be the 14th year of Tiberius (A. Kindler, 'More Dates on the Coins of the Procurators', *IEJ*, VI [1956], 56). But this suggestion is improbable for three reasons: (1) If one looks at the coin (cf. Madden, *Coins of the Jews*, p. 183; Kindler, no. 18, pl. 8) the inscription is clearly IH, and not IΔ as Kindler suggests. (2) On the reverse side the type is changed. It both has a wreath which was not used from A.D. 6 to 29/30, and excludes Livia (cf. Madden, *Coins of the Jews*, p. 183; Kindler, no. 18, pl. 8) who was otherwise included from the time of Tiberius' accession until her death in A.D. 29. It is unreasonable to suppose that they would stop one type of coin, introduce an entirely different type for only one year, then continue with the first type for another two or three years, and then reintroduce the coin type which was only used for one year as part of a series from A.D. 29 to 31/2. (3) On the obverse side of the coin (Madden, *Coins of the Jews*, p. 183) there is a crook curved to the right which identifies this coin with the type after Livia's death. Why would there be a coin type introduced for only one year when the same coin type is again used in a series of years? It seems more reasonable that this coin should read IH (as suggested by Madden, *Coins of the Jews*, p. 183) and thus be placed in the year 31/2 as the last of the series which began after Livia's death in 29/30. Therefore, one has no coins early in Pilate's rule to help establish the precise date of his accession.

[3] The words δέκα ἔτεσιν διατρίψας ἐπὶ Ἰουδαίας (Jos. *Ant.* xviii. 89) give a round figure probably calculated to the nearest year. It agrees well with Gratus' stay of 11 years (*Ant.* xviii. 35) which fits within the reign of

decessors were Coponius (*ca.* A.D. 6–9),[1] Marcus Ambivulus (or Ambibulus or Ambivius, *ca.* A.D. 9–12),[2] Annius Rufus (A.D. 12–15),[3] and Valerius Gratus (A.D. 15–26),[4] who ruled from the time of the deposition of Archelaus. They are only briefly mentioned and there is no account of their relationship with Antipas.

Pilate is described by his contemporary Philo,[5] and later by Josephus,[6] as being one who was greedy, inflexible, cruel, and resorted to robbery and oppression. Almost immediately upon his arrival in Palestine, he was at odds with the Jews. In both accounts of Josephus, his first act of provocation against the Jews was the introducing of Roman standards into Jerusalem.[7] This aroused great indignation on the part of the Jews, and as a result they sent a delegation to Caesarea, to plead for their removal.[8] Finally, when Pilate realized that the Jews would

Tiberius (*Ant.* xviii. 177). Holzmeister suggests that Gratus' accession should be dated in A.D. 15 rather than 16 because, when there was a change of emperors, the procurators of the former emperor lost their position. Tiberius' accession was so late in A.D. 14 that he did not appoint a successor to Rufus until the following year (U. Holzmeister, 'Wann war Pilatus Prokurator von Judaea?', *Biblica*, xiii [1932], 231). Smallwood rightly rejects this view with regard to procurators losing their position. She gives ample illustrations of new emperors confirming their predecessor's delegates in office (Smallwood, *JJS*, v, 12 n. 5). Therefore the exact date of Gratus' accession is not known.

[1] Jos. *Ant.* xviii. 2, 29, 31; *BJ* ii. 117–18.

[2] Jos. *Ant.* xviii. 31.   [3] Jos. *Ant.* xviii. 32–3.

[4] Jos. *Ant.* xviii. 32–5, 177.   [5] *Leg.* 301–2.

[6] *Ant.* xviii. 55–9; *BJ* ii. 169–77.

[7] *Ant.* xviii. 55–9; *BJ* ii. 169–74; cf. C. H. Kraeling, 'The Episode of the Roman Standards at Jerusalem', *HTR*, xxxv (1942), 263–89.

[8] Apparently it was not the standards *per se* but the embossed figures of the emperor (προτομὰς καίσαρος) that bothered the Jews (Jos. *Ant.* xviii. 55; cf. *BJ* ii. 169). The Jews had allowed other procurators to bring standards without images into Jerusalem (*Ant.* xviii. 56). Also, according to Jos. *Ant.* xviii. 59, the εἰκόνες were removed from Jerusalem (though in *BJ* ii. 174 the σημαῖαι were removed). It seems that the Jews objected in this case on the basis of a rigid interpretation of their Law against the making of images (cf. Exod. 20: 4; Deut. 4: 16; cf. also J.-B. Frey, 'La question des images chez les Juifs. A la lumière des récentes découvertes', *Biblica*, xv [1934], 273–82. Specifically the prohibition was against the production or use of any representation of men or animals, cf. Schürer, ii, 65; E. Bevan, *Holy Images* [London, 1940], pp. 48–9; E. Goodenough, *Jewish Symbols in the Greco-Roman Period*, iv [New York, 1954], 11–24).

rather die than transgress their laws, he ordered their removal. This probably occurred in his first year in Judaea.[1]

Josephus' second recorded conflict was when Pilate seized funds from the sacred treasury known as the Corbonas for constructing an aqueduct.[2] Later when Pilate visited Jerusalem, the Jews besieged him with angry clamour and he, seeing the possibility of an uprising, ordered his soldiers to mingle with the crowd dressed as civilians armed with hidden clubs (σκυτά-λας). When the protest became more pronounced the soldiers, on a pre-arranged signal, drew the clubs from under their tunics and began to beat them, killing many.[3]

Josephus records one final conflict as a result of which Pilate was dismissed.[4] In A.D. 36 a Samaritan false prophet promised his followers that he would show them the sacred vessels which according to tradition Moses had buried on Mount Gerizim. Believing him, his hearers gathered with arms at a village at the foot of the mountain,[5] named Tirathana.[6] When

---

[1] Josephus (*Ant.* xviii. 55) states that the troops were going to their winter quarters in Jerusalem. If *Megillat Taanit* ix (for text and discussion, see S. Zeitlin, 'Megillat Taanit as a source for Jewish Chronology and History in the Hellenistic and Roman Periods', *JQR*, x [1919–20], 239, 241, 259–61) is speaking of the same incident, it means that the standards were removed on 3 Chislev. According to Parker and Dubberstein (p. 46) 3 Chislev would have been 2 December in A.D. 26.

[2] *BJ* ii. 175–7; *Ant.* xviii. 60–2. With regard to this treasury, Zeitlin (*Judaean State*, II, 143) states: 'The money in this treasury was not in the same category as the communal money of the Temple, but was considered private property held as a religious trust. It consisted of the sums deposited by the Nazarites for their sacrifices and was not to be used for any other purpose.'

[3] Eus. *HE* ii. 6. 6–7 quotes Jos. *BJ* ii. 175–7 verbatim, except for an alteration in the length of the aqueduct.

[4] *Ant.* xviii. 85–9.

[5] The Samaritans believed that the *Taheb* (Messiah) would reveal the hidden vessels; cf. M. Gaster, *The Samaritans* (London, 1925), pp. 90–1; J. MacDonald, *The Theology of the Samaritans* (London, 1964), p. 365.

[6] J. A. Montgomery, *The Samaritans* (Philadelphia, 1907), p. 146 n. 15 suggests that this is the modern *Tire*, four miles southwest of Shechem. For different conjectures, see G. Hölscher, 'Tirathana', PW, 2. Reihe, VI, 2 (1937), 1431. H. G. May, R. W. Hamilton, and G. N. S. Hunt (eds.), *Oxford Bible Atlas* (London, 1962), p. 87, place Tirathana about one to one and a quarter miles northeast of Mount Gerizim or about three-quarters of a mile south of Sychar and about two miles southeast of Neapolis.

the pilgrimage was about to take place, Pilate blocked the projected route with a detachment of cavalry and heavily-armed infantry. Some they killed in battle, others were imprisoned, still others fled. The more prominent prisoners were later executed. The Samaritans complained to Vitellius, prefect of Syria, who shortly afterwards sent Marcellus to take temporary charge of Judaea, ordering Pilate to report to Tiberius.[1] Pilate probably left Palestine towards the end of A.D. 36 or the beginning of 37.[2]

There are two other incidents involving Pilate which are not mentioned in Josephus. Both of these would have had an effect upon the relationship between Pilate and Antipas.

The first is mentioned in Luke 13:1. Some people came to Jesus[3] and told of the Galilaeans whose blood Pilate had mingled with their sacrifices. Although this incident is not mentioned by Josephus, the character of Pilate portrayed in this act is in agreement with that of Josephus and Philo. It is not Josephus' purpose to give every incident of Pilate's brutality. It has been suggested that the story was fabricated by those reporting it to Jesus,[4] but there is no convincing reason to doubt its authenticity.[5]

There have been various attempts to harmonize this event with the incidents of the standards, the construction of the water conduit, the conflict with the Samaritans, and other incidents such as the revolt which Archelaus quelled after his father's death, and the slaughter by Alexander Jannaeus. But none of

---

[1] The power to depose a governor or to appoint a successor lay not with a legate but only with the emperor. Therefore the move made by Vitellius was only provisional (cf. S. J. De Laet, 'Le successeur de Ponce-Pilate', *L'Antiquité Classique*, VIII [1939], 413–19). The assumption of Mommsen and Dessau that Vitellius had extraordinary powers in the East similar to those of Gaius Caesar and Germanicus has little evidence to support it (cf. Magie, II, 1364, n. 39).

[2] See Appendix VIII.

[3] The words παρῆσαν δέ τινες are better translated 'they came' or 'they had come' rather than 'they were present' (cf. Plummer, *Luke*, pp. 337–8; Creed, *Luke*, p. 180; J. Blinzler, 'Die Niedermetzelung von Galiläern durch Pilatus', *NovT*, II [1957], 25 n. 2).

[4] For a brief discussion of this, see T. W. Manson, *Sayings*, p. 273.

[5] Cf. C. H. Dodd, *The Parables of the Kingdom*[3] (London, 1936), p. 65; J. Blinzler, *Der Prozess Jesu*[4] (Regensburg, 1969), p. 291; P. Winter, *On the Trial of Jesus*, *SJ*, I (Berlin, 1961), p. 176 n. 9.

these attempts are satisfactory.[1] Since the event most likely occurred at a Passover and since it was reported to Jesus (rather than Jesus giving the story as the one who had witnessed it), it is propounded by Blinzler that it occurred at the Passover of the year before his death – the one which Jesus did not attend in Jerusalem, remaining in Galilee (Jn. 6:4).[2] Whether or not these Galilaeans were Zealots, as some suggest,[3] is impossible to determine.[4] Nevertheless, Pilate's conduct toward the Galilaeans, whether or not justified, may well have caused enmity between himself and Antipas.

The second incident involving Pilate is described by Philo, who extols Tiberius' liberal policy towards the Jews.[5] According to Philo, Pilate distressed the people more than he honoured Tiberius in that he set up in the former palace of Herod the Great gilded votive shields bearing the name, though not the image, of the emperor. When Pilate refused to hear their request, the prominent Jews, including the four sons of Herod,

[1] It is beyond the scope of this chapter to treat the various attempts, but for a discussion on the various harmonizations Blinzler should be consulted (*NovT*, II, 32–7).

[2] J. Blinzler, 'Eine Bemerkung zum Geschichtsrahmen des Johannesevangeliums', *Biblica*, XXXVI (1955), 20–35; cf. also E. E. Ellis, *The Gospel of Luke* (London, 1966), p. 184.

[3] This suggestion has been made by Eisler, ΙΗΣΟΥΣ, II, 513–25 (Eng. trans. pp. 505–10); H. G. Wood, 'Interpreting This Time', *NTS*, II (1956), 263; O. Cullmann, *The State in the New Testament* (London, 1957), p. 14; Bultmann, pp. 54–5. Blinzler (*NovT*, II, 44–9) suggests that after Jesus' withdrawal, the Galilaean crowd went on to keep the Passover at Jerusalem, where, however, their messianic aspirations alarmed Pilate and caused him to suppress them. He argues that Jesus, foreseeing the 'messiaspolitische Demonstrationen', did not himself go to Jerusalem.

[4] M. Hengel, *Die Zeloten* (Leiden and Köln, 1961), p. 344; Grundmann, *Lukas*, p. 276. Corbishley puts forth the theory that the Galilaeans were some of the victims of the former massacre, and that the στάσις in Jerusalem which resulted in the imprisonment of the well-known brigand (λῃστής) Barabbas and his band (Mt. 27: 16; Mk. 15: 7; Lk. 23: 18–19; Jn. 18: 40) was a part of the disturbance (T. Corbishley, 'Pontius Pilate', *The Clergy Review*, XII [1936], 375–6). Although attractive, this theory has to assume too much. It has to assume that Barabbas was a Galilaean and that he was imprisoned for his part in the incident mentioned in Lk. 13: 1. If Barabbas was imprisoned because of this, Luke would probably have alluded to it when mentioning Barabbas, especially since he does give a vivid description of him.

[5] Philo *Leg.* 299–305.

appealed to the Emperor Tiberius. Whereupon Tiberius expressed the strongest disapproval of Pilate's action and ordered him to take down the shields and to have them transferred to the temple of Augustus at Caesarea.

Graetz,[1] and more recently Colson,[2] think that this incident, recorded by Philo, is only a variant tradition of the standard episode mentioned by Josephus. Pilate's actions are not altogether clear in Eusebius' writings. In *Historia Ecclesiastica* ii. 6. 4 he records the standard episode, stating Josephus as his source. In the *Demonstratio Evangelica* viii. 2. 122 he records that Pilate brought by night images of Caesar not merely into Jerusalem but into the ἱερόν.[3] In the very next verse (*DE* viii. 2. 123) Eusebius cites Philo along with Josephus as his source that Pilate took the σημαῖαι into the ἱερόν. Schürer thinks that this may mean that Philo had recorded the incident of the Roman standards, but that his record is no longer extant.[4] A more probable solution is that Eusebius assumed that Philo and Josephus were variants of a single episode.[5]

Certainly, if one compares the two accounts, it seems improbable that they are variants of the same incident. Some of these differences are summarized by Doyle:

The one concerns standards, the other shields; the standards bore images, the shields did not; the standards affair comes at the beginning of Pilate's term, Philo's story presupposes some years of previous misrule by Pilate; in Josephus the people appeal to Pilate at Caesarea, and successfully; in Philo first to Pilate unsuccessfully, apparently at Jerusalem, then by letter to Tiberius successfully.[6]

Thus it seems that Philo is recording an entirely different episode from that of Josephus.

In *Legatio ad Gaium* Philo is making a polemic directed against

[1] III, 285–6.

[2] F. H. Colson (trans.), *Philo*, vol. x of *LCL*, xix–xx.

[3] A similar exaggeration, to the effect that they were brought into the temple, is given in Eus. *Chron.* II, 149–50 and by Origen *Commentarii in Evangelium Matthaei* xvii. 27 (*MPG*, XIII, 1549) where ναός is used rather than ἱερόν; and by Jerome *Commentarii in Evangelium Matthaei* xxiv. 15 (*MPL*, XXVI, 177).

[4] III, 679–80.

[5] E. M. Smallwood (ed.), *Philonis Alexandrini* (Leiden, 1961), p. 302.

[6] A. D. Doyle, 'Pilate's Career and the Date of the Crucifixion', *JTS*, XLII (1941), 190–1.

Gaius, probably written to the new emperor Claudius, demonstrating that God protects the Jews. Gaius tried to uproot their religion but the end result was that he was assassinated by conspirators. In the matter of the shields, he is trying to prove that Tiberius was sympathetic towards the Jews, hoping for the same attitude from Claudius.[1] Hence the tendency would be to select incidents within Tiberius' reign to depict his liberal policy towards the Jews.[2]

The most interesting aspect of this episode of the shields is that four Herodian princes, with the head of the Jewish delegation, appealed to Pilate to remove the shields. Who these four Herodian princes were one can only guess. Antipas and Philip the tetrarch were almost certainly among them, also possibly Herod (Philip) who resided in Palestine and Agrippa I, Herodias' brother. Antipas may have been the spokesman of the group, for he was the most powerful as well as the one closest to Tiberius. The petition, stated in summary form by Philo, was to the effect that Pilate should not cause a revolt (μὴ στασίαϛε), nor destroy the peace (μὴ κατάλυε τὴν εἰρήνην), nor use Tiberius as a pretext for outraging the nation (μὴ πρόφασις τῆς εἰς τὸ ἔθνος ἐπηρείας ἔστω σοι Τιβέριος). Possibly a part of this petition was given by Antipas.[3] Pilate was then

---

[1] For a discussion on this, see E. R. Goodenough, *The Politics of Philo Judaeus* (New Haven, 1938), pp. 3–20; *An Introduction to Philo Judaeus*[2] (Oxford, 1962), pp. 57–60; S. Zeitlin, 'Did Agrippa write a Letter to Gaius Caligula?', *JQR*, LVI (1965), 29.

[2] Cf. *Leg.* 8, 14, 33, 158–61, 298–305, 308.

[3] Since Antipas, probably, was the spokesman of the Jews, could not at least part of the speech mentioned by Philo be attributed to him? If this is so, it is still difficult to know which part Antipas may have spoken and which part has been inserted as polemic by Philo. It is possible that at least those aspects of the speech which have to do with Tiberius were spoken by Antipas. In other words, he would have stated that disrespect to the Jewish Law brings no honour to the emperor and that Pilate should not use Tiberius as the pretext of his actions. Antipas, being a friend of Tiberius, would have known the wishes of the emperor on the religious issue. In fact, Antipas would have been on safe ground in reproving Pilate since Tiberius used to play down emperor worship (cf. L. R. Taylor, 'Tiberius' Refusals of Divine Honors', *TAPA*, LX [1929], 87–101). The other parts of the speech, about causing a revolt and destroying the peace, may have been a part of Philo's polemic or, if a part of Antipas' speech, possibly it was heightened by Philo. Again one must be extremely cautious, for one can do no more than conjecture.

challenged to produce authority for his action or else they would appeal to the emperor, whom they called their lord (δεσπότης).[1] Because of this Pilate became exasperated, for he did not want Tiberius to be informed, nor for that matter did he wish to appear penitent. However, this event was reported to Tiberius by letter, the result of which was that Pilate was ordered to take down the shields immediately.[2]

Two problems remain. Why were these shields offensive, and when did this occur? It is understandable that the standards would be taken as a violation of the Jewish Law since they bore images of the emperor, but in this incident the shields were aniconic. Smallwood suggests that the incident of the standards may have awakened the Jews to the fact that aniconic objects had religious significance for the Romans. Consequently the Jews would have wanted to keep them out of Jerusalem on the grounds that they were the thin end of the wedge.[3] But to aniconic standards the Jews seem to have had no objections. A more probable suggestion is that of Brandon who thinks that the inscription may have contained some reference to the divinity of the emperor, and that it was this which proved offensive to the Jews.[4]

The episode of the votive shields seems to have occurred later in Pilate's administration because: (1) the reference to Pilate's fear of impeachment implies it; (2) the fact that the Jewish embassy was able to report to Tiberius directly, rather than through Sejanus, would seem to indicate that it was after Sejanus' death on 18 October A.D. 31; (3) the fact that Pilate and Antipas, both friends of Sejanus, were opposing each other may also indicate that this event occurred after Sejanus' death. So long as Sejanus was in power Pilate had nothing to fear.

[1] Again because of Antipas being a friend of Tiberius, this seems significant.

[2] Smallwood (*Philonis*, p. 306) thinks that Tiberius' anger against Pilate was 'for having disregarded the instructions which he had issued after Sejanus' death to provincial governors to protect the Jews under their rule'.

[3] Smallwood, *Philonis*, p. 304.

[4] Brandon, *Jesus*, p. 74; cf. also Kraeling, *HTR*, xxxv, 277; Smallwood, *Latomus*, xv, 327. Maier suggests that Jerusalemites were not only oversensitive but Pilate's venture was badly timed politically, cf. P. L. Maier, 'The Episode of the Golden Roman Shields at Jerusalem', *HTR*, LXII (1969), 117–20.

With Sejanus removed, however, both leaders would have wanted at all costs to avoid identification with Sejanus, and each would have looked for opportunities to ingratiate himself with the emperor, and possibly to accuse the other in order to protect himself.[1]

Therefore, it seems most likely that this incident occurred sometime after Sejanus' death, or between 18 October A.D. 31 and the time of Pilate's return to Rome in the winter of 36/7.

There is a curious statement in Luke that the long-standing enmity of Antipas and Pilate was finally removed during the trial of Jesus. He states: ἐγένοντο δὲ φίλοι ὅ τε Ἡρῴδης καὶ ὁ Πιλᾶτος ἐν αὐτῇ τῇ ἡμέρᾳ μετ᾽ ἀλλήλων· προϋπῆρχον γὰρ ἐν ἔχθρᾳ ὄντες πρὸς αὐτούς.[2] Dibelius suggests that the friendship mentioned here was extracted from Psalm 2:1–2.[3] Is it then a separate tradition which Luke inserted here to finish off his pericope on Herod's trial of Jesus, demonstrating that both rulers were in agreement about Jesus?[4] This is possible, but the statement seems to imply more. If the crucifixion of Jesus was in A.D. 30, then the enmity stated here could, as mentioned above, refer to the massacre of the Galilaeans at the Passover in A.D. 29.

However, if the crucifixion was in 33, it could refer not only to the massacre but also to the incident of the votive shields. Doyle suggests that the shield episode occurred at the Passover of 32 and the reconciliation at the Passover of 33.[5] One objection to this is that it seems unlikely that Pilate would have tried to stir up trouble amongst the Jews so soon after hearing of Sejanus' death, especially since he may not have known about it until the winter of 31/2. He would no doubt have

---

[1] It is possible that Pilate was trying to promote emperor worship to ingratiate himself with the emperor (especially if Sejanus had already died). Pilate's name is in an inscription at Caesarea which seems to have been in connection with dedicating some important building in Tiberius' honour. It may well have been a temple (cf. J. Vardaman, 'A New Inscription which mentions Pilate as "Prefect"', *JBL*, LXXXI [1962], 70–1; H. Volkmann, 'Die Pilatusinschrift von Caesarea Maritima', *Gymnasium*, LXXV [1968], 124–35). Pilate may have thought it would benefit him if he introduced emperor worship in Jerusalem in a different way from that of the standards.

[2] Lk. 23:12.

[3] M. Dibelius, *From Tradition to Gospel*[2], trans. B. L. Woolf (London, 1934), p. 199.

[4] Cf. Conzelmann, p. 86 n. 2.   [5] *JTS*, XLII, 191–3.

waited long enough so as not to rock his own boat. If this incident was before A.D. 33, could it not have occurred at the Feast of Tabernacles in 32? This would have been around 10 October,[1] and would have given a little more breathing space for Pilate after Sejanus' death. Also, it would have allowed enough time for the Jewish delegation to have sent a letter to Tiberius, and for Pilate to have received instructions for the removal of the shields before the Passover of 33.

Hence, whether the crucifixion was in A.D. 30 or 33, the latter part of Luke's statement, asserting the existence of enmity, is historically valid. However, on the basis of the later date for the crucifixion, the enmity would be more realistic. The slaughter of the Galilaeans, which offended Antipas, could have occurred at the Passover of 32, and the votive shields incident, which offended the Jews as well as Antipas, at the Feast of Tabernacles of 32. In the winter of 32/3, or early 33, Pilate would have received Tiberius' orders. This would have placed Pilate in a very awkward position in relation to Tiberius, the Jews, and Antipas.

Pilate, having overstepped himself, was now anxious to appease. Certainly the picture presented of Pilate in the passion narrative of the Gospels is not the unbending and reckless character pictured in Josephus and Philo. On the contrary it is one of submissiveness. According to John 19:12, the Jews stated that unless he released Jesus he was not a friend of Caesar. The reverse implication is that he was still a friend of Sejanus and/or friendly toward his policies. Both Bammel[2] and Stauffer[3] have suggested that these words had tremendous significance for Pilate after Sejanus' death, for Pilate was now a man with a broken backbone who could not afford to be at odds with Tiberius. Thus they posit that Jesus was crucified in A.D. 32. However, there is no convincing reason why this would not have had equal effect in 33.[4] Moreover, if Pilate had just

---

[1] Based on the calculation of Parker and Dubberstein, p. 46.

[2] E. Bammel, 'Φίλος τοῦ Καίσαρος', *Theologische Literaturzeitung*, LXXVII (1952), 205–10.

[3] Stauffer, *Jerusalem*, p. 18; *Jesus and His Story*, trans. D. M. Barton (London, 1960), pp. 108–10.

[4] An A.D. 32 crucifixion is impossible from astronomical evidence, whereas either the year 30 or 33 has astronomical confirmation. Cf. J. K. Fotheringham, 'The Evidence of Astronomy and Technical Chronology for the Date

received the instructions from Tiberius to remove the shields, the Jews would have only recently learned of their success, and Pilate would have known all too well that he could not afford to quarrel with the emperor. For this reason he gave in to them by handing over Jesus.[1]

The same could be said about Antipas. According to Luke, after Pilate heard that Jesus was a Galilaean, he sent him to Herod.[2] Probably he did this primarily to get rid of an awkward case.[3] He may however have known that Antipas desired to see Jesus. At least Luke states that Antipas was very glad (ἐχάρη λίαν) to see him.[4] If this were the case, then handing him over to Antipas would have served not only to save face, but also to ingratiate himself with Antipas.[5] This would have been a wise move on the part of Pilate. Jesus was neutral ground as far as Pilate's and Antipas' relationship with each other was concerned. Yet he was the centre of controversy amongst the Jews. Hence, rather than taking a course of action which might again align Antipas and the Jews, he wisely handed Jesus over to Antipas. Possibly Pilate was hoping that Antipas would make a wrong move against either the Roman government, or the Jews, or both. Antipas accepted the courtesy gesture 'but was wise enough not to presume upon it'.[6] He sent Jesus back to Pilate. This exchange of courtesies may have sufficed to put an end to their grievances.

Luke's statement that they became friends in the same day is an emphatic one. Along with this is the impression that from

of the Crucifixion', *JTS*, xxxv (1934), 146–62; J. Jeremias, *The Eucharistic Words of Jesus*, trans. from 3rd German ed. by N. Perrin (London, 1966), pp. 36–41.

[1] Brandon dates Jesus' crucifixion at A.D. 30; cf. S. G. F. Brandon, *The Trial of Jesus of Nazareth* (London, 1968), pp. 146, 150. Hence, he thinks that the characterization of Pilate in the Gospels as being the weak, abject figure as opposed to that given in Josephus and Philo is ludicrous (*Trial*, pp. 99, 190 n. 100; cf. also pp. 35–41; *Jesus*, pp. 68–80, 248). However, if the crucifixion did occur in A.D. 33 (Brandon acknowledges in passing that some do hold to this date; *Jesus*, p. 75 n. 1), then the characterization of Pilate given in the Gospels is indeed very intelligible.

[2] Lk. 23: 6–7.   [3] This will be treated in more detail in ch. 9.

[4] Lk. 23: 8.

[5] According to Just. *Dial.* ciii. 4 (*MPG*, vi, 717) Pilate sent Jesus to Herod as a compliment.

[6] Bruce, *ALUOS*, v, 16.

that day they remained friends. It seems then that the enmity, which was caused probably by the Galilaean massacre, by the shields, and by the instructions from Tiberius, could well have arisen before the crucifixion, if that occurred in A.D. 33. Jesus' trial furnished an opportunity for reconciliation (as well as appeasing the Jews). Hence, Luke's statements have historical validity in that context. Luke's motive for their inclusion was due probably to the interest of his recipient, Theophilus, who may well have been interested in the relationship of the Herods with the Roman procurator of Judaea,[1] especially if there was a reconciliation between them.

To sum up: If Jesus died in 30, then the enmity mentioned by Luke may have been the result of the Galilaean massacre, possibly at the Passover of 29. The incident of the votive shields would not have contributed to the enmity unless Luke placed this tradition here for some other motive. However, if the crucifixion were in A.D. 33, which seems far more probable, then the enmity between the two leaders may have been caused by the Galilaean massacre, which could have happened at the Passover of 32, while the incident of the votive shields could have occurred at the Feast of Tabernacles of 32. Pilate probably received orders to remove the shields in the winter of 32/3, or early, 33, and thus Pilate would have been in the position of an appeaser at the Passover of 33. His handing over of Jesus to Antipas and his release of Jesus to the Jews would confirm this.[2] It seems best, then, to place the incident of the shields about a year after Sejanus' death in the autumn of 32.

In conclusion, during Pilate's ten years as procurator of Judaea he had provoked the Jews a number of times. However, there are only two recorded incidents which involved Antipas and which may have caused grievances between them. According to Luke the trial of Jesus was the occasion of their reconciliation. Nothing more is known about their relationship with each other.

---

[1] This is also seen in the relationship between Festus and Agrippa II (cf. Acts 25: 13–27; 26: 24–32).

[2] Two years after coming to the conclusion of an A.D. 33 crucifixion, it was confirmed in an article, using very similar lines of argument, by P. L. Maier, 'Sejanus, Pilate, and the Date of the Crucifixion', *Church History*, XXXVII (1968), 3–13.

CHAPTER 9

ANTIPAS AND JESUS

The relationship between Antipas and Jesus is difficult to determine with certainty. Yet there are a few references to justify a short study. The intention is not only to weigh the few specific passages mentioning the relationship but also to see whether or not Jesus' movements were determined by Antipas.

Most of John the Baptist's ministry took place in Antipas' territory of Peraea. After John's imprisonment, Jesus began his ministry in Galilee. Antipas would have viewed Jesus' movement as the continuation of John's.

ANTIPAS' HEARING OF JESUS

Apart from the possibility of indirect contact through the Herodians,[1] the first mention of any direct relationship between Antipas and Jesus is at the time of Antipas' hearing of Jesus.[2]

The problem of Mark 6 : 14–16 and parallels

Before dealing with this particular pericope a brief mention of its possible source is in order. This account of what the public thought of Jesus (as being the resurrected John) may have been drawn from general knowledge of public opinion in Jesus' day.[3]

---

[1] Mk. 3: 6. It seems that the Herodians were men of influence and standing, who in some circles were also known as the Boethusians. They were at one with the Sadducees religiously, but generally speaking were more pro-Herodian while the Sadducees were more pro-Hasmonaean. For a discussion on the Herodians, see Appendix X.

[2] Mt. 14: 1–2; Mk. 6: 14–16; Lk. 9: 7–9.

[3] If one accepts Marcan priority, then it may have been Peter who told Mark this opinion. This is more or less repeated in Mk. 8: 28. The sources of Herod's utterance may again have been from Joanna or Manaen, as mentioned in Chapter 7 and Appendix VI. In general the historicity of the pericope is not questioned, except by those who question the next pericope. The two stand and/or fall together.

Syntactical problems

Mark 6:14–16 is the longest of the three parallels and has fifty-four words. All three have six words in common, whereas Matthew and Mark have nine, Mark and Luke fourteen, and Matthew and Luke only ὁ τετράρχης in common. Those who accept Marcan priority find no real difficulty in Matthew and Luke having copied Mark, except that the last two sentences in Luke may have been 'a variant version of some lost continuation of this present section which disappeared from Mark and from the parallels which depend on Mark'.[1] Those who hold to Matthaean priority explain the phenomenon by saying: 'Mark, however, clearly turned to the Matthean parallel, for his account is a blending of Matthew's with that of Luke.'[2]

Among the synoptic parallels the great difficulty lies in Mark's account. First consideration must be given to a textual problem in 6:14. The reading ἔλεγεν has good attestation and is accepted by some commentators.[3] The reading ἔλεγον has few but weighty manuscripts and is preferred by most commentators.[4] The singular number is due perhaps to scribal assimilation to ἤκουσεν or possibly to influence from Matthew (14:2) εἶπεν. If Luke employed Mark, his reading in 9:7 διὰ τὸ λέγεσθαι ὑπό τινων ὅτι 'Ιωάννης ἠγέρθη... would confirm the plural reading in Mark.[5] Matthew's omission of the divergent views about Jesus offers no parallel or help. The plural fits better structurally for it would be parallel to the two ἔλεγον in verse 15, and this in turn would be parallel to the three opinions about Jesus in 8:28. Also, if it were singular, it would seem to be a needless repetition of verse 16. The plural reading is therefore preferable.[6]

---

[1] Creed, *Luke*, p. 127.

[2] W. R. Farmer, *The Synoptic Problem* (New York and London, 1964), p. 242.

[3] ℵ A C K L Δ Θ Π, f¹f¹³; e.g. O. Holtzmann, *Das Neue Testament*, 1 (Giessen, 1926), 27; Bultmann, p. 302.

[4] B D (ἔλεγοσαν) W, e.g. Field, p. 28; C. H. Turner, *JTS*, xxv, 380–1; Klostermann, *Markusevangelium*, p. 59; Lohmeyer, *Markus*, p. 115 n. 4; Taylor, *Mark*, p. 308; Cranfield, p. 206; Haenchen, *Der Weg Jesu*, p. 235; Schweizer, *Markus*, pp. 73–4.

[5] Turner, *JTS*, xxv, 380–1.

[6] For a brief discussion of the singular reading, see Achtemeier, *JBL*, LXXXIX, 269–70.

The second problem, and the main one, is the difficult grammatical structure of ἤκουσεν with no object. There are two possible solutions. According to Ljungvik, καὶ ἔλεγον is the object of ἤκουσεν and thus καί stands hypotactically for ὅτι, while the statement φανερὸν γὰρ ἐγένετο τὸ ὄνομα αὐτοῦ is parenthetical. It would thus read: 'And Herod the king heard (for his name had become known) that they (some) said that John the baptizer has been raised from the dead...'[1] Ljungvik finds support for this construction in modern Greek, analogous constructions in the New Testament, and one Koine papyrus of the second century. On the other hand, according to Blinzler, the object of ἤκουσεν must be supplied by some such phrase as 'of Jesus (works)', while the parenthesis begins with φανερόν (v. 14) and ends with τῶν προφητῶν (v. 15).[2] Blinzler finds it difficult to believe that Antipas would have decided in favour of John having been raised from the dead (v. 16) simply on the basis of other people's opinions. Rather, he would himself have sought the particulars of Jesus' works. He thinks that Ljungvik's view is weak linguistically and that the support from modern Greek, New Testament, and Koine is not convincing.[3] In view of φανερὸν γὰρ ἐγένετο τὸ ὄνομα αὐτοῦ, he holds that Antipas would have heard of Jesus (works) as other people had,[4] and therefore that the καί before ἔλεγον is explicative,[5] showing what the public opinion was.

While both views are plausible, Blinzler's is the more probable. Granting Marcan priority, it is evident that Matthew has supplied τὴν ἀκοὴν Ἰησοῦ as the object of ἤκουσεν.[6] In the next

---

[1] Ljungvik, ZNW, xxxiii, 90–2. This interpretation has been followed by most recent commentators, cf. Klostermann, Markusevangelium, p. 59; Lohmeyer, Markus, p. 115 n. 4; Grundmann, Markus, p. 126; J. Jeremias, ''Ηλ(ε)ίας', TDNT, ii (1964), 936 n. 64; Cranfield, p. 206; Taylor, Mark, p. 308; Bauer/AG, p. 393; BD/Funk, § 471 (4).

[2] J. Blinzler, 'Zur Syntax von Markus 6, 14–16', Philologus, xcvi (1943), 119–31.

[3] With regard to modern Greek Blinzler feels that the present day construction is seldom used and that although it is used today it does not mean it was used in NT times. With regard to the other NT usages (Mk. 9: 4; 15: 25; Rev. 6: 12; 15: 5) and the papyrus example, Blinzler thinks that other explanations are just as plausible if not more so (Blinzler, Philologus, xcvi, 121–6). [4] Cf. Mk. 3: 8; 5: 27; 7: 25.

[5] Bauer/AG, pp. 393–4. [6] Mt. 14: 1.

verse Matthew ascribes to Antipas the declaration that this is John the baptizer risen from the dead, and hence his ability to do mighty works. Although Matthew omits the clumsy Marcan structure, it seems nevertheless that he condensed the Marcan account for his own purpose. Luke also supplies an object to ἤκουσεν, namely, τὰ γινόμενα πάντα,[1] which refers back to the previously portrayed ministry of Jesus.[2] Granting Matthaean priority, it is not difficult to conceive Mark conflating Matthew and Luke.[3]

In conclusion, it seems that the plural reading (ἔλεγον) is to be preferred, so that the reference is to public opinion rather than to Antipas' private opinion. Blinzler's conjecture regarding the lack of an object to ἤκουσεν is the most satisfactory. The parenthesis beginning with φανερόν in 6:14 and ending with τῶν προφητῶν in 6:15 provides the reason for Jesus' fame coming to Antipas' ears. The seemingly needless repetition of ἀκούσας δὲ ὁ Ἡρῴδης in 6:16 is simply a resumption of the thought before the parenthesis and could be translated, 'Herod, then, on hearing about Jesus, said...'.[4]

Interpretative problems

The public opinion as to John's resurrection. This need not detain one since it is not directly related to the study of Antipas. The texts would indicate that Herod and some of the people believed that Jesus was in fact John resurrected[5] from the dead. Such a belief was known among the Jews.[6] Also, it was said that

---

[1] Lk. 9: 7. 　　　　[2] Blinzler, *Philologus*, xcvi, 130–1.

[3] Farmer, *Synoptic Problem*, p. 242.

[4] Turner, *JTS*, xxvi, 148.

[5] It is difficult to know which term is to be used. Wink (p. 10) does not like the term 'resurrection' because it implies that a body is brought back from heaven. Instead he prefers to think that John has been physically 'resuscitated' but he has to qualify it further by saying that John had actually been buried so as not to imply that John was revived after a brief lapse into death. The present author prefers the term 'resurrection' as long as it does not connote a spiritual resurrection in this context. It seems that it was more than resuscitation for it was a restoration of a decapitated man. For a discussion of resurrection in the present context, see O. Cullmann, *The Christology of the New Testament*[2], trans. by S. C. Guthrie and C. A. M. Hall (London, 1963), p. 33.

[6] Cf. Strack–Billerbeck, I, 679. 'Mt. 14: 1–2 gives a revealing insight into the religious expectations in Israel at the time: Jesus is considered "John

Jesus so resembled John that the people could not tell them apart. This did not mean that they resembled each other physically as suggested by Origen,[1] but possibly that their activities were similar. Yet it is more probable that the people who expressed this opinion were not in the immediate company of either John or Jesus.[2] Further, there is an implication that the activities of Jesus and John must be separated both chronologically and spatially. Although, according to the synoptics, Jesus' ministry did not begin until after John's arrest, the Gospel of John indicates that Jesus and John work simultaneously, but independently, for at least a short time. The opinion that Jesus was John resurrected may be due to the fact that Jesus' ministry between his baptism and John's imprisonment was overshadowed by that of the Baptist; but it is more probable that the people responsible for the opinion that Jesus was the risen John had not been personally acquainted with Jesus and/or John.[3] Finally, since Jesus is accounted to be John because of his mighty deeds (δυνάμεις), it is implied that John had himself performed mighty deeds before his death.[4] But there is no evidence of this in the narratives of the synoptics, and the fourth evangelist specifically states that John did no sign/miracle.[5] It may have been thought that the resurrected John was endued with powers not previously possessed by him,[6]

risen from the dead". Mt. gives this "parallel" to Jesus' resurrection as a matter of course' (K. Stendahl, 'Matthew', *PCB*, p. 786).

[1] Origen *Commentarii in Evangelium Joannis* vi. 30 (*MPG*, xiv, 285).

[2] Cullmann, *Christology*, pp. 32–3.

[3] *Ibid.* pp. 31–2; Wink, pp. 9, 94.

[4] Kraeling's theory that Jesus was thought to be using the spirit of John brought back from the dead to perform his miracles is not convincing, cf. C. H. Kraeling, 'Was Jesus Accused of Necromancy?', *JBL*, LIX (1940), 147–57. If this were the case, the evangelists would have stated clearly that public opinion maintained this view. After all, they clearly stated that Jesus had Beelzebub under his control and that he drove out demons by the prince of demons (Mt. 9: 34; 12: 24 = Mk. 3: 22 = Lk. 11: 15). Rather than Mark being wrong in reporting the opinion that Jesus *is* John, it is easier to believe that Kraeling is wrong in emending the opinion to 'Jesus *has* John'. Interestingly enough, this view of Kraeling's is never once mentioned in his book published eleven years after his article (*John the Baptist*, New York and London, 1951), which may indicate he did not find it convincing either!

[5] Jn. 10: 41. For an interpretation of this verse, see E. Bammel, 'John Did No Miracle', *Miracles*, ed. by C. F. D. Moule (London, 1965), pp. 181–202.

[6] Cf. Klostermann, *Markusevangelium*, p. 59.

but it is more probable that the people either confused the two
ministries or erred through not having known John intimately.
In conclusion, then, the popular opinion as to John's resurrection was probably inaccurate due to the people not having
intimately known or seen John and/or Jesus. Rather, it was
based on popular rumour and alarm.

Antipas' opinion as to John's resurrection. Whereas it is reasonable to
suppose that public opinion under the influence of Pharisaism
might hold to the resurrection of a prophet, this is not the case
with Herod Antipas, whose views on the after-life would probably
have been more Hellenistic and Sadducaean.[1] The passage in
Luke (9:9) avoids the dilemma by making Herod state: Ἰωάνην
ἐγὼ ἀπεκεφάλισα· τίς δέ ἐστιν οὗτος περὶ οὗ ἀκούω τοιαῦτα;
Hardly, however, did Matthew or Mark mean it as a question.[2]
Certainly, if it were a question, one would like to know how
he would have anwered it. Luke felt this need by answering
καὶ ἐζήτει ἰδεῖν αὐτόν, but there is no equivalent in the other
synoptics. Rather, in Mark (6:16), Antipas' statement[3] agrees
with one of the conjectures offered by the public. This statement,
however, seen in Matthew and Mark, may only be a literary
device by the evangelists to make a good starting point for the
story of how Antipas treated the Baptist.[4] This might explain

[1] The Sadducees did not believe in the resurrection of the body as may be
seen in Mt. 22: 23–8 = Mk. 12: 18–23 = Lk. 20: 27–33; Acts 4: 1–2; 23: 8;
Jos. *Ant.* xviii. 16. The attitude of the Greeks appears in Acts 17: 32; 1 Cor.
15: 12, 35.

[2] As advocated by G. Wohlenberg, *Das Evangelium des Markus*[1,2], *KNT*, ii
(Leipzig, 1910), p. 180 n. 55. The punctuation at the end of Mk. 6: 16 is
a question mark (;) only in some commentary sections of a manuscript
which differs from the reading of the Greek text. Clearly there is no MS
evidence for a question mark.

[3] Mark does not indicate to whom Antipas made his statement, whereas
Matthew states that it was to παισὶν αὐτοῦ (14: 2). In the orient, servants
were the courtiers or officers of the court and not household servants (Gen.
41: 10, 37–8; 1 Sam. 16: 17; 18: 22–6; Jer. 36 [43]: 31; 37 [44]: 2; 1 Macc.
1: 6, 8; Diodorus Siculus xvii. 36. 5; 76. 5; cf, M'Neile, p. 208; Lohmeyer,
Matthäus, p. 232 n. 1; P. Bonnard, *L'Évangile selon Saint Matthieu. Commentaire du Nouveau Testament*, ed. by J.-J. von Allmen *et al.*, i (Neuchâtel,
1963), p. 216. These παισίν may have been the transmitters of the story.

[4] Haenchen, *Der Weg Jesu*, p. 237; cf. also J. Bowman, *The Gospel of
Mark. The New Christian Jewish Passover Haggadah, Studia Post-Biblica*, ed. by
P. A. H. DeBoer, *et al.*, viii (Leiden, 1965), p. 153.

the omission of the statement in Luke,[1] for Luke does not include the story of the Baptist's death. Nevertheless, this statement would seem to be more than just a literary device of a transitional nature. It may be that a guilty conscience working on a superstitious mind convinced Antipas that John had really returned.[2] He was grieved that he was caught in Herodias' trap over the death of John.[3] Although he would be inclined towards Hellenistic and Sadducaean thought with respect to resurrection, his beliefs would have been difficult to formulate into watertight compartments, especially since a phenomenon such as this could have concerned him politically. This is not the first example in the history of the Herodian family of a belief in the possibility of supernatural working in their midst.[4] There are times in life when strange or inexplicable things occur which cause one to doubt one's own philosophy. It is more probable, however, that the statement is to be taken symbolically or perhaps ironically or in mockery. He had put an end to one dangerous movement, so he had thought, but now there appeared a still more remarkable and successful people's preacher. Symbolically, the idea would be that Jesus was the *alter ego* of the man whom Antipas had beheaded. Antipas may well have thought, 'it is John the Baptist all over again'.[5] Antipas had made use of irony and mockery at other times[6] and this may have been the case here – 'John I have beheaded and now he is resurrected.'[7] If it is irony or mockery the Matthaean parallel fits well. The Lucan parallel supple-

---

[1] It is interesting to notice that Luke's version is very concise. Herod's conclusion is: 'John I have killed – then who can this possibly be?' The mention of John's death is only incidental and Herod is not seen as propounding the resurrection of John. Again it may be, as mentioned above (p. 110), that Luke plays down John's ministry because he had finished with it in 3: 19–20 (cf. Conzelmann, pp. 21, 26).

[2] Grundmann, *Markus*, p. 127; Cranfield, p. 207; Bowman, p. 153.

[3] Mt. 14: 9; Mk. 6: 26,.

[4] A belief in ghosts and demons is seen in Jos. *BJ* i. 599, 607, possibly in *BJ* vii. 185 and Persius *Satura* v. 180–8, but these references may relate to the servants or attendants of Herod rather than to the Herodian family itself.

[5] Wellhausen, *Marci*, p. 46; Rawlinson, *Mark*, p. 79; Branscomb, p. 107; Taylor, *Mark*, p. 309; Manson, *Servant-Messiah*, p. 69.

[6] Cf. Lk. 23: 11; Jos. *Ant.* xviii. 150.

[7] Cf. Blinzler, *Philologus*, xcvi, 129 n. 22; Lohmeyer, *Markus*, p. 117; esp. the Ergänzungsheft, p. 11.

ments the irony by putting it into the form of a question, and adds sarcasm by saying that he would like to see him. Some critics feel that Luke 13:31–3 belongs immediately after Luke 9:9 of which the last statement should read 'and he sought to *kill* him', not 'and he sought to see him'.[1] But there is no evidence for this. It may be that Luke inserts this saying to lead up to the passion narrative (23:8) and also to 13:31–3.[2] It is an interesting development that on the only two occasions that Antipas is mentioned after Luke 9:7–9 it is in connection with his desire to see or kill Jesus. Yet there is no good reason for not accepting the statement as historically true. Antipas may well have wanted to see this wonder-worker who was operating in his territory, without wishing, however, to get into trouble with him as he had with John. Politically he had to be careful not to rouse public feeling, as again he had with John.[3] No doubt Antipas watched Jesus' movements to see if he would preach about the royal family's evil conduct and if he would initiate any insurrection with the large crowds. Since Jesus did not attempt either of these things, Antipas had no legitimate reason for seizing him. Furthermore, if Antipas had really wanted to seize Jesus he could have done so in the same way as he had seized John. He would have had ample scouts and military men to achieve this. It seems, therefore, that Antipas may have wanted to see the wonder-worker out of mere curiosity, rather than to coerce or harm him.

On the other hand, after Antipas had gained knowledge of Jesus' ministry, Jesus withdrew from his territories. It is thought by some that Antipas wanted to seize Jesus, but that he could not do so because Jesus had withdrawn from his territories. This is true to some extent, but that it is not the whole answer will be seen later in this chapter.

The setting of the pericope

Does the setting of the present pericope have any significance in the chronological sequence of Jesus' ministry? It would appear from Antipas' remarks that he had only recently heard

---

[1] Wellhausen, *Marci*, p. 48; M. Goguel, *The Life of Jesus*, trans. O. Wyon (London, 1933), p. 355.
[2] Cf. Conzelmann, p. 51; Haenchen, *Der Weg Jesu*, p. 237.
[3] Jos. *Ant.* xviii. 119.

of Jesus. But how can this be? According to the narratives of Jesus' ministry, he had already attracted great crowds and his fame was already widespread.[1] Also, very early in Jesus' ministry, Mark and Luke mention the great number of governmental workers that followed him,[2] while Mark indicates that the Herodians knew of him.[3] In addition to this, Jesus, early in his ministry, became well known at Capernaum[4] which is only ten miles from the coast of the Sea of Galilee. How can it be that Antipas had not heard of Jesus' works?

One possible solution is to assume that the pericope of Antipas' hearing of Jesus is out of chronological order and should be placed earlier in Jesus' ministry. A brief review of the context is in order. With regard to the broader context of the synoptic Gospels the block of material, beginning with Mark 4:1 (= Mt. 13:1 = Lk. 8:4) and ending with the last verse of the present pericope (Mk. 6:16 = Mt. 14:2 = Lk. 9:9), has the same general order.[5] As for the more immediate context, Mark 4:35 – 6:16 and Luke 8:22 – 9:9 are in the same order except that Luke omits Jesus' rejection at Nazareth, having already mentioned it in 4:16–30. Matthew's order is very

---

[1] Cf. Mt. 4: 23–5; 5: 1; 7: 28 – 8: 1, 16, 18; 9: 8, 26, 31, 35–6; 12: 15; 13: 2; Mk. 1: 28, 32–4, 37, 39, 45; 2: 1–2, 4, 13; 3: 7–9, 20, 32; 4: 1, 36; 5: 21, 24; Lk. 4: 14, 37, 40, 42; 5: 1, 15, 17, 19; 6: 17, 19; 7: 11, 17; 8: 1, 4, 19, 40, 42. Some, of course, are parallel while others are not.

[2] Mk. 2: 15; Lk. 5: 29; cf. also Mt. 9: 10.

[3] Mk. 3: 6.

[4] Mk. 1: 21, 28; 2: 1–2. Although before the sermon at Nazareth Luke gives no specific ministry at Capernaum it is mentioned that the people of Nazareth wanted him to perform for them as he had performed in Capernaum (4: 23). This ministry may be included in the general Galilaean ministry mentioned in Lk. 4: 14–15 or it may be that the pericope is chronologically out of order (cf. below, p. 193 n. 5).

[5] The exceptions are as follows. Matthew deviates from Mark and Luke on the pericope in which it is stated 'he having ears let him hear' (Mk. 4: 21–5 = Lk. 8: 16–18); on the pericope of stilling the storm, Gerasene demoniac, and Jairus' daughter (Mk. 4: 35 – 5: 43 = Lk. 8: 22–56); and on the pericope of the commissioning of the twelve (Mk. 6: 6b–13 = Lk. 9: 1–6). Luke deviates from the Matthaean–Marcan order in the parables of the mustard seed and of leaven (Mt. 13: 31–3 = Lk. 4: 30–2) and Jesus' rejection at Nazareth (Mt. 13: 53–8 = Mk. 6: 1–6a). Mark and Matthew deviate from Luke's order only in the paragraph on Jesus' true kindred (Lk. 8: 19–21). These changes in order are readily explainable by those who hold the Marcan priority (cf. Jeremias, *Eucharistic Words*, pp. 97–8) and by those who hold to the Matthaean priority (Farmer, *Synoptic Problem*, pp. 239–42).

broken in comparison with the other two synoptics in this section. He has only Jesus' rejection at Nazareth (13:53-8) which is placed immediately before the present pericope. Thus he omits the sending out of the twelve, which he treated earlier.[1] If the conjecture is correct that the object of ἤκουσεν in Mark 6:14 is something similar to that in Matthew (τὴν ἀκοὴν Ἰησοῦ) or Luke (τὰ γινόμενα πάντα), then the present pericope may be out of the proper chronological sequence of Jesus' ministry. In Mark and Luke the immediately preceding pericope is about the commissioning of the twelve. Mark indicates that Antipas had not heard of the twelve, but only of Jesus himself (φανερὸν γὰρ ἐγένετο τὸ ὄνομα αὐτοῦ). Whereas Luke is more general (τὰ γινόμενα πάντα) Matthew is more specific (τὴν ἀκοὴν Ἰησοῦ). Thus the evangelists appear to indicate that Antipas had heard of Jesus' ministry but not the ministry of the commissioned disciples. This is also substantiated by the fact that the two pericopes about Herod's hearing of Jesus and his executing John are only filling in the gap between the sending out and the return of the disciples.[2] Matthew's phrase ἐν ἐκείνῳ τῷ καιρῷ 'is loosely connected with the Galilaean ministry',[3] since the immediately preceding pericope is concerned with that and not with the disciples' commissioning. The pericope preceding this one in Mark is about Jesus' rejection at Nazareth. This is paralleled in Matthew,[4] but is omitted by Luke who had treated it earlier.[5] Luke places it almost at the beginning of Jesus' public ministry, whereas in Matthew and Mark it represents the last occasion that Jesus ministered in the synagogue before beginning to withdraw from Galilee. Hence, according to the synoptists' programme, the Galilaean ministry is climaxed at Nazareth, where Jesus is rejected. Because of this, he uses other means of proclaiming the message, sending out the twelve. Up to this point Jesus

---

[1] Mt. 10: 1 ff. Nowhere does Matthew specifically state their ministry or their return.

[2] Mk. 6: 6b-13, 30; Lk. 9: 1-6, 10a. Matthew's transition (14: 12-13) is different since the commissioning of the twelve is not in this context. Cf. also Achtemeier, *JBL*, LXXXIX, 270.

[3] M'Neile, p. 207. [4] Mk. 6: 1-6a; Mt. 13: 53-8.

[5] Lk. 4: 16-30. For a discussion on the setting of this pericope in the synoptics, see R. H. Lightfoot, *History and Interpretation in the Gospels* (London, 1935), pp. 182-205.

had a wide public ministry, but after it he must needs withdraw from Galilee. The pericope on Antipas' hearing of Jesus seems to hinge on these two phases of Jesus' ministry. Immediately before this incident is the healing of Jairus' daughter and the woman with a haemorrhage. It may have been these miracles of which Antipas had heard.[1]

Another possible hint may be the sentence immediately after the rejection at Nazareth: καὶ περιῆγεν τὰς κώμας κύκλῳ διδάσκων.[2] It may be to this that Mark refers when he speaks of Antipas' hearing of Jesus' works. Could this sentence serve as another clue referring to a similar statement early in Mark which says: καὶ ἦλθεν κηρύσσων εἰς τὰς συναγωγὰς αὐτῶν εἰς ὅλην τὴν Γαλιλαίαν καὶ τὰ δαιμόνια ἐκβάλλων?[3] The next thing Jesus does according to Mark is to heal a leper, who subsequently spread the news about Jesus ὥστε μηκέτι αὐτὸν δύνασθαι φανερῶς εἰς πόλιν εἰσελθεῖν, ἀλλ' ἔξω ἐπ' ἐρήμοις τόποις ἦν.[4] In other words, Jesus had a wide public ministry until the leper spread the news. Antipas may have heard about it and for this reason Jesus could not openly minister in the towns. The pericope concerning Antipas' hearing of Jesus (6:14–16) should be inserted between 1:45 a and b. Or possibly, since his popularity had already become known as early as his Capernaum ministry[5] and since Capernaum was so near to Tiberias, it was this earlier ministry of which Antipas had heard.[6]

Although these are attractive possibilities, there are two things that militate against them. First, Jesus had a wide and open ministry after this point. Secondly, and more pointedly, the pericope on Herod's hearing of Jesus presupposes the death of the Baptist. John's arrest is stated early in all the synoptics,[7] and only after it does Jesus begin his ministry. How long an interval there was between the beginning of Jesus' ministry and the death of the Baptist cannot be known, but there must have been a period of weeks, if not months, between the beginning of Jesus' ministry and the Baptist's enquiry regarding Jesus him-

---

[1] Cf. Bacon, *Mark*, p. 161.
[2] Mk. 6: 6 b.　　　　[3] Mk. 1: 39 = Mt. 4: 23 = Lk. 4: 44.
[4] Mk. 1: 45.
[5] Mk. 1: 21–8; Lk. 4: 31–7.
[6] Cf. K. Schmidt, *Der Rahmen der Geschichte Jesu* (Berlin, 1919), p. 173.
[7] Mt. 4: 12; Mk. 1: 14; Lk. 3: 20.

self.[1] There is also an indefinite period between John's enquiry and his death.[2] This means that the occasion of Antipas' first hearing of Jesus was not in the first days of his Galilaean ministry but at some later time.

Yet it seems incredible that Antipas did not hear of Jesus' ministry earlier. A possible explanation is offered by Edersheim[3] and Blinzler.[4] They feel that Antipas may have been in Peraea during the first days of Jesus' ministry and up to the time of John's death, but that he did not hear of Jesus until he returned to Galilee. Yet even in Peraea he would have received some reports, for his informants would not have been idle. On the other hand, Schofield[5] suggests that Antipas had left Palestine. He may have gone to Rome, or it may have been the time of his visit to Phoenicia, or again he may even have travelled to some of the islands between Greece and Asia Minor as did his father.[6] There are inscriptions attesting his presence in the islands of Cos and Delos[7] and a record of a visit to Phoenicia.[8] Could it be during this time that he made these visits? It is possible, but there is no evidence for it one way or the other. Several things make it difficult to accept Schofield's theory. First, he believes that Antipas wanted to take a holiday now that John had been arrested, the hazardous marriage with Herodias completed, the menace of Aretas settled down, and Pilate been tamed by the emperor.[9] However, it is doubtful whether he would want to leave so soon after his arrest of John for fear of a revolt by the Baptist's followers. If he had left the country, it would have been an opportune moment for Aretas to have struck and for Pilate to have attempted a new move. Secondly, according to Schofield, Antipas returned to Palestine in A.D. 29 and then

[1] Mt. 11: 2–6; Lk. 7: 18–23; cf. also J. Blinzler, *Herodes Antipas*, pp. 9–10.
[2] It was estimated to be a period of about a year between John's imprisonment and death (cf. above, pp. 170–1).
[3] I, 654, 657. Edersheim believes that Antipas resided in Peraea either at Julias or Machaerus for a period of nine or ten months, which would be time enough for Jesus' Galilaean ministry. He thinks that Antipas found out about Jesus as a result of the disciples' labours.
[4] *Herodes Antipas*, p. 11.   [5] Pp. 133–4.
[6] Jos. *BJ* i. 422–5.
[7] Above, p. 106 n. 3. Cf. Herod the Great's generosity towards the inhabitants of Cos (Jos. *BJ* i. 423).
[8] Jos. *Ant.* xviii. 150.
[9] P. 134.

went straight to Machaerus, where he executed the Baptist. He then returned to Galilee and was told of Jesus' works.[1] But there are inherent problems in this. To come back from Rome by boat at the time of the Passover of A.D. 29 (about 18 April)[2] would have meant his travelling during the doubtful period of sailing. It is unlikely that Antipas would have travelled during this period unless he thought it necessary to be present at the festival. Also, this would mean that Antipas was away for some eight or nine months – an incredibly long time when things were so unsettled in Palestine. It is unlikely that Antipas would have gone to Machaerus instead of his capital, Tiberias, immediately after visiting Jerusalem. Even if he did go directly to Machaerus, the officials who came from Galilee to Machaerus for the birthday celebration would surely have informed him of what had happened during his absence and especially of Jesus' movement, now that it had grown so large. Schofield seems to contradict himself. At one point he says that if Antipas were in Machaerus he would have been in constant communication with Tiberias; but later he suggests that Antipas received no communication when he returned to Machaerus after his long journey outside Palestine.[3] Although Schofield's theory explains some of the data, there are too many inherent problems to make it plausible.

It is difficult to know exactly what happened. It may be that Antipas watched the developments of the Baptist's movement after John's imprisonment. He may have been in Machaerus while Jesus' movement was gaining momentum, but was more concerned with what Aretas was up to, having by now married Herodias. He may have heard of Jesus' movement but was satisfied, at least in its early stages, that Jesus was causing no political disturbance. John's ministry did arouse Antipas' political suspicions,[4] but Jesus apparently tried to prevent this by avoiding publicity.[5] It may be that after John's execution

---

[1] Pp. 142–60, esp. pp. 142–4, 159–60.
[2] Cf. Parker and Dubberstein, p. 46.
[3] Pp. 133, 159–60.   [4] Jos. *Ant.* xviii. 118.
[5] Mk. 1: 44–5; cf. Mt. 8: 4 = Lk. 5: 14; Mk. 5: 43 = Lk. 8: 56; Mt. 9: 30; Mk. 3: 12. He did not try to prevent publicity after the commotion consequent on the healing at Gadarene/Gerasene/Gergesa. In fact Jesus told the demoniac to report to his house what had been done (Mk. 5: 19 = Lk. 8: 39). There is a good discussion on the problem of the designation of the

Antipas returned to Galilee. Probably many adherents of John joined up with Jesus. Antipas was now in a better position to observe this movement more closely. When it gained momentum, Antipas could only conclude that Jesus was John all over again. Antipas may have seen a need to curtail this, and yet he had to be careful how he did it lest he caused more resentment on the part of the people.

This view is similar to that of Edersheim and Blinzler except that their view presupposes that Antipas, being in Peraea, would not have heard anything of Jesus' movement. This is incredible.

Therefore the setting of this pericope may be out of chronological order in Jesus' ministry. Both Matthew and Mark seem to place it here to serve as an introduction to a new phase of his ministry. Before it he had success, after it he continually withdrew from a public ministry. It is probable that Antipas had heard of Jesus' ministry, and that the evangelists were not referring to the ministry of the twelve nor possibly to Jesus' being rejected at Nazareth. How far back one can place this pericope is difficult to say but it must be after John's death. It is probable that Antipas had heard of Jesus early in his ministry, but did not get seriously concerned about it until after the Baptist's death and after his own arrival in Galilee where he could observe it more closely. The healing of Jairus' daughter may have been the climax as far as Antipas was concerned and have led to his concluding that it was John all over again. Hence, this pericope is in its proper chronological setting. After this Jesus withdrew from Antipas' territory. Is this because he thought that Antipas was after him? It is to this consideration that the next portion of this chapter is devoted.

ANTIPAS AND THE WITHDRAWALS OF JESUS

Studying the movements of Jesus, it is natural to suppose a certain chronological sequence. From the outset Papias has stated that Mark, who received his information from Peter, did not write what Jesus said or did in chronological order.[1]

Gadarenes by T. Baarda, 'Gadarenes, Gerasenes, Gergesenes and the "Diatessaron" Traditions', *Neotestamentica et Semitica*, ed. by E. E. Ellis and M. Wilcox (Edinburgh, 1969), pp. 181–97.

[1] Eus. *HE* iii. 39. 15.

Schmidt argues that the Marcan outline of Jesus' ministry is irretrievably broken, apart from fragmentary episodes in some of the smaller sections and in the passion narrative.[1] On the other hand, there are some such as Stauffer who would attempt a very detailed chronology of Jesus' ministry.[2] A more moderate position is that of Cadman[3] and Dodd.[4] The latter argues that although Mark may not give a strict chronological order of Jesus' ministry, nevertheless he does give the broadest outlines of his ministry within which movement and development can be traced.[5] This does not preclude there being a theological or thematic purpose in the selection and arrangement of the pericopes. On the other hand, it does not seem likely that the evangelists regarded the historical order of key events as a matter of indifference.[6] 'The best reason for confidence in the

[1] Schmidt, *Der Rahmen der Geschichte Jesu*. The Form critics have left little room for confidence in Mark and think that the original tradition was made up almost entirely of brief simple units of sayings and short narratives (cf. Dibelius, *From Tradition to Gospel*, pp. 1–8, 287–301; Bultmann, pp. 1–7, 302–74, esp. pp. 338–50, 368–74; Nineham, *Mark*, pp. 35–8; cf. also Nineham, *JTS*, IX, 13–25, 243–52; XI, 253–64). For the same approach in Luke, cf. Conzelmann, pp. 9–17.

[2] *Jesus and His Story*, pp. 17–18.

[3] W. H. Cadman, *The Last Journey of Jesus to Jerusalem* (London, 1923).

[4] C. H. Dodd, 'The Framework of the Gospel Narrative', *ET*, XLIII (1932), 396–400 (reprinted by C. H. Dodd, *New Testament Studies* [Manchester, 1953], pp. 1–11). This has been challenged by D. E. Nineham, 'The Order of Events in St Mark's Gospel – an Examination of Dr Dodd's Hypothesis', *Studies in the Gospels*, ed. by Nineham (Oxford, 1955), pp. 223–39, which in turn has been challenged by C. F. D. Moule, 'Review of *Studies in the Gospels*, ed. by D. E. Nineham', *JTS*, N.S. VII (1956), 281–2; cf. also Moule, 'The Intention of the Evangelists', *New Testament Essays*, ed. by A. J. B. Higgins (Manchester, 1959), p. 169 (reprinted by Moule, *The Phenomenon of the New Testament*, SBT, 2nd series, no. 1 [London, 1967], Appendix II, pp. 104–5); H. Sawyerr, 'The Marcan Framework', *The Scottish Journal of Theology*, XIV (1961), 279–94.

[5] Burkitt states: 'In opposition to the opinion of many scholars I feel that Mark *is* a Biography, if by Biography we mean the chief outlines of a career, rather than a static characterization. In Mark there is movement and progression' (F. C. Burkitt, 'Review of *Die Zusammensetzung des Markusevangeliums*, by J. Sundwall', in *JTS*, XXXVI [1935], 187). Cf. also T. W. Manson, 'The Quest of the Historical Jesus – Continued', *Studies in the Gospels and Epistles*, ed. by M. Black (Manchester, 1962), pp. 5–6, 11–12; Taylor, *Mark*, pp. 145–9; Cranfield, pp. 17–18.

[6] Cf. Moule, *JTS*, N.S. VII, 282.

Markan itinerary of Jesus, again in its broadest outlines, is that it makes good historical sense.'[1] It is on this assumption that the present study will rest.

The broad outline in the first six chapters of Mark deals with the ministry in Galilee (the one exception being Gergesa: 5: 1–20): the last six chapters 11–16 deal with Jesus' ministry and passion in Jerusalem. The intervening portion (6: 31 – 10: 1) deals with the ministry beyond Galilee. It is this portion with which the present study will be concerned. In passing, it is interesting to notice that Mark 6: 32 – 10: 1 is paralleled in the same order in Matthew 14: 13 – 19: 2, with the exception of two healing stories and the episode of the strange exorcist which only occur in Mark (7: 33–7; 8: 22–6; and 9: 38–41). Matthew has in excess of Mark the incident of the payment of the temple tax (17: 24–7) and a section on the teaching of Jesus (18: 10–35). Luke has the feeding of the 5,000 (9: 10–17) but leaves out the other pericopes until Peter's confession, and from there follows the same order as the other synoptists (9: 18–50), except that he leaves out the passage concerning the coming of Elijah (Mt. 17: 10–13 = Mk. 9: 11–13) and a section on the teachings of Jesus (Mt. 18: 6–35; Mk. 9: 42–50).[2] Hence for this study the Marcan order can be adopted.

Before the incident of Herod's hearing of Jesus, there were according to the synoptists two withdrawals of Jesus, both of which were induced by the crowd.[3] On the first occasion he did not go outside of Galilee,[4] and on the second he returned to Galilee.[5] These two withdrawals need not concern the present study.

It is thought by some that after Antipas had heard of Jesus' works, he was intent on arresting him, and so Jesus took flight. Hence, these withdrawals were motivated by political expediency

[1] J. B. Tyson, 'Jesus and Herod Antipas', *JBL*, LXXIX (1960), 242.

[2] Where all three synoptists are parallel, the verbal agreements of Matthew are closer to Mark than Luke in the case of the feeding of the 5,000 (Mk. 6: 32–44) and in the events from Peter's confession up to the pericope on the transfiguration (8: 27 – 9: 10). In Mark 9: 14–50 the verbal agreements with Matthew and Luke are comparable, though in some cases closer to Luke than Matthew.

[3] Mk. 3: 7, 13 = Lk. 6: 12; cf. Mt. 12: 15; Mk. 4: 35 = Lk. 8: 22 = Mt. 8: 23.

[4] Mk. 3: 19*b*.   [5] Mk. 5: 21 = Lk. 8: 40 = Mt. 9: 18.

to escape from Antipas.[1] On the other hand, Blinzler[2] and Taylor[3] believe that the idea of Jesus' fleeing is entirely out of accord with the evidence in the Gospels.

This study is not concerned with the ministry of Jesus *per se* but only with his withdrawals and their relationship to Antipas. These can be known only by inference and consequently only a short survey is needed.[4] It will suffice to present a list of Jesus' movements and to draw some tentative conclusions from them. According to the synoptists, Jesus' wanderings after Antipas had heard of him were as follows: (1) to the eastern shore of the Sea of Galilee (Mk. 6: 31–2; Mt. 14: 3); (2) to Bethsaida and Gennesaret (Mk. 6: 45, 53; Mt. 14: 22, 34); (3) to Tyre (Mk. 7: 24; Mt. 15: 21); (4) to Sidon, the Sea of Galilee, and the Decapolis (Mk. 7: 31; Mt. 15: 21, 29); (5) to Dalmanutha (Mk. 8: 10) or Magadan (Mt. 15: 39); (6) to Bethsaida (Mk. 8: 22); (7) to Caesarea Philippi (Mk. 8: 27; Mt. 16: 13); (8) to the Mount of Transfiguration (Mk. 9: 2; Mt. 17: 1); (9) through Galilee to Capernaum (Mk. 9: 30, 33; Mt. 17: 22); (10) to Judaea and Transjordan (Mk. 10: 1; Mt. 19: 1–2).

Jesus' first three withdrawals seemed to be motivated primarily by a desire to be alone with his disciples for the purpose of rest and instruction,[5] and secondarily to avoid Antipas. After these three withdrawals Jesus remained outside of Antipas' territory (except for the brief visit to Dalmanutha – no. 5; and his secret journey through Galilee – no. 9). This would seem to point clearly to his avoidance of Antipas. This conclusion is supported by the fact that, when he finally left Galilee for Jerusalem (no. 10), he was again followed by a great crowd.

---

[1] Goguel, *Life of Jesus*, pp. 354–92; Harlow, pp. 148–60. Cf. also Cadman, pp. 27–52; Tyson, *JBL*, LXXIX, 239–46; F. C. Burkitt, *The Gospel History*, pp. 91–8. Burkitt admits in the preface of his 3rd ed. (pp. xii–xiv) that he may have overstated the case that Jesus withdrew on account of Antipas.

[2] *Herodes Antipas*, pp. 26–30.

[3] *Mark*, pp. 635–6; *Life*, pp. 118–19.

[4] For a more detailed analysis of this list of withdrawals of Jesus, see Appendix IX.

[5] Jesus' withdrawals to solitude and private teaching 'are two sides of the same coin'. This is seen not only in the Gospels but also in Jewish literature about Jesus, cf. E. Bammel, 'Christian Origins in Jewish Tradition', *NTS*, XIII (1967), 328.

Hence the paramount motives for his later withdrawals seem to have been the avoidance of Antipas and the desire to be alone with his disciples for at least part of the time.[1] Those who would make Jesus' withdrawals almost exclusively motivated by his desire to be alone or with his disciples do not give any weight to the fact of his leaving Antipas' domain. This is especially marked towards the end. Another interesting fact is that during the period of his withdrawals, the public preaching of the Kingdom of God in Galilee also ceased.[2] As soon as Jesus made his final departure from Galilee he began again to preach the Kingdom of God.[3] Jesus' kingdom was not in competition with that of Antipas or the Roman government. His avoidance of Antipas seems to have been not so much out of fear of Antipas *per se*, but rather to avoid giving Antipas the impression of a political insurrection or revolt against him when this was not his intention.[4] In short, Jesus was not to be classed with the rabble-rousers. This would allow for some ministry within Galilee,[5] but the multitudes were now drawn outside of Antipas' jurisdiction. On the other hand, it seems that Antipas could have arrested Jesus if he had so desired. If he did not so desire, it was because there was no evidence of Jesus causing a political revolt, and because Antipas was basically a coward.

Those who hold to the other point of view that Jesus' withdrawals were almost exclusively motivated by his fear of Antipas, gloss over the fact that some of his ministry was actually accomplished in Galilee (nos. 2, 5, 9). It seems more reasonable to think that these withdrawals were motivated not by an 'either/or' but by a 'both/and'. After all, most courses of action cannot be attributed to one overriding motive, but to a combination of two or more motives. In this case, to make Jesus'

---

[1] E.g. Mk. 8: 27–33; 9: 2–13.

[2] Whereas before the period of the withdrawals Jesus was constantly speaking of the Kingdom in public, during the withdrawals he only twice spoke of the Kingdom publicly, and both times outside of Antipas' domain (Mt. 16: 28 = Mk. 9: 1 = Lk. 9: 27; Lk. 9: 11). On four occasions he spoke privately to his disciples (Mt. 16: 19, 28; 18: 1, 3, 4, 24; Mk. 9: 47).

[3] E.g. Mt. 19: 12; 19: 14 = Mk. 10: 14; Lk. 9: 60, 62, etc.

[4] Cf. Jn. 6: 15. This is also seen in Jesus' rebuke of the disciples for their thinking in terms of a purely political kingdom (Mk. 8: 15–21; cf. 8: 32). Jesus stated that his kingship was not of this world (Jn. 18: 36).

[5] E.g. Mk. 7: 14–23.

withdrawals motivated by either his wanting to be alone with his disciples or his avoidance of Antipas is unrealistic. It is far more probable that he wanted first to get away from the multitude with his disciples, and secondly to avoid Antipas now that Antipas knew of his movements. Later, it seems, his primary reason for withdrawing was to avoid Antipas, since he remained nearly all the time outside of Antipas' territory. It may be that Antipas was now more earnestly seeking him.

It is stated in Luke 9: 9 that Antipas wanted to see Jesus and in 13: 31 that he wanted to kill him, but he took no action to do either. As with John, he wanted to kill Jesus but refrained from doing so for fear of the people.[1] This also points to his ambivalence of character.

ANTIPAS' AND JESUS' MUTUAL ATTITUDES

The attitude of Antipas and Jesus towards each other can only be deduced from the statements in the Gospels ascribed to them. There are two portions to be reviewed, namely, Jesus' warning about the leaven of the Pharisees and of Herod (Mk. 8: 15), and Antipas' threat to kill Jesus and Jesus' reply (Lk. 13: 31–3).

The leaven of the Pharisees and Herod

The saying

According to Mark 8: 15 Jesus says: Ὁρᾶτε, βλέπετε ἀπὸ τῆς ζύμης τῶν Φαρισαίων καὶ τῆς ζύμης Ἡρῴδου. This saying has long been a *crux interpretum*. The saying is undoubtedly genuine. It was current as an isolated logion in L.[2] Dibelius states that it is a traditional saying 'since there is no reason in this connection for naming Herod'.[3]

However, it is commonly maintained that this saying of Jesus is an artificial insertion into the context, induced by the connection between leaven and bread.[4] But, if this were the case, then Jesus' rebuke οὔπω νοεῖτε οὐδὲ συνίετε (v. 17) and οὔπω συνίετε (v. 21) would be unintelligible, for it presupposes

[1] Mt. 14: 5.
[2] Lk. 12: 1.
[3] *From Tradition to Gospel*, pp. 228–9.
[4] Wellhausen, *Marci*, p. 61; cf. also Dibelius, *From Tradition to Gospel*, pp. 228–9; R. H. Lightfoot, *History and Interpretation*, p. 115 n. 2.

a difficult saying which the disciples had failed to comprehend.[1] Also, Taylor states: 'it is not Mark's habit to insert sayings into the body of the narrative, as Matthew does (cf. ix. 13 a and xii. 5–7), but to append them to the end; cf. ii. 21 f., 27; iii. 27–9, etc.'[2] Further, Knox states: 'It goes back to a period in which the tradition preserved a memory of the facts independent of their value for purposes of edification.'[3] The saying, then, is genuine and is in its original setting.[4] Far from being an intrusion, it may well be the *raison d'être* of the story.[5]

There is a textual problem in that the majority of the texts have τῆς ζύμης 'Ηρῴδου,[6] but there are some that read τῶν 'Ηρῳδιανῶν.[7] The second reading is probably a correction influenced by Mark 3: 6 and 12: 13. But, in either case, the sense remains unchanged, for the leaven of the Herodians would be the same as the leaven of Herod.

The term ζύμη is used metaphorically in a bad sense in the New Testament,[8] while in rabbinical literature it generally has the idea of the evil inclinations of man.[9] This sense is appropriate to the Pharisees to whom many evil characteristics are ascribed in the Gospels, but the Gospels are not as specific about Herod's waywardness and thus this interpretation seems inappropriate in regard to the leaven of Herod. It is more probable that ζύμη conveys the neutral idea that each man has a leaven, that is, 'every man or teacher exerts influence, whether for good or for bad. The emphasis, then, is not on the ζύμη but on the genitive: τῶν Φαρισαίων.'[10] This is confirmed in

---

[1] T. W. Manson, 'Mark viii. 14–21', *JTS*, xxx (1929), 45–6; cf. also P. B. Emmet, 'St Mark viii. 15', *ET*, xlviii (1937), 332–3.

[2] *Mark*, p. 366; cf. also Mt. 18: 3–4.

[3] I, 57. Against this, see Bultmann, p. 403.

[4] Manson, *JTS*, xxx, 45–6.   [5] Cf. Bowman, p. 180.

[6] אABCDKLXΠ.   [7] 𝔓45, WAΘ,*f*1*f*13.

[8] I Cor. 5: 6, 7, 8; Gal. 5: 9. The most probable exception to this is in the parable of the leaven in Mt. 13: 33 = Lk. 13: 20–1. However, even this has been questioned by B. T. D. Smith, *The Parables of the Synoptic Gospels* (Cambridge, 1937), pp. 122–3. For a change of meaning, see *Gospel of Thomas*, logion 96; B. Gärtner, *The Theology of the Gospel of Thomas*, trans. E. J. Sharpe (London, 1961), pp. 230–2.

[9] Strack–Billerbeck, I, 728–9; I. Abrahams, *Studies in Pharisaism and the Gospels*, I, 51–3.

[10] H. Windisch, 'ζύμη', *TDNT*, II (1964), 906; cf. also Schlatter, *Matthäus*, p. 499. Another possible interpretation is that in Jesus' time the

Matthew 16: 12 where it explains the leaven as meaning 'teaching'. The word ζύμη precedes both *Pharisees* and *Herod*, which may indicate that the leaven of Herod is not the same in all details as the leaven of the Pharisees. Jesus, then, is warning his disciples to beware of the influence of the Pharisees and of the influence of Herod.

The interpretation of the saying

Possible historical setting. In this pericope the disciples were concerned because they had forgotten to bring bread. This is understandable since they were probably going to the sparsely populated east side of the Sea of Galilee. Immediately Jesus warned them to beware of the leaven of the Pharisees and Herod. The disciples apparently understood leaven to mean bread, and having missed the point of Jesus' statement began again to discuss their lack of bread. Jesus replied by asking them why they were concerned about the bread, and then he questioned their perception. 'The cross-examination which follows concerning the feeding of the multitudes has its object to show that the literal meaning of bread is out of the question.'[1]

However, since the Pharisees and Herod were opposed to each other, what would they have had in common which the disciples were warned to avoid? Wendt has plausibly suggested that both the Pharisees and Herod had set their hearts upon purely external-political power and upon a national-political kingdom.[2]

That the Pharisees were looking forward to the day when the Messiah would appear and set up his kingdom, is demonstrated in both canonical and uncanonical Jewish literature.[3]

Aramaic words 'leaven' (ḥămîrā) and 'teaching' or 'word' ('ămira) were homonyms, cf. A. Negoiţă and C. Daniel, 'L'énigme du levain', *NovT*, IX (1967), 306–14.

[1] Manson, *JTS*, XXX, 47.

[2] H. H. Wendt, *The Teaching of Jesus*, trans. J. Wilson, I (Edinburgh, 1909), 367–8. This view is also propounded by Lohmeyer, *Markus*, pp. 157–8; Blinzler, *Herodes Antipas*, pp. 13–16; G. H. Boobyer, 'The Miracles of the Loaves and the Gentiles in St Mark's Gospel', *The Scottish Journal of Theology*, VI (1953), 85–6.

[3] Strack–Billerbeck, I, 6–11; IV, 'Exkurs 29: Diese Welt, die Tage des Messias u. die zukünftige Welt', 799–976; W. D. Davies, 'The Jewish Background of the Teaching of Jesus: Apocalyptic and Pharisaism', *ET*, LIX (1948), 233–7; cf. also a thorough and up-to-date discussion on the

It seems, however, that their Messiah was expected to conform to the Torah. There has been a prolonged debate about the Torah in the Messianic age. This question is beyond the scope of the present study, though it may be safely stated that in Jesus' day it was thought that the existing Torah (not a new Messianic Torah) would continue into the Messianic age.[1] Thus it seems that anyone who claimed to be the Messiah must conform to the Torah. According to the synoptics, however, Jesus did not conform to the rabbinic understanding of the Law. He broke the written Torah by working and healing on the Sabbath.[2] He also broke the oral Torah by not conforming to the traditions of the elders.[3] Jesus himself, of course, taught that the Pharisees had missed the point of the Law by holding on to the traditions of man rather than to the commandments of God. The Pharisees, however, would have concluded that, since he had broken both the written and oral Law, he could not legitimately be the Messiah.

Another qualification for the coming Messiah was the ability to give a sign. In the Johannine account of the feeding of the 5,000, when the crowd had seen the sign,[4] they thought that

---

Jewish Messianic expectation in W. D. Davies, *The Setting of the Sermon on the Mount* (Cambridge, 1964), 109–90 (except for a few minor changes, this is a reprint of W. D. Davies, *Torah in the Messianic Age and/or the Age to Come*, *JBL* Monograph Series, VII [Philadelphia, 1952]).

[1] Cf. G. Barth, 'Matthew's Understanding of the Law', *Tradition and Interpretation in Matthew*, by G. Bornkamm, G. Barth and H. J. Held, trans. P. Scott (London, 1963), pp. 153–9. Barth states (p. 157 n. 4): 'It is difficult to deduce from the evidence that there is to be a new Torah, another Torah, or even the cessation of the Torah in the Messianic time. Such a thought is quite impossible for the Jew, who believes that God himself studies the law three hours daily (*Abodah Zarah* 3 b).' Davies (*Sermon on the Mount*, pp. 172–3, 183–4, 187–8) admits there is not much evidence for a new Messianic Torah. However, he concludes that there is a stream of tradition within Judaism which gives evidence for a New Torah to be established in the Messianic age. Both Barth (pp. 156–7 and n. 4) and E. Bammel, 'Νόμος Χριστοῦ', *SE*, III, *TU*, LXXXVIII (Berlin, 1964), 121–3, state that the evidence for a new Torah is weak. First, the rabbinic statements to this effect are usually minority voices contradicted by what follows, and, secondly, these statements are late and reveal an intensification and glorification of the Torah of the later period.

[2] Cf. Mt. 12: 1–14; Mk. 2: 23 – 3: 6; Lk. 6: 1–11.

[3] Mt. 15: 1–20; Mk. 7: 1–23.

[4] For a discussion on this, see Strack–Billerbeck, IV, 'Exkurs 30: Vorzeichen und Berechnung der Tage des Messias', 977–1015.

Jesus was the coming prophet and attempted to force him to be their king.[1] This fits perfectly with the mood of that day in Palestine. During the procuratorship of Cuspius Fadus (ca. A.D. 43–4), an impostor named Theudas persuaded the people to attempt an uprising, προφήτης γὰρ ἔλεγεν εἶναι, promising to divide the Jordan, no doubt as a 'sign' to authenticate his mission.[2] Later, under Felix (ca. A.D. 52–60), there were impostors who called the people into the desert to show them τέρατα καὶ σημεῖα which were according to God's designs.[3] Also, at that time there arose an Egyptian ψευδοπροφήτης, who, προφήτης εἶναι λέγων, led some 30,000 men from the desert to the Mount of Olives for an attack on Jerusalem, promising that the walls would fall down as they advanced to enter the city. He intended to overthrow the Roman garrison and rule over the people.[4] In all of these the chief characteristics were the prophet, the sign, and an attempted uprising, which characteristics are also found in the Johannine narrative. Although none of the passages in Josephus or in John specifically designates the prophet as Messiah, yet in the decades prior to the destruction of Jerusalem the concepts of the coming prophet and of the Deliverer–Messiah belonged together.[5] The attempt to make out that Jesus was the Deliverer at about the time of the Passover[6] is all the more significant in the light of the fact that it was at this time of year that Messiah was

---

[1] Jn. 6: 14–15.

[2] Jos. *Ant.* xx. 97; cf. Acts 5: 36.

[3] Jos. *Ant.* xx. 167–8; *BJ* ii. 258–60.

[4] Jos. *Ant.* xx. 169–70; *BJ* ii. 261–2; cf. Acts 21: 38.

[5] Strack–Billerbeck, II, 480; cf. also C. H. Dodd, *Historical Tradition in the Fourth Gospel* (Cambridge, 1963), pp. 214–15; C. K. Barrett, *The Gospel according to St John* (London, 1955), pp. 231–2; J. N. Sanders, *A Commentary on the Gospel according to St John*, ed. and completed by B. A. Mastin (London, 1968), pp. 180–2. Jeremias states: 'In Jn., too, there is reference to the later Jewish Moses/Messiah typology in 6: 14 f., where after the feeding of the five thousand the crowd wants to make Him king, and also in 6: 30 f., 34, where He is asked to repeat the miracle of the manna. In these passages not only is there ascribed to the crowds the popular expectation that the last time will bring a repetition of the miracle of the manna, but it is presupposed that this miracle will be expected of the Messiah' ('Μωυσῆς', *TDNT*, iv [1967], 862).

[6] Jn. 6: 4 specifically states that the Passover was approaching, and this is confirmed by Mark's mention (6: 39) of the green grass, which also points to the Passover time.

expected to manifest himself.[1] The Passover commemorated the time of deliverance from the foreign oppressor, Egypt, and it was still the hope of the Jews to overthrow the Roman oppressor. In their attempt to make Jesus king, Jesus himself forestalled any attempt at revolt by separating himself (as well as his disciples) from the crowd.[2] This is followed by a long discourse on the Bread of Life,[3] the beginning of which indicates that the multitude had misunderstood the mission of Jesus.

So also the Pharisees. According to the synoptics, they asked Jesus for a sign from heaven[4] which would convince them of his being the Messiah. It seems, however, that the Pharisees were not so much interested to see if Jesus was genuinely the Messiah, as to dispute with him (or question him)[5] with a view to putting him to the test.[6] It implies that they came expressly to disprove any popular notion as to his being the Messiah. This is confirmed by Jesus' reply to them and (if the next pericope belongs historically after the present one) by his discourse to his disciples in the boat. Nevertheless, the fact that they had asked for a sign from heaven would seem to indicate the desire for an extraordinary proof to determine whether or not he was the Messiah.[7]

The warning about the leaven of the Pharisees could easily refer to the Pharisaic concept of the Messiah and his kingdom, as merely an external-political force within the framework of their theology.

---

[1] Edersheim, I, 171.   [2] Jn. 6: 15.

[3] Jn. 6: 26–59.

[4] Mt. 16: 1–4; Mk. 8: 11–13. While Mk. 8: 11 has only the Pharisees, Mt. 16: 1 has both the Pharisees and Sadducees. This mention of both parties is carried through by Matthew into the next pericope (16: 6, 11, 12) and will be treated below.

[5] The term συζητέω is used only by Mark (1: 27; 8: 11; 9: 10, 14, 16; 12: 28) and Luke (22: 23; 24: 15; Acts 6: 9; 9: 29). It conveys the idea of disputing, arguing with, or questioning a person (cf. MM, p. 607; J. Schneider, 'συζητέω', *TWNT*, vii [1964], 747–8).

[6] Cf. Mt. 16: 1. The context must determine if πειράζω is friendly (cf. Jn. 6: 6) or hostile (cf. Mk. 10: 2; 12: 15). In the present case the intention must have been clear to anyone who knew the situation. They had ascribed his exorcism to Beelzebub (3: 22) and now they wanted to cast doubt on his claims.

[7] For a different interpretation, see O. Linton, 'The Demand for a Sign from Heaven', *Studia Theologica*, xix (1965), 112–29.

However, would this fit the second part of Jesus' statement about the leaven of Herod or of the Herodians? If anything, Herod Antipas would have been opposed to the Pharisaic concept of the Messianic kingdom which was liable to prove destructive to the existing government. This is illustrated by his treatment of John who caused a disturbance, and by his concern about the possible implications of Jesus' ministry. Rather, he would have supported the *status quo* in respect to political matters. Although he would have liked to gain the whole of Palestine like his father, as he made abundantly clear at the time of his father's death and of Archelaus' deposition, this he preferred to do through proper political channels. Hence, the leaven of Herod was his desire to maintain his position as sovereign by external-political means. In other words, the 'kingdom of Herod' was good enough for Herod!

In conclusion then, it seems that Jesus' warning referred to an influence exercised in the interests of an external-political kingdom – the Pharisees' concept within their theological framework, Herod's concept within his political framework. In contrast with these, Jesus' mission and message were concerned with a kingdom whose chief characteristics were neither political nor external.

Context. The wider context of this pericope lends further support to the above theory. The pericope itself (Mk. 8: 14–21) seems to be a summary of the two feedings. It is interesting to note that the order of the nine literary units from the feeding of the 5,000 (Mk. 6: 32–44) to the present pericope is identical in Mark and Matthew, though Matthew omits parts of the stories and Mark introduces a healing story (7: 32–7).[1]

Following the feeding of the 5,000, Jesus withdrew from the crowd. If the Johannine account is referring to the same feeding, and it seems likely that it is,[2] the reason for his with-

---

[1] The key word throughout this whole section seems to be ἄρτος. This is used in the feeding of the 5,000 (Mt. 14: 17, 19 (bis); Mk. 6: 37, 38, 41, 44; cf. also Mk. 6: 52); the tradition of the elders (Mt. 15: 2; Mk. 7: 2, 5); the Syro-Phoenician Woman (Mt. 15: 26; Mk. 7: 27), the feeding of the 4,000 (Mt. 15: 33, 34, 36; Mk. 8: 4, 5, 6); and the leaven of the Pharisees (Mt. 16: 5, 7, 8, 9, 10, 11, 12?; Mk. 8: 14, 16, 17, 19).

[2] Cf. S. Mendner, 'Zum Problem "Johannes und die Synoptiker"', *NTS*, iv (1958), 282–307.

drawal was that they wanted to make him king.[1] This withdrawal is followed by a long discourse on the Bread of Life,[2] the beginning of which indicates that the multitude had misunderstood his mission.

According to the synoptics, soon after the feeding, the Pharisees and scribes came from Jerusalem to question Jesus about his transgression of the tradition of the elders.[3] If this is the correct setting of the pericope, their appearance may have been a result of the feeding of the multitude, and their aim to test Jesus to see if he were in truth the coming prophet. This he could not be if he rejected the traditions of the elders. After this the Pharisees asked for a sign from heaven.[4] Again Jesus fails to meet their test of the true coming one. According to the synoptics, it was after this incident that Jesus told his disciples to beware of the leaven of the Pharisees and of Herod. In other words, they were to avoid the purely external-political nature of the kingdom propagated by both the Pharisees and Herod.

The context subsequent to this pericope favours this interpretation. In both Matthew and Mark the readers hear not only the negative instruction of this pericope, but also, immediately after, the positive teaching at Caesarea Philippi where Peter admits for the first time that Jesus is the Messiah.[5] Jesus charges his disciples to tell no one about his true character for this was bound to be interpreted by the public in the 'rebel' sense.[6] Jesus then reveals that he must suffer, for which Peter rebukes him. Moule states:

Instantly, Jesus recognizes the very same test as had come to him at the beginning of his ministry. In Matt. 4: 8–10, the tempter shows him all the kingdoms of the world, and invites him to possess them in the world's way (by force of arms, by violence). 'Begone, Satan', is Jesus's reply; 'Scripture says, "You shall do homage to the Lord your God and worship him alone"'. So now again, Jesus recognizes 'the Satan', 'the Opposition'. . . : *'Away with you, Satan,' he said; 'you*

---

[1] Jn. 6: 15. [2] Jn. 6: 26–59.
[3] Mt. 15: 1–20; Mk. 7: 1–23. [4] Mt. 16: 1–4; Mk. 8: 10–12.
[5] Mt. 16: 13–20. Mark has the short story of the healing of a blind man at Bethsaida (8: 22–6) before he gives the incident at Caesarea Philippi (8: 27–30).
[6] Cf. C. F. D. Moule, *The Gospel according to Mark*, *The Cambridge Bible Commentary*, ed. by P. R. Ackroyd, A. R. C. Leaney, and J. W. Packer (Cambridge, 1965), pp. 64–7.

think as men think, not as God thinks.' Several times already we have seen Jesus trying to keep his great authority a secret: now we gain some insight into the reason for this secrecy. He must at all costs fight the idea that victory is by the kind of Messiahship or kingship which the general public want.[1]

In other words, Jesus rebukes Peter for being on the side of Satan, that is, for regarding the Messiah and the Messianic kingdom in a purely external light. Peter was contemplating a Messiah that would fit within his own reasoning, as were the multitude in John 6, and the Pharisees and Herod(ians) in the previous pericope. Therefore, Peter is rebuked because his view was comparable with the leaven of the Pharisees and Herod of which Jesus had warned his disciples to beware. Jesus' mission and Messiahship were not merely an external-political force which would fit within the framework of men's reasoning and theology.[2]

In conclusion, then, the leaven of the Pharisees and Herod-(ians) is an influence exerted in the interests of an external-political Messiah and/or Messianic kingdom. The disciples were warned to beware of this influence, for the true Messiah was not to be a worldly figure who would upset kingdoms or maintain the political *status quo*.[3] This concept of the leaven of the Pharisees and Herod harmonizes with the emphases of Matthew and Mark, beginning with the feeding of the multitude and ending with the pericope of Jesus telling that he must

[1] *Ibid.* pp. 66–7; cf. also Cullmann, *Christology*, pp. 122–5. For a defence of the unity of the scene (presented in Mk. 8: 31–3) as opposed to the assumption that the prophecy of suffering is a later insertion and that the hypothesis of the whole scene is unhistorical, see E. Schweizer, *Lordship and Discipleship*, *SBT* no. 28 (London, 1960), p. 19; Cullmann, *Christology*, p. 63.

[2] Grant states that Jesus refused 'to use His Messiahship for His own personal ends, or to satisfy the bizarre political dreams of His people' (Grant, *Economic Background*, p. 126). See also O. Cullmann, *Jesus and the Revolutionaries*, trans. G. Putnam (New York, 1970), pp. 31–50, esp. pp. 41–2.

[3] Mánek's interpretation is that Jesus is warning his disciples against the influence of the religious teaching and discussion of the Pharisees and Herodians at the table. These sects, he is saying, do not help to solve the burning desires of humanity, for the solution of these is in the hands of Jesus who is the Bread of Life (J. Mánek, 'Mark viii 14–21', *NovT*, VII [1964], 12). This may be true, but it would seem that the evangelist's intention was also to answer the pressing problem as to the true character of the Messiah and of his relationship to his kingdom.

suffer. It shows that the multitude, the Pharisees, and the disciples were blinded to the true mission of Jesus.

The synoptic relationships

Whereas in Mark Jesus warns his disciples of the leaven of the Pharisees and Herod, in Luke he warns them of the leaven of the Pharisees which is hypocrisy.[1] For the purposes of the present study, Luke's variation is not important, since it comes in an entirely different context to that of either Matthew or Mark,[2] which is, as Manson suggests, genuine.[3] This may indicate that the saying itself is not just a variant of Mark 8: 15 and Matthew 16: 6 but was uttered on more than one occasion in slightly different forms.[4]

The real problem is the relationship between Matthew and Mark. Matthew substitutes the leaven of the Pharisees and Sadducees[5] for Mark's leaven of the Pharisees and Herod. Does this change alter the basic meaning of the saying? The Sadducees, who denied the resurrection and the immortality of the soul[6] and believed that man's fate was entirely in his own hands,[7] would also have rejected a future cataclysmic Messianic kingdom. It is possible that they thought the Messianic kingdom had already come in the shape of the Hasmonaean house. In their capacity as aristocrats and wealthy landowners, the last thing they would have wished was a revolution with the consequent loss of their position and wealth. Hence, they

---

[1] Lk. 12: 1.

[2] For a discussion of this, see Hawkins, *SSP*, pp. 71–2; Plummer, *Luke*, p. 318; Dibelius, *From Tradition to Gospel*, pp. 228–9; Creed, *Luke*, p. 170; Lagrange, *Luc*, p. 352; Grundmann, *Lukas*, p. 253; Knox, I, 56–8, 101–2; II, 64, 68.

[3] T. W. Manson, *Sayings*, pp. 269–70.

[4] Cf. Plummer, *Luke*, p. 318; N. B. Stonehouse, *The Witness of Luke to Christ* (London, 1951), p. 127 and n. 2. Manson, however, feels that Lk. 12: 1 is a fragment of Luke's separate tradition (L) which was inserted here in what seemed to be an appropriate context (*Sayings*, p. 105). On the other hand, even Manson (*Sayings*, p. 270) regards Luke's version of the saying as secondary, the words 'which is hypocrisy' are an explanatory comment by Luke or his source.

[5] Mt. 16: 6.

[6] Mt. 22: 23 = Mk. 12: 18 = Lk. 20: 27; Jos. *Ant.* xviii. 16–17; *BJ* ii. 164–5; cf. also Finkelstein, *Pharisees*, II, 748.

[7] Jos. *Ant.* xiii. 173.

'were anxious above all things to maintain the political status quo, and so to avoid conflict with the imperial power'.[1] In this context, therefore, the Matthaean inclusion of the Sadducees would not be essentially different from the Marcan usage of Herod(ians). The Matthaean habit of using the term Sadducees with the Pharisees (where the other evangelists are silent) may indicate in this case that his readers understood that the political implications of the Sadducees were the same as those of Herod(ians), namely, the maintaining of the political *status quo*. Thus Matthew's inclusion of the Sadducees in place of Herod is entirely legitimate and understandable.[2] On the other hand, Mark's readers in Rome may not have understood the political implications of the Sadducees since he mentions them elsewhere only in the context of a theological question on the resurrection (12: 18), whereas the name Herod would have been known.[3] Also if the term *Herodians* is the correct reading in 8: 15, his readers would have understood them as adherents of Herod as indicated in 3: 6 and 12: 13.

On the occasions that Matthew mentions the leaven of the Pharisees and Sadducees (16: 6, 11, 12) it is always in the form ἀπὸ τῆς ζύμης τῶν Φαρισαίων καὶ Σαδδουκαίων – the term *leaven* is not repeated as in Mark. This may indicate that Jesus was warning his disciples to beware of only one influence common to both, namely a purely external-nationalistic political kingdom, but not indicating that they have a different concept of the kingdom as Mark suggests by repeating ζύμη. The term διδαχή in the pericope refers probably to teaching concerning this one aspect which both held in common.

Therefore, in this context the inclusion of the Sadducees is

---

[1] Taylor, *Life*, p. 62.

[2] Knox' statement (i, 57) that Matthew did not understand the saying of Jesus and so changed the word *Herod* to *Sadducees* is untenable. This would be true only if the Herodians were a political party and the Sadducees strictly a religious sect. But if the Sadducees were a religious sect with political ideals as well as political adherents, then this argument breaks down. They were pro-government and this would mean at least in part pro-Herodian government (cf. Appendix X).

[3] Mark refers to Herod (Antipas) eight times (6: 14, 16, 17, 18, 20, 21, 22; 8: 15) whereas Matthew only mentions him three times (14: 1, 3, 6). Mark refers to the Herodians twice (3: 6; 12: 13) with the possibility of a third mention in 8: 15, whereas Matthew mentions them only in a strictly political context in opposition to the religious Pharisees (22: 15–16).

understandable. Although they and the Pharisees were poles apart, they too would have been glad to test Jesus with a view to disproving any notion that he was the coming prophet.

Conclusion

Mark 8: 15 has long presented a difficulty. If ζύμη means 'influence', then Jesus' warning would have been twofold. On the one hand he would be warning them against the influence of the Pharisees who were thinking in terms of a political Messiah who would deliver them from the Roman oppressor, a view which fits within the Pharisaic concept of the Torah and the tradition of the elders. On the other hand, he was warning them against the influence of the Herod(ians)/Sadducees' interest in maintaining a political *status quo*. It is, then, entirely legitimate for Jesus to have mentioned both the Pharisees and Herod(ians)/Sadducees in one breath. This he did without implying that the two were in any way agreed except on the policy of opposing Jesus, as seen in Mark 3: 6. Matthew's replacement of Herod by the Sadducees does not alter the meaning. The warning was to beware a wrong concept of an external Messianic kingdom brought about by force. In John, after the crowd had attempted to make him king, Jesus rebukes them for misunderstanding his mission. He shows them that the externals are not important, but rather that they should believe in the one whom God had sent.[1] They were to come to Jesus whose true character they could only hear and learn from the Father.[2] In the two synoptics Jesus rebukes the Pharisees for perverting the Law and the Prophets[3] and for their demand for a visible sign.[4] For this reason, he told his disciples to beware of their notions of a purely external-nationalistic political kingdom. Immediately after this Jesus rebuked Peter for misunderstanding the proper course of events in relation to the recently revealed Messiah.[5] The proper attitude for both the Messiah and his disciples, from this point onward, was to take up their crosses[6] in total disregard of nationalistic and political aspirations.

[1] Jn. 6: 26–9.
[2] Jn. 6: 45.
[3] Mt. 15: 1–20; Mk. 7: 1–23.
[4] Mt. 16: 1–4; Mk. 8: 11–13.
[5] Mt. 16: 13–23; Mk. 8: 27–33.
[6] Mt. 16: 24–8; Mk. 8: 34–8.

Antipas' threat to kill Jesus and Jesus' reply

The second passage in which the mutal attitudes of Antipas and Jesus appear is Luke 13: 31–3.

Introductory matters

This pericope is peculiar to Luke and is followed by a lament (vv. 34–5) which occurs also in Matthew 23: 37–9. On the one hand, the authenticity of Luke 13: 31–3 has been questioned by Dibelius who thinks that Luke inserted the Pharisees into the story as the usual opponents of Jesus (as in Lk. 16: 14 and 17: 20). He regards this insertion by Luke as a Chria-like formulation,[1] 'for it is very doubtful whether Jesus' word was directed against the "fox" Herod. Probably here also the introduction is the work of the evangelist, who is always interested in the great ones of the earth.'[2] However, it is hardly probable that the Pharisees are introduced as opponents;[3] rather, they are represented as friendly towards Jesus. In fact, as Goguel observes, the role of the Pharisees here contradicts so strongly the traditional picture of them in the Gospels that their mention here could hardly have been invented.[4] Moreover, if Luke

---

[1] I.e. 'words of Jesus in such a construction that they appear as answers to short questions or as assertions from the opposite standpoint' (*From Tradition to Gospel*, p. 162).

[2] *Ibid.* pp. 162–3.

[3] Knox, II, 81 n. 2; W. G. Kümmel, *Promise and Fulfilment*[3], trans. D. M. Barton, *SBT*, no. 23 (London, 1957), pp. 71–2 n. 173.

[4] Cf. Goguel, *Life of Jesus*, p. 350; Knox, II, 81; Tyson, *JBL*, LXXIX, 245; Bultmann, p. 35. This is all the more evident when one examines the pericope from the point of view of Luke's use of the Pharisees. Wherever the material of Matthew and Luke is common (Mt. 11: 7–19 = Lk. 7: 24–35; Mt. 23: 23–4, 27–8 = ?Lk. 11: 42–4) and of Mark and Luke (Mk. 2: 1 – 3: 6 = Lk. 5: 17 – 6: 11), the Pharisees are always set in a bad light in Luke. The same is true when there is a reference to the Pharisees in the material which is peculiar to Luke (cf. 11: 53 – 12: 2; 15: 2; 16: 14; 17: 20–1; 18: 9–14). Although sometimes they are represented as being friendly to Jesus (Lk. 7: 36–50; 11: 37–41; 13: 31–3; 14: 1–3), each time (except in 13: 31–3) the episode ends with the Pharisees put in a bad light. One can draw two conclusions: (1) that while Luke conveys a bad impression of the Pharisees, there are usually moments of friendly conversation with Jesus, which shows that Luke did not tamper with his sources; (2) that Lk. 13: 31–3 is the only place where the Pharisees are placed in a good light. Here they receive no rebuke from Jesus. This remarkable fact undoubtedly points to its authenticity.

or a later editor wished to find fault with Herod, why did he not do it in a similar manner in connection with the Baptist's death (3: 19–20; 9: 7–9) or, better, in the trial of Jesus by Antipas (23: 6–12)? In fact, there is no real reason why Jesus should not have made this reply (calling Herod a fox) in the shape of a threat, especially if he knew it was no more than that. On the other hand, Bultmann thinks that Luke 13: 31–3 is 'in the strict sense a piece of biographical material'.[1] However, he would argue that verse 33 is an isolated saying introduced *ad vocem*, σήμερον καὶ αὔριον, in view of verse 32, or that verse 32 *b* is secondary (constructed by the church), leaving only πλήν in verse 33 as an editorial insertion.[2] Yet although Kümmel regards the sayings both in verses 32 and 33 as original sayings of Jesus, he thinks the second one did not originally belong here.[3] If, however, it makes the text read more roughly, it is difficult to understand why a repetition was later inserted. Would not a later editor have wanted to smooth this over? Black has suggested that by translating these two verses back into Aramaic a parallelism emerges.[4] There would seem, therefore, to be reasonable grounds for thinking that both these sayings of Jesus were originally in this context. The two sayings are parallel, and they convey a sense of urgency which would not be apparent if one of the sayings were left out.

[1] P. 35; cf. also p. 388.

[2] P. 35. Wellhausen thinks that one should omit from v. 32 καὶ τῇ τρίτῃ τελειοῦμαι and σήμερον καὶ αὔριον from v. 33 (J. Wellhausen, *Das Evangelium Lucae* [Berlin, 1904], p. 76; followed by Creed, *Luke*, p. 187 and Knox, II, 82). Although this makes for a smoother text, it does so at the expense of the saying's originality and the note of urgency. Schmidt (pp. 265–7) thinks that the genuine tradition comprised vv. 31 and 32 *a* (up to and including αὔριον) which was enlarged by Luke with 32 *b* and 33 on the basis of a saying about the passion and the resurrection. Taylor (*Jesus*, p. 171 n. 2) observes that the above suggestions are precarious and arbitrary, 'which obviously offers no resting-place in the critical inquiry'.

[3] *Promise*, pp. 71–2.

[4] *Aramaic Approach*, pp. 206–7. It would read as follows:

> (32) Behold I cast out demons, and I do cures day by day,
> But one day soon I am perfected.
> (33) But day by day I must needs work,
> Then one day soon pass on.

Probable historical setting

Luke 13: 31–3 is located in the midst of Luke's central section (9: 51 – 18: 14 or 19: 44). There has been a great deal of discussion on this section of Luke.[1] For the purposes of this study, suffice it to conclude that though there are several indications that Jesus and his disciples were on the road to Jerusalem,[2] this section's primary intention and arrangement are thematic not chronological, to present Jesus as the teacher, not as the traveller.[3]

The introductory words ('Εν αὐτῇ τῇ ὥρᾳ) which are peculiar to Luke are identical or similar to those of Luke 10: 21; 12: 12; 20: 19; and 24: 33. It seems that it has little, if any, chronological connection with the preceding; rather, it has a thematic connection with 13: 27 by clarifying the 'workers of iniquity'. The Pharisees' warning to Jesus, Ἔξελθε καὶ πορεύου ἐντεῦθεν, as well as Jesus' reply, incidentally implies that Jesus was still in one of Antipas' territories.

[1] For a fairly comprehensive bibliography on this subject for the years 1910 to 1953, see J. Blinzler, 'Die literarische Eigenart des sogenannten Reiseberichts im Lukasevangelium', *SS*, pp. 20–1 n. 3; also pp. 20–52. Cf. also J. A. Robertson, 'The Passion Journey', *Exp*, 8th series, XVII (1919), 54–73, 128–43, 174–94, 322–44; Schmidt, pp. 246–73; H. E. Guilleband, 'The Travel in St Luke (IX: 51 – XVIII: 14)', *BS*, LXXX (1923), 237–45; Stonehouse, pp. 114–27. For literature from 1953, see J. Schneider, 'Zur Analyse des lukanischen Reiseberichtes', *SS*, pp. 207–29; C. F. Evans, 'The Central Section of St Luke's Gospel', *Studies in the Gospels*, ed. by D. E. Nineham (Oxford, 1955), pp. 37–53; B. Reicke, 'Instruction and Discussion in the Travel Narrative', *SE*, I, *TU*, LXXIII (1959), 206–16; Conzelmann, pp. 60–73; W. C. Robinson, Jr, 'The Theological Context for Interpreting Luke's Travel Narrative (9: 51 ff.)', *JBL*, LXXIX (1960), 20–31; J. H. Davies, 'The Purpose of the Central Section of St Luke's Gospel', *SE*, II, *TU*, LXXXVII (1964), 164–9; M. D. Goulder, 'The Chiastic Structure of the Lucan Journey', *SE*, II, *TU*, LXXXVII (1964), 195–202; E. Ellis, pp. 148–9; F. Stagg, 'The Journey Towards Jerusalem in Luke's Gospel. Luke 9: 51 – 19: 27', *Review and Expositor*, LXIV (1967), 499–512.

[2] Lk. 9: 51, 53; 13: 22, 33; 17: 11; 18: 31; 19: 11, 28, 41.

[3] To try to reconstruct a chronological sequence of this section is almost impossible. In 9: 51 Jesus starts out for Jerusalem and by 13: 31–5 he is either in Galilee or Peraea; yet the lament over Jerusalem is a Jerusalem saying according to Matthew (23: 37–9). In 17: 11 Jesus is still in the vicinity of Galilee and Samaria. It is not until 18: 15, where Luke is again parallel to the other two synoptists, that any chronological sequence is apparent.

Because of Mark's reference that Jesus had left Galilee, many commentators assume that Jesus was now in Peraea.[1] However, the Lucan testimony excludes Peraea[2] and implies that Jesus was still in Galilee.[3] Would the Pharisees have come to Peraea to warn Jesus? The Gospels usually portray the Pharisees in Galilee or Judaea and not in Peraea. If Jesus was in Galilee it is difficult to know in what part of his ministry it occurred. Manson suggests that it was before Jesus went to Caesarea Philippi,[4] but it seems unlikely that Jesus would have told the Pharisees of his impending death in Jerusalem before he told his disciples. Certainly Peter was surprised when Jesus told him at Caesarea Philippi, which would be strange if he had heard Jesus make this same pronouncement previously. Cadman is vague on this but he seems to synchronize this warning with Jesus' final departure from Galilee after the feeding of the 5,000 (Mk. 6: 45).[5] Assuming that the feeding did occur in Galilee (which is questionable) the same criticism can be levelled against this suggestion as Manson's. Also, the tenor of Jesus' reply would indicate that he was going to Jerusalem fairly soon, whereas there would seem to be quite an extensive time lapse between Mark 6: 31 and 10: 1. Besides, if he was going to Jerusalem, it is strange that he should go via Bethsaida. It is possible to place this warning at the time of Jesus' stay at Gennesaret[6] since his reply to the Pharisees was that he would go on healing until he left. It is the last recorded healing ministry of Jesus in Galilee unless one includes the healing of the boy possessed by a spirit after the transfiguration.[7] Also, in the following pericope[8] there were the Pharisees questioning Jesus, as there were Pharisees warning Jesus in Luke 13: 31–3. Although this

---

[1] Cf. Plummer, *Luke*, p. 348; Holtzmann, *Das Neue Testament*, I, 293; Lagrange, *Luc*, p. 392; N. Geldenhuys, *Commentary on the Gospel of Luke* (London, 1950), p. 382; K. H. Rengstorf, *Das Evangelium nach Lukas*[8], *NTD* III (Göttingen, 1958), p. 174; Tyson, *JBL*, LXXIX, 245. Dodd states that the difficulty of fitting this pericope into the Marcan framework points to its authenticity (*Parables*, p. 100 n. 1).

[2] Luke does not even mention Peraea in 3: 1.

[3] Cadman, pp. 29–56; Creed, *Luke*, p. 186; Stonehouse, p. 120; Blinzler, *SS*, p. 30 n. 24; Knox, II, 81; Conzelmann, p. 61.

[4] *Sayings*, p. 276.   [5] Pp. 44–9, 53–6.

[6] Mt. 14: 34–6 = Mk. 6: 53–6.

[7] Mt. 17: 14–21 = Mk. 9: 14–29 = Lk. 9: 37–43*a*.

[8] Mt. 15: 1–20 = Mk. 7: 1–23.

suggestion is attractive, it is open to the same criticism as that of Cadman. Tyre was in the opposite direction to Jerusalem. In addition, the Pharisees' questioning Jesus in Matthew and Mark was on a religious issue and their attitude toward him was not friendly as portrayed in Luke 13: 31. The same could be said of Jesus' landing at Dalmanutha in Mark 8: 10b–13.

It seems best to place this warning just before, or at the time of, Jesus' leaving Galilee; the scene may be identical with Mark 10: 1[1] (= Mt. 19: 1) or Luke 9: 51.[2] It is stated that Jesus came through Galilee[3] to Capernaum[4] but there is no geographical notice until Matthew 19: 1 or Mark 10: 1. It may have been while Jesus and his disciples were travelling through southern Galilee, perhaps near Tiberias, that this warning took place. The one difficulty is that in the travel narrative just prior to his leaving Galilee there is no mention of a healing ministry. But neither is there any in the context of Luke 13: 31–3. This, however, does not necessarily preclude there having been one. Certainly the later ministry in Galilee was characterized by private instruction to his disciples,[5] and by public healings,[6] but not discourses or preaching.[7] It seems, then, best to place this pericope (Lk. 13: 31–3) sometime near the end of Jesus' Galilaean ministry, probably just before he left Galilee for the last time.

[1] As Blinzler, *SS*, p. 31 n. 24.　　　[2] Schneider, *SS*, pp. 214–17.

[3] Mt. 17: 22 = Mk. 9: 30.　　　[4] Mt. 17: 24 = Mk. 9: 33.

[5] Mt. 16: 5–12 = Mk. 8: 14–21; Mt. 17: 22–3 = Mk. 9: 30–2; Mt. 17: 24–7; Mk. 9: 33–50.

[6] Mt. 14: 34–6 = Mk. 6: 53–6.

[7] Jesus' rebuke of the Pharisees when they wanted a sign (Mt. 16: 1–4 = Mk. 8: 11–13) does not seem to have been witnessed by a great crowd, and certainly there was no discourse. The only exception to this is after Jesus rebukes the Pharisees for keeping the traditions of men which nullify the commands of God (Mt. 15: 1–9; Mk. 7: 1–13) and instructs the crowd about the true nature of defilement (Mt. 15: 10–20 = Mk. 7: 14–23). But it is possible that the whole discourse on the clean and unclean is not in its original position in either Matthew (cf. M'Neile, p. 221) or Mark (cf. Taylor, *Mark*, p. 334).

Interpretation

The interpretation of this pericope[1] raises several problems. These will be treated in the order in which they occur.

Antipas' threat. First, did Antipas really make this statement or did the Pharisees invent it? It is probable that this was not an invention of the Pharisees. If the Pharisees had made it up, Jesus no doubt would have rebuked them for their hypocrisy and 'it is very unnatural to make τῇ ἀλώπεκι ταύτῃ refer to the inventor of the report, or to the Pharisees as a body, or indeed to anyone but Herod'.[2] Also, it seems unlikely that they would have dared to ascribe false intentions to Antipas to further their own ends.

Yet for Antipas to have conveyed his message by means of his enemies, the Pharisees, is singular. Indeed, it is almost incredible. There is, however, no reason why they could not have worked together to achieve a common goal. Mark records that the adherents of Herod and the Pharisees had previously plotted to kill Jesus.[3] Antipas had been displeased with John the Baptist, while Jesus he must have liked even less, for Jesus was drawing huge crowds in Antipas' main territory of Galilee. Yet as with John, he hesitated to kill him for fear of his subjects who reckoned Jesus as a prophet, especially since there was no valid evidence for Jesus having caused an insurrection against Antipas or the Roman government. Indeed, it is unlikely that he really intended to kill Jesus, for had that been the case he would hardly have made public his intentions. A friend of the police does not tell the thief that the police are coming! More

---

[1] Dodd has called attention to the fact that this pericope is similar in form to that of Jesus' dialogue with his brothers in Jn. 7: 3–8 (cf. Dodd, *Historical Tradition*, pp. 322–5).

[2] Plummer, *Luke*, p. 348. It has been thought that Jesus was making a reply to the Pharisees rather than to Antipas, for he said to go and tell *this* (ταύτῃ) fox rather than *that* (ἐκείνη) fox, cf. Cyril of Alexandria, *A Commentary upon the Gospel according to S. Luke*, trans. R. P. Smith, II (Oxford, 1859), 468 (*MPG*, LXXII, 781). It is felt that the demonstrative pronoun ταύτῃ must refer to someone nearer the spot than Antipas, namely, the Pharisees (cf. 'Notes of Recent Exposition', *ET*, XIX [1909], 391–4). But this is not natural to the context. If this were the case, it is most likely that Jesus would have rebuked the Pharisees directly as he had done in other places (cf. Lk. 11: 39 ff.).

[3] Mk. 3: 6.

probably, Antipas was only making a threat so that Jesus would move out of his jurisdiction. Jesus' reply seems to indicate that he accepted it as no more than that.[1]

On the other side, the Pharisees are pictured throughout the Gospels as consumed with an intense hatred for Jesus. They wanted to get rid of him for his teaching as well as for the embarrassment he had caused them on several occasions. But they must have known their weak-kneed leader, Antipas. It is possible that the Pharisees had arranged with Antipas to tell Jesus his danger in order to hasten his departure. If he went to Judaea, then the Pharisees may have thought that the Sanhedrin would take care of him.[2] Thus, it is conceivable that the Pharisees worked in conjunction with Antipas – if not directly, then indirectly through the Herodians – to get Jesus out of Antipas' domain.

Jesus' reply. The second problem is Jesus' defiant reply. After designating Antipas 'that fox', he went on to say that he would leave when, and only when, he was ready, and that would be not because he feared Antipas, but because his mission was accomplished. This reply indicates that Jesus saw through the Pharisees as not being the sympathizers they pretended but the semi-official agents of Antipas.[3]

The designation 'fox' has given rise to some discussion. The fox is often contrasted with the lion. The lion, being powerful, is an animal which attacks directly, whereas the fox, being weak, uses cunning deceit to achieve its aims.[4] The person described as a fox is looked down upon as weak and wily, and as lacking real power and dignity.[5] Whereas Antipas wanted to be re-

[1] It may be that Jesus knew Antipas' real attitude through his informant, Joanna, the wife of Antipas' financial minister (Lk. 8: 3).

[2] As suggested by F. A. Farley, 'A Text (Luke xiii. 33)', *ET*, xxxiv (1923), 430; J. W. Lightley, *Jewish Sects and Parties in the Time of Christ* (London, 1925), p. 133.

[3] Manson states: 'This stiff and uncompromising reply, together with the fact that the messengers are told to convey it to Herod, may incline us to think that Jesus regarded these Pharisees as semi-official emissaries of the Tetrarch rather than sympathizers with Himself' (Manson, *Sayings*, p. 276).

[4] For a study of the use of the word 'fox', see Appendix XI.

[5] A parallel to this use of fox is found in a proverbial saying by Esarhaddon as found by Meissner, '"Wohin kann der Fuchs vor der Sonne gehen?" d.i. der kleine Fürst, der nur in der Nacht seinem Raube nachgeht, kann am hellen Tage gegen den grossen König nichts ausrichten' (B. Meiss-

presented as a real threat, his true character and weakness are
laid bare by Jesus. Jesus may even have considered himself as
the lion (later he was called 'the lion out of the tribe of Judah')[1]
in contrast with that fox of low estate coming from the deserts of
Edom![2] In that case his irony had a sharper edge. In conclusion,
then, the cunning schemes of that petty potentate, the fox,
were futile before the Great King, the lion.

Jesus' intention. The third problem is the last part of verse 32:
ἐκβάλλω δαιμόνια καὶ ἰάσεις ἀποτελῶ σήμερον καὶ αὔριον, καὶ τῇ
τρίτῃ τελειοῦμαι. Jesus' intention was to continue his activity
no matter what Antipas said. In fact he even stated that it
would be for at least a short time. The time reference is
probably not to three actual days,[3] to Sabbath motif,[4] or to
the three years of Jesus' ministry. Rather, it seems to be a
semitic idiom for a short indefinite period, followed by an
indefinite but imminent and certain event,[5] and thus the
words 'today and tomorrow' may mean simply 'day by day'.[6]
The third day probably does not have reference to his resurrection, for in that case the first two days would be those of the
crucifixion, whereas here Jesus is speaking of the preceding
days as a period of casting out demons and performing cures.[7]

ner, 'Sprichwörter bei Asarhaddon', *Archiv für Orientforschung*, x [1936],
362).   [1] Rev. 5: 5; cf. Gen. 49: 9–10.

[2] In Jewish literature the Herods, being hated and half-foreign, resembled
Laban, who was designated 'the Aramaean'. This 'was regarded by the
Rabbis as referring not only to his origin but also to his character as "the
deceiver", *rammay* (Gen. Rabba on 25: 20); and there are numerous descrip-
tions of him stressing the same characteristic. Herod was "a fox"' (Daube,
The New Testament and Rabbinic Judaism, pp. 190–1).

[3] As held by Plummer, *Luke*, pp. 349–50; Blinzler, *SS*, pp. 42–5.

[4] As suggested by V. E. McEachern, 'Dual Witness and Sabbath Motif
in Luke', *CJT*, xii (1966), 276.

[5] Cf. Hos. 6: 2. This is similar to the German word *paar* which designates
'a few', though its literal meaning is 'a couple'. Also, the American usage of
'a couple of days' may mean a short time although literally it would mean
only two days. For a discussion of this verse, see A. H. Gilbert, 'Σήμερον
καὶ αὔριον, καὶ τῇ τρίτῃ (Luke 13: 32)', *JBL*, xxxv (1916), 315–18.

[6] Black, *Aramaic Approach*, p. 206; cf. A. Loisy, *Les Évangiles Synoptiques*, ii
(Paris, 1908), 126. Conzelmann's view that this signifies a lengthy journey
(pp. 62–3 n. 4, 68, 197 n. 1) or the three stages in Jesus' ministry: Galilee,
the journey, Jerusalem (pp. 65, 68, 154 n. 1), is unlikely.

[7] Taylor, *Jesus*, p. 168; Blinzler, *SS*, p. 44.

Surely, if an interpolator had wanted to insert something here about Jesus' resurrection he would have followed something in the order of Luke 9:22. The point is that Jesus intended to remain in Antipas' territory for a short period of time. 'The temporal expressions relate solely to duration of the ministry, and the question of locality does not arise until verse 33.'[1]

The verb τελειοῦμαι is probably passive[2] and means 'I am brought to completion'. If this has reference to his death then here is a prophecy of his death. If it has reference to his ministry, which is more probable in this context, it means that he will work a while longer in Herod's domain, and that his work will then be completed.[3] Jesus gives his word that his mission will not stop short of its end however near that end may be.

Jesus' reiteration of his intention. The fourth problem is in verse 33 which reads: πλὴν δεῖ με σήμερον καὶ αὔριον καὶ τῇ ἐχομένῃ[4] πορεύεσθαι, ὅτι οὐκ ἐνδέχεται προφήτην ἀπολέσθαι ἔξω Ἰερουσαλήμ. In attempting to interpret this, Blinzler suggests that Jesus was to come to the end of his ministry on the third day; but that on the following day (the fourth) he must go away.[5] However, this still does not seem to alleviate the problem of the repetition of the words 'today and tomorrow'.[6] As mentioned above, it seems best to take this as a case of parallelism. It denotes a sense of urgency. The realization that Jesus' ministry was essentially a travelling ministry[7] may help to explain the repetition. While

---

[1] Taylor, *Jesus*, p. 168.

[2] Cf. a study of the different voices of the verb in Blinzler, *SS*, p. 43 n. 61; cf. also C. J. Ellicott, *Historical Lectures on the Life of Our Lord Jesus Christ, being the Hulsean Lectures for the Year 1859*[2] (London, 1861), p. 264 n. 2. For a study of the word, see B. F. Westcott, *The Epistle to the Hebrews*[3] (London, 1903), pp. 64–6.

[3] Loisy (II, 126) translates it 'I am about to arrive at my end' (Je suis à mon terme) and believes it refers to Jesus' ministry being accomplished by his resurrection and exaltation as well as by his death. Cf. also Black, *Aramaic Approach*, pp. 233–4.

[4] The words τῇ ἐχομένῃ with the meaning 'the next day' occur elsewhere in biblical literature (Acts 20:15; 1 Chron. 10:8; 2 Macc. 12:39; cf. also Acts 21:26; MSS A E*, *pc*, vg of Acts 13:44; 1 Macc. 4:28).

[5] *SS*, pp. 44–6.

[6] Even Blinzler seems to concede this; cf. *ibid.* p. 44 n. 64.

[7] Cf. Manson, *Sayings*, p. 277.

Jesus was casting out devils and performing cures he was also travelling, and on the final day he would have finished his ministry of healing as well as having left Antipas' domain.

Jesus' necessity for moving. According to Luke, Jesus states that he is going to perform a ministry for a short period of time in Antipas' territory and yet it is necessary (πλὴν δεῖ) for him to move. Is it because he feared Antipas? No, it is ὅτι οὐκ ἐνδέχεται προφήτην ἀπολέσθαι ἔξω Ἰερουσαλήμ. This agrees well with the context. The Pharisees came to Jesus and conveyed this threat as he was moving southward through Galilee. Jesus replies by directing them to tell that fox that he will still be performing his ministry of healing for a short period of time. He adds, however, that it is necessary for him to continue his journey, not because he fears Antipas, but because he must go to Jerusalem.

Although the words οὐκ ἐνδέχεται are common in Greek, they are found only here in the New Testament. The Authorized and Revised Standard Versions translate this 'it cannot be', which would preclude John's being a prophet. But Jesus affirmed that John was a prophet,[1] and it is improbable that Luke thought that John had died in Jerusalem.[2] The expression can also be translated 'it is not fitting' or 'it is not appropriate'[3] for a prophet to perish outside of Jerusalem. There is irony here, and it seems to cut two ways: first at the Pharisees, implying that Jerusalem had the monopoly of murdering God's prophets[4] (whom, of course, it considered false prophets)[5] and secondly at Antipas. Antipas must not be selfish, he hints, for though John was not killed in Jerusalem, Jerusalem must not be denied this privilege a second time after so short an interval! Antipas does not control the fate of this prophet!

---

[1] Cf. Lk. 7: 26 = Mt. 11: 9.   [2] Derrett, *ZNW*, N.F. ix, 241.

[3] Cf. NEB, 'It is unthinkable'; Jerusalem Bible, 'it would not be right'; Philips' Translation, 'It would never do'.

[4] 2 Chron. 24: 20–2; Jer. 26 [33]: 20–3; cf. also Jer. 26 [33]: 8–9.

[5] The Sanhedrin had the right to try a prophet (Deut. 18: 20; cf. Dalman, *Jesus-Jeshua*, p. 53 n. 2), but whether Jesus was regarded as such by his opponents is disputable (it is thought that he was considered a false prophet by Jeremias, *Eucharistic Words*, p. 79; but *contra* this view see Blinzler, *Prozess*, pp. 187–8 n. 11).

Conclusion

Antipas had threatened to curtail Jesus' ministry by death. Jesus replied that he would continue his ministry for at least a short time. It seems that Antipas' threat was no more than that, otherwise he would have taken action against him as he had against John the Baptist. Probably he would have preferred to see Jesus outside his realm, for a popular movement like his was potentially dangerous. It is typical of Antipas that he should want to nip in the bud any possible trouble. Yet he apparently felt unable to take action against Jesus because he had no evidence of his causing political trouble. Also, the people had not forgiven him his treatment of John. Thus the best that he could do was to issue a threat. It seems that Jesus saw through this and called him a fox – a crafty coward. Jesus' attitude towards Antipas was one of disdain. He had a ministry to perform. His fate was not to be in Antipas' territory but in Jerusalem.

ANTIPAS' TRIAL OF JESUS

Introductory matters

Luke's passion narrative

The trial of Jesus is a study in itself[1] which is beyond the scope of this work. This study can be concerned only with Antipas' involvement in it.

Also, the recent study of the sources of Luke's passion narrative is beyond the scope of the present work except briefly to mention its development. Differences between Luke's and Mark's passion narratives have suggested that Luke's narrative is largely based on a non-Marcan tradition into which extracts of Mark have been inserted. Although Wilke may have been the first to make this observation,[2] the theory was first developed by Hawkins.[3] Hawkins' three main points are: (1) that whereas the verbal correspondence of Mark and Luke is 53 per cent in the account of the ministry, it is only 27 per cent in the passion

---

[1] For a discussion of this whole study, see Blinzler, *Prozess*; Winter, *Trial*; Brandon, *Trial*; W. R. Wilson, *The Execution of Jesus* (New York, 1970).

[2] C. G. Wilke, *Der Urevangelist* (Dresden and Leipzig, 1838), pp. 482–3.

[3] *SSP*, pp. 76–94.

account; (2) that the transpositions of Marcan material in Luke's passion narrative are four times greater than elsewhere in Luke; (3) that although Luke's passion narrative is two-fifths as long as Mark's, it contains twice as much again of new interwoven material which is important. Following Hawkins, Perry[1] made a more detailed study, and in turn was followed by Streeter,[2] and Taylor[3] (as a part of proto-Luke), and many others.[4] Although some have been unable to accept the theory that Luke's passion narrative is a non-Marcan tradition,[5] for the purposes of this study it is accepted as the most probable solution.

The Lucan narrative of the political trials (Lk. 23: 1–25) has out of 372 words only forty-nine, or 13·2 per cent, in common with Mark 15: 1–15 while, if Antipas' trial of Jesus (Lk. 23: 6–15) is omitted, the percentage of common material only rises to 25·5 per cent. Moreover, of the forty-nine words that are common to Luke and Mark, thirty-eight are accounted

---

[1] A. M. Perry, *The Sources of Luke's Passion-Narrative*, 2nd series, vol. IV, pt. II of *Historical and Linguistic Studies in Literature Related to the New Testament* (Chicago, 1920); cf. also A. M. Perry, 'Luke's Disputed Passion-Source', *ET*, XLVI (1935), 256–60.

[2] B. H. Streeter, *The Four Gospels* (London, 1936), pp. xvii–xxi, 201–22.

[3] Taylor, *Behind*; cf. also V. Taylor, 'Important Hypotheses Reconsidered. I. The Proto-Luke Hypothesis', *ET*, LXVII (1955), 12–16.

[4] R. P. C. Hanson, 'Does δίκαιος in Luke xxiii. 47 Explode the Proto-Luke Hypothesis?', *Hermathena*, LX (1942), 74–8; P. Winter and V. Taylor, 'Sources of the Lucan Passion Narrative', *ET*, LXVIII (1956), 95; J. Jeremias, 'Perikopen-Umstellungen bei Lukas?', *NTS*, IV (1958), 115–19; F. Rehkopf, *Die lukanische Sonderquelle* (Tübingen, 1959); J. B. Tyson, 'The Lukan Version of the Trial of Jesus', *NovT*, III (1959), 249–58; cf. also P. Winter, 'The Treatment of his Sources by the Third Evangelist in Luke XXI–XXIV', *Studia Theologica*, VIII (1955), 138–72.

[5] J. W. Hunkin, 'The Composition of the Third Gospel, with Special Reference to Canon Streeter's Theory of Proto-Luke', *JTS*, XXVIII (1927), 250–62, esp. 255–8; Creed, *Luke*, pp. 262; M. Goguel, 'Luke and Mark: With a Discussion of Streeter's Theory', *HTR*, XXVI (1933), 1–55, esp. 26–39; J. M. Creed, 'Some Outstanding New Testament Problems. II. "L" and the Structure of the Lucan Gospel: A Study of the Proto-Luke Hypothesis', *ET*, XLVI (1934), 101–7; G. D. Kilpatrick, 'A Theme of the Lucan Passion Story and Luke xxiii. 47', *JTS*, XLIII (1942), 34–6; A. Barr, 'The Use and Disposal of the Marcan Source in Luke's Passion Narrative', *ET*, LV (1944), 227–31; S. M. Gilmour, 'A Critical Re-Examination of Proto-Luke', *JBL*, LXVII (1948), 147–9, 151–2; G. D. Kilpatrick, 'Scribes, Lawyers, and Lucan Origins', *JTS*, N.S. I (1950), 56–60; Conzelmann, pp. 28 and n. 3, 125.

for by proper names, pronouns, the definite article, conjunctions, and the verb 'to crucify'. Also, no less than sixteen occur in a single verse of nineteen words (Lk. 23: 3).[1] This verse may have been in the original Lucan source, but it seems more probable that Luke inserted it from the synoptic parallel.[2] Further, if one takes the words of this section which occur nowhere else in the Lucan writings, but which are characteristic of the source for the Lucan passion narrative (173 verses out of 313) – that is, they are used at least twice in that section but not more frequently in the rest of Luke and Acts – then in Luke 23: 1–25 there are twenty-five[3] of these characteristic words in twenty-four verses[4] or 1·04 of such words for each verse, which is about average for the whole Lucan passion narrative. If one takes only the trial by Herod (23: 6–12) then one finds eight such words for seven verses or 1·14 words per verse. Moreover, if one looks at the Lucan characteristic words mentioned by Stanton[5] in this portion, there are thirty in twenty-four verses (23: 1–25 omitting v. 17) or about 1·25 per verse, and for 23: 6–12 there are around fifteen or about 2·14 per verse. The usage of words and certain Lucan characteristics of this section seem to point to the fact that this section is in keeping with the source of the whole of Luke's passion narrative. Moreover, the trial by Antipas, having a greater concentration of Lucan words and Lucan characteristics, would seem to indicate that Luke's source for this pericope was not different from that of the rest of his passion narrative.

Although the trial by Herod (23: 6–12) is peculiarly Luke's, it cannot be omitted because it is closely fused with the rest of the account. Since commentators vary as to where this pericope begins and ends, Luke 23: 1–25 must be one literary unit, not

---

[1] If one holds to Matthaean priority, the same general results apply, for out of the 372 words in Luke's narrative of the political trials, forty-one (or 11 per cent) are common to Mt. 27: 1–26; and if the Herodian trial be removed, the percentage would only rise to 21·4 per cent; also, fifteen of the words which are common occur in Lk. 23: 3.

[2] For pro and con arguments, see Taylor, *Behind*, pp. 52–3; Perry, *Sources*, p. 45.

[3] This is based on Perry's work (*Sources*, pp. 81, 110–15), but on p. 81 there should be for 23: 1–16 six words marked * instead of four, and for 23: 18–25 three words should be marked * instead of four.

[4] Of course, omitting 23: 17.   [5] Stanton, II, 288–9, 306–7.

pieced together from Marcan (or Matthaean) material with the insertion of the story of Antipas.[1]

Therefore, it is reasonable to conclude that Antipas' trial of Jesus is an inseparable part of the Lucan narrative, the whole of which, with few possible exceptions (e.g. 23: 3), is based on a non-Marcan (or Matthaean) tradition.

Its historicity

It is difficult to see any apologetic purpose in Luke for the inclusion of Jesus' trial by Antipas. With this episode, Luke apparently does not attempt to exonerate Rome and blame the Jews.[2] Since Antipas was not a Jew by birth, the Jews did not think of him or the Herodian family as representatives of the Jews.[3] This would be true at least before the times of either Agrippa I or II.[4] It would seem that if Antipas were responsible for Jesus' death, it would have been stated much more clearly, or Antipas would have had a greater part in the trial. Although the Gospels tend to emphasize the responsibility of the Jews for the death of Christ and to exculpate the Roman government, 'it is not obvious how a trial before Herod comes into line with this tendency'.[5] Rather, Luke pictures Antipas as being completely free from responsibility for the death of Jesus.[6] The extra-canonical books give the opposite picture, and this will be discussed below.[7]

Another reason for rejecting the Lucan story of the trial of Jesus before Antipas is its omission by Mark (or Matthew). However, 'in view of the strong presumption that Luke had access to an alternative tradition of the passion to that of Mark, this objection to its historicity now falls to the ground'.[8] Finegan's

[1] Taylor, *Behind*, pp. 53–4; cf. also Stanton, II, 307.

[2] As suggested by Loisy, II, 640.

[3] Tyson, *NovT*, III, 256.   [4] Cf. Sot. vii. 8.

[5] B. H. Streeter, 'The Trial of Our Lord before Herod: A Suggestion', *SSP*, p. 229.

[6] W. Bauer, *Das Leben Jesu im Zeitalter der neutestamentlichen Apokryphen* (Tübingen, 1909), p. 194; Conzelmann, p. 86 n. 2; Blinzler, *Prozess*, pp. 291–2.

[7] Below, pp. 245–9.

[8] M. Black, 'The Arrest and Trial of Jesus and the Date of the Last Supper', *New Testament Essays*, ed. by A. J. B. Higgins (Manchester, 1959), p. 24.

suggestion that Luke 23: 6–16 is constructed from the various parts of Mark as well as from a shortened copy of the trial before Pilate[1] is, as Blinzler notes, utterly impossible.[2]

Many scholars, who doubt its historicity, have argued[3] that this pericope is a legend that has developed out of Psalm 2: 1–2 which is quoted in Acts 4: 25–6. They argue that Herod and Pilate in verse 27 represent the βασιλεῖς and ἄρχοντες who in the psalm plot against the Lord's anointed.[4] But Luke never refers to this verse in the scene of the trial; and if he had thought it fulfilled a prophecy of Psalm 2, surely he would have made it clear to his readers.[5] Moreover, if Psalm 2 were the basis of this pericope it would seem that Antipas would have played a far more active role in the trial than he plays in Luke.[6] Thus, the assumption that the trial of Jesus by Antipas is derived from Acts 4: 25–6 is weak. The reverse is more likely to be the case. It seems that Acts 4: 27 takes for granted that Antipas was involved in the trial of Jesus and, 'in fact, assumes an acquaintance with the story of Luke 23: 5 ff.'[7] The whole prayer in Acts 4: 24b–30 is 'semitic through and through'.[8] The prayer

[1] J. Finegan, *Die Überlieferung der Leidens- und Auferstehungsgeschichte Jesu* (Giessen, 1934), pp. 27–9. Cf. Winter, *Trial*, p. 213 n. 1.

[2] Blinzler, *Prozess*, p. 292 n. 26.

[3] Cf. M. Dibelius, 'Herodes und Pilatus', *ZNW*, xvi (1915), 113–26, esp. pp. 123–6; G. Bertram, *Die Leidensgeschichte Jesu und der Christuskult*, *FRLANT*, xxxii (Göttingen, 1922), p. 65; Creed, *Luke*, p. 280; H. Lietzmann, 'Der Prozess Jesu', *SAB*, xiv (Berlin, 1931), 314; Goguel, *HTR*, xxvi, 36–7; *Life of Jesus*, p. 515 n. 1; Bultmann, p. 273 (Bultmann believes that this tradition was already in existence, whereas Dibelius believes it was created by Luke, cf. Dibelius, *ZNW*, xvi, 125–6); E. Lohse, *History of the Suffering and Death of Jesus Christ*, trans. by M. O. Dietrich (Philadelphia, 1967), p. 91; cf. Brandon, *Jesus*, p. 317 n. 5; Wilson, pp. 137–9.

[4] Tertullian, *De Resurrectione Carnis* xx (*MPL*, ii, 821) interprets it slightly differently: 'In the person of Pilate the heathen raged, and in the person of Israel the people imagined vain things; the kings of the earth in Herod, and the rulers in Annas and Caiaphas were gathered together against the Lord, and against his anointed.'

[5] Tyson, *NovT*, iii, 256.

[6] Cf. Blinzler, *Prozess*, p. 292.

[7] Black, 'Arrest', p. 24; cf. Winter, *Trial*, p. 202 n. 4; P. Benoit, *The Passion and Resurrection of Jesus Christ*, trans. B. Weatherhead (New York and London, 1969), pp. 144–5.

[8] H. F. D. Sparks, 'The Semitisms of Acts', *JTS*, N.S. 1 (1950), 24. Cf. also R. A. Martin, 'Syntactical Evidence of Aramaic Sources in Acts i–xv', *NTS*, xi (1964), 38–59, esp. pp. 38–9, 51–3.

has several close Septuagint parallels. Especially 4: 25–6 agrees verbatim with the Septuagint, and Sparks suggests that Luke may have heard the story in general terms and cast it in 'an appropriately biblical mould'.[1] The existence of some six Lucanisms favours Sparks' suggestion.[2] Wilcox concludes that the presence of so-called Septuagintisms may have been a feature of early Christian liturgical composition.[3] If this is a correct deduction, it would mean that Antipas' role in the trial of Jesus was acknowledged by the early church and is not just an invention of Luke's. Further, there is a different emphasis in Acts 4: 25–7 from that given in Luke and the other synoptics. Whereas in Acts 4: 25–7 the blame for Jesus' death is placed on Antipas and Pilate,[4] according to the evangelists the chief agents behind the condemnation were the Sanhedrin, while Pilate and Antipas are pictured as favourable to Jesus. However, this different emphasis in Acts 4: 25–7 does not force one to revise the impression gained from the Gospels, for it was the common practice of the early church to see as much as possible of the Messianic Psalm 2 as fulfilled in Christ.[5] The kings were identified with Antipas – he was called king by the common people – and Pilate, the head of the foreign power who joined forces against Jesus by adopting an antimessianic attitude – the

---

[1] *JTS*, N.S. i, 24.

[2] M. Wilcox, *The Semitisms of Acts* (Oxford, 1965), p. 70, cf. pp. 69–72. The six Lucanisms are 'ἐν τῷ with infin., μετὰ παρρησίας, ἅγιον, τε, ἡ βουλή (of God's will), τὸν λόγον σου (i.e. God's word, or the gospel)' (Wilcox, p. 70 n. 5).

[3] *Ibid.* p. 74.

[4] As also in Ignatius *Epistola ad Smyrnaeos* i. 2 (*MPG*, v, 708).

[5] The same could be said for Just. *I Apol.* xl. 5–6 (*MPG*, vi, 389). In discussing Lk. 23 in relation to Acts 4 Brandon states: 'But such a contradiction [i.e., statement in Acts 4: 26] in the evaluation of Pilate and Herod is puzzling; it warns us that Luke was more concerned with effect than with historical truth in his writings' (*Trial*, p. 122). However, Brandon's statement is fallacious on two accounts. First, the two statements are not identical but that does not mean they are contradictory, but seem only to reflect differences in emphasis or purpose. Secondly, to say that Luke is more concerned with effect than with historical truth is ludicrous for if that were the case Luke would have tried to make the two accounts identical so that both passages would have the same effect. Furthermore, in his Gospel Luke is giving the historical account of the trial while in Acts he is giving the historical account of the early church's (not his) view of Antipas' role in the trial.

one by mocking, the other by finally condemning Jesus.[1] This all points to the conclusion that the emphasis in Acts 4: 25–7 is quite different from that of Luke 23: 6–12, and that the origin of Luke 23 is not in Acts 4: 25–7. Rather, the early church, as seen in Acts 4, had an acquaintance with the story in Luke 23.

Finally, Wilson argues against its historicity and its being a part of the early passion narrative by noting that in Luke 23: 10 the Jewish authorities are said to be present at the trial before Antipas while in 23: 15 Pilate's words to these authorities assumed that they remained with him at the praetorium.[2] However, in observing the text, the group in 23: 15 does not seem to be identical with that of 23: 10. Luke specifically states in 23: 13 that, after Jesus returned from Antipas, Pilate called together the chief priests, the rulers, and the people, whereas the group that went to Antipas to accuse Jesus was composed of only the chief priests and scribes. Hence, the group before Pilate was more inclusive than that before Antipas. Furthermore, why would Pilate have to 'call together' a group of people if they all went to Antipas? Wilson's argument is therefore untenable.

There are reasonable grounds, then, for accepting the historicity of this pericope, and for believing that Jesus was actually tried by Herod Antipas.[3]

Luke's sources

It is impossible to know for certain what sources Luke used, but one can make a reasonable attempt towards a solution. Loisy suggests that Luke's sources resembled either the *Gospel of Peter* or possibly a former edition of that Gospel.[4] If one accepts the latter alternative, a check upon word resemblances would be very difficult since there may well have been many alterations. If one accepts the former view, then it would seem that a fair amount of the wording would be common to the *Gospel of Peter* and Luke. But if one examines the *Gospel of Peter* alongside

---

[1] Blinzler, *Prozess*, p. 434.

[2] Wilson, p. 138.

[3] Schneider notes: 'Dass der römische Statthalter den galiläischen Landesherrn Herodes Antipas heranzog, ist wahrscheinlich' (C. Schneider, *Geistesgeschichte des antiken Christentums*, 1 [München, 1954], 71; cf. also M. Radin, *The Trial of Jesus of Nazareth* [Chicago, 1931], p. 175).

[4] Loisy, 11, 640.

of Luke[1] one finds very few parallels with the whole of Luke,[2] and really no parallel at all with Luke's trial of Jesus by Antipas.[3] It seems, then, that Luke's source was not similar to that of the *Gospel of Peter*.[4]

Regarding this pericope Schleiermacher observes: 'the transaction is too circumstantially detailed to admit of a doubt, and our reporter seems to have had an acquaintance in the house of Herod who supplied him with this fact, as John seems to have had in the house of Annas'.[5] Though such an approach is not fashionable these days it should nevertheless be considered. Luke mentions in his own writings two people who would have had close ties with the court of the ruler of Galilee. The one is Joanna whose husband Chuza was an ἐπίτροπος, a financial minister of Antipas,[6] the other was Manaen who was the σύντροφος, an intimate friend of Antipas.[7] Both of these persons have been suggested earlier in this study as the possible sources for the account of John the Baptist's death.[8] Manaen was a prominent member of the church at Antioch, which church was familiar to Luke who probably came from that town.[9] Luke's interest in the Herods may be due to his acquaintance

---

[1] For a convenient synoptic parallel of Luke and of the *Gospel of Peter*, see H. von Schubert (ed.), *Das Petrusevangelium* (Berlin, 1893), pp. 4–29.

[2] E.g. *Gospel of Peter* 3 is parallel to Lk. 23: 52 but it is closer to Mk. 15: 43; *Gospel of Peter* 5 with Mk. 15: 15 b; Lk. 23: 25 b; *Gospel of Peter* 10 with Lk. 23: 32; *Gospel of Peter* 12 with Mk. 15: 24; Lk. 23: 34; *Gospel of Peter* 13 with Lk. 23: 41 ?; *Gospel of Peter* 20 with Mk. 15: 38; Lk. 23: 45; *Gospel of Peter* 50, 51 with Lk. 24: 1. If one observes these parallels, many of them are not word for word parallels but parallel only in sense.

[3] The closest parallels to Jesus' trial by Antipas are the following: *Gospel of Peter* 4 (καὶ ὁ Πιλᾶτος πέμψας πρὸς Ἡρῴδην) with Lk. 23: 6–7 (Πιλᾶτος δὲ...ἀνέπεμψεν...πρὸς Ἡρῴδην). In the former Pilate sent to Herod to ask for Jesus' body; in the latter Pilate sent Jesus to Herod. *Gospel of Peter* 10 (αὐτὸς δὲ ἐσιώπα) with Lk. 23: 9 (αὐτὸς δὲ οὐδὲν ἀπεκρίνατο). The former deals with Jesus' silence on the cross and the latter with Jesus' silence before Antipas; cf. also the parallel in the *Gospel of Peter* 6 with Lk. 23: 11.

[4] If Luke is the basis for the *Gospel of Peter*, then it goes beyond Luke in the attempt to exculpate Rome (cf. below, p. 246).

[5] F. Schleiermacher, *A Critical Essay on the Gospel of St Luke*, intro. and trans. by [C. Thirlwall] (London, 1825), pp. 303–4.

[6] Lk. 8: 3.   [7] Acts 13: 1.

[8] Above, pp. 120–1; Appendix VI.

[9] The Anti-Marcionite prologue to the Gospel of Luke states: Ἔστιν ὁ Λουκᾶς Ἀντιοχεὺς Σύρος (found in Adolf von Harnack, 'Die ältesten

with these two people. Luke mentions them very casually in contexts not specifically dealing with the Herodian house. This gives to it a more authentic ring than if he had mentioned these names when dealing with the Herods. For if the latter were the case, it might be suspected that he was conjuring up names so as to give added weight to his story. It seems much more natural to assume that, since he knew these people, his sources for the story of Jesus' trial by Herod were derived from them. The disciples had left Jesus by this time and so would not be able to relate any aspect of the story. Also, the story has some intimate details such as the following: Antipas being very glad to see Jesus, the reason for his wanting to see him, his lengthy questioning of Jesus, the placing of the bright robe on Jesus, and the development of the friendship between Pilate and Antipas.[1] This would seem to indicate that the story was from someone who had been an eyewitness. It seems reasonable, then, to think that Luke may have received this story from one of these two men. Either they were present at the scene or they knew someone within the Herodian household who had been present.

Evangelien-Prologe und die Bildung des Neuen Testaments', *SAB*, xxiv [1928], 324). This is at least as early as Irenaeus in the latter part of the second century (cf. R. G. Heard, 'The Old Gospel Prologues', *JTS*, N.S. vi [1955], 9–11; W. F. Howard, 'The Anti-Marcionite Prologues to the Gospels', *ET*, xlvii [1936], 536–7; *contra* Haenchen, *Die Apostelgeschichte*, pp. 8–10 n. 3). If the 'we' passage in D of Acts 11 : 28 were original then this would be a starting point for tradition, but it is more likely that this passage is itself due to a tradition which, however, must have been very early, perhaps about the same time as the Anti-Marcionite Prologue (as Heard, *JTS*, N.S. vi, 10) or even fifty years before the prologue (as F. F. Bruce, *The Acts of the Apostles*[2] [London, 1962], p. 7). This is confirmed in the later sources such as *Argumentum evangelii secundum Lucam* (cf. P. Corssen, *Monarchianische Prologe zu den Vier Evangelien*, *TU*, xv [1896], p. 7) which Harnack dates at the beginning of the third century (A. Harnack, *Luke the Physician*, trans. J. R. Wilkinson [London, 1907], p. 4 n. 1), Eus. *HE* iii. 4. 6; Jerome *De Viris Illustribus* vii (*MPL*, xxiii, 619); Jerome *Commentarii in Evangelium Matthaei*, prologus (*MPL*, xxvi, 18) 'Tertius Lucas medicus, natione Syrus Antiochensis'. Connolly argues that there are some northern Syrian idioms in Luke's writings for which he (and not his sources) is responsible (R. H. Connolly, 'Syriacisms in St Luke', *JTS*, xxxvii [1936], 375–85, esp. 381–3). Although the evidence is limited it is nevertheless early, and thus it is reasonable to conclude that Luke was a native or resident of Antioch, Syria (A. Strobel, 'Lukas der Antiochener', *ZNW*, xlix [1958], 131–4).

[1] Cf. Perry, *Sources*, p. 63.

The pericope itself[1]

The problem of jurisdiction

After his trial before the Sanhedrin, Jesus was brought to Pilate.[2] Pilate found him not guilty of any crime worthy of death, and, in fact, made three attempts to release him from the hands of his accusers.[3] Pilate, exasperated because Jesus would not answer him, stated that the Jewish leaders had many charges against him[4] of which Luke mentions three.[5] According to Luke, after Pilate had found Jesus not guilty, the Jews stated that Jesus was stirring up the people, teaching throughout all Judaea, from Galilee even to this place.[6] At the mention of Galilee, Pilate inquired if Jesus were from there.[7] Hearing that

[1] Pp. 233–9 originally appeared in *The Trial of Jesus*, ed. by E. Bammel, published by S.C.M. Press Ltd (London, 1970).

[2] Mt. 27: 1–2; Mk. 15: 1; Lk. 23: 1; Jn. 18: 28.

[3] Lk. 23: 4, 14–16, 20–2; cf. Mt. 27: 21–4; Mk. 15: 9–12, 14; Jn. 18: 38–9.

[4] Mt. 27: 12–13; Mk. 15: 3–4.

[5] Lk. 23: 2 (τοῦτον εὕραμεν διαστρέφοντα τὸ ἔθνος ἡμῶν καὶ κωλύοντα φόρους Καίσαρι διδόναι καὶ λέγοντα ἑαυτὸν Χριστὸν βασιλέα εἶναι).

[6] Lk. 23: 5 (οἱ δὲ ἐπίσχυον λέγοντες ὅτι ἀνασείει τὸν λαόν, διδάσκων καθ' ὅλης τῆς Ἰουδαίας, καὶ ἀρξάμενος ἀπὸ τῆς Γαλιλαίας ἕως ὧδε). The words καθ' ὅλης τῆς Ἰουδαίας seem to be a reference to the whole of Palestine like 'from Dan to Beersheba'. 'Judaea' is equivalent to the whole 'land of the Jews' (cf. Acts 10: 37 and 39; Haenchen, *Die Apostelgeschichte*, pp. 297 n. 6, 298; cf. also Creed, *Luke*, p. 281; Grundmann, *Lukas*, p. 422). The words καθ' ὅλης which are repeatedly used in Luke and Acts (Lk. 4: 14; 23: 5; Acts 9: 31, 42; 10: 37; 13: 49) denote geographic extent, 'throughout' (cf. BD/Funk, § 225; Bauer/AG, p. 406. For a discussion on Lk. 23: 5 and its geographical significance, see W. C. Robinson, Jr, *The Way of the Lord* (D. Theol. dissertation, University of Basel, 1962), pp. 43–56.

[7] Lk. 23: 6. Bickermann argues that there is a contradiction within Luke, for earlier Luke (2: 4–7) has Jesus born in Bethlehem of Judaea (E. Bicker-mann, 'Utilitas crucis. Observations sur les récits du procès de Jésus dans les Évangiles canoniques', *RHR*, cxii [1935], 205). Certainly Pilate was not interested in his origin but his residence (cf. A. Steinwenter, 'Il processo di Gesù', *Jus*, N.S. iii [1952], 486 n. 4). As will be seen below, the prosecution of a criminal was to be in the place of the crime and not in the territory of his origin. Since it was stated by the Jews that Jesus was stirring up the people (with his teaching) in Galilee, as well as Judaea, possibly Pilate thought he could legitimately get rid of him by handing him over to Antipas. Antipas could then try him for stirring up the people in Galilee. On the other hand, undoubtedly Pilate knew that Jesus' origin was in Judaea, for

he was, he sent him to Antipas who happened to be in Jerusalem for the Passover[1] – something which is entirely probable, since Josephus records the fact that Antipas went with Vitellius to Jerusalem during a Jewish festival.[2]

It is thought by some that the verb ἀναπέμπω (or its Latin equivalent *remittere*) is used by Luke as a technical term for remanding to a higher authority.[3] But this is incorrect as is shown by Steinwenter.[4] Also, it occurs in juridical texts as merely meaning 'to send'.[5] Of the five occurrences of this word in the New Testament,[6] only in Acts 25: 21, where Paul is to be sent to Caesar, does it have a technical connotation. Certainly, by its usage within the pericope, it is unlikely that it is used technically, 'for it is used both when Pilate refers to Herod

according to official protocol personal particulars came at the beginning of the proceedings (cf. Acts 23: 34; T. Mommsen, 'Die Rechtsverhältnisse des Apostels Paulus', *ZNW*, II [1901], 92 and n. 2; Bertram, *FRLANT*, XXXII, 65–6; Steinwenter, *Jus*, III, 475 n. 1). This is certainly implied in Eus. *HE* v. 1. 20; cf. also J. Geffcken, 'Die christlichen Märtyrien', *Hermes*, XLV (1910), 488–90. Since it was the normal procedure, Luke would have had no interest in writing it (Bertram, *FRLANT*, XXXII, 65), but the mention of Galilee would be of interest to both Pilate and Luke: to the former as providing an excuse to get rid of an awkward case; to the latter as showing the reason for the transition to Antipas. Blinzler argues that his Galilaean activity was mentioned as well in the preliminaries, and that Pilate reverted to it in the attempt to get rid of an embarrassing case (Blinzler, *Prozess*, p. 285 n. 5). This is possible but it seems more likely that Galilee was mentioned in passing, and that Pilate seized upon it to get himself out of the dilemma. Certainly the Jewish leaders would not want to prolong the trial by having Jesus go to Antipas and by having a new trial. Also, the Jewish leaders could manipulate Pilate more easily than Antipas.

[1] Lk. 23: 7.

[2] *Ant.* xviii. 122. Although he does not specifically state which Jewish festival it was, he does state that Antipas had attended one. Because of Pilate's attack on the Galilaean pilgrims of the previous Passover (Lk. 13: 1; cf. above, pp. 175–6), Antipas may have wanted to be present personally in Jerusalem (cf. Blinzler, *Prozess*, pp. 284–5 n. 4).

[3] Cf. Creed, *Luke*, p. 281; Bickermann, *RHR*, CXII, 206; Harlow, pp. 173 n. 23, 234–5; cf. also Jos. *Ant.* iv. 218; *BJ* ii. 571.

[4] Steinwenter, *Jus*, III, 486–7; cf. also Blinzler, *Prozess*, p. 207 n. 9.

[5] E.g. Macer *D.* xlviii. 3. 7; Venuleius *D.* lxviii. 3. 9; Celsus *D.* lxviii. 3. 11 (cf. Sherwin-White, *Roman Society*, p. 29). Blinzler (*Prozess*, p. 287 n. 11) states that there is a parallel in Jos. *BJ* iii. 540–1, but the verb ἀναπέμπω is not used.

[6] Lk. 23: 7, 11, 15; Acts 25: 21; Philem. 12.

and later when Herod refers Jesus to Pilate (Luke xxiii. 11)'.[1]
It is, then, to be taken as meaning merely 'to send'.

The reason Pilate sent Jesus to Herod is that he learned that
Jesus came from the region of Herod's authority (ἐπιγνοὺς
ὅτι ἐκ τῆς ἐξουσίας Ἡρῴδου ἐστίν).[2] Mommsen proposed that
in the earlier principate a trial was conducted in the province of
the domicile of the accused (*forum domicilii*) after a preliminary
examination. This practice was later changed so that a
criminal was tried in the province in which his misdeeds
were committed (*forum delicti*).[3] The latter is based upon an
early second-century text of Celsus: 'without doubt, whatever
be the native province of a man who is brought forth from
custody, the trial must be conducted by the governor of the
province in which the relevant actions are done'.[4] Sherwin-
White has challenged Mommsen by stating that the *forum
delicti* was in operation in the early principate and the *forum
domicilii* came in later.[5] Therefore, if this is correct, it would be
normal in Antipas' time for a criminal to be tried in the province where the misdeed was done,[6] and, as Celsus states, only
for special circumstances would the criminal be transferred
from one jurisdiction to another.[7] This procedure is in line with
other parts of the New Testament where Paul – less than three
decades after the trial of Jesus – was sent to the procurator
Felix at Caesarea. Felix asked to which province he belonged

[1] H. J. Cadbury, 'Roman Law and the Trial of Paul', *BC*, v (1933),
p. 309. Cf. also Lk. 23: 15.

[2] Lk. 23: 7. It was thought by some early writers that Jesus' being sent to
Herod was a fulfilment of Hosea 10: 6: 'And having bound him they brought
him to Assyria for a gift to King Jarim (or Jareb)' (LXX: καὶ αὐτὸν εἰς
Ἀσσυρίους δήσαντες ἀπήνεγκαν ξένια τῷ βασιλεῖ Ἰαρίμ); cf. Just. *Dial.*
ciii. 4 (*MPG*, vi, 717); Irenaeus *The Proof of the Apostolic Preaching* lxxvii
(*PO*, xii, 717); Tertullian *Adversus Marcionem* iv. 42 (*MPL*, ii, 464); Cyril of
Jerusalem *Catecheses* xiii. 14 (*MPG*, xxxiii, 792).

[3] T. Mommsen, *Römisches Strafrecht* (Leipzig, 1899), pp. 356–7; Mommsen, *ZNW*, ii, 92.

[4] *D.* lxviii. 3. 11 (Non est dubium, quin, cuiuscumque est provinciae
homo, qui ex custodia producitur, cognoscere debeat is, qui ei provinciae
praeest, in qua provincia agitur).

[5] *Roman Society*, pp. 28–31.   [6] Cf. Paulus *D.* i. 18. 3.

[7] *D.* lxviii. 3. 11 (ex causa faciendum est). Mommsen (*Römisches Strafrecht*),
p. 357 n. 1, wishes to delete the phrase *ex causa* as a gloss or interpolation
since it does not fit in with his interpretation (Sherwin-White, *Roman Society*,
p. 30).

and when Paul replied that he was a Cilician, Felix apparently made no move to refer the case to the legate of Syria–Cilicia but dealt with it himself. The offence was the alleged violation of the sanctity of the temple in Jerusalem which was in Felix' domain.[1] Festus, who followed Felix, tried Paul himself rather than referring him to Syria–Cilicia.[2] Also, Gallio, the proconsul of Achaia, tried Paul rather than returning him to his home province.[3] It seems, then, that Pilate was under no obligation to hand Jesus over to Antipas.[4] On the contrary, he did this of his own volition.

It appears, then, that Pilate handed Jesus over to Herod not because he was obliged to do so, but because he wanted to.[5] One cannot imagine Pilate doing this out of kindness. Rather, he did it to free himself from an awkward case. He found no guilt in Jesus and yet the Jews were insisting on his execution. To give in to the Jews would be a sign of Roman injustice and a weakness on Pilate's part. To withstand the Jews might well have spelled trouble, as it had previously. Thus by handing the case over to Antipas he could save face.[6] The second reason for handing Jesus over to Antipas may have been a diplomatic courtesy in order to improve his relations with Antipas, which were strained at this time. As mentioned in the previous chapter, it is probable that Pilate at the Passover of 32 had offended Antipas in the Galilaean massacre (Lk. 13: 1) and

[1] Acts 23: 34 – 24: 26. For a different point of view, see Winter, *Trial*, pp. 76–82.

[2] Acts 25: 1–2. Paul's appeal was not to his home province but to Caesar.

[3] Acts 18: 12–17.

[4] Juster observed that Herod the Great had, according to Josephus (*BJ* i. 474), the unusual privilege of reclaiming offenders who fled from his kingdom to other parts of the Roman Empire (Juster, II, 145 n. 2). Sherwin-White (*Roman Society*, p. 31) thinks that some remnant of this privilege may underlie Jesus' being sent to 'the second Herod', since most of Jesus' activities had taken place in Galilee. However, there is no hint of this in the present pericope. Rather, the tone is entirely voluntary. Also, if he had such rights, Bruce rightly observes that they would have to be invoked before they could be granted (*ALUOS*, v, 16).

[5] Justin (*Dial.* ciii. 4 [*MPG*, VI, 717]) states that Pilate sent Jesus bound to Herod as a compliment.

[6] Bajsić thinks this incident must be related to the Easter amnesty of the political offenders. Pilate's handing Jesus over to Herod would not only allow him to save face but also confirm his decision to release Jesus; cf. A. Bajsić, 'Pilatus, Jesus und Barabbas', *Biblica*, XLVIII (1967), 21–3.

at the Feast of Tabernacles in 32 had offended both the Jews and Antipas in the setting up of votive shields in Jerusalem (Philo *Leg.* 299–304).[1] The last incident was reported to Tiberius, who ordered Pilate to remove the shields immediately. Pilate probably received these instructions around the winter of 32/3 or early 33. He had overstepped himself and now at the Passover of 33 was anxious to appease. He may have known that Antipas desired to see Jesus. At least Luke states that Antipas was very glad to see him (Lk. 23: 8). If this were the case, then handing him over to Antipas would have served not only to save face, but also to ingratiate himself with Antipas.[2] This would have been a wise move on the part of Pilate. Jesus was neutral ground as far as Pilate's and Antipas' relationship with each other was concerned. Yet he was the centre of controversy amongst the Jews. Hence, rather than take a course of action which might again align Antipas and the Jews, he wisely handed Jesus over to Antipas. At any rate Luke states that the two potentates were reconciled from that time as a result of the gesture.

What result Pilate expected from this gesture is difficult to determine. Although it was forbidden in principle for Roman governors to exercise any official function outside their own province,[3] there may have been exceptions to this rule. Certainly Agrippa II had a trial of Paul in Festus' territory.[4] First, one can assume that the governor of the province where the criminal was being tried could allow a Roman governor of another province to conduct a trial. This may have been the case here, for Luke certainly gives a picture of a trial in that

[1] Above, pp. 176–83.

[2] Brandon cannot understand why Pilate would hand Jesus over to Antipas (*Trial*, p. 121). However, if one dates the crucifixion in A.D. 33 (Brandon dates it in A.D. 30, cf. *Trial*, pp. 146, 150), then it is easy to understand that Pilate's relationship with Antipas was strained because of the votive shields incident and that Pilate would want to be friendly towards Antipas.

[3] Paulus *D.* i. 18. 3. This is illustrated in Jos. *Ant.* xviii. 163 where Herennius Capito could not sue or recover the money from Agrippa I because he had fled from the territory of Capito's jurisdiction.

[4] Acts 25: 23 – 26: 30. It is interesting to note in passing that it was Agrippa who desired to hear Paul, and Festus agreed to do it (Acts 25: 22). In other words, it was not Festus who asked the outsider to hear Paul but the outsider (Agrippa) who asked Festus.

οἱ ἀρχιερεῖς καὶ οἱ γραμματεῖς εὐτόνως κατηγοροῦντες αὐτοῦ.[1] Secondly, it may be that Antipas was allowed to sit in judgement on the people of his territory in his Jerusalem palace if the procurator of Judaea permitted it. In this case, it is probable that there would be a sort of preliminary trial, and that if he wanted to try the accused further he would take him to his own territory. But to assume that Pilate had counted on Antipas to judge Jesus in his own territory, as does Blinzler,[2] seems to presume too much, for there is nothing in Luke to suggest this. Rather, it seems that Pilate expected an immediate trial by the tetrarch in Jerusalem, for why else would the chief priests and scribes have gone to the tetrarch's Jerusalem palace to accuse Jesus vehemently or vigorously at that time if the trial were to take place in his territory at some later date?

Pilate, no doubt, expected that Antipas would come to the same conclusion as himself; otherwise why did he send Jesus to him? It seems unlikely that Pilate thought Antipas would be convinced by the accusers of Jesus. Also, the procurator probably assumed that Antipas would have taken measures against Jesus earlier if he were a dangerous agitator.[3] If Antipas disagreed with Pilate then the Jews would have had one more mark against Pilate's leadership. Pilate would not have taken such a risk. It is almost certain that Pilate expected the tetrarch to acquit Jesus. At the end of the episode where Jesus is again brought before Pilate, Pilate declared that Herod did not find him guilty for he sent him back.[4] At least Pilate draws the conclusion that Antipas, having sent him back, must have considered him innocent. This not only confirms Pilate's decision but also, in the end, absolves him from the responsibility of Jesus' death.

---

[1] Lk. 23: 10.   [2] *Prozess*, pp. 286–7.

[3] *Ibid.* p. 287.

[4] Lk. 23: 15. The oldest and best attested reading is the Alexandrian one (ἀνέπεμψεν γὰρ αὐτὸν πρὸς ἡμᾶς) found in 𝔓[75] ℵ B K L T Θ Π, 892 1071 1079 1216 1241 1546 1646 2175, it-aur f, cop-sa bo (Plummer, *Luke*, p. 524; Creed, *Luke*, p. 283). The Western reading (ἀνέπεμψα γὰρ ὑμᾶς πρὸς αὐτόν) is found in A D W X Δ Ψ, 063, *f*[1], 28 565 700 1009 1010 1195 1230 1242 1344 1365 2148, *Byz Lect* (*l*[47] ἀνέπεμψεν, *l*[547] ἐνέπεμψα and ἡμᾶς), it-a b c d e ff[2] (1) q r[1], vg, syr[h], (eth). This reading gives a very weak sense. There are some (Wellhausen, *Lucae*, pp. 131–2; Grundmann, *Lukas*, p. 425 n. 15) who accept the reading ἀνέπεμψα γὰρ αὐτὸν πρὸς αὐτόν (274, *l*[183],

In conclusion, it seems that Pilate was not obligated to hand Jesus over to Antipas. Probably he did this for diplomatic reasons, for at this time his relationship with Antipas was strained. It may be that the tetrarch was in Jerusalem at this feast because of Pilate's maltreatment of some Galilaeans on another occasion. The trial of Jesus presented itself as an awkward case for Pilate, and since Jesus' activities were in Galilee it was an opportune time for him to make diplomatic gestures. He had nothing to lose and everything to gain. In the end he gained, for he and Antipas became friends from that day.[1]

The role of Antipas in the trial

According to Luke. After Pilate's hearing that Jesus was from Galilee, Luke switches the scene to Jesus' being tried by Herod. He was no doubt escorted by some guards as well as by some of the Sanhedrin from Pilate's residence[2] to the Hasmonaean palace,[3] which was Antipas' Jerusalem residence, located west of the temple. When Jesus appeared before Antipas, Antipas was very glad to see him (ἐχάρη λίαν), not because a fugitive had been caught[4] but because ἐξ ἱκανῶν χρόνων θέλων ἰδεῖν

---

syr-c s p, arm, geo). But this seems to be a conflation of the two above readings (cf. Dibelius, *ZNW*, xvi, 122). Verrall suggests that the original should read ἀνέπεμψε γὰρ αὐτὸν πρὸς ὑμᾶς (A. W. Verrall, 'Christ before Herod', *JTS*, x [1909], 349–52). Although ingenious, it is unconvincing.

[1] Lk. 23: 12.

[2] There has been much debate as to whether this was Antonia, which stood northwest of the temple of the palace of Herod on the west hill of Jerusalem, south of the Jaffa Gate. For a discussion on the various views and the relevant literature, see E. Lohse, 'Die römischen Statthalter in Jerusalem', *ZDPV*, lxxiv (1958), 69–78; Blinzler, 'Exkurs XI: Wo lag das Prätorium des Pilatus?', *Prozess*, pp. 256–9; A. Vanel, 'Prétoire', *Dictionnaire de la Bible*, Supplément, ed. by L. Pirot, *et al.*, viii (1969), 513–54; cf. also M. Ita of Sion, 'The Antonia Fortress', *PEQ*, c (1968), 139–43.

[3] Jos. *BJ* ii. 344. This seems to be the most logical place for Antipas' residence, for it was also Agrippa II's place of residence when Judaea was under Roman governorship (cf. *Ant.* xx. 189–90).

[4] As suggested by Harlow, pp. 174, 231; Tyson, *NovT*, iii, 258. As stated above, if Antipas had wanted to catch Jesus there was no reason for not doing so. Antipas did not do so because he was afraid. He wanted to see Jesus at no expense to himself. The whole trial scene indicates that Antipas was glad to see him, not because the fugitive had at last been caught but because he wanted to see this man about whom he had heard so much. If

αὐτὸν διὰ τὸ ἀκούειν περὶ αὐτοῦ, καὶ ἤλπιζέν τι σημεῖον ἰδεῖν ὑπ' αὐτοῦ γινόμενον.[1] This desire to see Jesus had been announced earlier, in Luke 9: 9 and possibly in 13: 31. But typically, Antipas did not do anything to fulfil his desire for fear of agitating the people. Pilate now presented him with an excellent opportunity for seeing Jesus without any responsibility or repercussions on the part of his subjects. There is no indication that his delight was to see Jesus because of some past misconduct. Perhaps he hoped that Jesus would perform some sort of sign – possibly to show that he was a prophet,[2] or at least act as a court magician. He wanted to see him perform, and perhaps felt that Jesus would do what he was asked in order to gain the tetrarch's favour. But to a man so disposed Jesus answered not a word.[3]

In the embarrassment of silence Antipas proceeded with the legal business which was necessary. He allowed the chief priests and scribes who were present to make their accusations.[4] This they did 'vigorously' or 'at full pitch' (εὐτόνως).[5] It is not stated what the specific charges were, but probably they were the same as those given before Pilate in Luke 23: 2. Apparently, only one of the charges concerned Antipas and that was Jesus' claim to kingship. For around this charge the mockery centres.

Antipas had taken it seriously, there would hardly have been a mocking scene but only a condemnation. [1] Lk. 23: 8.

[2] According to TJ: Sanh. xi. 6, a prophet appearing for the first time could be given a hearing only if he showed signs and wonders.

[3] Lk. 23: 9. Harlow (p. 233) argues that within this verse the phrase ἐν λόγοις ἱκανοῖς does not mean 'in many words' but, besides 'many', ἱκανοῖς means 'strong, powerful, vigorous, violent'. 'In this instance it may well add to the sense of mere number, which the word usually has in the New Testament, the violent character of the speech which Herod addressed to this man who had disturbed his dominions.' But the context does not suggest of Herod a violent manner so much as a jovial one, asking Jesus many questions about his great capacities. Certainly, ἱκανός, in the previous verse (v. 8), bears the meaning 'many'.

[4] Lk. 23: 10. For the Syr^cur version, see F. C. Burkitt, *Evangelion Da-Mepharreshe*, II (Cambridge, 1904), 303–4. The portion Lk. 23: 10–12 is omitted by Syr^s (cf. A. Merx, *Die Evangelien des Markus und Lukas* [Berlin, 1905], pp. 484–5). Its omission has slight textual attestation and it leaves much to be desired for a smooth reading of the passage if left out. In omitting verses 10–12, there is no transition from Antipas' palace to Pilate's palace as is assumed in Lk. 23: 13 ff.

[5] In the NT this word is used only here and in Acts 18: 28. Cf. also Jos. *BJ* ii. 593; iv. 423.

Blinzler imagines, and rightly so, that the rather aged tetrarch may well have mocked Jesus by saying: 'So you are already a king, are you? Well, you have attained more than I have.'[1]

It is believed by some that the mockery scene in Luke has been carried over from the other synoptic accounts, especially since Luke omits the mockery scene of the Roman soldiers in Mark 15: 16–20.[2] On the other hand, many scholars think it is a totally different scene because there are so many dissimilarities.[3] For example, there is nothing said of the purple robe and the crown of thorns, nothing of the scourging and reviling of Jesus by Gentiles, but only the mocking of Jesus' Jewish captors and the rough horse-play of Herod's bodyguards. The only resemblances are the verb ἐμπαίζω in both scenes and the soldiers' clothing their prisoner. It is inconceivable that the story in Luke is the equivalent or even a condensation of the other.

The scene ends with Herod and his bodyguard[4] treating

---

[1] *Prozess*, pp. 289–90.

[2] E.g. E. Klostermann, *Das Lukasevangelium*[2], *HNT*, v (Tübingen, 1929), p. 223; Creed, *Luke*, p. 280; A. T. Olmstead, *Jesus in the Light of History* (New York, 1942), p. 234 n. 27; Winter, *Trial*, p. 102; Wilson, pp. 33 n. c, 138–9, 147.

[3] E.g. Verrall, *JTS*, x, 345; J. Weiss (ed.), *Die Schriften des Neuen Testaments*[3], i (Göttingen, 1917), 504–5; R. Delbrueck, 'Antiquarisches zu den Verspottungen Jesu', *ZNW*, xli (1942), 137; Knox, i, 139; cf. also Benoit, *Passion*, pp. 150–1.

[4] Lk. 23: 11 (ὁ Ἡρῴδης σὺν τοῖς στρατεύμασιν αὐτοῦ). The word στράτευμα has the meaning of an *expedition, campaign, army*, or *host* (LSJ, p. 1651). Here it is used in the plural and would almost suggest at first sight that Antipas had *armies* in Jerusalem. Foakes Jackson and Lake think that Antipas had a sizeable armed force with him because there was fear of a serious disturbance (*BC*, i, 8). It is unlikely that Antipas would have had a large force in Jerusalem. Also, it is unlikely that a large armed force would be mocking Jesus, for it seems to have been quite a private affair. Verrall's suggestion (*JTS*, x, 340) that there is a lack of precision in military matters on the part of Luke does not seem to be a plausible solution to the problem. Luke was much closer to the situation than the present generation. Rather, the plural may indicate only a modest detachment of soldiers on duty, as in Acts 23: 10 (cf. O. Baurnfeind, 'στρατεύομαι', *TWNT*, vii [1964], 709 n. 34; Bruce, *Acts*, p. 412). The plural usage here may be just a generalizing plural as so often found in the NT (cf. Jeremias, *ZNW*, xxxviii, 115–16). The most probable explanation is that it is not only a generalizing plural but a semitism and that the στρατεύματα should be regarded as Herod's *bodyguard*, as in 4 Macc. 5: 1 and Mt. 22: 7 (cf. K. H. Rengstorf, 'Die Stadt der Mörder (Mt. 22: 7)', Beiheft to *ZNW*, xxvi [1960], 108).

Jesus with contempt,[1] and mocking him[2] by placing a bright robe upon him and then sending him back to Pilate.[3] Bornhäuser's interpretation that Herod placed the robe upon Jesus and accompanied or conducted him back to Pilate, and that Antipas then witnessed the last phase of the trial,[4] is untenable. The term περιβαλών when in the active voice is only used in the transitive sense in the New Testament, and the term ἀνέπεμψεν undoubtedly means 'he sent back' and not 'he accompanied back'.[5] Bornhäuser asks: 'What happened to the bright robe when it was put on Jesus?'[6] Blinzler rightly asks the counter-question: 'What became of Herod who was present at the last phase of the trial?', for of this there is no hint in Luke or the other synoptics.[7] Therefore, he sent Jesus back to Pilate

[1] Bauer/AG, p. 277. Harlow (p. 233) argues that since the verb οὐθενέω means to set at *nought, make no value, hold in contempt*, the compound ἐξουθενέω is the intensive form meaning *of no value whatever*. It is true that at times the compound form intensifies the simple form (Moule, *Idiom*, pp. 87–9) but this is not always the case. This is especially true here, for there is no simple form of the verb οὐθενέω to be found in LSJ. Harlow's definition is entirely unfounded. Here Antipas, being embarrassed by his subject's refusal to answer his petty questions, tries to turn the situation to his advantage again by treating his subject with contempt.

[2] Although there is no pronoun in the original to indicate that the mocking was against Jesus, it seems that this is what is meant. Verrall (*JTS*, x, 341–2) supplies the word 'thereupon' and believes the mocking was not directed against Jesus but against his accusers. If this were the case it would seem that Luke would have made this more explicit. The whole context indicates that the mocking was against Jesus, and since the pronoun αὐτόν at the beginning of the sentence refers to Jesus, it is unlikely that the object of the mocking is different from the one being treated with contempt.

[3] If the participle περιβαλών is subordinate to the main verb ἀνέπεμψεν then the draping of the robe was after the mocking (cf. Blinzler, *Prozess*, pp. 290–1 n. 19). If περιβαλών supplements the participle ἐμπαίξας then the mockery was in the wearing of the robe (cf. Delbrueck, *ZNW*, XLI, 135–6; Grundmann, *Lukas*, p. 425). It is difficult to know which is intended. Grammatically the first is more probable; however, the latter gives more content to the mockery. 'Die Differenz der Auffassungen wäre übrigens für die hier besprochenen Fragen nicht wesentlich' (Delbrueck, *ZNW*, XLI, 136).

[4] Bornhäuser, 'Die Beteiligung des Herodes am Prozesse Jesu', *NKZ*, XL (1929), 714–18; K. Bornhaeuser, *The Death and Resurrection of Jesus Christ*, trans. A. Rumpus (Bangalore, India, 1958), pp. 143–4.

[5] Cf. Blinzler, *Prozess*, pp. 299–300.

[6] *NKZ*, XL, 717.

[7] *Prozess*, p. 300.

after placing upon him a bright robe,[1] which not only confirmed Pilate's verdict that he was innocent of the charges of his accusers but also indicated to Pilate that Antipas regarded Jesus' kingship with contempt and ridicule.[2] The king in all his glory is handed back to you!

Antipas' role, according to Luke, is very small indeed. There is no indication of the verdict reached by Antipas except from the mockery and his sending Jesus back to Pilate. When Pilate resumed the trial[3] he gathered that Antipas considered

[1] One cannot determine the colour of this robe with certainty. Tatian *Diatessaron* i. 8 (Arabic version) states that it was scarlet but there is nothing in Luke to indicate this. Tatian may have transferred this from the mocking by Pilate's soldiers in Mt. 27: 28. Certainly among royalty bright robes meant white for Solomon (Jos. *Ant.* viii. 186), Archelaus (*BJ* ii. 1–2), and Vitellius (Tac. *Hist.* ii. 89); and silver for Agrippa I (Jos. *Ant.* xix. 344; Acts 12: 21). For those who think ἐσθῆτα λαμπράν means a white robe, cf. A. Oepke, 'λάμπω', *TDNT*, IV (1967), 17, 27; P. Joüon, 'Luc 23, 11: ἐσθῆτα λαμπράν', *Recherches de Science Religieuse*, XXVI (1936), 80–5 sees it as a symbol of innocence and royalty; and Delbrueck, *ZNW*, XLI, 135–7, 140–2 suggests the ridiculous appearance of a Jewish national king's vestment. Actually no colour is mentioned in Lk. 23: 11 but at least the garment symbolizes royalty as in Acts 12: 21 and *Ant.* xix. 344 (cf. H. Riesenfeld, *Jésus Transfiguré*, XVI of *Acta Seminarii Neotestamentici Upsaliensis* [Lund, 1947], p. 267 n. 5; cf. also p. 122 n. 37; Blinzler, *Prozess*, p. 290 n. 18). This would also be true of the Lucan addition of ἐξαστράπτων for Jesus' garment at the Mount of Transfiguration (Lk. 9: 29). It is possible that the ridicule was directed against Jesus in the sense that λαμπρά ἐσθής was used especially for the *toga candida* of the candidate for office (cf. Polybius x. 4. 8 – 5. 1). Jesus was paraded in mockery by Antipas as the candidate for the kingship of the Jews! He had the vestment of Messiah.

[2] Verrall's suggestion (*JTS*, x, 344) that Antipas' placing the brilliant robe upon Jesus was not out of contempt but rather out of respect towards Jesus is unconvincing. This is not the impression one gains from Luke. It is most unlikely that Antipas would feel respect towards Jesus after his refusal to answer a word to his many questions (λόγοις ἱκανοῖς).

[3] The participle συγκαλεσάμενος is a middle form where an active is expected (i.e., the middle is followed by an accusative) and has the meaning 'he called (or summoned) them to or about himself' (cf. Bauer/AG, p. 780; K. L. Schmidt, 'καλέω', *TDNT*, III [1965], 496; BD/Funk, § 316 (1); Moulton–Turner, p. 55). According to Jaubert, this term implies that the resumption of the trial before Pilate was on the following day, that is, on Friday morning. This means that the trial before Herod was on Thursday afternoon (cf. A. Jaubert, *The Date of the Last Supper*, trans. I. Rafferty [Staten Island, New York, 1965], pp. 104–5, 112–15; E. Ruckstuhl, *Chronology of the Last Days of Jesus*, trans. V. J. Drapela [New York, 1965], pp. 33–4, 55, 137–8; cf. also N. Walker, 'Pauses in the Passion Story and

Jesus innocent, ἀνέπεμψεν γὰρ αὐτὸν πρὸς ἡμᾶς. If Antipas had reckoned him guilty then he would have either kept him or declined to put the robe of mockery on him. At least he would have been more explicit in what he said to Pilate.

Bornhäuser would have Antipas play a greater role in the trial. He argues that he not only accompanied Jesus back to Pilate, but also, since he did not protest against Pilate's final decision, that he shared the guilt and responsibility of Jesus' death.[1] In addition to Blinzler's refutation of Bornhäuser[2] (part of which was mentioned above), it is probable that if Antipas were in the last phase of the trial, Pilate's statement would not have been παιδεύσας οὖν αὐτὸν ἀπολύσω[3] but παιδεύσαντες οὖν αὐτὸν ἀπολύσομεν. Harlow also has Antipas play a greater role in the trial. He proposes that Pilate declared Jesus innocent whereas Antipas declared him guilty. Harlow suggests that in verse 15, instead of reading ἀλλ' οὐδὲ Ἡρῴδης (but also not Herod), it should read ἀλλ' οὐ δὲ Ἡρῴδης (but not Herod). Therefore Pilate, not Herod, acquitted Jesus, ἀνέπεμψεν γὰρ αὐτὸν πρὸς ἡμᾶς.[4] As Blinzler points out, the duplication of the adversative particle, suggested by Harlow, would be most singular. If Antipas thought Jesus to have been guilty then he would not have sent him back to Pilate but would have had a further trial and pronounced a sentence of guilt.[5] Secondly, if this were the case, then Antipas' verdict would have been of vital significance to the progress of the trial, and it would seem at least one of

their Significance for Chronology', *NovT*, VI [1963], 17–18). There is nothing in the text to suggest that the trial before Pilate was resumed the next morning. Rather, it seems that the trial before Herod was quite hurried and that Pilate summoned the chief priests, rulers, and the people around him to make his sentence which included Herod's verdict (cf. G. Ogg, 'Review of Mlle Jaubert, *L date de la Cène*', *NovT*, III [1959], 159). Therefore, there is no convincing reason for not believing that Pilate pronounced the sentence and handed Jesus over to the Jews about midday as suggested by Jn. 19: 14 (cf. B. Weiss, *Das Johannes-Evangelium*[9], *KEK* [Göttingen, 1902], pp. 502–3; Lagrange, *Marc*, pp. 428–9).

[1] Bornhäuser, *NKZ*, XL, 718.
[2] *Prozess*, pp. 298–300.   [3] Lk. 23: 16 and 22.
[4] Harlow, pp. 236–9. Tyson (*NovT*, III, 257) also believes that the reason for sending Jesus back to Pilate was because he was guilty, otherwise he would have been freed and not sent back (cf. also J. S. Kennard, *Render to God* [New York, 1950], p. 133).
[5] Blinzler, *Prozess*, p. 296–7.

the other evangelists would have mentioned Herod's verdict. Thirdly, it seems from the pericope that Antipas does not consider Jesus guilty, for he apparently ignores the accusations raised by the Jewish leaders. Finally, if Antipas did pronounce Jesus guilty it would seem that the Jewish leaders would have used this to influence Pilate and/or at least brought it to the attention of the crowd. But there is no hint of this. On the contrary, Pilate, with reluctance, hands Jesus over to the Jewish leaders,[1] and in Matthew Pilate's washing of the hands[2] clearly indicates that he was not responsible. Also the other evangelists very pointedly place the responsibility on the shoulders of the Jewish leaders and the crowd. Therefore, Antipas cannot be blamed for taking part in the condemnation of Jesus. Harlow musters his evidence from Acts 4: 27 and from extra-canonical material.[3] But one cannot draw this conclusion from Acts 4: 27. As mentioned above, it only shows that the early community did have knowledge of Antipas' being involved in the trial and sought to find as much as possible of the messianic Psalm 2 fulfilled in Christ. With regard to the extra-canonical literature, it does not provide a reliable source of information, as will be seen below.

In conclusion, then, Antipas' role in the trial was small. Pilate handed Jesus over to Antipas as a diplomatic gesture of courtesy. Antipas treated it as no more than that. He was glad to see Jesus, since he had heard about him previously and wanted him to perform a sign. Jesus, refusing to do what his leader wanted, was then treated with contempt, and was mocked by the placing of the bright vestment of Messiah upon him. He was then sent back to Pilate. Pilate interpreted the mockery as a confirmation of Jesus' innocence. As a result of this courtesy gesture the two potentates became friends from that day. Pilate's aim was accomplished, for he was not benevolent enough to do anything out of simple kindness, but always hoped for something in return.

According to extra-canonical literature. First a brief mention will be made of the literature that gives a different emphasis from that of the canonical Gospels. Ignatius mentions Antipas and

---

[1] Cf. Lk. 23: 14–25; Mt. 27: 17–23; Mk. 15: 8–15; Jn. 18: 38–40; 19: 12–16.   [2] Mt. 27: 24–5.   [3] Pp. 178–9.

Pilate only in passing (ἐπὶ Ποντίου Πιλάτου καὶ Ἡρῴδου τετράρχου).[1] Since there is no article before τετράρχου, the phrase ἐπὶ. . . Ἡρῴδου τετράρχου could be translated 'when Herod was tetrarch'.[2] In other words, Ignatius is not stating Herod's and Pilate's joint responsibility for Jesus' death as much as saying that it took place during their reigns.

As mentioned above, Justin Martyr's remark that Pilate, Herod, and the Jews met together against Jesus[3] is similar to that of Acts 4: 27 in that he is trying to see every aspect of Psalm 2 fulfilled in the trial of Jesus. This would be true as well for Tertullian,[4] and the same can be said to some extent for Irenaeus' mention of Herod with Pilate. Yet Irenaeus goes beyond this by stating that Herod and the Jews compelled Pilate to deliver Jesus to death rather than to act contrary to Caesar by releasing a man who was called a king.[5] Here, one can see already Pilate being exonerated and the blame being shifted to Herod and the Jews. This is very evident in the latter part of the second century in the *Gospel of Peter*, which is very anti-Jewish.[6] It states that neither the Jews nor Herod would wash their hands when Pilate did, and that Herod commanded Jesus to be taken and crucified.[7] This same attitude of exonerat-

---

[1] *Epistola ad Smyrnaeos* i. 2 (*MPG*, v, 707).

[2] J. B. Lightfoot, *The Apostolic Fathers*[2], ii, ii (London, 1889), 291.

[3] Just. *I Apol.* xl. 5–6 (*MPG*, vi, 389). On the other hand, Just. *Dial.* ciii. 4 (*MPG*, vi, 717) gives about the same information as Lk. 23: 7–12, for he states there that Pilate showed favour to Herod by sending Jesus to him.

[4] *De Resurrectione Carnis* xx (*MPL*, ii, 821).

[5] *The Proof of the Apostolic Preaching* lxxiv, lxxvii (*PO*, xii, 715, 717).

[6] Cf. H. B. Swete (ed.), *The Akhmîm Fragment of the Apocryphal Gospel of St Peter* (London, 1893), p. xxxviii; M. R. James (trans.), *The Apocryphal New Testament* (5th impression, Oxford, 1953), p. 90; Chr. Maurer, *Gospel of Peter, New Testament Apocrypha*, ed. by W. Schneemelcher, Eng. trans. ed. by R. McL. Wilson, i (London, 1963), 182. For an interesting development of this anti-semitism, see A. F. Findlay, *Byways in Early Christian Literature* (Edinburgh, 1923), pp. 81–2, 104–7. From the middle of the second century onwards it was the general belief that the Jews carried out the crucifixion of Jesus (cf. Just. *I Apol.* lxiii (*MPG*, vi, 424–5); Just. *Dial.* xvi–xvii (*MPG*, vi, 509–14). In addition the Talmud shows the same view for it knows nothing of Jesus' execution by the Romans but makes it solely an act of the Jews (R. T. Herford, *Christianity in Talmud and Midrash* [London, 1903], p. 86; Bauer, *Das Leben Jesu*, pp. 199–203).

[7] *Gospel of Peter* 1–2. This attitude can also be seen in the *Acts of Peter* viii (Schneemelcher, ii, 290) in the late second century (*ibid.* ii, 275).

ing Pilate and blaming Herod continues into the third,[1] fourth,[2] fifth,[3] and sixth (?) centuries,[4] and many centuries later.[5] But in all these one can see the apologetic motive of trying to convince the Roman government that Christianity was worthy of their benevolent regard, and that the governor before whom the case of Jesus was brought was friendly to Christianity and refused to have any part in putting Jesus to death. Thus Herod and the Jews are blamed totally for the death of Christ. This is in direct contradiction to the canonical Gospels, for although there was a reluctance on Pilate's part, it is never suggested that Pilate had no responsibility in the matter. It is by no means clear that the inclusion of the trial before Herod in Luke has the same apologetic motive as in the apocryphal literature. On the contrary, in Luke Herod is seen in an equally good light as Pilate in that neither is regarded as responsible for Jesus' death. Because of the marked apologetic motive within the contents of

---

[1] Herod commands Jesus to be crucified in *Didascalia Apostolorum* xxi. 19 (trans. by R. H. Connolly [Oxford, 1929], p. 190); Herod shared in the execution of Jesus in *Acts of Thomas* xxxii (Schneemelcher, II, 460); A. F. J. Klijn, *The Acts of Thomas, Supplements to NovT*, v [1962], 80, 226).

[2] Herod judges Jesus in *Dialogue of Adamantius* v. 1 (ed. by W. H. van de Sande Bakhuyzen [Leipzig, 1901], pp. 174–5). Eus. *HE* ii. 4. 1 does not put any blame on Herod but only records that he was the Herod of the passion. It serves only to inform the reader about which Herod Eusebius is writing.

[3] Herod was bribed by the Jewish leaders and he bribed the Roman authorities to go against Jesus in the *Coptic Narratives of the Ministry and the Passion* (James, pp. 148–9). *The Gospel of Gamaliel* is dated in either the fifth or sixth century (Schneemelcher, I, 508–10). Within it there are two homilies, namely, *The Lament of the Virgin* and *The Martyrdom of Pilate*. The Coptic has been translated into Arabic, which has been translated into English and ed. by A. Mingana, 'Woodbrooke Studies', with introductions by R. Harris, *BJRL*, XII (1928), 411–580; for references regarding Herod's responsibility, see pp. 439, 441, 500–2, 504–5, 507–8, 522. This work of Gamaliel which has been translated from the Coptic into Arabic has also been translated from the Arabic into Ethiopic, from which it has been translated into German by M.-A. van den Oudenrijn, *Gamaliel: Äthiopische Texte zur Pilatusliteratur* (Freiburg, 1959). For Herod's responsibility for Jesus' death, see *Die Marienklage* ii. 16, 29, 54–5; iii. 1; xi. 15, 20; *Martyrium Pilati* ii. 1–5; iii. 11; v. 22.

[4] Herod slew Jesus according to *Acts of Andrew and Matthias* xxvi (James, p. 457).

[5] E.g. in a fifteenth(?)-century writing Pilate appears to put blame on the Jews and Herod. Caesar asks Pilate why he yielded to them, and Pilate replies that the nations are disobedient and rebellious; cf. *Report of Pilate* (*Anaphora*) (James, p. 154; Schneemelcher, I, 482).

the apocryphal literature, its historical value and its reliability for source material with respect to Herod's part in the trial are questionable.

Recently the apocryphal Gospels by 'Abd al-Jabbār, who wrote in A.D. 995 in order to prove that Maḥummad was a true prophet, have gained notice both on the popular and scholarly levels.[1] In it the Jews tell Herod, a subordinate of King Pilate, of Jesus' misconduct and so Herod orders his arrest. After examining Jesus, Herod thinks that the accusations brought against Christ by the Jews are invented, and he washes his hands of the blood of Jesus.[2] Jesus is then sent to Pilate, who also declares his innocence, after which Herod orders him to be put in prison for the night. The next morning *the Jews* take Jesus, parade him and torture him.[3] In the end it is not Jesus but another man who is crucified.[4] This is typical of the Islamic tradition which adopts the docetic teaching that Jesus was not really crucified.[5] With regard to the trial, one can see many differences from that of the Gospel accounts.[6]

---

[1] On the popular level, see S. M. Stern, 'New Light on Judaeo-Christianity?', *Encounter*, xxviii (1967), 53–7. For the scholars, see S. M. Stern, 'Quotations from Apocryphal Gospels in 'Abd al-Jabbār', *JTS*, N.S. xviii (1967), 34–57; E. Bammel, 'Excerpts from a New Gospel?', *NovT*, x (1968), 1–9; R. McL. Wilson, 'The New *Passion of Jesus* in the Light of the New Testament and Apocrypha', *Neotestamentica et Semitica*, ed. by E. E. Ellis and M. Wilcox (Edinburgh, 1969), pp. 264–71.

[2] Similar to *Gospel of Peter* 1.

[3] Stern, *JTS*, N.S. xviii, 42–4, 54–6.

[4] Cf. *JTS*, N.S. xviii, 45.

[5] A good example of this is found in the *Gospel of Barnabas* which was written by a fifteenth- or sixteenth-century renegade from Christianity to Islam (James, p. 22). In the *Gospel of Barnabas* (ed. and trans. from Italian MS by L. and L. Ragg, Oxford, 1907), Judas was leading the soldiers to Jesus, but just before they reached him Jesus was taken up. At the same time Judas' speech and face so changed that the guards believed him to be Jesus (cf. 221 *b*–222 *a*) and so Judas was brought before the Sanhedrin (223 *a*–224 *a*) and before Pilate, who secretly loved Jesus (224 *a*–225 *a*). Later he was brought before Herod who was bribed to write to Pilate asking him not to fail in justice to the people of Israel (225 *a*–226 *a*). After the crucifixion of Judas (226 *a*) God allowed Jesus to re-appear (228 *a*), after which Jesus had his 'post-resurrection ministry' (228 *b*–231 *a*).

[6] Stern (*JTS*, N.S. xviii, 44) mentions some differences when he writes: 'The arrest of Jesus is ordered not by the High Priest, but Herod. Judas Iscariot does not go to the authorities with the offer to betray Jesus, but meets the guards and the crowd on the way...Jesus is brought to Herod, not

One obvious thing is that the Jews are held responsible for Jesus' death.

One can clearly see the Muslim polemics against Christianity in this work and can safely conclude that nothing goes back to the first century.[1] Certainly there is no reliable source material for the trial of Jesus by Herod in this work.

Conclusion

Luke's trial of Jesus by Herod is unique. Herod is brought into the trial but adds nothing to the progress of the trial. It has been thought by some that since there has been no progress in the trial of Jesus, this pericope has no point and therefore is not authentic.[2] On the contrary, if this pericope makes no specific point, it would argue for its authenticity. If something were mentioned in this pericope that drastically altered or showed great progress in the trial, it would cast doubt on the authenticity of the pericope in that it mentioned a special incident not included in the rest of Luke's trial narrative and the other Gospel accounts. Moreover, because no development in the trial of Jesus is evident in the trial before Herod, this may have been the reason for its exclusion by the other evangelists.

The one point of interest in the pericope is the reconciliation accomplished by Pilate's diplomatic courtesy. It may be that Theophilus, who was probably a Roman officer,[3] would have been deeply interested in the relationship of the Herods with the procurators of Judaea.[4] If this be the case, one can see the reason for its inclusion[5] and yet at the same time the reason for

the council of the High Priest, and then sent to Pilate; but it is Herod, and not Pilate, who washes his hands of his blood.'

[1] These are the same conclusions reached by Stern, *Encounter*, xxviii, 57. Bammel (*NovT*, x, 8) concludes that this work incorporated Toledoth Jeshu traditions.

[2] Cf. Goguel, *Life of Jesus*, p. 515 n. 1; C. H. Dodd, *Historical Tradition*, p. 117 n. 2.

[3] Weiss thinks that Theophilus was equivalent to Pilate or Felix in governmental rank (*Die Schriften des Neuen Testament*, i, 395); cf. also W. M. Ramsay, *St Paul the Traveller and Roman Citizen*[14] (London, 1920), p. 388 and n. 1.

[4] This is seen also in the relationship between Festus and Agrippa II (cf. Acts 25: 13–27; 26: 24–32).

[5] McEachern's (*CJT*, xii, 27) suggestion that Luke included the pericope because 'Herod is counterbalanced in Luke's system of dual witness by Caiaphas – i.e. Rome by Israel', is not convincing.

its exclusion by the other evangelists, since it gives no help in the progress of Jesus' trial. The other evangelists did not seem to have a real interest in the Herodian house as did Luke, and thus saw no need for including this pericope. But on the other hand, although it does not add anything to the progress of the trial *per se*, Luke himself thought of the incident as a sort of a climax to Jesus' trial in the sense that it gave support to Pilate's view of Jesus' innocence. In other words, Luke shows that it was not only Pilate's verdict but also Herod's.[1] Luke takes great pains to show that the condemnation by Pilate was forced on him by the crowd.[2]

[1] Cf. Lk. 23: 15.

[2] T. W. Manson, 'The Life of Jesus: A Study of the Available Materials', *BJRL*, xxviii (1944), 396.

THE LAST YEARS OF
ANTIPAS' REIGN

The last years of Antipas' life can be centred around his relationships with three people, namely Artabanus, Aretas, and Agrippa I.

ARTABANUS

Antipas' brother, Philip, the tetrarch, died in A.D. 34 and was buried in the tomb he had prepared at Bethsaida-Julius.[1] His widow, Salome, who was Herodias' daughter, married her first cousin, Aristobulus[2] (who was the son of Herod, king of Chalcis,[3] a full brother of Herodias), who in the time of Nero was to become king of Armenia Minor[4] and later of Chalcidice.[5] They had three children.[6]

Since Philip and Salome had no children to inherit the land, Tiberius annexed his tetrarchy to Syria, but he ordered the tribute collected to be held on deposit. It may be that Antipas was hoping to acquire Philip's territory in reward for his faithfulness towards, and confidence in, Tiberius. To have made it a part of Syria (later under Vitellius' jurisdiction), which was already so large, would not have suited Antipas at all.

In A.D. 35 Lucius Vitellius became the governor of Syria.[7]

---

[1] Jos. *Ant.* xviii. 106–8. Since he died in the twentieth year of Tiberius' reign he died sometime between 19 Aug. A.D. 33 and 19 Aug. A.D. 34. It is probable that in *Ant.* Josephus reckoned according to the Julian calendar (cf. Appendix V). In this case, since Philip had reigned for 37 years, i.e. he was in his thirty-eighth year, Josephus is referring to the Julian year of 1 Jan. to 31 Dec. of A.D. 34. Therefore one can conclude that Philip died sometime between 1 Jan. and 18 Aug. of 34.

[2] Jos. *Ant.* xviii. 137.

[3] Jos. *BJ* ii. 221; *Ant.* xviii. 134; xx. 104, 158.

[4] Jos. *BJ* ii. 252; *Ant.* xx. 158; Tac. *Ann.* xiii. 7; cf. also xiv. 26.

[5] Jos. *BJ* vii. 226.　　　　　　　　[6] Jos. *Ant.* xviii. 137.

[7] Tac. *Ann.* vi. 32; Suet. *Vit.* ii. 4; Dio lix. 27. 3; Pliny *NH* xv. 83, 91. Although Lewin (pp. 242–3, cf. also Zeitlin, *JQR*, LV, 186) believes that he began his governorship in Syria in 34, this is unconvincing, for it is based on

Tacitus tells how in A.D. 35, at the instigation of Vitellius, the subjects of the Parthian king, Artabanus III, became discontented and transferred their allegiance to Tiridates III. Artabanus was compelled to retire with only a band of foreign mercenaries to the remote districts adjoining Scythia. Soon after, with the aid of Dahae and Sacae contingents, he made a comeback, and Tiridates and a handful of men were forced to flee to Syria. Artabanus quickly reoccupied the country.[1]

Tiberius wanted the struggle formally ended and instructed Vitellius to that effect[2] sometime in the latter part of A.D. 36.[3] Antipas was asked to take part in the negotiations. It may be that he was needed because he spoke Aramaic, the *lingua franca* of the whole region.[4] Possibly Tiberius wanted to show his confidence in Antipas and to heal any ill feeling Antipas may have had towards him and Vitellius for not inheriting Philip's territory. At any rate the Roman government thought that Antipas would be a useful negotiator in this endeavour.

The conference took place in the middle of a specially constructed bridge that spanned the Euphrates.[5] A treaty was signed and Artabanus sent his son Darius as a hostage to Tiberius, along with many gifts, among which was a Jewish giant called Eleazar about ten and a half feet tall.[6] After the negotiations, Antipas gave a feast for both sides in a specially con-

the assumption that Flaccus died in A.D. 33 and on the possible implication in Jos. *Ant.* xviii. 96 that Vitellius was in Syria before Tiberius asked him to establish friendship with the Parthian king, Artabanus III. These are only assumptions that cannot be proved. Schürer (I, 332–4) makes a far better case for the rule of Vitellius commencing in A.D. 35 shortly after Flaccus' death.

[1] Tac. *Ann.* vi. 31–7, 41–4; cf. Dio lviii. 26. 1–4; Jos. *Ant.* xviii. 96–100; cf. also G. Rawlinson, *The Sixth Great Oriental Monarchy* (London, 1873), pp. 229–39; N. C. Debevoise, *A Political History of Parthia* (Chicago, 1938), pp. 155–63; U. Kahrstedt, *Artabanos III. und seine Erben* (Bern, 1950), pp. 34–5.

[2] Jos. *Ant.* xviii. 101.

[3] The fixing of the date arises from a statement of Tac. *Ann.* vi. 38 to the effect that the Parthian conflicts occurred during two summers. These would be the summers of 35 and 36, and so the negotiations would have been in the late summer or autumn of 36.

[4] As suggested by Perowne, *Later Herods*, p. 56.

[5] Jos. *Ant.* xviii. 101–5; cf. also Suet. *Calig.* xiv. 3; *Vit.* ii. 4; Dio lix. 27. 3.

[6] Jos. *Ant.* xviii. 102–3. Besides Josephus, Suet. *Calig.* xix. 2 and Dio lix. 17. 5 speak of Darius as being present in Rome in A.D. 39.

structed pavilion. This was typical of the Herodian family. Antipas, being very elated with his success, wanted to be the first to communicate the news to Tiberius. He wrote a detailed report. Antipas may have done this so that Tiberius would see the value of his mediation. The reason that he wrote so quickly may be due to the fact that he was anxious that Tiberius should not receive another's interpretation first. He may have wanted to impress Tiberius and thus gain his favour, with the possibility of acquiring Philip's territory. At any rate, although Tiberius was pleased, Vitellius was furious when he received a letter from Tiberius that he already had the full details of the successful negotiations before Vitellius' official report had arrived. Wisely Vitellius said nothing at the time.

Although it has been assumed above that the treaty was made during Tiberius' rule, Suetonius[1] and Dio Cassius[2] place it after Gaius had become emperor. Tacitus' *lacuna* at this point in his *Annals* does not offer any evidence for placing it in Gaius' reign.[3] Rawlinson argues that the terms and circumstances of the peace treaty were worked out during Tiberius' reign, but the treaty did not arrive at Rome until Tiberius had been succeeded by Gaius.[4] But this is unacceptable because, according to Josephus, Tiberius had received Antipas' letter. There can be no absolute certainty on this point. However, although there are scholars who favour the later date,[5] most scholars feel that it occurred while Tiberius was still reigning.[6] Täubler has argued with a high degree of probability that Suetonius and Dio, who were hostile to Tiberius, begrudged him his success.[7] Moreover, since

[1] *Calig.* xiv. 3.

[2] Dio lix. 27. 3.

[3] *Contra*, J. P. V. D. Balsdon, *The Emperor Gaius* (Oxford, 1934), p. 198 n. 2.

[4] Rawlinson, *Sixth Great Oriental Monarchy*, p. 239 and n. 3.

[5] Schürer, I, 446–7; H. Willrich, 'Caligula', *Klio*, III (1903), 300 n. 3; Balsdon, pp. 117, 198.

[6] E. Täubler, *Die Parthernachrichten bei Josephus* (Inaugural dissertation, Friedrich-Wilhelms-Universität zu Berlin, 1904), pp. 33–40; Mommsen, *Provinces*, II, 44–5; Otto, cols. 193–4; H. Dessau, *Geschichte der römischen Kaiserzeit*, I (Berlin, 1924), 87–8; J. G. C. Anderson, 'The Eastern Frontier from Tiberius to Nero', *CAH*, x (Cambridge, 1934), 749–50; Jones, *Herods*, p. 182; Debevoise, p. 163; Reicke, *New Testament Era*, p. 191; Bruce, *ALUOS*, v, 19.

[7] Täubler, *Parthernachrichten*, pp. 39–40.

Josephus' bias was towards Agrippa I (and Agrippa II)[1] he would have credited this success not to Tiberius but to Gaius, Agrippa I's friend. However, since Josephus does place this achievement within Tiberius' reign, it strongly suggests that it occurred then. Finally, as Bruce observes: 'in a matter where Josephus's personal interests were not engaged, and in a context where the circumstantial details so strongly favour his account of the affair, there is no reason for doubting his accuracy'.[2] This means that Vitellius returned to Antioch around the autumn of A.D. 36. Possibly he made the 'first' journey to Jerusalem mentioned in Josephus[3] on his way back from the Euphrates to Antioch or soon after his arrival at Antioch, to be assured that all was well within his jurisdiction.

ARETAS

Antipas' triumph did not last long. Aretas long awaited an opportunity for revenge for the insult Antipas had offered to the Nabataean royal family when he divorced Aretas' daughter. Aretas attacked Antipas on the pretext of a border dispute about boundaries of Gabalis[4] in south-eastern Peraea. Antipas'

---

[1] Cf. Hölscher, PW, IX, 1987; cf. also Thackeray, *Josephus*, p. 49.

[2] Bruce, *ALUOS*, V, 19.

[3] *Ant.* xv. 405. The Jews gave Vitellius a splendid reception, possibly because of his success with the Parthian treaty. In return for their kindness he allowed them to express a wish and they asked for the vestments of the high priest to be put into their authority. What better time for this request, after such a success as Vitellius had accomplished with the Parthians?

[4] Jos. *Ant.* xviii. 109, 113–14. Niese's Josephus text (*Ant.* xviii. 113) has Γαμαλικῆ and the variant reading of Γαμαλῖτις in codices Medicaeus, Vaticanus, and Epitome; and *Gamalica* (*Gamalitica* in Ambrosianus) in Latin. Gamala is located within what had been the tetrarchy of Philip. Harlow (pp. 188, 244–5) accepts this reading, although he wants the location of the controversy more to the east so that Aretas' territory would be included. Surely Gamala could not have been the subject of contention between Aretas and Antipas. Gamala was now a part of Syria (after Philip's death) and so Vitellius, not Antipas, would have been involved. If this were the case, why then was Vitellius reluctant to go against Aretas and why would he have gone towards Petra via Judaea? Would he not have gone via Gamala? Schürer's (I, 445 and n. 36; cf. also Abel, *Géographie*, II, 158) emendation, Galaaditis (Gilead) is possible, but Jones' (*CERP*, p. 449 n. 19) suggestion that it should read Γαβαλῖτις (a district south of Moabitis in Idumaea) seems more plausible (cf. Jos. *Ant.* ii. 6; iii. 40; ix. 188). Its loca-

army was disastrously defeated owing to the defection of a part of the army; those from the tetrarchy of Philip felt more sympathetic towards the Arab brethren than towards Antipas.

Exactly when it occurred is difficult to say, but since Rome was involved with Parthia it was an ideal time to strike. It may have been during Antipas' absence on the Euphrates,[1] but more likely it was after the conference, 'since Antipas would have had little time for diplomatic negotiations once his quarrel with Aretas had become serious'.[2] Also, if it occurred during the conference it would seem that Antipas would have mentioned Aretas' attack in the dispatch he sent to Tiberius. The ideal time for Aretas to strike would have been immediately after the conference, just as Antipas arrived back or shortly thereafter, and just before Vitellius returned to Antioch. Things would not have been settled for either Antipas or Vitellius. Also, Vitellius would have been far enough away for it to have taken some time for a dispatch to reach him and for him to return with his troops. Thus, sometime in the autumn of 36 seems probable.

Josephus states that some Jews saw in this defeat a divine retribution upon Antipas for his execution of John.[3] As mentioned above,[4] the Jews felt that God's revenge did not always occur immediately at the time of the misdeed. The time between John's death and Antipas' defeat was only a period of five or six years.

Although Josephus clearly puts the blame on him,[5] Antipas

tion is vague, for Eusebius (*Onomast.* pp. 102: 24, 25; 103: 24) locates it in the area of Petra, but elsewhere he uses the same name for the area above the River Arnon (pp. 128: 17, 18; 129: 17). Also, Josephus has it twice (*Ant.* ii. 6; iii. 40), once as synonymous with the Amalekites and the other time (*Ant.* ix. 188) as something distinct from the Amalekites and Edomites. At any rate Gabalis is probably a district on the Peraean frontier. It would have brought Antipas into the contention. Also, it is probable that Vitellius would have wanted to conquer this district on the way to Petra to regain lost ground. At least the location of Gabalis justifies Vitellius' direction of travel much better than Gamala.

[1] As suggested by Jones, *Herods*, p. 182; Perowne, *Later Herods*, p. 56.

[2] Smallwood, *JJS*, v, 19 n. 2.

[3] *Ant.* xviii. 116–19. Chrysostom errs by saying that Josephus ascribed the ultimate destruction of Jerusalem to John's execution (Chrysostom *Commentarii in S. Joannem* homily xiii. 1 [*MPG*, LIX, 87]).

[4] P. 126 n. 1.   [5] *Ant.* xviii. 109–14.

managed to make Tiberius believe that he was the injured party, and consequently Tiberius ordered Vitellius to declare war on Aretas and to send him or his head to Rome.[1] Vitellius mustered two legions (8,400 troops)[2] and a number of auxiliary forces and proceeded towards Petra. To avoid offending the Jewish religious convictions with regard to the images attached to the military standards, Vitellius, according to Josephus, sent his troops around Judaea while he himself with Antipas went to Jerusalem where a feast was being celebrated.[3] Also, possibly, he went up to Jerusalem to support Marcellus, the newly appointed governor, in case of any trouble.[4] But on the fourth day after his arrival at Jerusalem, he received the news of Tiberius' death which was on 16 March 37.[5] As a result of this news, Vitellius called off the expedition against Aretas. Before he left Jerusalem he obliged the Jews to take an oath of allegiance to the new emperor.[6]

There is a chronological problem here. To which feast is Josephus referring? As discussed in Appendix VIII, most scholars think it refers to the Passover, although Lewin, Jeremias, and Blinzler believe it refers to the feast of Pentecost. The last view is preferable for several reasons: (1) It avoids the reversing or the reordering of the feasts in Josephus as suggested by Holzmeister[7] and Smallwood.[8] (2) It better accounts for the speed of the couriers in delivering the message. The distance between Rome and Jerusalem on Roman roads was 2,413 Roman miles.[9] Over such great distances a courier would

---

[1] Jos. *Ant.* xviii. 115.

[2] Cf. above, pp. 119–20 n. 3; H. M. D. Parker, *The Roman Legions* (Cambridge, 1958), p. 14.

[3] *Ant.* xviii. 121–2.

[4] E. M. Smallwood, 'The Relations between the Jews and the Roman Government from 66 B.C. to the Foundation of the Christian Empire' (unpublished Ph.D. dissertation, University of Cambridge, 1950), p. 192.

[5] Tac. *Ann.* vi. 50; Suet. *Tib.* lxxiii. 1; Dio erred in placing it on 26 March (Dio lviii. 28. 5; cf. Clinton, *Fasti Romani*, I, 20; W. F. Synder, 'On the Chronology in the Imperial Books of Cassius Dio's Roman History', *Klio*, N.F. xv (1940), 45–6.

[6] Jos. *Ant.* xviii. 120–4. Later, according to Philo (*Leg.* 231), the Jews claimed that they were the first of all the inhabitants of Syria to rejoice in Gaius' accession.

[7] *Biblica*, XIII, 231. [8] *JJS*, V, 17–21.

[9] For calculation, see above, pp. 34 nn. 2, 5; 36 n. 2.

not average more than fifty miles a day, and hence it is reasonable to think that the feast mentioned refers to Pentecost of 37.[1] Then the chronological scheme would be as follows:

Struggle with the Parthians	35–6
Peace treaty with the Parthians	summer/autumn 36
Vitellius' first Jerusalem visit	
(Jos. *Ant.* xv. 405)	autumn 36
Aretas' war against Antipas	autumn 36
Pilate returned to Rome	winter 36/7
Tiberius died	16 Mar. 37
Vitellius (2nd Jerusalem visit) deposed	
Caiaphas and appointed Jonathan	
(Jos. *Ant.* xviii. 90–5)	Passover 37
Vitellius (3rd Jerusalem visit) deposed	
Jonathan and appointed Theophilus	
(Jos. *Ant.* xviii. 123)	Pentecost 37
Vitellius heard of Tiberius' death	Pentecost 37

(3) Within this scheme there is enough time to allow for Vitellius' correspondence with Tiberius about the high priest's garments, and for Tiberius' reply, before the Passover of 37. (4) It also allows enough time for Antipas' correspondence with Tiberius and the latter's instruction to Vitellius.

Vitellius left Jerusalem to return to Antioch. He did not carry out Tiberius' command to conquer Aretas now that he was under the new emperor, Gaius. Tiberius may have wanted to help out his loyal friend Antipas but there were no such instructions from Gaius. Moreover, because of Vitellius' personal grievance against Antipas, he would not have been anxious to help the tetrarch out of his dilemma.

AGRIPPA I

The beginning of the end came with the accession of Gaius. This was due partly to the hostility of his nephew and newly acquired brother-in-law, Agrippa, and partly to the frivolous ambition of his wife Herodias.

Agrippa, born in 10 B.C.,[2] was the son of Berenice (the daughter of Salome – Herod the Great's sister – and Costo-

---

[1] This is treated more fully in Appendix VIII.
[2] Cf. above, p. 154 n. 7.

barus) and the ill-fated Aristobulus (son of Herod the Great and Mariamme I). After his father's death, and before that of Herod the Great, Agrippa moved to Rome. His mother was a close friend of Antonia, widow of Drusus the Elder (brother of Tiberius). Agrippa was brought up with their son Claudius (the future emperor), and with the son of Tiberius who also was named Drusus, as well as with the members of the imperial family. Like many sons of the wealthy he was a spendthrift, and after his mother's death he spent so freely that he was reduced to poverty. With Sejanus being more favoured by Tiberius, 'Sejanus looked with little favour on the hangers-on of his principal rivals, Germanicus' widow Agrippina and her sons'.[1] Moreover, when the younger Drusus died in A.D. 23 (poisoned by Sejanus),[2] Tiberius forbade the visits of his deceased son's friends lest they should remind him of his grief. As a result of these circumstances Agrippa was forced to retire quietly to Malatha, a fortress in Idumaea, leaving many angry creditors behind him in Rome.[3]

Being utterly depressed over his humiliation, he had even thought of committing suicide. But his wife, Cypros, told his sister, Herodias, about his depression and asked for help. Apparently, Herodias' influence on Antipas on behalf of Agrippa was quite great, because he was given a home, a guaranteed income, and a small civil service position as inspector of markets (ἀγορανόμος) in Antipas' new capital, Tiberias.[4] Agrippa accepted his uncle's offer but soon became dissatisfied with it. For Agrippa the income was not enough,[5] and the thought of being dependent upon his uncle was humiliating. On the other hand, Antipas was not favourably disposed towards his spendthrift nephew and constantly reminded him where he

---

[1] Jones, *Herods*, p. 185. For a discussion of the bitter party struggles in Rome, see F. B. Marsh, 'Roman Parties in the Reign of Tiberius', *The American Historical Review*, XXXI (1926), 233–50.

[2] Tac. *Ann.* iv. 8; Suet. *Tib.* lxii. 1; Dio lvii. 22. 1–4.

[3] Jos. *Ant.* xviii. 143–7, 165.

[4] Above, p. 98.

[5] Here one can readily see Josephus' prejudice in favour of Agrippa and against Antipas, for the fault is almost entirely with Antipas (*Ant.* xviii. 148–50). Certainly Antipas was generous enough to help him out of his plight but Agrippa remained ungrateful. He wanted to get rich and powerful quickly rather than by the normal means of patient endurance as his uncle Antipas had done.

would have been if his uncle had not stepped in to help. Matters came to a head one evening at Tyre during a feast. Both Antipas and Agrippa drank too much and began quarrelling. Finally, Antipas reproached Agrippa for his poverty and pointed out to the guests that the very food he was eating he owed to Antipas. Agrippa could stand no more. He left and became attached to L. Pomponius Flaccus, legate of Syria (32–5?)[1] whom he had known intimately at Rome. Although Flaccus received him gladly, later he and Agrippa quarrelled and so Agrippa returned to Rome. He repaid his old debts by incurring new ones.[2]

Although at first the relationship between Agrippa and Tiberius was strained, this was later corrected. Agrippa came to Rome to curry favour, or to transact some business, with the emperor.[3] Perhaps now that his uncle Philip had died he was enquiring of Tiberius about the future of Philip's tetrarchy. In any case Agrippa tried to convince Tiberius of Antipas' treason but Tiberius refused to believe the charge made against his faithful servant in the East.[4] Nevertheless, Tiberius appointed Agrippa as companion to his grandson, Tiberius Gemellus (son of the younger Drusus), who was about seventeen years old at this time.[5] Also, at this time he became a friend of Tiberius' nephew, Gaius, who succeeded him as emperor (he was twenty-five years old[6] and was Tiberius Gemellus' rival). Being able to borrow more money he was able to pay court to Gaius, and consequently their friendship became intimate. Agrippa made an unwise remark to Gaius, stating that he wished Tiberius would relinquish his office to Gaius who was much more capable of ruling. A servant of Agrippa overheard the

---

[1] Cf. Schürer, I, 332–3. This would mean that Agrippa probably left Rome between A.D. 24 and 26 and arrived in Idumaea in 25 or as late as 27. He may have come to Tiberias shortly after Antipas' and Herodias' marriage, or as early as 27 but preferably in 29 or 30, and remained there until 32 or 33 at which time he went to Syria. Thus he was under Antipas' support for a period of two to four (or possibly even six) years.

[2] Jos. *Ant.* xviii. 151–60. His return to Rome was around A.D. 36 (*Ant.* xviii. 126: ἐνιαυτῷ πρότερον ἢ τελευτῆσαι Τιβέριον). Cf. Eus. *Chron.* II, 150, 151.

[3] Jos. *Ant.* xviii. 126. [4] Jos. *BJ* ii. 178.

[5] Tac. *Ann.* ii. 84 (of the twin brothers, only Tiberius Gemellus survived); cf. E. Kornemann, *Tiberius* (Stuttgart, 1960), p. 218.

[6] Suet. *Calig.* viii. 1.

conversation and reported it to the emperor. Tiberius, hearing this, cast Agrippa into prison where he remained until Tiberius' death six months later.[1]

The tables turned for Agrippa when Gaius became emperor. He was released from prison and was given a golden chain equal in weight to the iron chain he had worn in prison. In addition to this, Gaius conferred upon him the region of his uncle Philip, together with the more northerly territory which had formerly been the tetrarchy of Lysanias, and he was given the title of king.[2] The senate also conferred on him the honorary rank of praetor[3] and subsequently consular rank.[4]

However, it was not until the second year of Gaius' reign (16 March A.D. 38 to 16 March A.D. 39) that Agrippa received permission to set sail and make his rule secure.[5] According to Philo, Gaius advised him that, rather than take the long route to Syria, he should wait for the etesian (ἐτησίαι) or annual winds and take the short route via Alexandria.[6] For this reason, he probably went at the earliest possible time. Since his stay in Alexandria was short, he probably arrived in Palestine in early/middle August 38.

His arrival in Palestine roused Antipas' jealousy, but his sister Herodias became even more greatly incensed and she induced Antipas to aspire to the title of king. She reproached Antipas for his indolence and argued that if a commoner (ἰδιώτης) were able to attain the title of king, then surely the emperor would confer the same title upon a tetrarch. Moreover, if the emperor gave the honour to a worthless spendthrift, surely he would bestow the same honour on one who had faithfully served the Roman government so long. But, typical of Antipas' ambivalent attitude, he was content with his tranquillity. Possibly when Archelaus was deposed, he asked for the title

---

[1] Jos. *Ant.* xviii. 161–236; *BJ* ii. 178–80; cf. also Dio lix. 8. 2.

[2] Jos. *Ant.* xviii. 237; *BJ* ii. 181. Regarding Lysanias, cf. also *Ant.* xiv. 330–2; xv. 92, 344; xix. 275; xx. 138; *BJ* i. 248, 398, 440; ii. 215, 247; Lk. 3: 1.

[3] Philo *Flacc.* 40.   [4] Dio lx. 8. 2.

[5] Jos. *Ant.* xviii. 238–9.

[6] Philo *Flacc.* 26. Beginning on 19 July these winds blow for thirty days (Pliny *NH* ii. 47. 124) and one is able to sail from Puteoli to Alexandria in about nine days (*ibid.* xix. 1. 3). From Alexandria to Palestine it should not have taken more than five to seven days (cf. Casson, *TAPA*, LXXXII, 145).

of king[1] and was refused, but as a concession he was allowed to use the dynastic title *Herod*.[2] Hence he may have felt it unwise to ask again, especially since the new emperor was a personal friend of Agrippa. However, due to Herodias' insistence he gave way and prepared to go to Rome.[3] Having heard of their preparations, Agrippa also made preparations to go to Rome. Immediately after Antipas had left Palestine, Agrippa dispatched one of his freedmen, Fortunatus, to Rome to accuse Antipas.[4]

Both parties were at the same time before Gaius at Baiae, about three miles south of Puteoli. While engaged in interviewing Antipas, Gaius was perusing the letter of Agrippa which accused him of his conspiracy with Sejanus against the government of Tiberius, and of his being at the present time in league with the Parthians against the government of Gaius.[5] The first of these accusations was never raised since Gaius would not have been interested in the past administration. Nevertheless, it would seem unlikely that Agrippa would make up an accusation that would prove wrong. It is possible that he gathered such information while residing in Tiberias and intended to inform Tiberius of it in A.D. 36, but found Tiberius unwilling to listen to him.[6] The second accusation was raised, and Antipas could not deny it. As to when the alliance was made, it is hard to say. However, it is possible that, when Gaius became emperor and Agrippa received the title of king, Antipas may have thought that there was no future for him in the Roman government and so made a pact with the Parthians (possibly also for his protection). This would give ample time (two years) for acquiring equipment for 70,000 soldiers. Undoubtedly Antipas knew of the bond of friendship between Gaius and Agrippa. Although this pact may have been made before 37, most likely it was made after Gaius' accession and thus against Gaius' government. Possibly Antipas thought that if he were

---

[1] Cf. Dio lv. 27. 6.   [2] Above, pp. 103–9.

[3] Jos. *Ant.* xviii. 240–6; *BJ* ii. 181–3.

[4] According to Jos. *BJ* ii. 183, Agrippa went personally to Rome to accuse Antipas, but this is unlikely since he did not return to Rome until the autumn of 40 (cf. below, pp. 262–3 n. 4). Rather, Agrippa's accusations were by letter and not by personal appearance (cf. Otto, col. 195).

[5] Jos. *Ant.* xviii. 247–52.

[6] Jos. *BJ* ii. 178; *Ant.* xviii. 126.

called to Rome, as Pilate had been, he could, with the Parthians, resist Rome.

Gaius sentenced Antipas to exile at Lugdunum Convenarum (a town in Gaul situated on the right bank of the Garonne, now Saint-Bertrand de Comminges).[1] As a proof of his imperial favour, Antipas' tetrarchy and property were handed over to Agrippa. When Gaius learned that Herodias was the sister of Agrippa,[2] he made the offer that she should keep all her personal property and be regarded as a sister of his friend Agrippa and not the wife of his enemy Antipas. But she replied that she would be loyal to her husband, for it would only be proper for her to share in his exile as she had shared in his prosperity. Being angered at her haughtiness, he confiscated her property and granted it to Agrippa.[3]

The summer of 39[4] began a new era for Agrippa I, while Antipas and Herodias pass from the scene of history.

[1] Jos. *Ant.* xviii. 252. According to Jos. *BJ* ii. 183, Antipas died in Spain, which apparently, judging from the context, was the land of his exile. Therefore a town on the frontiers would satisfy both passages. Although Schürer (I, 448 n. 45, cf. also Baron, III, 47) prefers Lyons, surely Lugdunum Convenarum is to be preferred, cf. J. Sacaze, *Inscriptions Antiques des Pyrénées* (Toulouse, 1892), pp. 150–1; O. Hirschfeld, 'Zur Geschichte des Christenthums in Lugudunum vor Constantin', *SAB*, no. xix (Berlin, 1895), 399 n. 1 (*KS*, pp. 173–4 n. 2); R. Lizop, *Les Convenae et les Consoranni* (Toulouse and Paris, 1931), pp. 31–6; H. Crouzel, 'Le lieu d'exil d'Hérode Antipas et d'Hérodiade selon Flavius Josèphe', *Studia Patristica*, x, *TU*, cvii (Berlin, 1970), 275–80; cf. also Eisler, ΙΗΣΟΥΣ, II, 127 n. 1; Friedländer, III, 213; Jones, *Herods*, p. 195; Perowne, *Later Herods*, p. 69. Niese's emendation of ἐν Σπανίᾳ to ἐν Γαλλίᾳ in *BJ* ii. 183 is an attempt to conform to *Ant.* xviii. 252, but there is no manuscript evidence for it at all. If one accepts Lugdunum Convenarum, then there is no need for such an emendation. Finally, Eusebius' (*HE* i. 11. 4) statement that Antipas' banishment was to Vienna of Gaul is due to a confusion between Antipas and Archelaus.

[2] It is interesting that he did not already know this relationship, since he was so intimate with Agrippa. This may reveal the hatred of Agrippa towards both Antipas and Herodias in that he never mentioned them to Gaius. Of course, Agrippa was furthering his own cause with Gaius and would not have had time to talk about anyone else.

[3] Jos. *Ant.* xviii. 253–5; *BJ* ii. 183.

[4] The earliest possible time for Antipas and Herodias to be in Baiae was some time in A.D. 39, for there are coins extant for the forty-third year of Antipas. This would have begun some time around Nisan 39 since this was the time of year in which his father had died in 4 B.C. (for this coin, see Madden, *History of Jewish Coinage*, p. 99; De Saulcy, *Mélanges de Numisma-*

tique, II, 93; Madden, *Coins of the Jews*, pp. 121–2; Hill, *Catalogue*, p. 230; Reifenberg, *Ancient Jewish Coins*, p. 45). A coin has been published by Eckhel after Vaillant and Galland bearing the date MΔ = year 44 (J. Eckhel, *Doctrina Numorum Veterum*, III [Vienna, 1794], 486–9). This coin was rejected in Madden's earlier work (*History of Jewish Coinage*, p. 99) as possibly a misreading, but in the light of Lewin's comments (pp. 260–1, 266–8) Madden later accepted the reading of the coin (*Coins of the Jews*, p. 122). Thus Antipas was deposed in A.D. 40. But since there have never been any other coins found with the date MΔ, one suspects a misreading by Vaillant and Galland (Eckhel, pp. 486–9; Schürer, I, 488–9 n. 46; Reifenberg, *Ancient Jewish Coins*, p. 19). No numismatist, except for Madden, makes any reference to a coin published with the year MΔ. Also, to construct a chronology, as does Lewin, seems to go beyond the plain meaning of Josephus. Finally, since according to Lewin, Antipas had two hearings, one at Baiae in 39 and the other at Gaul in the spring of A.D. 40, it seems highly unlikely that Antipas would have minted coins between the two hearings, especially since his forty-fourth year did not commence until the spring of 40. Therefore, the earliest year for Antipas to have been banished would have been A.D. 39–40. The last possible time for his deposition would have been in the autumn of 39, for two reasons: (1) Twice in A.D. 39 there is mention of Gaius' being in the vicinity of Baiae (Campania, Dio lix. 13. 7 and Puteoli and Bauli, Dio lix. 17. 1–4, cf. also Suet. *Calig.* xix; Jos. *Ant.* xviii. 249). After these visits the next mentioned chronological item is his birthday, 31 August 39 (Dio lix. 20. 1; his birthday was on 31 August, cf. Suet. *Calig.* viii. 1). Immediately after his birthday, Gaius was away from Rome (since the roads were still dusty when he started for Gaul, it must have been before the winter, Suet. *Calig.* xliii) until 31 August 40, on an expedition to Gaul, Germany, and Britain (Dio lix. 21. 1 – 25. 4; Suet. *Calig.* xvii, xliii–xlix). (2) According to Josephus, in A.D. 39 Agrippa was in Palestine and not with Gaius, and thus he sent Fortunatus to Rome on his behalf (*Ant.* xviii. 238–9, 247; *BJ* ii. 181). However, from the autumn of A.D. 40 until Gaius' death, Agrippa was with Gaius (*Ant.* xviii. 289, xix. 236–9; *BJ* ii. 204–6; Dio lix. 24. 1; lx. 8. 2; cf. also Philo *Leg.* 261–8, 326). Therefore the deposition would have had to occur in A.D. 39, probably late in the summer. Although Josephus implies in *Ant.* xviii. 252 that the domains of Antipas were given over immediately to Agrippa, Josephus states later (*Ant.* xix. 351) that these territories were given to him in the fourth year of Gaius, or between 16 March 40 and 21 January 41. It is probable that several months elapsed between the deposition of Antipas and the conferring of the tetrarchy upon Agrippa, and the latter event may not have occurred until the spring/summer of 40 or possibly as late as the autumn of that year when Agrippa returned to Rome and rejoined Gaius. Finally, although not entirely clear, Dio (lix. 8. 2) may imply that Gaius executed Antipas. It was a common practice of Gaius to execute those whom he had banished (cf. Suet. *Calig.* xxviii; Dio lix. 18. 3; Philo *Flacc.* 184–91; Lewin, p. 261; Schürer, I, 449–50 n. 47). But it is more likely that Dio is not referring to Antipas but to Tiberius Gemellus (cf. Philo *Leg.* 28–31; Willrich, *Klio*, III, 304 n. 1).

CONCLUSION

Herod Antipas, the son of Herod the Great and Malthace, was the tetrarch of Galilee and Peraea from 4 B.C. to A.D. 39. He had hoped at one time to be the sole ruler over all of his father's realm, but owing to a change in his father's will was not able to attain to this. Upon his return from Rome in 4 B.C., his land was ravaged by war and hence he rebuilt the cities of Sepphoris and Livias. At the time of Archelaus' deposition, it seems that he acquired the dynastic title of Herod. Later in his rule he built a new capital city called Tiberias, setting it up on the general lines of a Hellenistic city. On a smaller scale than that of his father, he was a city builder.

He was a good ruler. His imprisonment of John the Baptist was a precautionary measure to avoid a possible insurrection. He was also anxious about Jesus' growing influence but only threatened him, probably because he was apprehensive of public reactions, since he was held responsible for John's death. Both of these instances show that he was anxious to destroy any seeds of rebellion at the early stage. He may have learned that, immediately following his father's death, procrastination proved fatal to Archelaus. Indeed, the length of Antipas' rule with only one recorded incident of trouble (the defeat by Aretas) demonstrates his able leadership. It is to be noted that his brother Archelaus lasted for only ten years in Judaea and that the procurators of Judaea experienced much trouble.

Yet, on the other hand, Antipas seems to have been much milder than Herod the Great, though it must be granted that there is not as much written concerning him as there is about his father. Certainly, he did not have the numerous wives and the manifold intrigues within his family as had his father. He was not power-hungry like his father but seemed to be more casual and ambivalent in his attitudes and aspirations. Seeing Archelaus' misrule and learning from his own bad experience with John the Baptist, he tended to be indecisive and at times uttered threats rather than taking any action. He seemed to lack political ambition. It was Herodias who induced him to try to gain the whole of his father's kingdom. He himself probably would not have attempted such an ambitious plan.

A main source of trouble was the ambition of his wife, causing the death of John the Baptist, which led the people to believe that his defeat by Aretas was God's revenge. Her selfish ambitions were responsible also for his exile to Lugdunum Convenarum. Of course, his conspiracy with Sejanus and later a pact with Parthia, revealed to the emperor by Agrippa, were integral parts of his downfall. However, the plots probably would not have been revealed if Herodias had not pressed him to make a bid for the title of king.

He was an able ruler. He lived peaceably with his people. Except for Agrippa II, he reigned longer than any other Herod. All of this is to his credit.

Appendices

THE WILLS OF HEROD

According to Schürer, Herod the Great made three testaments or wills,[1] while Otto[2] and Perowne[3] think there were four. Actually it seems that Herod made six wills.[4] These will be mentioned briefly.

THE FIRST WILL

Although not explicitly stated by Josephus, it seems that Herod made his first will in 22 B.C. when he brought his sons, Alexander and Aristobulus, to Rome for their education.[5] There are several factors which substantiate this. First, while he was in Rome this will seems to have been a topic of discussion, for it was at this time that Augustus granted Herod the right to give his kingdom to whichever son he pleased.[6] Secondly, when the emperor again told him in 12 B.C. that he had the right to choose his successor, Herod proceeded to do so immediately.[7] It is most likely that he had acted just as promptly after Augustus' permission in 22 B.C. Thirdly, when later Antipater had convinced his father of the evil intentions of Alexander and Aristobulus, Herod declared Antipater to be his heir in his next will.[8] This implies that he had made an earlier will. Fourthly, when writing to Augustus, Herod praised his son Antipater, and his intention may have been to convince the emperor that Antipater should be heir in preference to his other sons previously named.[9]

---

[1] I, 374.

[2] According to Otto they were made in the years 13, 7, 5 and 4 B.C., cf. cols. 135, 136, 144, 149, 201, Zeittafel für Herodes I.

[3] Perowne, *Herod the Great*, follows Otto, cf. pp. 161, 167, 170, 173, 182–3.

[4] According to Roman law, one could invalidate a will when a new one was made, cf. *Gai Inst.* ii. 144; *Ulp. Reg.* xxiii. 2.

[5] Jos. *Ant.* xv. 342–3; above, p. 9 n. 4.

[6] Jos. *Ant.* xv. 343.　　　[7] Jos. *Ant.* xvi. 129, 133; *BJ* i. 454, 458.

[8] Jos. *BJ* i. 451. Although this was a will (the second one), it seems that it had yet to be ratified by Augustus just as Archelaus had to have Herod's last will ratified (cf. *Ant.* xvii. 202–3, 209; *BJ* ii. 2–3, 17). This may have been one reason for Herod's going to Rome (cf. fifth point in the text above).

[9] Jos. *Ant.* xvi. 85.

Fifthly, why should Herod go to Rome just to prove his sons' guilt and their need of punishment? Is it not more likely that he went also to prove that they were not fit to succeed him? This seems to be the emphasis of the whole trial, for Herod told his two sons that he was at liberty to give his throne to whomsoever he chose. This may imply that he was willing to change his original intention.[1] Sixthly, even before the trial the sons had forfeited their position and power to Antipater.[2] This may indicate the invalidation of an older will and its replacement by another one. Finally, in the trial itself the sons, Alexander and Aristobulus, apparently defended their former assumption that Herod had designated at least one of them to be his successor, thus making it unnecessary for them to resort to subversive methods (Herod was accusing them of plotting to obtain the throne).[3]

Therefore it seems not impossible that Herod made his first will in 22 B.C. when he brought his sons, Alexander and Aristobulus, to Rome. At this time the emperor granted him the right to give his kingdom to whichever son he chose.

THE SECOND WILL

The second will is mentioned by Josephus in *Bellum Judaicum* i. 451. When he became suspicious of his sons, Alexander and Aristobulus, Herod, in 14 B.C., brought back his eldest son, Antipater,[4] into favour, so as to curb the reckless attitude of Mariamme's two sons. Antipater used this occasion to better his position by acting as a loyal son to his father and by reporting in an exaggerated form the misconduct of his two half-brothers. Thus in 13 B.C. Herod made a will publicly declaring Antipater as his heir. Then he sent Antipater, accompanied by Agrippa, to Rome, where he went in princely style and with every mark of royalty except for the diadem. Herod also sent many gifts to Augustus so that Antipater might become Καίσαρι

[1] Jos. *Ant.* xvi. 90–9; *BJ* i. 452–3.
[2] Jos. *BJ* i. 450; cf. *Ant.* xvi. 86–7.
[3] Jos. *Ant.* xvi. 112–17.
[4] It is interesting to note that according to Josephus Antipater was born to Herod when Herod was yet a commoner, before he had become king (cf. Jos. *Ant.* xvii. 192; *BJ* i. 665). Later Herod brought back Antipater's mother, Doris, into the household.

φίλος.[1] It may have been with Antipater and Agrippa that
Herod sent his second will to Rome for its ratification.[2] At any
rate, it seems to have been at the time that Alexander and
Aristobulus were excluded from the inheritance of Herod's
domain.[3] But Antipater realized all too well that Herod could
again change his mind and so he constantly wrote letters to him
from Rome, kindling his father's anger against Alexander and
Aristobulus and ingratiating himself. This finally led Herod
himself to come to Rome with a view to proving that Alexander
and Aristobulus were not worthy of the throne. The outcome of
the trial was that Herod and his sons were reconciled.[4]

THE THIRD WILL

The third will was made immediately after the trial while
Herod was still in Rome in 12/11 B.C.[5] There is a new facet to
this will. Whereas previously the emperor had allowed only one
successor,[6] now he allowed Herod to divide his kingdom among

---

[1] Jos. *Ant.* xvi. 85–6; *BJ* i. 451. Cf. also φίλους Καίσαρος in *BJ* i. 623.

[2] Cf. Jos. *Ant.* xvii. 202–3, 209; *BJ* ii. 2–3, 17. Ratification of a Roman
will was not normally necessary, but in this case the emperor was allowing
one of his subjects to distribute his own land!

[3] Jos. *Ant.* xvi. 86.

[4] It is interesting to notice that Augustus still favoured Alexander and
Aristobulus. He may well have been influenced by Alexander's father-in-
law, Archelaus, king of Cappadocia, who had written letters in order to
assist Alexander (Jos. *BJ* i. 456). Also, it may be that the emperor personally
liked the two sons for Alexander at least he seems to have known quite
intimately. When someone tried to pass himself off as Alexander nine or ten
years after Alexander's and Aristobulus' death, it is said that he had an
exact recollection of Alexander's features and was able to remember who in
his court knew Alexander the best (cf. Jos. *BJ* ii. 106–9; *Ant.* xvii. 332–3).
Thus, it may be that Augustus never actually ratified the will and this may
explain why Herod wrote him so many letters informing him how good
a son Antipater was and hoping that he would become a friend of the emperor. Finally he himself came to Rome to prove that Antipater really was
the only son worthy of the throne.

[5] Cf. Schürer, I, 371; Otto, cols. 125–6 n.; Corbishley, *JTS*, xxxv, 30–2.

[6] The wording in Jos. *Ant.* xv. 343 is καὶ δίδωσιν Ἡρῴδῃ τήν τε βασι-
λείαν ὅτῳ βούλεται βεβαιοῦν τῶν ἐξ αὐτοῦ γεγονότων. This is substantiated; first, at the time when Herod was in Rome making accusations
against his sons, Alexander and Aristobulus, he stated that Augustus gave
him authority not by compulsion but by choice to bestow the throne on the
one who remained most dutiful to him (*Ant.* xvi. 92). Again, in *Ant.* xvi. 95,

his sons if he so desired. When however Herod wished to give his kingdom immediately to his sons, rather than waiting until he died, Augustus would not allow it.[1] Herod accepted the emperor's ruling, and publicly proclaimed before his subjects all three as kings, stating that Antipater deserved it because of his age and Alexander and Aristobulus because of their noble birth.[2]

THE FOURTH WILL

After killing Alexander and Aristobulus by strangulation, Herod made a fourth will, as is clearly mentioned by Josephus. By this will he made Antipater the sole heir.[3] The situation in Judaea having made a turn for the worse, Antipater, around 6 B.C.,[4] wrote to his friends in Rome requesting them to instruct Herod to send him to Augustus as soon as possible. Antipater no doubt wanted to have the will ratified so that when Herod died there would be no dispute about the succession.[5] On

Herod said that he held out the throne as a prize for filial dutifulness to the (one) son who would show such concern for his father. Also, in *Ant.* xvi. 115, Alexander hints that there was only one throne to be given. This would suggest that the whole of Herod's possession would go to only one son. Secondly, when Herod made his second will he again assigned the throne to only one son, Antipater (*BJ* i. 451). Thirdly, when Augustus stated that Herod could either designate one successor or split up his kingdom, Herod immediately accepted the proposal that all three should be kings (*Ant.* xvi. 129, 133; *BJ* i. 458). It is true that in *BJ* i. 454 there is no indication of Augustus giving the option of allowing Herod to divide his kingdom among his sons, but Josephus' *Antiquitates Judaicae* gives a fuller account of the events. Also, the very fact that Herod did designate all three sons as kings, as recorded in the same context (*BJ* i. 458), would indicate that Augustus permitted it.

[1] Jos. *Ant.* xvi. 129. Possibly the transference of ownership to the sons during the lifetime of the parents was not allowed by Roman law as it was by Jewish and Hellenistic laws (for Jewish Law, see R. Yaron, 'Dispositions in Contemplation of Death: Some Formulas', *SH*, v [1958], 252–9, or R. Yaron, *Gifts in Contemplation of Death in Jewish and Roman Law* [Oxford, 1960], pp. 114–16, 120–4; I. Herzog, *The Main Institutions of Jewish Law*, I [London, 1936], 137–62; for Hellenistic law, see R. Taubenschlag, *The Law of Greco-Roman Egypt in the Light of the Papyri 332 B.C.–640 A.D.*[2] [Warsaw, 1955], p. 208).

[2] Jos. *Ant.* xvi. 132–4; *BJ* i. 458–60. Nobility was important to Herod the Great, for in such consisted the right to succeed; cf. *Ant.* xvii. 113.

[3] Jos. *Ant.* xvii. 53; *BJ* i. 573.

[4] Schürer, I, 374.   [5] Jones, *Herods*, p. 141.

receiving instructions to this effect, Herod immediately sent
Antipater to Rome with a brilliant retinue, a large sum of
money, and also a will naming him as successor to the throne,
and Herod (Philip), Mariamme II's son, successor in the event
of Antipater's death.[1] But when Herod discovered the plots
against him and found that Mariamme II was also involved in
them, he divorced her and struck Herod (Philip) out of the
will.[2] Why, it may be asked, was she involved in these plots
when she stood to gain no advantage from them? It was due
probably to Antipater and his mother, Doris. Antipater realized
that if she were not involved, she would, when she heard of the
plots, report them to Herod, and so provide for her own son to

[1] Jos. *Ant.* xvii. 52–3; *BJ* i. 573. There is some confusion between the two
texts. In *Ant.* xvii. 53 (and again in *Ant.* xvii. 67) Josephus states that Herod
(Philip) would be Herod the Great's successor only if Antipater died before
Herod the Great. In *BJ* i. 573 (and in *BJ* i. 588) Josephus states that Herod
(Philip) would be Antipater's successor, and there is no mention whether
this was only to be the case if Antipater died before Herod the Great. If the
account in *Ant.* is correct then one can argue that it is a fuller account and
thus is filling in the details of *BJ*. At any rate, one can see why Antipater
complained about the long life of his father (cf. *Ant.* xvii. 66–7; *BJ* i. 587),
for once Herod was dead Antipater would have no longer to worry about the
succession. It would go to whomsoever he wanted. This is supported by
Augustus' statement that Herod could choose his successors, though there is
no mention of choosing heirs beyond his own sons, e.g. his grandchildren.
Also in support of this view is the fact that Antipater took no action against
Herod (Philip). There was no need to, for once his father was gone, Antipater could control the succession. If the account in the *BJ* is correct, then
one can see why Antipater thought that Herod was senile, for when and if
he became king, he planned to destroy all of Herod's family (*BJ* i. 588, 637)
so that Herod (Philip) would not be his successor. In all probability this is
why he needed to get Herod (Philip) and his mother, Mariamme II,
involved in the plots against Herod the Great (*Ant.* xvii. 78; *BJ* i. 599–600).
He wanted to make them scapegoats for Herod's death (see text below), and
then by accusing them of his death to cause Herod (Philip) to be excluded
from the succession. In conclusion, whichever view one accepts, Antipater
wanted to get rid of his father before his own death so that he could have the
throne himself and control the succession after him.

[2] Jos. *Ant.* xvii. 78; *BJ* i. 599–600. According to Roman law, if a father
wished to exclude a son from his will, he must insert a clause which expressly
disinherited him, otherwise he would receive an equal part of the inheritance
with his brothers (cf. *Gai Inst.* ii. 123–9; *Ulp. Reg.* xxii. 14–16). So the very
act of striking his name out of the will may have been enough to satisfy the
law. This at least shows that he was not just forgotten or passed over in
the will.

be appointed Herod's heir in place of himself. Hence it may well be that Antipater persuaded his mother, Doris, who seems to have been one of the chief engineers of the plots,[1] to involve Mariamme II as an accomplice, urging upon her the utmost secrecy.[2] During the conspiracy Antipater made sure of his own safety by staying far away in Rome.

THE FIFTH WILL

The fifth will[3] was made around 5 B.C.[4] In this will Herod designated his youngest son, Antipas, to succeed him as king. Josephus states in this connection that he passed over his two eldest sons, Archelaus and Philip, because of his hatred toward them as the result of Antipater's calumnies. Could it not be as well that, the eldest son being so undutiful, he now went to the other extreme and chose one who was young and malleable? His choice of Antipas is a significant landmark in that it was the first time he had selected someone who was not in any way connected with the Hasmonaean house (as were Alexander, Aristobulus, and Antipater – through his wife, the daughter of Antigonus). Instead he chose a son whose mother was a Samaritan!

In this will Herod made new additions. He pledged himself to give a thousand talents and other gifts to Augustus; five hundred talents to the empress, her children, friends, and

---

[1] Cf. Jos. *Ant.* xvii. 64; *BJ* i. 584.

[2] In *Ant.* xvii. 78 Josephus states that she was zealous or eager to conceal these plots.

[3] Jos. *Ant.* xvii. 146–7; *BJ* i. 646. From *BJ* i. 646 one gets the impression that this was not a new will but only an alteration of the fourth will, because Josephus states that he called for the will and modified (μετέγραφεν) it (could it be that one of the papers Antipater brought to Herod from Augustus, when justifying himself before Herod, was the ratified will? *Ant.* xvii. 104; *BJ* i. 634). Also, Josephus makes the statement that this was what the will now contained after it was altered. But in *Ant.* xvii. 146, Josephus definitely implies that a new will was made. May it not be that he called for the previous will only to compare it when making the new will? Again when Herod altered his will for the last time, Josephus states in both accounts that he again altered his will (*Ant.* xvii. 188; *BJ* i. 664). This would indicate that both the fifth and sixth wills were only alterations of the fourth will. But this seems to be only a general reference, for Herod had changed his will so many times. In all probability the fifth will was an entirely new one.

[4] Cf. Schürer, I, 374.

freedmen; money, revenues, and tracts of land to his own sons; and considerable riches to Salome because of her faithfulness to him. Thus to others of his family he gave tracts of land and their revenues, but to Antipas he gave the kingdom.

THE SIXTH WILL

The sixth will consists only of the codicils[1] of the fifth will.[2] For the sake of clarity these codicils will be called Herod's sixth will. This will was drawn up in five days between Herod's execution of Antipater and his own death in March/April of 4 B.C.[3] In it Antipas was to be tetrarch of Galilee and Peraea, and Archelaus king over the whole realm. Philip was to be tetrarch over Gaulanitis, Trachonitis, Batanaea, and Paneas. To Salome he gave Jamnia, Azotus, and Phasaelis, along with

---

[1] Technically the term *codicil* should always be plural, cf. M. Kaser, *Das römische Privatrecht* (München, 1955), I, 579.

[2] Jos. *Ant.* xvii. 188–90; *BJ* i. 664. It was argued previously (above, p. 274 n. 3) that the fifth will of Herod the Great was a new will, but there are several indications that the sixth will was not entirely new but consisted only of codicils to the fifth will. In the first place, after Herod's death, Ptolemy read 'the codicils' (τὰς ἐπιδιαθήκας), cf. *BJ* i. 668. Secondly, Josephus specifically mentions in the same context that all the remaining particulars of the previous will (τὰς προτέρας διαθήκας – this is most likely referring to the fifth will), which were not altered by the codicils, were to hold good (*BJ* i. 669). Although Josephus states in *Ant.* xvii. 195 that Ptolemy read aloud Herod's *will*, one must remember that the codicils to a will are really one's last will. Thus, in this connection Josephus is more specific in the *BJ* account by using the term ἐπιδιαθήκη. Thirdly, when Antipas considered sailing to Rome, it says specifically that the will in which he had been named king had greater validity than the codicils (*BJ* ii. 20). Regarding the same event, Josephus in *Ant.* xvii. 224 makes a very general statement to the effect that Antipas believed that the earlier will was more binding than the later one. Although his words are very general, Josephus in the same context (cf. *Ant.* xvii. 226) makes a specific comparison between the two wills, when some people told Antipas that he should give way to Archelaus because of the codicils (ἐπιδιαθήκαι). This is also mentioned in *BJ* ii. 20. Fourthly, in Antipater's defence of Antipas in Rome, he states that Herod inscribed Archelaus' name in the codicils in contrast to the previous will wherein Antipas was named. Furthermore, in reply to Antipas Nicolaus of Damascus also refers to 'codicils' (*BJ* ii. 31, 35). Thus it can be concluded that the sixth will was only the codicils to the fifth will.

[3] Herod's death is recorded in Jos. *Ant.* xvii. 191–2; *BJ* i. 665–6. Regarding the date one should see above, p. 10 n. 5.

500,000 pieces of coined silver. The other relatives were to be endowed with gifts of money and sundry revenues. To Augustus he left 10,000,000 pieces of coined silver besides gold and silver vessels and some very valuable garments, and to the empress and others 5,000,000 pieces of silver. The basic difference in this will is that, whereas Antipas was previously designated king, now Archelaus is, while Antipas and Philip are given tetrarchies. Why did Herod make this change? Possibly, now that he had discovered Antipater's intrigues against his life, he may have surmised or have been informed that Antipater's slander of Archelaus and Philip was false. Also, now that they had resided in Palestine for the best part of a year, Herod could have seen that their conduct was not that of villains, as made out by Antipater, and thus realized that he had been unjust towards them in the fifth will. Finally, it is probable that the Roman government would not have found it acceptable for Antipas, a lad of only about sixteen years of age, to have been the sole ruler of such a vast realm as Herod's.

In conclusion, it seems likely that there were six wills of Herod. The fourth one was the last to be ratified by the emperor before Herod died, and since both Antipater and Herod (Philip) were by then removed from the scene, it was no longer valid. Neither the fifth nor sixth wills (or the codicils of the fifth) had been ratified by Augustus, yet no one could claim to be Herod's successor until some sort of ratification had been accomplished. Hence the necessity of the sons' journey to Rome.

THE BOUNDARIES OF
ANTIPAS' TERRITORIES

This Appendix elaborates and substantiates the territorial boundaries of Antipas' territories as given in Chapter 3.

THE BOUNDARIES OF GALILEE

In tracing the borders of Galilee, the order will be first the southern boundary, and then the eastern, northern, and western boundaries.

The southern boundary

The southwestern corner of Galilee would begin with the town of Gaba, modern *el-Harithiyye*.[1] Josephus mentions next that Galilee borders Samaria.[2] Josephus states that Xaloth (Exaloth) is in Galilee[3] while the village of Ginaea is to be considered the first northern village of Samaria.[4] These two

---

[1] Jos. *Ant.* xv. 294; *BJ* iii. 36; *Vita* 115. It is called *Geba* by Pliny *NH* v. 17. 75. There has been much controversy over the past years as to whether or not Gaba should be considered as a part of Galilee because of Josephus' reference in *Vita* 115 that Simonias is the village on the Galilaean frontier, which seems to exclude Gaba. This is so argued by Oehler, *ZDPV*, xxviii, 65; Schürer, ii, 199–200. Cf. also A. Alt, 'Die Reiterstadt Gaba', *ZDPV*, lxii (1939), 3–21; G. Dalman, 'Nach Galiläa vom 30. September bis 13. Oktober 1921', *PJB*, xviii–xix (1922–3), 31, 38–9; A. Alt, 'Das Institut im Jahre 1924', *PJB*, xxi (1925), 41; M. Avi-Yonah, 'Map of Roman Palestine', *QDAP*, v (1936), see enclosed map; E. G. Kraeling, *Rand McNally Bible Atlas* (London, 1956), map xvi. But now that Gaba has been identified with *el-Harithiyye*, it should be included within Galilee. For a discussion on this, cf. B. Maisler, 'Beth She'arim, Gaba, and Harosheth of the Peoples', *HUCA*, xxiv (1952–3), 75–84; cf. also M. Avi-Yonah, *Map of Roman Palestine²* (London, 1940), p. 38 n. 1, and see also the enclosed map where he now includes Gaba within the borders of Galilee. So also G. E. Wright and F. V. Filson (eds.), *The Westminster Historical Atlas to the Bible* (London, 1946), p. 85; pl. xiv. Hence it is most likely that Gaba was a part of Antipas' Galilee.

[2] *BJ* iii. 37.

[3] *BJ* iii. 39. Japha, 3 miles west of Xaloth, was a fortified village of Josephus in the war of 66–70 and must be considered a part of Galilee (cf. *BJ* ii. 573; *Vita* 188).

[4] *BJ* iii. 48, cf. also *Ant.* xx. 118. In *BJ* ii. 232 it is called Gema (Γῆμα).

points were around thirteen or fourteen miles apart as the crow flies – a considerable distance. There remains some confusion regarding the possession of the Great Plain.[1] It is thought by some that the whole Plain of Esdraelon belonged to the territory of Galilee.[2] Oehler[3] believes that the political border ran in the middle of the Great Plain of Esdraelon, whereas Dalman[4] believes that the Great Plain was neutral ground and that Galilee and Samaria proper only began at the mountainous regions on either side. Hence, one can only estimate where the border passed between Galilee and Samaria. Although the whole Plain of Esdraelon could have been a part of Galilee, it is reasonable to claim that the border ran about halfway between Xaloth and Ginaea which should include Nain[5] which was located on the southern frontier of Galilee.

Last to be considered in connection with Galilee's southern border is the city-state Scythopolis which went right up to the Jordan River. Hölscher believes that Scythopolis was a part of Galilee.[6] He draws support for his argument from sources other than Josephus. First, Strabo says ἡ περὶ Γαλιλαίαν Σκυθόπολις,[7] that is, 'Scythopolis [is] in Galilee'. Secondly, Hölscher argues from 1 Maccabees 12: 47 that since Jonathan and Trypho met in Beth-shan and Jonathan agreed to meet Trypho in Ptolemais, Jonathan left 2,000 troops in Galilee, that is, in Beth-shan. From this he draws his third argument, namely, that the Alexandrian text of 1 Maccabees 12: 49 says that Trypho sent his troops into Galilee into the Great Plain (εἰς Γαλιλαίαν εἰς πεδίον τὸ μέγα). Therefore, the Great Plain must have belonged to Galilee. His fourth reason is based on the preceding two arguments, namely that Judith 1: 8–9 states that since the Plain of Esdraelon is to be considered as a part of Upper Galilee one is to conclude that the Valley of Jezreel would be Lower Galilee of which Scythopolis is a part.

It seems that Hölscher is proving too much. First, if one

---

[1] G. Hölscher, 'Palästina in der persischen und hellenistischen Zeit', *Quellen und Forschungen zur alten Geschichte und Geographie*, ed. by W. Sieglin (Berlin, 1903), pp. 78–9.

[2] L. Haefeli, 'Samaria und Peräa bei Flavius Josephus', *Biblische Studien*, ed. by O. Bardenhewer, XVIII, 66–120.

[3] *ZDPV*, XXVIII, 67. [4] *SSW*, pp. 211–12.

[5] Lk. 7: 11; Dalman, *SSW*, p. 192.

[6] 'Palästina', pp. 79–80. [7] Strabo XVI. 2. 40.

carefully considers Strabo, it will be evident that περί should not be translated *in* but rather it should read as it is normally translated, as *around* or *about* or, in this context, *in the neighbourhood of*. For previously in the same sentence Strabo uses περί and it is also best translated as *in the neighbourhood of* (καὶ τὰ περὶ τὴν Φιλαδελφίαν καὶ ἡ περὶ Γαλιλαίαν Σκυθόπολις – 'and those in the neighbourhood of Philadelphia and Scythopolis in the neighbourhood of Galilee'). Secondly, although Jonathan and Trypho had met in Beth-shan and at the same time Jonathan had left the 2,000 troops in Galilee at the time he went to Ptolemais (1 Macc. 12: 47), one cannot argue that 'Galilee' here refers to Beth-shan. This is an *argumentum ex silentio*. It is more likely that if the author meant Beth-shan he would have specified it. Thus the reference to Galilee could well mean anything but Scythopolis.

Thirdly, in the LXX only the Alexandrian MSS (and no more than a fourth of all these MSS) have the εἰς after Γαλιλαίαν. Most MSS have nothing, but καί is supplied to make better sense. Thus it would read 'Trypho sent troops and cavalry into Galilee and the Great Plain' (RSV). Fourthly, it does not state in Judith 1: 8–9 that the Plain of Esdraelon is a part of Upper Galilee; it is only listed with Upper Galilee. Even if it were the case one cannot argue that the Valley of Jezreel is a part of Lower Galilee. This is also an *argumentum ex silentio*. Since Judith was written about the middle of the second century before Christ[1] and 1 Maccabees around 100 B.C.,[2] the borders of Galilee may have varied considerably by the time of Antipas. It was not until the time of Pompey, who founded the Decapolis,[3] that Scythopolis was excluded from Galilee. Thus Hölscher's use of the Apocrypha would not be applicable in the time of Herod Antipas.

It is best to accept Scythopolis as a part of the Decapolis in this time and separate from Galilee[4] for it is so designated or

---

[1] B. M. Metzger, *An Introduction to the Apocrypha* (New York, 1957), p. 43.

[2] *Ibid.* p. 130.

[3] Jos. *BJ* i. 156; cf. also *Ant.* xiv. 75. H. Bietenhard, 'Die Dekapolis von Pompeius bis Traian, ein Kapitel aus der neutestamentlichen Zeitgeschichte', *ZDPV*, LXXIX (1963), 33–9; Schürer, II, 170–3.

[4] Jos. *Vita* 318 (cf. also § 126); *BJ* ii. 595. It is to be considered a wedge between Samaria and Galilee, cf. Dalman, *SSW*, p. 6; T. Schlatter, 'Im Gebiet der Zehnstädte', *PJB*, XIV (1918), 106–8; Polybius v. 70. 3–4.

assumed by Josephus after Pompey's invasion.[1] In fact it was considered as the largest city of the Decapolis.[2] The problem is to determine the border between Scythopolis and Galilee. On the Galilaean side there was Mount Tabor, where Josephus built one of his fortifications for Galilee in the war of 66–70.[3] Also, Sennabris[4] and Philoteria[5] located on the southwestern tip of the Sea of Galilee are to be considered in the territory of Galilee.[6] Actually they are situated just west of the Jordan River's outlet at the Sea of Galilee. Although these two adjoining towns were politically independent for most of the time, it is thought with good reason by Albright that in the Roman period they were considered as one under the name of Sennabris,[7] and thus there is no mention of Philoteria by Josephus at the time of the war of 66–70.[8]

[1] *BJ* i. 156; iii. 37, 446; *Vita* 42, 121 (cf. also *BJ* ii. 458, 466–8, 470–2, 477; vii. 364).

[2] Jos. *BJ* iii. 446. For a history of this city, see A. Rowe, *The Topography and History of Beth-Shan* (Philadelphia, 1930), pp. 7–62, especially pp. 44–9; H. O. Thompson, 'Tell el-Husn – Biblical Beth-Shan', *BA*, xxx (1967), 110–35.

[3] Jos. *Vita* 188; *BJ* ii. 573; iv. 54–6.

[4] Jos. *BJ* iii. 447; W. F. Albright, 'Contributions to the Historical Geography of Palestine', *AASOR*, ii–iii (1921–2), 36–8; Dalman, *PJB*, xviii–xix, 47; S. Klein, *Beiträge zur Geographie und Geschichte Galiläas* (Leipzig, 1909), 90–1; Dalman, *SSW*, pp. 180–1. It was one time called Kinneret (Chinnereth); cf. A. Saarisalo, 'The Boundary between Issachar and Naphtali', *Annales Academiae Scientiarum Fennicae*, series B, xxi (1927), 81–2. Kinneret is to be identified with *Tell el-'Oreimeh*, cf. W. F. Albright, 'The Jordan Valley in the Bronze Age', *AASOR*, vi (1924–5), 24–6.

[5] Polybius v. 70. 3–4; L. Sukenik, 'The Ancient City of Philoteria (Beth-Yerah)', *JPOS*, ii (1922), 101–8; B. Maisler, M. Stekelis, and M. Avi-Yonah, 'The Excavations at Beth Yerah (Khirbet el-Kerak) 1944–6', *IEJ*, ii (1952), 165–73, 219–29; Dalman, *SSW*, p. 180; Klein, *Beiträge*, p. 91. There has been a great deal of controversy as to whether or not Beth Yerah (modern Khirbet el-Kerak) was to be identified with Tarichaeae. Scholars now believe that Tarichaeae was located at Mejdel and that Philoteria was located at Beth Yerah. For a good history of the discussion, see Albright, *AASOR*, ii–iii, 29–46; Sukenik, pp. 102–3. Cf. also Albright, 'Some Archaeological and Topographical Results of a Trip through Palestine', *BASOR*, no. 11 (1923), 12–14.

[6] This is the consensus of scholarly opinion, although Schlatter believes that Philoteria was a part of the Decapolis; cf. Schlatter, *PJB*, xiv, 95–6.

[7] Albright, *AASOR*, ii–iii, 35–6.

[8] In fact Philoteria had been in ruins since its capture by Alexander Jannaeus (cf. Georgius Syncellus *Chronographiae*, ed. by G. Dindorf in the

It is rather difficult to be more definite than this in Herod Antipas' time. Thus the southern boundary runs from south of Nain to somewhere south of Sennabris. There is only one other place to be considered, and that is Agrippina, which is identified with *Kaukab el-Hawa*.[1] Although Josephus never mentions this as one of his fortresses, Avi-Yonah believes it should be considered one of them, otherwise 'the front between Mount Tabor and the Jordan would be dangerously open'.[2] If this is true, it is possible that the border ran east from Nain to Agrippina and north and east from Agrippina to somewhere south of Sennabris. It is very possible that the road connecting Scythopolis and Damascus[3] was in existence at the time of Herod Antipas. If this were the case then it is probable that the border between Scythopolis and Galilee was north of the place where the road crossed the Jordan, or at *Jis el Majāmi*,[4] for it would seem to have been the most sensible course for the main road to remain within the borders of the Decapolis. Thus the border would have gone north as far as *Jis el Majāmi* and then run east into the Jordan above that point.[5]

Thus, the southern boundary would have run eastwards somewhere south of Gaba and around the middle of the Plain of Esdraelon (or at most the whole of the plain) and then south of Xaloth, Nain, and Agrippina and then it would have proceeded north near the Scythopolis–Damascus road and finally run east to the Jordan somewhere south of Sennabris.

Corpus Scriptorum Historiae Byzantinae, ed. by B. G. Niebuhr, i [Bonn, 1829], 558–9) and apparently for some reason Pompey did not restore it, for its name is missing from all four lists in Josephus (*Ant.* xiv. 74–6, 88; *BJ* i. 155–6, 166).

[1] R.H. ii. 4; cf. Dalman, *PJB*, xviii/xix, 43–4.

[2] M. Avi-Yonah, 'The Missing Fortress of Flavius Josephus', *IEJ*, iii (1953), 95.

[3] P. Thomsen, 'Die römischen Meilensteine der Provinzen Syria, Arabia und Palaestina', *ZDPV*, xl (1917), 33–4, 70–1, see map after p. 264; Avi-Yonah, *Map*, p. 44; M. Avi-Yonah, 'The Development of the Roman Road System in Palestine', *IEJ*, i (1950–1), 56–7.

[4] Saarisalo, pp. 24, 70 n. 2.

[5] There is the bridge at *Khirbet Buk'ah* which lies about three-quarters of a mile north of the Yarmuk River (cf. Saarisalo, p. 71). If this were in the territory of Scythopolis as Avi-Yonah includes it (cf. *Map*, p. 31, see also his map), then the border would have run somewhere between that bridge and Sennabris (the distance between them is five miles).

The eastern boundary

The southern portion of the eastern boundary is that short distance of the Jordan River between the southern boundary and the Sea of Galilee's outlet to the Jordan River. From there the eastern border ran northward along the Sea of Galilee.[1] Gadara and Hippos were those territories east of the Jordan and Sea of Galilee which bordered Galilee and Scythopolis.[2] Capernaum was considered a city of Galilee.[3] In the north Gaulanitis was the territory east of the Jordan which bordered Galilee from the Sea of Galilee to Lake Hula.[4] Gaulanitis belonged to Philip, the tetrarch.[5] Thella is a north-eastern boundary point of Galilee[6] which is identified with *et-Tell* on the southwestern corner of Lake Hula around three-quarters of a mile from the mouth of the Jordan.[7]

Josephus mentions that the kingdom of Agrippa II bordered Galilee.[8] Later Agrippa took over the lands Batanaea, Trachonitis, and Gaulanitis from Philip and the territory of Lysanias.[9] Caesarea Philippi remained the capital of the domain, for it was enlarged in honour of Nero.[10] Caesarea Philippi was in the territory of Paneas and this is associated by Josephus with Ulatha[11] which is the plain north of Lake Hula.[12]

[1] Jos. *BJ* iii. 37.

[2] *Ibid.*; *Vita* 42. At the time when Herod the Great's will was being deciphered, Augustus separated Gadara and Hippos from Herod's domain and they came under Syria (cf. *Ant.* xvii. 320; *BJ* ii. 97).

[3] Jos. *Vita* 403.   [4] Jos. *BJ* iii. 37.

[5] Jos. *BJ* ii. 168; *Ant.* xvii. 189; xviii. 106.

[6] Jos. *BJ* iii. 40.

[7] Dalman, *SSW*, p. 197. Oehler, p. 51; S. Klein, *Neue Beiträge zur Geschichte und Geographie Galiläas*, pp. 50–1.

[8] *BJ* iii. 37.

[9] Jos. *BJ* ii. 247.

[10] Jos. *Ant.* xx. 211. For details on sources of this city, see Thomsen, *Loca Sancta*, p. 75.

[11] Jos. *Ant.* xv. 360; A. H. M. Jones, 'The Urbanization of the Ituraean Principality', *JRS*, xxi (1931), 267. Notice that Ulatha in *Ant.* xv. 360 is not to be confused with the city having the same name mentioned in *Ant.* xvii. 24–5, cf. C. H. Kraeling, 'The Jewish Community at Antioch', *JBL*, li (1932), 133–5 (esp. p. 135 n. 32), 143–5.

[12] Avi-Yonah, *Map*, p. 8; Oehler, pp. 68–9. Smith (*HGHL*, pp. 480 n. 5, 542 n. 4) identifies Ulatha as Lake Hula. This territory north of Lake Hula may well have been the territory of the house of Zenodorus which Augustus

This would mean that the border of Galilee would have run from Thella up along the southwestern side of Lake Hula up to the most western tip of that lake.

The eastern boundary of Galilee was thus the Jordan River and the two bodies of water, namely, the Sea of Galilee and Lake Hula. It started somewhere south of Sennabris and terminated at the most western tip of Lake Hula.

The northern boundary

If Ulatha is the plain north of Hula and if it is on both sides of the Jordan, then it would border the eastern portion of Galilee's northern boundary.[1] In all probability Ulatha's land area west of the Jordan would extend only a very short distance and this may be the reason Josephus did not mention it. Josephus mentions only Tyre as that which borders Galilee on the north.[2] Kedesh (or Cadasa) is in Tyre[3] and so the border would be south of this town. In Galilee the fortress town of Gischala was the most northerly location given by Josephus.[4] Between Kedesh and Gischala runs *Wādi 'Ōba*, which may have served, in whole or in part, as the boundary between Galilee and Tyre.[5]

gave to Philip after Herod's death (cf. Jos. *Ant.* xvii. 319; Dio liv. 9. 3) or Zeno's domain (Jos. *BJ* ii. 95); see also Smith, *HGHL*, p. 546 n. 1, as well as pp. 474 n. 4, 542 n. 6, 647; Jones, *JRS*, xxi, 266.

[1] Cf. the map included with Avi-Yonah, *Map*; see also Kraeling, *Rand McNally*, map. xvi; Y. Aharoni and M. Avi-Yonah, *The Macmillan Bible Atlas* (New York, 1968), p. 140.

[2] Jos. *BJ* iii. 38.

[3] Κάδασα – Jos. *BJ* ii. 459; Κύδασα – *BJ* iv. 104; Κέδασα – *Ant.* xiii. 154, 162. In the last reference Kedesh is considered between Galilee and Tyre, which may indicate that the border ran very near Kedesh. For references to Kedesh in different periods of Israel's history, see Thomsen, *Loca Sancta*, p. 74. For more information on Kedesh, see G. Dalman, 'Jahresbericht des deutschen evangelischen Instituts für Altertumswissenschaft des heiligen Landes für das Arbeitsjahr 1913/14', *PJB*, x (1914), 46–7; W. F. Albright, 'A Tour on Foot through Samaria and Galilee', *BASOR*, no. 4 (1921), 11.

[4] *BJ* ii. 575; iv. 84–96; cf. also *BJ* ii. 585, 621–32; iv. 1, 123–30, 208; *Vita* 43–5, 70–7, 101–2, 122, 189, 235, 271, 308, 317. For description of Gischala's involvement in the war of 66–70, see Oehler, pp. 25–6.

[5] Dalman, *SSW*, p. 199; Alt, *PJB*, xxxiii (1937), 85 n. 1 (or *KS*, ii, 392 n. 3). Alt states that Avi-Yonah has insufficient evidence for placing the border above *Wādi 'Ōba* (cf. Avi-Yonah, *QDAP*, v, 175 and see attached map). Avi-Yonah included the village Aithalu which is mentioned in the Talmud corresponding to 'Aitarūn (three miles west of Kedesh) as a part of

It is probable that the northern boundary went from the westernmost point of Lake Hula directly west to the two northern tips or bends of *Wādi 'Ōba.*

Josephus mentions Baca as the most northerly or north-westerly village of Galilee.[1] Where this was located is anyone's guess.[2] Buhl believes it was the ruin *Tabaka*[3] just north-north-west of *Kura* or about eight or ten miles northwest of Gischala. Klein suggests confidently that it should be identified with *Ter Bīchā*[4] which is about eleven or twelve miles west-northwest from Gischala. Both of these seem to be too far north and west for Galilee and Dalman feels that Klein's suggestion is geographically improbable and linguistically impossible.[5] Dalman suggests that *el Jermak* may be the correct location for Baca for the natives stated that the ancient name of Jermak was *el-Baka* and nearby is the cave of Peka or Beka where R. Shim'on ben Jochai hid himself.[6] This is only two miles southwest of Gischala and is just east of the end of *Wādi 'Ōba.* This may well be the case, for it would be the most northwestern point of Galilee.[7]

If this be the case, then the northern boundary of Galilee would have been from the most western tip of Lake Hula to the northern tips of *Wādi 'Ōba* which was between Kedesh and Gischala and ended somewhere in the vicinity of *el Jermak.*

Galilee. Alt (cf. *Where Jesus Worked*, trans. K. Grayston [London, 1961], p. 29 n. 83) along with Klein (*Beiträge*, pp. 46–8) believe that Aithalu belonged to Tyre. Avi-Yonah did change in his second edition to the position of having Aithalu as a part of Tyre and he brought the northern border of Galilee down to *Wādi 'Ōba's* northern bends, cf. the changes in Avi-Yonah, *Map*, p. 38 and see the change of border in the attached map.

[1] *BJ* iii. 39. [2] Oehler, p. 69, see also p. 51.

[3] F. Buhl, *Geographie des Alten Palästina* (Freiburg and Leipzig, 1896), p. 231.

[4] Klein, *Neue Beiträge*, p. 38. Earlier Klein identified בקע near Tiberias, cf. S. Klein, 'Hebräische Ortsnamen bei Josephus', *MGWJ*, LIX (1915), 159–60.

[5] *SSW*, p. 197 n. 1.

[6] *Ibid.* p. 197; cf. also I. Ben-Zevil, 'Discoveries at Pekiin', *PEFQS*, LXII (1930), 210–14.

[7] It seems that most geographers (cf. Kraeling, *Rand McNally*, map xvi; Avi-Yonah, *Map*, p. 39 and see attached map) want to include *Kefr Bir'im* (it is about three miles northwest of Gischala) which has the remains of a synagogue of around second or third century, cf. H. Kohl and C. Watzinger, *Antike Synagogen in Galilaea* (Leipzig, 1916), pp. 89–100, 154–6, 172–3.

The western boundary

According to Josephus, Meroth (Μηρώθ) is the most westerly town in Galilee, at least in northern Galilee.[1] This was a fortified village in the war of 66–70.[2] Since Meroth (modern Meiron) was on the eastern slope of Jebel Jermak, Dalman believes one can include *Beit Jenn*, which is on the western side, within Galilee.[3] The only other reference to the breadth of Galilee is Lower Galilee which extends from Tiberias to Chabulon (Χαβουλών)[4] which is today *Kabul*.[5]

Bersabe (Khirbet Abu esh Sheba) is considered by Josephus as the most northern point of Lower Galilee[6] and was a fortified town,[7] about four miles south-southwest of Meroth. Selame (Sellamiya) – five miles southwest of Bersabe, Sogane (Sukhnin) – five miles west-southwest of Selame and five miles east of Chabulon, and Sepphoris – six miles south of Jotapata, were all fortress cities under Josephus' jurisdiction.[8] Avi-Yonah tries to identify a fortress ('Caphareccho') mentioned by Josephus, the location of which has been disputed amongst scholars, at *Khirbet et-Tayyibe* just southwest of *Shefar'am*.[9] If this is true then the border was west of this location and then ran south to the west of Gaba, the most western village on the southern border considered in this study.

Therefore the western boundary would have started around *el Jermak* and run west of Meroth, Chabulon, and Jotapata, somewhere in the vicinity of *Shefar'am* and then continued to the west of Gaba where it joined the southern boundary. This, then, completes Herod Antipas' territory of Galilee.

[1] *BJ* iii. 40. One should consider this as the most westerly village only in the north for Josephus is showing the breadth of Galilee with Thella as the most easterly location.

[2] Jos. *BJ* ii. 573; *Vita* 188.

[3] *SSW*, p. 196.

[4] Jos. *BJ* iii. 38; *Vita* 234; Josephus mentions the fact that Chabulon is in the vicinity of Ptolemais (Acre) which is actually only ten miles west-north-west from Chabulon.

[5] Klein, *Beiträge*, pp. 55–6; S. Klein, 'Kabul', *EJ*, ix (1932), 733–4.

[6] *BJ* iii. 39.

[7] *Vita* 188; *BJ* ii. 573.

[8] *Ibid.*

[9] Avi-Yonah, *IEJ*, iii, 94–8.

THE BOUNDARIES OF PERAEA

In tracing the borders of Peraea, the order will be the same as that for Galilee, namely, the southern, and then the eastern and northern boundaries. The Jordan River and the Dead Sea serve as its western boundary.

The southern boundary

The Herodian fortress, Machaerus, marks the most southern point.[1] Glueck's explorations of the Transjordan have confirmed the southern boundary as having run 'eastward from the Dead Sea on a line with Machaerus to the top of the western edge of the Moabite plateau'.[2] At the time Antipas' wife, daughter of Aretas IV, was about to be divorced, she asked to be sent to Machaerus, which Josephus describes correctly as being on the border between the lands of Aretas IV and Antipas, but incorrectly places the fortress in the territory of Aretas.[3] Moab bordered Peraea on the south and the *Wâdī el-Môjib* (River Arnon) branching off north with the *Wâdī el Wâlā* (River Wala), which in its lower stretch is called *Seil Heidân*, could have served as a boundary between Peraea and Moab.[4] If these two rivers were the boundaries, Machaerus remains close to the boundary and Antipas' wife would not have had a great distance to travel.

The eastern boundary

The eastern boundary was bordered by Philadelphia, Gerasa, Arabia, and Hesbonitis.[5] Hesbonitis ('Εσεβωνῖτις), which is the district of Heshbon,[6] was a part of Jewish territory in Jannaeus' time[7] and in Herod the Great's time,[8] but may have fallen into the hands of the Arabians after the death of Herod.[9]

---

[1] This is certainly implied in Jos. *BJ* iv. 439.

[2] N. Glueck, 'Explorations in Eastern Palestine, III', *AASOR*, XVIII–XIX (1937–9), 140·

[3] *Ant.* xviii. 111–12; cf. Glueck, *AASOR*, XVIII–XIX, 140.

[4] At least this is what seems to have been established by Wright and Filson (pl. xiv) and L. H. Grollenberg, *Atlas of the Bible*, trans. and ed. by J. M. H. Reid and H. H. Rowley (London, 1956), map 34, p. 116; Aharoni and Avi-Yonah, *Bible Atlas*, pp. 140, 145.

[5] Jos. *BJ* iii. 46–8.   [6] Schürer, II, 201 n. 441.

[7] Jos. *Ant.* xiii. 397.   [8] Jos. *Ant.* xv. 294.

[9] Aretas helped Varus, and it could be that Varus gave him some territory when he dismissed him (cf. Jos. *Ant.* xvii. 287–96; *BJ* ii. 68–76).

At the beginning of the war of 66–70 Hesbonitis was not a part of Jewish territory.[1] Thus Hesbonitis was either partitioned or, more likely, it was a state which was outside the borders of Peraea in Antipas' time.

Both Philadelphia and Gerasa were cities of the Decapolis. Glueck believes that Josephus' description of the breadth of Peraea as being 'from Philadelphia to the Jordan' should probably be changed to 'from the Jordan to about half way to Philadelphia'.[2] But is this necessary? In mentioning Philadelphia he may have been making reference to the whole city-state of Philadelphia and to the fact that the breadth of Peraea ran from the border of the city-state of Philadelphia to the Jordan River. A boundary along this line seems to be indicated in the case of the border dispute between the inhabitants of Philadelphia and Zia, a village fifteen Roman miles west of Philadelphia.[3] The border-line, then, is not the city's but along the border of the territory connected with the city. Possibly the border of the city-state of Philadelphia would be approximately half way between the city of Philadelphia and the Jordan. The same thing would apply to the city-state of Gerasa.

The term *Arabia* is too general to justify a specific border distinction. It is difficult, therefore, to establish the eastern boundary with real exactness. Glueck states that the eastern border, at least in the former Moabite territory, could be fixed by a north–south line somewhat west of Mâdebā,[4] a town which is about twelve miles east-southeast of the north end of the Dead Sea. This may well have been the same in Antipas' day.

The northern boundary

According to Josephus the northern frontier of Peraea was Pella.[5] According to Eusebius it was located six miles from

---

[1] Jos. *BJ* ii. 458.

[2] Glueck, *AASOR*, xviii–xix, 140.

[3] Jos. *Ant.* xx. 2. The village Zia is a reading for μία (i.e. 'one'). The name of the village, according to Niese, had dropped out. Several scholars, beginning with Reland and followed by Havercamp, Tuch, and Schürer (ii, 146 n. 348), have accepted Zia as the correct reading. Eusebius mentions a village Zia as being fifteen miles west of Philadelphia (Eus. *Onomast.* pp. 94: 3–4; 95: 3–4).

[4] Glueck, *AASOR*, xviii–xix, 140.   [5] *BJ* iii. 46.

Jabesh on the road which led to Gerasa.[1] Since Gerasa lay south of *Wadi Jabis*, Pella must have been north of it. Pella is identified with the entire site of *Khirbet Fahil*[2] and is five miles southeast of Scythopolis.[3] Pliny[4] and Ptolemy[5] as well as Epiphanius[6] attest that Pella was a part of the Decapolis. Because of this fact most scholars assume that Pella was not a part of Peraea.[7] Actually there is no evidence to support this idea, for being a part of the Decapolis does not necessarily imply that it was not somehow and at times under someone else's rule. Certainly this was the case for the Decapolis cities of Dion, Raphana, and Canatha, which were in Philip's territory,[8] and Damascus, which was in Aretas IV's territory,[9] as well as the cities of Gadara and Hippos, which were at one time a part of Herod the Great's domain[10] and after his death were not given to Archelaus but were placed under Syria's rule.[11] Thus there is no reason not to take Josephus' statement at face value and include Pella within Peraea.

But there is one final fact that should be considered before one can conclude that Pella should be included within Peraea. Very early in the war of 66–70 (*ca.* Sept. 66) the Syrians massacred the Jews in Caesarea, and in revenge the Jews sacked the Syrian villages and the neighbouring cities, Philadelphia, Heshbon and its district, Gerasa, Gadara, Hippos, and Gaulanitis.[12] The interesting fact is that the progression of the attacks was from the south to the north and all of the cities were those outside Peraea and within the Decapolis. Since

---

[1] Eus. *Onomast.* pp. 32: 5–7; 33: 5–7.

[2] G. Schumacher, *Pella* (London, 1888); S. Merrill, *East of the Jordan* (London, 1881), pp. 442–7; J. Richmond, 'Khirbet Fahil', *PEFQS*, LXVI (1934), 18–31; N. Glueck, 'Explorations in Eastern Palestine, IV', *AASOR*, XXV–XXVIII (1945–9), 254–7; R. W. Funk and H. N. Richardson, 'The 1958 Sounding at Pella', *BA*, XXI (1958), 82–96.

[3] From Ptolemy *Geographia* v. 15. 23, Ritter calculates that Pella was five miles southeast of Scythopolis, cf. C. Ritter, *Die Erdkunde*, xv (Berlin, 1851), 1025.

[4] *NH* v. 16. 74.   [5] Ptolemy *Geographia* v. 15. 23.

[6] Epiphanius *Adversus Octoginta Haereses* xxix. 7 (*MPG*, XLI, 402).

[7] Schürer, II, 175–6.

[8] They were in Philip's territory of Batanaea and Auranitis (or Trachonitis), cf. Jos. *Ant.* xvii. 319; *BJ* ii. 95.

[9] 2 Cor. 11: 32.   [10] Jos. *Ant.* xv. 217; *BJ* i. 396.

[11] Jos. *Ant.* xvii. 320; *BJ* ii. 97.   [12] Jos. *BJ* ii. 457–9.

Pella was one of these attacked towns, it is quite reasonable to argue that it was not a part of Peraea. Another fact to be observed from this list of cities is that they were all near the border of Jewish territories whether under the Roman procurator, Gessius Florus, or under Herod Agrippa II,[1] which may indicate a sort of terrorist attack and then a quick retreat to their own land. If this were the case then Pella could have been very close to the northern border of Peraea. In all probability there would have been no geographical change between Antipas' time and the time of the war of 66–70. At least Josephus makes no mention of any such change whereas he does enumerate changes in the cases of both Agrippa I's and II's reigns. Finally, the description that Pella extended ἀπὸ Μαχαιροῦντος εἰς Πέλλαν[2] may indicate the inclusion of Machaerus and the extension of the land 'unto' (or 'up to') Pella, and thus would exclude Pella. The northern boundary of Peraea, then, probably ran just south of Pella or at *Wadi Jabis*.[3]

Before one can finish discussion of Peraea's northern border, there is one other item to be considered, namely, that Gadara is, according to Josephus, Peraea's capital.[4] Gadara is the modern *Umm Keis* or *Mukes* southeast of the Sea of Galilee, and was principal city of the Decapolis. Dalman[5] and especially Haefeli[6] have ably argued that Josephus does not make reference to the Decapolis city Gadara but to Gador (or Gadara), which is the present-day *es Salt*, located about 18 miles north-northwest of the northern tip of the Dead Sea and about eleven miles east of the Jordan.[7] Therefore, the northern boundary would be located just south of Pella.

---

[1] In the same context Josephus lists the other cities which are not relevant to the Decapolis but confirms the fact that border towns were attacked, e.g. Kedesh, Ptolemais, Gaba (a pro-Roman town in Galilee), and Caesarea (*BJ* ii. 459).

[2] Jos. *BJ* iii. 46.

[3] So Wright and Filson, pl. xiv; Grollenberg, map 34, p. 116; Aharoni and Avi-Yonah, *Bible Atlas*, p. 140.

[4] *BJ* iv. 413.

[5] G. Dalman, 'Jahresbericht des deutschen evangelischen Instituts für Altertumswissenschaft des heiligen Landes', *PJB*, vi (1910), 21–2; Dalman, *SSW*, p. 238.

[6] Haefeli, pp. 107–10.

[7] In a footnote to *BJ* iv. 413 Thackeray gives strong objections to identifying the reference to Gadara with *Umm Keis* or *Mukes* by writing, '(1)

Peraea, then, comprises the territory bounded on the south by the rivers Arnon and Wala, on the east by the north–south line just west of Mâdebā (a town twelve miles east southeast of the north end of the Dead Sea), and west of Hesbonitis and the city-states of Philadelphia and Gerasa; and bounded on the north by the Jabesh River just south of Pella.

Mukes was in Decapolis whereas the Gadara here mentioned is called the capital or metropolis of Peraea, of which district Pella, some 15 miles S. of *Mukes*, was the northern boundary (*B.* iii. 46 f.); (2) Gadora (Gadara?) *es Salt*, is actually in Peraea and satisfies the other data, for (3) it is not far from the village to which the Gadarene fugitives fled (§ 420 note – which states that Bethennabris is "doubtless Beth-Nimrah, *Tell Nimrin*, some 12 miles S.W. of the Peraean Gadara, and on the direct line for Jericho, which lay nearly opposite it on the other side of the Jordan"); (4) that village was on the direct line to Jericho, for which they were making (§ 431), an unnatural refuge for fugitives from the northern Gadara; (5) Vespasian was marching southwards from Caesarea upon Jerusalem (§ 412), not north-wards towards Galilee, which was already subdued', H. St J. Thackeray, *Josephus, LCL*, III (London, 1928), 120–1. See also A. Schlatter, 'Gadara nicht Geser', *ZDPV*, XVIII (1895), 75–6; I. Benzinger, 'Gadara', PW, VII, 1 (1910), 438.

THE POPULATION

There have been many attempts to estimate the number of people living in Galilee and/or Palestine at the time of Jesus. On this score a final conclusion is impossible for the data are just not available. Indeed, Rostovtzeff not only refuses to state any definite figure, but avows that there cannot be even an approximation of the density of the population of the Hellenistic world.[1]

GALILEE

According to Josephus the population of Galilee was in his time around 3,000,000.[2] In determining above[3] the approximate borders of Galilee, it was estimated that at the time of Antipas the land area of Galilee was about 750 square miles. Assuming this figure to be correct, there were about 4,000 persons to the square mile. This however is incredibly high, for the population of Israel today is only 2,737,900 for 7,993 square miles,[4] or a little over 355 persons to the square mile. West Jordan alone has 805,450 persons for 5,650 square kilometres (2,151 sq. m.),[5] or about 374 persons to the square mile. On average there are 349 persons to the square mile for Israel and West Jordan.

Although Merrill believes Josephus' statement to be acceptable, especially since he calculates the land area of Galilee as having 2,000 square miles,[6] most scholars believe that Josephus' figure is a gross exaggeration. Certainly if today's Palestine has only 349 inhabitants to the square mile with modern methods of agriculture and industry, it is most unlikely that Josephus' figure is correct.

[1] *SEHHW*, II, 1140–3. [2] *BJ* iii. 43; *Vita* 235.
[3] Cf. Chapter 3 and Appendix II.
[4] Based on the 1968 statistics in S. H. Steinberg and J. Paxton (eds.), *The Stateman's Year-Book, 1969–1970* (London, 1969), p. 1072.
[5] *Ibid.* p. 1104. This includes the refugees but excludes nomads.
[6] S. Merrill, 'Galilee in the Time of Christ', *BS*, XXXI (1874), 34–7. Graetz also estimates Galilee's population as being 3,000,000; cf. H. Graetz, *Geschichte der Juden³*, III (Leipzig, 1878), 529.

There have been various estimates from Harnack's 500,000[1] up to Juster's 5,000,000 for the Jewish population in Palestine.[2] Masterman, who lived there for several years, demonstrates that Josephus' figure is impossible and believes that in Antipas' time there was an average of 1,000 inhabitants to each of the 200 villages (this being double that of his own day), and an average of 50,000 in the four great cities of Sepphoris, Tiberias, Tarichaeae, and Scythopolis. This makes a total of 400,000 for an area of 900 square miles, or a density of about 440 to the square mile.[3] Using Masterman's figures, but eliminating Scythopolis and its area of around 150 to 175 square miles, the average population to the square mile for Galilee alone would be slightly higher than 440. Masterman admits that probably his 'estimate errs on the side of excess'.[4]

Beloch estimates for Galilee about 400,000 inhabitants to 3,200 square kilometres (or 1,235 sq. m.), that is, about 325 persons to the square mile. This he admits is high, but Galilee, he says, was not only very productive but also the wealthiest district in Palestine.[5] Beloch's calculations, which include all of Syria and Palestine, have caused much discussion. On the basis of Theodoret's statement regarding the Orthodox Greek community of Cyrrhus (in the fifth century A.D.), Cumont believes that Beloch's estimate of Syria's population is too small.[6] On the other hand McCown believes that it is far too high. According to him, there would in Antipas' day have been at most 150 persons to the square mile.[7]

McCown bases his calculations on the population figures

---

[1] A. Harnack, *Die Mission und Ausbreitung des Christentums*[4], 1 (Leipzig, 1924), 12.

[2] J. Juster, *Les Juifs dans l'empire Romain* (Paris, 1914), 1, 210 n. 2.

[3] E. W. G. Masterman, *Studies in Galilee* (Chicago, 1909), pp. 133–4.

[4] *Ibid.* p. 134.

[5] J. Beloch, *Die Bevölkerung der griechisch-römischen Welt* (Leipzig, 1886), pp. 246–7. This figure is also accepted by F. M. Heichelheim, 'Roman Syria', *An Economic Survey of Ancient Rome*, ed. by T. Frank, IV (Baltimore, 1938), p. 158.

[6] F. Cumont, 'The Population of Syria', *JRS*, XXIV (1934), 187–90. Beloch (p. 249) estimates that there were 5–6,000,000 in Syria and Palestine, whereas Heichelheim (p. 158) using Cumont's calculation would estimate around 10,000,000 people for 80,000 square miles.

[7] C. C. McCown, 'The Density of Population in Ancient Palestine', *JBL*, LXVI (1947), 436.

between the 1920s and the 1940s, which show that the average population density in Palestine in 1940, excluding the Beersheba subdistrict, was 290 persons to the square mile.[1] Because of antiquated methods of agriculture and industry in the first century, he implies that this figure is too high, and says that for western Palestine there could not have been much more than a million[2] (that of the 1931 census taken just before the decade of mass migration).[3] In fact, McCown believes that in Antipas' day there were considerably less than a million persons in western Palestine. He estimates no more than 90 to 100 persons to the square mile in Judaea and 150 to the square mile in Galilee.[4]

Actually McCown proves no more than anyone else would prove who attempts to estimate the population in Antipas' day. In determining the population of Galilee at that time one can do no more than make an estimate. It would seem that McCown has estimated too little. Although what he says is exaggerated, Josephus points out that Galilee was both very productive and densely populated.[5] Jesus and his disciples were always able to gather a crowd quickly in Galilee, and during the war of 66–70 Josephus was able to muster an army of nearly 100,000 Galilaeans quite easily.[6] Galilee, moreover, stood up well against the Romans. These considerations suggest a dense population. Josephus states in addition (though he may be exaggerating) that Galilee and Peraea were liberally covered with many kinds of trees.[7] In warfare, to cut down the trees in the enemy's territory was considered an effective retaliation.[8] Josephus mentions that during the war of 66–70, vast tracts were denuded of trees, some of which were used for defence purposes by the enemy.[9] Around Jerusalem where many trees had previously beautified the countryside, it was now like a desert.[10] Wars have

---

[1] *Ibid.* pp. 427–34.

[2] Actually the official census of 1931 has a population of 1,035,821, cf. E. Mills, *Census of Palestine 1931* (Alexandria, 1932), I, 18.

[3] Cf. F. W. Notestein and E. Jurkat, 'Population Problems of Palestine', *The Milbank Memorial Fund Quarterly*, XXIII (1945), 313–15.

[4] McCown, *JBL*, LXVI, 435–6.   [5] *BJ* iii. 42–3.

[6] Jos. *BJ* ii. 576; *Vita* 98–9; cf. also *BJ* ii. 598. Again, this may be an exaggerated figure.

[7] *BJ* iii. 42, 45.   [8] Jos. *Ant.* ix. 36; *BJ* vii. 211.

[9] *BJ* v. 107, 264, 523.   [10] Jos. *BJ* vi. 6.

taken their toll in Palestine. The wars of the Moslems and Crusaders have destroyed many a flourishing district.[1] During the Crusades there were great forests that do not exist today.[2] As a result of deforestation, much that was once arable land is now eroded and bare,[3] and this in turn has had its effect on the population.

To reckon population density it is only proper to calculate from the same general areas which were a part of Antipas' Galilee rather than modern Galilee, which is much larger. The census figures for 1931 make the density of Galilee about 187 persons to the square mile,[4] and if the same density obtained in Antipas' day, the total population would have been slightly over 140,000. According to the 1961 census the density of Galilee was about 253 persons to the square mile,[5] and if it were the same density in Antipas' time, the population of the area would have been about 190,000. Clearly there have been changes and shifts in the population. Whereas in the first century Sepphoris was the largest city in Galilee,[6] in 1961 it had only 7,225 people, as compared with Tiberias (20,792) and Nazareth (25,047).[7] When Antipas was in Palestine, Tiberias and Sepphoris were probably larger than at the present time,

[1] Smith, *HGHL*, pp. 38–9, 262–3 n. 4, 359–60.

[2] *Ibid.* pp. 120, 146.

[3] D. Baly, *The Geography of the Bible* (London, 1958), pp. 70–6. It may be a combination of soil erosion, mismanagement on the part of the declining Roman Empire and 13 centuries of Muslim misrule, cf. S. W. Baron, *A Social and Religious History of the Jews*[2], 1 (New York, 1952), 371.

[4] E. Mills, *Census of Palestine 1931. Population of Villages, Towns and Administrative Areas* (Jerusalem, 1933), p. 21. The sub-districts of Acre, Safad, Tiberias, Nazareth, and the portion of Haifa north of Carmel give a total area of 1,055 square miles and a population of 197,577. The population for the same area in 1922 was 158,184, or 150 persons to the square mile, cf. J. B. Barron (comp.), *Palestine: Report and General Abstracts of the Census of 1922* (Jerusalem, 1923), p. 32. If the density of the population were the same in Antipas' time there would have been 112,500 residents in Galilee.

[5] State of Israel, Central Bureau of Statistics, *The Division of the State of Israel into Regions for Statistical Purposes. Population and Housing, 1961*, pub. no. 20 (Jerusalem, 1967), pp. 22–3. This calculation includes the demographic regions of Eastern Upper and Lower Galilee, Western Upper and Lower Galilee, Hazor, Kinerot, Kokhav Plateau, and the Nazareth–Tiran Mountains. These give a total area of 797 square miles and a population of 201,876 persons.

[6] Jos. *BJ* iii. 34; *Vita* 232; cf. also, *BJ* ii. 511; *Vita* 346.

[7] State of Israel, Central Bureau of Statistics, pp. 22–3.

for they were seats of government. Reckoning an average of 25,000 persons for each of these two cities together with Gabara and Tarichaeae,[1] and an average of 500 persons for each of the remaining 200 villages, the population of Galilee would have been about 200,000 or about 266 persons to the square mile. It is true their agricultural methods were primitive but so too, no doubt, were their living standards. A population of 200,000 would seem to be a reasonable estimate for Antipas' time.

PERAEA

It is almost impossible to estimate the population of Peraea. Before 1961 there was no census, but it is estimated that the population of Transjordan (which exceeds 20,000 sq. m.) in the

[1] This is a reasonable estimate for these four cities. Josephus specifically states that the three largest cities in Galilee at the time of the war of 66–70 were Sepphoris, Tiberias, and Gabara (*Vita*, 123, 203). Tarichaeae is not listed as one of the largest cities, yet Cassius (53–51 B.C.) reduced 30,000 of its inhabitants to slavery (Jos. *Ant.* xiv. 120; *BJ* i. 180). During the war of 66 Josephus states that there were 40,000 Tarichaeans (*BJ* ii. 608). These figures may be exaggerated and may include also some of the people outside the city belonging to the jurisdiction of Tarichaeae. It is not, however, unreasonable to estimate that Tarichaeae had around 25,000 inhabitants. Certainly Tiberias, which is listed as the second largest (*Vita*, 346), and had a governing council of 600 men (*BJ* ii. 641), would have had at least 23–30 thousand people. Avi-Yonah, after comparing other Hellenistic capitals, estimates that Tiberias must have numbered between 30 and 40 thousand people, cf. M. Avi-Yonah, 'The Foundation of Tiberias', *IEJ*, 1 (1950–1), 164–5. Sepphoris was the largest (Jos. *BJ* iii. 34; *Vita* 232) and the strongest (*BJ* ii. 511) city in Galilee. It seems improbable that Vespasian would have sent 1,000 cavalry and 6,000 infantry to Sepphoris if it had been less than 30–40 thousand. Again, an exaggeration on Josephus' part must be reckoned with, as well as the fact that in war there was always a gathering to the cities for protection. Taking into account these factors, an estimate of 25,000 inhabitants for each of these four cities is not unreasonable. According to Jeremias, Jerusalem had only 25–30 thousand inhabitants in the first century (J. Jeremias, 'Die Einwohnerzahl Jerusalems zur Zeit Jesus', *ZDPV*, LXVI [1943], 24–31; *Jerusalem in the Time of Jesus*, trans. from the 3rd German ed. [with the author's rev. to 1967] by F. H. and C. H. Cave [London, 1969], p. 84). This would give Jerusalem the same population as the four cities of Galilee mentioned above. Jeremias' estimate 'is based upon an assumed lower density of the population per square kilometer than is justified in oriental cities then and now, and upon the equally unwarranted assumption that but relatively few Jews resided outside the city walls', Baron, 1, 370 n. 5. Therefore the estimate of 25,000 for each of the four largest Galilaean cities is justifiable.

1930s was between 300,000 and 350,000.[1] This means an average of 15 to 18 people to the square mile. Much of this is desert, of course, and the area is much larger than the Peraea of Antipas.

From the discussion above[2] concerning Peraea's borders, it is estimated that the area was about 850 square miles.[3] Today, the Jordanian districts of Amman and Balqa occupy the same area as ancient Peraea though these districts overlap. They have a total population of 496,576 over an area of 1,393 square miles (excluding the desert area of Amman),[4] or about 356 persons to the square mile. Hence, these two areas are more densely populated than present-day Galilee. But this is explained by the fact that the two largest cities of the entire kingdom of Jordan are situated in Amman. These are Amman itself, population 246,475, and Zarqa, population 96,080:[5] total 342,555, or 111 persons to the square mile over the two districts. If the one other major town of Balqa is deducted, namely Salt (population of 16,176),[6] then the rural population of the two districts would be 137,845, or 99 persons to the square mile. If this rural density is taken and multiplied by the area in Antipas' day, the population of the rural area of Peraea would be 84,150.

Josephus specifically states that Peraea, though larger than Galilee, was mostly desert, having only a few places of good productivity.[7] It is also described as being covered with rugged mountains.[8] The implication is that the population of Peraea was less than Galilee. Thus, a population of around 80 to 85 thousand for the rural area would seem reasonable. There were really no major cities, comparatively speaking, in Antipas' day. Gadara[9] and Amathus[10] were probably very small. It is possible

[1] H. Luke and E. Keith-Roach, *The Handbook of Palestine and Trans-Jordan*[3] (London, 1934), p. 435.

[2] Chapter 3 and Appendix II.

[3] That Peraea was larger than Galilee is confirmed by Josephus' statement to that effect, *BJ* iii. 44.

[4] This is based on the figures of the Hashemite Kingdom of Jordan, Department of Statistics, *First Census of Population and Housing, 18th November, 1961* (Amman, 1964), Table 1.12, p. 30. A 1963 estimate which one must use with caution is 549,832 or about 395 persons to the square mile.

[5] *Ibid.* Table 1.7, p. 13 (cf. also Table 1.2, p. 4).   [6] *Ibid.*

[7] *BJ* iii. 44–5.   [8] Pliny *NH* v. 15. 70.   [9] Jos. *BJ* iv. 413–19.

[10] Jos. *Ant.* xiii. 356, 374; xiv. 91; *BJ* i. 86, 89, 170.

that Julias[1] was a little larger, and Machaerus[2] the largest of all. It is reasonable to suppose that these four towns/cities would not have exceeded 45 to 50 thousand inhabitants all told.[3] This would give a total of 125 to 135 thousand, which would be about 147 to 159 persons to the square mile. This does not seem to be an unreasonable figure.

[1] Jos. *Ant.* xvii. 277; xviii. 27; *BJ* ii. 59, 168, 252; iv. 438.

[2] Jos. *Ant.* xiii. 417; xiv. 83, 89, 94, 96; xviii. 111–12, 119; *BJ* i. 161, 167, 171–2; ii. 485–6; iii. 46; iv. 439, 555; vii. 164–210.

[3] From Jos. *BJ* ii. 485–6, vii. 190-5 one gets the impression, since the Romans feared the Jews at Machaerus, that the city was very large. But if there were a great number of Jews there, it may be that they fled there from other districts as the last stronghold of the war of 66–70. Besides, the Romans' fear may not have been due only to the number of inhabitants but also to the fortress' position which made it difficult to defeat.

THE PROBLEM OF TRIBUTE

Herod's financial obligation to Rome presents a puzzling problem. On returning to the East (late 39 B.C.), Antony set up client kings, each of whom had to pay a prescribed tribute, and Herod was responsible for ᾿Ιδουμαίων...καὶ Σαμαρέων...[1] Momigliano interprets this to mean that in 39 B.C. Samaria was restored to Judaea and an extra part of Idumaea was also added, and since Judaea was already paying tribute it is only natural that the new acquisition would be under the same obligations.[2] Jones states that this is a 'fantastic' explanation and thinks that it is simpler to accept either of the alternatives which Momigliano does not favour,[3] namely, that either Appian has confused ᾿Ιδουμαίων with ᾿Ιουδαίων or that καὶ ᾿Ιουδαίων has slipped out of the text by haplography with ᾿Ιδουμαίων. The latter seems more probable, and would simply mean that Herod, as king of Judaea, Idumaea, and Samaria, paid tribute. Besides 'Idumaea and Samaria had been a part of Judaea for many years and Appian's statement cannot mean that they were new acquisitions specifically made tributary'.[4] Also, Momigliano confuses the district of Samaria, which had been a part of the Jewish territory for many years, with the city of Samaria which was independent of the Jewish territory from the time of Pompey–Gabinius to 30 B.C.[5]

Taking Appian literally, as Otto does,[6] would mean that in

[1] Appian BC v. 75.

[2] A. Momigliano, 'Ricerche sull'Organizzazione della Giudea sotto il Dominio Romano (63 a.C – 70 d.C)', Annali della R. Scuola Normale Superiore di Pisa – Lettere, Storia e Filosofia, series II, vol. III (1934), 348–50; CAH, x, 320 n. 2.

[3] A. H. M. Jones, 'Review and Discussion of "Ricerche sull'Organizzazione della Giudea sotto il Dominio Romano (63 a.C. – 70 d.C.)", by A. Momigliano', JRS, xxv (1935), 229.

[4] E. M. Smallwood, 'The Relations between the Jews and the Roman Government from 66 B.C. to the Foundation of the Christian Empire' (unpublished Ph.D. dissertation, University of Cambridge, 1950), p. 114.

[5] Jones, JRS, xxv, 229–30.

[6] Col. 58; cf. also Mommsen, Provinces, II, 175 n. 1.

39 B.C. Idumaea and Samaria were tributary, while Judaea was not. This deduction clearly is based on the *argumentum ex silentio*. 'There is no evidence for the exemption of Judaea in 39, and for the years after 30 the evidence strongly suggests that Judaea *was* tributary.'[1] The census taken at Augustus' orders at the time of Jesus' birth was probably for financial purposes and this would substantiate the idea that the Herods paid tribute.[2]

Since the sources are silent about Herod's financial obligations after 30 B.C., there have been some scholars who think Herod paid no tribute after that date.[3] Instead it is thought that Herod may have given voluntary contributions to Rome as he did give 800 talents to Augustus in 30 B.C.[4] This, of course, does not prove that Herod had not paid regular tribute to the Roman government. In the republican era it was a practice not to impose tribute on client kings, but Pompey had made Palestine tributary and Julius Caesar, although altering some aspects of the tribute, did not abolish it.[5] If there was an abolition of tribute for Palestine, it seems incredible that Josephus would not have mentioned that fact. There is no evidence for Augustus altering the existing system and the *argumentum ex silentio* in this case is an argument in favour of the continued system of tribute.

[1] Smallwood, p. 114.

[2] *Ibid.* p. 115. Although Lk. 2: 1-5 has been questioned, Luke's accuracy has recently been vindicated by M.-J. Lagrange, 'Où en est la question du recensement de Quirinius?', *RB*, VIII (1911), 60-84; W. M. Ramsay, *The Bearing of Recent Discovery on the Trustworthiness of the New Testament*[4] (London, 1920), pp. 238-300; J. W. Jack, 'The Census of Quirinius', *ET*, XL (1929), 496-8; L. R. Taylor, 'Quirinius and the Census of Judaea', *AJP*, LIV (1933), 120-33; R. Syme, 'Galatia and Pamphylia under Augustus: the Governorships of Piso, Quirinius and Silvanus', *Klio*, XXVII (1934), 131-8; T. Corbishley, 'Quirinius and the Census: A Restudy of the Evidence', *Klio*, XXIX (1936), 81-93; A. G. Roos, 'Die Quirinius-Inschrift', *Mnemosyne*, 3rd series, IX (1941), 306-18; Smallwood, Appendix A, pp. 1004-26; A. N. Sherwin-White, *Roman Society*, pp. 162-71; L. Dupraz, *De l'association de Tibère au principat à la naissance du Christ*, vol. (N.S.) XLIII of *Studia Friburgensia* (Fribourg, 1966), pp. 143-220; G. M. Lee, 'The Census in Luke', *CQR*, CLXVII (1966), 431-6; A. J. B. Higgins, 'Sidelights on Christian Beginnings in the Graeco-Roman World', *The Evangelical Quarterly*, XLI (1969), 198-201.

[3] Otto, cols. 29, 58; Schürer, I, 528-9; Heichelheim, p. 233. Mommsen, *Provinces*, II, 175 n. 175; Abel, *Histoire*, I, 361; Perowne, *Herod the Great*, p. 177.

[4] Jos. *Ant.* xv. 200.   [5] Smallwood, p. 115.

The practice of paying tribute as a client king existed even during Antony's rule, for Herod had to pay tribute on the districts assigned to Cleopatra.[1] The census taken by P. Sulpicius Quirinius in Judaea after Archelaus' deposition in A.D. 6 caused an insurrection by Judas of Galilee saying that they should consider only God and not the Romans as their master.[2] This may seem to imply that they previously were not under Roman tribute but now were coming under it. But this is not necessarily so. This census was not the regular periodic one (occurring every fourteen years, i.e. in 9 B.C., A.D. 6, 20, 34, 48, etc.), but a special one to assess more accurately the financial capabilities of the new province for the purposes of the Roman administration. With this it is probable that the taxes were increased. Probably it was conducted by Roman rather than Jewish officials and this marked the end of Jewish independence and the beginning of the domination of the great Roman Empire. All of these factors would have been adequate to provoke the disturbances mentioned by Josephus.

It seems, then, most probable that the Herods had to pay tribute but that they were to be free from financial support of the auxiliary troops and from the burdens of soldiers extracting money from them.[3]

[1] Jos. *Ant.* xv. 96, 106–7, 132–3.
[2] Jos. *Ant.* xviii. 1–10; *BJ* ii. 118, 433; vii. 253; Acts 5: 37.
[3] Jos. *Ant.* xiv. 204.

ARCHELAUS' LENGTH OF RULE

Josephus contradicts himself. In *Antiquitates Judaicae* xvii. 342 he states that Archelaus was deposed in his tenth year and in *Bellum Judaicum* ii. 111 that he was deposed in his ninth year. The fixed point of this chronology is Archelaus' banishment in the consulship of Aemilius Lepidus and Lucius Arruntius, or in A.D. 6.[1] One solution to the problem is that Josephus was mistaken in *Bellum Judaicum* and that he corrected himself in his later work *Antiquitates Judaicae*.[2] This may be true but it does not explain why in *Bellum Judaicum* Josephus places the event in the ninth year. Another approach to the problem is to enquire whether Josephus may have started from a different point in reckoning Archelaus' rule, such as would account for the differences in the two accounts. It is difficult to determine Josephus' method of reckoning, but it is probable that he used the same method as his sources.[3] If his source for *Bellum Judaicum* was primarily his own memory rather than outside sources,[4] it would mean that the Jews reckoned the first year of Archelaus' or Antipas' rule from the time of their appearance in the spring of 3 B.C. On the other hand if they reckoned the reign of Archelaus from his accession date in the Jewish calendar they would have reckoned his first year from the middle of November 4 B.C. to 1 Tishri 3 B.C., and his ninth year from 1 Tishri A.D. 5 to 1 Tishri A.D. 6.[5] On this reckoning,

---

[1] Dio lv. 27. 6. [2] Schürer, I, 416 n. 167.

[3] Schürer, I, 757; K. Lake, 'The Chronology of Acts', *BC*, v, 447.

[4] *BJ* i. 15. This is a debatable point, see Thackeray, *Josephus*, pp. 36–41; Shutt, *Studies in Josephus*, pp. 26–9. Thackeray thinks that Josephus used the *Commentaries* of Vespasian for the war of 66–70 and Nicolaus of Damascus for the greater portion of Book i of *BJ* (*contra*, cf. Schürer, I, 757–60). But these sources would only cover the period up to Archelaus' and Antipas' accession and from the outbreak of the war of 66–70. The deposition of Archelaus would not be included in either of them. For this event Josephus was probably relying on his memory based on an unknown Palestinian source.

[5] According to Josephus the Jews reckoned the religious year from 1 Nisan and the civil year from 1 Tishri; cf. *Ant.* i. 80–1; J. Wellhausen,

Bellum Judaicum is correct in placing Archelaus' deposition in his ninth year. It is known that Josephus used sources for his later work *Antiquitates Judaicae*, and if these sources were Roman ones based on the Julian calendar then Archelaus' first year would have been reckoned from the middle of November to 31 December 4 B.C. (or it may have been reckoned from Herod the Great's death to the end of the Julian year, i.e. March/April to 31 December 4 B.C.), and his tenth year from 1 January to 31 December A.D. 6.[1] Or alternatively, if in *Antiquitates Judaicae* Josephus reckoned from the death of Herod the Great using the Jewish calendar, it would make the first year from March/April 4 B.C. to 1 Tishri 4 B.C. and the tenth year from 1 Tishri A.D. 5 to 1 Tishri A.D. 6.

In conclusion, it seems probable that in *Bellum Judaicum* Josephus used Palestinian sources reckoned on the Jewish calendar, starting either at Archelaus' accession in November 4 B.C., or at his appearance in Palestine sometime after that date, possibly in the spring of 3 B.C. On the other hand, in *Antiquitates Judaicae*, he may have used Roman sources reckoned on the Julian calendar and starting either at Herod's death or at Archelaus' accession. Finally, if he used the Jewish calendar for both works, it is possible that in *Bellum Judaicum* he reckoned as above, but that his starting point in *Antiquitates Judaicae* was Herod's death.

Prolegomena zur Geschichte Israels[6] (Berlin, 1905), pp. 103–7; I. Abrahams, 'Time', *HDB*, iv (1902), 763–5. It is thought by some scholars that *BJ* followed the Tyrian calendar (beginning with Tishri), cf. B. Niese, 'Zur Chronologie des Josephus', *Hermes*, xxviii (1893), 197–208; E. Schwartz, 'Christliche und jüdische Ostertafeln', *AGG*, N.F. viii (Berlin, 1905), 138–50.

[1] His work *Vita* which forms an appendix to *Ant.* (*Vita* 430; *Ant.* xx. 266) agrees with *Ant.* that Archelaus reigned until at least his tenth year (*Vita* 5).

POSSIBLE SOURCES OF THE STORY
OF JOHN'S DEATH

The purpose of this appendix is to set forth the *possible* sources of the story of John the Baptist's death. There are at least two people who might have divulged reliable information not only of John's death but also of Jesus' trial by Antipas (Lk. 23: 6–12).

The first is Joanna, who was one of the women who ministered to Jesus and his disciples.[1] Her husband, Chuza,[2] was the ἐπίτροπος of Herod Antipas. The term ἐπίτροπος is used of procurators, who, at least in Augustus' time, were personal agents of the emperor and were responsible for the supervision of his property and financial business.[3] Magie states that the procurator was not a public official but a personal agent of the emperor much like the steward in a private household.[4] In the New Testament the ἐπίτροπος is one who is concerned

---

[1] Lk. 8: 3, and also mentioned in 24: 10.

[2] As to Chuza, Blass thought that this name did not occur anywhere outside the NT and that he was probably a Jew who had both a Greek and an Aramaic name (F. Blass, *Philology of the Gospels* [London, 1898], pp. 152–3), but the name does occur in a Nabataean inscription (*CIS*, II, i, 227; cf. F. C. Burkitt, 'Chuza', *Exp*, 5th series, IX [1899], 118–22), and from a Nabataean inscription found at Petra, the name is conjecturally restored by E. Littmann, 'Zu den nabatäischen Inschriften von Petra', *Zeitschrift für Assyriologie*, XXVIII (1914), 275; and also in a Syrian inscription, cf. Littmann, 'Eine altsyrische Inschrift', *ibid.* XXVII (1912), 380–1. This shows that Chuza is found independently of Luke's reference. If Chuza were a Nabataean, he would have been of the same origin as the Herods (*contra* this, see H. J. Cadbury, 'Some Semitic Personal Names in Luke–Acts', *Amicitiae Corolla*, ed. by H. G. Wood (London, 1933), p. 54.

[3] For a study of the development of the procurator and his duties, see O. Hirschfeld, *Die kaiserlichen Verwaltungsbeamten*[2] (Berlin, 1905), pp. 70–1, 410–65, esp. 411–12; H. Mattingly, *The Imperial Civil Service of Rome* (Cambridge, 1910), pp. 102–49; A. N. Sherwin-White, 'Procurator Augusti', *Papers of the British School at Rome*, XV (1939), 14–15; M. Rostovtzeff, *SEHRE*, I, 49, 82; Jones, *Studies in Roman Government and Law*, pp. 119–25.

[4] Magie, I, 489.

with the finances and personal property of an owner.[1] In Josephus it is used of Antipater (Herod the Great's father),[2] of other procurators,[3] of Thaumastus as a manager of Agrippa I's personal estates,[4] and of Syllaeus as manager of the estate of Obadas, king of Arabia.[5] In the Talmud ἐπίτροπος (אֲפִּיטְרוֹפּוֹס) is used by Eliezer (ca. A.D. 90) with reference to Agrippa II's steward.[6] It is very probable that Chuza[7] was Antipas' financial minister, or manager of his estates, and therefore may have been one of the μεγιστᾶνες[8] or πρῶτοι τῆς Γαλιλαίας of Mark 6: 21. As such he would have been an eyewitness of the events.

Although his wife, Joanna, is not specifically mentioned by Mark or Matthew, she is associated in Luke with Mary Magdalene and other women who were ministering to Jesus

[1] Mt. 20: 8; Gal. 4: 2. Gal. 4: 2 is problematic as commentators indicate. Besides the commentaries, one should consult in this connection S. Belkin, 'The Problem of Paul's Background', *JBL*, LIV (1935), 52–5; O. Eger, 'Rechtswörter und Rechtsbilder in den paulinischen Briefen', *ZNW*, XVIII (1917), 105–6.

[2] Jos. *Ant.* xiv. 143; *BJ* i. 199.

[3] Jos. *Ant.* xv. 406; xx. 107; *BJ* ii. 117, 223.

[4] Jos. *Ant.* xviii. 194.

[5] Jos. *BJ* i. 487; Strabo xvi. 4. 23. That he was in charge of the finances of Arabia is seen in Jos. *Ant.* xvi. 279–82, 291, 295–6, 343, 353. That he was called 'brother' of the king, as Lagrange suggests, is unfounded, cf. M.-J. Lagrange, *Évangile selon Saint Luc*[8], p. 235 n. 3.

[6] TB: Shab. 121 a; Suk. 27 a. Cf. Klein, *Beiträge*, p. 66 n. 1; H. Graetz, 'Agrippa II und der Zustand Judäas nach dem Untergang Jerusalems', *MGWJ*, xxx (1881), 484.

[7] It is thought by some that Chuza was the nobleman of Jn. 4: 46–53, cf. F. Godet, *A Commentary on the Gospel of St Luke*[5], trans. from 2nd French ed. by E. W. Shalders (Edinburgh, n.d.), I, 365; T. Zahn, *Das Evangelium des Lukas*[1,2], *KNT*, III (Leipzig, 1913), p. 340 n. 8.

[8] The δεκάπρωτοι seem to have been the finance committee of the πόλις council in the first century A.D.; cf. A. H. M. Jones, *GC*, p. 139. It is used in connection with Tiberias (cf. Jos. *Vita* 69, 296) and also referred to, though not in the technical sense, in *Vita* 168 = *BJ* ii. 639. Could it not be that the ἄρχων was the head of the city's council (e.g. Sapphias over Tiberias, *Vita* 134, 271, 278, 294; *BJ* ii. 599, who presides over the meetings of the council, *Vita* 276–9, 300) whereas the ἐπίτροπος was the head of the finance committee and the actual manager of the estates? He would hold, therefore, a very influential position in Antipas' government. It is possible that the ἐπίτροπος could be considered one of the χιλίαρχοι because the procurator was involved with the militia (cf. Mattingly, pp. 137–49). This seems unlikely here. The first suggestion seems more probable.

and his disciples.[1] In the passion narrative both Matthew and Mark specifically mention Mary Magdalene and Mary the mother of James, among other women, as those who followed Jesus from Galilee and ministered to him.[2] In the parallel passage Luke mentions these women but omits their names.[3] Apparently he felt that it was unnecessary to mention their names since he had done so already in 8: 2–3.[4] On the other hand, he does mention Mary Magdalene and Mary the mother of James, together with Joanna, as those who went to Jesus' tomb and reported back to the disciples.[5] Thus, Luke also associates Joanna with those women who ministered to Jesus and his disciples. It is not improbable that she may have given a first-hand report of John's death to Peter, who later passed it on to Mark. Granting an early date for Matthew,[6] it is generally felt that the author of the Gospel was Jesus' disciple of that name. If this was the case, then Matthew may have received the story direct from Joanna.

The second person who may have divulged reliable information is Manaen, the σύντροφος Ἡρῴδου τοῦ τετράρχου.[7] As mentioned above,[8] the term σύντροφος means a person who was a companion in education or one who was an intimate friend. Hence Manaen, being an intimate friend of Antipas, may well have been asked by the Christian community to tell what had happened on the occasion of John's execution. Although Manaen is placed in Antioch, one cannot preclude that he was not with Antipas during his rule, and he may have been an actual eyewitness of the banquet. On the other hand, whether or not he was at the banquet himself, he would have known something about it from Antipas. Again, Mark may

---

[1] Lk. 8: 2–3.

[2] Mt. 27: 55–6; Mk. 15: 40–1. For a discussion on this, see M. Hengel, 'Maria Magdalena und die Frauen als Zeugen', *Abraham unser Vater, Festschrift für O. Michel*, ed. by O. Betz, M. Hengel, and P. Schmidt (Leiden and Köln, 1963), pp. 243–56.

[3] Lk. 23: 49.

[4] J. M. Creed, *The Gospel according to St Luke* (London, 1930), p. 288; Lagrange, *Luc*, p. 594; Grundmann, *Lukas*, p. 436.

[5] Lk. 24: 10.

[6] As does B. C. Butler, *The Originality of Matthew* (Cambridge, 1951), pp. 165–9. The problem of the Matthaean authorship is beyond the scope of this study. See, however, Kümmel, *Introduction*, pp. 84–6; Guthrie, pp. 33-44.

[7] Acts 13: 1.   [8] P. 14 n. 2.

have received the story first-hand from Manaen when he was in Antioch[1] with Paul and Barnabas, or possibly from Peter who also visited Antioch.[2] On the assumption of a later date for Matthew (A.D. 80–100), the author of that Gospel must have been someone other than Jesus' disciple, and it is generally felt that its composition was outside of Palestine. Most scholars agree with Streeter that it was written in Antioch, or in Syria more generally.[3] If this were the case, then the author of this Gospel may have received his story from the Antiochean church where Manaen had been a member.

[1] Acts 12: 25; 15: 37.
[2] Gal. 2: 11.
[3] B. H. Streeter, *The Four Gospels* (London, 1936), pp. 500–27; Kümmel, p. 84.

THE COMMENCEMENT OF JOHN THE BAPTIST'S MINISTRY

The logical place to begin a discussion on the commencement of John the Baptist's ministry is Luke 3: 1–2[1] where six chronological facts[2] are listed. Five of these give only the broadest limits: Pilate was procurator of Judaea from A.D. 26 to late 36 or early 37;[3] Herod Antipas was deposed in A.D. 39; Philip died in A.D. 34;[4] Lysanias tetrarch of Abilene cannot be dated;[5] and Caiaphas was high priest from A.D. 18 until not later than the Passover of A.D. 37.[6] Hence, the broad limits for the beginning of John's ministry are A.D. 26 and the Passover of 37. The

---

[1] It is thought by Grant that the reason for this chronological notice was to prevent the chronological confusion respecting the Lord's ministry which was so evident in the following centuries. Grant thinks this confusion had already begun in the first century, as is seen in Jn. 8: 57 (R. M. Grant, 'The Occasion of Luke III: 1–2', *HTR*, xxxiii [1940], 151–4). However, it is doubtful if Jn. 8: 57 was intended to serve as a chronological landmark. Moreover, the accuracy of Lk. 3: 1 cannot be challenged (cf. Sherwin-White, pp. 166–7). For a theological rather than a chronological interpretation, see V. E. McEachern, 'Dual Witness and Sabbath Motif in Luke', *CJT*, xii (1966), 267–9, 272.

[2] Similarly Thucydides introduces his account of the Peloponnesian Wars by a sextuple dating, Thucydides ii. 2. 1 (cf. also Polybius i. 3. 1–5). Luke may have taken over a form used by secular historiographers, who used to make prominent important events, especially those with which the narrative begins, by means of circumstantial datings and synchronisms (E. Schwartz, 'Noch einmal der Tod der Söhne Zebedaei', *ZNW*, xi [1910], 102).

[3] Schürer, i, 487–8 n. 141. Numismatically it could not have been before A.D. 26, cf. Hedley, *JTS*, xxxv, 56–8. Smallwood thinks that Josephus' figure of ten years (*Ant.* xviii. 89) is a round number and thus dates his departure sometime between mid-December 36 and the end of February 37, cf. Smallwood, *JJS*, v, 12–14, 19–21; cf. Appendix VIII, below, pp. 313–16.

[4] Jos. *Ant.* xviii. 106; Schürer, i, 431 n. 11; above, p. 251 and n. 1.

[5] The inscription which records a temple dedication by the freedman of Lysanias the tetrarch (*CIG*, 4521) is dated between A.D. 14 and 29. For a discussion of the problem, see Schürer, i, 716–20; Creed, *Luke*, Additional Note, pp. 307–9; G. Ogg, *The Chronology of the Public Ministry of Jesus* (Cambridge, 1940), pp. 171–2.

[6] Jos. *Ant.* xviii. 35, 95. Jeremias, *Jerusalem*, p. 195 n. 153.

one precise date is the fifteenth year of Tiberius, and this is interpreted in five different ways.

Augustus died on 19 August A.D. 14. The first method of reckoning would be the normal Roman method, according to which Tiberius' fifteenth year would have run from 19 August A.D. 28 to 18 August A.D. 29. The second method grows out of the first. Some think that the above date is too late, and so they suggest that Luke was counting from the decree by which Tiberius became co-regent with Augustus.[1] On the basis of Velleius Paterculus ii. 121 Mommsen dates the decree at the end of A.D. 11,[2] which would make A.D. 25/6 the fifteenth year of Tiberius. The consensus of scholarly opinion is that neither of these two methods was used. The first method is rejected because it would be too complicated and confusing to reckon according to dynastic years.[3] It was almost essential to measure against some regular calendar. The second method is rejected because there is no historical evidence for its employment.[4] There is need, therefore, of some standard method of reckoning the reigns of emperors, and it is here that the third, fourth, and fifth methods of reckoning come into play.

The third method is that used by Syria from the time of Augustus to Nerva. According to this the regnal years of the Roman emperors were reckoned from 1 Tishri as were those of

---

[1] For a discussion on this argument, see K. Wieseler, *Beiträge*, pp. 195–6; W. M. Ramsay, *Was Christ Born at Bethlehem?* [2] (London, 1898), pp. 199–202, 221; Zahn, *Lucas*, pp. 183–8.

[2] T. Mommsen, *Römisches Staatsrecht*[3], ii, ii (Leipzig, 1887), 1159 n. 3.

[3] Niese, *Hermes*, xxviii, 210–11; Ogg, *Chronology*, p. 187. Lewin states: 'the reign of Tiberius, as beginning from 19th Aug. A.D. 14, was as well-known a date in the time of Luke as the reign of Queen Victoria in our own day, and that no single case has ever been or can be produced in which the years of Tiberius were reckoned in any other way' (Lewin, p. liii). The government officials may have calculated from the date of Tiberius' accession, but would the average subject have known the date?

[4] Madden, *Coins of the Jews*, p. 177 n. 1; K. Wieseler, *A Chronological Synopsis of the Four Gospels*[2], trans. by E. Venables (London, 1877), p. 172. Note Wieseler abandoned this position later in his life; cf. Wieseler, *Beiträge*, pp. 177–96. For a thorough discussion on this, see H. Dieckmann, 'Die effektive Mitregenschaft des Tiberius', *Klio*, xv (1918), 339–75. J. K. Fotheringham, 'The Evidence of Astronomy and Technical Chronology for the Date of the Crucifixion', *JTS*, xxxv (1934), 151–2. Even among those who hold to the co-regency theory there is no agreement as to the beginning of the co-regency, cf. Ogg, *Chronology*, pp. 174–83.

the old Syro-Seleucids.[1] Thus, the first year of Tiberius would have extended from 19 August A.D. 14 to 1 Tishri 14, and his fifteenth year from 1 Tishri 27 to 1 Tishri 28,[2] or more exactly from 21 September 27 to 8 October 28.[3] The adherents of this view believe that since Luke was from Antioch,[4] he would have calculated the reigns of emperors according to the calendar with which he was there familiar.[5] Also, the official Jewish New Year, except possibly during the exilic period, commenced with the autumn equinox (especially after Nehemiah's reformation).[6] Would it not be natural to reckon regnal years from the New Year? Moreover, this method agrees well with other chronological factors in the life of Jesus. If Jesus was born around the winter of 5/4 B.C.,[7] then the beginning of his ministry could have been soon after the beginning of John's, possibly before the Passover of A.D. 28 (Jn. 2: 13). At this time he would have been only 30 or just 31, which fits in well with the statement that he was 'about 30 years of age' at the commence-

---

[1] Mommsen, *Römisches Staatsrecht*, II, ii, 802–4; M. Dibelius, *From Tradition to Gospel*[2], trans. by B. L. Woolf (London, 1934), pp. 293–4. For a discussion of Syrian calendars, see Finegan, *Handbook*, pp. 61–8.

[2] C. Cichorius, 'Chronologisches zum Leben Jesu', *ZNW*, XXII (1923), 17–19; G. Hölscher, 'Die Hohenpriesterliste bei Josephus und die evangelische Chronologie', *Sitzungsberichte der Heidelberger Akademie der Wissenschaften – Philosophisch-historische Klasse*, XXX (Heidelberg, 1940), 27; C. H. Kraeling, 'Olmstead's Chronology of the Life of Jesus', *ATR*, XXIV (1942), 346; G. Bornkamm, *Jesus of Nazareth*, trans. I. and F. McLuskey (London, 1960), p. 45; G. B. Caird, 'The Chronology of the NT', *IDB*, I (1962), 601.

[3] Parker and Dubberstein, p. 46.

[4] W. M. Ramsay, *St Paul the Traveller and the Roman Citizen*[14] (London, 1920), pp. 389–90; D. Smith, *The Life and Letters of St Paul* (London, 1919), Appendix IV, pp. 667–70; above, pp. 231–2 n. 9.

[5] W. M. Ramsay, 'Numbers, Hours, Years, and Dates', *HDB*, Extra Volume (1904), 481; Cichorius, *ZNW*, XXII, 18–19; Kraeling, *ATR*, XXIV, 344–6.

[6] J. F. McLaughlin, 'New Year', *JE*, IX (1895), 254–6; J. Morgenstern, 'New Year', *IDB*, III (1962), 544–6; J. Morgenstern, 'Year', *IDB*, IV (1962), 923–4. Also, cf. Jos. *Ant.* i. 80–1; Wellhausen, *Prolegomena*, pp. 103–7; Abrahams, *HDB*, II, 763–5.

[7] This is the very latest date for the birth of Jesus. Ogg thinks he was born sometime between 11 and 9 B.C. (G. Ogg, 'Chronology of the New Testament', *PCB* [London, 1962], p. 728); Stauffer at 7 B.C. (E. Stauffer, *Jesus and His Story*, trans. by D. M. Barton [London, 1960], pp. 36–43); and Montefiore and Finegan in 5 B.C. or early 4 B.C. (H. Montefiore, *Josephus and the New Testament* [London, 1962], p. 12; Finegan, *Handbook*, pp. 215–48).

ment of his ministry.[1] Also, if Jesus indeed died on 7 April
A.D. 30, it would allow at least three Passovers (Jn. 2: 12; 6: 4;
11: 55) to be included.[2] If this method was employed, John's
ministry would have commenced between 1 Tishri 27 and
1 Tishri 28.

The fourth opinion is that Luke reckoned from 1 Nisan. This
would make the first year of Tiberius last from 19 August 14
to 1 Nisan 15, and his fifteenth year from 1 Nisan 28 to
1 Nisan 29,[3] or 15 April A.D. 28 to 4 April A.D. 29.[4] The
reasons for this view are several. First, it is felt that Luke
was drawing on sources from the Baptist's circle, and since
this was centred on Palestine, he would have used the Jewish
method of reckoning, which for the regnal years of their rulers
commenced with 1 Nisan.[5] Without any supporting evidence
Ogg assumes this to be true. Although the Mishnaic tractate
Rosh ha-Shanah specifically states that the regnal years were
reckoned from 1 Nisan,[6] a discussion on this in the Talmud
shows that it was not universally accepted. After a considerable
discussion it is decided that the kings of Israel were reckoned
from 1 Nisan and the non-Israelite kings from 1 Tishri, citing
Nehemiah 1: 1 and 2: 1 as proof texts.[7] R. Joseph objects by
showing that this was not always the case. One cannot therefore
count on Talmudic sources for a settled method of reckoning
regnal years.[8]

Neither is it any help to see how the reckoning was calculated
during the Maccabaean times, for both the Nisan and Tishri
New Years were used. While 2 Maccabees always uses the
Seleucid era (which reckons from October), 1 Maccabees seems
to imply, although not at all clearly, that the author used the
years beginning with Nisan when following Palestinian sources,
and years beginning with Tishri when following a Syrian

---

[1] Lk. 3: 23.

[2] Kraeling, *ATR*, xxiv, 346. Jeremias uses this method, cf. Jeremias,
Eucharistic Words, p. 39 n. 1.

[3] Ogg, *Chronology*, pp. 200–1.

[4] Parker and Dubberstein, p. 46.

[5] Ogg, *Chronology*, pp. 196–200.   [6] R.H. i. 1.

[7] TB: R.H. 3*a–b*, 8*a*; for a discussion of this see Finegan, *Handbook*,
pp. 88–91.

[8] TB: R.H. 3*b*; cf. J. Morgenstern, 'The New Year for Kings', *Occident
and Orient*, ed. by B. Schindler (London, 1936), pp. 439–40.

source.[1] Frank thinks both books reckon according to the Seleucid method, but that 1 Maccabees started year 1 in autumn 313 B.C. whereas 2 Maccabees started year 1 in 312 B.C.[2] In fact he believes that the Talmudic teaching (mentioned in the previous paragraph) that non-Jewish kings were reckoned from Tishri has reference to the Seleucid era.[3] The two books of Maccabees could be used as evidence for a 1 Nisan reckoning only if one agrees with Bickermann's or Dancy's theory.[4] Weightier is the evidence in favour of a 1 Tishri reckoning, but it cannot be pressed too far.

If one goes back to Old Testament times in order to determine regnal years, as Ogg does, one cannot conclude as he does that the Jews reckoned from 1 Nisan. In fact, reckoning in the Old Testament varied a great deal both in respect of their own kings and of foreign kings. Thus it is difficult to determine whether they used the accession-year system or the non-accession-year system, and whether they reckoned from Nisan or Tishri.[5] It seems, however, that the Tishri to Tishri regnal year is the more plausible view for post-captivity Judah.[6]

The fifth opinion is that Luke used the Julian Calendar, and therefore that he reckoned Tiberius' first year from 19 August A.D. 14 to 31 December A.D. 14, and his fifteenth year from 1 January to 31 December A.D. 28. The chief argument in favour of this view is that since the combined work of Luke–Acts is addressed to Theophilus (Lk. 1: 3) who is saluted as κράτιστε, a term Luke otherwise employs only as a form of address to a Roman official (Acts 23: 26; 24: 3; 26: 25), it is probable therefore that the writing is addressed to Roman readers or to those under Roman dominion, who would be familiar with the Julian Calendar.[7] This method was used by the Roman historians such as Tacitus and Suetonius.

If the fourth and fifth views are to be accepted, then the terminology of 'about 30 years' in Luke 3: 23 is used in a

---

[1] Bickermann, 'Makkabäerbücher', PW, XIV, 1 (1928), cols. 781–4; J. C. Dancy, *A Commentary on I Maccabees* (Oxford, 1954), pp. 50–1.

[2] E. Frank, *Talmudic and Rabbinical Chronology* (New York, 1956), pp. 30–2.

[3] *Ibid.* p. 35.

[4] As does Fotheringham, *JTS*, XXXV, 154.

[5] For a discussion on these problems, see E. R. Thiele, *The Mysterious Numbers of the Hebrew Kings*[2] (London, 1966), pp. 16–38, 161.

[6] *Ibid.* p. 30.   [7] Finegan, *Handbook*, p. 273.

broader sense than would be necessary on the third method; for if Jesus was born in the winter of 5/4 B.C. then he would have been around thirty-two or -three at the beginning of his ministry.[1]

In conclusion, of the five methods, the second and fourth are the least likely. If one were to accept A.D. 30 as the crucifixion date, then the third method would be the most probable. On the other hand, if one thinks that Jesus was crucified in A.D. 33 as the present author does, then either the first or fifth method would be preferable. Whichever of these last three methods (i.e. first, third, or fifth) is accepted, it follows that John's ministry would not have begun before 1 Tishri A.D. 27 nor after 18 August A.D. 29.

[1] Ogg doubts whether Lk. 3: 23 can serve any chronological purpose and thinks that the statement about Jesus not yet being 50 years old (Jn. 8: 57) is more significant. Jesus, then, was probably born sometime between 11 and 9 B.C. (Ogg, *PCB*, p. 728). It seems that because Lk. 3: 23 does not fit well into Ogg's system, he rejects it and uses Jn. 8: 57. But is not John's reference much more vague and thus far less likely to serve specifically as a chronological landmark than Lk. 3: 23?

THE DATE OF PILATE'S RETURN TO ROME

There has been much debate over the date of Pilate's return to Rome. Schürer suggests that he was recalled before the Passover of A.D. 36.[1] Since, however, this would have involved a journey of more than a year, it seems highly unlikely, and the more so if Augustus' rule that a retiring magistrate had to return within three months[2] was still in force. Also, Josephus specifically states that Pilate 'hurried' to Rome.[3] This would mean that the emperor's confirmation of a new procurator was delayed for well over a year, which is very unlikely.

Another suggestion, made by Holzmeister, is that Pilate left for Rome before the Feast of Tabernacles in A.D. 36. It was at this festival that Vitellius paid his first visit,[4] at which time he deposed Caiaphas and appointed Jonathan to officiate at the festival. Just before the Passover of 37 Vitellius paid his second visit[5] to Jerusalem, at which time he deposed Jonathan and appointed Theophilus.[6] The difficulty with this view is that Josephus calls the feast at which Caiaphas was deposed the Passover, but the feast at which Jonathan was deposed he leaves unspecified. Vitellius, moreover, would not have been able to depose Caiaphas and appoint Jonathan in time for the latter to officiate at the Feast of Tabernacles, because a week was needed for the ceremonies of consecration.

A third suggestion, made by Smallwood, is that Pilate's departure from Judaea occurred in the latter half of December 36, that Vitellius' first visit to Jerusalem was at the end of 36 or the beginning of 37, and that his second visit was at the Passover of 37.[7] Again, she has to assume that Josephus is

---

[1] I, 493–4 n. 152.　　　　　　　　　[2] Dio liii. 15. 6.
[3] *Ant.* xviii. 89.　　　　　　　　　　[4] Jos. *Ant.* xviii. 90–5.
[5] Jos. *Ant.* xviii. 122–5.
[6] Holzmeister, *Biblica*, XIII, 231; followed by De Laet, *L'Antiquité Classique*, VIII, 414.
[7] Smallwood, *JJS*, V, 12–21, esp. 17–21.

mistaken when he states that Vitellius' first visit to Jerusalem was at a Passover while the second visit is left unspecified.

A fourth view is that, since Pilate arrived in Rome after the death of Tiberius (16 March 37) and since he hurried to Rome (Jos. *Ant.* xviii. 89; Dio liii. 15. 6), he must have been deposed at the end of 36 or the beginning of 37. Vitellius came to Jerusalem at the time of the unspecified feast. Since Vitellius received the news of Tiberius' death on his fourth day there,[1] it seems that this feast was that of Pentecost, 37.[2] The difficulty with this view is the seemingly long time between the death of Tiberius and Vitellius' receiving the news of it. Since it was at a time in the year when sailing was not feasible, it is most likely that the news went by land. It was concluded above that the average speed of the Roman Imperial Post was no more than fifty miles a day on long journeys.[3] Hence it would be impossible for the news of Tiberius' death to have arrived in time for the Passover. If the Passover were on 19 April,[4] then the courier would have travelled the distance of 2,413 Roman miles[5] at an average of seventy-five miles a day. This speed is virtually impossible over such a great distance. Also, during the spring, travel was more difficult than in winter because of the melting snow,[6] and therefore even an average of fifty miles a day is unlikely.[7] Yet if it were speaking of Pentecost (9 June) it would mean only an average of twenty-nine miles a day. This

[1] Jos. *Ant.* xviii. 122–4.

[2] Lewin, pp. 247–51; also held by Jeremias, *Jerusalem*, p. 195 n. 143; J. Blinzler, *Der Prozess Jesu*[4] (Regensberg, 1969), pp. 271–3.

[3] Above, p. 34.

[4] Based on Parker and Dubberstein, p. 46.

[5] Above, pp. 34 nn. 2, 5; 36 n. 2.

[6] Cf. Ammianus Marcellinus xv. 10. 4, where the difficulties of crossing the Alps in the spring which are described would also apply in the mountainous regions of Asia Minor.

[7] Bruce reckons only 2,000 miles and thinks that the couriers travelled sixty miles a day (*ALUOS*, v, 18, 23 n. 65). However, his calculation of 2,000 miles is a gross underestimation and his reckoning of sixty miles a day would be subject to the same criticism as mentioned above. His note regarding the accession of Galba as being known in twenty-seven days (found in U. Wilcken, *Griechische Ostraka*, i [Leipzig and Berlin, 1899], 800) is irrelevant, for this was in the summer and would have been sent by sea, a journey which under ordinary conditions need not have taken more than ten to thirteen days (cf. Pliny *NH* xix. 1. 3; cf. also L. Casson, 'Speed under Sail of Ancient Ships', *TAPA*, LXXXII [1951], 146).

is rather slow unless the couriers delivered the news to other provincial governors on the way, as opposed to having a special courier for each governor. This would slow down the average considerably. Also, it could be that the courier was unable to locate Vitellius immediately, either thinking that he would be with his soldiers or that he would be near Petra. On the other hand, if Pentecost in A.D. 37 were a month earlier,[1] on 11 May, then the courier would have averaged forty-five miles a day. Considering all factors, this last hypothesis is very reasonable.

There is one final problem which deserves mention. In an entirely different context Josephus mentions a visit made by Vitellius to Jerusalem.[2] Smallwood makes this journey the same as that mentioned in *Antiquitates Judaicae* xviii. 90–5, and concludes that since Tiberius replied to Vitellius concerning the restoration of the high priest's vestments to Jewish custody, the visit of Vitellius could not have been at the Passover but must have occurred in late December.[3] Lewin thinks that Josephus was in error and that Gaius rather than Tiberius must have sent the reply.[4] Jeremias and Blinzler do not even mention the problem. Thus both Smallwood and Lewin think that Josephus was in error. This may well be the case, but is it necessary to hold that the visits mentioned in the two different contexts of Josephus are the same? Is it not more probable that in *Antiquitates Judaicae* xv. 405 Josephus may be referring to a visit of Vitellius in the autumn (or earlier) of 36, and in this context may he not be speaking proleptically of what actually occurred later? It seems, then, that Vitellius visited Jerusalem some time in A.D. 36, that he wrote to Tiberius, received a reply, and then restored the vestments to the custody of the Jews at the Passover of 37.

If the above conclusions are correct, the chronological sequence would be as follows:

Vitellius' first Jerusalem visit (Jos. *Ant.* xv. 405)	autumn 36
Pilate returns to Rome	winter 36/7
Tiberius dies	16 March 37

[1] As supposed by Lewin (p. 255), and as mentioned by Holzmeister (*Biblica*, xiii, 299) and Blinzler (*Prozess*, p. 273).

[2] *Ant.* xv. 405.

[3] *JJS*, v, 17–19.

[4] P. 249.

Vitellius (2nd Jerusalem visit) deposed
Caiaphas and appointed Jonathan
(Jos. *Ant.* xviii. 90–5)   Passover 37
Vitellius (3rd Jerusalem visit) deposed
Jonathan and appointed Theophilus
(Jos. *Ant.* xviii. 123)   Pentecost 37
Vitellius heard of Tiberius' death   Pentecost 37

THE WITHDRAWALS OF JESUS

The purpose of this appendix is only to elaborate on the ten withdrawals of Jesus mentioned above.[1] As stated there,[2] in discussing these withdrawals two things must be kept in mind. First, the scope of this study is not the life and ministry of Jesus but only his withdrawals and their possible relationship to Antipas. Secondly, the Marcan outline of the itinerary of Jesus (which is basically paralleled in the other two synoptics) in its broadest outlines makes good historical sense. Having stated these assumptions, a review of the relevant passages is in order. Each section will be numbered to correspond with the numbers in Chapter 9.

I. TO THE EASTERN SHORE OF THE SEA OF GALILEE
MARK 6: 31–2; MATTHEW 14: 13

The first withdrawal according to the synoptists comes immediately after the return of the twelve, and the reason given for it is that he might be alone with his disciples. Matthew, who says nothing of the commissioning of the twelve in this context, states that Jesus departed[3] when he heard of John's fate, or, if this is parenthetical, that he departed because he had heard that Antipas knew of his activities.[4] Whichever view is correct, Matthew's text seems to imply that he left because of Antipas.[5] Although Matthew does not specifically state that Jesus left Antipas' domain, this is implied in the fact that he left by boat. It is corroborated by Luke who states that Jesus came to Bethsaida,[6] and by John who says that he went to the other

---

[1] P. 200.

[2] Pp. 197–200.

[3] Mt. 14: 13.

[4] Jesus may have known Antipas' feelings through informants such as Joanna, the wife of Chuza, Antipas' financial minister (Lk. 8: 3).

[5] See M'Neile, p. 213; against this see Lohmeyer, *Matthäus*, p. 235; *Markus*, p. 123; Grundmann, *Matthäus*, p. 363.

[6] Lk. 9: 10.

side of the Sea of Galilee.[1] Hence, one cannot exclude the possibility that Jesus left because of Antipas, but at the same time one cannot conclude that this was the only reason for his departure. It seems more likely that he left primarily to seek an opportunity for a rest with his disciples and secondarily because of Antipas.[2] This is substantiated by the fact that, although Matthew does not mention the return of the twelve in the immediate context (the disciples are with him as indicated later in the pericope),[3] the stated purpose of his withdrawal is to go to a lonely place. That he was fleeing from Antipas is not directly stated, but the implication is too strong to be ignored. Neither is this implication lacking in Mark and Luke, for when Antipas heard of Jesus' ministry, Jesus is said to have withdrawn from Antipas' territory, and this by the shortest possible route.

In conclusion, it seems that Jesus withdrew to a lonely place with his disciples primarily to get away from the crowd, but secondarily because he knew of Antipas' desire to see him.

2. TO BETHSAIDA AND GENNESARET
MARK 6: 45, 53; MATTHEW 14: 22, 34

After the feeding of the 5,000, Jesus constrained (ἠνάγκασεν) his disciples to enter a boat to travel towards Bethsaida,[4] while he

[1] Jn. 6: 1. The exact place is not certain but Smith argues that it was a desert place in the vicinity of Bethsaida. This was reached by the multitudes on foot by the fords over the Jordan (Smith, *HGHL*, p. 457). Dalman locates it near the middle of the eastern side of the Lake of Galilee between *Wady es-Samak* and *Wady en-Nkeb* which was only 6–10 miles south of Bethsaida (Dalman, *SSW*, p. 173).

[2] Cf. Klostermann, *Matthäusevangelium*, pp. 127–8.

[3] Mt. 14: 15. It is in the same point in the other two synoptists (Mk. 6: 35; Lk. 9: 12) that they again pick up the reference to the disciples.

[4] There are two basic problems in connection with Bethsaida. First, John refers to Bethsaida in Galilee (Jn. 12: 21), so leading to the conjecture that there were two Bethsaidas. This view is now generally abandoned (cf. Smith, *HGHL*, p. 458; Dalman, *SSW*, p. 165; C. McCown, 'The Problem of the Site of Bethsaida', *JPOS*, x [1930], 32–58; C. H. Dodd, *Historical Tradition in the Fourth Gospel*, p. 310 n. 1). The second is the phrase εἰς τὸ πέραν (Mt. 14: 22; Mk. 6: 45). Although this is generally thought of as implying east–west or west–east travel (this may account for the omission of the phrase from Mark in 𝔓45–*vid*, W*f*1 q, sy-s. This is favoured by F. C. Burkitt, 'The Chester Beatty Papyri', *JTS*, xxxiv [1933], 367–8; Taylor, *Mark*, p. 327. Against it, see P.-L. Couchoud, 'Notes sur le texte de St. Marc dans

dismissed the people.[1] The motive for a sudden departure is made clearer in John 6: 15.[2] Because of the wind[3] they never landed at Bethsaida but went instead to Gennesaret.[4] Jesus landed in Antipas' territory and conducted a healing ministry in the area.[5] It is supposed by Burkitt that the intention to go to Bethsaida was politically motivated, for Bethsaida was outside of Galilee.[6] But if Jesus and his disciples had really wanted to avoid Antipas' territory, why did they land at Gennesaret? Why did they not change direction and go to Bethsaida when the wind had abated? According to Loisy, Jesus supposed that

le codex Chester Beatty', *JTS*, xxxv [1934], 8–9), it can also mean across the lake on the same side, as when Josephus crossed over from Tiberias to Tarichaeae, both of which were on the same side of the lake (*Vita* 304; cf. also 153; cf. Smith, *HGHL*, p. 457). The preposition πρός following προάγω can probably be translated 'to' or 'towards' (Taylor, *Mark*, pp. 327–8).

[1] Schmidt (p. 193) argues that the dismissal of the crowd, the constraint placed upon the disciples, and the reference to the feeding of the 5,000 in Mk. 6: 25, were already a connected series of events before the evangelist's own composition.

[2] Cf. Goguel, *Life of Jesus*, p. 377; H. Montefiore, 'Revolt in the Desert? (Mark vi. 30 ff.)', *NTS*, VIII (1962), 135–41.

[3] Mt. 14: 24; Mk. 6: 48; Dalman, *SSW*, pp. 175–6; Taylor, *Mark*, p. 332.

[4] Mt. 14: 34; Mk. 6: 53. In both Gospels there is an inferior reading Γεννησάρ in D. The place is variously identified. There was a plain called Gennesaret located on the western shore of the Sea of Galilee between Tiberias and Capernaum just north of Tarichaeae. This is about thirty by twenty stadia (or *ca.* three and a half by two and a half miles) in area (cf. Jos. *BJ* iii. 516–21; G. L. Robinson, 'Land of Gennesaret', *A Dictionary of Christ and the Gospels*, I [1906], 640–1). It is thought that there was a town by this name which is identified with the Kinnereth of Jewish tradition (cf. Deut. 3: 17; Josh. 11: 2) and is located on the site of *el-'Oremeh* (cf. Dalman, *SSW*, pp. 130–1; Simons, pp. 52, 358; cf. also pp. 198, 274). It seems best to refer the synoptist's Gennesaret to the plain, though in accepting this there is difficulty in translating καὶ διαπεράσαντες ἐπὶ τὴν γῆν ἦλθον εἰς Γεννησαρὲτ καὶ προσωρμίσθησαν which seems to be redundant. It may be an Aramaic idiom which could be literally rendered 'and when they had crossed over, they came to land on the other side, to Gennesaret'. Torrey would omit 'on the other side' as mere tautology (Torrey, *The Four Gospels*, p. 300).

[5] Mt. 14: 35–6; Mk. 6: 55–6. Lagrange (*Marc*, p. 178) suggests that Mark may have described here, in abbreviated form, what transpired *en route* from the lake to Tyre (7: 24). This may have some validity but cannot be proved one way or the other.

[6] Burkitt, *Gospel History*, pp. 91–2.

he would not be recognized by the people, and that he and his disciples would be able to move quietly outside of Antipas' territory. After all, he would not want to attract attention in a district so near to Tiberias, Antipas' capital.[1] But the description of Jesus' healing ministry would suggest otherwise. Goguel's contention that everything about Jesus' ministry at Gennesaret betrays a note of haste, Jesus being in a hurry to get out of Antipas' territory,[2] finds little support in either Mark or Matthew.[3]

Those who conjecture that Jesus was fleeing from Antipas are seriously embarrassed by Jesus' landing at Gennesaret. Explanations have been offered but most of them go beyond the evidence. There is no suggestion here that Jesus was in flight from, or in fear of, Antipas.

3. TO TYRE
MARK 7: 24; MATTHEW 15: 21

In both Matthew and Mark, Jesus, after his controversy with the Pharisees,[4] goes to the territory of Tyre.[5] There is no reason for this stated or implied, except possibly that it was a continuation of his withdrawal from the crowds. Manson states: 'I regard this withdrawal as a flight, but far more a flight from the dangerous enthusiasm of his friends than from the suspicions and fears of his enemies.'[6] In Tyre, Jesus intended no public

---

[1] A. Loisy, *Les Évangiles Synoptiques*, I (Paris, 1907), 947–8; cf. Lagrange, *Marc*, p. 178.

[2] Goguel, *Life of Jesus*, pp. 363–4; cf. also Cadman, pp. 39–40.

[3] Cf. Taylor, *Mark*, p. 332.

[4] Mt. 15: 1–20; Mk. 7: 1–23.

[5] Mt. 15: 21; Mk. 7: 24. Matthew has Jesus and his disciples enter into the territories of both Tyre and Sidon at this point of the narrative, whereas Mark has only Tyre (although there is textual support for καὶ Σιδῶνος in Mk. 7: 24, it is omitted by D L W Δ Θ). Mark has Sidon later on in Jesus' journey (7: 31). There is a divergence of opinion over the setting of this pericope. Dibelius (*From Tradition to Gospel*, p. 261) suggests that it should be placed along with the scene in Mk. 12: 35–7, which speaks of the Messiah as the Son of David. Schmidt (p. 198) states only that it may have originally stood in connection with another series of events. However, if Jesus' desire was to get away from the multitude, its place here makes good historical sense.

[6] Manson, *Servant-Messiah*, p. 71. In a similar manner, Dodd states: 'It is probable that the withdrawal from Galilee was due not simply to the menace of death from Herod and the Pharisees, but even more to the fact that the Galilean populace responded in a wrong way to the proclamation of the

ministry[1] and there is none recorded except in connection with the Syrophoenician woman.

It seems then that according to the synoptists his going to Tyre was a continuation of his withdrawal from the multitudes. He pauses long enough in Gennesaret for some ministry but then hastens on to Tyre. The main motive implied by the evangelists is a desire to get away from the multitude, for he did not want to be known even in Tyre. Yet one has to ask his reason for going outside Antipas' territory to do this. Parts of Peraea would have been just as sparsely populated as Tyre. Possibly Jesus thought that in Peraea he would not be able to get away from the people, but would pick up a crowd, as did John. In the region of Tyre neither John nor Jesus had previously ministered, although he seems to have been known in Tyre and Sidon as well as Peraea.[2] Possibly to avoid the multitudes, it was thought best to go to a non-Jewish territory. Nevertheless, Jesus' leaving Antipas' territory must not be overlooked or ignored.

4. TO SIDON, SEA OF GALILEE, THE DECAPOLIS
MARK 7: 31; MATTHEW 15: 21, 29

According to Mark, Jesus went from Tyre through Sidon[3] to the

Kingdom of God. They surrounded Jesus with a mistaken enthusiasm, but did not "repent". If He was to remain in Galilee, the only alternative to falling a victim to the plots of His enemies was to throw Himself upon an excited and morally worthless popular movement, which would rapidly become a revolt' (C. H. Dodd, 'The Life and Teaching of Jesus Christ', *A Companion to the Bible*, ed. by T. W. Manson [Edinburgh, 1939], p. 383).

[1] Mk. 7: 24.
[2] Mk. 3: 8; cf. also Mt. 4: 24–5; Lk. 6: 17.
[3] There is the reading καὶ Σιδῶνος ἦλθεν in 𝔓⁴⁵, A K W X Π, $f^1 f^{13}$. Although an easier reading, it 'is probably a very early attempt to relieve the geographical difficulty' (Taylor, *Mark*, p. 353). Schmidt (p. 200) suggests that Mark awkwardly expressed himself and meant the region of Tyre and Sidon. Wellhausen (*Marci*, p. 58) conjectures that διὰ Σιδῶνος is a mistranslation of בצידן and that it should have been rendered εἰς Βηθσαιδάν, as it is in D in Mk. 6: 45, meaning Bethsaida. Allen (*Mark*, p. 110) and Taylor (*Life*, p. 132) accept this conjecture because it makes much more sense to go south directly after Tyre. Schmidt (p. 201 n. 1) and Lohmeyer (*Markus*, p. 149 n. 1) feel it cannot be verified, and Howard (Moulton–Howard, p. 471) that it is an unnecessary geographical correction (cf. also M'Neile, p. 232). Matthew omits a reference to Sidon here (15: 29) but

Lake of Galilee through[1] the region of Decapolis. Matthew does not mention Sidon and the Decapolis, but only that Jesus travelled παρὰ τὴν θάλασσαν τῆς Γαλιλαίας.[2] Still, Matthew's omission does not exclude the possibility of Mark's route. The problem is that Mark's route is circuitous and uncertain. Some have suggested that this journey is incredible for it would have been like going from Cornwall to London via Manchester.[3] This does not necessarily prove anything. If Jesus were in a hurry it would be right to question it. However, there is nothing in the text to imply this. Some have suggested that from Tyre he went north to Sidon, and then southeast across the Leontes by the natural bridge, passed through the tetrarchy of Abilene in the direction of Damascus (including possibly Damascus itself), turned south, and finally reached the lake from the east in the northern part of the Decapolis.[4] Dalman suggests that he crossed the Jordan north of the Hula district 'reaching the Golan from Caesarea Philippi, then turning from el-Ḳuneṭra, and joining the Damascus road at *Tell Tshochadar*, which passes to the lake through the Hippos district'.[5]

Whatever route was taken it was circuitous, and the time it would have taken is difficult to ascertain. Burkitt suggests that it may have taken up to eight months, for 'the grass was still

includes it earlier (15: 21), when Jesus was in the vicinity of Tyre and Sidon. The words διὰ Σιδῶνος may not necessarily mean that he actually entered the city of Sidon (Cranfield, p. 250). There is no reason why Jesus should not have gone from Tyre to Sidon, a distance of about twenty-five miles, unless he was in a real hurry. But there is nothing in the text to indicate this.

[1] The double preposition ἀνὰ μέσον (with genitive) is found outside of this verse in Mt. 13: 25; 1 Cor. 6: 5; Rev. 7: 17. Its exact meaning is problematic here, but generally it means 'in the midst of'. Here possibly it means 'right through' (Moule, *Idiom*, p. 67).

[2] Mt. 15: 29.

[3] Rawlinson, p. 101; or in Germany 'von Darmstadt über Frankfurt nach Mannheim mitten durchs Neckartal' (Schweizer, *Markus*, p. 87); or in U.S.A. from Dallas to Miami via Chicago!

[4] Swete, p. 159, cf. the map facing p. 408. Burkitt has a similar route but, in preference to Jesus' going east towards Damascus after crossing the Leontes, he would have him continue south past Caesarea Philippi, east of the Jordan to the northern part of the Decapolis (Burkitt, *Gospel History*, p. 92 n. 1; cf. the map facing p. 92; cf. also E. G. Kraeling, *Rand McNally Bible Atlas* [London, 1956], pp. 387–8; Aharoni and Avi-Yonah, *Bible Atlas*, p. 147).

[5] Dalman, *SSW*, p. 201.

green when the Five Thousand were fed, but now we have arrived almost at the time of S. Peter's confession and the start for Jerusalem to keep the last Passover'.[1] Certainly there is nothing in the text to indicate that this journey was done in haste, yet it seems strange, if it took as long as eight months, that there is so little known about Jesus during this period. Moreover, seeing that Jesus coupled the two feedings,[2] the implication is that the interval between them was not very great. The main purpose of the journey, probably, was to keep away from the crowds. This could be achieved by not remaining for long in any one place. It was not until he arrived at the east side of the Lake of Galilee that the crowds again gathered.

Thus it seems that the main purpose of the roundabout journey was to be away from the crowds. Yet one cannot help noticing that he stayed outside of Antipas' territories. It seems, then, that at least part of the reason for the roundabout journey was to avoid Antipas.[3] Swete correctly observes: 'The long *détour* may have served the double purpose of defeating the immediate designs of His enemies and providing for the Apostles the rest which He had desired to give them before.'[4]

5. TO DALMANUTHA OR MAGADAN
MARK 8: 10; MATTHEW 15: 39

While on the eastern side of the lake, Jesus instructed the crowd not to tell anyone of the healing of the deaf mute, whereupon the people proclaimed it all the more.[5] According to Matthew, he healed many others as well.[6] After the crowds had been with Jesus for three days, he had compassion on them and saw their need of sustenance.[7] This section is called the feeding of the 4,000, and is generally held to be the same incident as the feeding of the 5,000. It is also observed that the events which follow the two feedings are similar in character, and consequently

---

[1] Burkitt, *Gospel History*, p. 93; cf. M'Neile, p. 232.

[2] Mk. 8: 19–20; cf. also Mt. 16: 9–10.

[3] Cf. Burkitt, *Gospel History*, pp. 93–4; cf. also F. C. Burkitt, 'W and Θ: Studies in the Western Text of St Mark', *JTS*, XVII (1915), 14.

[4] Swete, p. 159.

[5] Mk. 7: 32–7.

[6] Mt. 15: 30–1.

[7] Mt. 15: 32–8 = Mk. 8: 1–9.

they are considered to be doublets.[1] But the differences between the two feedings are considerable, and they are expressly mentioned as two separate events by both evangelists (Mt. 16: 9–10 = Mk. 8: 19–20).[2] The same can be said for the sequence of events after the feedings. It would seem, moreover, improbable that Matthew would naively copy Mark's (or *vice versa* if one holds to a Matthaean priority) two series of events when actually they were one series of events, especially since they took up valuable space on the papyrus roll. At any rate, for the present study it is assumed that there are two series of events. This will make it possible to inspect each movement of Jesus more minutely.

After the feeding of the 4,000 Mark states that Jesus went εἰς τὰ μέρη Δαλμανουθά,[3] and Matthew, εἰς τὰ ὅρια Μαγα-

---

[1] The correspondences outlined by Dodd are as follows:

	Mark A		Mark B
vi. 30.	Return of the xii.		
vi. 31–44.	Feeding the People.	viii. 1–9.	Feeding the People.
vi. 45–52.	Voyage and Storm.	viii. 10 a	Voyage.
vi. 53.	Landing.	viii. 10 b.	Landing.
vi. 54–6.	Reunion with the People: healing.		
vii. 1–23.	Controversy with the Pharisees (washing).	viii. 11–12.	Controversy with the Pharisees (sign).
vii. 24.	Departure from Galilee.	viii. 13.	Departure from Galilee.
		viii. 14–21.	Sayings about bread and leaven.
vii. 25–30.	Healing in Phoenicia.		
vii. 31–7.	Healing in Decapolis.	viii. 22–6.	Healing in Gaulanitis.

(C. H. Dodd, 'The Close of the Galilaean Ministry', *Exp*, 8th series, XXII [1921], 273–80; cf. also Goguel, *Life of Jesus*, pp. 359–60 n. 2; M'Neile, pp. 237–8; Taylor, *Mark*, pp. 628–32).

[2] Moule states it well when he writes: 'it is impossible to prove even that the two stories spring from one and the same root: there are a number of differences in detail. One thing is clear, and that is that the evangelist himself intended to convey the impression of two distinct incidents, for in 8: 19–20 they are both expressly mentioned' (C. F. D. Moule, *The Gospel according to Mark*, p. 60; cf. also Swete, pp. 163–6; R. A. Cole, *The Gospel according to St Mark, Tyndale New Testament Commentary*, ed. by R. V. G. Tasker [London, 1961], pp. 125–6; Bowman, p. 174; Plummer, *Luke*, pp. 218–20; R. V. G. Tasker, *The Gospel according to St Matthew, Tyndale New Testament Commentary*, ed. by R. V. G. Tasker [London, 1961], pp. 153–4).

[3] Mk. 8: 10. The various readings are: τὰ μέρη Δαλμανουθά ℵ A (B Δαλμανουνθά) C K L X Δ Π, 0131 33 700 892 1009 1010 1079 1195 1216

δάν.[1] The identification of these two places is uncertain.[2] It is probable, however, that Jesus landed on the western side of the Lake of Galilee. Once again he was in a hurry to get away. As after the feeding of the 5,000, his flight was more from the dangerous enthusiasm of his friends and followers than from the suspicions and fears of his enemies. On the basis of Dalman's conjecture that the site was Magdala, Blinzler thinks that Jesus was not afraid of Antipas because he would have been, according to the Talmud,[3] only about a twenty minute walk from Tiberias.[4] But either the Talmud must be referring to another place[5] or has calculated the distance incorrectly,[6] for Dalman's[7] Magdala was a little over three miles from Tiberias, and it would have taken about an hour to travel that distance. In the last resort, it is difficult to know how far Magadan was from Tiberias. Here, the only exchange in which Jesus took part was to rebuke the Pharisees who had asked for a sign. After this he

1242 1253 1344 1365 1546 1646 2148 2174, *Byz Lect*, it-l q, vg, syr-(p) h (h^{gr}), Cop-sa bo (arm Δαλμανοῦναι), geo[1]; τὰ ὄρη Δαλμανουθά 1071^c; τὸ ὄρος Δαλμοῦναι W; τὰ ὅρια Δαλμανουθά 1241; it-f; τὸ ὄρος Μαγεδᾶ 28 (syr-s Μαγεδᾶν); τὰ ὅρια Μελεγαδᾶ D^{gr}* (D^b Μαγαδᾶ, it-aur *Magedan*, it-c k *Mageda*); τὰ μέρη Μάγδαλα θ (565 Μαγεδᾶ), f^1f^{13}, l^{80} (it-a d *Magedan*, it-b ff² r¹ *Magedam*, it-i *terra Magedam*), syr-pal, goth, geo². Schmidt (p. 203) states that it is difficult to determine whether Mk. 8: 10 (= Mt. 15: 39) belongs at the end of this pericope or at the beginning of the following pericope. He favours the latter.

[1] Mt. 15: 39. The various readings are: Μαγαδάν אּ* B D, it-d (syr-c *Magadon*, syr-pal *Magadin*, syr-p *Magdu*; Μαγεδάν אּ^{c}, it-aur c f ff¹ g¹ (it-a ff² *Magedam*), vg, syr-s, cop-sa, eth-ms, Eusebius, Jerome, Augustine; *Magedan* or *Magedam* it-b e l; Μαγεδαλ eth-pp; Μαγδαλάν C W 33 565 1079 1195 1546 $l^{5\ 292}$, it-q; cop-bo; Μαγδαλά K L X Δ^{gr} Θ Π, f^1f^{13}, 700 892 1009 1010 1071 1216 1230 1241 1242 1253 1344 1356 1646 2174, *Byz Lect*, syr-h, arm, eth-ro, geo, Chrysostom.

[2] For a discussion of these place names, see Eus. *Onomast.* pp. 134: 18–20; 135: 22–4; N. Herz, 'Dalmanutha', *ET*, VIII (1897), 563; E. Nestle, 'Dalmanutha', *ET*, IX (1897), 45; Herz, 'Dalmanutha', *ET*, IX (1897), 95; cf. also *ET*, IX (1898), 426; Burkitt, *JTS*, XVII, 16; J. Sickenberger, 'Dalmanutha (Mk. 8, 10)', *ZDPV*, LVII (1934), 281–5; Dalman, *SSW*, p. 128; Abel, *Géographie*, II, 373; Kraeling, *Bible Atlas*, p. 388. The presence of these obscure names would suggest the use of primitive tradition and not an invention of the evangelists (cf. Schmidt, p. 210; Taylor, *Mark*, p. 361).

[3] Cf. TB: Pes. 46 a.   [4] *Herodes Antipas*, p. 28.
[5] Cf. Albright, *AASOR*, II–III (1921–2), 42–5.
[6] Cf. Klein, *Beiträge*, pp. 76–84.
[7] Dalman, *SSW*, pp. 126–8.

again left. Could it be that this question by the Pharisees was designed to trick him into making an unguarded statement against the government, so giving them a legitimate excuse for seizing him?[1] If it were a trap he did not fall into it, but rebuked the Pharisees and left.

It seems that Jesus' ministry there was short indeed. Certainly, in the later portion of his ministry, Jesus spent longer periods outside of Antipas' territory than within it. He may have gone to the western side only to get away from the crowd, and the best way to accomplish this was to cross the lake in a boat. Having done this, he was soon off again to the eastern side of the lake. The short duration of his stay on the west coast may indicate his avoidance of Antipas.

6. TO BETHSAIDA
MARK 8: 22

From the western side of the Lake of Galilee Jesus now travelled to Bethsaida in Philip's territory.[2] Blinzler states that the motive for this journey was to get away from the Pharisees rather than from Herod.[3] This may be true, yet curiously, while crossing the lake, Jesus discussed the leaven not only of the Pharisees but also of Herod.[4] Why did Jesus mention Herod as well as the Pharisees? Could it have been his relationship with Herod, as well as his disgust for the Pharisees, which made him leave the western shore? Certainly his short stay on the western coast could point to this. Hence, Blinzler's suggestion may not be wholly correct. Not only the Pharisees but also Antipas may have been a reason for Jesus' swift departure from the western coast.

[1] Matthew uses the term πειράζω (16: 1) and Mark συζητέω (8: 11) which may suggest this.

[2] It is difficult to know whether Mk. 8: 22 belongs to this pericope (8: 22–6) or the preceding one. Schmidt (p. 206) thinks it belongs to the present story, and that Mark found Bethsaida as part of the story in the tradition.

[3] *Herodes Antipas*, p. 28.

[4] Mk. 8: 15. Cf. above, pp. 202–13.

7. TO CAESAREA PHILIPPI
MARK 8: 27; MATTHEW 16: 13

After healing the blind man at Bethsaida, Jesus and his disciples went to the region of Caesarea Philippi.[1] No purpose is given by the evangelists for his going there. After Peter's confession, Jesus instructed both the multitude and his disciples.[2] Primarily, it seems, he ministered to his disciples, and only incidentally to the crowd. This ministry continued six days before he left for the Mount of Transfiguration.[3] Being once again outside of Antipas' territory, he now assumed a more leisurely pace.

8. TO THE MOUNT OF TRANSFIGURATION
MARK 9: 2; MATTHEW 17: 1

Only three of his disciples went with Jesus up the mount.[4] This was to be a unique occasion such as alone would justify his being away from the crowd and his other disciples.

Coming down from the mountain Jesus healed a boy possessed by a spirit.[5] Again there was a crowd of people. Thus Jesus did not entirely cut himself off from the multitude in order to spend all his time with the disciples.

9. THROUGH GALILEE TO CAPERNAUM
MARK 9: 30, 33; MATTHEW 17: 22

After the healing, Jesus and his disciples passed through Galilee, but he did not wish anyone to know it. The fact that Jesus did not want anyone to know it is significant. Taylor maintains that he wanted to instruct his disciples concerning his suffering, 'but behind this motive lies the fact that the public ministry in Galilee is now ended'.[6] This may have been so, but the possibility cannot be ruled out that he wanted to avoid the attention of Herod Antipas. The fact that he resumed the public ministry after he left would substantiate this.[7]

---

[1] Mt. 16: 13–28; Mk. 8: 27 – 9: 1. For debate of place name, cf. Taylor, *Mark*, pp. 374–6.

[2] Mk. 8: 34; cf. also Lk. 9: 23.   [3] Mt. 17: 1; Mk. 9: 2.

[4] Mt. 17: 1–13; Mk. 9: 2–13; Lk. 9: 28–36.

[5] Mt. 17: 14–21; Mk. 9: 14–29; Lk. 9: 37–43 *a*.

[6] Taylor, *Mark*, p. 402.   [7] Mt. 19: 1–2; Mk. 10: 1.

In conclusion, therefore, Jesus did want to be alone with his disciples, and so he was before leaving Antipas' territory.[1] Nevertheless, one cannot exclude the possibility that one of his reasons for leaving was to avoid Antipas' attention.

10. TO JUDAEA AND TRANSJORDAN
MARK 10: 1; MATTHEW 19: 1–2

Mark 10: 1 is self-contained and is called a *Sammelbericht* by Schmidt.[2] The words καὶ ἐκεῖθεν ἀναστάς serve as a connecting link with the last place mentioned, namely, Capernaum (9: 33). It seems, then, that Jesus left Galilee to go to Judaea and the Transjordan.

There are two textual problems to be discussed. The first concerns the reading εἰς τὰ ὅρια τῆς Ἰουδαίας καὶ πέραν τοῦ Ἰορδάνου. The western, Caesarean, and Antiochian authorities omit the καί between Ἰουδαίας and πέραν[3] and would translate 'the territory of Judaea beyond Jordan'.[4] This reading may have been influenced by Matthew 19: 1. Its supporters maintain that no part of Judaea was on the east side of the Jordan but that nevertheless part of the country east of the Jordan belonged to the Jews.[5] Certainly the east of the Jordan

---

[1] Mt. 17: 24 – 18: 35; Mk. 9: 30–50.

[2] Schmidt, pp. 238–9.   [3] Attested in C² D W Δ Θ, *f*¹, *f*¹³.

[4] This is accepted by Wellhausen, *Marci*, p. 77; Burkitt, *Gospel History*, p. 96 n. 1; E. Meyer, *Ursprung und Anfänge des Christentums* I (Stuttgart and Berlin, 1924), 119 n. 1. See also a discussion of this by A. Schlatter, *Markus: Der Evangelist für die Griechen* (Stuttgart, 1935), p. 185.

[5] Cf. Strabo xvi. 2. 21. Burkitt conjectures that in order to avoid Antipas' domain Jesus, John and James travelled through Samaria, as Luke relates, while Peter and the rest went via Peraea, meeting Jesus at the place where the pilgrims crossed the Jordan into Judaea. Hence the words πέραν τοῦ Ἰορδάνου describe the west side from Peter's point of view (Burkitt, *Gospel History*, pp. 96–7 n. 1; F. C. Burkitt, 'The Peraean Ministry: A Reply', *JTS*, xi [1910], 412–15). As Burkitt himself admits, it is only a conjecture, and it labours under the disadvantage that πέραν τοῦ Ἰορδάνου has to be understood of the area west of the Jordan. As a result, it has never been widely accepted (cf. Rawlinson, p. 132; Taylor, *Life*, pp. 156–67; Haenchen, *Der Weg Jesu*, p. 336). Lenski gives another plausible solution when commenting on Mt. 19: 1: 'The phrase with πέραν does not modify "Judea" but the verb ἦλθεν, and states that Jesus took this road "beyond Jordan" to reach the boundaries of Judea, instead of the road through Samaria' (R. C. H. Lenski, *Interpretation of St Matthew's Gospel* [Columbus, Ohio, 1932], p. 706).

was not considered part of Judaea until so called by Ptolemy, the astronomer, about A.D. 130–60.[1] The second reading, which retains the καί between 'Ιουδαίας and πέραν, is exclusively Alexandrian[2] and would be translated 'he came into the territories of Judaea and Transjordan'. It may be that the καί was added as a correction. Taylor argues that this reading is seriously weakened by the fact that Judaea is mentioned first.[3] It gives the impression that Jesus first went through Judaea and then crossed the Jordan into Peraea, as in fact he did according to Luke 17: 11; John 7: 10; 10: 40; and 11: 54.[4] The inversion of order (Judaea and beyond Jordan) is thought by Klostermann to rule out the possibility of this reading[5] but a similar inversion occurs in Mark 11: 1.[6] Hence, this reading makes good sense, as well as being the reading most widely held. The third reading, διὰ τοῦ πέραν, is attested mainly by later authorities[7] and would require the translation 'he came into the territories of Judaea via Transjordan'. This would seem to be an obvious correction to explain Jesus journey.[8] It is difficult to choose between the first and second variants, though the first reading is intrinsically the better. Perhaps as Manson states: '*Mk x. 1 does not describe a trip from Galilee to Jerusalem but a ministry in Judaea and Peraea.*'[9]

The second textual problem is concerned with καὶ συνπορεύονται πάλιν ὄχλοι πρὸς αὐτόν. Although there is a variant reading of this (συνέρχεται πάλιν ὁ ὄχλος πρὸς αὐτόν),[10] the main considerations for the present study are the words ὄχλοι and πάλιν. The plural ὄχλοι is preferred,[11] but this is the only example of its plural usage in Mark out of thirty-seven

---

[1] Cf. Abel, *Géographie*, II, 164.   [2] In ℵ B C* L Ψ.

[3] Taylor, *Mark*, p. 416.

[4] Cf. Swete, p. 214; Lagrange, *Marc*, p. 256; Dodd, *Exp*, 8th series, XXII, 286–90.

[5] *Markusevangelium*, p. 98.

[6] Lagrange, *Marc*, p. 256; Taylor, *Mark*, p. 416.   [7] In A K X Π.

[8] Klostermann, *Markusevangelium*, p. 98. Taylor, *Mark*, p. 416 and most other commentators.

[9] T. W. Manson, 'The Cleansing of the Temple', *BJRL*, XXXIII (1951), 273.

[10] In D Θ (W f[1] f[13] pc), it. For a discussion on this, see C. H. Turner, 'Western Readings in the Second Half of St Mark's Gospel', *JTS*, XXIX (1927), 4–5; Manson, *BJRL*, XXXIII, 273–4.

[11] For a discussion on the various readings, see above, n. 10.

occurrences. The plural may suggest different crowds on the different occasions[1] and this would be natural if Mark 10: 1 were a *Sammelbericht*.[2] The term πάλιν is used twice within the same verse (καὶ συνπορεύονται πάλιν ὄχλοι πρὸς αὐτόν, καὶ ὡς εἰώθει πάλιν ἐδίδασκεν αὐτούς). Although it may mean 'as elsewhere', referring back to a similar activity in Galilee or to a previous ministry in Judaea and Peraea, it seems more probable that it means 'as before', meaning that Jesus resumed his public teaching which he had discontinued while in Galilee (Mk. 9: 30). This is supported by the fact that 'the imperfect ἐδίδασκεν may well signify that Jesus was again occupied with teaching',[3] and by ὡς εἰώθει which also denotes resumption (πάλιν) of the customary teaching ministry.[4] Thus it was not that Jesus passed through Judaea and Peraea, teaching as he went; but that when he arrived in Judaea and Peraea he again began teaching.

Blinzler thinks that it does not lie within the scope of a study on Antipas to enquire why Jesus turned to the people again. He feels that the change here has nothing to do with Antipas.[5] But, on the contrary, this would seem to be ruinous to Blinzler's argument. Although Peraea may be a part of Antipas' territory, yet some of the journey was in Judaea. The geographical reference in Mark 10: 1 is too vague to determine on whose territory most of Jesus' ministry took place. It is probable that he won over many of the people of that area who formerly had been under the influence of John the Baptist. Nevertheless, one cannot just pass off this reference as irrelevant, but must consider it in the light of the whole picture. It seems then that when Jesus left Galilee he again conducted a public teaching ministry, similar to that of the earlier Galilaean period but dissimilar to that of the later Galilaean period.

It is concluded that Jesus did want to avoid Antipas' attention while in Galilee, at least in the latter portion of that ministry, and for this reason he avoided the crowds. When he left Galilee, both the gathering of crowds around him and his teaching ministry were resumed.

---

[1] Cf. Manson, *BJRL*, XXXIII, 274; Cranfield, p. 318; Turner once held this view (*JTS*, XXVI, 237) but later abandoned it (*JTS*, XXIX, 4–5); cf. also Grundmann, *Markus*, p. 203.

[2] Taylor, *Mark*, p. 417.

[3] Manson, *BJRL*, XXXIII, 274.

[4] Taylor, *Mark*, p. 417.

[5] *Herodes Antipas*, p. 29.

APPENDIX X

THE HERODIANS

THE USAGE OF THE TERM IN THE GOSPELS

The Ἡρῳδιανοί are mentioned in three passages of the Gospels, dealing with two incidents,[1] one in Galilee and one in Jerusalem, and they are associated with the Pharisees in their opposition to Jesus. In Mark 3: 6, after the healing of the man with the withered hand, the Pharisees went out and took counsel with the Herodians to destroy Jesus; in Matthew 22: 16 and Mark 12: 13 the Pharisees and Herodians combined against Jesus to entangle him with their question as to the lawfulness of paying taxes to Caesar. The Herodians are never mentioned in either Luke or John.

THE MEANING OF THE TERM

Over the centuries there have been many views on the Herodians. The modern consensus of opinion is that they were political supporters of the Herodian dynasty rather than a religious sect or party. Within the present century there have been four substantial discussions on this problem. Otto believes that they had their origins in the days of Herod the Great, and are to be identified with those mentioned in Josephus as Ἡρῴδειοι[2] and οἱ τὰ Ἡρῴδου φρονοῦντες[3] (which incidentally come in the contexts of Galilee and Judaea respectively). He thinks that they wanted to have Rome's authority exercised mediately through the Herods rather than immediately through a Roman official.[4] Bickerman observes that the Latin (not the Greek) ending -ianus is appended to three adjectives employed as substantives in that period of Greek literature. These are Χριστιανοί, Ἡρῳδιανοί, and Καισαριανοί, the last of which is clearly based on the Latin Caesariani, the word used of Caesar's domestic

---

[1] Mk. 3: 6; 12: 13 = Mt. 22: 16.

[2] *BJ* i. 319 – Thackeray translates this 'Herodians', *Josephus, LCL*, II, 151.

[3] *Ant.* xiv. 450 – Markus translates this 'partisans of Herod', *Josephus, LCL*, VII, 681–2.

[4] Otto, PW, Supp. II, 201–2.

servants. By analogy, therefore, Ἡρῳδιανοί should apply to the members of Herod's household. Bickerman also observes that the true Greek ending, which corresponds to *-iani*, is -ειοι (as *Caesariani* is equivalent to Καισάρειοι, and *Augustiani* to Αὐγούστειοι), and thus Josephus' term Ἡρῴδειοι is equivalent to Ἡρῳδιανοί of the Gospels.[1] Joüon, while adopting a similar view to Bickerman, holds that the term implies the responsible officers or agents of Herod, similar to *Caesariani*, which by the end of the third century had become the technical term for a class of fiscal officers.[2]

The most comprehensive review of both ancient and recent interpretation is provided by Rowley.[3] He continues the argument of Bickerman, but demonstrates from Josephus and classical literature that terms ending in Latin with *-iani* and in Greek with -ειοι or -ιανοί had the general meaning of *adherents* or *partisans* of a person. Therefore the term may have the meaning of members of the household, officials, soldiers, or supporters of Herod. From an examination of the Gospel narratives, Rowley argues that they were neither domestic servants nor official agents of Herod, but men of standing and influence whose outlook was friendly to the Herodian rule and consequently to the Roman rule upon which that rested.[4] This view would seem to square with the evidence.

It is probable that they preferred Herod Antipas' rule to the direct rule of the procurators. The rule of the procurators originated from the Jews' desire to escape the hated Herodian dynasty but they later found that procuratorial rule was even less bearable than dynastic rule.[5] Because of this the Herodians' position was undoubtedly strengthened, and they hankered

---

[1] E. Bickerman, 'Les Hérodiens', *RB*, XLVII (1938), 192, 193–7. For Latin suffixes see also Moulton–Howard, pp. 359–60; BD/Funk, § 5 (2).

[2] P. Joüon, 'Les "Hérodiens" de l'Évangile (Marc 3, 6; 12, 13 = Matthieu 22, 16)', *Recherches de Science Religieuse*, XXVIII (1938), 587–8.

[3] H. H. Rowley, 'The Herodians in the Gospels', *JTS*, XLI (1940), 14–27.

[4] *Ibid.* XLI, 26–7. Cf. also Lagrange, *Marc*, p. 60; Jones, *Herods*, p. 179; Bonnard, p. 322; Taylor, *Mark*, p. 224; Haenchen, *Der Weg Jesu*, p. 124. Schalit (*König Herodes*, pp. 479–81) goes even further by thinking that Herod bought their friendship. The Herodians would serve as good public relations men, trying to pacify the people's hatred toward the Herodian house.

[5] Momigliano, *CAH*, x, 339.

after a reconstitution of a single united nation under Antipas as in the days of Herod the Great.[1] This may account for their being in Judaea, as well as in Galilee.[2]

THE INCLUSION AND OMISSION OF THE TERM IN THE SYNOPTICS

Mark mentions the Herodians in connection with both the incident of healing the man with the withered hand on the Sabbath (3: 1–6) and with the question of the tribute (12: 13–17). In both cases they are seen in a bad light. The first case shows them as plotting with the Pharisees[3] in order to destroy Jesus. Mark may mean to indicate that Jesus was hated by both the religious and political men of his day. In connection with the question of the tribute, Brandon argues that the Roman Christians would have known of the Herodians because of the notorious liaison of Titus and Berenice, the sister of Agrippa.[4] But it is doubtful if they would have first learned of the Herodians at such a late date. It is more probable, since the Herods were so long in power, that Mark would have been understood by his readers to be speaking of Herod's supporters in Antipas' day.[5] It is highly doubtful whether the Herodians

[1] Otto, PW, Supp. II, 202.

[2] Another possible explanation for the Herodians' appearance in Jerusalem at the time of the tribute question is that according to Lk. 23: 7 Herod was in Jerusalem at this particular Passover season, cf. Cadman, p. 122 n. 1; Taylor, *Mark*, p. 478 n. 1.

[3] Bacon argues that the alliance of the Pharisees and Herodians could only have happened after A.D. 41. Mark includes it here due to his knowledge of the formidable danger to the infant church arising from an alliance of Herod Agrippa with the Pharisees to extirpate Christianity (B. W. Bacon, 'Pharisees and Herodians in Mark', *JBL*, XXXIX [1920], 102–12). Although the Herodians were opposed to the Pharisees this view ignores the fact that strange unions are created when there is a common hostility (cf. Taylor, *Mark*, p. 224).

[4] *Jesus*, pp. 200 n. 4; 249.

[5] Knox (I, 10) argues that the Herodians were those who regarded the rule of the Herodian dynasty as the best solution of the Jewish problem. This would not have been true after Herod Agrippa I's death 'when it still seemed possible that the Roman government might reconstitute the kingdom of Herod the Great' (*ibid.*). Knox believes, then, that this mention of the Herodians points to a time between A.D. 6 and 44. This is weak on two accounts. First, if the Herodians as a group were to have disappeared at the

would have been introduced if they were unknown and were of no interest to the readers. 'The Herodians figure in the primitive tradition because they belong to, were indeed an important factor in, the historical situation of the Jewish people in the reign of Tiberius.'[1]

Mark (as well as Matthew) includes the Herodians in 12: 13 no doubt as the opposite numbers of the Pharisees with regard to the tribute, a burning question of the day.[2] Matthew includes this reference but omits the Herodians in connection with the healing of the man with the withered hand.[3] Matthew merely states that the Pharisees took counsel against Jesus in order to destroy him. This does not absolutely exclude the Herodians, but there is a tendency in Matthew to place the responsibility of Jesus' persecution on the religious leaders of the day.[4] His inclusion of the Herodians in the debate with

time when a Herod was restored to the kingdom of Herod the Great, then they would have disappeared around A.D. 41 when Claudius gave to Agrippa I the domains of Herod the Great (Jos. *Ant.* xix. 274–5; 351–2). According to Knox' reasoning there would have been no need of the Herodians from A.D. 41 to 44, but there would have been a need after A.D. 44 during Agrippa II's reign. Secondly, there is no reason for the disappearance of a group adhering to the Herods at a time when one of the Herods controlled the same area as Herod the Great. After all there were adherents of Herod during the reign of Herod the Great himself (Jos. *BJ* i. 319; *Ant.* xiv. 450).

[1] Wood, *NTS*, II, 263.

[2] Brandon argues that Mark includes the pericope of the tribute money because the Roman Christians would have been concerned about such a matter, for the Jewish revolt (A.D. 66–70) against Rome was symbolized by the Jewish refusal to pay tribute, cf. S. G. F. Brandon, 'The Date of the Markan Gospel', *NTS*, VII (1961), 139–40; *Jesus*, pp. 224–5, 270–1. It seems more probable that paying tribute was always a question for the Jews from the time of Archelaus' deposition (as even Brandon concedes, *Jesus*, p. 224 n. 1), and that not only the Roman Christians would have been interested in it (Rom. 13: 7), but any Christian group. This could account for Matthew's and Luke's inclusions as well. This question was of interest, therefore, not only to the Jews in Jesus' day but also to Christians in the various parts of the world. This pericope reveals not only Jesus' attitude to the paying of the tribute but also his attitude toward human government and the proper relationship one should have toward it and God.

[3] Mt. 12: 9–14.

[4] Matthew is more specific about the Pharisees as being the ones who persecuted Jesus, whereas Mark in place of the word 'Pharisees' has 'the scribes of the Pharisees' (Mt. 9: 11 = Mk. 2: 16), 'disciples of the Pharisees'

Jesus over the tribute[1] may be 'merely out of mechanical copying of Mark'.[2] Since however this involved a governmental question, the Herodians would be well suited as representatives of governmental thought as the Pharisees were of religious thought.

Luke never mentions the Herodians at all. He seems more vague with regard to the opponents of Jesus in both the healing of the man with the withered hand on the Sabbath[3] and the question of the tribute.[4] Concerning the tribute, he states that the opponents were the spies of the chief priests[5] and scribes.[6] It is possible that Luke is preparing for his passion narrative where he makes the tribute question the main accusation before Pilate.[7] This may also account for the absence of the term 'Herodians'. It seems strange for Luke to have omitted the Herodians since he has an interest in Herod. Knox thinks that 'his interest in Herod is simply due to his sources, in view of his omission of the Herodians...here'.[8] This is possible, although he probably had a copy of Mark (or Matthew if one accepts a Matthaean priority) before him. It may be that he did not know anything about them, but this seems unlikely in view of their existence in the other synoptists and of his interest in Herod. It seems more likely that his readers may not have known about, or been interested in, the Herodians.

THE POSSIBLE AFFILIATIONS OF THE HERODIANS

Were the Herodians an entirely separate group, or were they affiliated in some way to another party or sect? The problem comes to the fore when dealing with the problem of the leaven of Herod in Mark 8: 15 and its replacement by the leaven of the

(Mt. 9: 14 = Mk. 2: 18 b), or only 'scribes' (Mt. 9: 34/12: 24 = Mk. 3: 22; Mt. 22: 41 = Mk. 12: 35). For another approach, cf. Walker, *FRLANT*, XCI, 11–29.

[1] Mt. 22: 16.   [2] Knox, I, 9–10.
[3] Lk. 6: 6–11.   [4] Lk. 20: 20–6.
[5] The chief priests, rather than a specific party, are predominant in the trial of Jesus (A. F. J. Klijn, 'Scribes Pharisees High-Priests and Elders in the New Testament', *NovT*, III [1959], 265–6).
[6] Lk. 20: 19–20.
[7] Lk. 23: 1–2; cf. Conzelmann, p. 139.
[8] I, 57 n. 1.

Sadducees in Matthew 16: 6. This becomes more acute if Mark's secondary reading of the leaven of the Herodians is the correct one. The problem here is not the interpretation of the passage[1] but whether there is any connection between the Herodians and the Sadducees. First, as mentioned above, it is the tendency of Matthew to label the religious leaders as the opponents of Jesus, whereas Mark emphasizes that his opponents were both religious and political. Secondly, Matthew is the only evangelist who uses the term Sadducees outside of their discussion with Jesus about the resurrection.[2] In doing so, he tends to group them with the Pharisees. In Matthew 3: 7 both the Pharisees and Sadducees are mentioned, whereas in the parallel in Luke (3: 7) the multitudes are prominent. In Matthew 16: 1 both parties are mentioned, whereas in Mark (8: 1) only the Pharisees. In Matthew 16: 6, 11, 12 both parties are again mentioned, but in Mark (8: 15) the Pharisees and Herod(ians). Matthew seems to concentrate more on the religious leaders than the other synoptics. 'Clearly the danger apprehended by Mt is Jewish unbelief in general, of which the Pharisees, but also and especially the worldly and sceptical Sadducees, are representative.'[3]

However, having observed this tendency in Matthew's Gospel, what is the significance for the present study in Matthew's use of the leaven of the Sadducees in place of Mark's leaven of Herod or of the Herodians? In accepting the reading Ἡρῳδιανοί in Mark 8: 15, some maintain that they were a political party composed principally of Sadducees.[4] Some have even identified them with the Sadducees,[5] and others identify

---

[1] Cf. above, p. 203.

[2] The term Sadducees is used in the resurrection dispute in Mt. 22: 23 = Mk. 12: 18 = Lk. 20: 27. The other places in Matthew where it is found are Mt. 3: 7; 16: 1, 6, 11, 12; 22: 34.

[3] B. W. Bacon, *Studies in Matthew* (London, 1930), p. 512. Schalit (*König Herodes*, pp. 480–1) thinks that the hypocrites among the Pharisees were paid with good money to be his followers and consequently lived a double life.

[4] H. Ewald, *Die drei ersten Evangelien und die Apostelgeschichte*[2], 1 (Göttingen, 1871), 242–3; W. P. Armstrong, 'Herodians', *A Dictionary of Christ and the Gospels*, 1 (1906), 723.

[5] J. Harduini *De Nummis Herodiadum* (Paris, 1693), pp. 96–107, esp. 105, 107; J. Le Clerc, *The Harmony of the Evangelists* (London, 1701), pp. 114, 426.

them with the Boethusians[1] whose name, more often than not, was used interchangeably with that of the Sadducees.[2] However, although the two parties were theologically indistinguishable, it would seem that the Sadducees remained loyal to the memory of the Hasmonaeans,[3] whereas the Boethusians were attached to the Herodian house, and consequently were called Herodians.[4] Thus their political affiliations were with the Herodian house while their religious affiliations were with the Sadducees. As mentioned above, the Herodians were men of standing and influence, and this would also be true of the Sadducees as being the aristocrats of Palestine.[5]

It is very possible that the political differences of the Boethusians/Herodians and the Sadducees had become less clear-cut at the time of Jesus' ministry owing to the marriage of Antipas to Herodias, a Hasmonaean on her mother's side. That Agrippa I, Herodias' brother, was considered by the Jews to be the best of kings,[6] was due perhaps to the influence of the

---

[1] E. Renan, *The Life of Jesus* (London, 1867), p. 243; K. Kohler, 'Herodians', *JE*, VI (1894), 360; Momigliano, *CAH*, x, 324 n. 1. Against this, see Keim, 'Herodianer', *Bibel-Lexikon*, III (1871), 67.

[2] L. Ginzberg, 'Boethusians', *JE*, III (1892), 285; A. Schlatter, *Geschichte Israels*[3] (Stuttgart, 1925), p. 167; M.-J. Lagrange, *Le Judaïsme avant Jésus-Christ*, EB (Paris, 1931), p. 403; H. Danby (trans.), *The Mishnah*, (Oxford, 1933), p. 506 n. 1; Finkelstein, *The Pharisees*, II, 835 n. 20; R. Meyer, 'Σαδδου-καῖος', *TWNT*, VII (1964), 45.

[3] Finkelstein, *Pharisees*, II, 821 n. 3.

[4] *Ibid.* II, 770. Herod the Great from the beginning of his rule in 37 B.C. sought to discredit the Hasmonaean house, for he never selected a high priest from that house (cf. Jos. *Ant.* xv. 22, 39–41, 56, 322). From 23 B.C. to A.D. 6 the high priests were selected almost always from the house of Boethus – never from the Hasmonaeans (cf. Jos. *Ant.* xv. 320–2; xvii. 78, 164–7, 339, 341; xviii. 3). From A.D. 6 to 41 most of the high priests were from the house of Ananus – never from either the Hasmonaeans or Boethusians (cf. Jos. *Ant.* xviii. 26, 34, 35, 95, 123). However, when Agrippa I gained Judaea in A.D. 41 he selected a new high priest, Simon Cantheras of the house of Boethus (Jos. *Ant.* xix. 297–8). For the list of high priests, with references to their appointments as well as a concise discussion on the family of Boethus, see Smallwood, *JTS*, N.S. XIII, Appendices A and B, pp. 31–3. It seems that in general the Herods were pro-Boethusians and in turn that the Boethusians were pro-Herodian. The anti-Hasmonaean attitude in the Herod family became less marked as the years passed, especially when Antipas married Herodias, a descendant of the Hasmonaeans on her mother's side, and when Agrippa I (Herodias' brother) became king. [5] Jos. *Ant.* xiii. 298.

[6] Jos. *Ant.* xix. 328–31; cf. also xix. 332–52. Cf. Sot. vii. 8.

Sadducees. It is even possible that Antipas married Herodias to gain the support of the Sadducees. The Herodians and Sadducees would have been on the same side of the political fence in opposition to the Pharisees; the former being pro-government[1] while the Pharisees were both anti-Hasmonaean and anti-Herodian.[2] In Matthew 16: 12 and Mark 8: 15 they represent opposite parties against Jesus.

Rowley raises the following objections:

That the term Herodians is to be equated with Sadducees is in every way improbable, since in that case the use of a name not elsewhere attested for this party would be strange in three passages in works which elsewhere regularly use the normal name. Moreover, immediately following the incident of the questioning of our Lord by Pharisees and Herodians, we read that He was questioned by Sadducees. It is very unlikely that in the same context an author would conceal the identity of the party to which the two groups of questioners belonged by using these different names. And since the Boethusians were so closely associated with the Sadducees that the two names are not infrequently interchanged in rabbinical literature, this consideration would apply with almost equal weight against Renan's view. Further, there is nothing in the passages where the Herodians appear to suggest any particular religious interest of theirs, and, if they did form a party of Herod's supporters, it is improbable that they consisted principally, or even largely, of members of one of the great religious parties of the day.[3]

The first objection is invalid in so far as the present writer does not equate the Sadducees and the Herodians as being identical in every respect. Although it is difficult to understand how the evangelists interpreted the various groups, in this case Mark uses the term *Sadducees* only once (12: 18),[4] in connection with their questioning Jesus about the resurrection. Mark mentions the Herodians three times (if this reading is accepted in 8: 15) in connection with the Pharisees, whereas Matthew and Luke tend to omit them.[5] The second objection can be answered

---

[1] Finkelstein, *HTR*, XXII, 248–53.   [2] Allon, *SH*, VII, 53–78.

[3] Rowley, *JTS*, XLI, 17–18.

[4] This is the only time the term Sadducees is used in Luke's Gospel (20: 27), and the only time they are mentioned alone in Matthew (22: 23). Otherwise in Matthew they are always found in conjunction with the Pharisees (3: 7; 16: 1, 6, 11, 12; 22: 34).

[5] Cf. Klijn, *NovT*, III, 259–67, esp. 261–4.

from the context of Matthew 22: 16 and Mark 12: 13. The question concerning the tribute is a political one and thus the term *Herodians* is natural, whereas the next question, concerning the resurrection, is a theological one where the term *Sadducees* is appropriate. The third objection is specifically against Renan's view that the Boethusians were a religious sect closely associated with the Sadducees. But the present author does not hold that the Boethusians were a separate religious sect from the Sadducees, and so this objection does not apply. The fourth objection is based on an argument from silence. Moreover, it was natural for the Herodian supporters and the Sadducees to be closely associated, for they were the aristocrats of the day. Their position materially as well as religiously would have been dependent on a close relationship with the Herodian house.[1]

It seems, therefore, that the Herodians were men of influence and standing, who in some circles were also known as the Boethusians. They were at one with the Sadducees religiously, but generally speaking were more pro-Herodian than they. Due to the marriage of Antipas and Herodias the two groups may have been brought closer together.

Before concluding this section, it should be noted that a new theory has been proposed by Daniel, who in several recent articles[2] identifies the Herodians with the Essenes. He thinks that the prophecy by Menahem, an Essene, regarding Herod the Great's

[1] Avi-Yonah states: 'Hand in Hand mit den Herodianern gingen die neuen Sadduzäer, (die übrigens mit den Sadduzäern aus der hasmonäischen Zeit kaum mehr als den Namen gemeinsam hatten). Es waren dies die aristokratischen Familien (zum Teil Babylonier und Idumäer), die sich um die vom König begünstigten Hohepriesterfamilien scharten. Diese Familien bildeten eine geschlossene Sippe, in deren Händen die Verwaltung des "königlichen Landes" (*Chorê*) lag, d.h. jenes Teiles des Königreiches, der nicht zu den von Herodes beherrschten Griechenstädten gehörte' (M. Avi-Yonah, *Geschichte der Juden im Zeitalter des Talmud in den Tagen von Rom und Byzanz, SJ*, II [Berlin, 1962], 10).

[2] C. Daniel, 'Les "Hérodiens" du Nouveau Testament sont-ils des Esséniens?', *RQ*, VI (1967), 31–55; Daniel, 'Le Esséniens et "Ceux qui sont dans les maisons des rois" (*Matthieu* 11, 7–8 et *Luc* 7, 24–25)', *RQ*, VI (1967), 261–77; A. Negoiţă and C. Daniel, *NovT*, IX (1967), 306–14; C. Daniel, '"Faux Prophètes": surnom des Esséniens dans le Sermon sur la Montagne', *RQ*, VII (1969), 45–79, esp. pp. 68–71; Daniel, 'Nouveau arguments en faveur de l'identification des Hérodiens et des Esseniens', *RQ*, VII (1970), 397–402.

kingship, Herod's building a special gate in Jerusalem for the Essenes, and the fact that Herod waived their having to make a vow of loyalty to him all point to their being connected with Herod and his house.[1] He then goes on to substantiate his hypothesis by showing that some of the characteristics of the Herodians seem to fit well with Essene characteristics. Some examples will only briefly be mentioned.

Antipas' statements of John the Baptist's resurrection reveal the Essene belief in the resurrection and angelic powers (Mt. 14: 2).[2] However, this reveals not so much Antipas' belief but rather an element of surprise, and Daniel stretches the meaning of δυνάμεις as meaning 'angelic' power in this context.

Another example is when the Pharisees warned Jesus to leave Antipas' territory because the tetrarch desired to kill him (Lk. 13: 31). Luke states that Jesus told the Pharisees to tell 'that fox' that he was going to cast out demons and heal people and eventually leave. Daniel says that what Jesus was really saying was that since Herod admired the Essenes for their ability to cure illness and exorcize, and he allowed them to stay in his territory, then Antipas should admire Jesus more because he is doing the same thing in only two days.[3] But does Luke really say this? This is inserting something into the text which is not at all obvious. Also, is it possible that so many Essenes were in Antipas' territory?

Another argument Daniel gives is that, since the Pharisees and Sadducees were hated by the Essenes and the Herodian family, it must be that the Essenes and the Herodians were the same party.[4] This is like saying that since Christians are hated by the Communists and humanists, it would mean that the humanists were Communists.

One could go on but rather than cite specific examples it would be best to examine some basic considerations. It is true that the Essenes did not make a loyalty oath[5] but neither did some of the Pharisees. Rather than say that this is evidence that Herod was friendly towards the Essenes and thus the Herodians were Essenes, it is more probable that since Herod had gone against the Hasmonaean house it would be good politics to be friendly with a religious group who had the same

---

[1] Daniel, *RQ*, VI, 31–5.   [2] *Ibid.* 35–6.   [3] *Ibid.* 37–8.
[4] *Ibid.* 39.   [5] Jos. *Ant.* xv. 371.

feelings.[1] Also, if the Essenes were Herodians, why did Herod the Great have to excuse them from the loyalty oath as he had some of the Pharisees?[2] Would he have to excuse his own adherents? But more important is the fact that it is exceptionally strange for Josephus who had not only submitted to the training of the Essenes[3] but also gives a long description of this sect[4] never once mentions their close collaboration with Herod or the fact that they were Herodians. Also, when he speaks of the adherents of Herod,[5] Josephus never mentions the fact that they are Essenes. Although this is an argument from silence, it is a very strong one here.

Furthermore, the Essenes were ascetics and shunned the worldly pleasures,[6] which was just the opposite of the Herodian dynasty with their great building enterprises in conjunction with the Hellenistic philosophy. Their views regarding marriage, though there were some variances among them, were quite restrictive.[7] In fact they protected themselves against women's wantonness.[8] Herod's house was just the opposite. There were many marriages with many children. Although the Essenes adopted other people's children[9] it is unlikely that they adopted the children of the Herodian house.

Also, could the Essenes who hated and even fought against injustice[10] be the ones who were associated with the Herodian house, which was not particularly known for justice? In addition, Josephus writes that the Essenes were martyred by the Romans.[11] If they were pro-Herodian and consequently pro-Roman, why would they have been martyred by Rome?[12]

In conclusion, one cannot identify the Essenes with the Herodians. The present author agrees with Daniel that the Herodians were related to a religious group. However, they

---

[1] Cf. W. R. Farmer, 'Essenes', *IDB*, II (1962), 145.

[2] Jos. *Ant.* xv. 371.   [3] Jos. *Vita* 10–11.

[4] Jos. *BJ* ii. 119–61; *Ant.* xviii. 18–22.

[5] Jos. *BJ* i. 319; *Ant.* xiv. 450.

[6] Jos. *BJ* ii. 119.   [7] Jos. *BJ* ii. 120–1; *Ant.* xviii. 21–2.

[8] Jos. *BJ* ii. 121.   [9] Jos. *BJ* ii. 120.

[10] Jos. *BJ* ii. 139.   [11] *BJ* ii. 152.

[12] Since Negoitsa holds to the position of identifying the Essenes with the Herodians he tries, although not convincingly, to overcome this difficulty; A. Negoitsa, 'Did the Essenes Survive the 66–71 War?', *RQ*, VI (1969), 517–30.

are not to be identified with the Essenes but rather with the Boethusians. This is all the more striking when in Matthew 16: 12 the term 'Sadducees' replaces the term 'Herodians' in Mark 8: 15. If they were Essenes why was it not mentioned by Matthew? Daniel never adequately deals with the Matthaean passage. It is rather a difficult one to work with if the Herodians were Essenes.

THE MEANING OF 'FOX'

A brief study of the usage of the word *fox* will help to determine what was meant when Jesus called Antipas 'that fox'.

ITS USE IN THE OLD TESTAMENT

The word *fox* occurs six times in the Massoretic text of the Old Testament.[1] Four of these references offer no help in the study of the meaning. The two references that are helpful are Ezekiel 13: 4 and Song of Solomon 2: 15.

First, Ezekiel is prophesying against the false prophets of Israel and states that they are like foxes in desolate places, who attempt to undermine Israel's theocracy.[2] The fox is one who is insidiously destructive. Secondly, the reference in Song of Solomon 2: 15. Although there are many variations of interpretation of this verse,[3] the fact remains that foxes spoil the vines and eat young grapes. The adjective קְטַנִּים indicates their smallness or insignificance.[4] It is interesting that the Midrash, when commenting on this verse, identifies the foxes as the Egyptians who were cunning but yet insignificant compared to other nations, being defeated by their burial in the Red Sea.[5]

Although the Septuagint translates the Hebrew word שׁוּעָל by ἀλώπηξ in all six instances, it does have two other occurrences of the word[6] which offer no help to this study. In conclusion one

[1] Judg. 15: 4; Ezek. 13: 4; Ps. 63 [62]: 11; S. of S. 2: 15; Lam. 5: 18; Neh. 4: 3 [3: 35].
[2] Cf. G. A. Cooke, *A Critical and Exegetical Commentary on the Book of Ezekiel*, ICC (Edinburgh, 1936), p. 139; C. F. Keil, *Biblical Commentary on the Prophecies of Ezekiel*, trans. J. Martin, 1 (Edinburgh, 1876), 165.
[3] Cf. A. Robert and R. Tournay (eds.), *Le Cantique des Cantiques*, EB (Paris, 1963), pp. 123–4.
[4] *Ibid.* p. 123. [5] Cant. R. ii. 15. 1.
[6] The first is in Judg. 1: 35 where ἀλώπηξ is derived from שַׁעַלְבִים. This has reference to a place and not to the animal. For a succinct discussion regarding this, cf. G. F. Moore, *A Critical and Exegetical Commentary on Judges*[2], ICC (Edinburgh, 1908), p. 54. The second reference is in 1 Kgs. 20: 10

can draw the inferences that the fox is destructive (Ezek. 13:4), insignificant, and cunning (S. of S. 2:15).

ITS USE IN CLASSICAL LITERATURE

Since there are so many references to the fox, one must concentrate on those references which mention the characterizations of a fox.

The pre-Christian era

Archilochus of the seventh century B.C. describes a fox as being sagacious as well as mischievous. Its wisdom is elevated.[1]

Aesop, who lived about the seventh or sixth century B.C., devotes much space to the fox in his fables. Out of 420 fables observed, thirty-nine deal with the fox, thirty-seven with the lion, twenty-six with the dog, and twenty-one with man. He devotes more fables to the fox than any other creature. Another interesting observation is that in the fables dealing with the fox, the lion is contrasted more often than any other animal (out of the thirty-nine fables on the fox, the lion is mentioned in twelve).

The most prominent theme in the fables is the sagacity of the fox.[2] The second main theme of the fox fables is its inferiority to

(LXX 21:10). Here Ben-Hadad boasts that there were more men in his army than there were handfuls of dust in Samaria or that Ben-Hadad felt that the Syrian army could carry away the whole city by handfuls, cf. J. A. Montgomery and H. S. Gehman (eds.), *A Critical and Exegetical Commentary on the Books of Kings, ICC* (Edinburgh, 1951), p. 321. The LXX reading שׁוּעָלִים (*foxes*) instead of שְׁעָלִים (*handfuls*) has εἰ ἐκποιήσει ὁ χοῦς Σαμαρείας ταῖς ἀλώπεξιν παντὶ τῷ λαῷ τοῖς πεζοῖς μου, which really makes no sense. Klostermann thinks that there would not be enough earth left to serve as foxholes, cf. A. Klostermann, *Die Bücher Samuelis und der Könige. Kurzgefasster Kommentar*, ed. by H. Strack and O. Zöckler (Nordlingen, 1887), p. 375. Josephus seems to have misunderstood the Hebrew for he considers this to be the erection of a mound by means of handfuls of dust, the mount rising higher than the walls of the city of Samaria (*Ant.* viii. 371). Whatever the reading may be in this incident, it does not help this present study for if one accepted the LXX reading as referring to foxes, this would give only the normal usage for the word *fox.*

[1] *Fragments* 197.

[2] The fable number is according to *Aesop without Morals*, trans. and ed. by L. W. Daley (New York, 1961). Cf. fables nos. 9, 124, 142; cf. also nos. 12, 17, 27, 41, 81, 107, 126, 147, 241, 252, 275, 333, 408.

the lion but its use of wisdom to outwit other animals to gain something for itself and to escape being devoured by the lion.[1] The fox is unprincipled in its use of wisdom.

Solon, of the sixth century B.C., makes one reference to the fox, where it is again credited with the idea of sagacity.[2] Plato, in the fifth century B.C., demonstrates that the fox obtains a superior position by craft and subtlety.[3] Pindar, of the same century, shows that dominance is obtained either by power, as in the case of the lion, or by craftiness, as in the case of the fox.[4] Aristotle, of the fourth century B.C., states that the fox is cunning and has an evil disposition.[5]

The characterization of the fox in the pre-Christian era is mainly about its craftiness. It uses its power of craft to outwit other animals for its own benefit. It is interesting to observe that throughout its development, the fox is contrasted with the lion – the lion is the king of the animals by its own power, and the fox seeks the lion's favour by use of its wisdom. It is obvious that the fox is inferior to the lion.

New Testament times

During New Testament times again there is an emphasis on the craftiness[6] of the fox and its capability to outwit other animals.[7] When persons were identified with animals, the person identified with a lion was powerful while the one identified with a fox was a degraded, as well as crafty, individual.[8] Thus in this further development it appears that a person identified as a fox is looked down upon. Another new idea is given by Suetonius, where Vespasian is called a fox by his slave because of his greed.[9] Therefore, the word *fox* carries the idea of craftiness, degradation, and greed.

---

[1] Cf. fables nos. 10, 188, 191, 257, 258, 409; cf. also nos. 146, 149, 394, 406.

[2] *Fragments* (of a poem) xiv. 1–7.   [3] *Respublica* ii. 365a–c.

[4] *Isthmia* iv. 40–51 (or iv. 72–84).

[5] *Historia Animalium* i. 1. 488b: 20.

[6] Pliny *NH* viii. 42. 103. This is also seen in Aelian *De Natura Animalium* vi. 24.

[7] Plutarch *Solon* xxx. 1–3; *Sulla* xxviii. 1–3.

[8] Epictetus *Dissertationes ab Arriano* i. 3. 7.

[9] *Ves.* xvi. 3.

ITS USE IN JEWISH LITERATURE

The earliest reference in Jewish literature is from the second generation of Tannaim (*ca.* A.D. 90–130). One reference shows the fox's inferiority; to be the tail of a lion is held to be more honourable than to be the head of a fox.[1] Another reference to the fox states that the fox's cleverness is really foolishness.[2] Possibly also belonging to this period is R. Benjamin b. Japhet's comment on a saying of R. Eleazar (*ca.* A.D. 90–130) 'a fox in its hour – bow down to it'.[3] It is difficult to interpret this saying but Strack–Billerbeck think it means that the base man (i.e. the fox) rises to power and prestige when the time favours him and everyone must bow down to him.[4]

In the fourth generation of Tannaim (A.D. 160–90) there is again a reference to the fox's inferiority to the lion.[5] Later references in Jewish literature do not change the basic meaning[6] and are not really helpful in that they are so far removed in time from the object of this study.

CONCLUSION

One can conclude from a study of Greek, Latin, and Jewish literature that the fox is both crafty and inferior in its position. It is interesting to observe that in the earliest Greek writings the emphasis is on its sagacity and its capability to outwit other creatures. In later Greek writings the idea of the inferiority of the fox in comparison with other beasts, especially the lion, is emphasized. Around the first century, the man who was called a fox was considered degraded or base in his character.

In Jewish writings the concept of inferiority is always the prevalent one. The craftiness of the fox is not emphasized at all.

It is interesting to observe that when a fox is contrasted with another animal, it is for the most part with the lion. The lion is pictured as the one who had its position because of its power,

---

[1] Ab. iv. 15; cf. also TB: Sanh. 37 a.

[2] TB: Ber. 61 b. [3] TB: Meg. 16 b.

[4] II, 201.

[5] TB: B.M. 84 b. Cf. also Ecc. R. xi. 2. 1; Cant. R. ii. 15. 1.

[6] E.g. in the third century, cf. TB: Hag. 14 a; B.K. 117 a; and in the fourth century cf. Est. R. vii. 3 (this is the only occurrence in Jewish literature where the fox is considered wise, as in classical writings).

whereas the fox only gained a high position by the deceitful means of outwitting the other animals. The fox is pictured as being fearful of the lion and recognizing its position as the leader of the animal kingdom.

Therefore, one can conclude that a person who is designated a fox is an insignificant or base person.[1] He lacks real power and dignity, using cunning deceit to achieve his aims.

[1] This is in agreement with Strack–Billerbeck, II, 201.

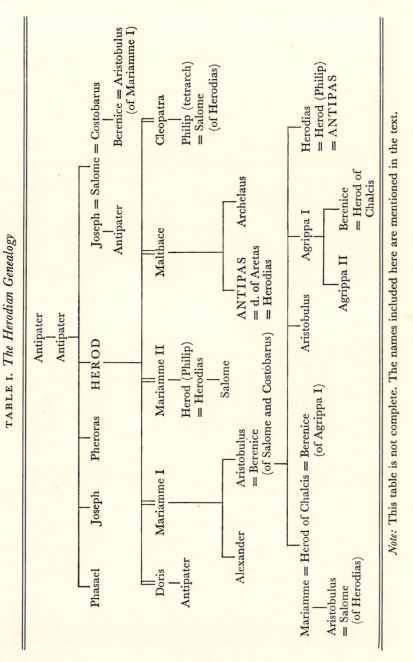

TABLE I. *The Herodian Genealogy*

Note: This table is not complete. The names included here are mentioned in the text.

349

TABLE II. *Chronology of Antipas' life*

Antipas' birth	20 B.C.
Antipas went to Rome for education	late 8/early 7 B.C.
Antipas returned to Palestine	late 5/early 4 B.C
Herod the Great's death	Mar./Apr. 4 B.C.
Passover	12–19 Apr.
Archelaus in Caesarea	*ca.* 23 Apr.
Antipas and Archelaus departed for Rome	*ca.* early May
Pentecost and dispatch (*re* revolt) to Rome	May/June
Antipas and Archelaus arrived in Rome	early July
First trial concerning Herod's will	middle of July
Dispatch from Varus arrived in Rome	middle of July
Dispatch to Varus arrived in Palestine	early Aug.
End of revolt in Palestine	July/Aug.
Delegation and Philip departed for Rome	middle/late Aug.
Delegation and Philip arrived in Rome	middle/late Oct.
Second trial concerning Herod's will	Oct./Nov.
Decision of Augustus	early/middle Nov.
Pseudo-Alexander arrived in Rome	late Nov.
Antipas returned to Palestine	spring, 3 B.C.
Sepphoris rebuilt	3 B.C.–A.D. 8–10
Antipas received dynastic title at the time of Archelaus' deposition	A.D. 6
Foundation of Livias	A.D. 13
Foundation of Tiberias	A.D. 23
Pilate arrived in Judaea	A.D. 26
Commencement of John the Baptist's ministry	A.D. 28 or 29
Antipas went to Rome	A.D. 29
Antipas married Herodias	A.D. 29/30
Antipas befriended Agrippa	A.D. 29/30
Antipas imprisoned John	A.D. 30 or 31
John's death	A.D. 31 or 32
Massacre of the Galilaeans	Passover 32
Votive shields incident	Feast of Tabernacles 32
Antipas' trial of Jesus	Passover 33
Agrippa left Antipas	A.D. 32/3
Rome's struggle with the Parthians	A.D. 35–6
Antipas as negotiator for peace treaty between Rome and Parthia	summer/autumn 36
Antipas defeated by Aretas	autumn 36
Pilate returned to Rome	winter 36/7
Tiberius died	16 Mar. 37
Vitellius heard in Jerusalem of Tiberius' death	Pentecost 37
Agrippa returned to Palestine	early/middle Aug. 38
Antipas deposed and exiled	summer 39

BIBLIOGRAPHY

BIBLIOGRAPHY

PRIMARY SOURCES

The Acts of Augustus. With Eng. trans. by F. W. Shipley (*LCL*). London, 1924.

Aelian, *The Characteristics of Animals.* 3 vols., with Eng. trans. by A. F. Scholfield (*LCL*). London, 1958–9.

Aesop Without Morals. Trans. and ed. by L. W. Daly. New York, 1961.

Ammianus Marcellinus. 3 vols., with Eng. trans. by J. C. Rolfe (*LCL*). London, 1935–9.

Die Apologie des Aristides. Ed. by E. Hennecke, *TU*, IV. Leipzig, 1893.

Appian, *Roman History.* 4 vols., with Eng. trans. by H. White (*LCL*). London, 1912–13.

Archilochus, *The Fragments of Archilochus.* Trans. by G. Davenport. Los Angeles, 1964.

Aristotle, *Historia Animalium.* 3 vols., with Eng. trans. by A. L. Peck (*LCL*). London, 1965–.

The Babylonian Talmud. 18 vols., trans. and ed. by I. Epstein. London, 1961.

Der Babylonische Talmud. 8 vols., ed. by L. Goldschmidt. Berlin and Leipzig, 1899–1922.

Caesar, *The Civil Wars.* With Eng. trans. by A. G. Peskett (*LCL*). London, 1914.

Cicero, *The Speeches.* 6 vols., with Eng. trans. by N. H. Watts, *et al.* (*LCL*). London, 1923–58.

    The Verrine Orations. 2 vols., with Eng. trans. by L. H. G. Greenwood (*LCL*). London, 1943–53.

The Code of Maimonides. Book XIV: The Book of Judges. Trans. by A. M. Hershman. Vol. III of *Yale Judaica Series*, ed. by J. Obermann, L. Ginzberg, and H. A. Wolfson. New Haven, 1949.

Corpus Inscriptionum Graecarum. 4 vols., ed. by A. Boeckhius, *et al.* Berlin, 1828–77.

Corpus Inscriptionum Judaicarum. 2 vols., ed. by J.-B. Frey. Rome and Paris, 1936–52.

Corpus Inscriptionum Semiticarum. 4 pts. Paris, 1881.

Corpus Iuris Civilis. 3 vols., ed. by P. Krueger, T. Mommsen, and R. Schoell. Berlin, 1872–95.

Cyril of Alexandria, *A Commentary upon the Gospel according to S. Luke.* Trans. by R. P. Smith. Oxford, 1859.

Der Dialog des Adamantius. Ed. by W. H. van de Sande Bakhuyzen. Leipzig, 1901.

Didascalia Apostolorum. Syriac version trans. by R. H. Connolly. Oxford, 1929.

Dio Cassius, *Roman History.* 9 vols., with Eng. trans. by E. Cary (*LCL*), London, 1914–27.

Diodorus Siculus. 12 vols., with Eng. trans. by C. H. Oldfather, *et al.* (*LCL*). London, 1933–67.

Epictetus, *The Discourses as Reported by Arrian, the Manual, and Fragments.* 2 vols., with an Eng. trans. by W. A. Oldfather (*LCL*). London, 1926–8.

Εὐαγγέλιον κατὰ Πέτρον. *The Akhmîm Fragment of the Apocryphal Gospel of St Peter,* ed. with intro., notes by H. B. Swete. London, 1893.

Eusebius, *Chronica.* 2 vols., ed. by A. Schoene. Berlin, 1867–75.
  Die Demonstratio Evangelica. Ed. by I. A. Heikel. Leipzig, 1913.
  The Ecclesiastical History. 2 vols., with Eng. trans. by K. Lake and J. E. L. Oulton (*LCL*). London, 1926–32.
  Das Onomastikon der biblischen Ortsnamen. Ed. by E. Klostermann. Leipzig, 1904.

Fayûm Towns and their Papyri. Ed. by B. P. Grenfell, A. S. Hunt, and D. G. Hogarth. London, 1900.

The First Book of Maccabees. Eng. trans. by S. Tedesche with intro. and comm. by S. Zeitlin of *Jewish Apocryphal Literature,* ed. by S. Zeitlin, *et al.* New York, 1950.

Fragments of a Zadokite Work. Vol. 1 of *Documents of Jewish Sectaries,* ed. and trans. by S. Schechter. Cambridge, 1910.

Gamaliel: Äthiopische Texte zur Pilatusliteratur. Trans. by M.-A. van den Oudenrijn. Freiburg, 1959.

Georgii Cyprii, *Descriptio Orbis Romani.* Ed. and comm. by H. Gelzer. Leipzig, 1890.

Gospel of Barnabas. Trans. from Italian MS in the Imperial Library at Vienna by L. and L. Ragg. Oxford, 1907.

The Greek New Testament. Ed. by K. Aland, *et al.* Stuttgart, 1966.

Hegesippi qui Dicitur Historiae Libri V. Ed. by V. Ussani. Vol. LXVI of *Corpus Scriptorum Ecclesiasticorum Latinorum.* Vienna, 1932.

Herodotus. 4 vols., with Eng. trans. by A. O. Godley (*LCL*). London, 1921–5.

Homer, *The Iliad.* 2 vols., with Eng. trans. by A. T. Murray (*LCL*). London, 1924–5.

Itineraria Antonini Augusti et Burdigalense. Ed. by O. Cuntz. Leipzig, 1929.

Jacoby, F., *Die Fragmente der griechischen Historiker.* 3 pts, 14 vols. Berlin, 1925–58.

James, M. R. (trans.), *The Apocryphal New Testament.* 5th impression, Oxford, 1953.

The Jerusalem Talmud. Ed. by B. Behrend. Krotoshin, 1866.

Joseph ben Gurion. Trans. into Latin by S. Münster. Basel, 1541, 1559.
The Wonderful and Most Deplorable History of the Latter Times of the Jews. Trans. by P. Morwyn from Hebrew of A. B. David's abridgement ed. by J. Howell. London, 1671.
Josephi, Flavii, *Opera.* 7 vols., ed. by B. Niese. Berlin, 1887–95.
Œuvres complètes. 7 vols., trans. into French under direction of Th. Reinach. Paris, 1900–29.
Opera Omnia. 6 vols., ed. by S. A. Naber. Leipzig, 1888–96.
9 vols., with Eng. trans. by H. St J. Thackeray, R. Marcus, L. H. Feldman (*LCL*). London, 1926–65.
Justin Martyr, *The Dialogue with Trypho.* Trans., intro., and notes by A. L. Williams. London, 1930.
Kittel, R. (ed.), *Biblia Hebraica*[3]. Stuttgart, 1954.
Lightfoot, J. B., *The Apostolic Fathers*[2]. 2 pts, 5 vols. London, 1889–90.
Livy. 14 vols., with Eng. trans. by B. O. Foster, F. G. Moore, E. T. Sage, and A. C. Schlesinger (*LCL*). London, 1919–59.
Midrasch Tannaim zum Deuteronomium. Ed. by D. Hoffmann. Berlin, 1908–9.
Midrash Rabbah. 10 vols., trans. and ed. by H. Freedman and M. Simon. London, 1961.
The Mishnah. Trans. by H. Danby. London, 1933.
Novum Testamentum Graece[25]. Ed. by E. Nestle and K. Aland. Stuttgart, 1963.
Orientis Graeci Inscriptiones Selectae. 2 vols., ed. by W. Dittenberger. Leipzig, 1903–5.
The Oxyrhynchus Papyri. 31 vols., ed. with trans. and notes by B. P. Grenfell and A. S. Hunt, *et al.* London, 1898–1963.
Patrologia Graeca. Ed. by J.-P. Migne. Paris, 1857–1936.
Patrologia Latina. Ed. by J.-P. Migne. Paris, 1844–1963.
Patrologia Orientalis. Ed. by R. Graffin and F. Nau. Paris, 1907–.
Pausanias, *Description of Greece.* 5 vols., with Eng. trans. by W. H. S. Jones and H. A. Ormerod (*LCL*). London, 1918–35.
Persius, *The Satires.* With Eng. trans. by G. G. Ramsay (*LCL*). London, 1918.
Das Petrusevangelium. Ed. by H. von Schubert. Berlin, 1893.
Philo. 10 vols., with Eng. trans. by F. H. Colson, G. H. Whitaker, and R. Marcus (*LCL*). London, 1929–53.
Philonis Alexandrini, *Legatio ad Gaium.* Ed. with intro., trans., and comm. by E. M. Smallwood. Leiden, 1961.
Pindar, *The Odes of Pindar including the Principal Fragments.* Trans. by J. E. Sandys (*LCL*). London, 1915.
Plato, *Laws.* 2 vols., with Eng. trans. by R. G. Bury (*LCL*). London, 1926.

Plato, *The Republic.* 2 vols., with Eng. trans. by P. Shorey (*LCL*). London, 1930–5.

Pliny, *Natural History.* 10 vols., with Eng. trans. by H. Rackham (*LCL*). London, 1938–63.

Plutarch, *Lives.* 10 vols., with Eng. trans. by B. Perrin (*LCL*). London, 1914–26.

Polybius, *The Histories.* 6 vols., with Eng. trans. by W. R. Paton (*LCL*). London, 1922–7.

Ptolemaei, Claudii, *Geographia.* 3 vols., ed. by C. F. A. Nobbe. Leipzig, 1888–1913.

Rahlfs, A. (ed.), *Septuaginta*[5]. 2 vols. Stuttgart, 1952.

Répertoire d'Épigraphie Sémitique. 2 vols., ed. by J. B. Chabot, *et al.* Paris, 1900–.

Schneemelcher, W. (ed.), *New Testament Apocrypha.* 2 vols., Eng. trans. ed. by R. McL. Wilson. London, 1963–5.

Seneca, *Epistulae Morales.* 3 vols., with Eng. trans. by R. M. Gummere (*LCL*). London, 1917–25.

Solon. Trans. by I. M. Linforth. Berkeley, California, 1919.

Stephanus Byzantinus. 4 vols., ed. by L. Holstein, A. Berkel, and T. de Pinedo. Leipzig, 1825.

Strabo, *The Geography of Strabo.* 8 vols., with Eng. trans. by H. L. Jones (*LCL*). London, 1917–32.

Suetonius, *The Lives of the Caesars and the Lives of Illustrious Men.* 2 vols., with Eng. trans. by J. C. Rolfe (*LCL*). London, 1914.

Syncellus, Georgius, *Chronographiae.* 2 vols., ed. by G. Dindorf. *Corpus Scriptorum Historiae Byzantinae*, ed. by B. G. Niebuhr. Bonn, 1829.

Synopsis Quattuor Evangeliorum[4]. Ed. by K. Aland. Stuttgart, 1965.

Tacitus, *Agricola.* With Eng. trans. by M. Hutton (*LCL*). London, 1932.

The Annals. 3 vols., with Eng. trans. by J. Jackson (*LCL*). London, 1931–7.

The Histories. 2 vols., with Eng. trans. by C. H. Moore (*LCL*). London, 1925–31.

Le Talmud de Jérusalem. 12 vols., trans. by M. Schwab. Paris, 1871–90.

Tatiani, *Evangeliorum Harmoniae.* Ed. and trans. into Latin by P. A. Ciasca. Rome, 1888.

Thucydides, *History of the Peloponnesian War.* 4 vols., with Eng. trans. by C. F. Smith (*LCL*). London, 1919–23.

Tosephta[2]. Based on the Erfurt and Vienna codices with parallels and variants by M. S. Zuckermandel. Jerusalem, 1937.

The Twelve Tables. Vol. iii of *Remains of Old Latin*, ed. and trans. by E. H. Warmington. London, 1938.

Vegetius Renatus, *De re Militari*[2]. Ed. by C. Land. Leipzig, 1885.

C. Velleius Paterculus, *History of Rome.* With Eng. trans. by F. W. Shipley (*LCL*). London, 1924.

Wilcken, U. (ed.), *Griechische Ostraka*. 2 vols. Leipzig and Berlin, 1899.

BOOKS

Abel, F. M., *Géographie de la Palestine*[2]. *EB.* 2 vols. Paris, 1933–8.
Histoire de la Palestine. *EB.* 2 vols. Paris, 1952.
Abrahams, I., *Studies in Pharisaism and the Gospels.* 2 vols. Cambridge, 1917–24.
Aharoni, Y. and Avi-Yonah, M., *The Macmillan Bible Atlas.* New York, 1968.
Allen, W. C. *The Gospel according to Saint Mark.* London, 1915.
A Critical and Exegetical Commentary on the Gospel according to S. Matthew[3]. *ICC.* Edinburgh, 1912.
Alt, A., *Kleine Schriften zur Geschichte des Volkes Israel.* 3 vols. München, 1953–9.
Where Jesus Worked. Trans. by K. Grayston. London, 1961.
André, J., *La vie et l'œuvre d'Asinius Pollion.* Vol. VIII of *Études et Commentaires.* Paris, 1949.
Avi-Yonah, M. *Geschichte der Juden im Zeitalter des Talmud in den Tagen von Rom und Byzanz. SJ,* II. Berlin, 1962.
The Holy Land. Grand Rapids, 1966.
Map of Roman Palestine[2]. London, 1940.
Bachi, R., *et al.*, *Registration of Population (8 ix, 1948).* Pt A. *Towns, Villages and Regions.* Jerusalem, 1955.
Bacon, B. W., *The Gospel of Mark: Its Composition and Date.* New Haven, 1925.
Studies in Matthew. London, 1930.
Bailey, J. A., *The Traditions Common to the Gospels of Luke and John.* *Supplements to NovT,* VII. Leiden, 1963.
Balsdon, J. P. V. D., *The Emperor Gaius (Caligula).* Oxford, 1934.
Baly, D., *Geographical Companion to the Bible.* London, 1963.
The Geography of the Bible. London, 1958.
Barnard, L. W., *Justin Martyr: His Life and Thought.* Cambridge, 1967.
Baron, S. W., *A Social and Religious History of the Jews*[2]. 14 vols. New York, 1952–70.
Barrett, C. K., *The Gospel according to St John.* London, 1955.
Barron, J. B. (comp.), *Palestine: Report and General Abstracts of the Census of 1922.* Jerusalem, 1923.
Bauer, W., *A Greek–English Lexicon of the New Testament and Other Early Christian Literature.* Trans. and adaptation of the 4th rev. and augmented ed. by W. F. Arndt and F. W. Gingrich. Cambridge, 1957.
Das Leben Jesu im Zeitalter der neutestamentlichen Apokryphen. Tübingen, 1909.

Beloch, J., *Die Bevölkerung der griechisch-römischen Welt*. Leipzig, 1886.

Belser, J. E., *History of the Passion, Death, and Glorification of Our Saviour Jesus Christ*. Trans. by F. A. Marks. London, 1929.

Bengel, J. A., *Gnomon of the New Testament*[7]. 4 vols., trans. by J. Bandinel, A. R. Fausset, and J. Bryce. Edinburgh, 1873.

Benoit, P., *The Passion and Resurrection of Jesus Christ*. Trans. by B. Weatherhead. New York and London, 1969.

Bertram, G., *Die Leidensgeschichte Jesu und der Christuskult. FRLANT*, xxxii. Göttingen, 1922.

Bevan, E., *Holy Images*. London, 1940.

Jerusalem Under the High-Priests. London, 1904.

Bienert, W., *Der älteste nichtchristliche Jesusbericht Josephus über Jesus*. Halle, 1936.

Bishop, E. F. F., *Jesus of Palestine: The Local Background to the Gospel Documents*. London, 1955.

Black, M., *An Aramaic Approach to the Gospels and Acts*[3]. Oxford, 1967.

The Scrolls and Christian Origins. London, 1961.

Blakiston, A., *John the Baptist and his Relation to Jesus*. London, 1912.

Blass, F., *Philology of the Gospels*. London, 1898.

and Debrunner, A. *A Greek Grammar of the New Testament and Other Early Christian Literature*. Trans. and rev. of the 9–10th German ed. by R. W. Funk. Cambridge, 1961.

Blinzler, J., *Herodes Antipas und Jesus Christus*. Stuttgart, 1947.

Der Prozess Jesu[4]. Regensburg, 1969.

Bonnard, P., *L'Évangile selon Saint Matthieu. Commentaire du Nouveau Testament*, ed. by J.-J. von Allmen, *et al.*, 1. Neuchâtel, 1963.

Bonsirven, J., *Le judaïsme palestinien du temps de Jésus-Christ*. 2 vols. Paris, 1924.

Bornhaeuser, K., *The Death and Resurrection of Jesus Christ*. Trans. by A. Rumpus. Bangalore, India, 1958.

Bornkamm, G., *Jesus of Nazareth*. Trans. by I. and F. McLuskey with J. M. Robinson. London, 1960.

Bousset, W., *Die Religion des Judentums im späthellenistischen Zeitalter*[3], ed. by H. Gressmann. *HNT*, xxi. Tübingen, 1926.

Bowman, J., *The Gospel of Mark. The New Christian Jewish Passover Haggadah. Studia Post-Biblica*, ed. by P. A. H. DeBoer, *et al.*, viii. Leiden, 1965.

Brandon, S. G. F., *The Fall of Jerusalem and the Christian Church*[2]. London, 1957.

Jesus and the Zealots. Manchester, 1967.

The Trial of Jesus of Nazareth. London, 1968.

Branscomb, B. H., *The Gospel of Mark. The Moffatt New Testament Commentary*, ed. by J. Moffatt. London, 1937.

Brown, F., Driver, S. R., and Briggs, C. A., *A Hebrew and English Lexicon of the Old Testament*. Oxford, 1906.

Brown, R. E., *The Gospel according to John*. 2 vols. *The Anchor Bible*, ed. by W. F. Albright and D. N. Freedman. Garden City, New York, 1966–70.

Bruce, F. F., *The Acts of the Apostles*[2]. London, 1962.
New Testament History. London, 1969.

Büchler, A., *Der galiläische 'Am-ha 'Ares des zweiten Jahrhunderts*. Wien, 1906.
The Political and Social Leaders of the Jewish Community of Sepphoris in the Second and Third Centuries. London, n.d.
Types of Jewish-Palestinian Piety from 70 B.C.E. to 70 C.E. London, 1922.

Buckland, W. W., *A Text-Book of Roman Law from Augustus to Justinian*[3]. Rev. by P. Stein. Cambridge, 1963.

Buhl, F., *Geographie des Alten Palästina*. Freiburg and Leipzig, 1896.

Bultmann, R., *The History of the Synoptic Tradition*. Trans. by J. Marsh. Oxford, 1963.

Burkitt, F. C., *Evangelion Da-Mepharreshe*. 2 vols. Cambridge, 1904.
The Gospel History and its Transmission[3]. Edinburgh, 1911.

Burney, C. F., *The Aramaic Origin of the Fourth Gospel*. Oxford, 1922.

Busch, F. O., *The Five Herods*. Trans. by E. W. Dickes, London, 1958.

Bussmann, W., *Synoptische Studien*. 3 vols. Halle, 1925–31.

Butler, B. C., *The Originality of Matthew*. Cambridge, 1951.

Buzy, D., *The Life of S. John the Baptist*. Trans. by J. M. T. Barton. London, 1933.

Cadbury, H. J., *The Making of Luke–Acts*. London, 1927.

Cadman, W. H., *The Last Journey of Jesus to Jerusalem*. London, 1923.

Caney, R. W. and Reynolds, J. E. (comps.), *Reed's New Marine Distance Tables*. Sunderland, 1965.

Carmichael, J., *The Death of Jesus*. London, 1963.

Case, S. J., *Jesus: A New Biography*. Chicago, 1927.

Charlesworth, M. P., *Five Men: Character Studies from the Roman Empire*. Vol. vi of *Martin Classical Lectures*. Cambridge, Massachusetts, 1936.
Trade-Routes and Commerce of the Roman Empire[2]. Cambridge, 1926.

Christie, W. M., *Palestine Calling*. London, n.d.

Le Clerc, J., *The Harmony of the Evangelists*. London, 1701.

Clinton, H. F., *Fasti Hellenici*. 3 vols. Oxford, 1834.
Fasti Romani. 2 vols. Oxford, 1845–50.

Cole, R. A., *The Gospel according to St Mark. Tyndale New Testament Commentary*, ed. by R. V. G. Tasker. London, 1961.

Conder, C. R. and Kitchener, H. H., *The Survey of Western Palestine*. 3 vols. London, 1881–3.

Conzelmann, H., *The Theology of St Luke*. Trans. G. Buswell. London, 1960.

Cooke, G. A., *A Critical and Exegetical Commentary on the Book of Ezekiel. ICC.* Edinburgh, 1936.

A Text-book of North-Semitic Inscriptions. Oxford, 1903.

Corbett, P. E., *The Roman Law of Marriage.* Oxford, 1930.

Corssen, P., *Monarchianische Prologe zu den Vier Evangelien. TU*, xv. Leipzig, 1896.

Cranfield, C. E. B., *The Gospel according to Saint Mark². The Cambridge Greek Testament Commentary*, ed. by C. F. D. Moule. Cambridge, 1963.

Creed, J. M., *The Gospel according to St Luke.* London, 1930.

Crook, J., *Consilium Principis.* Cambridge, 1955.

Cullmann, O., *The Christology of the New Testament².* Trans. by S. C. Guthrie and C. A. M. Hall. London, 1963.

Jesus and the Revolutionaries. Trans. by G. Putnam. New York, 1970.

The State in the New Testament. London, 1957.

Dalman, G., *Aramäische Dialektproben².* Leipzig, 1927.

Arbeit und Sitte in Palästina. 7 vols. Gütersloh, 1928–42.

Grammatik des jüdisch-palästinischen Aramäisch². Leipzig, 1905.

Jesus-Jeshua. Trans. by P. P. Levertoff. London, 1929.

Sacred Sites and Ways. Trans. by P. P. Levertoff. London, 1935.

The Words of Jesus. Trans. by D. M. Kay. Edinburgh, 1902.

Dancy, J. C., *A Commentary on I Maccabees.* Oxford, 1954.

Daniélou, J., *The Work of John the Baptist.* Trans. by J. A. Horn. Baltimore, 1966.

Daube, D., *The New Testament and Rabbinic Judaism.* London, 1956.

The Sudden in the Scriptures. Leiden, 1964.

Davies, W. D., *Christian Origins and Judaism.* London, 1962.

Invitation to the New Testament. London, 1967.

Paul and Rabbinic Judaism. London, 1955.

The Setting of the Sermon on the Mount. Cambridge, 1964.

Torah in the Messianic Age and/or the Age to Come. JBL Monograph Series, vii. Philadelphia, 1952.

Debevoise, N. C., *A Political History of Parthia.* Chicago, 1938.

Deissmann, A., *Bible Studies².* Trans. by A. Grieve. Edinburgh, 1903.

Dessau, H., *Geschichte der römischen Kaiserzeit.* 2 vols. Berlin, 1924–30.

Dibelius, M., *From Tradition to Gospel².* Trans. by B. L. Woolf. London, 1934.

Die urchristliche Überlieferung von Johannes dem Täufer. FRLANT, xv. Göttingen, 1911.

Dickey, S., *The Constructive Revolution of Jesus.* London, 1923.

Dodd, C. H., *Historical Tradition in the Fourth Gospel.* Cambridge, 1963.

History and the Gospel. London, 1938.
New Testament Studies. Manchester, 1953.
*The Parables of the Kingdom*³. London, 1936.
Domaszewski, A. von, *Die Rangordnung des römischen Heeres*². Rev. by B. Dobson. Köln, 1967.
Downey, G., *A History of Antioch in Syria from Seleucus to the Arab Conquest.* Princeton, 1961.
Driver, S. R., *Notes on the Hebrew Text and Topography of the Books of Samuel*². Oxford, 1913.
Dubnow, S., *Die alte Geschichte des jüdischen Volkes.* Vol. II of *Weltgeschichte des jüdischen Volkes.* Trans. by A. Steinberg. Berlin, 1925.
Dupraz, L., *De l'association de Tibère au principat à la naissance du Christ. Studia Friburgensia*, N.S. XLIII. Fribourg, 1966.
Easton, B. S., *The Gospel according to St Luke.* Edinburgh, 1926.
Eckhel, J., *Doctrina Numorum Veterum.* 8 vols. Vienna, 1792–8.
Edersheim, A., *The Life and Times of Jesus the Messiah*³. 2 vols. London, 1886.
Eisler, R., ΙΗΣΟΥΣ ΒΑΣΙΛΕΥΣ ΟΥ ΒΑΣΙΛΕΥΣΑΣ. 2 vols. Heidelberg, 1929.
The Messiah Jesus and John the Baptist. Trans. by A. H. Krappe. London, 1931.
Ellicott, C. J., *Historical Lectures on the Life of Our Lord Jesus Christ, being the Hulsean Lectures for the Year 1859*². London, 1861.
Elliott-Binns, L. E., *Galilean Christianity. SBT*, no. 16. London, 1956.
Ellis, E. E., *The Gospel of Luke.* New ed. of *The Century Bible.* London, 1966.
Epstein, L. M., *The Jewish Marriage Contract.* New York, 1927.
Marriage Laws in the Bible and Talmud. Cambridge, Massachusetts, 1942.
Ewald, H., *Die drei ersten Evangelien und die Apostelgeschichte*². 2 vols. Göttingen, 1871–2.
*Geschichte des Volkes Israel*²,³. 7 vols. Göttingen, 1864–8.
Farmer, W. R., *The Synoptic Problem.* New York and London, 1964.
Farrar, F. W., *The Herods.* London, 1898.
Feldman, L. H., *Scholarship on Philo and Josephus.* Vol. I of *Studies in Judaica*, ed. by L. D. Stitskin. New York, n.d.
Felten, J., *Neutestamentliche Zeitgeschichte.* 2 vols. Regensburg, 1910.
Field, F., *Notes on the Translation of the New Testament*². Being the Otium Norvicense (Pars Tertia), ed. by A. M. Knight. Cambridge, 1899.
Findlay, A. F., *Byways in Early Christian Literature.* Edinburgh, 1923.
Finegan, J., *Handbook of Biblical Chronology.* Princeton, 1964.
*Light from the Ancient East*². Oxford, 1959.

Finegan, J., *Die Überlieferung der Leidens- und Auferstehungsgeschichte Jesu*. Beiheft to *ZNW*. Giessen, 1934.

Finkel, A., *The Pharisees and the Teacher of Nazareth*. Leiden, 1964.

Finkelstein, L., *Akiba: Scholar, Saint and Martyr*. Philadelphia, 1936.
The Pharisees: The Sociological Background of their Faith[3]. 2 vols. Philadelphia, 1962.

Foakes Jackson, F. J., *Josephus and the Jews*. London, 1930.
and Lake, K. (eds.), *The Beginnings of Christianity*. 5 vols. London, 1920–33.

Foerster, W., *Palestinian Judaism in New Testament Times*. Trans. from 3rd rev. German ed. by G. E. Harris. Edinburgh, 1964.

Frank, E., *Talmudic and Rabbinical Chronology*. New York, 1956.

Frank, T. (ed.), *An Economic Survey of Ancient Rome*. 6 vols. Baltimore, 1933–40.

Frend, W. H. C. *Martyrdom and Persecution in the Early Church*. Oxford, 1965.

Frey, J., *Der slavische Josephusbericht*. Dorpat, 1908.

Friedländer, L., *Darstellungen aus der Sittengeschichte Roms*[10]. 4 vols. Leipzig, 1921–3.

Fullard, H. (ed.), *The Mercantile Marine Atlas*[16]. London, 1959.

Gams, B., *Johannes der Täufer im Gefängnisse*. Tübingen, 1853.

Gärtner, B., *The Theology of the Gospel of Thomas*. Trans. by E. J. Sharpe. London, 1961.

Gaster, M., *The Samaritans: Their History, Doctrines and Literature*. Schweich Lectures. London, 1925.
(comp.), *Studies and Texts in Folklore, Magic, Mediaeval Romance, Hebrew Apocrypha and Samaritan Archaeology*. 3 vols. London, 1925–8.

Geiger, A., *Urschrift und Uebersetzungen der Bibel*. Breslau, 1857.

Geldenhuys, N., *Commentary on the Gospel of Luke*. London, 1950.

Ginsburg, M., *Rome et la Judée*. Paris, 1928.

Ginzberg, L., *Eine unbekannte jüdische Sekte*. New York, 1922.
The Legends of the Jews. 7 vols. Trans. by H. S. Zold. Philadelphia, 1909–38.

Glueck, N., *Deities and Dolphins: The Story of the Nabataeans*. London, 1966.

Godet, F., *A Commentary on the Gospel of St Luke*[5]. Trans. from 2nd French ed. by E. W. Shalders and M. D. Cusin. Edinburgh, n.d.

Goguel, M., *The Life of Jesus*. Trans. by O. Wyon. London, 1933.
Au seuil de l'Évangile: Jean-Baptiste. Paris, 1928.

Goodenough, E. R., *An Introduction to Philo Judaeus*[2]. Oxford, 1962.
Jewish Symbols in the Greco-Roman Period. 13 vols. New York, 1953–68.

The Politics of Philo Judaeus with *A General Bibliography of Philo* by H. L. Goodhart and E. R. Goodenough. New Haven, 1938.

Gould, E. P., *A Critical and Exegetical Commentary on the Gospel according to St Mark. ICC.* Edinburgh, 1896.

Graetz, H., *Geschichte der Juden*[3]. 11 vols. Leipzig, 1897–1911.

Grandmaison, L. de, *Jesus Christ.* 3 vols. Trans. by D. B. Wheelan, A. Lane, and D. Carter. London, 1930–4.

Grant, F. C. *The Economic Background of the Gospels.* London, 1926.

Grollenberg, L. H. *Atlas of the Bible.* Trans. and ed. by J. M. H. Reid and H. H. Rowley. London, 1956.

Shorter Atlas of the Bible. Trans. by M. F. Hedlund. Edinburgh, 1959.

Grundmann, W., *Das Evangelium nach Lukas*[2]. *THNT*, III. Berlin, 1961.

Das Evangelium nach Markus[2]. *THNT*, II. Berlin, 1959.

Das Evangelium nach Matthäus. THNT, I. Berlin, 1968.

Guignebert, C., *Jesus.* Trans. by S. H. Hooke. London, 1935.

The Jewish World in the Time of Jesus. Trans. by S. H. Hooke. London, 1939.

Gulak, A., *Das Urkundenwesen im Talmud.* Jerusalem, 1935.

Guthe, H., *Bibelatlas.* Leipzig, 1911.

Die griechisch-römischen Städte des Ostjordanlandes. Vol. II of *Das Land der Bibel.* Leipzig, 1918.

Guthrie, D., *New Testament Introduction*[3]. London, 1970.

Haenchen, E., *Die Apostelgeschichte. KEK*[15]. Göttingen, 1968.

Der Weg Jesu. Berlin, 1966.

Harduini, J., *Chronologiae ex Nummis Antiquis Restitutae Prolusio. De Nummis Herodiadum.* Paris, 1693.

Harlow, V. E., *The Destroyer of Jesus: The Story of Herod Antipas, Tetrarch of Galilee.* Oklahoma City, 1954.

Harnack, A., *Luke the Physician.* Trans. by J. R. Wilkinson. London, 1907.

Die Mission und Ausbreitung des Christentums[4]. 2 vols. Leipzig, 1924.

Harris, R., *Testimonies.* 2 pts. Cambridge, 1916.

The Hashemite Kingdom of Jordan, Department of Statistics, *First Census of Population and Housing, 18th November, 1961.* Amman, 1964.

First Census of Population and Housing, 18th November, 1961. Interim Report no. 4. *Distribution and Characteristics of Population, Al-Balqa District.* N.p., 1963.

First Census of Population and Housing, 18th November, 1961. Interim Report no. 6. *Distribution and Characteristics of Population, Amman District.* N.p., 1963.

Hatch, E. and Redpath, H. A., *A Concordance to the Septuagint and Other Greek Versions of the Old Testament.* 3 vols. Oxford, 1897–1906.

Hausrath, A., *A History of the New Testament Times: The Time of Jesus*[2,3]. Trans. by C. T. Poynting and P. Quenzer. London, 1878–80.

Hawkins, J. C. *Horae Synopticae*[2]. Oxford, 1909.

Head, B. V., *Historia Numorum*[2]. Oxford, 1911.

Headlam, A. C., *The Life and Teaching of Jesus Christ.* London, 1923.

Hengel, M., *Die Zeloten.* Leiden and Köln, 1961.

Herford, R. T., *Christianity in Talmud and Midrash.* London, 1903.
Judaism in the New Testament Period. London, 1928.
The Pharisees. New York, 1924.

Herzog, I., *The Main Institutions of Jewish Law.* 2 vols. London, 1936–9.

Hildesheimer, H., *Beiträge zur Geographie Palästinas.* Berlin, 1886.

Hill, G. F., *Catalogue of the Greek Coins of Palestine.* London, 1914.

Hill, J. H., *The Earliest Life of Jesus ever Compiled from the Four Gospels being the Diatessaron of Tatian.* Edinburgh, 1894.

Hirschfeld, O., *Die kaiserlichen Verwaltungsbeamten bis auf Diocletian*[2]. Berlin, 1905.

Hölscher, G., *Die Quellen des Josephus.* Leipzig, 1904.

Holtzmann, H. J., *Die Synoptiker.* Vol. 1 of *Hand-Commentar zum Neuen Testament.* Freiburg, 1889.

Holtzmann, O., *Das Neue Testament.* 2 vols. Giessen, 1926.

Hultsch, F., *Griechische und römische Metrologie*[2]. Berlin, 1882.

Husband, R. W., *The Prosecution of Jesus.* Princeton, 1916.

Hyamson, A. M., Mason, K., and Myres, J. L., *Palestine and Transjordan.* Oxford, 1943.

Jack, J. W., *The Historic Christ: An Examination of Dr Eisler's Theory according to the Slavonic Version of Josephus.* London, 1933.

Jastrow, M. (comp.), *A Dictionary of the Targumim, the Talmud Babli and Yerushalmi, and the Midrashic Literature.* 2 vols. London, 1903.

Jaubert, A., *The Date of the Last Supper.* Trans. by I. Rafferty. Staten Island, New York, 1965.

Jeremias, J., *The Eucharistic Words of Jesus.* Trans. from 3rd German ed. by N. Perrin. London, 1966.
Jerusalem in the Time of Jesus. Trans. from the 3rd German ed. (with the author's rev. to 1967) by F. H. and C. H. Cave. London, 1969.

Johnson, S. E., *Jesus in His Own Times.* London, 1957.

Jolowicz, H. F., *Historical Introduction to the Study of Roman Law*[2]. Cambridge, 1952.

Jones, A. H. M., *Cities of the Eastern Roman Provinces.* Oxford, 1940.

The Greek City from Alexander to Justinian. Oxford, 1940.

The Herods of Judaea. Oxford, 1938.

Studies in Roman Government and Law. Oxford, 1960.

Juster, J., *Les Juifs dans l'empire Romain.* 2 vols. Paris, 1914.

Kahrstedt, U., *Artabanos III. und Seine Erben.* Bern, 1950.

Kammerer, A., *Pétra et la Nabatène.* 2 vols. Paris, 1929.

Kaser, M., *Das römische Privatrecht.* 2 vols. München, 1955–9.

Kaster, K., *Jesus vor Pilatus: ein Beitrag zur Leidensgeschichte des Herrn.* Vol. IV of *Neutestamentliche Abhandlungen* ed. by M. Meinertz. Münster, 1914.

Keil, C. F., *Biblical Commentary on the Prophecies of Ezekiel.* 2 vols. Trans. by J. Martin. Edinburgh, 1876.

Keim, T., *The History of Jesus of Nazara.* 6 vols. Trans. by E. M. Geldart and A. Ransom. London, 1873–83.

Kennard, J. S., *Render to God: A Study of the Tribute Passage.* New York, 1950.

Kilpatrick, G. D., *The Trial of Jesus.* Sixth lecture of Friends of Dr Williams's Library, 1952. London, 1953.

Kindler, A., *The Coins of Tiberias.* Tiberias, 1961.

Kittel, G., *Die Probleme des palästinischen Spätjudentums und des Urchristentums.* Stuttgart, 1926.

Klausner, J., *Jesus of Nazareth.* Trans. by H. Danby. London, 1929.

Klein, S., *Beiträge zur Geographie und Geschichte Galiläas.* Leipzig, 1909.

Neue Beiträge zur Geschichte und Geographie Galiläas. Heft 1 of *Palästina-Studien.* Wien, 1923.

Klijn, A. F. J., *The Acts of Thomas. Supplements to NovT,* v. Leiden, 1962.

Klostermann, A., *Die Bücher Samuelis und der Könige. Kurzgefasster Kommentar,* ed. by H. Strack and O. Zöckler. Nordlingen, 1887.

Klostermann, E., *Das Lukasevangelium².HNT,* v. Tübingen, 1929.

Das Markusevangelium³.HNT, III. Tübingen, 1936.

Das Matthäusevangelium².HNT, IV. Tübingen, 1927.

Knox, W. L., *The Sources of the Synoptic Gospels.* 2 vols. Cambridge, 1953–7.

Kohl, H. and Watzinger, C., *Antike Synagogen in Galilaea.* Leipzig, 1916.

Kopp, C., *The Holy Places of the Gospels.* Trans. by R. Walls. Freiburg, 1963.

Kornemann, E., *Tiberius.* Stuttgart, 1960.

Kraeling, C. H., *John the Baptist.* New York and London, 1951.

Kraeling, E. G., *Rand McNally Bible Atlas.* London, 1956.

Krauss, S., *Griechische und lateinische Lehnwörter im Talmud, Midrasch und Targum.* 2 vols. Berlin, 1898–9.

Talmudische Archäologie. 3 vols. Leipzig, 1910–12.

Kuhn, E., *Die städtische und bürgerliche Verfassung des römischen Reichs bis auf die Zeiten Justinians*. 2 vols. Leipzig, 1864–5.

Über die Entstehung der Städte der Alten. Komenverfassung und Synoikismos. Leipzig, 1878.

Kümmel, W. G., *Introduction to the New Testament*. Trans. from 14th rev. ed. by A. J. Mattill. London, 1966.

Promise and Fulfilment[3]. Trans. by D. M. Barton. *STB*, no. 23. London, 1957.

Lagercrantz, O., *Papyrus Graecus Holmiensis. Recepte für Silber, Steine und Purpur*. Uppsala and Leipzig, 1913.

Lagrange, M.-J., *Évangile selon Saint Luc*[8]. *EB*. Paris, 1948.

Évangile selon Saint Marc[4]. *EB*. Paris, 1928.

The Gospel of Jesus Christ. 2 vols. Trans. by the Members of the English Dominican Province, 1938.

Le Judaïsme avant Jésus-Christ. *EB*. Paris, 1931.

Lampe, G. W. H. (ed.), *A Patristic Greek Lexicon*. Oxford, 1961–9.

Laqueur, R., *Der jüdische Historiker Flavius Josephus*. Giessen, 1920.

Lenski, R. C. H., *Interpretation of St Matthew's Gospel*. Columbus, Ohio, 1932.

Levick, B., *Roman Colonies in Southern Asia Minor*. Oxford, 1967.

Levy, J., *Chaldäisches Wörterbuch über die Targumim und einen grossen Theil des rabbinischen Schriftthums*. Leipzig, 1867.

Neuhebräisches und Chaldäisches Wörterbuch über die Talmudim und Midrashim. 4 vols. 1889.

Lewin, T., *Fasti Sacri or a Key to the Chronology of the New Testament*. London, 1865.

Liberty, S., *The Political Relations of Christ's Ministry*. London, 1916.

Liddell, H. G. and Scott, R. (comps.), *A Greek–English Lexicon*[9]. New ed. rev. and augmented by H. S. Jones. Oxford, 1940.

Lightfoot, J., *Horae Hebraicae et Talmudicae*. 4 vols. New ed. by R. Gandell. Oxford, 1859.

Lightfoot, R. H., *History and Interpretation in the Gospels*. London, 1935.

Lightley, J. W., *Jewish Sects and Parties in the Time of Christ*. London, 1925.

Lizop, R., *Histoire de deux cités Gallo-Romaines, Les Convenae et les Consoranni*. 2nd series, vol. xxv of *Bibliothèque Méridionale*. Toulouse and Paris, 1931.

Loewe, H., *Render unto Caesar*. Cambridge, 1940.

Lohmeyer, E., *Das Evangelium des Markus*, with Ergänzungsheft ed. by G. Sass. *KEK*[12]. Göttingen, 1953.

Das Evangelium des Matthäus[3], ed. by W. Schmauch. *KEK*. Göttingen, 1962.

Das Urchristentum, I. Johannes der Täufer. Göttingen, 1932.

Lohse, E., *History of the Suffering and Death of Jesus Christ*. Trans. by M. O. Dietrich. Philadelphia, 1967.

Loisy, A., *Les Évangiles Synoptiques*. 2 vols. Paris, 1907–8.

Löw, I., *Die Flora der Juden*. Vol. II. Wien and Leipzig, 1924.

Luke, H. and Keith-Roach, E., *The Handbook of Palestine and Trans-Jordan*[3]. London, 1934.

MacDonald, J., *The Theology of the Samaritans*. London, 1964.

M'Neile, A. H., *The Gospel according to St Matthew*. London, 1915.

Madden, F. W., *Coins of the Jews*. Vol. II of *The International Numismata Orientalia*. London, 1881.

   History of Jewish Coinage and of Money in the Old and New Testament. London, 1864.

Magie, D., *Roman Rule in Asia Minor*. 2 vols. Princeton, 1950.

Manson, T. W., *The Sayings of Jesus*. London, 1949.

   The Servant-Messiah. Cambridge, 1953.

   The Teaching of Jesus[2]. Cambridge, 1935.

Marañón, G., *Tiberius: A Study of Resentment*. Trans. by W. B. Wells. London, 1956.

Marriott, H., *The Sermon on the Mount*. London, 1925.

Marsh, F. B., *The Reign of Tiberius*. London, 1931.

Masterman, E. W. G., *Studies in Galilee*. Chicago, 1909.

Matthews, B., *A Life of Jesus*[2]. London, 1934.

Mattingly, H., *The Imperial Civil Service of Rome*. Cambridge, 1910.

May, H. G., Hamilton, R. W., and Hunt, G. N. S. (eds.), *Oxford Bible Atlas*. London, 1962.

Mayer, L. A., *A Bibliography of Jewish Numismatics*. Jerusalem, 1966.

Merrill, S., *East of the Jordan*. London, 1881.

   Galilee in the Time of Christ. London, 1885.

Merx, A., *Die Evangelien des Markus und Lukas*. Berlin, 1905.

   Das Evangelium Matthaeus. Berlin, 1902.

Metzger, B. M., *An Introduction to the Apocrypha*. New York, 1957.

Meyer, A., *Jesu Muttersprache*. Freiburg and Leipzig, 1896.

Meyer, E., *Ursprung und Anfänge des Christentums*. 3 vols. Stuttgart and Berlin, 1923–5.

Meyer, H. A. W., *Critical and Exegetical Handbook to the Gospels of Mark and Luke*. Trans. from 5th German ed. by R. E. Wallis, trans. rev. and ed. by W. P. Dickson. Edinburgh, 1880.

   Critical and Exegetical Handbook to the Gospel of Matthew. 2 vols. Trans. from 6th German ed. by P. Christie, trans. rev. and ed. by F. Crombie and W. Stewart. Edinburgh, 1877–9.

Meyer, R., *Der Profet aus Galiläa, eine Studie zum Jesusbild der ersten drei Evangelien*. Leipzig, 1940.

Mielziner, M., *The Jewish Law of Marriage and Divorce*. Cincinnati, 1884.

Mills, E., *Census of Palestine 1931*. 2 vols. Jerusalem and Alexandria, 1932–3.

Minkin, J. S., *Herod, King of the Jews*. New York, 1936.

Mionnet, T. E., *Description de médailles antiques grecques et romains*. 6 vols. Paris, 1806–37.

Mommsen, T., *Epigraphische und numismatische Schriften*. Vol. VIII of *Gesammelte Schriften*. Berlin, 1913.

Geschichte des römischen Münzwesens. Berlin, 1860.

The Provinces of the Roman Empire. 2 vols. Trans. by W. P. Dickson. London, 1909.

Römisches Staatsrecht[3]. 2 vols. Leipzig, 1887.

Römisches Strafrecht. Leipzig, 1899.

Montefiore, C. G. (ed.), *The Synoptic Gospels*[2]. 2 vols. London, 1927.

Montefiore, H., *Josephus and the New Testament*. London, 1962.

Montgomery, J. A., *The Samaritans*. Philadelphia, 1907.

and Gehman, H. S. (eds.), *A Critical and Exegetical Commentary on the Books of Kings*. ICC. Edinburgh, 1951.

Moore, G. F. *A Critical and Exegetical Commentary on Judges*[2]. ICC. Edinburgh, 1908.

Judaism. 3 vols. Cambridge, Massachusetts, 1927–30.

Morison, F., *And Pilate Said: A New Study of the Roman Procurator*. London, 1939.

Morrison, W. D., *The Jews under Roman Rule*. London, 1890.

Moule, C. F. D., *The Gospel according to Mark. The Cambridge Bible Commentary*, ed. by P. R. Ackroyd, A. R. C. Leaney, and J. W. Packer. Cambridge, 1965.

An Idiom Book of New Testament Greek[2]. Cambridge, 1959.

The Phenomenon of the New Testament. SBT, N.S. no. 1. London, 1967.

Moulton, J. H., Howard, W. F., and Turner, N., *A Grammar of New Testament Greek*. 3 vols. Edinburgh, 1908–63.

Moulton, J. H. and Milligan, G., *The Vocabulary of the Greek Testament*. London, 1930.

Moulton, W. F. and Geden, A. S. (eds.), *A Concordance to the Greek Testament*[2]. Edinburgh, 1899.

Muirhead, J., *Historical Introduction to the Private Law of Rome*[2]. Rev. and ed. by H. Goudy. London, 1899.

Neubauer, A., *La Géographie du Talmud*. Paris, 1868.

Neusner, J., *A Life of Rabban Yohanan ben Zakkai Ca. 1–80 C.E. Studia Post-Biblica*, ed. by P. A. H. DeBoer, *et al.*, VI. Leiden, 1962.

Nineham, D. E., *The Gospel of St Mark*[2]. London, 1968.

Ogg, G., *The Chronology of the Public Ministry of Jesus*. Cambridge, 1940.

Olmstead, A. T., *Jesus in the Light of History*. New York, 1942.

Otto, W., *Herodes: Beiträge zur Geschichte des letzten jüdischen Königshauses*. Stuttgart, 1913.

Pallis, A., *A Few Notes on the Gospels according to St Mark and St Matthew*. Liverpool, 1903.

Parker, H. M. D., *The Roman Legions*. Cambridge, 1958.

Parker, R. A. and Dubberstein, W. H., *Babylonian Chronology 626 B.C. – A.D. 75*[2]. Providence, 1956.

Parrot, A., *Land of Christ*. Trans. by J. H. Farley. Philadelphia, 1968.

Perowne, S., *The Later Herods*. London, 1958.
The Life and Times of Herod the Great. London, 1957.

Perrin, N., *Rediscovering the Teaching of Jesus*. London, 1967.

Perry, A. M., *The Sources of Luke's Passion-Narrative*. 2nd series, vol. IV, pt II of *Historical and Linguistic Studies in Literature Related to the New Testament*. Chicago, 1920.

Peterson, E., *Theologische Traktate*. München, 1951.

Pfeiffer, R. H., *History of New Testament Times*. London, 1949.

Pickl, J., *Messiaskönig Jesus in der Auffassung seiner Zeitgenossen*[2]. München, 1935.

Plummer, A., *A Critical and Exegetical Commentary on the Gospel according to St Luke*[4]. ICC. Edinburgh, 1905.
An Exegetical Commentary on the Gospel according to S. Matthew[2]. London, 1909.

Podro, J., *The Last Pharisee*. London, 1959.

Prosopographia Imperii Romani[2]. 4 vols., ed. by E. Groag and A. Stein. Berlin and Leipzig, 1933–66.

Rabin, C., *Qumran Studies*. London, 1957.

Radin, M., *The Jews Among the Greeks and Romans*. Philadelphia, 1915.
The Trial of Jesus of Nazareth. Chicago, 1931.

Ramsay, W. M., *The Bearing of Recent Discovery on the Trustworthiness of the New Testament*[4]. London, 1920.
St Paul the Traveller and the Roman Citizen[14]. London, 1920.
Was Christ Born at Bethlehem?[2]. London, 1898.

Rawlinson, A. E. J., *St Mark*[5]. Westminster Commentaries. London, 1942.

Rawlinson, G., *The Sixth Great Oriental Monarchy; or the Geography, History, and Antiquities of Parthia*. London, 1873.

Rehkopf, F., *Die lukanische Sonderquelle*. Vol. v of *Wissenschaftliche Untersuchungen zum Neuen Testament*, ed. by J. Jeremias and O. Michel. Tübingen, 1959.

Reicke, B., *The New Testament Era*. Trans. by D. E. Green. Philadelphia, 1968.

Reifenberg, A., *Ancient Jewish Coins*[2]. Jerusalem, 1947.
Israel's History in Coins. London, 1953.
Portrait Coins of the Herodian Kings. London, 1935.

Reimarus, S. (pseud.), *Stoffgeschichten der Salome-dichtungen, nebst einer Analyse des Marcus-evangeliums*. Leipzig, 1913.

Renan, E., *The Life of Jesus*. London, 1867.

Rengstorf, K. H., *Das Evangelium nach Lukas*[8]. *NTD*, III. Göttingen, 1958.

Riddle, D. W., *Jesus and the Pharisees*. Chicago, 1928.

Riesenfeld, H., *Jésus Transfiguré*. Vol. XVI of *Acta Seminarii Neotestamentici Upsaliensis*. Lund, 1947.

Ritter, C., *Die Erdkunde im Verhältniss zur Natur und der Geschichte des Menschen oder Allgemeine vergleichende Geographie*[2]. 19 vols. 1822–59.

Robert, A. and Tourney, R. (eds.), *Le Cantique des Cantiques*. *EB*. Paris, 1963.

Robertson, A. T., *A Grammar of the Greek New Testament in the Light of Historical Research*[3]. London, 1919.

John the Loyal. London, 1912.

The Pharisees and Jesus. London, 1920.

Robinson, E., *Biblical Researches in Palestine and Adjacent Regions*[3]. 3 vols. London, 1867.

Robinson, L., 'Judaea under the Procurators'. Unpublished M.Litt. dissertation, University of Cambridge, 1926.

Robinson, W. C., Jr, *The Way of the Lord. A Study of History and Eschatology in the Gospel of Luke*. D.Theol. dissertation, University of Basel, 1962.

Rogers, E., *A Handy Guide to Jewish Coins*. London, 1914.

Romanoff, P., *Jewish Symbols on Ancient Jewish Coins*. Philadelphia, 1944.

Rostovtzeff, M., *Caravan Cities*. Trans. by D. and T. Talbot Rice. Oxford, 1932.

The Social and Economic History of the Hellenistic World. 3 vols. Oxford, 1941.

The Social and Economic History of the Roman Empire[2]. 2 vols., rev. by P. M. Fraser. Oxford, 1957.

Rostowzew [=Rostovtzeff], M., *Studien zur Geschichte des römischen Kolonates*. Beiheft 1 to *Archiv für Papyrusforschung und verwandte Gebiete*. Leipzig and Berlin, 1910.

Rowe, A., *The Topography and History of Beth-Shan*. Philadelphia, 1930.

Ruckstuhl, E., *Chronology of the Last Days of Jesus*. Trans. by V. J. Drapela. New York, 1965.

Rushbrooke, W. G., *Synopticon*. London, 1880.

Sacaze, J., *Inscriptions Antiques des Pyrénées*. 2nd series, Vol. II of *Bibliothèque Méridionale*. Toulouse, 1892.

Sanders, J. N., *A Commentary on the Gospel according to St John*. Ed. and completed by B. A. Mastin. London, 1968.

Sandmel, S., *Herod: Profile of a Tyrant*. Philadelphia, 1967.

De Saulcy, C., *Histoire d'Hérode, roi des Juifs*. Paris, 1867.

Mélanges de Numismatique. 3 vols. Paris, 1875–82.

Numismatique de la Terre Sainte. Paris, 1874.

Schalit, A., *König Herodes: Der Mann und sein Werk. SJ*, IV. Berlin, 1969.

Namenwörterbuch zu Flavius Josephus. Leiden, 1968.

Schlatter, A., *Die Evangelien nach Markus und Lukas.* Stuttgart, 1947.

Der Evangelist Matthäus. Stuttgart, 1948.

Das Evangelium des Lukas. Stuttgart, 1931.

Geschichte Israels[3]. Stuttgart, 1925.

Markus: Der Evangelist für die Griechen. Stuttgart, 1935.

Schleiermacher, F., *A Critical Essay on the Gospel of St Luke.* Intro. and trans. by [C. Thirlwall]. London, 1825.

Schmidt, K. L., *Der Rahmen der Geschichte Jesu.* Berlin, 1919.

Schnackenburg, R., *The Moral Teaching of the New Testament.* Trans. from 2nd rev. ed. by J. Holland-Smith and W. J. O'Hara. Freiburg and London, 1965.

Schneider, C., *Geistesgeschichte des antiken Christentums.* 2 vols. München, 1954.

Schniewind, J., *Das Evangelium nach Markus*[8]. *NTD*, I. Göttingen, 1958.

Das Evangelium nach Matthäus[8]. *NTD*, II. Göttingen, 1956.

Schofield, G., *Crime before Calvary: Herodias, Herod Antipas, and Pontius Pilate; a New Interpretation.* London, 1960.

Schonfield, H. J., *The Passover Plot.* London, 1965.

Schulz, F., *Classical Roman Law.* Oxford, 1951.

Schumacher, G., *Pella.* London, 1888.

Schürer, E., *Geschichte des jüdischen Volkes im Zeitalter Jesu Christi*[4]. 3 vols. Leipzig, 1901–9.

Schütz, R., *Johannes der Täufer. Abhandlungen zur Theologie des Alten und Neuen Testaments.* L. Zürich and Stuttgart, 1967.

Schweizer, E., *Das Evangelium nach Markus. NTD*, I. Göttingen, 1967.

Lordship and Discipleship. SBT, no. 28. London, 1960.

Scobie, C. H. H., *John the Baptist.* London, 1964.

Sevenster, J. N., *Do You Know Greek? How much Greek could the first century Jewish Christians have known?* Supplements to *NovT*, XIX. Leiden, 1968.

Sherwin-White, A. N., *Roman Society and Roman Law in the New Testament.* Oxford, 1963.

Shutt, R. J. H., *Studies in Josephus.* London, 1961.

Simons, J., *The Geographical and Topographical Texts of the Old Testament.* Leiden, 1959.

Smallwood, E. M., 'The Relations between the Jews and the Roman Government from 66 B.C. to the Foundation of the Christian Empire.' Unpublished Ph.D. dissertation, University of Cambridge, 1950.

Smith, B. T. D., *The Parables of the Synoptic Gospels*. Cambridge, 1937.

Smith, D., *The Days of His Flesh*. London, 1905.

The Life and Letters of St Paul. London, 1919.

Smith, G. A., *Historical Atlas of the Holy Land*. London, 1936.

The Historical Geography of the Holy Land[25]. London, 1931.

Snaith, N. H., *The Jewish New Year Festival*. London, 1947.

Spitta, F., *Streitfragen der Geschichte Jesu*. Göttingen, 1907.

Stanton, V. H., *The Gospels as Historical Documents*. 3 pts. Cambridge, 1903–20.

Stapfer, E., *Palestine in the Time of Christ*[3]. Trans. by A. H. Holmden. London, 1886.

State of Israel, Central Bureau of Statistics, *Demographic Characteristics of the Population*. Pt 1. *Population and Housing Census, 1961*. Publication no. 7. Jerusalem, 1962.

The Division of the State of Israel into Regions for Statistical Purposes. Population and Housing, 1961. Publication no. 20. Jerusalem, 1964.

Statistical Yearbook. The Hashemite Kingdom of Jordan, Department of Statistics. Amman, 1963.

Stauffer, E., *Jerusalem und Rom im Zeitalter Jesu Christi*. Bern and München, 1957.

Jesus and His Story. Trans. D. M. Barton. London, 1960.

Steinberg, S. H. and Paxton, J. (eds.), *The Statesman's Year-Book, 1969–1970*, London, 1969.

Steinmann, J., *Saint John the Baptist*. Trans. by M. Boyes. London, 1958.

Stevenson, G. H., *Roman Provincial Administration till the Age of the Antonines*. Oxford, 1939.

Stonehouse, N. B., *The Witness of Luke to Christ*. London, 1951.

Strack, H. L., *Introduction to the Talmud and Midrash*. Trans. from 5th German ed. Philadelphia, 1931.

and Billerbeck, P., *Kommentar zum Neuen Testament aus Talmud und Midrasch*. 6 vols. München, 1922–61.

Le Strange, G., *Palestine under the Moslems*. London, 1890.

Streeter, B. H., *The Four Gospels*. 5th impression. London, 1936.

Sutcliffe, E. G., *A Two Year Public Ministry Defended*. London, 1938.

Swete, H. B., *The Gospel according to St Mark*[3]. London, 1909.

Tasker, R. V. G., *The Gospel according to St Matthew. Tyndale New Testament Commentary*, ed. by R. V. G. Tasker. London, 1961.

Taubenschlag, R., *The Law of Greco-Roman Egypt in the Light of the Papyri 332 B.C. – 640 A.D.*[2]. Warsaw, 1955.

Täubler, E., *Die Parthernachrichten bei Josephus*. Inaugural dissertation, Friedrich-Wilhelms-Universität zu Berlin, 1904.

Taylor, V., *Behind the Third Gospel*. Oxford, 1926.

*The Gospel according to St Mark*². London, 1966.

Jesus and His Sacrifice. London, 1959.

The Life and Ministry of Jesus. London, 1954.

Thackeray, S. St J., *Josephus: The Man and the Historian*. New York, 1929.

Thiele, E. R., *The Mysterious Numbers of the Hebrew Kings*². London, 1966.

Thomas, J., *Le mouvement Baptiste en Palestine et Syrie*. Gembloux, 1935.

Thomsen, P., *Loca Sancta*. Halle, 1907.

Torrey, C. C., *The Four Gospels*. London, n.d.

Tristram, H. B., *The Land of Moab*². London, 1874.

Turner, H. E. W., *Jesus Master and Lord*. London, 1953.

Turner, N., *Grammatical Insights into the New Testament*. Edinburgh, 1965.

Unger, M. F., *Archaeology and the New Testament*. London, 1964.

Vincent, L. H. and Steve, M. A., *Jérusalem de l'Ancien Testament. Recherches d'Archéologie et d'Histoire*. 3 pts. Paris, 1956.

Vogelstein, H., *Die Landwirtschaft in Palästina*. Berlin, 1894.

Wacholder, B. Z., *Nicolaus of Damascus*. Vol. LXXV of the *University of California Publications in History*. Berkeley and Los Angeles, 1962.

Walker, R., *Die Heilsgeschichte im ersten Evangelium*, FRLANT, XCI. Göttingen, 1967.

Waterman, L., *Preliminary Report of the University of Michigan Excavations at Sepphoris, Palestine, in 1931*. Ann Arbor, 1937.

Weiss, B., *Die Evangelien des Markus und Lukas. KEK*⁹. Göttingen, 1901.

*Das Johannes-Evangelium. KEK*⁹. Göttingen, 1902.

The Life of Christ. 3 vols. Trans. by J. W. Hope. Edinburgh, 1883–4.

*Das Matthäus-Evangelium. KEK*⁷. Göttingen, 1898.

Weiss, J. (ed.), *Die Schriften des Neuen Testaments*³. 4 vols., ed. by W. Bousset and W. Heitmüller. Göttingen, 1917–20.

Wellhausen, H., *Einleitung in die drei ersten Evangelien*². Berlin, 1911.

Das Evangelium Lucae. Berlin, 1904.

*Das Evangelium Marci*². Berlin, 1909.

*Israelitische und jüdische Geschichte*⁷. Berlin, 1914.

*Prolegomena zur Geschichte Israels*⁶. Berlin, 1905.

Wendt, H. H., *The Teaching of Jesus*. 2 vols. Trans. by J. Wilson. Edinburgh, 1909–11.

Westcott, B. F., *The Epistle to the Hebrews*³. London, 1903.

Wickes, D. R., *The Sources of Luke's Perean Section*. 2nd series, vol. II, pt II of *Historical and Linguistic Studies in Literature Related to the New Testament*. Chicago, 1912.

Wieseler, K., *Beiträge zur richtigen Würdigung der Evangelien und der evangelischen Geschichte*. Gotha, 1869.

A Chronological Synopsis of the Four Gospels[2]. Rev. and corrected, trans. by E. Venables. London, 1877.

Wilcox, M., *The Semitisms of Acts*. Oxford, 1965.

Wilke, C. G., *Der Urevangelist*. Dresden and Leipzig, 1838.

Willet, W. M., *Herod Antipas: Sequel to Herod the Great*. New York, 1866.

Williams, A. L., *St Matthew. The Pulpit Commentary*. 2 vols., ed. by H. D. M. Spence and J. S. Exell. London, 1906.

Williamson, G. A., *The World of Josephus*. London, 1964.

Willrich, H., *Das Haus des Herodes*. Heidelberg, 1929.

Wilson, W. R., *The Execution of Jesus*, New York, 1970.

Wink, W., *John the Baptist in the Gospel Tradition*. Vol. VII of *Society for New Testament Studies Monograph Series*, ed. by M. Black. Cambridge, 1968.

Winter, P., *On the Trial of Jesus. SJ*, I. Berlin, 1961.

Wohlenberg, G., *Das Evangelium des Markus*[1,2]. *KNT*, II. Leipzig, 1910.

Wright, G. E. and Filson, F. V. (eds.), *The Westminster Historical Atlas to the Bible*. London, 1946.

Yaron, R., *Gifts in Contemplation of Death in Jewish and Roman Law*. Oxford, 1960.

Zahn, T., *Das Evangelium des Lucas*[1,2]. *KNT*, III. Leipzig, 1913.

Das Evangelium des Matthäus. KNT, I. Leipzig, 1903.

Introduction to the New Testament. 3 vols., trans. from 3rd German ed. under the direction of M. W. Jacobus and C. S. Thayer. Edinburgh, 1909.

Zeitlin, S., *The Rise and Fall of the Judaean State*. 2 vols. Philadelphia, 1962–7.

PERIODICAL ARTICLES

Abbott, W. G. M., 'Did Jesus Speak Aramaic?', *ET*, LVI (1945), 305.

Abel, F. M., 'Exploration du sud-est de la vallée du Jourdain', *RB*, XL (1931), 214–26.

Achtemeier, P. J., 'Toward the Isolation of Pre-Markan Miracle Catenae', *JBL*, LXXXIX (1970), 265–91.

Albright, W. F., 'Bronze Age Mounds of Northern Palestine and the Havron: The Spring Trip of the School in Jerusalem', *BASOR*, no. 19 (1925), 5–19.

'Contributions to the Historical Geography of Palestine', *AASOR*, II–III (1921–2), 1–46.

'The Jordan Valley in the Bronze Age', *AASOR*, VI (1924–5), 13–74.

'Review of *Preliminary Report of the University of Michigan Excavations at Sepphoris, Palestine, 1931*', by L. Waterman, *et al.*, *Classical Weekly*, XXI (1938), 148.

'Some Archaeological and Topographical Results of a Trip through Palestine', *BASOR*, no. 11 (1923), 3–14.

'Some Observations favoring the Palestinian Origin of the Gospel of John', *HTR*, XVII (1924), 189–95.

'A Tour on Foot through Samaria and Galilee', *BASOR*, no. 4 (1921), 7–13.

Allen, W. C., 'The Aramaic Element in St Mark', *ET*, XIII (1902), 328–30.

Allon, G., 'The Attitude of the Pharisees to the Roman Government and the House of Herod', *SH*, VII (1961), 53–78.

Alt, A., 'Galiläische Probleme', *PJB*, XXXIII (1937), 52–88.

'Das Institut im Jahre 1924', *PJB*, XXI (1925), 5–58.

'Die Reiterstadt Gaba', *ZDPV*, LXII (1939), 3–21.

Argyle, A. W., 'Did Jesus Speak Greek?', *ET*, LXVII (1955), 92–3.

'Did Jesus Speak Greek?', *ET*, LXVII (1956), 383.

Avi-Yonah, M., 'The Development of the Roman Road System in Palestine', *IEJ*, I (1950–1), 54–60.

'The Foundation of Tiberias', *IEJ*, I (1950–1), 160–9.

'Map of Roman Palestine', *QDAP*, V (1936), 139–93.

'The Missing Fortress of Flavius Josephus', *IEJ*, III (1953), 94–8.

Bacon, B. W., 'Aenon near to Sâlim', *BW*, XXXIII (1909), 223–38.

'The Baptism of John – Where was it?', *BW*, XXX (1907), 39–50.

'Pharisees and Herodians in Mark', *JBL*, XXXIX (1920), 102–12.

Bajsić, A., 'Pilatus, Jesus und Barabbas', *Biblica*, XLVIII (1967), 7–28.

Balsdon, J. P. V. D., 'Notes concerning the Principate of Gaius', *JRS*, XXIV (1934), 13–24.

Bammel, E., 'Die Bruderfolge im Hochpriestertum der herodianisch-römischen Zeit', *ZDPV*, LXX (1954), 147–53.

'Christian Origins in Jewish Tradition', *NTS*, XIII (1967), 317–35.

'Excerpts from a New Gospel?', *NovT*, X (1968), 1–9.

'Is Luke 16: 16–18 of Baptist's Provenience?', *HTR*, LI (1958), 101–6.

'The Organization of Palestine by Gabinius', *JJS*, XII (1961), 159–62.

'Die Rechtsstellung des Herodes', *ZDPV*, LXXXIV (1968), 73–9.

'Syrian Coinage and Pilate', *JJS*, II (1951), 108–10.

'Φίλος τοῦ Καίσαρος', *Theologische Literaturzeitung*, LXXVII (1952), 205–10.

Barnes, T. D., 'The Date of Herod's Death', *JTS*, N.S. XIX (1968), 204–9.

Barr, A., 'The Use and Disposal of the Marcan Source in Luke's Passion Narrative', *ET*, LV (1944), 227–31.

Barr, J. 'Which Language did Jesus Speak? – Some Remarks of a Semitist', *BJRL*, LIII (1970), 9–29.

Belkin, S., 'The Problem of Paul's Background', *JBL*, LIV (1935), 41–60.

Benoit, P., 'Prétoir, Lithostroton et Gabbath', *RB*, LIX (1952), 531–50.

Ben-Zevil, I., 'Discoveries at Pekiin', *PEFQS*, LXII (1930), 210–14.

Bickerman (n), E., 'Les Hérodiens', *RB*, XLVII (1938), 184–97.

'Utilitas crucis. Observations sur les récits du procès de Jésus dans les Évangiles canoniques', *RHR*, CXII (1935), 169–241.

Bietenhard, H., 'Die Dekapolis von Pompeius bis Traian, ein Kapitel aus der neutestamentlichen Zeitgeschichte', *ZDPV*, LXXIX (1963), 24–58.

Black, A., 'The Leaven of Herod. St Mark viii. 15', *Exp*, 5th series, IX (1899), 173–86.

Black, M., 'The Recovery of the Language of Jesus', *NTS*, III (1957), 305–13.

'Second Thoughts. IX. The Semitic Element in the New Testament', *ET*, LXXVII (1965), 20–3.

Blinzler, J., 'Eine Bemerkung zum Geschichtsrahmen des Johannesevangeliums', *Biblica*, XXXVI (1955), 20–35.

'Die Niedermetzelung von Galiläern durch Pilatus', *NovT*, II (1957), 24–9.

'Zur Syntax von Markus 6, 14–16', *Philologus*, XCVI (1943), 119–31.

Boddington, A., 'Sejanus, Whose Conspiracy?', *AJP*, LXXXIV (1963), 1–16.

Bonner, C., 'Addition and Corrections, Mark 6. 20', *HTR*, XXXVIII (1944), 336.

'Note on Mark 6. 20', *HTR*, XXXVII (1944), 41–4.

Boobyer, G. H., 'Galilee and Galileans in St Mark's Gospel', *BJRL*, XXXV (1953), 334–48.

'The Miracles of the Loaves and the Gentiles in St Mark's Gospel', *The Scottish Journal of Theology*, VI (1953), 77–87.

Bornhäuser, 'Die Beteiligung des Herodes am Prozesse Jesu', *NKZ*, XL (1929), 714–18.

Bowker, J. W., 'The Origin and Purpose of St John's Gospel', *NTS*, XI (1965), 398–408.

Bradley, W. P., 'John the Baptist as Forerunner', *BW*, XXXV (1910), 327–38.

Brandon, S. G. F., 'The Date of the Markan Gospel', *NTS*, VII (1961), 126–41.

'Herod the Great: Judaea's Most Able but Most Hated King', *History Today*, XII (1962), 234–42.

Brann, M., 'Die Söhne des Herodes', *MGWJ*, XXII (1873), 241–56, 305–21, 345–60, 407–20, 459–74, 497–507.

Brown, D., 'Herod the Tetrarch: A Study of Conscience', *Exp*, 4th series, VI (1892), 305–12.

Bruce, F. F., 'Did Jesus Speak Aramaic?', *ET*, LVI (1945), 328.

'Herod Antipas, Tetrarch of Galilee and Peraea', *ALUOS*, V (1963–5), 6–23.

'History and the Gospel', *Faith and Thought*, XCIII (1964), 121–45.

Bunn, L. H., 'Herod Antipas and "that Fox"', *ET*, XLIII (1932), 380–1.

Burkitt, F. C., 'The Chester Beatty Papyri', *JTS*, XXXIV (1933), 363–8.

'Chuza', *Exp*, 5th series, IX (1899), 118–22.

'The Peraean Ministry: A Reply', *JTS*, XI (1910), 412–15.

'Review of *Die Zusammensetzung des Markusevangeliums*, by J. Sundwall', *JTS*, XXXVI (1935), 186–8.

'St Mark and Divorce', *JTS*, V (1904), 628–30.

'W and Θ: Studies in the Western Text of St Mark', *JTS*, XVII (1915), 1–21.

Case, S. J., 'Jesus and Sepphoris', *JBL*, XLV (1926), 14–22.

Casson, L., 'The Isis and Her Voyage', *TAPA*, LXXXI (1950), 43–56.

'Speed under Sail of Ancient Ships', *TAPA*, LXXXII (1951), 136–48.

Charlesworth, M. P., 'Tiberius and the Death of Augustus', *AJP*, XLIV (1923), 145–57.

Christie, W. M., 'Ḳuṣr bint el-Melek', *Glasgow University Oriental Society Transactions*, V (1930), 36–7.

Cichorius, C., 'Chronologisches zum Leben Jesu', *ZNW*, XXII (1923), 16–20.

Cohen, B., 'Concerning Divorce in Jewish and Roman Law', *Proceedings of American Academy for Jewish Research*, XXI (1952), 3–34.

Cohon, S. S., 'The Place of Jesus in the Religious Life of His Day', *JBL*, XLVIII (1929), 82–108.

Coleman-Norton, P. R., 'St Chrysostom's Use of Josephus', *Classical Philology*, XXVI (1931), 85–9.

Conder, C. R., 'The Fertility of Ancient Palestine', *PEFQS*, VIII (1876), 120–32.

Connolly, R. H., 'Syriacisms in St Luke', *JTS*, XXXVII (1936), 375–85.

Corbishley, T., 'The Chronology of the Reign of Herod the Great', *JTS*, XXXVI (1935), 22–32.

'A Note on the Date of the Syrian Governorship of M. Titus', *JRS*, XXIV (1934), 43–9.

Corbishley, T., 'Pontius Pilate', *The Clergy Review*, XII (1936), 368–81.
'Quirinius and the Census: A Restudy of the Evidence', *Klio*, XXIX (1936), 81–93.
Couchoud, P.-L., 'Notes sur le texte de St Marc dans le codex Chester Beatty', *JTS*, XXXV (1934), 3–32.
'Les textes relatifs à Jésus dans la version slave de Josèphe', *RHR*, XCIII (1926), 44–64.
Creed, J. M., 'Josephus on John the Baptist', *JTS*, XXIII (1921), 56–60.
'The Slavonic Version of Josephus' History of the Jewish Wars', *HTR*, XXV (1932), 277–319.
'Some Outstanding New Testament Problems. II. 'L' and the Structure of the Lucan Gospel: A Study of the Proto-Luke Hypothesis', *ET*, XLVI (1934), 101–7.
Cronin, H. S., 'Abilene, the Jewish Herods and St Luke', *JTS*, XVIII (1917), 147–51.
Cumont, F., 'The Population of Syria', *JRS*, XXIV (1934), 187–90.
Daget, M. B. 'The Habbakuk Scroll and Pompey's Capture of Jerusalem', *Biblica*, XXXII (1951), 542–8.
Dalman, G., 'Jahresbericht des deutschen evangelischen Instituts für Altertumswissenschaft des heiligen Landes', *PJB*, VI (1910), 1–24.
'Jahresbericht des deutschen evangelischen Instituts für Altertumswissenschaft des heiligen Landes für das Arbeitsjahr 1913/14', *PJB*, X (1914), 1–50.
'Nach Galiläa vom 30. September bis 13. Oktober 1921', *PJB*, XVIII–XIX (1922–3), 10–80.
'Zum Tanz der Tochter der Herodias', *PJB*, XIV (1918), 44–6.
Daniel, C., 'Les Esséniens et "Ceux qui sont dans les maisons des rois" (*Matthieu* 11, 7–8 et *Luc* 7, 24–25)', *RQ*, VI (1967), 261–77.
'"Faux Prophètes": surnom des Esséniens dans le Sermon sur la Montagne', *RQ*, VII (1969), 45–79.
'Les "Hérodiens" du Nouveau Testament sont-ils des Esséniens?', *RQ*, VI (1967), 31–53.
'Nouveaux arguments en faveur de l'identification des Hérodiens et des Esséniens', *RQ*, VII (1970), 397–402.
Davies, W. D., 'The Jewish Background of the Teaching of Jesus: Apocalyptic and Pharisaism', *ET*, LIX (1948), 233–7.
Delbrueck, R., 'Antiquarisches zu den Verspottungen Jesu', *ZNW*, XLI (1942), 124–45.
Delling, G., 'Josephus und die heidnischen Religionen', *Klio*, XLIII–XLV (1965), 263–9.
Denney, J., 'Caesar and God. Mk xii. 13–17', *Exp*, 5th series, III (1896), 61–9.

Derrett, J. D. M., 'Herod's Oath and the Baptist's Head', *BZ*, N.F. IX (1965), 49–59, 233–46.

Dibelius, M., 'Herodes und Pilatus', *ZNW*, XVI (1915), 113–26.

Dieckmann, H., 'Die effektive Mitregenschaft des Tiberius', *Klio*, XV (1918), 339–75.

'Das fünfzehnte Jahr des Caesar Tiberius', *Biblica*, VI (1925), 63–7.

Dimont, C. T., 'The Synoptic Evangelists and the Pharisees', *Exp*, 8th series, I (1911), 231–44.

Dobschütz, E. von, 'Jews and Antisemites in Ancient Alexandria', *The American Journal of Theology*, VIII (1904), 728–55.

Dodd, C. H., 'The Close of the Galilaean Ministry', *Exp*, 8th series, XXII (1921), 273–91.

'The Framework of the Gospel Narrative', *ET*, XLIII (1932), 396–400.

Downing, J., 'Jesus and Martyrdom', *JTS*, N.S. XIV (1963), 279–93.

Doyle, A. D., 'Pilate's Career and the Date of Crucifixion', *JTS*, XLII (1941), 190–3.

Draper, H. M., 'Did Jesus Speak Greek?', *ET*, LXVII (1956), 317.

Duncan, J. G., 'The Sea of Tiberias and its Environs', *PEFQS*, LVIII (1926), 15–22, 65–74.

Dupont-Sommer, A., 'Le "Commentaire d'Habacuc" découvert près de la Mer Morte', *RHR*, CXXXVII (1950), 129–71.

Easton, B. S., 'The Trial of Jesus', *The American Journal of Theology*, XIX (1915), 430–52.

Eger, O., 'Rechtswörter und Rechtsbilder in den paulinischen Briefen', *ZNW*, XVIII (1917), 84–108.

Eisler, R., 'Flavius Josephus on Jesus Called the Christ', *JQR*, XXI (1930–1), 1–60.

'Jésus d'après la version slave de Flavius Josèphe', *RHR*, XCIII (1926), 1–21.

'The Newly Rediscovered Witness of Josephus to Jesus', *The Quest*, XVII (1925), 1–15.

'The Present Position of the Slavic Josephus Question', *The Quest*, XX (1928), 1–19.

'Recherches sur la chronologie évangélique', *Revue Archéologique*, série V, XXXII (1930), 116–26.

Eliot, C. W. J., 'New Evidence for the Speed of the Roman Imperial Post', *The Phoenix*, IX (1955), 76–80.

Emerton, J. A., 'Did Jesus Speak Hebrew?', *JTS*, N.S. XII (1961), 189–202.

Emmet, P. B., 'St Mark viii. 15', *ET*, XLVIII (1937), 332–3.

Farley, F. A., 'A Text (Luke xiii. 33)', *ET*, XXXIV (1923), 429–30.

Farmer, W. R., 'Jesus, Simon, and Athronges', *NTS*, IV (1958), 147–55.

Feldman, L. H., 'Asinius Pollio and his Jewish Interests', *TAPA*, LXXXIV (1953), 73–80.

Filmer, W. E., 'The Chronology of the Reign of Herod the Great', *JTS*, N.S. XVII (1966), 283–98.

Fink, R. O., 'Jerash in the First Century A.D.', *JRS*, XXIII (1933), 109–24.

Finkelstein, L., 'The Pharisees: Their Origin and their Philosophy', *HTR*, XXII (1929), 185–261.

Fitzmyer, J. A., 'The Languages of Palestine in the First Century A.D.', *Catholic Biblical Quarterly*, XXXII (1970), 501–31.

Fotheringham, J. K., 'The Evidence of Astronomy and Technical Chronology for the Date of the Crucifixion', *JTS*, XXXV (1934), 146–62.

Frey, J.-B., 'Les communautés Juives à Rome', *Recherches de Science Religieuse* XX (1930), 269–97.
'La question des images chez les Juifs. À la lumière des récentes découvertes', *Biblica*, XV (1934), 265–300.

Friedlander, M., 'Jewish Lulab and Portal Coins', *JQR*, I (1889), 282–4.

Fulford, H. W., 'This Fox', *ET*, XIX (1908), 523.

Funk, R. W. and Richardson, H. N., 'The 1958 Sounding at Pella', *BA*, XXI (1958), 82–96.

Geffcken, J., 'Die christlichen Märtyrien', *Hermes*, XLV (1910), 481–505.

Gibson, J. C. L., 'John the Baptist in Muslim Writings', *MW*, XLV (1955), 334–45.

Gihon, M., 'Idumea and the Herodian Limes', *IEJ*, XVII (1967), 27–42.

Gilbert, A. H., 'Σήμερον καὶ αὔριον, καὶ τῇ τρίτῃ (Luke 13: 32)', *JBL*, XXXV (1916), 315–18.

Gilmour, S. M., 'A Critical Re-Examination of Proto-Luke', *JBL*, LXVII (1948), 143–52.

Glueck, N., 'Explorations in Eastern Palestine, I', *AASOR*, XIV (1934), 1–113.
'Explorations in Eastern Palestine, III', *AASOR*, XVIII–XIX (1937–9), xxiv+288.
'Explorations in Eastern Palestine, IV', *AASOR*, XXV–XXVIII (1945–9), xix+711.
'Nabataean Syria and Nabataean Transjordan', *JPOS*, XVIII (1938), 1–6.
'Some Ancient Towns in the Plains of Moab', *BASOR*, no. 91 (1943), 7–26.

Godolphin, F. R. B., 'A Note on the Marriage of Claudius and Agrippina', *Classical Philology*, XXIX (1934), 143–5.

Goguel, M., 'Juifs et Romains dans l'histoire de la passion', *RHR*, LXII (1910), 165–82, 295–322.

'Luke and Mark: With a Discussion of Streeter's Theory', *HTR*, XXVI (1933), 1–55.

'Notes d'histoire évangélique. Le problème chronologique', *RHR*, LXXIV (1916), 1–47.

Graetz, H., 'Agrippa II und der Zustand Judäas nach dem Untergang Jerusalems', *MGWJ*, XXX (1881), 481–99.

Grant, F. C., 'On the Trial of Jesus: A Review Article', *The Journal of Religion*, XLIV (1964), 230–7.

Grant, R. M., 'The Occasion of Luke III: 1–2', *HTR*, XXXIII (1940), 151–4.

Greig, J. C. G., 'εὔκαιρος', *ET*, LXV (1954), 158–9.

Grether, G., 'Livia and the Roman Imperial Cult', *AJP*, LXVII (1946), 222–52.

Griffiths, J. G., 'Did Jesus Speak Aramaic?', *ET*, LVI (1945), 327–8.

Grintz, J. M., 'Hebrew as the Spoken and Written Language in the Last Days of the Second Temple', *JBL*, LXXIX (1960), 32–47.

Guilleband, H. E., 'The Travel in St Luke (IX: 51 – XVIII: 14)', *BS*, LXXX (1923), 237–45.

Gundry, R. H., 'The Language Milieu of First-Century Palestine. Its Bearing on the Authenticity of the Gospel Tradition', *JBL*, LXXXIII (1964), 404–8.

Gutmann, J., 'The "Second Commandment" and the Image in Judaism', *HUCA*, XXXII (1961), 161–74.

Hammond, P. C., 'Review of *Deities and Dolphins: The Story of the Nabataeans* by N. Glueck', *JBL*, LXXXV (1966), 90–2.

Hanson, R. P. C., 'Does δίκαιος in Luke xxiii. 47 Explode the Proto-Luke Hypothesis?', *Hermathena*, LX (1942), 74–8.

Harder, G., 'Herodes-Burgen und Herodes-Städte im Jordangraben', *ZDPV*, LXXVIII (1962), 49–63.

Harris, J. R., 'Osiris in Galilee', *ET*, XL (1929), 188–9.

Harrison, J., 'The Head of John the Baptist', *The Classical Review*, XXX (1916), 216–19.

Hart, J. H. A., 'Possible References to the Foundation of Tiberias in the Teaching of Our Lord', *Exp*, 8th series, I (1911), 74–84.

Heard, R. G., 'The Old Gospel Prologues', *JTS*, N.S. VI (1955), 1–16.

Hedley, P. L., 'Pilate's Arrival in Judaea', *JTS*, XXXV (1934), 56–8.

Heinen, H., 'Zur Begründung des römischen Kaisercults von 48 v. bis 14 n. Chr.', *Klio*, XI (1911), 129–77.

Héring, J., 'Review of *The Destroyer of Jesus: The Story of Herod Antipas* by V. E. Harlow', *Revue d'Histoire et de Philosophie Religieuses*, XXXVI (1956), 85–6.

'Herodias and Salome,' *ET*, XXIX (1917), 122–6.

Herz, J., 'Grossgrundbesitz in Palästina im Zeitalter Jesu', *PJB*, XXIV (1928), 98–113.

Herz, N., 'Dalmanutha', *ET*, VIII (1897), 563.

'Dalmanutha', *ET*, IX (1897), 95; (1898), 426.

Higgins, A. J. B., 'Sidelights on the Christian Beginnings in the Graeco-Roman World', *The Evangelical Quarterly*, XLI (1969), 197–206.

'The Words of Jesus according to St John', *BJRL*, XLIX (1967), 363–86.

Holzmeister, U., 'Wann war Pilatus Prokurator von Judaea?', *Biblica*, XIII (1932), 228–32.

Horsfield, G. and A., 'Sela-Petra, the Rock, of Edom and Nabatene', *QDAP*, VII (1938), 1–42; VIII (1938), 87–115; IX (1941), 105–204.

'The House of Herod in History and Art', *Edinburgh Review or Critical Journal*, CCXV (1912), 291–317.

Howard, W. F., 'The Anti-Marcionite Prologues to the Gospels', *ET* XLVII (1936), 534–8.

Hultsch, F., 'Das hebräische Talent bei Josephus', *Klio*, II (1902), 70–2.

Hunkin, J. W., 'The Composition of the Third Gospel, with Special Reference to Canon Streeter's Theory of Proto-Luke', *JTS*, XXVIII (1927), 250–62.

'St Luke and Josephus', *CQR*, LXXXVIII (1919), 89–108.

Husband, R. W., 'The Year of the Crucifixion', *TAPA*, XLVI (1915), 5–28.

Ita of Sion, M., 'The Antonia Fortress', *PEQ*, C (1968), 139–43.

Jack, J. W., 'The Census of Quirinius', *ET*, XL (1929), 496–8.

Jeremias, J., 'Beobachtungen zu neutestamentlichen Stellen an Hand des neugefundenen griechischen Henoch-Texts', *ZNW*, XXXVIII (1939), 115–24.

'Die Einwohnerzahl Jerusalems zur Zeit Jesu', *ZDPV*, LXVI (1943), 24–31.

'Perikopen-Umstellungen bei Lukas?', *NTS*, IV (1958), 115–19.

'Zöllner und Sünder', *ZNW*, XXX (1931), 293–300.

Jones, A. H. M., 'Review and Discussion of "Ricerche sull'Organizzazione della Giudea sotto il Dominio Romano (63 a.C. – 70 d.C.)", by A. Momigliano', *JRS*, XXV (1935), 228–31.

'The Urbanization of the Ituraean Principality', *JRS*, XXI (1931), 265–75.

'The Urbanization of Palestine', *JRS*, XXI (1931), 78–85.

Jones, H. S., 'Claudius and the Jewish Question at Alexandria', *JRS*, XVI (1926), 17–35.

Jones, J. L., 'References to John the Baptist in the Gospel according to St Matthew', *ATR*, XLI (1959), 298–302.

Joüon, P., 'Les "Hérodiens" de l'Évangile (Marc 3, 6; 12, 13 = Matthieu 22, 16)', *Recherches de Science Religieuse*, XXVIII (1938), 585–8.

'Luc 23, 11: ἐσθῆτα λαμπράν', *Recherches de Science Religieuse*, XXVI (1936), 80–5.

Kahane, P., 'Pottery Types from the Jewish Ossuary-Tombs around Jerusalem. An Archaeological Contribution to the Problem of Hellenization of Jewry in the Herodian Period', *IEJ*, II (1952), 125–39; III (1953), 48–54.

Kanael, B., 'Ancient Jewish Coins and their Historical Importance', *BA*, XXVI (1963), 38–62.

'The Coins of King Herod of the Third Year', *JQR*, XLII (1952), 261–4.

'The Partition of Judea by Gabinius', *IEJ*, VII (1957), 98–106.

Keim, T., 'Drei christliche Chronologen', *Protestantische Kirchenzeitung*, XVI (1869), 1174–80, 1214–20.

Kelso, J. L., 'New Testament Jericho', *BA*, XIV (1951), 34–43.

Kennard, J. S., Jr, 'The Jewish Provincial Assembly', *ZNW*, LIII (1962), 25–51.

Kilpatrick, G. D., 'Scribes, Lawyers, and Lucan Origins', *JTS*, N.S. 1 (1950), 56–60.

'A Theme of the Lucan Passion Story and Luke xxiii. 47', *JTS*, XLIII (1942), 34–6.

Kindler, A., 'More Dates on the Coins of the Procurators', *IEJ*, VI (1956), 54–7.

Klein, S., 'Hebräische Ortsnamen bei Josephus', *MGWJ*, LIX (1915), 156–69.

'Zur Topographie des alten Palästina (Ergänzungen und Berichtigungen zu Thomsen Loca Sancta)', *ZDPV*, XXXIII (1910), 26–43.

Klijn, A. F., 'Scribes Pharisees High-priests and Elders in the New Testament', *NovT*, III (1959), 259–67.

Knox, W. L., 'Church and State in the New Testament', *JRS*, XXXIX (1949), 23–30.

Kraeling, C. H., 'The Episode of the Roman Standards at Jerusalem', *HTR*, XXXV (1942), 263–89.

'The Jewish Community at Antioch', *JBL*, LI (1932), 130–60.

'Olmstead's Chronology of the Life of Jesus', *ATR*, XXIV (1942), 334–54.

'Was Jesus Accused of Necromancy?', *JBL*, LIX (1940), 147–57.

Krieger, N., 'Ein Mensch in weichen Kleidern', *NovT*, 1 (1956), 228–30.

De Laet, S. J., 'Le successeur de Ponce-Pilate', *L'Antiquité Classique*, VIII (1939), 413–19.

Lagrange, M.-J., 'Jean-Baptiste et Jésus d'après le texte slave du livre de la guerre des Juifs de Josèphe', *RB*, XXXIX (1930), 29–44.

'Où en est la question du recensement de Quirinius?', *RB*, VIII (1911), 60–84.

Lake, K., 'The Date of Herod's Marriage with Herodias, and the Chronology of the Gospels', *Exp*, 8th series, IV (1912), 462–77.

La Potterie, I. de, 'Mors Johannis Baptistae', *Verbum Domini*, XLIV (1966), 142–51.

Lauterbach, J. Z., 'The Pharisees and their Teachings', *HUCA*, VI (1929), 69–139.

Lee, G. M., 'The Census in Luke', *CQR*, CLXVII (1966), 431–6.

Liberty, S., 'Pharisees, Herodians, and "Just Men", as the Questioners about the Tribute', *ET*, XXVIII (1917), 522–3.

Lichtenstein, H., 'Die Fastenrolle. Eine Untersuchung zur jüdisch-hellenistischen Geschichte', *HUCA*, VIII–IX (1931–2), 257–351.

Lillie, W., 'Salome or Herodias?', *ET*, LXV (1954), 251.

Linton, O., 'The Demand for a Sign from Heaven', *Studia Theologica*, XIX (1965), 112–29.

Littmann, E., 'Eine altsyrische Inschrift', *Zeitschrift für Assyriologie*, XXVII (1912), 379–82.

'Zu den nabatäischen Inschriften von Petra', *Zeitschrift für Assyriologie*, XXVIII (1914), 263–79.

Ljungvik, H., 'Zum Markusevangelium 6. 14', *ZNW*, XXXIII (1934), 90–2.

Lohse, E., 'Die römischen Statthalter in Jerusalem', *ZDPV*, LXXIV (1958), 69–78.

McArthur, H. K., 'A Survey of Recent Gospel Research', *Interpretation*, XVIII (1964), 39–55.

McCown, C. C., 'The Density of Population in Ancient Palestine', *JBL*, LXVI (1947), 425–36.

'The Geography of Jesus' Last Journey to Jerusalem', *JBL*, LI (1932), 107–29.

'The Geography of Luke's Central Section', *JBL*, LVII (1938), 51–66.

'Gospel Geography, Fiction, Fact, and Truth', *JBL*, LX (1941), 1–25.

'The Problem of the Site of Bethsaida', *JPOS*, X (1930), 32–58.

'Scene of John's Ministry and its Relation to the Purpose and Outcome of His Mission', *JBL*, LIX (1940), 113–31.

McEachern, V. E., 'Dual Witness and Sabbath Motif in Luke', *CJT*, XII (1966), 267–80.

MacGregor, W. M., 'Christ's Three Judges', *Exp*, 6th series, I (1900), 407–14; II, 59–68, 119–29.

MacLeish, K., 'The Land of Galilee', *National Geographic Magazine*, CXXVIII (1965), 832–65.

Madden, F. W., 'Jewish Numismatics', *The Numismatic Chronicle*, N.S. XIV (1874), 281–316; XV (1875), 41–80, 101–39, 165–95, 298–333; XVI (1876), 45–70, 81–132, 177–234.

'Rare or Unpublished Jewish Coins', *The Numismatic Chronicle*, N.S. XIX (1879), 13–22.

Magoun, H. W., 'The Testimony of Josephus concerning Jesus', *BS*, LXIX (1912), 288–309.

Maier, P. L., 'The Episode of the Golden Roman Shields at Jerusalem', *HTR*, LXII (1969), 109–21.

'Sejanus, Pilate, and the Date of the Crucifixion', *Church History*, XXXVII (1968), 3–13.

Maisler, B., 'Beth She'arim, Gaba, and Harosheth of the Peoples', *HUCA*, XXIV (1952–3), 75–84.

Stekelis, M., and Avi-Yonah, M. 'The Excavations at Beth Yerah (Khirbet el-Kerak) 1944–46', *IEJ*, II (1952), 165–73.

Mallon, A., 'Deux forteresses au pied des monts de Moab', *Biblica*, XIV (1933), 400–7.

Mánek, J., 'Mark viii 14–21', *NovT*, VII (1964), 10–14.

Manson, T. W., 'The Cleansing of the Temple', *BJRL*, XXXIII (1951), 271–82.

'John the Baptist', *BJRL*, XXXVI (1954), 395–412.

'The Life of Jesus: A Study of the Available Materials', *BJRL*, XXVII (1943), 323–37; XXVIII (1944), 119–36, 382–403.

'Mark viii 14–21', *JTS*, XXX (1929), 45–7.

Marcus, R., 'Notes on Torrey's Translation of the Gospels', *HTR*, XXVII (1934), 211–39.

'The Pharisees in the Light of Modern Scholarship', *The Journal of Religion*, XXXII (1952), 153–64.

'A Selected Bibliography (1920–45) of the Jews in the Hellenistic-Roman Period', *American Academy for Jewish Research*, XVI (1946–7), 97–181.

Marmorstein, A., 'Some Remarks on the Slavonic Josephus', *The Quest*, XVII (1926), 145–57.

Marsh, F. B., 'Roman Parties in the Reign of Tiberius', *The American Historical Review*, XXXI (1926), 233–50.

Martin, R. A., 'Syntactical Evidence of Aramaic Sources in Acts i–xv', *NTS*, XI (1964), 38–59.

Mead, G. R. S., 'John the Baptizer and Christian Origins', *The Quest*, XIII (1922), 466–91.

'The Slavonic Josephus' Account of the Baptist and Jesus', *The Quest*, XV (1924), 457–79.

Meecham, H. G., 'St Mark X. 51', *ET*, LII (1941), 437.

Meeks, W. A., 'Galilee and Judea in the Fourth Gospel', *JBL*, LXXXV (1966), 159–69.

Meissner, B., 'Sprichwörter bei Asarhaddon', *Archiv für Orientforschung*, X (1936), 361–2.

Mendner, S., 'Zum Problem "Johannes und die Synoptiker"', *NTS*, IV (1958), 282–307.

Merrill, S., 'Galilee in the Time of Christ', *BS*, XXXI (1874), 29–73, 235–65.

Meyer, R., 'Die Figurendarstellung in der Kunst des späthellenistischen Judentums', *Judaica*, V (1949), 1–40.

Milligan, W., 'Some Recent Critical Readings in the New Testament', *Exp*, 1st series, VII (1878), 123–37.

Mingana, A. (ed. and trans.), 'Woodbroke Studies', *BJRL*, XII (1928), 411–580.

Moffatt, J., 'Jesus and the Four Men', *ET*, XXXII (1921), 486–9.

Momigliano, A., 'Ricerche sull'Organizzazione della Giudea sotto il Dominio Romano (63 a.C. – 70 d.C.)', *Annali della R. Scuola Normale Superiore di Pisa – Lettere, Storia e Filosofia*, series II, vol. III (1934), 183–221, 347–96.

Mommsen, T., 'Die Rechtsverhältnisse des Apostels Paulus', *ZNW*, II (1901), 81–96.

Montefiore, H., 'Revolt in the Desert? (Mark vi. 30 ff.)', *NTS*, VIII (1962), 135–41.

Moule, C. F. D., 'Review of *Studies in the Gospels: Essays in Memory of R. H. Lightfoot*, ed. by D. E. Nineham', *JTS*, N.S. VII (1956), 280–2.

Mowry, L., 'A Greek Inscription at Jathum in Transjordan', *BASOR*, no. 132 (1953), 34–41.

'Settlements in the Jericho Valley during the Roman Period (63 B.C. – A.D. 134)', *BA*, XV (1952), 26–42.

Negoiṭā, A. and Daniel, C., 'L'énigme du levain', *NovT*, IX (1967), 306–14.

Negoitsa [=Negoiṭā], A., 'Did the Essenes Survive the 66–71 War?', *RQ*, VI (1969), 517–30.

Nestle, E., 'Dalmanutha', *ET*, IX (1897), 45.

'The Lake of Tiberius', *ET*, XXIII (1911), 41.

'A Little Mistake in the Revised Version', *ET*, XV (1903), 95.

'Der Name des Sees Tiberias', *ZDPV*, XXXV (1912), 48–50.

'Stadt und See des Tiberius', *Berliner philologische Wochenschrift*, XXXI (1911), 1486–7.

Neuman, A. A., 'A Note on John the Baptist and Jesus in *Josippon*', *HUCA*, XXIII (1950–1), 137–49.

Nicklin, T., 'Matthew xiv. 12', *ET*, LV (1944), 110.

Niese, B., 'Zur Chronologie des Josephus', *Hermes*, XXVIII (1893), 194–229.

Nineham, D. E. 'Eye-Witness Testimony and the Gospel Tradition', *JTS*, N.S. IX (1958), 13–25, 243–52; XI (1960), 253–64.

Nock, A. D., 'The Roman Army and the Roman Religious Year', *HTR*, XLV (1952), 187–252.

'Notes of Recent Exposition', *ET*, X (1899), 483–4.

'Notes of Recent Exposition', *ET*, XIX (1909), 391–4.

'Notes of Recent Exposition', *ET*, XXVII (1915), 3–7.

'Notes of Recent Exposition', *ET*, XXXII (1921), 197–9.

'Notes of Recent Exposition', *ET*, LXIV (1953), 289–90.

Notestein, F. W. and Jurkat, E., 'Population Problems of Palestine', *The Milbank Memorial Fund Quarterly*, XXIII (1945), 307–52.

Oehler, W., 'Die Ortschaften und Grenzen Galiläas nach Josephus', *ZDPV*, XXVIII (1905), 1–26, 49–74.

Oepke, A., 'Das Bevölkerungsproblem Galiläas', *Theologische Literaturblatt*, LXII (1941), 201–5.

Ogg, G., 'Review of Mlle Jaubert, *La date de la Cène*', *NovT*, III (1959), 149–60.

O'Hara, J., 'Question and Answer: Two Bethsaidas or One?', *Scripture*, XV (1963), 24–7.

Olmstead, A. T., 'The Chronology of Jesus' Life', *ATR*, XXIV (1942), 1–26.

Ott, H., 'Um die Muttersprache Jesu; Forschungen seit Gustaf Dalman', *NovT*, IX (1967), 1–25.

Perry, A. M., 'Luke's Disputed Passion-Source', *ET*, XLVI (1935), 256–60.

Petersen, H., 'Real and Alleged Literary Projects of Josephus', *AJP*, LXXIX (1958), 259–74.

Pick, B., 'John the Baptist and Christ in the Slavic Translation of Josephus' "Jewish Wars"', *BW*, XLIII (1914), 172–7.

Plummer, A., 'Review of *The Gospel according to St Mark, the Greek Text, with Introduction, Notes and Indices*, by H. B. Swete', *JTS*, I (1900), 613–19.

Ramsay, A. M., 'The Speed of the Roman Imperial Post', *JRS*, XV (1925), 60–74.

Rasp, H., 'Flavius Josephus und die jüdischen Religionsparteien', *ZNW*, XXIII (1924), 24–47.

Rees, W., 'Archelaus, Son of Herod', *Scripture*, IV (1951), 348–55.

Reicke, B., 'Herodes der Grosse', *Reformatio*, IX (1960), 24–34.

Reifenberg, A., 'Unpublished and Unusual Jewish Coins', *IEJ*, I (1950–1), 176–8.

Reinach, S., 'Jean Baptiste et Jésus suivant Joséphus', *Revue des Études Juives*, LXXXVII (1929), 113–31.

Réville, A., 'Les Hérodes et le rêve Hérodien', *RHR*, XXVIII (1893), 283–301; XXIX (1894), 1–24.

Revillout, E., 'La sage-femme Salomé', *Journal Asiatique*, 10th series, v (1905), 409–61.

Richards, G. C. and Shutt, R. J. H., 'Critical Notes on Josephus' *Antiquities*', *The Classical Quarterly*, XXXI (1937), 170–7.

Richmond, J., 'Khirbet Fahil', *PEFQS*, LXVI (1934), 18–31.

Robertson, J. A., 'The Passion Journey', *Exp*, 8th series, XVII (1919), 54–73, 128–43, 174–94, 321–44.

Robinson, J. A. T., 'The Destination and Purpose of St John's Gospel', *NTS*, VI (1960), 117–31.

'Elijah, John and Jesus: An Essay in Detection', *NTS*, IV (1958), 263–81.

Robinson, T. H., 'Jesus and the Pharisees', *ET*, XXVIII (1917), 550–4.

Robinson, W. C., Jr, 'The Theological Context for Interpreting Luke's Travel Narrative (9: 5 ff.)', *JBL*, LXXIX (1960), 20–31.

Rogers, R. S., 'The Conspiracy of Agrippina', *TAPA*, LXII (1931), 141–68.

'Tiberius' Travels, A.D. 26–37', *The Classical Weekly*, XXIX (1945), 42–4.

Romanoff, P., 'Jewish Symbols on Ancient Jewish Coins', *JQR*, XXXIII (1942), 1–15; (1943), 435–44; XXXIV (1943), 161–77; (1944), 299–312, 425–44.

Roos, A. G., 'Die Quirinius-Inschrift', *Mnemosyne*, 3rd series, IX (1941), 306–18.

Rosenthal, F., 'Die Erlässe Cäsars und die Senatsconsulte im Josephus Alterth. XIV, 10 nach ihrem historischen Inhalte untersucht', *MGWJ*, XXVIII (1869), 176–83, 216–28, 300–22.

Rostovtzeff, M., '*Vexillum* and Victory', *JRS*, XXXII (1942), 92–106.

Roth, C., 'An Ordinance against Images in Jerusalem, A.D. 66', *HTR*, XLIX (1956), 169–77.

Rowley, H. H., 'The Herodians in the Gospels', *JTS*, XLI (1940), 14–27.

Rüger, H. P., 'Zum Problem der Sprache Jesu', *ZNW*, LIX (1968), 113–22.

Saarisalo, A., 'The Boundary between Issachar and Naphtali', *Annales Academiae Scientiarum Fennicae*, series B, XXI (1927), viii + 139.

Sanford, E. M., 'Propaganda and Censorship in the Transmission of Josephus', *TAPA*, LXVI (1935), 127–45.

De Saulcy, F., 'Catalogue raisonné de monnaies judaïques recueillies à Jérusalem en novembre 1869', *The Numismatic Chronicle*, N.S. XI (1872), 235–55.

Savignac, R. and Starcky, J., 'Une inscription Nabatéene provenant du Djôf', *RB*, LXIV (1957), 196–215.

Sawyerr, H., 'The Marcan Framework', *The Scottish Journal of Theology*, xiv (1961), 279–94.

Schalit, A., 'Die frühchristliche Überlieferung über die Herkunft der Familie des Herodes', *ASTI*, i (1962), 109–60.

'Die "herodischen" Patriarchen und der "davidische" Herodes', *ASTI*, vi (1968), 114–23.

Schille, G., 'Die Topographie des Markusevangeliums, ihre Hintergründe und ihre Einordnung', *ZDPV*, lxxiii (1957), 133–66.

Schlatter, A., 'Gadara nicht Geser', *ZDPV*, xviii (1895), 73–81.

Schlatter, T., 'Im Gebiet der Zehnstädte', *PJB*, xiv (1918), 90–110.

Schonfield, H., 'Some Jottings on the Slavonic Josephus', *The Quest*, xviii (1927), 133–9.

Schulze, W., 'Ahd. *suagur*', *Zeitschrift für vergleichende Sprachforschung*, xl (1906), 400–18.

Schumacher, G., 'Researches in the Plain North of Caesarea', *PEFQS*, xix (1887), 78–90.

Schürer, E., 'Epigraphische Beiträge zur Geschichte der Herodäer', *Zeitschrift für wissenschaftliche Theologie*, xvi (1873), 248–55.

Schützinger, H., 'Die arabische Legende von Nebukadnezar und Johannes dem Täufer', *Der Islam*, xl (1965), 113–41.

Schwartz, E., 'Noch einmal der Tod der Söhne Zebedaei', *ZNW*, xi (1910), 89–104.

Scott, R. B. Y., 'Weights and Measures of the Bible', *BA*, xxii (1959), 22–40.

Sealey, R., 'The Political Attachments of L. Aelius Seianus', *The Phoenix*, xv (1961), 97–114.

Selwyn, E. C., 'The Trial-Narratives Based on the Oracles', *Exp*, 8th Series, ix (1915), 254–71.

Sharps, Pixley Limited, Bullion Brokers, London, May 1970.

Sherwin-White, A. N., 'Procurator Augusti', *Papers of the British School at Rome*, xv (1939), 11–26.

Sickenberger, J., 'Dalmanutha (Mk. 8, 10)', *ZDPV*, lvii (1934), 281–5.

Skånland, V., 'Spiculator', *Symbolae Osloenses*, Fasc. xxxviii (1963), 94–119.

Smallwood, E. M., 'The Date of the Dismissal of Pontius Pilate from Judaea', *JJS*, v (1954), 12–21.

'High Priests and Politics in Roman Palestine', *JTS*, N.S. xiii (1962), 14–34.

'Some Notes on the Jews under Tiberius', *Latomus*, xv (1956), 314–29.

Smith, D. H., 'An Exposition of Mark viii. 14–21', *ET*, lix (1948), 125–6.

Smith, G. A., 'Callirrhoe and Machaerus', *PEFQS*, xxxvii (1905), 219–30.

Sollertinsky, S., 'The Death of St John the Baptist', trans. by Orloff, *JTS*, i (1900), 507–28.

Solmsen, F., 'Eigennamen als Zeugen der Stammesmischung in Böotien', *Rheinisches Museum für Philologie*, lix (1904), 481–505.

Solomon, D., 'Philo's Use of ΓΕΝΑΡΧΗΣ in *In Flaccum*', *JQR*, lxi (1970), 119–31.

Sparks, H. F. D., 'The Semitisms of the Acts', *JTS*, N.S. i (1950), 16–28.

Stagg, F., 'The Journey towards Jerusalem in Luke's Gospel. Luke 9: 57 – 19: 27', *Review and Expositor*, lxiv (1967), 499–512.

Starcky, J., 'The Nabataeans: A Historical Sketch', *BA*, xviii (1955), 84–106.

Stauffer, E., 'Zur Münzprägung und Judenpolitik des Pontius Pilatus', *La Nouvelle Clio*, i/ii (1950), 495–514.

Steinwenter, A., 'Il processo di Gesù', *Jus*, N.S. iii (1952), 471–90.

Stern, S. M., 'New Light on Judaeo-Christianity?', *Encounter*, xxviii (1967), 53–7.

'Quotations from Apocryphal Gospels in 'Abd al-Jabbār', *JTS*, N.S. xviii (1967), 34–57.

Stevens, W. A., 'Aenon near to Salim', *JBL*, iii (1883), 128–41.

Stewart, Z., 'Sejanus, Gaetulicus, and Seneca', *AJP*, lxxiv (1953), 70–85.

Strobel, A., 'Lukas der Antiochener', *ZNW*, xlix (1958), 131–4.

'Der Termin des Todes Jesu', *ZNW*, li (1960), 69–101.

Sukenik, L., 'The Ancient City of Philoteria (Beth Yerah)', *JPOS*, ii (1922), 101–8.

Syme, R., 'Galatia and Pamphylia under Augustus: The Governorships of Piso, Quirinius and Silvanus', *Klio*, xxvii (1934), 122–48.

Synder, W. F., 'On the Chronology in the Imperial Books of Cassius Dio's Roman History', *Klio*, N.F. xv (1940), 39–56.

Täubler, E., 'Zur Beurteiling der constantinischen Excerpte', *Byzantinische Zeitschrift*, xxv (1925), 33–40.

Taylor, L. R., 'Quirinius and the Census of Judaea', *AJP*, liv (1933), 120–33.

'Tiberius' *Ovatio* and *Ara Numinis Augusti*', *AJP*, lviii (1937), 185–93.

'Tiberius' Refusal of Divine Honors', *TAPA*, lx (1929), 87–101.

Taylor, R. O. P., 'Did Jesus Speak Aramaic?', *ET*, lvi (1945), 95–7.

Taylor, V., 'Important Hypotheses Reconsidered. I. The Proto-Luke Hypothesis', *ET*, lxvii (1955), 12–16.

Thompson, H. O., 'Tell el-Husn – Biblical Beth-Shan', *BA*, xxx (1967), 110–35.

Thomsen, P., 'Die römischen Meilensteine der Provinzen Syria, Arabia und Palaestina', *ZDPV*, xl (1917), 1–103.

Trilling, W., 'Die Täufertradition bei Matthäus', *BZ*, N.F. iii (1959), 271–89.

Turner, C. H., 'Markan Usage: Notes, Critical and Exegetical, on the Second Gospel', *JTS*, xxv (1924), 377–86; xxvi (1924), 12–20; (1925), 145–56, 225–40, 337–46; xxvii (1925), 58–62; xxviii (1926), 9–30, 349–62; xxix (1928), 275–89, 346–61.

'Western Readings in the Second Half of St Mark's Gospel', *JTS*, xxix (1927), 1–16.

Tyson, J. B., 'Jesus and Herod Antipas', *JBL*, lxxix (1960), 239–46.

'The Lukan Version of the Trial of Jesus', *NovT*, iii (1959), 249–58.

Vardaman, J., 'A New Inscription which Mentions Pilate as "Prefect"', *JBL*, lxxxi (1962), 70–1.

Verrall, A. W., 'Christ before Herod', *JTS*, x (1909), 321–53.

Vincent, L. H., 'Chronique', *RB*, xxx (1921), 434–43.

'Le lithostrotos évangélique', *RB*, lix (1952), 513–30.

Volkmann, H., 'Die Pilatusinschrift von Caesarea Maritima', *Gymnasium*, lxxv (1968), 124–35.

Walker, N., 'Pauses in the Passion Story and their Significance for Chronology', *NovT*, vi (1963), 16–19.

Wansbrough, H., 'Suffered under Pontius Pilate', *Scripture*, xviii (1966), 84–93.

Warfield, B. B., 'The Scenes of the Baptist's Work', *Exp*, 3rd series, i (1885), 267–82.

Webster, C. A., 'St Mark vi. 20', *ET*, xlix (1937), 93–4.

Wendling, E., 'Synoptische Studien', *ZNW* (1909), 46–58.

West-Watson, C., 'The Peraean Ministry', *JTS*, xi (1910), 269–74.

Willrich, H., 'Caligula', *Klio*, iii (1903), 85–118, 288–317, 397–470.

Windisch, H., 'Kleine Beiträge zur evangelischen Überlieferung', *ZNW*, xviii (1917), 73–83.

Winter, P., 'The Treatment of his Sources by the Third Evangelist in Luke XXI–XXIV', *Studia Theologica*, viii (1954), 138–72.

and Taylor, V., 'Sources of the Lucan Passion Narrative', *ET*, lxviii (1956), 95.

Wirgin, W., 'Bemerkungen zu dem Artikel über "Die Herkunft des Herodes"', *ASTI*, iii (1964), 51–4.

'A Note on the "Reed" of Tiberias', *IEJ*, xviii (1968), 248–9.

'Two Notes: (2) On King Herod's Messianism', *IEJ*, xi (1961), 151–4.

Wood, H. G., 'Interpreting This Time', *NTS*, ii (1956), 262–6.

Wright, G. E., 'Herod's Nabataean Neighbor', *BA*, i (1938), 1–4.

Yaron, R., 'Dispositions in Contemplation of Death: Some Formulas', *SH*, v (1958), 245–59.

Zeitlin, S. 'The Crucifixion of Jesus Re-examined', *JQR*, xxxi (1941), 327–69; xxxii (1941), 175–89; (1942), 279–301.

'Did Agrippa Write a Letter to Gaius Caligula?', *JQR*, lvi (1965), 22–31.

'The Duration of Jesus' Ministry', *JQR*, lv (1965), 181–200.

'Herod: A Malevolent Maniac', *JQR*, liv (1963), 1–27.

'Megillat Taanit as a Source for Jewish Chronology and History in the Hellenistic and Roman Periods', *JQR*, ix (1918), 71–102; x (1919), 49–80; (1919–20), 237–90.

'The Slavonic Josephus and the Dead Sea Scrolls: An Exposé of Recent Fairy Tales', *JQR*, lviii (1968), 173–203.

'Studies in the Beginnings of Christianity', *JQR*, xiv (1923–4), 111–39.

ESSAYS

Albright, W. F., 'Recent Discoveries in Palestine and the Gospel of St John', *The Background of the New Testament and its Eschatology*. Ed. by W. D. Davies and D. Daube. Cambridge, 1956, pp. 153–71.

Anderson, J. G. C., 'The Eastern Frontier from Tiberius to Nero', *CAH*, x. Cambridge, 1934, pp. 743–80.

Baarda, T., 'Gadarenes, Gerasenes, Gergesenes and the "Diatessaron" Traditions', *Neotestamentica et Semitica*. Ed. by E. E. Ellis and M. Wilcox. Edinburgh, 1969, pp. 181–97.

Bammel, E., 'John Did No Miracle', *Miracles: Cambridge Studies in their Philosophy and History*. Ed. by C. F. D. Moule. London, 1965, pp. 181–202.

'Νόμος Χριστοῦ', *SE*, iii, *TU*, lxxxviii. Berlin, 1964, pp. 120–8.

'Die Täufertradition bei Justin', *Studia Patristica*, viii. Ed. by F. L. Cross, *TU*, xciii. Berlin, 1966, pp. 53–61.

Barth, G., 'Matthew's Understanding of the Law', *Tradition and Interpretation in Matthew*. By G. Bornkamm, G. Barth, and H. J. Held, trans. P. Scott. London, 1963, pp. 58–164.

Bartlett, J. V., 'The Sources of St Luke's Gospel', *SSP*. Oxford, 1911, pp. 315–66.

Bauer, W., 'Jesus der Galiläer', *Festgabe für Adolf Jülicher*. Tübingen, 1927, pp. 16–34.

Berendts, A., 'Die Zeugnisse vom Christentum im slavischen "De Bello Judaico" des Josephus', *TU*, xxix. Leipzig, 1906, 79 pp.

Birkeland, H., 'The Language of Jesus', *Avhandlinger utgitt av det Norske videnskaps-akademi*, i, Oslo ii. *Hist.-filos. klasse*. Oslo, 1954, 40 pp.

Black, M., 'The Arrest and Trial of Jesus and the Date of the Last Supper', *New Testament Essays: Studies in Memory of Thomas Walter Manson*. Ed. by A. J. B. Higgins. Manchester, 1959, pp. 19–33.

'The Development of Judaism in the Greek and Roman Empire', *PCB*. London, 1962, pp. 693–8.

Blinzler, J., 'Die literarische Eigenart des sogenannten Reiseberichts im Lukasevangelium', *SS*. München, 1953, pp. 20–52.

Botha, F. J., 'The Date of the Death of Jesus and the Conversion of Paul', *Biblical Essays*. Ed. by A. H. van Zyl. Stellenbosch, Union of South Africa, 1966, pp. 181–90.

Cadbury, H. J., 'The Family Tree of the Herods', *BC*, v. London, 1933, pp. 487–9.

'Roman Law and the Trial of Paul', *BC*, v. London, 1933, pp. 297–338.

'Some Semitic Personal Names in Luke–Acts', *Amicitiae Corolla. A Volume of Essays Presented to J. R. Harris on the Occasion of his Eightieth Birthday*. Ed. by H. G. Wood. London, 1933, pp. 45–56.

Charlesworth, M. P., 'Tiberius', *CAH*, x. Cambridge, 1934, pp. 607–52.

Crouzel, H., 'Le lieu d'exil d'Hérode Antipas et d'Hérodiade selon Flavius Josèphe', *Studia Patristica*, x. Ed. by F. L. Cross, *TU*, CVII. Berlin, 1970, pp. 275–80.

Davies, J. H., 'The Purpose of the Central Section of St Luke's Gospel', *SE*, II, *TU*, LXXXVII. Berlin, 1964, pp. 164–9.

Dodd, C. H., 'The Life and Teaching of Jesus Christ', *A Companion to the Bible*. Ed. by T. W. Manson. Edinburgh, 1939, pp. 367–89.

Evans, C. F., 'The Central Section of St Luke's Gospel', *Studies in the Gospels: Essays in Memory of R. H. Lightfoot*. Ed. by D. E. Nineham. Oxford, 1955, pp. 37–53.

Goldin, J., 'The Period of the Talmud (135 B.C.E. – 135 C.E.)', *The Jews, Their History, Culture, and Religion*[3]. Ed. by L. Finkelstein, I. London, 1960, pp. 115–215.

Goulder, M. D., 'The Chiastic Structure of the Lucan Journey', *SE*, II, *TU*, LXXXVII. Berlin, 1964, pp. 195–202.

Grundmann, W., 'Das palästinensische Judentum im Zeitraum zwischen der Erhebung der Makkabäer und dem Ende des jüdischen Krieges', *Darstellung des neutestamentlichen Zeitalters*, vol. I of *Umwelt des Urchristentums*. Ed. by J. Leipoldt and W. Grundmann. Berlin, 1965, pp. 143–291.

Haefeli, L., 'Samaria und Peräa bei Flavius Josephus', *Biblische Studien*, XVIII. Ed. by O. Bardenhewer. Freiburg, 1913, pp. x + 120.

Harnack, A. von, 'Die ältesten Evangelien-Prologe und die Bildung des Neuen Testaments', *SAB*, xxiv. Berlin, 1928, pp. 322–41.

Harper, G. M., 'Village Administration in the Roman Province of Syria', *Yale Classical Studies*, i. Ed. by A. M. Harmon. New Haven, 1928, pp. 101–68.

Hawkins, J. C., 'Three Limitations of St Luke's Use of St Mark's Gospel', *SSP*. Oxford, 1911, pp. 29–94.

Heichelheim, F. M., 'Roman Syria', *An Economic Survey of Ancient Rome*. Ed. by T. Frank, iv. Baltimore, 1938, pp. 121–257.

Hengel, M., 'Maria Magdalena und die Frauen als Zeugen', *Abraham unser Vater: Juden und Christen im Gespräch über die Bibel, Festschrift für Otto Michel zum 60. Geburtstag*. Ed. by O. Betz, M. Hengel, and P. Schmidt. Leiden and Köln, 1963, pp. 242–56.

Hirschfeld, O., 'Zur Geschichte des Christenthums in Lugudunum vor Constantin', *SAB*, no. xix. Berlin, 1895, pp. 381–409.

Hölscher, G., 'Die Hohenpriesterliste bei Josephus und die evangelische Chronologie', *Sitzungsberichte der Heidelberger Akademie der Wissenschaften – Philosophisch-historische Klasse*, xxx. Heidelberg, 1940, pp. 1–33.

'Palästina in der persischen und hellenistischen Zeit', *Quellen und Forschungen zur alten Geschichte und Geographie*. Ed. by W. Sieglin, v. Berlin, 1903, pp. xii + 99.

Howard, W. F., 'John the Baptist and Jesus: A Note on Evangelic Chronology', *Amicitiae Corolla. A Volume of Essays Presented to J. R. Harris on the Occasion of his Eightieth Birthday*. Ed. by H. G. Wood. London, 1933, pp. 118–32.

Kingdon, H. P., 'Messiahship and the Crucifixion', *SE*, iii, *TU*, lxxxviii. Berlin, 1964, pp. 67–86.

Krauss, S., 'Die Ehe zwischen Onkel und Nichte', *Studies in Jewish Literature. Issued in Honor of Professor Kaufmann Kohler*. Berlin, 1913, pp. 165–75.

Lake, K., 'The Chronology of Acts', *BC*, v. London, 1933, pp. 445–74.

Lieberman, S., 'How Much Greek in Jewish Palestine?', *Biblical and Other Studies*. Ed. by A. Altmann. Cambridge, Massachusetts, 1963, pp. 123–41.

Lietzmann, H. 'Der Prozess Jesu', *SAB*, xiv. Berlin, 1931, pp. 313–22.

Manson, T. W., 'The Quest of the Historical Jesus – Continued', *Studies in the Gospels and Epistles*. Ed. by M. Black. Manchester, 1962, pp. 3–12.

Marcus, R., 'Recent Literature on Philo (1924–34)', *Jewish Studies in Memory of George A. Kohut*. Ed. by S. W. Baron and A. Marx. New York, 1935, pp. 463–91.

Meyshan, J., 'The Coins of the Herodian Dynasty', *The Dating and Meaning of Ancient Jewish Coins and Symbols*. Vol. II of *Numismatic Studies and Researches*. Jerusalem, 1958, pp. 29–41.

'The Monetary Pattern of the Herodian Coinage', *The Patterns of the Monetary Development in Phoenicia and Palestine. International Numismatic Convention*. Proceedings ed. by A. Kindler. Tel-Aviv, 1967, pp. 220–6.

Momigliano, A. 'Herod of Judaea', *CAH*, x. Cambridge, 1934, pp. 316–39.

Morgenstern, J., 'The New Year for Kings', *Occident and Orient. Being Studies in Semitic Philology and Literature, Jewish History and Philosophy and Folklore in the Widest Sense in Honour of Haham Dr. M. Gaster's 80th Birthday*. Ed. by B. Schindler. London, 1936, pp. 439–56.

Moule, C. F. D., 'The Intention of the Evangelists', *New Testament Essays: Studies in Memory of Thomas Walter Manson*. Ed. by A. J. B. Higgins. Manchester, 1959, pp. 165–79.

Moulton, J. H., 'New Testament Greek in the Light of Modern Discovery', *Cambridge Biblical Essays*. Ed. by H. B. Swete. London, 1909, pp. 461–505.

Neubauer, A., 'On the Dialects Spoken in Palestine in the Time of Christ', *Studia Biblica: Essays in Biblical Archaeology and Criticism and Kindred Subjects*, I. Oxford, 1885, pp. 39–74.

Neuman, A. A., 'Josippon: History and Pietism', *Alexander Marx Jubilee Volume on the Occasion of his Seventieth Birthday*. New York, 1950, pp. 637–67.

Nineham, D. E., 'The Order of Events in St Mark's Gospel – an Examination of Dr Dodd's Hypothesis', *Studies in the Gospels: Essays in Memory of R. H. Lightfoot*. Ed. by D. E. Nineham. Oxford, 1955, pp. 223–39.

Ogg, G., 'Chronology of the New Testament', *PCB*. London, 1962, pp. 728–32.

Parsons, E. W., 'John the Baptist and Jesus. An Essay in Historical Reconstruction', *Studies in Early Christianity*. Ed. by S. J. Case. New York and London, 1928, pp. 151–70.

Reicke, B., 'Instruction and Discussion in the Travel Narrative', *SE*, I, *TU*, LXXIII. Berlin, 1959, pp. 206–16.

Rengstorf, K. H., 'Die Stadt der Mörder (Mt. 22: 7)', *Judentum, Urchristentum, Kirche. Festschrift für Joachim Jeremias*. Ed. by W. Eltester. Beiheft to *ZNW*, XXVI. Berlin, 1960, pp. 106–29.

Riesenfeld, H., 'Nachträge I. Lagercrantz' Beiträge zum N.T.', *Coniectanea Neotestamentica*, III. Ed. by A. Fridrichsen. Uppsala and Leipzig, 1938, pp. 22–7.

Rostovtzeff, M., 'Ptolemaic Egypt', *CAH*, VII. Cambridge, 1928, pp. 109–54.

'Seleucid Babylonia: Bullae and Seals of Clay with Greek Inscriptions', *Yale Classical Studies*, III. Ed. by A. M. Harmon. New Haven, 1932, pp. 1–114.

Rostowzew [= Rostovtzeff], M., 'Geschichte der Staatspacht in der römischen Kaiserzeit bis Diokletian', *Philologus*, Supp. IX. Leipzig, 1904, pp. 329–512.

Sanders, M. and Nahmad, H., 'A Judeo-Arabic Epitome of Yosippon', *Essays in Honor of Solomon B. Freehof*. Pittsburgh, 1964, pp. 275–99.

Schneider, J., 'Zur Analyse des lukanischen Reiseberichtes', *SS*. München, 1953, pp. 207–29.

Schwartz, E., 'Christliche und jüdische Ostertafeln', *AGG*, N.F. VIII. Berlin, 1905, pp. 1–197.

Scramuzza, V. M., 'The Policy of the Early Roman Emperors towards Judaism', *BC*, V. London, 1933, pp. 277–97.

Stauffer, E., 'Der Stand der neutestamentlichen Forschung', *Theologie und Liturgie. Eine Gesamtschau der gegenwärtigen Forschung in Einzeldarstellungen*. Ed. by L. Hennig. Kassel, 1952, pp. 35–105.

Stendahl, K., 'Matthew', *PCB*. London, 1962, pp. 769–98.

Streeter, B. H., 'The Trial of Our Lord before Herod: A Suggestion', *SSP*. Oxford, 1911, pp. 228–31.

Styler, G. M., 'The Priority of Mark', *The Birth of the New Testament*, by C. F. D. Moule, Excursus IV. London, 1962, pp. 223–32.

Till, W. C., 'Johannes der Täufer in der koptischen Literatur', *Mitteilungen des deutschen archäologischen Instituts, Abteilung Kairo, Festschrift zum 80. Geburtstage von Professor Dr. Hermann Junker*, XVI. Wiesbaden, 1958, pp. 310–32.

Turner, H. E. W., 'The Chronological Framework of the Ministry', *Theological Collections VI: Historicity and Chronology in the New Testament*. London, 1965, pp. 59–74.

Volkmann, H., 'Zur Rechtsprechung im Principat des Augustus. Historische Beiträge', *Münchener Beiträge zur Papyrusforschung und antiken Rechtsgeschichte*. München, 1935, pp. xiii+227.

Wellhausen, J., 'Der arabische Josippus', *AGG*, N.F. I. Berlin, 1897.

Wilson, R. McL., 'The New *Passion of Jesus* in the Light of the New Testament and Apocrypha', *Neotestamentica et Semitica*. Ed. by E. E. Ellis and M. Wilcox. Edinburgh, 1969, pp. 264–71.

Zeitlin, S., 'The Pharisees and the Gospels', *Essays and Studies in Memory of Linda R. Miller*. Ed. by I. Davidson. New York, 1938, pp. 235–86.

DICTIONARY AND ENCYCLOPAEDIA ARTICLES

Abrahams, I., 'Time', *HDB*, IV (1902), 762–6.

Armstrong, W. P., 'Herodians', *A Dictionary of Christ and the Gospels*. Ed. by J. Hastings, I (1906), 723.

Avi-Yonah, M., 'Aenon', *IDB*, I (1962), 52.

Bammel, E., 'Salome', *Encyclopædia Britannica*, XIX (1970), 952.

Bauernfeind, O., 'στρατεύομαι', *TWNT*, VII (1964), 701–13.

Benzinger, I., 'Gadara', PW, VII, I (1910), 435–6.

Bertram, G., 'νήπιος', *TDNT*, IV (1967), 912–23.

Bickermann, 'Makkabäerbücher', PW, XIV (1928), 779–800.

Caird, G. B., 'The Chronology of the NT', *IDB*, I (1962), 599–607.

Cassuto, U., 'Josippon', *EJ*, IX (1932), 420–5.

Farmer, W. R., 'Essenes', *IDB*, II (1962), 143–9.

Ffoulkes, E. S., 'Herodias', *A Dictionary of the Bible*[2]. Ed. by W. Smith and J. M. Fuller, I, ii (1893), 1346–7.

Foerster, W., 'Herodes und seine Nachfolger', *Die Religion in Geschichte und Gegenwart*[3]. Ed. by K. Galling, III (1959), 266–9.

Ginzberg, L., 'Boethusians', *JE*, III (1892), 284–5.

Grant, R. M., 'Tiberius', *IDB*, IV (1962), 640.

Gutmann, J., 'Antipas (Herodes Antipas)', *EJ*, II (1928), 947–51.

Hauck, F. and Bammel, E. 'πτωχός', *TDNT*, VI (1968), 885–915.

Hölscher, 'Josephus', PW, IX (1916), 1934–2000.

'Tirathana', PW, 2nd series, VI (1937), 1431.

Jeremias, J., ''Ηλ(ε)ίας', *TDNT*, II (1964), 928–41.

'Μωυσῆς', *TDNT*, IV (1967), 848–73.

John, W., 'P. Quinctilius Varus', PW, XXIV (1963), 907–84.

Keim, 'Herodes Söhne und Enkel', *Bibel-Lexikon*. Ed. by D. Schenkel, III (1871), 38–65.

'Herodianer', *Bibel-Lexicon*. Ed. by D. Schenkel, III (1871), 65–7.

Kennedy, A. R. S., 'Money', *HDB*, III (1900), 417–32.

Klein, S., 'Kabul', *EJ*, IX (1932), 733–4.

Kohler, K., 'Herodians', *JE*, VI (1894), 360.

Lehmann-Haupt, 'Talent', PW, Supp. VIII (1956), 791–848.

McLaughlin, J. F., 'New Year', *JE*, IX (1895), 254–6.

Meyer, R., 'Σαδδουκαῖος', *TWNT*, VII (1964), 35–54.

Morgenstern, J., 'New Year', *IDB*, III (1962), 544–6.

'Year', *IDB*, IV (1962), 923–4.

Oepke, A., 'λάμπω', *TDNT*, IV (1967), 16–28.

'παῖς', *TDNT*, V (1967), 636–54.

Otto, W., 'Herodes', PW, Supp. II (1913), 1–200.

Ramsay, W. M., 'Numbers, Hours, Years, and Dates', *HDB*, Extra Volume (1904), 473–84.

Ramsay, W. M., 'Roads and Travel (in NT)', *HDB*, Extra Volume (1904), 375–402.

Reicke, B., 'Herodes', *Biblisch-historisches Handwörterbuch*. Ed. by B. Reicke and L. Rost, II (1964), 696–703.

'Herodianer', *Biblisch-historisches Handwörterbuch*. Ed. by B. Reicke and L. Rost, II (1964), 703.

Robinson, G. L., 'Land of Gennesaret', *A Dictionary of Christ and the Gospels*. Ed. by J. Hastings, I (1906), 640–1.

Sanday, W., 'Jesus Christ', *HDB*, II (1900), 603–53.

Sandmel, S., 'Herod (Family)', *IDB*, II (1962), 585–94.

'Herodians', *IDB*, II (1962), 594–5.

Schmidt, K. L., 'καλέω', *TDNT*, III (1965), 487–536.

Schneider, J., 'συζητέω', *TWNT*, VII (1964), 747–8.

Smith, G. A., 'Trade and Commerce', *EncB*, IV (1903), 5145–99.

Vanel, A., 'Prétoire', *Dictionnaire de la Bible*, Supplément. Ed. by L. Pirot, *et al.*, VIII (1969), 513–54.

Wellmann, M., 'Fuchs', PW, VII (1910), 189–92.

Westcott, B. F., 'Herod', *A Dictionary of the Bible*². Ed. by W. Smith and J. M. Fuller, I, ii (1893), 1340–6.

'Herodians', *A Dictionary of the Bible*². Ed. by W. Smith and J. M. Fuller, I, ii (1893), 1346.

Wilcken, U., 'Antipatros', PW, I (1894), 2509–13.

Windisch, H., 'ζύμη', *TDNT*, II (1964), 902–6.

INDICES

I. INDEX OF PASSAGES CITED

A. BIBLICAL SOURCES

I. OLD TESTAMENT ([ ] = LXX)

Genesis
24: 2, *118 n. 3*; 40: 20, *160–1 n. 5*; 41: 10, 37–8; *189 n. 3*; 49: 9–10, *221 n. 1*; 49: 20, *66 n. 8*; 49: 23, *158 n. 2*

Exodus
19: 11–16, *96 n. 6*; 20: 4, *96 n. 4*, *173 n. 8*; 35: 34, *164 n. 4*

Leviticus
18: 16; 20: 21, *137 n. 4*, *137–8 n. 4*; 21: 14; 22: 13, *143 n. 7*

Numbers
30: 10, *143 n. 7*; 32: 36, *88 n. 3*

Deuteronomy
4: 16, *173 n. 8*; 6: 7, *164 n. 4*; 18: 20, *223 n. 5*; 24: 1, *139 n. 1*; 25: 5, *137–8 n. 4*; 33: 24, *66 n. 8*

Joshua
146 n. 6; 1: 18, *159 n. 4*; 12: 6; 13: 8–28, *54 n. 9*; 13: 27, *88 n. 2*; 18: 7, *54 n. 9*; 19: 35, *92 nn. 2, 3*; 20: 8; 22: 1–4, 9, *54 n. 9*

Judges
1: 30, 33, *53 n. 2*; 1: 35, *343 n. 6*; 15: 4, *343 n. 1*; 18: 7, 28, *53 n. 3*

Ruth
2: 8, 22, 23, 3: 2, *155 n. 11*

1 Samuel
9: 11, 12, *155 n. 11*; 13: 7, *54 n. 9*; 16: 17, 18: 22–6, *189 n. 3*; 20: 30, *156 n. 2*

2 Samuel
12: 1–12, *118 n. 1*; 16: 5, 7, 9, *159 n. 4*

1 Kings
9: 1, *162 n. 1*; 9: 13, *64 n. 3*; 10: 13, *162 n. 1*; 11: 31, *54 n. 10*; 12: 24, *155 n. 9*; 12: 25, *54 n. 10*; 13: 8, *151 n. 6*; 19: 2, 10, 14, *162 n. 2*; 20 [21]: 10, *343–4 n. 6*; 21: 1–29, *162 n. 5*; 21: 17–24, *118 n. 1*

2 Kings
146 n. 6; 10: 33, *54 n. 11*; 15: 29, *53 n. 5, 55 n. 1*; 17: 24–7, *53 n. 5*

1 Chronicles
5: 26, *55 n. 1*; 10: 8, *222 n. 4*

2 Chronicles
24: 20–2, *223 n. 4*

Nehemiah
1: 1; 2: 1, *310*; 4: 3 [3: 35], *343 n. 1*

Esther
2: 2, 3, 7, 8, 9, 12, *156 n.*

1; 5: 3, 6, *151 n. 3*; 7: 1–10, *118 n. 1*; 7: 2, *151 n. 3*

Psalms
2, *228, 229, 245, 246*; 2: 1–2, *180, 228*; 15 [14]: 4, *167 n. 5*; 42 [41]: 5, *164 n. 4*; 63 [62]: 11, *343 n. 1*; 115: 3 [113: 11], *162 n. 1*

Song of Solomon
2: 15, *343 and n. 1, 344*

Isaiah
8: 23 [9: 1], *43 n. 4, 46 n. 5, 53 n. 4*; 38: 15, *164 n. 4*

Jeremiah
26 [33]: 8–9, 20–3, *223 n. 4*; 36 [43]: 31, 37 [44]: 2, *189 n. 3*

Lamentations
5: 18, *343 n. 1*

Ezekiel
13: 4, *343 and n. 1, 344*

Daniel
5: 23, *102 n. 3*; 8: 4, *162 n. 1*

Hosea
6: 2, *221 n. 5*; 10: 6, *235 n. 2*

Joel
4: 3, *155 n. 10*

Zechariah
8: 5, *155 n. 10*

2. OLD TESTAMENT APOCRYPHA AND PSEUDEPIGRAPHA

Judith, *279*
1: 8–9, *278–9*

1 Maccabees, *279, 310–11*
1: 6, 8, *189 n. 3*; 1: 29, 54,

126 n. 1; 4: 28, *222 n. 4*; 5: 14–17, *53 n. 7*; 5: 15, *43 n. 5, 53 n. 8*; 5: 20–3, *53 n. 7*; 5: 45–54, *55 n. 3*;

5: 55, *53 n. 7*; 6: 8–13, *126 n. 1*; 10: 30, *75 n. 7*; 12: 47, *278, 279*; 12: 49, *278*

Mark (cont.)

139 n. 2, 217; 6: 31-2, 200, 317; 6: 31-44, 324 n. 1; 6: 31 - 10: 1, 199; 6: 32-44, 199 n. 2, 208; 6: 32 - 10: 1, 199; 6: 35, 318 n. 3; 6: 37, 38, 208 n. 1; 6: 39, 206 n. 6; 6: 41, 44, 208 n. 1; 6: 45, 200, 217, 318 and n. 4, 321 n. 3; 6: 45-52, 324 n. 1; 6: 48, 319 n. 3; 6: 52, 208 n. 1; 6: 53, 200, 318, 319 n. 4, 324 n. 1; 6: 53-6, 217 n. 6, 218 n. 6; 6: 54-6, 324 n. 1; 6: 55-6, 319 n. 5; 7: 1-13, 218 n. 7; 7: 1-23, 59 n. 5, 205 n. 3, 209 n. 3, 213 n. 3, 217 n. 8, 320 n. 4, 324 n. 1; 7: 2, 5, 208 n. 1; 7: 14-23, 201 n. 5, 218 n. 7; 7: 24, 200, 319 n. 5, 320 and n. 5, 321 n. 1, 324 n. 1; 7: 24 ff., 139 n. 2; 7: 25, 186 n. 4; 7: 25-30, 324 n. 1; 7: 27, 208 n. 1; 7: 31, 92 n. 1, 200, 320 n. 5, 321; 7: 31-7, 324 n. 1; 7: 32-7, 208, 323 n. 5; 7: 33-7, 199; 8: 1, 336; 8: 1-9, 323 n. 7, 324 n. 1; 8: 4, 5, 6, 208 n. 1; 8: 10, 200, 323, 324-5 n. 3, 325 n. 2; 8: 10a, b, 324 n. 1; 8: 10-12, 209 n. 4; 8: 10b-13, 218; 8: 11, 207 nn. 4, 5, 326 n. 1; 8: 11-12, 324 n. 1; 8: 11-13, 207 n. 4, 213 n. 4, 218 n. 7; 8: 13, 324 n. 1; 8: 14, 208 n. 1; 8: 14-21, 203 n. 1, 208, 210 n. 3, 218 n. 5, 324 n. 1; 8: 15, 202, 203 n. 1, 211, 212 and n. 3, 213, 326, n. 4, 335, 336, 338, 342; 8: 15-21, 201 n. 4; 8: 16, 208 n. 1; 8: 17, 202, 208 n. 1; 8: 19, 208 n. 1; 8: 19-20, 323 n. 2, 324; 8: 21, 202; 8: 22, 200, 326 and n. 2; 8: 22-6, 199, 209 n. 5, 324 n. 1, 326 n. 2; 8: 27, 200, 327; 8: 27-30, 209 n. 5; 8: 27-33, 201 n. 1, 213 n. 5; 8: 27 - 9: 1, 327 n. 1; 8: 27 - 9: 10, 199 n. 2; 8: 27 - 9: 29, 139 n. 2; 8: 28, 184 n. 3, 185; 8: 31-3, 210 n. 1; 8: 32, 201 n. 4; 8: 34, 327 n. 2; 8: 34-8, 213 n. 6; 9: 1, 201 n. 2; 9: 2, 200, 327 and n. 3; 9: 2-13, 201 n. 1, 327 n. 4; 9: 4, 186 n. 3; 9: 10, 207 n. 5; 9: 11-13, 199; 9: 13, 162 n. 1; 9: 14, 207 n. 5; 9: 14-29, 217 n. 7, 327 n. 5; 9: 14-50, 199 n. 2; 9: 16, 207 n. 5; 9: 30, 139 n. 2, 200, 218 n. 3, 327, 330; 9: 30-2, 218 n. 5; 9: 30-50, 328 n. 1; 9: 33, 200, 218 n. 4, 327, 328; 9: 33-50, 218 n. 5; 9: 38-41, 42-50, 199; 9: 47, 201 n. 2; 10: 1, 139 n. 2, 200, 217, 218, 327 n. 7, 328, 329, 330; 10: 1-12, 55 n. 7; 10: 2, 207 n. 6; 10: 10-12, 12, 139 n. 2; 10: 13-16, 55 n. 8; 10: 14, 201 n. 3; 10: 17-23, 71-2 n. 17; 10: 17-22, 55 n. 9

11-16, 199; 11: 1, 329; 11: 18, 163 n. 6; 11: 27-33, 141; 11: 32, 145 n. 5, 163 n. 4; 12: 1-11, 71 n. 10; 12: 12, 145 n. 5, 163 n. 6; 12: 13, 203, 212 and n. 3, 331 and n. 1, 332 n. 2, 334, 339; 12: 13-17, 333; 12: 15, 207 n. 6; 12: 18, 211 n. 6, 212, 336 n. 2, 338; 12: 18-23, 189 n. 1; 12: 19, 137-8 n. 4; 12: 28, 207 n. 5; 12: 28-34, 113 n. 1; 12: 35, 334-5 n. 4; 12: 35-7, 320 n. 5; 12: 37, 114 n. 6; 12: 42-4, 72 n. 6; 14: 1-2, 163 n. 6; 14: 3-9, 113 n. 1; 14: 5, 202 n. 1; 14: 70, 63 n. 8; 15: 1, 233 n. 2; 15: 1-15, 225; 15: 3-4, 233 n. 4; 15: 7, 176 n. 4; 15: 8-15, 245 n. 1; 15: 9-12, 14, 233 n. 3; 15: 15b, 231 n. 2; 15: 16-20, 241; 15: 24, 231 n. 2; 15: 25, 186 n. 3; 15: 38, 231 n. 2; 15: 40-1, 305 n. 2; 15: 43, 231 n. 2

Luke

1: 3, 311; 1: 5, 149 n. 5; 2: 1-5, 299 n. 2; 2: 4-7, 233 n. 7; 3: 1, 33 n. 4, 107 n. 6, 113 n. 4, 125, 131 n. 4, 135 n. 7, 149 n. 5, 149 n. 5, 217 n. 2, 260 n. 2, 307 n. 1; 3: 3, 146 n. 6; 3: 7, 336; 3: 12, 141; 3: 12-13, 78 n. 5; 3: 14, 141 and n. 1; 3: 19, 33 n. 4, 132, 135 n. 7, 149 nn. 4, 5, 159 n. 3; 3: 19-20, 110 and n. 4, 112, 113, 136 n. 5, 215; 3: 20, 159 n. 1, 194 n. 7; 3: 23, 310 n. 1, 311, 312 n. 1; 4: 14, 170 n. 6, 192 n. 1, 233 n. 6; 4: 14-15, 192 n. 4; 4: 15-16, 54 n. 4, 58 n. 5; 4: 16-30, 193 n. 5; 4: 23, 192 n. 4; 4: 30-2, 192 n. 5; 4: 31-7, 194 n. 5; 4: 37, 40, 42, 192 n. 1; 4: 44, 54 n. 4, 58 n. 5, 194 n. 3; 5: 1, 92 n. 1, 192 n. 1; 5: 1-11, 68 n. 4; 5: 14, 196 n. 5; 5: 15, 192 n. 1; 5: 17, 54 n. 5, 58 n. 6, 192 n. 1; 5: 17 - 6: 11, 214 n. 4; 5: 19, 192 n. 1; 5: 27, 76 n. 4, 78 n. 3;

4. NEW TESTAMENT APOCRYPHA AND QUMRAN

B. RABBINIC SOURCES

1. THE MISHNAH

2. THE BABYLONIAN TALMUD

Sanhedrin (*cont.*)
  78 n. 5; 25*b*–26*a*, *78 n.
    9*; 37*a*, 346 *n. 1*; 49*a*,
    159 *n. 4*
Shabbath
  47*a*, *66 n. 8*; 78*b*, *78 n. 9*;
    120*b*, *68 n. 11*; 121*a*, *304
    n. 6*; 147*b*, *66 nn. 6, 11*

Shebiith
  39*a*, *78 n. 9*
Sotah
  41*b*, *107 n. 13*
Sukkah
  20*a*–*b*, *68 n. 7*; 27*a*, *107
    n. 13*, *137 n. 4*, *304
    n. 6*

Taanith
  24*b*–25*a*, *60 n. 3*
Yebamoth
  15*a*, *137 n. 4*, *137–8 n. 4*;
    55*a*, 55*b*, *137–8 n. 4*;
    121*a*, *67 n. 8*
Yoma
  20*b*, *107 n. 13*

3. THE JERUSALEM TALMUD

Ketuboth
  iv. 12, *64 n. 4*; iv. 12 [or
    14], *69 n. 8*
Maaseroth
  iii. 2, *66 n. 4*

Megillah
  i. 1, *92 nn. 2, 3*
Sanhedrin
  xi. 6, *240 n. 2*
Shabbath
  xvi. 8, *58–9 n. 8*

Shebiith
  38*d*, *88 n. 4*
Taanith
  iv. 5, *65 n. 5*
Yebamoth
  xvi. 4, *67 n. 8*; i. 4 [or 6],
    137 n. 4

4. THE TOSEPHTA

Menahoth
  ix. 5, *66 nn. 8, 13*
Sanhedrin
  ix. 3, *159 n. 4*

Sukkah
  iv. 1–4, *157 n. 6*
Yebamoth
  i. 10, *137 n. 4*

5. THE MIDRASH

Genesis Rabbah
  xx. 6 (iii. 16), *66 n. 9*;
    xxiii. 1 (iv. 17), *93 n. 8*;
    xliii. 4 (xxv. 20), *221
    n. 2*; lxxxvi. 5 (xxxix.

3), *68 n. 12*; xcviii. 17
  (xlix. 21); xcix. 12
  (xlix. 20), *65 n. 2*
Esther Rabbah
  vii. 3, *346 n. 6*

Ecclesiastes Rabbah
  i. 18, *68 n. 5*; ii. 8. 2, *68
    n. 6*; xi. 2. 1, *346 n. 5*
Canticles Rabbah
  ii. 15.1, *343 n. 5*, *346 n. 5*

6. OTHER WORKS

The Code of Maimonides:
  Mishnah Torah
    xiv. 5. 3. 8, *159 n. 4*
Megillat Taanit
  ix, *174 n. 1*

Midrash Tannaim: Deuter-
  onomy
    33: 24, *66 nn. 8, 10, 13*
Sifre: Deuteronomy
  33: 24, *66 n. 8*

C. CLASSICAL SOURCES

I. INSCRIPTIONS AND PAPYRI

*Corpus Inscriptionum Graeca-
  rum* 4521, *307 n. 5*
*Corpus Inscriptionum Semiti-
  carum*
  II, i, 160: 2, *49 n. 4*; 161,
    143–4 n. 9; 161: 3, 6;
    169: 2; 173: 5; 195: 2,
    49 n. 4; 195: 2–4, *143–4*

n. 9; 195: 4, *49 n. 4*;
  196, *143–4 n. 9*; 196: 2,
  49 n. 4, *143–4 n. 9*; 196:
  3, 5; 207: 2, 4, *49 n. 4*;
  213, *143–4 n. 9*; 213: 2,
  49 n. 4; 214, *143–4 n. 9*;
  214: 1, 2; 221: 1, *49
  n. 4*; 224, *143–4 n. 9*;

224: 7, *49 n. 4*; 227,
  303 n. 2; 234, *143–4 n.
  9*; 234: 3, *49 n. 4*; 235,
  143–4 n. 9; 235: A, *49
  n. 4*; 238, *49 n. 4*, *143–4
  n. 9*; 387; 790: 2, *49
  n. 4*
II, iii, 3913, *76 n. 9*

Die Fragmente der griechischen Historiker
IIa, 326 (Testimony 8), *30 n. 5*; 381 (90 Frag. 96), *5 n. 2*; 420–1 (90 Frag. 131), *30 n. 5*; 423 (90 Frag. 136.1), *14 n. 7*; 424 (90 Frag. 136.8), *29 n. 3*; 424 (90 Frag. 136.8–9), *20 n. 1*; 424 (90 Frag. 136.9), *12 n. 2, 20 n. 5, 26 n. 3, 27 nn. 2, 4, 33 n.*

Contra Apionem
i: 50, *62 n. 4*; i. 51, *108–9 n. 6*; i. 60, *14 n. 4*; ii. 178, *14 n. 3*
Vita
5, *150 n. 2, 301–2 n. 5*; 10–11, *341 n. 3*; 16, *38 n. 6*; 30, *85 n. 5, 86 n. 6*; 32, *71 n. 3*; 33, *71 n. 5, 98 n. 3*; 33–4, *101 n. 6*; 33–6, *97 n. 2*; 34, *97 n. 5*; 36–7, *101 n. 7*; 37, *85 n. 5, 87 n. 5, 97–8 n. 8, 106 n. 1*; 37–9, *85 n. 5*; 38, *85 n. 5, 86 n. 6, 97–8 n. 8*; 39, *108 n. 6*; 42, *280 n. 1, 282 n. 2*; 43–5, *283 n. 4*; 46, *98 n. 3, 108 n. 6*; 64, *85 n. 5, 97 n. 7*; 65, *96 n. 4, 106 n. 1*; 65–6, *97 n. 4, 96 n. 3*; 66, *72 n. 5, 98 n. 1*; 66–7, *71 n. 3*; 67, *54 n. 8, 97 n. 3, 98 n. 1*; 68, *96 n. 3*; 69, *97 n. 8, 304 n. 8*; 70–3, *71 n. 13*; 70–6, *71 n. 4*; 70–7, *283 n. 4*; 71–3, *66 n. 1, 70 n. 4*; 74, *98 n. 3*; 74–6, *67 n. 1, 71 n. 14*; 82, *85 n. 5*; 85, *92 n. 2*; 86, *98 n. 3*; 92, *61 n. 2, 96 n. 1*; 98–9, *293 n. 6*
101–2, *283 n. 4*; 103–4, *85 n. 5*; 104, *86 n. 6*; 111, *85 n. 5*; 112,

3, *35 n. 4*; 424 (90 Frag. 136.10), *30 n. 6*, *33 n. 4*; 425 (90 Frag. 136.11), *28 n. 4, 29 n. 3*; 424–5 (90 Frag. 136.11), *29 n. 3, 31 n. 3*
IIc, 255, *5 n. 2*; 290, *30 n. 5*
Fragments of a Zadokite Work, *137–8 n. 4*
Orientis Graeci Inscriptiones Selectae

2. JOSEPHUS

102 n. 3; 114, *108 n. 6*; 115, *44 n. 6, 277 n. 1*; 118–19, *66 n. 2*; 119, *70 n. 3*; 121, *280 n. 1*; 122, *283 n. 4*; 123, *46 n. 1, 295 n. 1*; 123–4, *85 n. 5*; 126, *279 n. 4*; 134, *98 n. 1, 304 n. 8*; 149, *102 n. 3*; 153, *318–19 n. 4*; 154, *108 n. 6*; 168, *97 n. 8, 304 n. 8*; 169, *97 n. 7*; 180, 182, *108 n. 6*; 187–8, *44 n. 3*; 188, *45 n. 7, 85 n. 5, 95–6 n. 3, 277 n. 3, 280 n. 3, 285 nn. 2, 7, 8*; 189, *283 n. 4*
203, *85 n. 5, 295 n. 1*; 230, *56 n. 3*; 232, *45 n. 11, 85 n. 5, 86 n. 6, 294 n. 6, 295 n. 1*; 232–3, *85 n. 5*; 234, *45 n. 8, 285 n. 4*; 235, *52 n. 1, 283 n. 4, 291 n. 2*; 271, *98 n. 1, 283 n. 4, 304 n. 8*; 276–9, *98 n. 1, 304 n. 8*; 277, *96 n. 2*; 278, *98 n. 1, 304 n. 8*; 280, *96 n. 2*; 284, *97 n. 7*; 293, *96 n. 2*; 294, *98 n. 1, 304 n. 8*; 295, *96 n. 3*; 296, *71 n. 3, 97 n. 8, 304 n. 8*
300, *97 n. 7, 98 n. 1, 304 n. 8*; 304, *318–19 n. 4*; 308, *283 n. 4*; 313, *97*

1, 416; 417, *106 n. 3*; 419, *108 n. 5, 108–9 n. 6*; 420; 424, *108–9 n. 6*
Papyri Fayum
114: 20, *160–1 n. 5*
Papyri Holm, *153, n. 10*
The Oxyrhynchus Papyri
736: 56; 57, *160–1 n. 5*
Répertoire d'Épigraphie Semitique
II, 1104: 1, 2; 1108: 1, 8; 1196; 2024: 2, *49 n. 4*

n. 7; 317, *283 n. 4*; 318, *279 n. 4*; 331, *61 n. 2, 96 n. 1*; 343, *108 n. 6*; 345, *108–9 n. 6*; 346, *45 n. 12, 86 n. 6, 294 n. 6, 295, n. 1*; 346–7, *85 n. 5*; 349, 351–4, 355, 359, 362, 364, 365, 366, *108–9 n. 6*; 373–4, *85 n. 5*; 376–7, *87 n. 4*; 379–80, *85 n. 5*; 381, *97 n. 7*; 382, *97 n. 2*; 384, 394–6, *85 n. 5*
403, *282 n. 3*; 407, 408, 409, *108–9 n. 6*; 411, *85 n. 5*; 414–15, *137 n. 4*; 422–5, 429, *71 n. 6*; 430, *301–2 n. 5*
Antiquitates Judaicae
i. 80–1, *301 n. 5, 309 n. 6*; ii. 6, *50 n. 3, 254–5 n. 4*; iii. 40, *254–5 n. 4*; iv. 176, *48 n. 10*; iv. 209–11, *14 n. 4*; iv. 218, *234 n. 3*; v. 4, *48 n. 10*; vii. 230, *102 n. 3*; viii. 141–3, *64 n. 3*; viii. 186, *243 n. 1*; viii. 371, *343–4 n. 6*; ix. 36, *293 n. 8*; ix. 188, *254–5 n. 4*; ix. 235, *53 n. 5, 55 n. 1*; xi. 37, 141, *102 n. 3*; xii. 167–85, *77 n. 4*; xii. 186–9, *137–8 n. 4*; xii. 196, *160–1 n. 5*; xii. 248–53, 357, *126 n. 1*

3. OTHER CLASSICAL AUTHORS

Suetonius (cont.)
 xiv. 3, *252 n. 5, 253 n. 1*;
 xvi. 3, *89 n. 6*; xvii,
 xix, *262–3 n. 4*; xix. 2,
 252 n. 6; xxviii, xliii,
 xliii–xlix, *262–3 n. 4*
Divus Claudius
 xxvi. 3, *137–8 n. 4*
Tiberius
 xxxvi, *101 n. 1*; xxxix–xl,
 129 n. 3; lxii. 1, *258
 n. 2*; lxxiii. 1, *256
 n. 5*
Vespasian
 xvi. 3, *345 n. 9*
Vitellius
 ii. 4, *251 n. 7, 252 n. 5*
Georgius Syncellus *Chronographiae, 280 n. 8*

Tacitus *Agricola*
 xv, *73 n. 8*
Annales
 i. 8, *89 n. 6*; i. 9, *91 n. 8*;
 i. 14, *89 n. 6*; ii. 42, *73
 n. 8, 77 n. 3*; ii. 84, *259
 n. 5*; ii. 85, *101 n. 1*;
 iv. 8, *258 n. 2*; iv. 41,
 129 n. 3; iv. 66, *29 n. 9*;
 iv. 67, *129 n. 3*; v. 1,
 89 n. 6, 91 n. 5; vi. 5,
 91 n. 2; vi. 18, *160–1
 n. 5*; vi. 31–7, *252 n. 1*;
 vi. 32, *251 n. 7*; vi. 38,
 252 n. 3; vi. 41–4, *252
 n. 1*; vi. 50, *256 n. 5*;
 xii. 6–7, *137–8 n. 4*;
 xii. 23, *108 n. 1*; xiii.
 7, *108 n. 1, 108–9 n. 6,*

 251 n. 4; xiv. 26, *251
 n. 4*; xv. 27, *102 n. 3*
Historiae
 i. 24–5, ii. 73, *119–20 n. 3*;
 ii. 81, *108 n. 1*; ii. 89,
 243 n. 1; ii. 95, *160–1
 n. 5*; v. 1, *108 n. 1*;
 v. 5, *157 n. 3*; v. 9,
 *6 n. 3, 7 n. 2, 19 n. 1.
 31 n. 3, 33 n. 4, 83 n. 4*
Thucydides
 ii. 2.1, *307 n. 2*
Vegetius Renatus *De re
 militari*
 iv. 39, *35 n. 1, 38 nn. 3, 9*
Velleius Paterculus *His-
 toriae Romanae*
 ii. 37.5, *73 n. 5*; ii. 121,
 308

4. ROMAN LAW

Codex Iustinianus
 v. 17.5–6; viii. 38.2, *139
 n. 1*
Gai Institutiones
 i. 93, 94, *18 n. 2*; ii. 112,
 18 n. 1; ii. 123–9, *273
 n. 2*; ii. 135a, *18 n. 2*; ii.
 144, *269 n. 4*; ii. 147,
 18 n. 1; iii. 2, 20, 71,
 18 n. 2

Iustiniani Digesta
 i. 18.3, *235 n. 6, 237 n. 3*;
 xlviii. 3.7; lxviii. 3.9,
 234 n. 5; lxviii. 3.11,
 234 n. 5, 235 nn. 4, 7
Iustiniani Institutiones, 22
 ii. 12.1, *22 n. 3*; ii. 17.6,
 18 n. 1
Pauli Sententiae, 22
 iii. 4a, 5, 11, *22 n. 3*

The Twelve Tables
 v. 7, *22 n. 6*
*Ulpiani Liber Singularis Regu-
 larum, 22*
 xx. 10–16, *18 n. 1*; xx. 13,
 22 n. 3; xxii. 14–16,
 273 n. 2; xxiii. 2,
 269 n. 4

D. EARLY CHRISTIAN SOURCES

Julius Africanus *Epistola ad
 Aristidem, 5 n. 2*
Anti-Marcionite prologue
 to the Gospel of Luke,
 231–2 n. 9
*Argumentum Evangelii Secun-
 dum Lucam, 231–2 n. 9*
Chrysostom *Commentarii in
 Matthaeum*
 homily lxi. 2–4, *72 n. 6*
Commentarii in S. Joannem
 homily xiii. 1, *255 n. 3*
Cyril of Jerusalem *Cate-
 cheses*
 xiii. 14, *235 n. 2*
Epiphanius *Adversus Octoginta Haereses*
 xxix. 7, *288 n. 6*

Eusebius *Chronica*
 II. 146–7, *32 nn. 2, 3, 107
 n. 5*; 148–9, *93 n. 9*; 149–
 50, *177 n. 3*; 150, 151,
 259 n. 2
Demonstratio Evangelica
 viii. 2.122, 123, *177*
Historia Ecclesiastica
 i. 6.2; 7.11, *5 n. 2*; i. 7.12,
 106 n. 1; i. 9.1, *32 n. 3*;
 i. 10.1, *106 n. 1, 107 n.
 9*; i. 11.1, 2, 3, *106 n. 1*;
 i. 11.4, *262 n. 1*; i. 11.5,
 106 n. 1; i. 11.6, *106
 n. 1, 137 nn. 1, 2*; i. 11.7,
 106 n. 1; ii. 4.1, *106 n.
 1, 107 n. 9, 247 n. 2*;
 ii. 6.4, *177*; ii. 6.6–7,

 174 n. 3; ii. 10.9, *106
 n. 1, 107 n. 9*; ii. 19.2
 108 n. 6; iii. 4.6, *231–2
 n. 9*; iii. 10.10, *108–9
 n. 6*; iii. 39.15, *197
 n. 1*; v. 1.20, *233–4
 n. 7*
Onomasticon
 p. 12: 24–5; p. 13: 24–5;
 p. 16: 26–18: 1; p. 17:
 27, *88 n. 8*; p. 22: 23–8,
 p. 23: 25–31, *48 n. 7*;
 p. 32: 5–7; p. 33: 5–7,
 288 n. 1; p. 48: 4, *88
 n. 7*; p. 48: 13, *88 n. 5*;
 p. 48: 15, *89 n. 3*;
 p. 49: 4, *88 n. 7*; p. 49:
 14, *88 n. 5, 89 n. 3*;

Eusebius (*cont.*)
p. 94: 3–4; p. 95: 3–4,
287 n. 3; p. 102: 24, 25;
p. 103: 24; p. 128: 17,
18; p. 129: 17, *254–5
n. 4*; p. 134: 18–20;
p. 135: 22–4, *325 n.
2*
Ignatius *Epistola ad Smyrnaeos*
i. 2, *229 n. 4, 246 n. 1*
Irenaeus *The Proof of the
Apostolic Preaching*
lxxiv, *246 n. 5*; lxxvii,
235 n. 2, 246 n. 5
Jerome *Commentarii in Joelem*
3: 18, *88 n. 7*

*Commentarii in Evangelium
Matthaei*
prologus, *231–2 n. 9*;
xxiv. 15, *177 n. 3*
De Viris Illustribus
vii, *231–2 n. 9*
Justin Martyr *I Apologiae*
i. 1, *86 n. 1*; xl. 5–6, *229
n. 5, 246 n. 3*; lxiii, *246
n. 6*
II Apologiae
ii. 8, *86 n. 1*
*Dialogus cum Tryphone
Judaeo*
xvi–xvii, *246 n. 6*; xlix. 4,
*149 n. 1, 151 n. 7, 153
nn. 2, 8, 164 n. 2*; xlix.
5, *162 n. 1*; lii. 3,

5 n. 2; ciii. 4, *32 n. 1,
107 n. 4, 182 n. 5, 235
n. 2, 236 n. 5, 246 n. 3*;
cxxxiv. 1; cxli. 4, *137–
8 n. 4*
Origen *Commentarii in Evangelium Matthaei*
xvii. 27, *177 n. 3*
*Commentarii in Evangelium
Joannis*
vi. 30, *188 n. 2*
Tatian *Diatessaron*
i. 8, *243 n. 1*
Tertullian *Adversus Marcionem*
iv. 42, *235 n. 2*
De Resurrectione Carnis
xx, *228 n. 4, 246 n. 4*

II. INDEX OF AUTHORS

Abel, F.-M., 11 n. 3, 66 n. 12, 88 n. 7,
89 n. 2, 254 n. 4, 299 n. 3, 325 n. 2,
329 n. 1
Abrahams, I., 72 n. 1, 78 n. 7, 203 n. 9,
301–2 n. 5, 309 n. 6
Achtemeier, P. J., 114 n. 1, 185 n. 6,
193 n. 2
Aharoni, Y. and Avi-Yonah, M., 69 n. 1,
283 n. 1, 286 n. 4, 289 n. 3, 322
n. 4
Aland, K., 115 n. 4
Albright, W. F., 86 n. 2, 147 n. 2,
280 nn. 4, 5, 7, 283 n. 3, 325 n. 5
Allen, W. C., 116–17 n. 2, 118 n. 3,
152 n. 2, 321 n. 3
Allon, G., 26 n. 6, 338 n. 2
Alt, A., 43 n. 3, 53 nn. 5, 8, 277 n. 1,
283–4 n. 5
Anderson, J. G. C., 253 n. 6
André, J., 15 n. 2
Argyle, A. W., 63 n. 1
Armstrong, W. P., 336 n. 4
Avi-Yonah, M., 44 n. 4, 45 n. 13, 46 n. 2,
68 nn. 9, 10, 89 n. 7, 90 and n. 3,
91 n. 11, 92 n. 5, 94 and n. 4, 95–6 n. 3,
97 n. 6, 98 n. 3, 99 n. 1, 147 n. 2, 277
n. 1, 280 n. 5, 281 nn. 2, 3, 5, 282
n. 12, 283 n. 1, 283–4 n. 5, 284 n. 7,
285 n. 9, 295 n. 1, 339 n. 2; *see also*
Aharoni and Avi-Yonah

Baarda, T., 196–7 n. 5
Bacon, B. W., 147 nn. 2, 3, 149 n. 2,
194 n. 1, 333 n. 3, 336 n. 3
Bajsić, A., 236 n. 6
Balsdon, J. P. V. D., 253 nn. 3, 5
Baly, D., 69 n. 5, 294 n. 3
Bammel, E., 19 n. 2, 72 n. 1, 102 n. 3,
106–7 n. 5, 107 n. 5, 122 n. 3, 123 n. 3,
137 n. 1, 142 n. 2, 181 n. 2, 188 n. 5,
200 n. 5, 205 n. 1, 248 n. 1, 249
n. 1
Barnard, L. W., 123 n. 3
Barnes, T. D., 10 n. 5
Baron, S. W., 56–7 n. 5, 58 n. 8, 71 n. 7,
72 n. 4, 77 n. 2, 124 n. 2, 262 n. 1,
294 n. 3, 295 n. 1
Barr, A., 225 n. 5
Barr, J., 62–3 n. 5
Barrett, C. K., 206 n. 5
Barron, J. B., 294 n. 4
Barth, G., 205 n. 1
Bauer, W., 53 n. 8, 78 n. 6, 116 n. 2,
119–20 n. 3, 155 n. 8, 164 n. 5, 186
nn. 1, 5, 227 n. 6, 233 n. 6, 242 n. 1,
243 n. 3, 246, n. 6
Baurnfeind, O., 241 n. 4
Belkin, S., 304 n. 1
Beloch, J., 292 and n. 5
Bengel, J. A., 159 n. 6
Benoit, P., 228 n. 7, 241 n. 3

III. INDEX OF NAMES AND SUBJECTS